Unpublished Materials Of Ellen G. White

1

Spalding And Magan Collection: Unpublished Manuscript Testimonies

Original Edition

Ellen G. White

Copyright ©2023

LS COMPANY

ISBN: 978-1-0881-7474-6

Table of Contents

Chapter 1—Copy of Three Early Visions 15

Chapter 2—Praying for the Sick 19

Chapter 3—The Bible in the Public Schools 23

Chapter 4—Domestic Education 25

Chapter 5—Authors and Subjects in Our Schools 27

Chapter 6—Battle Creek and the Southern Field 30

Chapter 7—Sunday Labor And the Way to Oppose Error 37

Chapter 8—Methods of Work in the Southern Field 45

Chapter 9—Letter from W. W. Prescott 49

Chapter 9.1—Diet for Workers and Sick 51

Chapter 10—Forwardness and Consolidation 54

Chapter 11—Temperance in Diet 60

Chapter 13—Meat Eating 69

Chapter 14—The Essential Education 73

Chapter 15—Our School Work 78

Chapter 16—True Education 82

Chapter 17—Controlling Brethren 87

Chapter 18—Exercise Versus Amusement 97

Chapter 18.1—Behavior of Students 105

Chapter 19—Words to the Young 107

Chapter 20—Hearing and Doing 110

Chapter 21—Unity in Work and in Counsel 118

Chapter 22—Dress Reform 122

Chapter 23—Study for Time and Eternity 125

Chapter 24—Short Work in School 127

Chapter 25—Rational Education 129

Chapter 26—Training an Army of Missionaries 133

Chapter 27—To Teachers 138

Chapter 28—Adopting Infant Children 150

Chapter 29—Principles of Finance 154

Chapter 30—The Need of Harmonious Action Among Teachers 157

Chapter 31—Life in Medical Missionary Work 161

Chapter 32—Practical Missionary Work a Branch of Education 164

Chapter 34—Financial, Social, and Spiritual Education 168

Chapter 35—School Finance 172

Chapter 36—The Education Our Schools Should Bring 175

Chapter 37—A Satanic Program 182

Chapter 38—Bible Teaching in our Schools 184

Chapter 39—Dealing with Delinquent Students 186

Chapter 40—The Review and Herald and the College Debt 191

Chapter 41—School Diet 196

Chapter 41.1—W.C. White to P.T. Magan (1899) 199

Chapter 41.2—W.C. White to G.A. Erwin (1899) 199

Chapter 42—Help to be Given to our Schools 199

Chapter 43—Kingly Power 201

Chapter 44—The Regular Lines 214

Chapter 45—Neglect of the Southern Field 218

Chapter 46—The Work of COL & the Barrien Springs School 222

Chapter 47—The Church School 225

Chapter 48—Lines Regular and Irregular 230

Chapter 48.1—St. Helena, Aug 6, 1901 233

Chapter 49—Student Teachers 236

Chapter 50—The School at Berrien Springs 238

Chapter 51—Faith Under Discouragements 241

Chapter 52—Help for Berrien Springs 244

Chapter 53—The Necessity of a Close Walk with God 246

Chapter 54—Results of Indulgence in Meat-Eating 250

Chapter 55—Meat Diet and Life in Cities 253

Chapter 56—Selection of Sanitarium Workers 255

Chapter 57—Systematic Giving 258

Chapter 58—The Use of the Tithe 259

Chapter 59—The Work in Nashville 261

Chapter 60—Instruction Regarding the Southern Work 265

Chapter 61—The Use of Talents 269

Chapter 62—The Trees of the Lord 275

Chapter 63—The Mantle of Christ 277

Chapter 64—Counsels In Reform 280

Chapter 65—Unwise Changes 282

Chapter 66—The Work at Berrien Springs 283

Chapter 67—A Call to Service 286

Chapter 68—The School of the Home 288

Chapter 69—Consolidation and Control 296

Chapter 70—September 3 298

Chapter 71—The Influence of Diet on Council-Meetings 301

Chapter 72—Establishing Schools in the South 305

Chapter 73—Instruction in Regard to Sanitariums 309

Chapter 74—Strong Minds and Weak Stomachs 312

Chapter 75—Counsels on Health and the Southern Field 314

Chapter 76—Points in Diet 316

Chapter 77—The Work of Our Fernando School 317

Chapter 78—Professionalism Versus Simplicity 323

Chapter 79—The Work in the South 326

Chapter 80—Our Attitude Toward the Work and Workers in the Southern Field 331

Chapter 81—Principles for the Guidance of Men in Positions of Responsibility ... 337

Chapter 82—The Work in the Southern Field 341

Chapter 83—To the Teachers of the Fernando School 354

Chapter 84—To Those in Charge of the Fernando School 356

Chapter 85—To the Students of the Fernando School 358

Chapter 86—Right Principles of Management 359

Chapter 87—To Those in Council at Battle Creek 363

Chapter 88—To Our Brethren in Council at Battle Creek 366

Chapter 89—Be Strong, and of Good Courage 368

Chapter 90—The Reopening of Battle Creek College and the Fault of Large Institutions 370

Chapter 91—Bound Not to Men But to God 372

Chapter 92—To the Leaders in Our Medical Work 375

Chapter 93—Be Not Weary in Well-Doing 380

Chapter 94—The Training of Medical Missionaries 382

Chapter 95—The Development of the Medical Missionary Work 385

Chapter 96—Teach the Word 388

Chapter 97—A Warning of Danger 392

Chapter 98—The Battle Creek College Debt 394

Chapter 99—Giving Heed to Seducing Spirits 397

Chapter 100—Proposed Plan for Book Education 400

Chapter 101—Stepping Off the Platform 402

Chapter 102—The Specious Working of Satan 411

Chapter 103—A New Conversion Needed 414

Chapter 104—God Above All 417

Chapter 105—Work Misrepresented 419

Chapter 106—Unify 422

Chapter 106.1—Remarks Made at Berrien Springs 426

Chapter 106.2—Extracts from Talks at the Lake Union Conference 430

Chapter 107—The Huntsville School 434

Chapter 108—The Necessity of Harmony 437

Chapter 109—The Signing of Agreements 442

Chapter 110—The Closing of the Southern Field 448

Chapter 111—The Work in the Southern States 449

Chapter 112—Will You Help 453

Chapter 113—Unity Not Consolidation 455

Chapter 114—Pioneers in the South 457

Chapter 115—The Conditions in Nashville 461

Chapter 116—Judge Not 463

Chapter 117—The Madison Sanitarium 466

Chapter 118—Harmonize As Christian Workers 468

Chapter 119—We Must Not Pull Apart 469

Chapter 120—Simplicity in Treatments 471

Chapter 121—Local Health Foods 473

Chapter 122—The Work At Madison 474

Chapter 123—Silence is Eloquence 476

Chapter 124—Cautions to a Reformer 477

Chapter 125—Help the Workers 479

Chapter 126—Awake! Awake! Awake! 481

Chapter 127—Do Not Colonize 483

Chapter 128—Helping the Madison School 485

Chapter 129—Support to Be Given Madison 487

Chapter 130—Encourage the Workers 488

Chapter 131—The Right Use of Means 490

Chapter 132—A Broader Work 494

Chapter 133—A Missionary Field 498

Chapter 134—All Ye Are Brethren 500

Chapter 135—The Work God Has Appointed 502

Chapter 136—The Right of Way to the Footstool of Christ 504

Chapter 137—Go Not to Human Agencies 506

Chapter 138—Health Reform Essential for These Times 511

Chapter 139—To Those Bearing Responsibilities in Washington and Other Centers 513

Chapter 140—An Appeal For the Madison School 519

Chapter 141—Backsliding in Health Reform 521

Chapter 142—Home Schools 525

Chapter 143—The Aim of Our School Work 527

Chapter 144—Is Man to be a Dictator 530

Chapter 144.1—On Degrees 533

Chapter 145—Work For Every Member of the Family 533

Chapter 146—Call Your Forces Into Action 534

Chapter 147—A Division of Large Companies 536

Chapter 148—The True Higher Education 538

Chapter 149—The Hillcrest School 543

Chapter 150—To Our People in the Southern States 546

Chapter 151—W.C.W. The Work in the South 548

Chapter 152—The Last Days of Mrs E. G. White 551

Chapter 153—A Message For Our Young People 554

Chapter 154—"I Know My Work is Done" 556

Chapter 155—"I Go Only a Little Before the Others" 558

Chapter 156—« Unto Him Be Glory » 559

Chapter 156.1—Longs For Rest 561

Chapter 156.2—Extremes 562

Chapter 157—We Are Laborers Together... 564

Chapter 158—Who Has Told Sister White?.. 568

Chapter 158.1—The Integrity of the Testimonies to the Church..................... 570

Chapter 158.2—A Sure Basis of Beliefs 582

Chapter 159—A Messenger 587

Chapter 159.1—The Discerning of Spiritual Things....................................... 591

Chapter 159.2—The Use and Abuse of the Testimonies................................. 594

Chapter 1—Copy of Three Early Visions

I saw that we must wake up, wake, and cry earnestly for the arm of the Lord to be revealed. It is fatal to sleep now. Time is almost finished. I saw that it was a shame for us to refer to the scattering for examples to govern us now in the gathering time; for if God does no more for us now than He did then, we shall never be gathered. In the scattering, Israel were torn and smitten, but now God will bind up and heal them.

I saw that God had stretched out His hand the second time to recover the remnant of His people. They are these who have been covered up in the "rubbish" since 1844. I saw that efforts to spread the truth should now be put forth, such as in 1843 and 1844. In the scattering, efforts to spread the truth had but little effect--accomplished but little or nothing--but now in the gathering time, when God has set His hand to gather His People, efforts to spread the truth will have their designed effect; and all should be zealous and united in the work. I saw that a paper was needed, and all should feel interested in it.

I saw that the truth should be made plain upon tables, that the earth and the fullness thereof is the Lord's, and that necessary means should not be spared to make it plain. I saw that the old chart was directed by the Lord, and that not a figure of it should be altered except by inspiration. I saw that the figures of the chart were as God would have them, and that His hand was over and hid a mistake in some of the figures, so that none should see it till His hand was removed.

I saw that the two-horned beast had a dragon's mouth, and that his power was in his head, and that the decree would go out of his mouth. Then I saw the Mother of Harlots; that the mother was not the daughters, but separate and distinct from them. She has had her day, and it is past, and her daughters, the Protestant sects, were the next to come on the stage and act out the same mind that the mother had when she persecuted the saints. I saw that as the mother has been declining in power, the daughters had been growing, and soon they will exercise the power once exercised by the mother.

I saw the nominal church and nominal Adventists, like Judas, would betray us to the Catholics to obtain their influence to come against the truth. The saints then will be an obscure people, little known to the Catholics; but the churches and nominal Adventists who know of our faith and customs (for they hated us on account of the Sabbath, for they could not refute it) will betray the saints and report them to the Catholics as those who disregard the institutions of the people; that is, that they keep the Sabbath and disregard Sunday.

Then the Catholics bid the Protestants to go forward, and issue a decree that all who will not observe the first day of the week, instead of the seventh day, shall be slain. And the Catholics, whose numbers are large, will stand by the Protestants. The Catholics will give their power to the image of the beast. And the Protestants will work as their mother worked before them to destroy the saints. But before their decree bring or bear fruit, the saints will be delivered by the Voice of God. Then I saw that Jesus' work in the sanctuary will soon be finished. And after His work there is finished, He will come to the door of the first apartment, and confess the sins of Israel upon the head of the Scape Goat. Then He will put on the garments of vengeance. Then the plagues will come upon the wicked, and they do not come till Jesus puts on that garment, and takes His place upon the great white cloud. Then while the plagues are falling, the Scape Goat is being led away. He makes a mighty struggle to escape, but he is held fast by the hand that leads him. If he should effect his escape, Israel would lose their lives. I saw that it would take time to lead away the Scape Goat into the land of forgetfulness after the sins were put on his head.

The great white cloud I saw was not the holy place, but entirely separate from the holy and most holy place, entirely separate from the sanctuary.

Then the angel repeated these words, and said, "This is the time spoken of in Isaiah. He saw that there was not man, and wondered that there was no intercessor. He had no mediator between God and man, and these plagues could be withheld no longer, for Jesus had ceased to plead for Israel, and they were covered with the covering of the Almighty God, and then they could live in the sight of a holy God, and those who were not covered, the plagues fell upon them, for they had nothing to shelter or protect them from the wrath of God."

The Nations

Thou wouldst not want him to step out if thou knewest thy situation. That desire is to disenthrone those kings, but that could not be, for kings must reign till Christ begins to reign.

I saw in Europe just as things were moving to accomplish their desires, there would seemingly be a slackening up once or twice: thus the hearts of the wicked would be relieved and hardened; but the work will not settle down, only seem to, for the minds of kings and rulers were intent on overthrowing each other, and the minds of the people to get the ascendency.

I saw that all things are intensely looking and stretching their thoughts on the impending crisis before them. The sins of Israel must go to judgment beforehand. Every sin must be confessed at the sanctuary, then the work will move. It must be done now. The remnant in the time of trouble will cry, My God, My God, why hast Thou forsaken me?

The latter rain is coming on those that are pure -- all then will receive it as formerly.

When the four angels let go, Christ will set up His kingdom. None receive the latter rain but those who are doing all they can. Christ would help us. All could be overcomers by the grace of God, through the blood of Jesus. All heaven is interested in the work. Angels are interested.

Think ye that He will bring His hand unto Himself until He has accomplished the object for which He stretched it out? Yea, more bitter hatred against those that keep the law than against the Catholics. Truth, the truth, let it shine. Hold them by the side of truth. What are they rich in? They seek falsehood, deception and cunning. Behold where is their strength? Is it in the truth? A mere knowledge of the truth will never save.

How long then, angel of God, before the message will go with a loud voice? Other things to be accomplished. They must make themselves more vile. If Jesus should make His appearance in their midst, they would despise Him. They advocate their errors for awhile, until the people get disgusted with it, then they add another. Nights upon their beds, horror gets hold upon them. Can ye not see it? Live unto God. He has got them safe in the snare. The honest are getting disgusted. Satan works at the very ones that do Him the most harm. God can make them a host against their enemies. Ye give up too quick. Ye let go too soon. That arm, the arm of God is mighty. Satan works in different ways to steal the mind off from God.

Victory! victory, we must have it over every wrong. A solemn sinking into God. Get ready! Set thine house in order.

March 18, 1852.

Vision of August 24, 1850

Said the angel, Can ye stand in the battle in the day of the Lord? Ye need to be washed, and live in nearness of life to God.

Then I saw those whose hands are engaged in making up the breach and are standing in the gap, that have formerly since 1844 broken the commandments, and have so far followed the pope as to keep the first day instead of the seventh, and who have since the light shone out of the Most Holy Place, changed their course, given up the institution of the pope, and are keeping God's Sabbath, would have to go down into the water, and be baptized in the faith of the sanctuary, and keeping the commandments of God and the faith of Jesus.

I saw those who have been baptized as a door into the churches, would have to be baptized again as a door into the faith. Those who have not been baptized since 1844 will have to be before Jesus comes. And some I saw would not make progress till the duty was performed.

The angel said, some tried too hard to believe. Faith is so simple they look above it. Satan has deceived some, and got them to looking at their own unworthiness. I saw they must look away from self to the worthiness of Jesus, and throw themselves just as they are, needy, dependent upon His mercy, and draw by faith strength and nourishment from Him.

Said the angel, The desolations of Zion are accomplished -- the scattering time is past. Should the living go to the dead for knowledge? The dead know not anything. They have departed from the living God to converse with the dead. I saw that our minds must be stayed upon God, and we must not fear the fear of the wicked. Evil angels are around us trying to invent a new way to destroy us. The Lord would lift up a standard against him (the devil). We must take the shield of faith.

Washington, N. H., September, 1852.

You are getting the coming of the Lord too far off. I saw the latter rain was coming as [suddenly as] the midnight cry, and with ten times the power.

Chapter 2—Praying for the Sick

The Need of Instruction on Health Principles

During my sickness I have thought much in reference to praying for the sick, and I believe that if prayer should be offered for the sick at any place (and it certainly should), it should be offered at the Sanitarium for the relief and restoration of the suffering.

But in this matter of praying for the sick, I should not move in exactly the same lines as have my brethren. I have been considering many things that have been presented to me in the past in reference to this subject. Suppose that twenty men and women should present themselves as subjects of prayer at some of our camp-meetings. This would not be unlikely, for those who are suffering will do anything in their power to obtain relief and to regain their health. Of these twenty, few have regarded the light on the subject of purity and health reform. They have neglected to practice right principles in eating and drinking, and in taking care of their bodies: and those who are married have formed gross habits, and indulged in unholy practices, while those who are unmarried have been reckless of life and health. In clear rays the light has shone upon them; but they have not had respect to the light, nor have they walked circumspectly; yet they solicit the prayers of God's people, and call for the elders of the church. Should they regain the blessing of health, many of them would pursue the same course of heedless transgression of nature's laws, unless enlightened and thoroughly transformed.

They solicit the prayers of God's people, and call for the elders, of the church; but little is known of their private life. Sin has brought many of them where they are, to a state of feebleness of mind and debility of body. Shall prayer be offered to the God of heaven for His healing power to come upon them then and there, without specifying any conditions? I say No! decidedly no!

What then shall be done? Present their cases before Him who knows every individual by name. Present their cases to Him who so loved the world that He gave His only begotten Son, that whosoever believeth in Him should not perish but have everlasting life. Present these thoughts to the persons who come asking for your prayers. We are human, we can not read the mind or heart or know the secrets of your life. These are known only to yourself and God. If you now repent of your sin, if you can see that in any instance you have walked contrary to the light given you of God, and have neglected to give honor to the body, the temple of God, and by wrong habits have degraded the body which is Christ's property, make confession of these things to God.

Unless you are wrought upon by the Spirit of God in a special manner to confess your sins of a private nature to man, do not breathe them to any human soul. Christ is your Redeemer, He will take no advantage of your humiliating confessions. If you have a sin of a private character, confess it to Christ, who is the only Mediator between God and man. "If any man sin, we have an advocate with the Father, Jesus Christ the righteous." If you have sinned by withholding from God His own in tithes and offerings, confess your guilt to God and to the church, and heed the injunction that has been given you, "Bring ye all the tithes into the storehouse, that there may be meat in my house, and prove me now herewith, saith the Lord of Hosts, if I will not open you the windows of heaven, and pour you out a blessing, that there shall not be room enough to receive it."

Praying for the sick is a most solemn thing, and we should not enter upon this work in any careless, hasty way. Examination should be made as to whether those who would be blessed with health have indulged in evil speaking, alienation, and dissension. Have they sowed discord among the brethren and sisters in the church? If these things have been committed, they should be confessed, before God and the church. When wrongs have been confessed, the subjects for prayer may be presented before God in earnestness and faith, as the Spirit of God may move upon you.

But it is not always safe to ask for (un?) conditional healing. Let your prayer include this thought, "Lord, Thou knowest every secret of the soul. Thou art acquainted with these persons, for Jesus their advocate gave His life for them. He loved them better than we possibly can. If therefore it is for Thy glory, and the good of these afflicted ones to raise them up to health, we ask in the name of Jesus, that health may be given them at this time."

In a petition of this kind, no lack of faith is manifested. There are cases that are clear, and the Lord works with His divine power in their restoration. The will of God is evidenced too plainly to be misunderstood. The Lord does not afflict willingly nor grieve the children of men. Like as a father pitieth his children, so the Lord pitieth them that fear Him. For He knoweth our frame, He remembereth what we are dust. He knoweth our hearts, for He reads every secret of the soul. He knows whether or not those for whom petitions are offered would be able to endure the trial and test that would come upon them if they lived. He knows the end from the beginning.

Many will be laid away to sleep in Jesus before the fiery ordeal of the time of trouble shall come upon our world. This is another reason why we should say after our earnest petition, "Nevertheless, not my will, but Thine, O Lord, be done." Such a petition will never be registered in heaven as a faithless prayer. The Apostle was bidden to write: "Blessed are the dead which die in the Lord from henceforth; Yea saith the Spirit, that they may rest from their labors; and their works do follow them." From this we can see that every one is not to be judged as unworthy of eternal life. If Jesus, the world's Redeemer, prayed, "O My Father, if it be possible, let this cup pass from me," and then added, "Nevertheless not as I will, but as Thou wilt," how very appropriate is it for poor, infinite mortals to make surrender to the wisdom and will of God.

In praying for the sick, we are to pray that if it be God's will, they may be raised up, but if not, that He will give them His grace to comfort, His presence to sustain them in their suffering. Many who should set their house in order, neglect to do it when they have hope that they will be raised to health in answer to prayer. Buoyed up by a false hope, they do not feel the need of saying words of exhortation to their children, parents, or friends, and it is a great misfortune. Accepting the assurance that they should be healed when prayed for, they dare not make a reference as to how their property should be disposed of, how their family is to be cared for, or express any wish concerning their matters of which they would speak if they thought they should be removed by death. In this way disasters are brought upon the family and friends. For many things are left unmentioned, because they fear expressions on these points would be a denial of their faith that should be understood. Believing that they will be raised to health by prayer, they fail to make use of hygienic measures that are in their power to use, fearing that it would be a denial of their faith. I thank the Lord that it is our privilege to cooperate with Him in the work of restoration, availing ourselves of all possible advantages in the recovery of health. It is no denial of our faith to place ourselves in the condition most favorable to recovery.

The use of drugs has not been specified as in the Lord's order, but He has given special light concerning our health institutions, directing His people to practice and cultivate hygienic principles. Such should be taught those who are in ignorance as to how to live in accordance with pure principles, practicing those things that will preserve the body in a healthful condition. Man is to cooperate with God-given ability. He is not to be ignorant as to what are right practices in eating and drinking, and in all his habits of life. The Lord designs that His human agents shall act as rational, accountable beings in every respect.

But though light upon this matter has been shining upon the pathway of our people for nearly thirty years, yet a large number are far behind the light. Our churches are ignorant of hygienic principles and practices. We ought to be far advanced in wisdom, understanding what the will of the Lord is. We ought to know how to keep our minds pure and our bodies in a healthful condition.

But though we have sinned, we may come to Christ in penitence, and find pardon. We can not afford to neglect one ray of light God has given. To be sluggish in the practice of those things which require diligence, is to commit sin. The human agent is to cooperate with God, and keep under those passions which should be in subjection. To do this he must be unwearied in his prayers to God, ever obtaining grace to control his spirit, temper, and actions.

Ellen G. White - July 5, 1892

Chapter 3—The Bible in the Public Schools

Battle Creek, Michigan, May 17, 1893.

Dear Will:--I received a Testimony from Sister White today, and I copy the following and send to you:--

Elder A. T. Jones,

Dear Brother: There is a subject which greatly troubles my mind: While I do not see the justice nor light in enforcing by law the bringing the Bible to be read in the public schools, yet there are some things which burden my mind in regard to our people making prominent their ideas on this point.

These things, I am sure, will place us in a wrong light before the world. Cautions were given me as to this point. There were some things shown me in reference to the words of Christ "Render therefore unto Caesar the things that are Caesar's and unto God the things which are God's" -- placing the matter where the church would have no right to enforce anything of a religious character upon the world. Yet in connection with this were given words of caution. If such a law should go into effect, the Lord would overrule it for good; that an argument should be placed in the hands of those who keep the Sabbath, in their favor, to stand on the Bible foundation in reference to the Sabbath of the fourth commandment; and the book which the State and Christian world have forced upon the notice of the people to be read in the schools, shall it not speak, and shall not the words be interpreted just as they read?

My brother, this objecting to the passing of a law to bring the Bible into the schools will work against us, those of our faith who are making so much of the Bible. A year ago there was something presented before me in reference to those things, and we shall have to use the Bible for our evidence to show the foundation of our faith. We should be exceedingly cautious in every particular lest we shut out a single ray of the light from those who are in darkness.

I remember particularly this point: That anything that should give the knowledge of God and Jesus Christ whom He hath sent, should not be obstructed at all. Some things I can not present in distinct lines, but enough is clear to me that I want you to be very careful on what ground you tread; for our enemies will make a decided argument against us, if we shall give them a semblance of a chance.

I think the law-making powers will carry their point in this particular; if not now, a short period ahead. And it is very essential that as a people in a future crisis we take the greatest care that no provocation shall be given our enemies which they will make capital of against us as a people, in the matter of opposing so good a work as the introduction of the Bible into the public schools.

I wish I could lay my hand on something I wrote on this point at the last General Conference that I attended. But I can not bring it to light. I hope that the Lord will help us not to make a wrong move; but please be cautious on this point."

Ellen G. White.

Chapter 4—Domestic Education

Bismark, Tasmania, April 22, 1895.

Dear Brother Olsen:--

I have written largely with reference to students spending an unreasonably long time in gaining an education; but I hope I shall not be misunderstood in regard to what is essential education. I do not mean that a superficial work should be done, that may be illustrated by the way in which some portions of the land are worked in Australia. The plow was put into the soil to the depth of only a few inches, the ground was not prepared for the seed, and the harvest was meager, corresponding to the superficial preparation that was given to the land.

God has given inquiring minds to youth and children. Their reasoning powers are entrusted to them as precious talents. It is the duty of parents to keep the matter of their education before them in its true meaning: for it comprehends many lines. They should be used in the service of Christ for the uplifting of fallen humanity. Our schools are the Lord's special instrumentality to fit up the children and the youth for missionary work. Parents should understand their responsibility, and help their children to appreciate the great blessings and privileges that God has provided for them in educational advantages.

But their domestic education should keep pace with their education in literary lines. In childhood and youth, practical and literary training should be combined, and the mind stored with knowledge. Parents should feel that they have solemn work to do, and should take hold of it earnestly. They are to train and mold the characters of their children. They should not be satisfied with doing a surface work. Before every child is opened up a life involved with highest interests; for they are to be made complete in Christ through the instrumentalities which God has furnished. The soil in the heart should be preoccupied, the seeds of truth should be sown there in the earliest years. If parents are careless in this matter, they will be called to account for their unfaithful stewardship. Children should be dealt with tenderly and lovingly, and taught that Christ is their personal Saviour, and that by the simple process of giving their hearts and minds to Him, they become His disciples.

Children should be taught to have a part in domestic duties. They should be instructed how to help father and mother in little things that they can do. Their minds should be trained to think, their memories tasked to remember their appointed work, and in the training to habits of usefulness in the home, they are being educated in doing practical duties appropriate to their age. If children have proper home training, they will not be found upon the streets receiving the haphazard education that so many do. Parents who love their children in a sensible way will not permit them to grow up with lazy habits, and ignorant of how to do home duties. Ignorance is not acceptable to God, and is unfavorable for the doing of His work. To be is not to be considered a mark of humility, or something for which men should be praised. But God works for His people in spite of their ignorance. Those who have had no opportunity for acquiring knowledge (or who have had opportunity and have failed to improve it), and become converted to God, can be useful in the service of the Lord through the operation of His Holy Spirit. But those who have education, and who consecrate themselves to the service of God, can do service in a greater variety of ways and can accomplish a much more extensive work in bringing souls to the knowledge of the truth than can those who who are uneducated. They are on vantage ground, because of the discipline of mind which they have had.

We should not depreciate education in the least; but would counsel that it be carried forward with a full sense of the shortness of time and the great work that has to be accomplished before the coming of Christ. We would not have the students receive the idea that they can spend many years in acquiring an education. Let them use the education that they can acquire in a reasonable time in carrying forward the work of God. ...

Ellen G. White

Chapter 5—Authors and Subjects in Our Schools

Granville, N.S.W., June 12, 1895.

I have some matter which I wish to present before you in regard to education. The teachers in our schools have great respect for authors and books that are current in most of our educational institutions. All heaven has been looking upon our institutions of learning, and asking you what is the chaff to the wheat. The Lord has given us the most precious instructions in His Word, teaching us what characters we must form in this life to prepare us for the future immortal life. It has been the custom to exalt books and authors that do not present the proper foundation for true education. From what source did these authors obtain their wisdom, a large share of which does not deserve our respect, even if the authors are regarded as being wise men? Have they taken their lessons from the greatest Teacher that the world ever knew? If not, they are decidedly in the fault. Those who are preparing for the heavenly abodes should be recommended to make the Bible the chief book of their study.

These popular authors have not pointed out to the students the way that leads to eternal life. "For this is life eternal, that they might know Thee the only true God, and Jesus Christ, whom thou has sent." John 17:3. The authors of these books current in our schools are recommended and exalted as learned men; their education is in every way deficient, unless they themselves have been educated in the school of Christ, and by practical knowledge bear witness to the Word of God as the most essential study for children and youth. "The fear of the Lord is the beginning of wisdom." Books should have been prepared to place in the hands of students that would educate them to have a sincere reverent love for truth and steadfast integrity. The class of studies which are positively essential in the formation of character to give them a preparation for the future life, should be kept ever before them. Christ should be uplifted as the first great Teacher, the only begotten Son of God, who was with the Father from eternal ages. ...

The prophecies are to be studied and the life of Christ compared with the writings of the prophets. He identifies Himself with the prophecies, stating over and over again, They wrote of me; they testify of me. The Bible is the only book giving a positive description of Christ Jesus, and if every human being would study it as his lesson book and obey it, not a soul would be lost.

All the rays of light shining in the Scriptures point to Jesus Christ, and testify of Him, linking together the Old and the New Testament Scriptures. Christ is presented as the Author and Finisher of their faith, Himself the one in whom their hopes of eternal life are centered. "For God so loved the world that he gave his only begotten Son, that whosoever believeth in Him should not perish, but have everlasting life."

What book can begin to compare with the Bible? It is essential, for every child, for youth, and for those of mature age to understand, for it is the Word of God, the Word to guide all the human family to heaven. Then why does not the Word from God contain the chief elements which constitute education? Uninspired authors are placed in the hands of children and youth in our schools as a lesson book - books from which they are to be educated. They are kept before the youth, taking up their precious time in studying those things which they can never use. Many books have been introduced into the schools which should never have been placed there. These books do not in any sense voice the words of John, "Behold the Lamb of God that taketh away the sin of the world." The whole line of studies in our schools should be to prepare the people for the future immortal life. ...

How necessary that this mine of truth be explored, and the precious treasures of truth be discovered and secured as rich jewels. The incarnation of Christ His divinity, His atonement, His wonderful life in heaven as our Advocate, the office of the Holy Spirit, all these living, vital themes of Christianity are revealed from Genesis to Revelation. The golden links of truth form a chain of evangelical truth, and the first and staple link is found in the great teachings of Christ Jesus. Why then should not the Scriptures be ennobled and exalted in every school in our Land? ...

The doctrines of grace and truth are not really understood by the larger number of our students and church members. Blindness of mind has happened to Israel. For human agents to misconstrue and put a forced, half-truthful, and mystical construction upon the oracles of God, is an act which endangers their own souls, and the souls of others. ...

How many can truthfully answer this question, What is the essential education for this time? Education means much more than many suppose. True education embraces physical, mental, and moral training, in order that all the powers shall be fitted for the best development to do service for God, and to work for the uplifting of humanity. To seek for self-recognition, for self-glorification, will leave the human agent destitute of the Spirit of God, destitute of that grace which will make him a useful, efficient worker for Christ. Those who desire only to glorify God will not be striving to bring their supposed merits into notice, or striving for recognition or for the highest place. They that hear the call of the world's Redeemer, and obey that call, will be recognized as a distinct, self-sacrificing, holy people. ...

The youth are in need of educators who shall keep the Word of God ever before them in living principles. If they will keep Bible precepts ever as their text-book, they will have greater influence over the youth: for the teachers will be learners, having a living touch with God. All the time they are inculcating ideas and principles that will lead to a greater knowledge of God, and earnest growing faith in their behalf in the blood of Jesus, and the power and efficacy of the grace of our Lord Jesus Christ to keep them from falling; because they are constantly seeking the strongholds of a healthful and well-balanced Christian experience, carrying with them qualifications for future usefulness, and intelligence, and piety. The teachers see and feel that they must labor not to dwarf and taint the minds of their associates with a sickly, half-religious service. There is need of separating from our educational institutions an erroneous, polluted literature, so that ideas will not be received as seeds of sin. Let none suppose that education means a study of books that will lead to the reception of ideas of authors, that will sow seed and spring up to bear fruit that must be bound up in bundles with the world. Separating them from the source of all wisdom, all efficiency, and all power, leaving them the sport of Satan's arch-deceiving power. A sure seduction for youth in our schools, undiluted with heathen philosophy, is a positive necessity in literary lines. ...

Ellen G. White

Chapter 6—Battle Creek and the Southern Field

Norfolk Villa, Granville, July 24, 1895.

To my Brethren in Responsible Positions in America:

I am deeply concerned in regard to the disregard of warning and appeals that have been made by the Spirit of God through the humble instrument. Much time is devoted to large gatherings for the instruction of those who know the truth, when, if these very ones would with contrition of heart forsake their selfishness, and go earnestly, prayerfully to work to communicate light to those who are in spiritual darkness, they would receive strength far superior to anything they can obtain through spending so much money and labor for themselves. They have the benefits of the campmeetings and many other opportunities for instruction. If these do not accomplish the work for them, large, expensive institutes will not accomplish it. The time thus spent by those in attendance might better be employed in going into some of the dark, unworked fields, and proclaiming the truth to those who are ready to perish.

The money spent in enlarging the institutions in Battle Creek might far better be devoted to planting the truth in cities and places where it has not yet taken hold. Money has been entrusted to human agents, to be invested in the Lord's work, put out to the exchangers and increased with use. Again and again the men in positions of trust have had laid before them the necessity of the Lord's vineyard's being more equally worked. The vineyard is the world, every part of it is the Lord's, and it should receive due attention. No one locality is to swallow up every resource that can be obtained to enrich and magnify and multiply its facilities, while the largest portions of the field are left destitute. This policy is not inspired of God. The gracious calls of mercy are to be given to all parts of the world. God's field is the world. ...

In the parable of the good Samaritan, the priest and the Levite looked on the wretched man who had been robbed and wounded but it did not seem to them desirable for them to help the one who most needed help because he was helpless and forsaken. That priest and Levite represent many, many in Battle Creek. ... The Lord has presented to me the fact that thousands of souls are longing for something better than they have. Many can be saved if the Southern field can have simply a small part of the means expended so lavishly in Battle Creek, to make things more convenient. ... The Lord's heritage has been strangely neglected, and God will judge His people for this thing. Pride and the love of display are gratified by the accumulated advantages while new fields are left untouched. The rebuke of God is upon the managers for their partiality and selfish appropriation of His goods.

Something has been done in foreign missions, and something in home missions; but altogether too much territory has been left unworked. The work is too much centralized. The interests in Battle Creek are overgrown, and this means that other portions of the field are robbed of facilities which they should have had. The larger and still larger preparations, in the erection and enlargement of buildings, which have called together and hold so large a number in Battle Creek, are not in accordance with God's plan, but in direct contravention of His plan. It has been urged that there were great advantages in having so many institutions in close connection; that they could be a strength to one another, and could afford help to those seeking education and employment. This is according to human reasoning. It will be admitted that from a human point of view, many advantages are gained by crowding so many [responsibilities in Battle Creek; but the vision needs to be extended. These interests should be broken up into many] parts, in order that the work may start in cities which it will be necessary to make centers of interest. Buildings should be erected and responsibilities centered in many localities that are now robbed of vital, spiritual interest in order to swell the overplus already in Battle Creek. The Lord is not glorified by this management on the part of those who are in responsible positions. "The earth shall be full of the knowledge of the glory of God, as the waters cover the sea." "For this is life eternal, that they might know thee, the only true God, and Jesus Christ whom Thou hast sent."

The salvation of the heathen has long been deemed a matter that should engage the interests of Christians; and it is no more than justice to bring light to their dark borders; but home missionary work is just as much needed. The heathen are brought to our very shores. Idolatrous ignorance is in the very shadow of our homes. Something is being done for the colored people, but next to nothing compared to others receive who have a knowledge of the truth, who have had opportunities innumerable, but who have not half appreciated their advantages. To those who know not the truth, let the love of Jesus be presented, and it will work like leaven for the transformation of character.

What are we doing for the Southern field? I have looked most anxiously to see if some plan would not be set in operation to redeem the sinful neglect of that field, but I see not a proposition or a resolution to do anything. Perhaps something has been planned that I have not seen. I hope so, and praise the Lord if it is so. But though for years our duty has been laid out in a most decided manner, yet the Southern field has been only touched with the tip ends of our fingers. I now feel deeply in earnest in again bringing before you this neglected portion of the Lord's vineyard. The matter is brought before me again and again. I have been awakened in the night season, and the command has come, "Write the things I have opened before you, whether men will hear, or whether they will forbear."

Men and women are sent to far-off lands, to labor at great expense, and often at the sacrifice of their lives for heathen savages; but here are heathen at our very doors. The nation of slaves who are treated as though they had no souls, but were under the control of their masters, were emancipated at immense cost of life on both sides, the North seeking to restrict, the South to perpetuate and extend slavery. If, after the war, the Northern people had made the South a real missionary field, if they had not left the negroes to ruin through poverty and neglect, thousands of souls would have been brought to Christ. But it was an unpromising field, and the Catholics have been more active in it than any other class.

Will our brethren explain what their course means? Will the men in charge of the work of God sense their neglect? Will the people in Battle Creek show how much zeal, how much true missionary spirit they have received? With the great privileges you have had to learn line upon line and precept upon precept. With precious outpouring of the Spirit of God, what lessons have you learned? How much self-denial will our institutions manifest in binding about their imaginary wants? Will they continue to spread themselves, and strive to obtain more and still more conveniences for their accommodation, while the means to be expended for the down-trodden colored race is so little and meager? Here are your neighbors, poor, beaten, oppressed: thousands of human beings suffering for want of educational advantages; many, so many who need to hear the gospel preached in its purity.

I appeal to families who understand the truth. What are you doing? You can be God's ministers, taking up the work in this neglected field that needs to be plowed and to be sowed with the gospel seed of truth. Who for Christ's sake will give themselves to this work? You could have had missionaries in this hard field many years ago. God has called upon you to go labor in His vineyard, but the most miserable, unpromising portions of the vineyard have been passed by. Human beings, who are the Lord's by creation and by redemption, have been left for wolves to devour, while you have lived at ease, eating from the abundant supply which God gave you to share with those in need.

In the past some attempts have been made to present the truth to the colored people, but those among the white people who claim to believe the truth have wanted to build a high partition between themselves and the colored race. We have one Saviour, who has died for the black man as well as for the white man, and those who possess the Spirit of Christ will have love and pity for all who know not the precious Saviour. They will labor to the utmost of their ability to wipe away the reproach of ignorance from white and black alike.

From the light God has given me, the blood of souls will surely be found upon the garments of those who, like the priest and Levite, are passing by on the other side. This is just what our people are doing. They have been eating of the large loaf, and left the suffering, distressed people of the Southern regions starving for education, starving for spiritual advantages. While feeding from a well supplied table, they have not allowed even the crumbs that fall from the table to be bestowed upon the colored people. By their action they have said, Am I my brother's keeper? Where are those who have had so much light, so much food, that they have lost their appetite, and do not appreciate the bread of life? These rich treasures, if imparted to others, would give life and hope and salvation to them.

It is not merely the white people in the Southern field that are to receive the message of truth. Methods and plans must be devised to reach the colored people. Divine illumination must come to them. This kind of work calls for laborers, and the duty rests upon our responsible men to set men to work in that field, and to sustain the work with a portion of the means supplied by tithes and offerings, from the believers in all parts of our world. The Bible, the precious Bible, is not to be chained to any one place. It is to go to all parts of our world; its sacred truth is to be everywhere studied.

You can not send laborers into the Southern field, and merely say to one, You may work there, or to another, You may work there. Facilities must be provided, and workmen sent who can plan for these states. I beseech you, brethren, do not take the work out of the hands of those who would work every chance they may have, to obtain means to work in the Southern field. It is not your privilege to grasp every title to dispose of as you see fit. God has been teaching me, and I will not rest, I dare not hold my peace. I urge you to supply the people of this long-neglected field with food out of your abundance.

God will not commend selfishness in your planning and managing. Do not act as though you feared some other one of his instrumentalities would have a few crumbs from God's table. Those who are struggling with all their might to do a work for the most depressed and discouraging class of people, need encouragement. If men or women have entrusted talents, and use these talents to advance the work of God, regarding their Lord's money as a sacred trust, to use to His glory, they are doing a work that God approves. Those who are converted in the South will work with their own families, with their relatives, with their friends, and so we may hope for increase from the seed sown. If you should send many laborers to the most destitute part of this vineyard, and yet tie their hands by neglecting to furnish them with necessary means, for any real work of uplifting, do you think this would please God. Are not the ways of the Lord equal? Shall Battle Creek be supplied with every facility, and thousands of dollars be spent in making things a little more convenient?

Your already abundant facilities in Battle Creek, your buildings, your large wages, will witness against you in that day when everyone shall be judged according to the deeds done in the body. The managers of the College and publishing house will not look with such proud satisfaction on their wide-spreading advantages, when God shall make inquiry in regard to the souls they have left without regard, without labor, without light. Those whom you might have helped to receive the truth, would in their turn have labored to help others that are in darkness. Do not continue to dishonor God by your indolence, your neglect, by passing by on the other side.

The colored people might have been helped with much better prospects of success years ago than now. The work is now ten-fold harder than it would have been then. But do not, I beseech you, look upon the hard field, groan a little, set two or three at work in one locality, and a few in another, providing them only enough for the bare necessities of life. Those who labor in the Southern field will have to stand amid the most discouraging, hopeless poverty, and they need encouragement and help. They see the needs of the work, and from the abundant supply in Battle Creek means should be furnished them to supply the people with advantages they can not otherwise obtain.

Men of ability are willing to work for a meager sum, two or three dollars a week, to sustain their families. They have souls as precious as those of the men who, because of their selfishness and covetousness, have received thirty dollars a week. Will those who have an abundance put their hands into their pockets, and out of their plentiful supply impart something to furnish their neighbors with facilities? Will they make provision to help men to do the work they can do for a few dollars a week? Most earnest work should have been done many years ago. There might have been an altogether different presentation from what we now see.

God's means are not to be abundantly bestowed on a few privileged ones, so that they shall become exalted in pride, spreading themselves like a green bay tree, while the most needy, suffering ones are left without succor. Let not those who are in positions of responsibility rest satisfied with saying to the needy, Be ye warmed and clothed and fed, doing nothing to relieve the temporal and spiritual necessities of the suffering ones.

The reproach of indolence will never be wiped away from the church till every one who believes the truth shall be willing to labor as did our self-sacrificing Redeemer. Christ can not pronounce those good and faithful servants who have had the greatest advantages, the richest blessings, and yet have allowed a nation of helpless, dependent beings to remain degraded and unenlightened. Brethren, when you seek to help the ones who need education, that they may read the Word of God, when you say to every man, from the least to the greatest, Know the Lord, know Him for yourself, then your reproach will be wiped away. The Spirit of God will bless the means employed, even now. ...

Suppose that our people should practice the self-denial and love for souls that Jesus manifested while here on earth. Suppose that they should make the experiment of bearing much fruit to the glory of God, instead of studying how to absorb all the profits of the institutions (which were established in poverty), in enlarging and enriching themselves. Suppose that they should regard these institutions as God's instrumentalities, and provide facilities whereby destitute places should be provided with meeting places, and, in a limited degree, with the advantages that are so abundant in Battle Creek. Would not such a course be attended by the blessing of God, whose means they are handling? Would it not be far safer to experiment in right doing than in selfishly grasping so much where there is no real need, which means robbery and want to other fields.

The colored people have been neglected because the vexed question of how to build a wall of distinction between the whites and the blacks has been agitated. Some have thought it best to reach the white people first, for if we should labor for the colored people, we could do nothing for the white population. This is not the right position to assume. Christ's followers are to learn all about the woes of the poor in their immediate vicinity, and in their own country. The poor, friendless. Those who have a dark, disagreeable life are the very ones we should bid to hope because Christ is their Saviour. God has jewels in the rough, and his true followers will find them.

All who possess the Spirit of Christ will have a tender, sympathetic heart, and an open, generous hand. Nothing can be really selfish that has Christ for its absorbing object. True faith works by love, and purifies the soul from all moral defilement. It is a holy faith, superior to sensual delights. It is a power enabling the soul to apply itself resolutely to irksome tasks and self-sacrifice for the Master's sake.

Those who press close to the bleeding side of Christ will have the Spirit of Christ, and a nature that will be quickly responsive to his call. They will work to relieve the necessities of suffering humanity, as Christ worked before the world fallen, the worlds unfallen, and all the heavenly hosts, representing the way and works of God. In the life of Christ we see what a Christian can do in relieving distress, ministering to both physical and spiritual wants. Among the colored people, many, even of those who profess to be Christians, are sadly ignorant, not only of Bible doctrines, but of Christian principles. Their religion is mingled with earthliness and sensuality. Justice, mercy, and the Love of God, demand that those who have learned of Christ shall impart to others, the very ones in the greatest need. The light is to shine forth amid the corruptions that will be found in the Southern field.

It is not ordained ministers that are required for most of the labor in this field. Another minister will be just as effectual. Those who work here should have a thorough knowledge of the condition of the field. An occasional visit from a minister will accomplish but little unless there are those who can follow up and continue the work. Missionaries are needed through whom God can work in His own appointed way, according to their several ability. Missionaries are needed who are full of tender sympathy, who with hearts softened and subdued by the love of God, can talk and pray with the people, showing an interest in their welfare, and obtaining a knowledge of their home life and their religious life.

There is need of shepherds who, under the direction of the Chief Shepherd, will visit and present the truth in the simplicity of Christ. This means physical discomfort, and the sacrifice of ease. It means that the workers are to represent the Great Shepherd, leaving ninety and nine, and seeking for the stray sheep and lambs. It means a tender solicitude for the erring, the forbearance of Christ, a divine compassion, because the human agent is a partaker of the divine nature. It means an ear that can listen to heart-breaking recitals of wrongs, of degradation, of falling under temptation, of despair and misery. This kind of work means self-sacrifice. Is this why so little has been done for the negro race?

E. G. White.

Chapter 7—Sunday Labor And the Way to Oppose Error

On the morning of November 20, 1895, a council meeting was called at the large tent on the Avondale campground to consider some questions arising from the discussions of our brethren regarding the religious liberty work. The positions recently taken by some of our brethren indicated that there was a necessity for a more thorough understanding of the principles which must govern our work.

There were present Brethren W. W. Prescott, A. G. Daniells, W. C. White, H. C. Israel, L. J. Rousseau, W. A. Colcord, M. C. Kellogg, W. D. Salisbury, James Smith, and Sisters E. G. White and E. J. Burnham.

Several letters were read with reference to the questions at issue, then Sister White read a letter which she had written to Elder A. T. Jones in May, 1894, which had been unavoidably withheld until very recently.

In this letter reference was made to the necessity of our speakers presenting the truth in such a simple manner that even the small children could comprehend the lessons which it was designed to teach. Remarking on this, Sister White said: "According to the light which has been given to me, when the heavenly intelligences see that men will no longer present the truth in simplicity as did Jesus, the very children will be moved upon by the Spirit of God, and will go forth proclaiming the truth for this time."

The brethren were invited to discuss the points treated in the letters, but all were desirous of hearing further from Sister White, and she made the following remarks:--

"There is a terrible crisis just before us, through which all must pass, and especially will it come and be felt in ____. My mind has been much troubled over the positions which some of our brethren are liable to take in regard to the work to be done among the colored people in the Southern States. There is one point that I wish to lay before those who work in the Southern field. Among the colored people, they will have to labor in different lines from those followed in the North. They can not go to the South and present the real facts in reference to Sunday-keeping being the mark of the beast, and encourage the colored people to work on Sunday: for the same spirit that held the colored people in slavery is not dead, but alive today, and ready to spring into activity. The same spirit of oppression is still cherished in the minds of many of the white people of the South and will reveal itself in cruel deeds, which are the manifestation of their religious zeal. Some will oppose in every possible way any action which has a tendency to uplift the colored race, and teach them to be self-supporting.

"When the white people try to educate the colored people in the truth, jealousy is aroused, and ministers, both colored and white, will bitterly oppose the truth. The colored ministers think that they know how to preach to their own race better than the white ministers can, and they feel that the whites are taking the work out of their hands. By falsehood they will create the most decided opposition, and those among the white people who are opposed to the truth will help them and will make it exceedingly hard for the work of the message to advance.

"When the truth is proclaimed in the South, a marked difference will be shown by those who oppose the truth in their greater regard for Sunday, and great care must then be exercised not to do anything to arouse their prejudice. Otherwise, we may just as well leave the field entirely, for the workers will have all the white people against them. Those who oppose the truth will not work openly, but through secret organizations, and they will seek to hinder the work in every possible way. Our laborers must move in a quiet way, striving to do everything possible to present the truth to the people, remembering that the love of Christ will melt down opposition.

"From the light that I have received, I see that if we would get the truth before the Southern people, we must not encourage the colored people to work on Sunday. There must be a clear understanding regarding this, but it need not be published in our papers. Not a word should be spoken to create prejudice, for if by any careless or impulsive speech to the colored people in regard to the whites any prejudice is created in their minds against the whites, or in the minds of the white people against them the spirit of the enemy will work in the children of disobedience. Thus an opposition will be aroused which will hinder the work of the message, and will endanger the lives of the workers and of the believers.

"We are not to make efforts to teach the Southern people to work on Sunday. That which some of our brethren have written upon this point is not based upon right principles. When the practices of the people do not come into conflict with the law of God, you may conform to them. If the workers fail to do this, they will not only hinder their own work, but they will place stumbling blocks in the way of those for whom they labor, and hinder them from accepting the Truth. On Sunday there is the very best opportunity for those who are missionaries to hold Sunday schools, and come to the people in the simplest manner possible, telling them of the Love of Jesus for sinners, and educating them in the Scriptures. There are many ways of reaching all the classes, both dark or white. We are to interest them in the life of Christ from His childhood up to manhood, and through His life of ministry to the cross. We can not work in all localities in the same way. We must let the Holy Spirit guide; for men and women can not convince others of the wrong traits of character. While laboring to introduce the truth, we must accommodate ourselves as much as possible to the field, and the circumstances of those for whom we labor."

Question: Should not those in the Southern Field work on Sunday?

"If they do this, there is danger that as soon as the opposing element can get the slightest opportunity, they will stir up one another to persecute those who do this, and to pick off those whom they hate. At present Sunday-keeping is not the test. The time will come when men will not only forbid Sunday work, but they will try to force men to labor on the Sabbath. And men will be asked to renounce the Sabbath and to subscribe to Sunday observance or forfeit their freedom and their lives. But the time for this has not yet come, for the truth must be presented more fully before the people as a witness. What I have said about this should not be understood as referring to the action of old Sabbath-keepers who understand the truth. They must move as the Lord shall direct them, but let them consider that they can do the best missionary work on Sunday.

"Slavery will again be revived in the Southern States; for the spirit of slavery still lives. Therefore it will not do for those who labor among the colored people to preach the truth as boldly and openly as they would be free to do in other places. Even Christ clothed His lessons in figures and parables to avoid the opposition of the Pharisees. When the colored people feel that they have the Word of God in regard to the Sabbath question, and the sanction of those who have brought them the truth, some who are impulsive will take the opportunity to defy the Sunday laws, and by a presumptuous defiance of their oppressors they will bring to themselves much sorrow. Very faithfully the colored people must be instructed to be like Christ, to patiently suffer wrongs, that they may help their fellow men to see the light of truth.

"A terrible condition of things is certainly opening before us. According to the light which is given me in regard to the Southern Field, the work there must be done as wisely and carefully as possible, and it must be done in the manner in which Christ would work. The people will soon find out what you believe about Sunday and the Sabbath, for they will ask questions. Then you can tell them, but not in such a manner as to attract attention to your work. You need not cut short your work by yourself laboring on Sunday. It would be better to take that day to instruct others in regard to the love of Jesus and true conversion."

Question: Should the same principles govern our work and our attitude toward the Sunday question in foreign fields where the prejudices of the people are so strong?

"Yes, just the same. The light that I have is that God's servants should go quietly to work, preaching the grand, precious truths of the Bible--showing that the reason why Christ died is because the law of God is immutable, unchangeable, eternal. The Spirit of the Lord will awaken the conscience and the understanding of those with whom you work, bringing the commandments of God to their remembrance. I can hardly describe to you the way in which this has been presented to me. The Lord says in (Rev. 22:16): "I Jesus have sent mine angel to testify unto you these things in the churches." Have any of you seen this angel? The messengers from heaven are close beside those who stand before the people, holding forth the word of life. In preaching the truth, it is not always best to present those strong points of truth that will arouse prejudice, especially where such strong feelings exist as are felt in the Southern States. The Sabbath must be taught in a decided manner, but be cautious how you deal with the idol, Sunday. "A word to the wise is sufficient.""

"I have given you the light which has been presented to me. If followed, it will change the course of many, and will make them wise, cautious teachers. Refraining from work on Sunday is not receiving the mark of the beast: and where this will advance the interests of the work, it should be done. We should not go out of our way to work on Sunday.

"After the Sabbath has been sacredly observed, in places where the opposition is so strong as to arouse persecution if work is done on Sunday, let our brethren make that day an occasion to do genuine missionary work. Let them visit the sick and the poor, ministering to their wants, and they will find favorable opportunities to open the Scriptures to individuals and to families. Thus most profitable work can be done for the Master. When those who hear and see the light on the Sabbath take their stand upon the truth to keep God's holy day, difficulties will arise, for efforts will be brought to bear against them to compel men and women to transgress the law of God. Here they must stand firm, that they will not violate the law of God, and if the opposition and persecution is determinedly kept up, let them heed the words of Christ, "When they persecute you in one city, flee ye into another; for verily I say unto you, ye shall not have gone over the cities of Israel, till the Son of Man be come."

"The time has not yet come for us to work as though there were no prejudice. Christ said, "Be ye wise as serpents, and harmless as doves." If you see that by doing certain things which you have a perfect right to do, you hinder the work of the truth, refrain from doing those things. Do nothing that will close the minds of others against the truth. There is a world to save, and we gain nothing by cutting loose from those we are trying to help. All things may be lawful, but all things are not expedient. We have no right to do anything that will obstruct the light which is shining from heaven; yet by a wrong course of action we may imperil the work, and close the door which God has opened for the entrance of the Truth.

The final issue of the Sabbath question has not yet come, and by imprudent action we may bring on a crisis before the time. You may have all the truth, but you need not let it all flash at once upon minds, lest it become darkness to them. Even Christ said to His disciples, "I have many things to say unto you, but ye can not hear them now." We must not go into a place, open our satchel, show all we have, and tell everything we know at once. We must work cautiously, presenting the truth by degrees, as the hearers can bear it, and keeping close to the Lord. "The Waldensians entered the schools of the world as students. They made no pretensions. Apparently they paid no attention to any one; but, they lived out what they believed. They never sacrificed principle, and their principles put into practice soon became known to other students. This was different from anything the other students had ever seen, and they began to ask among themselves, what does this all mean? While they were considering this, they heard them praying in their rooms, not to the Virgin Mary but to the Saviour, whom they addressed as the only mediator between God and man. The worldly students were encouraged to make inquiries, and as the simple story of the truth as it is in Jesus was told, their minds grasped it.

"These things I tried to present at Harbor Heights. These who have the Spirit of God, who have the truth wrought into their very being, prudent men, wise in their methods of reaching others, should be encouraged to enter colleges, as students live the truth, as did Joseph in Egypt, and Daniel, and Paul. Each one should study the situation and see what is the best way to represent the truth in the school, that the light may shine forth. Let them show that they respect all the rules and regulations of the schools. The leaven will begin to work; for we can depend much more upon the power of God manifested in the lives of His children than upon any words that can be spoken. But they should also tell inquirers, in as simple language as they can, of the Bible doctrines.

"There are those who, after becoming established, rooted, and grounded in the truth, should enter these institutions of learning as students. They can keep the living principles of the truth, and observe the Sabbath, and yet they will have opportunity to work for the Master by dropping seeds of truth in minds and hearts. Under the influence of the Holy Spirit, those seeds will spring up to bear fruit for the glory of God, and will result in the saving of souls. The students need not go to these institutions of learning in order to become enlightened upon theological subjects; for, the teachers of the school need themselves to become Bible students. No open controversies should be entered into, but opportunity given for questions upon Bible doctrines, and light will be flashed into many minds, and a spirit of investigation will be aroused.

"But I scarcely dare present this method of labor; for there is danger that those who have no decided connection with God will place themselves in these schools, and instead of correcting error and diffusing light, will themselves be led astray. But this work must be done; and it will be done by those who are led and taught of God.

"Jesus was a teacher when He was but twelve years old. He went in before the rabbis and doctors of the law as a learner, asking questions that surprised the learned doctors, and showing eagerness to obtain information. By every question he poured light into their darkened minds. Had He allowed them to suspect that He was trying to teach them, they would have spurned Him. So it was all through His life. By His purity, His humility, His meekness, He rebuked sin. Those around Him could not find a single thing for which to blame Him, yet He was at work all the time. He worked in His own home until He had no home. His lot was no more pleasant than that of the young people who today are trying to walk in His footsteps.

"If all our people would work in Christ's way, what a blessing it would be. There are many ways in which to diffuse light, and a great work can be done in many lines that is not now done. "Let your light so shine before men, that they may see your good works, and glorify your Father which is in heaven." This spirit will inspire others to do the will of the Lord also, in earnest, self-sacrificing effort.

"This world is God's property. Wicked men are only permitted to live in it till they have filled up the cup of their iniquity. It was deeded to Abraham and His children, and ere long God's people shall take possession of it. In our work for the saving of souls, we must not think that we can receive help from those around us; by a close connection with Jesus, we must be in that place where we can help them. Advance truth! Give those with whom you may come in contact an opportunity to learn what is truth, and to become converted. But do not think that your light gives you license to make a raid on those who are in error.

"When we begin to work with parliaments, and with men holding high positions in governments, the enemy is aroused to exert all his strength against us, and he will make the work hard. Do not let your work be known any more than is necessary: the best course to follow is that which will avoid opposition. The least said about the foolish errors of others, the better. Do not speak disrespectfully of ministers. Satan and all his hosts are working to make of none effect the law of God and when we begin to work on controversial lines, he will lead men to believe that we do not regard their laws or obey their decrees. Believing this, they will make it as hard as possible for all who will not worship their idol Sunday.

"We are not to reveal all our purposes and plans to men. Satan will take advantage of any indiscretion shown on this point. He does not work openly and above-board. He works in an underhanded manner, and will continue to do so. Before the people are prepared for it, he leads men to set a powerful movement on foot by working on their minds.

Question: Can we not get the truth before the minds of the members of parliament in a quiet way, by furnishing them with reading matter?

"From the light that has been given me, I see that we should fear lest rulers take their position against our work. If they do this, they will act like the enemy of all good. Every opportunity to become acquainted with these men should be embraced: but we should do nothing that will produce anything like prejudice. It means a great deal to be as wise as serpents and as harmless as doves. We have so much determination in us that often we do things unguardedly and rashly. We must appear before these men as trying to help others, working on the lines of the Christian help work. As they see the good work we do in these lines, their prejudice in a measure will be removed; their hearts will be opened to the truth. Do not present the Sabbath abruptly: present Christ. Should they begin to oppose you, saying, "Oh, he is a Seventh-day Adventist,'lift up Christ higher, and still higher."

Question: Would it not be as well for us to present principles, rather than to dwell upon what the government will do?

"We should have nothing to do with the actions of the government. Our duty is to obey God. When you are arrested, take no thought what you shall say or do. You are to follow Christ step by step. You need not commence weeks beforehand to examine the question and lay plans as to what you will do when the powers shall do this or that, neither need you think what you are to say. Study the truth, and the Spirit of the Lord will bring to your remembrance what you shall say. Our minds should be a treasure house, filled with the Word of God.

"When the enemy begins to work, we need not allow our feelings to control, and resort to strange fire. We need not become combative. By doing this, we may thus betray the cause at the very point where victory is ours. If we let go our hold of Jesus, and trust in ourselves, it may take months, or perhaps years, to counteract that one wrong move. Unless we are converted, and become as little children, we shall never see the kingdom of God. These are the lessons we need to bring into our schools. The students do not need science as much as they need these principles. Teach them how to advance the truth as it is in Jesus.

"The world is not to be condemned until after it has had the light. We must tell people the simple story of the cross. They are to be pitied, and just as much as possible we must soften the message we bring to them. This will soften their hearts, so that the Spirit of the Lord can mold them. In all their past life they have been receiving false ideas. If we come close to them, and tell them of the love of Christ, we can do much for them."

Question: Is it wrong for our brethren to work out their fines?

"Christ, the King of Glory, carried the cross upon which He was about to be crucified. The people had not the slightest semblance of right to inflict this upon Him, but He did not refuse to submit. Christ suffered and died for us. Shall we refuse to be partaker of His sufferings? Let the servants pay tribute as the Master did, lest others be offended.

"When brought before courts, we are to give up our rights, unless by so doing we are brought into collision with God. We are not pleading for our right, but for God's right to our service. Instead of resisting the penalties imposed unjustly upon us, it would be better to take heed to the Saviour's word, 'When they persecute you in this city, flee ye into another: for verily I say into you, Ye shall not have gone over the cities of Israel, till the Son of Man be come.'"

Mrs. E. G. White

Chapter 8—Methods of Work in the Southern Field

Armadale, Melbourne, Victoria, Nov. 20, 1895.

Elder A. O. Tait,

Battle Creek, Michigan, U. S. A.

Dear Brother.--

This morning I attended a meeting where a select few were called together to consider some questions that were presented to them by letter, soliciting consideration and advice on these subjects. Of some of these things I could speak, because at sundry times and in diverse places many things have been presented to me in reference to some matters of labor that required great caution in speech as well as in the expression of thoughts with the pen. The advice given to our brethren in the Southern field has been diverse. It would bring in confusion.

As my brethren read the selections from letters, I know what to say to them for this matter has been presented to me again and again in regard to the Southern field. I have not felt at liberty to write out the matter until now. I will endeavor to make some brief statements at this time, hoping soon to have an opportunity to speak more clearly and at length.

The light that the Lord has given me at different times has been, that the Southern field, where the greatest share of the population of the colored race is, can not be worked after the same methods as others fields. They are excitable, and outward actions in bodily exercise is wrought up to a high strain of fanaticism, and exercises are more to them than inward piety and compose their religion. Should the colored people in the Southern States be educated as they receive the truth, that they should work on Sunday there would be excited a most unreasonable and unjust prejudice. Judges and Jurors, lawyers and citizens, would if they had a chance, bring decisions which would bind about them rites which would cause much suffering, not only to the ones whom they term guilty of breaking the laws of their state, but all the colored people everywhere would be placed in a position of surveillance, and under cruel treatment of the white people, that would be no less than slavery. They have been treated as chattels, regarded as not much above the dumb animals, to do just as their masters told them to do. This has degraded all their powers, and different methods of labor altogether must be pursued toward them than where the colored people have had greater advantages of schooling, and have learned to read.

As the colored people have not been educated to read and have not been uplifted, their religion is more of bodily exercise than inward piety. There can not be anything like the kind of labor pursued toward them as that bestowed upon the people whose religion is not outward workings. The Lord will look upon this poor, neglected, downtrodden race with great compassion. Everything of a character to set them in a position of opposition to authorities, as working on Sunday, would cause the colored people great suffering, and cut off the possibility of white laborers going among them; for the workers that intended to do them good would be charged with raising insurrections.

I do not want anything of this character to appear, for I know the result. Tell them they need not provoke their neighbors by doing work on Sunday; that this will not prevent them from observing the Sabbath. The Sabbath should not be introduced until they know the first principles of the religion of Jesus Christ. The truth as it is in Jesus it to be made known little by little, line upon line, and precept upon precept.

Punishment for any offence would be visited unsparingly and unmercifully upon the colored people. Here it is a neglected field where medical missionary work can be one of the greatest blessings. In this line the truth may be introduced, but the very first principles of Christianity are to be taught in the A B C. The schools are to be established, having not only children, but fathers and mothers learning to read. Teaching the truth is involving great liabilities. It is essential, then, that there be families to settle in the South, and as missionary workers they can, by precept and example, be a living power. There can not be much preaching. The least notice possible should be given to the point of what is doing, and what is to be done: for it will create suspicion and jealousy in the minds of men, who, with their fathers and grandfathers, have been slaveholders. There has been so little done for the South that they are in moral degradation, and are looked upon as slaves to the white population still, although they have been emancipated at terrible cost.

We are to study the situation with great care: for the Lord is our enlightener. The Lord has given men capabilities to exercise, but there is too little deep thinking, and too little earnest praying that the Lord would give wisdom at all times, and show how to work difficult fields. We are under obligation to God, and if we love God, we are in duty bound, not only on the general ground of obligation and obedience to obey the orders of our Spiritual Leader, and to save as many souls as we can to present them as slaves to Jesus Christ, who gave Himself a living sacrifice to ransom them, and make them free servants of Jesus Christ. There is not to be one word uttered which would stir up the slumbering enmity and hatred of the slaves against discipline and order, or to present before them the injustice which has been done them. Nothing can be done at first in making the Sabbath question prominent, and if the colored people are in any way educated to work on Sunday, there will be unsparing, merciless oppression brought upon them. Already there has been too much printed in regard to the persecution of the Sabbath-keepers in the Southern States, and those who are bitter against the law of God, trampling it under their feet, are all the more earnest to make human laws a power. Their religious prejudice and bigotry would lead them to do any acts of violence, verily thinking they were doing God's service: for they are in great error. A blind zeal under false religious theories, is the most violent and merciless. There are many who are stirred up by the representations in our papers, to do just as their neighboring states are doing. All these things give them the appearance of defying the law. In Christ's day, when persecuted in one city, they fled to another. It may be the duty of those persecuted to avail themselves of finding refuge in another city or another country. (Matt. 10:22, 23) "And ye shall be hated of all men for my name's sake; but he that endureth to the end, shall be saved. But when they persecute you in this city, flee ye into another: for verily I say unto you, ye shall not have gone over the cities of Israel, till the Son of Man be come." "The disciples is not above his master, nor the servant above his lord."

At present, persecution is not general, but let the Southern element have word come to them of a nature to raise their excitable disposition, and the whole cause of truth would suffer, and the great missionary field be closed. Let all be warned. Let the instruction be given to this much oppressed class that the keeping of the Sabbath does not necessitate their working on Sunday: for, if they should do this, they would have instigated against them all the powers of the white population, who are transgressors of the law of God. Church members and priests and rulers will combine to organize secret societies to work in their hand to whip, imprison, and destroy the lives of the colored race. History will be repeated. Let efforts be made in as silent manner as possible, but this people need not be told that the observance of Sunday is the mark of the beast until this time shall come. If the Southern people get some of the ideas in their minds of the mark of the beast, they would misconstrue, and give honestly the most false impressions on these subjects, and do strange things. As many of the people can not read for themselves, there are plenty of professed leaders who will read the Bible falsely and make it testify to a lie. Many are working in this line among those who are poor scholars, and have not a knowledge of the Scripture. Our publications also will be misread. Things will be read out of the books that were never there, advocating the most objectionable things. An excitement could be easily worked up against the Seventh-day Adventists. The most successful methods are to encourage families who have a missionary spirit to settle in the Southern states and work with the people without making any noise.

In such places as the Southern field, there should be established sanitariums. There should be those who believe the truth, colored servants of God, under training to do work as medical missionaries, under the supervision of white managers: for this combination will be much more successful. The medical missionary workers, cooperating with families who shall make their home in the South, need not think that God will condemn them if they do not work on Sunday: for the Lord understands that every effort not to create prejudice, must be made if the truth finds standing place in the South. The words of truth can not go forth with great publicity, but schools should be started by families coming into the South, and working in schools, not with a large number congregated in one school, but, as far as possible, in connection with those who have been working in the South. Dwell particularly upon the love of God, the righteousness of Christ, and upon the treasure house of God, presenting the truth in clear lines upon personal piety. There will be bad influences of the white people upon the blacks as there has been in the past. Evil angels work with their own spirit upon evil men. Those cooperating with those who work in any place to uplift Jesus and to exalt the law of God, will find to all intents and purposes that they wrestle not against flesh and blood, but against principalities, against powers, against the rulers of the darkness of this world, and against spiritual wickedness in high places. "Wherefore, take unto you the whole armor of God, that ye may be able to withstand in the evil day, and having done all, to stand. Stand therefore, having your loins girt about with truth, and having on the breastplate of righteousness and your feet shod with the preparation of the gospel of peace; above all, taking the shield of faith, wherewith ye shall be able to quench all the fiery darts of the wicked. And take the helmet of salvation, and the sword of the spirit which is the Word of God." ...

(I would not advise that this be published in our papers, but let the workers have it in leaflets, and let them keep their own counsels.)

Ellen G. White

Chapter 9—Letter from W. W. Prescott

April 29, 1896

Prof. E. A. Sutherland,

College Place, Washington, U.S.A.

Dear Brother:--

Your letters of February 27th And March 20th both came by the last Vancouver mail and reached me last Thursday, just as I was closing up the work of our institute and preparing to go to Sydney to attend the sessions of the New South Wales Conference. I returned yesterday and took the first opportunity yesterday afternoon to have a talk with Sister White with reference to the matter of the degrees, as you requested.

I am in great haste this morning, as we are packing up to go to Sydney this afternoon, and we sail for Africa on Friday, but I am anxious to give you a reply before leaving the country, as you wish the information in planning future work.

Sister White says that she is not aware that she has ever written anything about the question of degrees, and in fact she seemed to know very little about their significance, and so she said she was quite sure that she had never written about them. She said, however, as she has said many times, before, that our schools should give a better class of education than the schools of the world, but that it should be of an entirely different character. I explained to her the significance of the degrees and the meaning which was attached to them and the general course of study which was implied by them in the eyes of other educators, and her idea seemed to be that there was no need that we should pay attention to those things, that what we wanted to do was to educate for usefulness here and the eternal kingdom hereafter, and that the question with our people was not whether a young man had a degree, but whether he had suitable preparation so that he could be a blessing to others in this work.

You ask me whether I would advise you to secure a charter so that you could grant degrees. For myself I should say, No. If I were in your place, I should want to feel perfectly free to arrange the work just as I thought would be best for the young people and for the work, without being bound by the idea that you must maintain a course of study so that you could consistently grant degrees.

If I had more time at my disposal now, I would write my views more fully, but I have but little time and many things to receive attention. I have not had time to examine your correspondence work, but shall do as soon as possible. I am interested in the plan. Excuse a hasty letter this time. White me when you can get time. With kind regards to all.

Yours faithfully in the work,

W. W. Prescott

Chapter 9.1—Diet for Workers and Sick

"Sunnyside," Cooranbong, July 10, 1896.

Dr. J. H. Kellogg,

Battle Creek, Michigan.

Dear Brother:--

... There are those associated with you that should ever have kept before them their aptness and inclination to use poisonous drugs, that kill if they do not cure. The light that God has given upon the subject of disease and its causes, needs to be dwelt upon largely for it is the wrong habit of indulgence of appetite and careless, reckless inattention to properly care for the body that tells upon the people. Habits of cleanliness, care in regard to that which is introduced into the mouth, should be observed.

You are to make no prescription that no flesh meats shall never be used, but you are to educate the mind, and let the light shine in. Let the individual conscience be awakened in regard to self-preservation and self-purity from every perverted appetite. The variety of food at one meal causes unpleasantness, and destroys the good which each article, if taken alone, would do the system. This practice causes constant suffering, and often death.

You have too little care and feel too lightly the burden of providing an orderly, ample repast for your workers. They are the ones who need an abundance of fresh, wholesome provision. They are constantly taxed: their vitality must be preserved. Their principles should be educated. They, of all in the Sanitarium should be abundantly furnished with the best and most wholesome strength-giving food. The table of your helpers should be furnished not with meat, but with an abundant supply of good fruit, grains, and vegetables, prepared in a nice, wholesome way. Your neglect to do this has increased your income at altogether an expense to the strength and souls of your workers. This has not pleased the Lord. The influence of the entire fare does not recommend your principles to those that sit at the helpers' tables. If they are worthy to compose your family, they are worthy of the very best and most strength-giving diet, that seeds may not be planted in their breasts which will germinate and bring forth a harvest to the dishonor of God. But this has been done: and this must have attention. Equality must be practiced as well as talked.

The God who gave His only begotten Son to die for the redemption of the sinful race, will not approve the management of the table for workers at the Sanitarium. The money saved by limiting the table supplies, by not providing fresh, wholesome food, and not taking pains to get a right preparation in food, but to provide odds and ends, is a loss. The ones who give the treatment and care for the sick are taxed in their labor, and must have greater privileges than have been given them, if their hearts are to be kept from temptation and corruption. This line of work has been neglected. Let the education be given line upon line, precept upon precept, that we all are servants. All work done is serving ministers of the gospel.

All the servants of God are to be respected, loved, cared for. There are servants who work in caring for the sick, who need to have vital force to do their work intelligently and thoroughly, and with good cheer in their hearts. All the time they are to feel that their labors are appreciated, and that they must be kind, cheerful, hopeful, full of faith, having words they can speak to poor suffering ones. ...

There are many things that need to be corrected and made wholesome and beautiful, so that the angels of God may not see preference for one and dishonor for another. Eating of the flesh of dead animals is deleterious to the health of the body, and all who use a meat diet are increasing their animal passions and are lessening the susceptibility of the soul to realize the force of truth and the necessity of its being brought into their practical life. This meat-eating question needs to be guarded. When one changes from the stimulating diet of meat-eating to the fruit and vegetable diet, there will always be a sense of weakness and a lack of vitality, and many urge this as an argument for the necessity of a meat diet. ...

The change should not be urged to be made too abruptly, especially for those who are taxed with continuous labor. Let the conscience be educated, the will energized, and the change can be made much more readily and willingly.

The consumptives who are going steadily down to the grave should not make particular changes in this respect, but care should be exercised to obtain the most of healthy animals (that) can be found.

Persons with tumors ruining their life away should not be burdened with the question as to whether they should leave meat eating or not. Be careful to make no stringent resolutions in regard to this matter. It will not help the case to force changes, but will do injury to the non-meat-eating principles. Give lectures in the parlor. Educate the mind, but force no one: for such reformation made under pressure is worthless, and they will surely go back to a meat-eating diet. Enlighten the mind, that God would be pleased to have the body free from disease. The greatest cause of disease is in the food taken into the system in large meat-eating. When you remove the meat from the table, you have a work to do to substitute articles of food tasteful and appetizing in fruits and grains. Meat will soon be forgotten in arousing the conscience and the determined will brought into action. There is to be no forcing the mind, but educating it to view the subject from a right standpoint.

There needs to be presented to all students and physicians, and by them to others, that the whole animal creation is more or less diseased. Diseased meat is not rare, but common. Every phase of disease is brought into the human system through subsisting upon the flesh of dead animals. That feebleness and weakness in consequence of change from meat diet will soon be overcome, and physicians ought to understand that they should not make the stimulus of meat-eating essential for health and strength. All who leave it alone intelligently will have, after becoming accustomed to the change, health of sinews and muscles. More again.

Ellen G. White

Chapter 10—Forwardness and Consolidation

Sunnyside, Cooranbong, N.S.W., May 31, 1896.

Elder O. A. Olsen,

Battle Creek, Michigan, U.S.A.

My dear Brother;--

Scenes that were a shame to Christians, have been presented to me, as taking place in the council meetings held after the Minneapolis meeting. The loud voice of dispute, the hot spirit, the harsh words, resembled a political meeting more than a place where Christians were met for prayer and counsel. These meetings should have been dismissed as an insult to heaven. The Lord was not revered as an honored guest by those assembled in council, and how could they expect divine light to shine upon them; how could they feel that the presence of Jesus was molding and fashioning their plans? The place of meeting was not held as sacred, but was looked upon as a common business place. Then how could those assembled receive an inspiration which would lead them to enthrone truth in their hearts, to speak words in the tender, loving spirit of the Master?

In your council meetings and committee meetings, decisions are made, plans devised and matured, which, when put into practice, leave an impression on the work at large; and no vestige of a spirit of harshness should appear. Loud, impatient words should never be heard. Remember that in all your council meetings there is a heavenly Watcher. Do not allow one word of vanity to be spoken: for you are legislating for God, and He says to you, "Be still, and know that I am God."

If your committee meetings and council meetings are not under the direct supervision of the spirit of God, your conclusions will be earth-born, and worthy of no more consideration than are any man's expressions. Christ says, "Without Me ye can do nothing." If He is not honored in your assemblies as chief Counsellor, your planning comes from no higher source than the human mind.

Brother Olsen, you speak of my return to America. For three years I stood in Battle Creek as a witness for the truth. Those who then refused to receive the testimony given me by God for them, and rejected the evidences attending these testimonies, would not be benefited should I return.

I shall write to you: but should I return to Battle Creek and bear my testimony to those who love not the truth, the ever ready words would rise from unbelieving hearts, "Somebody has told her." Even now unbelief is expressed by the words, "Who has written these things to Sister White?" But I know no one who knows them as they are, and no one could write that which he does not suppose has an existence. Some one has told me - He who does not falsify, misjudge, or exaggerate any case. While at Minneapolis He bade me follow Him from room to room that I might hear what was spoken in the bed chamber. The enemy had things very much his own way. I heard no word of prayer, but I heard my name mentioned in a slurring, criticising way.

I shall never, I think, be called to stand under the direction of the Holy Spirit as I stood at Minneapolis. The presence of Jesus was with me. All assembled in that meeting had an opportunity to place themselves on the side of truth by receiving the Holy Spirit which was sent by God in such a rich current of love and mercy. But in the rooms occupied by some of our people, we heard ridicule, criticism, jeering, laughter. The manifestations of the Holy Spirit were attributed to fanaticism. Who searched the Holy Scriptures as did the noble Bereans, to see if the things they heard were so? Who prayed for divine guidance? The scenes which took place at this meeting made the God of Heaven ashamed to call those who took part in them, His brethren. All this the heavenly Watcher noticed, and it is written in the book of God's remembrance.

The Lord will blot out the transgression of those who, since that time, have repented with a sincere repentance, but every time the same spirit wakens in the soul, the deeds done on that occasion are endorsed, and the doers of them are made responsible to God, and must answer for them at His judgment throne. The same spirit that actuated the rejectors of Christ, rankles in their hearts, and had they lived in the days of Christ, they would have acted toward Him in a manner similar to that of the godless and unbelieving Jews.

God's servants have no tame testimony to bear at this time, whether men will hear or whether they will forbear. He who rejects the light and evidence God has been liberally bestowing upon us, rejects Christ: and for him there is no other Saviour.

The Work at Battle Creek

The spirit of the Lord has outlined the condition of things at the Review and Herald Office. Speaking through Isaiah God says, "I will not contend forever, either will I be always wroth: for the spirit should fail before me, and the souls which I have made. For the iniquity of his covetousness was I wroth, and smote him: I hid me, and was wroth, and he went on frowardly in the way of his heart."

This is precisely what has been done in the Office of Publication at Battle Creek. Covetousness has been woven into nearly all the business transactions of the institution, and has been practiced by individuals. This influence has spread like the leprosy, until it has tarried and corrupted the whole. As the publishing house has become corrupted, the General Conference Association has stepped in, and proposed to take the diseased child off its hands, and care for it. But it is a snare for the General Conference Association to take the publishing work on its shoulders. This puts no special sanctity upon the work, but upon the General Conference Association a burden which will weigh it down, cripple it, and weaken its efficiency, unless men who have firm principle, mingled with love, shall conduct the business lines.

In this step there has been a change of responsibility, but the wrong principles remain unchanged. The same work that has been done in the past will be carried forward under the guise of the General Conference Association. The sacred character of this Association is fast disappearing. What will then be respected as pure, holy, and undefiled? Will there be any voice that God's people can regard as a voice they can respect? There certainly is nothing now that bears the divine credentials. Sacred things are mixed and mingled with earthly business that has no connection with God.

To a large degree the General Conference Association has lost its sacred character, because some connected with it have not changed their sentiments in any particular since the Conference held in Minneapolis. Some in responsible positions go on "frowardly" in the way of their own hearts. Some who came from South Africa and from other places to receive an education which would qualify them for the work, have imbibed this spirit, carried it with them to their homes, and their work has not borne the right kind of fruit. The opinions of men which were received by them, still cleave to them like the leprosy; and it is a very solemn question whether the souls who became imbued with the spiritual leprosy in Battle Creek, will ever be able to distinguish the impressions received in Battle Creek, have done much to retard the work in South Africa.

As things now exist in Battle Creek, the work of God can not be carried forward on a correct basis. How long will these things be? When will the perceptions of men be made clear and sharp by the ministration of the Holy Spirit? Some there do not detect the injurious effects of the plans which for years have been working in an underhanded manner. Some of the managers at the present time are walking in the light they have received and are doing the best they can, but their fellow workers are making things so oppressive for them that they can do but little. The enslaving of the souls of men by their fellow men is deepening the darkness which already envelopes them. Who can now feel sure that they are safe in respecting the voice of the General Conference Association? If the people in our churches understood the management of the men who walk in the light of the sparks of their own kindling, would they respect their decisions? I answer, No, not for a moment. I have been shown that the people at large do not know that the heart of the work is being diseased and corrupted at Battle Creek. Many of the people are in a lethargic, listless, apathetic condition, and assent to plans which they do not understand. Where is the voice, from whence will it come, to whom the people may listen, knowing that it comes from the true Shepherd? I am called upon by the Spirit of God to present these things before you, and they are correct to the life, according to the practice of the past few years. ...

Consolidation of the Publishing Work

The Lord has presented before me matters that cause me to tremble for the institutions at Battle Creek. He has laid these things before me, and I shall not be consistent if I do not seek to repress the spirit in Battle Creek, which reaches out for more power, when for years there have not been men who were qualified to preside, with Christian truthfulness, over the charge they already have.

The scheme for consolidation is detrimental to the cause of present truth. Battle Creek has all the power she should have. Some in that place have advanced selfish plans, and is any branch of the work promised a measure of success, they have not exercised the spirit which lets well enough alone, but have made an effort to attach these interests to the great whole. They have striven to embrace altogether too much, and yet, they are eager to get more. When they can show that they have made these plans under the guidance of the Holy Spirit, then confidence in them may be restored.

Twenty years ago, I was surprised at the cautions and warnings given me in reference to the Publishing house on the Pacific Coast-- that it was ever to remain independent of all other institutions: that it was to be controlled by no other institutions but was to do the Lord's work under His guidance and protection. The Lord says, "All ye are brethren;" and the Pacific Press is not to be envied and looked upon with jealousy and suspicion by the stronger publishing house at Battle Creek. It must maintain its own individuality, and be strictly guarded from any corruption. It must not be merged into any other institution. The hand of power and control at Battle Creek must not reach across the continent to manage it.

At a later date, just prior to my husband's death, the minds of some were agitated in regard to placing these institutions under one presiding power. Again the Holy Spirit brought to my mind what has been stated to me by the Lord. I told my husband to say in answer to this proposition, that the Lord had not planned any such action. He who knows the end from the beginning, understands the matter better than erring man.

At a still later date the situation of the publishing house at Oakland was again presented to me. I was shown that a work was to be done by this institution which would be to the glory of God if the workers should keep His honor ever in view; but that an error was being committed by taking in a class of work which had a tendency to corrupt the institution. I was also shown that it must stand in its own independence, working out God's plans under the control of none other but God.

The Lord presented before me that branches of this work would be planted in other places, and carried on under the supervision of the Pacific Press, but that if this proved a success, jealousy, evil surmisings, and covetousness would arise. Efforts would be made to change the order of things, and embrace the work among other interests at Battle Creek. Men are very zealous to change the order of things, but the Lord forbids such a consolidation, Every branch should be allowed to live and do its own work.

Mistakes will occur in every institutions, but if the managers will learn the lessons all must learn - to move guardedly - these errors will not be repeated, and God will preside over the work. Every worker in our institutions needs to make the Word of God his rule of action. Then the blessing of God will rest on him. He can not with safety dispense with the truth of God as his guide and monitor. If man can take one breath without being dependent upon God, then he may lay aside God's pure, holy Word, as guide book. The truth must take control of the conscience and the understanding in all the work that is done. The Holy Spirit must preside over thought and word and deed. It is to direct in all temporal and spiritual actions.

It is well pleasing to God that we have praise and prayer, and religious services, but Bible religion must be brought into all we do, and give sanctity to each daily duty. The Lord's will must become men's will in everything. The Holy One of Israel has given rules of guidance to all, and these rules of guidance are to be strictly followed, for they form the standard of character. No one can swerve from the first principles of righteousness without sinning. But our religion is misinterpreted and despised by (un?) believers because so many who profess to hold the truth, do not practice its principles in dealing with their fellow men.

To my brethren at Battle Creek, I would say, You are not in any condition to consolidate. This means nothing less than placing upon the institutions at Battle Creek the management of all the work, far and near. God's work cannot be carried forward successfully by men, who, by their resistance to light, have placed themselves where nothing will influence them to repent or change their course of action. There are men connected with the work at Battle Creek whose hearts are not sanctified and controlled by God.

If those connected with the work of God will not hear His voice and do His will, they should be separated entirely from the work. God does not need the influence of such men. I speak plainly, for it is time that things were called by their right name. Those who love and fear God with all their hearts are the only men that God can trust. But those who have separated their souls from God, should themselves be separated from the work of God, which is so solemn and so important.

E.G. White

Chapter 11—Temperance in Diet

Sunnyside, Cooranbong, N. S. W., Aug. 30.

Dear Brother and Sister:--

You have the light which the Lord has given our people and kept before them for many years. The Lord does not say Yea and Nay to his people, but Yes and Amen. I will send you the testimonies given to others upon the subject of health reform. This is a large subject. I am now revising the book entitled. Christian Temperance."

I was somewhat surprised at your argument as to why a meat-eating diet kept you in strength, for if you put yourself out of the question, your own reason will teach you that a meat diet is not of such advantage as you suppose. You know how you would answer the tobacco devotee if he urged as a plea for the use of tobacco, the arguments you have advanced as a reason why you should continue to use the flesh of dead animals for food.

In California there is an abundance for the table, in the shape of fresh fruit, vegetables, and grains, and there is no necessity that meat be used. The weakness you experience without the use of meat is one of the strongest arguments I could present to you as a reason why you should discontinue its use. Those who eat meat feel stimulated after eating this food, and they suppose they are made stronger. After he discontinues the use of meat, he may for a time feel a weakness but when his system is cleansed from the effect of this diet, he no longer feels the weakness, and will cease to wish for that which he has pleaded for as an essential to strengthen him.

I have a large family which often numbers sixteen. In it there are men who work at the plow, and who fell trees. These have most vigorous exercise, but not a particle of the flesh of animal is placed on our table. Meat has not been used by us since the Brighton Campmeeting. It was not my purpose to have it on my table at any time, but urgent pleas were made that such an one was unable to eat this or that, and that their stomach could take care of meat better than it could anything else. Then I was enticed to place it on my table. The use of cheese began to creep in, because some liked cheese; but I soon controlled that. But when the selfishness of taking lives of animals to gratify a perverted appetite was presented to me by a Catholic woman, kneeling at my feet, I felt ashamed and distressed. I saw it in a new light, and I said, I will no longer patronize the butcher; I will not have the flesh of corpses on my table.

You have told me what the advantage of a meat diet is to you. I must tell you what a non-flesh diet has done for me. Ever since the stone was thrown in my face, when I was nine years old, I have had difficulty. At that time I nearly lost my life through the loss of blood. Dropsy then set in, and since I have suffered very much from kidney affliction.

After a long sickness of eleven months of malarial fever and rheumatism, I was not able to ride without the most easy spring seat. Even when this was made as easy as possible, with soft cushions, it was a torture to my hip and lower part of my spine to ride.

I prayed much over this matter. I sought the Lord during the night hours, and He heard me. Some months ago a new spring seat was made for me. One day I said, "Take that spring seat and put it in the store room; I shall not need it any more." This was done by faith, and never since have I needed it. The difficulty which made it agony for me to sit in meeting or in the carriage, was taken away. After I had suffered for years, the Lord healed me. My hip continues to trouble me, but I think my health is better than it has been all through my lifetime. I prayed much in regard to the affliction of the kidneys, and I am healed of that trouble also. Some four years I was dependent upon the use of a syringe in order to make a movement of the bowels, but after the lower part of my spine was healed, I have no need to resort to artificial means.

I eat only two meals, and can not eat vegetables or grains. I do not use meat: I can not go back on this. When tomatoes, raised on my land were placed on my table, I tried using them, uncooked and seasoned with a little salt or sugar. These I found agreed with me very well, and from last February until June they formed the greater part of my diet. With them I ate crackers, here called biscuits. I eat no dessert but plain pumpkin pie. I use a little boiled milk in my simple homemade coffee, but discard cream and butter and strictly adhere to a limited amount of food. I am scarcely ever hungry, and never know what it is to have a feverish, disagreeable feeling in my stomach. I have no bad taste in my mouth.

All who come to my table are welcome, but I place before them no meat. Grains, vegetables, and fresh and canned fruit constitute our table fare. At present we have plenty of the best oranges, also plenty of lemons. This is the only fresh fruit we can get at this season of the year, which is winter. We ride about five miles into the country to get this fruit, for which we pay three pence per dozen (six cents in American money). We enjoy picking the large golden fruit from the trees. Lemons in California, I should enjoy them far more than I do the oranges. I manage to keep a box of apples for my own use, but they are inferior to the apples we get in America. I pay $1.75 at this season of the year for a box of apples, holding less than a bushel.

I have written this to give you some idea of how we live. I never enjoyed better health than at the present time, and never did more writing. I rise at three in the morning, and do not sleep any during the day. I am often up at one o'clock, and when my mind is especially burdened, I rise at twelve o'clock to write out matters that are urged upon my mind. I praise the Lord with heart and soul and voice for the great mercy toward me.

I have felt urged by the Spirit of God to set before several the fact that their suffering and ill health were caused by a disregard of the light given them upon the health reform. I have shown them that their meat diet, which was supposed to be essential, was not necessary, and that as they were composed of what they ate, brain, bone, and muscle were in an unwholesome condition because they lived on the flesh of dead animals. Their blood was being corrupted by this improper diet. The flesh which they ate was diseased, and their entire system was becoming gross and corrupted. More than this, I set before them the fact that by placing several kinds of food in the stomach at one meal, they were causing disease which was not attributed to the food eaten. I told them that they would realize much benefit if they would eat only two meals a day.

There is an alarming lethargy shown on the subject of unconscious sensualism. It is customary to eat the flesh of dead animals. The human family is under the despotism of custom and false education, of hereditary and cultivated habits. Appetite reigns as a king over the mind and reason. The animal propensities are allowed to become a controlling power. And proportionately as nature's laws are transgressed, physical suffering and disease of every stripe and type is seen; for every transgression of the laws of physical life is a transgression of the laws of God.

If appetite, which should be strictly guarded and controlled, is indulged to the injury of the body, the penalty of transgression will surely be the result. As nature's laws are transgressed, mind and soul become enfeebled.

Christians should regard a transgression of these laws as a sin against God, to be accounted for in the day of Judgment, when every case shall come in review before God.

The world today is full of pain and suffering and agony. But is it the will of God that such a condition shall exist? -- No. God, the Creator of our bodies, has arranged every fiber and nerve, and sinew and muscle, and has pledged himself to keep the machinery in order, if the human agent will cooperate with him, and refuse to work contrary to the laws which govern the physical system.

God's law is written by His own finger upon every nerve, every muscle, every faculty which has been entrusted to man. These gifts were bestowed upon him, not to be abused, corrupted and abased, but to be used to His honor and glory. Every misuse of any part of our organism is a violation of the law which God designs shall govern us in these matters, and by violating this law human beings corrupt themselves; sickness and disease of every kind, ruined constitutions, premature decay, untimely deaths, these are the results of a violation of nature's laws.

The living organism is God's property. It belongs to Him by creation and by redemption: and by a misuse of any of our powers we rob God of the honor due Him.

The need of healthful habits is a part of the gospel which must be presented to the people by those who hold forth the word of Life.

The importance of the health of the body is to be taught as a Bible requirement. "I beseech you, brethren, therefore," writes Paul, "That ye present your bodies a living sacrifice, holy, acceptable unto God, which is your reasonable service. And be not conformed to this world, but be ye transformed by the renewing of your mind, that ye may prove what is that good, and acceptable, and perfect will of God. For I say through the grace given unto me, to every man that is among you, not to think of himself more highly than he ought to think; but think soberly, according as God has dealt to every man the measure of faith. For as we have many members in one body, and all members have not the same office, so we, being many, are one body in Christ, and every one members one of another."

This is a sermon which needs to be presented to the people. The question of health reform is not agitated as it must and will be. A simple diet, and the entire absence of drugs, leaving nature free to recuperate the wasted energies of the body, would make our sanitariums far more effectual in restoring the sick to health. The intellectual and moral energies of Christians need to be awakened. Far less money and time should be given to the table, and more to the advancement of missionary work in our land. Cooks should be thought of, and their strength saved as much as possible, for they have souls to save. The many dishes usually prepared for dessert should be dispensed with.

Every minister who preaches the gospel to the people should study the laws of physical health. He should carefully consider what effect eating and drinking have upon the health of the soul. By precept and example, by a life of obedience to nature's laws, he can present the truth in a favorable manner. The teachers and workers in our sanitariums should not only preach, but practice, abstinence from food which stimulates fleshly lusts which war against the soul.

"Ye are not your own; for ye are bought with a price: therefore glorify God in your body and in your spirit, which are God's." Nearly all of the human family eat more than the system requires. This excess decays, and becomes a putrid mass. Catarrhal difficulties, kidney disease, headache, and heart troubles, are the result of immoderate eating. Even so-called health reform needs reforming upon this point. When men and women cease to indulge their appetites by eating too largely of food of a questionable quality, when they treat their stomach as respectfully as it deserves to be treated, when they relieve it of one-half to two-thirds of the laborious task they require it to perform, when nature is more respected than taste and perverted appetite, then there will be a change for the better in health and morals.

If more food, even of a simple quality, is placed in the stomach than the living machinery requires, this surplus becomes a burden. The system makes a desperate effort to dispose of it, and this extra work causes a tired, weary feeling. Some who are continually overeating call this all-gone feeling hunger, but it is caused by the overworked condition of the abused digestive organs.

At too many tables, when the stomach has received all that it requires to properly carry on its work of nourishing the system, another course, consisting of pies, puddings, and highly flavored sauces, is placed upon the table. Society has sought out many inventions and she has decreed that the food be placed upon the table in different courses. Not knowing what is coming next, one may partake of a sufficiency of food which perhaps is not the most suited to him. Then the last course is brought on. This may be composed of articles of food which, if they had been placed on the table at the first, would have added much to his enjoyment of the food. Many, though they have already eaten enough, will overstep the bounds, and eat the tempting dessert, which, however, proves anything but good to them.

The custom of placing different courses of food upon the table would better never have been invented. Let that which is provided for the meal be placed upon the table at the beginning, and then let each one eat that which will be the most healthful for him. Let each have an opportunity to choose what shall compose his meal. If the extras which are provided for dessert were dispensed with altogether it would be a blessing.

Another custom which has been instituted is, that which requires all to keep their places at the table till the last one has finished. But this makes eating a burden to those who eat no more than they feel their stomachs can properly care for. Health reformers need not observe these inventions of fashion. If you are where those eating to excess continually pass the tempting dishes, it is well to break human rules and pass quietly from the table.

Eating merely to please the appetite is a transgression of nature's laws. Often this intemperance is felt at once in the form of headache and indigestion and colic. A load has been placed upon the stomach that it cannot care for, and a feeling of oppression comes.

The head is confused, the stomach is in rebellion. But these results do not always follow overeating. In some cases the stomach is paralysed. No sensation of pain is felt, but the digestive organs lose their vital force, the foundation of the human machinery is gradually undermined, and life is rendered very unpleasant.

By indulging in a wrong course of action in eating and drinking, thousands upon thousands are ruining their health. And not only is health ruined, but their morals are corrupted, because diseased blood flows through their veins.

I have a suggestion to make to those who have moral courage and self-control enough to try it. If your work is sedentary, take exercise every day, and at each meal eat only two or three kinds of simple food, taking no more of these than will satisfy the demands of hunger. Make up your mind that this is all the food you will give your stomach. For some days perseveringly carry out your determination to eat less than you have in the past. See how this will work. Strong, hearty men, who are engaged in active physical labor, can eat food which those of sedentary habits can not eat without injury to their health. Those engaged in active physical labor are not compelled to be so careful as to the quantity or quality of their food. But even this class of people could have better health by practicing earnest self-control in eating and drinking. But one's stomach cannot be made the rule for measuring the diet of every one else.

It is the positive duty of physicians to educate, educate, educate, by pen and voice, all who have the responsibility of preparing food for the table. Teach them to bind about their ambitious desires to place before their family and before visitors a variety of tempting dishes. It would be much better to eat only two or three different kinds of food at each meal, than to overload the stomach with many varieties.

There are many kinds of intemperance in this world. Overeating is intemperance just as surely as liquor-drinking. Intemperate eating mars the system, producing a morbid appetite, which enslaves men and women. The stomach must have careful attention. It must not be kept in continual operation. Give this much used and much abused organ some peace and quiet and rest. After it has done its work for one meal, do not crowd more work upon it before it has had a chance to rest, and before a sufficient quantity of gastric juice is provided. Five hours at least should be given between each meal, and always bear in mind that if you would give it a trial, you would find that two meals would be better than three.

The sin of the Noetic world was intemperance, and today this sin, exhibited by intemperance in eating and drinking, is so marked that God will not always tolerate it. By eating and drinking we sustain life, and in themselves, if kept within the bound of temperance, they are of no harm, but a blessing. But when eating and drinking are carried to excess they come under the head of intemperance. Man carries to excess that which is lawful, and his whole being suffers the results of the violation of the laws which the Lord established.

Intemperance in eating and drinking is on the increase. Tables are spread with all kinds of food, with which to satisfy the epicurean appetite. Suffering must follow this course of action. The vital forces of the system can not bear up under the tax placed upon it, and it finally breaks down.

God is greatly dishonored by the way in which man treats his organs, and He will not work a miracle to counteract a perverse violation of the laws of health. The Lord Jesus purchased man, paying for him the infinite price of His own life. Man should estimate himself by the price which has been paid for him. When he places this value upon himself, he will not knowingly abuse one of his physical or mental faculties. It is an insult to the God of heaven for man to abuse his precious powers, by placing himself under the control of Satanic agencies, and besotting himself by indulging in that which is ruinous to health, to piety and spirituality. "Know ye not that ye are the temple of God, and that the Spirit of God dwelleth in you? If any man defile the temple of God, him will God destroy; for the temple of God is holy, which temple ye are."

When man educates the appetite to desire the flesh of dead animals and to love wine and strong drink he becomes a body of corruption. Oh, how little God is honored by them, how little He is brought into their thoughts. Gluttony and strong drink degrade the beings who are God's property by creation, His property because He has given His only begotten Son for their redemption. Look at that party of judges, lawyers, and ministers, who claim to be the servants of God and co-workers with Jesus Christ, united at the festive board. Through the indulgence of perverted appetites, they have made themselves a set of driveling fools bereft of reason. And these are men for whom Christ died that it might be possible for them to have a life of usefulness, to wear Christ's yoke, and to show their loyalty to God.

Satan is the destroyer; and God is the restorer. He calls upon us to cooperate with Him by doing our utmost, by precept and example, to restore the moral image of God in man. It is our duty to engage in the work of helping our fellow men to stand in their God-given freedom, men of self-control, vessels unto honor. We can show ourselves of much value as colaborers with God by elevating the standard of temperance, by trying to raise our brethren from degradation, so that Christ shall not have died for them in vain. Thus we show our nobility as sons of God, and joint heirs with Jesus Christ, and manifest our fitness for the immortal inheritance, which Christ has gone to prepare for us. All this we may be and do if we submit to the control of God.

But oh, how fast the world is rushing on in their madness, hastening the day of retribution. "As the days of Noah were, so also shall the days of the coming of the Son of Man be." Each day man is forming his own destiny. Every day his account is passed by the heavenly Watcher into the record books of heaven. The time will come when each one must meet the history of his life. But how much of the money which God has given to man, the money which should be used to restore the obliterated image of Jesus, is used to gratify appetite and ambition, to prepare extravagant festivals, and to build and furnish grand houses.

One soul saved for Jesus Christ is of more value than the whole world. Then how God would be honored if He could see that the physical, mental, and moral powers of men and women were kept free from every unnatural appetite, every wrong practice, every species of intemperance, tobacco-using, liquor drinking, or gluttony. Let men and women obey the work of God and they will bring heaven very near to earth.

I feel deeply over the existing state of things. It is today "as it was in the days of Noah." Then they ate and drank and planted and builded, with an enthusiasm from beneath stirring them. This made them intensely active to follow the evil imaginations of their own heart, and that continually. There was violence in the land. What do we see now in 1896? Men work in the same manner as in Noah's day, forgetful of God, educating themselves in habits and practices which corrupt soul and body. We see terrible calamities coming upon our world because of iniquity. Thousands are being killed by floods, by terrible tornadoes, by earthquakes. Ships that are upon the great deep perish in the angry billows. Yet in spite of this men continue to act in opposition to God.

My brother, there is need that economy be practiced in every line of our work. There is need of prayer, earnest, heartfelt, sincere prayer. There is need that temperance in eating, drinking and building shall be practiced. There is need to educate the people in right habits of living. Put no confidence in drug medicine. If every particle of it were buried in the great ocean, I would say Amen. Our physicians are not working on the right plan. A reform is needed which will go deeper and be more thorough. Meat-eating is doing its work, for the meat is diseased. We may not long be able to use even milk. The very earth is groaning under the corrupted inhabitants. We need to consider closely our habits and practices, and banish our sinful, darling indulgences. I have had light from God on this subject, and I have been endeavoring to give this light to our people in this country. I could write you pages upon pages of this; but I feel so deeply over these things that I scarcely dare to take my pen in my hands.

I tell you, my brother and sister, we are living in the Laodicean state of the church. If any ever needed to fall upon the rock and be broken, it is the people of California and all through our church in America. We need to arouse and act as one man. We need to be earnest and alive. Horrors upon horrors are following upon the destruction of human life. Yet these things receive only a few remarks. The world will not be warned: but the day of the Lord is coming unawares, as a thief in the night.

E. G. White.

Chapter 13—Meat Eating

Sunnyside, Cooranbong, Nov. 5, 1896.

Dear Brother and Sister Maxson:--

I have had the letter of August 12, written to you for a long time, but I decided to send that which I have already sent you, withholding that which I now send. You cannot understand how much more effectual your services in the religious interest would be, and how much more satisfactory to yourself, if you would follow the light which has been given you. But it is a phase of your character to strenuously hold to your own ideas, and if possible, carry them out. Every soul of us is in danger, and if we refuse the light, darkness will come upon all. We never proposed to establish sanitariums to have them run in nearly the same grooves as other institutions. If we do not have a sanitarium which is in many things decidedly contrary to other institutions, we can see nothing gained. Shall our appetites, habits, and practices be of that order that you will educate those who are connected with you to make excuses similar to those you have made for the indulgence of eating the flesh of animals?

The Lord intends to bring His people back to live upon simple fruits, vegetables, and grains. He led the children of Israel into the wilderness where they could not get a flesh diet; and He gave them bread from heaven. Man did eat angel's food. But they craved the flesh pots of Egypt, and mourned and cried for flesh, notwithstanding that the Lord had proposed that if they would submit to His will, He would carry them into the land of Canaan, and establish them there, a pure, holy, happy people, and there would not be a feeble one in all their habitations, for He would take away all sickness from among them. But although they had a plain "thus saith the Lord," they mourned, and wept, and murmured, and complained, it displeased the Lord; and the Lord burnt among them and consumed them that were in the uttermost part of the camp. And the people cried unto Moses; and when Moses prayed unto the Lord, the fire was quenched. And he called the name of the place Taberah, because the fire of the Lord burnt among them. And the mixed multitude that was among them fell a lusting and the children of Israel also wept again, and said, Who shall give us flesh to eat? We remember the fish we did eat in Egypt so freely; and the cucumbers, and the melons, and the leeks, and the onions, and the garlic. But now our soul is dried away; and there is nothing at all besides this manna before our eyes." Because they were so determined to have the flesh of dead animals, He gave them the very diet He had withheld from them.

The Lord would have given them flesh had it been essential for their health, but He who created and redeemed them led them the long journey in the wilderness to educate, discipline, and train them in correct habits. The Lord understood what influence flesh-eating would have upon the human system. He would have a people that would, in their physical appearance, bear the divine credentials, notwithstanding their long journey.

When I read your letter, I was forcibly reminded of the complaining of the children of Israel because they were not favored with a meat diet. The diet of the animals is vegetables and grains. Must the vegetables be animalized, must they be incorporated in the systems of animals before we get them? Must we obtain our vegetable diet by eating the flesh of dead creatures? God provided fruit in its natural state for our first parents. He gave to Adam charge of the garden, to dress it and to care for it, saying, "To you it shall be for meat." One animal was not to destroy another animal for food. After the fall, the eating of flesh was suffered, in order to shorten the period of the existence of the long-lived race. It was allowed because of the hardness of the hearts of men. One of the great errors that many insist upon is that muscular strength is dependent upon animal food. But the simple grains, fruits of trees, and vegetables have all the nutrition necessary to make good blood. This a flesh diet can not do.

When a limb is broken, physicians recommend their patients not to eat meat, as there would be danger of inflammation setting in. Condiments and spices used in the preparation of food for the table, and in the digestion (cause indigestion?) in the same way that tea, coffee, and liquor are supposed to help a laboring man to prepare his tasks. After the immediate effects are gone, they drop as low correspondingly below par as they were elevated above par by those stimulating influences. The system is weakened, the blood is contaminated, and inflammation is the sure result.

The less condiments and desserts are placed on our tables the better it will be for all who partake of the food. All mixed and complicated foods are injurious to the health of human beings. Dumb animals would never eat such a mixture as is placed in the human stomach. Hot bread and biscuit, fresh from the oven, is not healthful. The heated gases need to be evaporated. Hot soda biscuits are often spread with butter and eaten as a choice diet. But the enfeebled digestion can not but feel the abuse placed upon it. Unhealthful habits of eating are killing their thousands and ten thousands. Food should be thoroughly cooked, nicely prepared, and appetizing. My brother, after all the light that has been given on the diet question, your lamentations because you can not exercise freedom in meat-eating is apparently similar to the complaining lamentations and weeping children of Israel in the ears of the Lord. I tell you that from the light the Lord has been pleased to give me there is a continual taxing of the human stomach with a wrong quality of food, also with too large a quantity. The stomach is overloaded and worn out when it should be capable of performing good work. The amount of cooking done is not at all necessary, neither should there be any poverty-stricken diet, either in quality or quantity, but the richness of the food and complicated mixtures are destroying. Highly seasoned meats, followed by rich pastry, is wearing out the vital organs of digestion of children. Were they accustomed to plain, wholesome food, their appetites would not crave unnatural luxuries and mixed preparations. Education, habit, and custom make it difficult to reconstruct the family arrangements. Meat given to children is not the best thing to insure success. Make fruit the article of diet to be placed upon your table which shall constitute the bill of fare. The pieces of fruit mingled with the bread will be highly enjoyed. Good, ripe, undecayed fruit is the thing we should thank God for because it is beneficial to the health. Try it. To educate your children to subsist upon a meat diet would be hurtful to them. It is much easier to create an unnatural appetite than to correct and reform the taste after it has become second nature.

Our sanitariums should never be conducted after the fashion of a hotel, I am very sorry that it is such a difficult matter for you to deny your appetite and reform your habits of eating and drinking. A meat diet changes the disposition, and strengthens the animalism. We are composed of what we eat, and eating much flesh will diminish intellectual activity. Students would accomplish much more in their studies if they never tasted meat. When the animal part of the human agent is strengthened by meat-eating, the intellectual diminish proportionately. A religious life can be more successfully gained and maintained if meat is discarded; for this diet stimulates into intense activity lustful propensities and enfeebles the moral and spiritual nature. The flesh warreth against the spirit and the spirit against the flesh. We need to greatly encourage and cultivate pure, chaste thoughts and to strengthen the moral powers, rather than the lower and carnal powers. God help us to wake from our self-indulgent appetites.

The idea of eating dead flesh is abhorrent to me. One living animal eating the flesh of another animal is shocking. There is no call for it. All your excuses made in regard to faintness is an argument why you should eat no more meat. Cancer, tumors, and all inflammatory diseases are largely caused by meat-eating. From the light which God has given me, the prevalence of cancers, and tumors is due to gross living on dead flesh. I sincerely and prayerfully hope that as a physician you will not forever be blind upon this subject. For blindness mingled with a want of moral courage to deny your appetite, to lift the cross, which means to take up the very duties that cut across the natural appetite and passion. Feeding on flesh the juices and fluids of what we eat passes into the circulation of our blood, and as we are composed of what we eat, we become animalized.

Thus a feverish condition is created because the animals are diseased and by partaking of their flesh we plant the seeds of disease in our own tissue and blood. Then when exposed to the changes in a malarious atmosphere, these are more sensibly felt. Also when we are exposed to prevailing epidemics and contagious diseases, the system is not in a condition to resist the disease. I have the subject presented to me in different aspects. The mortality caused by meat-eating is not discerned. If it were, we should hear no more arguments and excuses in favor of the indulgence of the appetite for dead flesh. We have plenty of good things to satisfy hunger without bringing corpses upon our tables to compose our bill of fare. I might go on to any length upon this subject, but I will forbear.

I do hope that you, as a physician, will come to your senses, and will not, by precept and example, counterwork that which the Lord has given to enlighten minds and bring in thorough reforms. I am working earnestly on these lines and shall never cease to work against the practice of meat-eating. I have had opened before me the stumbling blocks which this diet question has been to your spiritual advancement, and what a stumbling block you have placed in the way of others and all because your own sensibilities were blunted through selfish gratification of appetite. For Christ's sake look deeper; study deeper, and act in accordance with the light God has been pleased to give you and others on this subject. I forbear writing more. I love your souls, and I want you both to accept every ray of light that the Lord has been pleased to give, and then cooperate with the Great Teacher by giving that light to others.

In love,

E. G. White

Chapter 14—The Essential Education

"Sunnyside", Cooranbong, N. S. W., Dec. 20, 1896.

In the night season some things were opened before me in reference to the work and the school that will soon be opened in this locality. The light given me was that we must not pattern after the similitude of any school that has been established in the past. We must study the Word of God critically as the great lesson book, in order to know what the school may become under the receiving and doing of the Word of God. Unless we are guarded, we shall experience those hindrances to the spiritual education that have retarded the work of our schools in America, by misapplication and miscalculation of the work most essential.

When Christ was working in our world, He had but few followers, and those whom He called His disciples were, by the maxims and customs of the scribes and Pharisees, constantly kept back from the advancement they might have made in supplying their great want and becoming efficient in usefulness. Through the rabbis, customs had come down from generation to generation and these were made all-essential, even of more force than the ten commandments. Thus the precepts of men were taught and dwelt upon as of more value than a "Thus saith the Lord."

I have been warned not to travel over the ground that many of the Battle Creek teachers have gone over in their experience. The amusement question was brought in there under a deceptive garb. Satan approached as an angel of light, and he worked most actively. If he could obtain the sanction of the teachers in the school at the great heart of the work, every school established would follow in its tread. The leaven of evil, introduced and sanctioned by Battle Creek, would spread the properties introduced to all with whom it had any connection.

The Lord has thought it essential to give reproof, correction, and instruction in righteousness on many things in regard to the management of schools among Seventh-day Adventists. All the light that has been given must be carefully heeded. No man or woman should be connected with our schools as educators, who have not had an experience in obeying the Word of God. That which the Lord has spoken in the instruction given to our schools is to be strictly regarded: for if there is not, in some respects, an education of altogether a different character in our schools than has been given in Battle Creek, then we need not get to the expense of purchasing land, and erecting school buildings.

In every school Satan has tried to make himself the guide of the teachers who instruct the students. It is he who has introduced the idea that selfish amusements are a necessity. Students sent to school for the purpose of receiving an education to become evangelists, ministers and missionaries to foreign countries, have received the idea that amusements are essential to keep them in physical health, while the Lord has presented before them that the better way is to embrace in their education manual labor in the place of amusements. This amusement question, if practiced, will soon become a passion that gives disrelish to useful, healthful exercise of mind and body, which makes students useful to themselves and others.

This education, in felling trees, tilling soil, erecting buildings, as well as in literature, is the education our youth should each seek to obtain. Further on, a printing-press should be connected with our school, in order to educate in this line. Tent-making also should be taken hold of. Buildings should be erected, and masonry should be learned. There are also many things in which the lady students may be engaged. There is cooking, dressmaking, and gardening to be done. Strawberries should be planted, plants and flowers cultivated. This the lady students may be called out of doors to do. Thus they may be educated to useful labor. Bookbinding also, and a variety of trades should be taken up. These will not only be putting into exercise brain, bone, and muscle but will also be gaining knowledge. The greatest curse of our world in this our day is idleness. It leads to amusements merely to please and gratify self. The students have had a superabundance of this way of passing their time; they are now to have a different education, that they may be prepared to go forth from the school with an all-around education.

The proper cooking of food is a most essential acquirement, especially where meat is not made the staple article of diet. Something must be prepared to take the place of meat, and these foods must be well prepared, so that meat will not be desired. Culture on all points of practical life will make our youth useful after they shall leave school to go to foreign countries. They will not then have to depend upon the people to whom they go to cook and sew for them, or build their habitations. They will be much more influential if they show that they can educate the ignorant how to labor with the best methods, and to produce the best results. This will be appreciated where means are difficult to obtain. They will reveal that missionaries can become educators in teaching them how to labor. A much smaller fund will be required to sustain such missionaries, because they have put to the very best use their physical powers in useful, practical labor combined with their studies. And wherever they may go, all that they have gained in this line will give them standing room. If the light God has given were cherished, students would leave schools free from the burden of debt.

It is also essential to understand the philosophy of medical missionary work. Wherever the students shall go, they need an education in the science of how to treat the sick; for this will give them a welcome in any place, because there is suffering of every kind in every part of the world.

The education given in our schools is one-sided. Students should be given an education that will fit them for successful business life. The common branches of education should be fully and thoroughly taught. Bookkeeping should be looked upon as of equal importance with grammar. This line of study is one of the most important for use in practical life; but few leave our schools with a knowledge of how to keep books correctly. The reason that today so many mistakes are made in accounts is not because those in charge of them are dishonest, but because they do not have a thorough knowledge of bookkeeping. They are not prompt in making a faithful, daily estimate of their outgo. These mistakes have placed them in the ranks of dishonest men, when designedly, they are not dishonest. Many a youth, because ignorant of how to keep accounts, has made mistakes which have caused him serious trouble. Those who have a living interest in the cause and work of God should not allow themselves to settle down with the idea that they are not required to know how to keep books.

Education, true education, means much. The time devoted in school to learning how to eat with your fork in place of your knife is not the most essential. These little matters of form and ceremony should not occupy time and strength. Those students who are at first coarse and awkward will soon overcome this. If the teachers are themselves courteous and kind and attentive, if they are true in heart and soul, if they do their work as in the sight of the whole universe of heaven, if they have the mind of Christ and are molded and fashioned by the Holy Spirit, they will behave not in a simpering, affected manner, but as ladies and gentlemen. And if students have before them the teachers' example of propriety, they will day by day be educated in proper manners.

To establish our school in this out-of-the-way place seemed to surprise some. It has required some hard work to make a beginning. If the work is well begun, it will cost time and money. But a thing begun right is half done. It is the first steps that cost. But in holding what is already gained, we make a continual advance in the right direction. All are not wise to see this.

By the blessing of the Lord the work has been started, and now the help of every one is needed. The students must be taught how to begin. The educators must be men and women who have had experience, and who will lead the students in the right way at every step they advance. Teach Bible manners; teach purity of thought the strictest integrity. This is the most valuable instruction that can be given. Keep Jesus, the Pattern, ever before your students by your example. This will act a prominent part in restoring the moral image of God in those under your charge. Teachers, you have no time, no duty to teach students the forms and ceremonies of this age of corruption, when everything is perverted to outward appearance and display. This must never find a place in our school. This reform is not to be brought in as essential.

All religious exercises are to be treated with the greatest solemnity and reverence. The teaching given should be of a high class, of a more sacred and religious character, than has been given in schools generally. Human nature is worth working for, and it is to be elevated and refined. There is a work which God alone can do for those who are deficient. They must be fitted with the inward adorning which is in the sight of God of great price. But the teachers can cooperate with God. Through the grace of God in Jesus Christ, which bringeth salvation and immortality to light, teachers may cooperate with God, and His heritage may be educated, not in the minuteness of etiquette, but in the science of salvation and godliness; this will prepare the sons and daughters of God to be finally transformed by the finishing touch of immortality, and in heaven they will carry forward more thoroughly the education begun in the schools here below. We shall be learners through all eternity.

Every student should aspire to obtain a fitness by the inward adorning of a meek and quiet spirit which is in the sight of God of great price. Therefore he should in this life make diligent use of every opportunity and privilege to obtain all the knowledge possible for a qualification for that higher life in the future world. God requires of every youth the full development and cultivation of all his powers. Every faculty of mind, soul, and body is to be taxed to the highest to understand the Word of God, and have a correct knowledge of the people and their manners, who are chosen the elect of God, and who will receive the "Well done" from the lips of their Master, and compose the family of God in heaven. This is work that every one can do. Some are incapable of managing or organizing, but these can cooperate with those who have a talent for this.

The teachers are to educate the youth to realize that if they receive Christ and believe in Him, they will be brought into close relationship with God. He gives them power to become the sons of God, to associate with the highest dignitaries in the kingdom of heaven, to unite with Gabriel, with cherubim and seraphim, with angels and the archangel. "And he showed me a pure river of water of life, clear as crystal, proceeding out of the throne of God and of the Lamb. In the midst of the street of it, and on either side of the river, was there the tree of life, which bare twelve manner of fruits, and yielded her fruit every month; and the leaves of the tree were for the healing of the nations. And there shall be no more curse; but the throne of God and of the Lamb shall be in it; and his servants shall serve him. And they shall see His face, and His name shall be in their foreheads. And there shall be no night there; and they need no candle, neither light of the sun; for the Lord God giveth them light; and they shall reign forever and ever."

In His teaching our Savior did not encourage any to attend the rabbinical schools of His day, for the reason that their minds would be corrupted with the continually repeated, "They say," or, "It hath been said." The Lord can do more with minds that have no connection with schools where infidel authors are perused. These lesson books He reaches out His hand to remove, and in their stead places the Old and New Testament Scriptures. Those who will search the Scriptures for themselves, because it is the Word of God, who are willing to dig for the truth as for hidden treasures, will receive for their prize that wisdom which cometh from God. If they will not rely upon their own smartness, not trust in their own inventions and fruitful minds, if they will give the working of the mind into the Lord's hands, and yoke up with Jesus Christ, they will not take steps where Jesus does not lead the way.

The aim of life should be to obey the call of Christ, "Follow me." Those whose minds are kept pure and uncrowded with too many small items, who will let their mind give its strength to those things that will be received not from their standpoint, but from the light that God has given, will be continually gaining in knowledge. And this knowledge will direct them in straightforward channels. By their aftersight they will be able to give thanks to God that they had studiously chosen to know and understand what saith the Lord to His servant.

The Word of God is to be studied and taught. Converse with God through the medium of His Word. Thus our characters will be transformed. The ideas and habits once thought essential, will be changed. God's Word is to be our lesson book. It is through the medium of this Word that we are to learn all about that better country, and the preparation essential for every one to obtain an entrance into the kingdom of God. That word obeyed cheerfully and willingly, will ennoble your whole being. ...

Mrs. E. G. White

Chapter 15—Our School Work

Economy in regard to the outlay of means should be practiced in our school in Cooranbong, This must be done, or the same mistake will be made here that has been made in our schools in America. Those who stand at the head of the schools here need to guard carefully every point and bind about every needless expense, that the burden of debt may not fall upon the school. As colaborers with Christ, every student who loves God supremely will help to bear responsibility in this matter. ...

Light has been given you in clear lines in regard to the mistakes made in the education of teachers. The education which teachers might gain may regard as nonessential. They do not gain a knowledge of practical life, a knowledge of how to work as well as of how to study. This mistake must not be allowed to influence the youth who attend the school we are trying to establish.

Many look upon a study of books as the principal purpose of their scholastic life. They know very little of practical business management, and are therefore one-sided. Their faculties have not been developed proportionately. They have not plowed deep, to understand the weak points in their character-building, and they do not realize their own deficiency. They start wrong. They feel too unconcerned in regard to becoming involved in debt. They do not look critically at the outcome of this. What is faith? True faith takes in the whole man. It enables the soul to rise out of an imperfect, undeveloped state, and to understand what wisdom is. (See Prov. 8)

If education had been carried on in accordance with the mind and will of God, the dark shadow of heavy debt would not today be hanging over our institutions. If the students had developed brain, bone, and muscle harmoniously, they could have studied better. But many students have followed their own idea as to what constitutes education, and therefore they have not placed themselves where their determination was to be self-made men and women. Many have failed because they have not reasoned from cause to effect. They are contented to be carried rather than to work their own way. And many follow their example.

When students are carried through years of study on the means of others, they lose that experience of practical life that it will be difficult for them to recover. One who has so often appeared as my instructor, placed His hand on the shoulder of a young man, and said, "You have yet to sink the shaft deeper if you obtain the heavenly treasure. You must learn to cling to the truth by faith in Jesus Christ. Associate with men of experience, who have been taught by God, and who have experimental knowledge of saving faith.

Notwithstanding all that has been written in regard to God's plan for the education of our schools, this subject has not been fully taken in. It is today as it was in the days of Christ. The sayings of the priests and rabbis were then frequently brought forward as if they were truth and light. Their words were repeated with assurance, because they had been handed down from rabbi to rabbi. Men departed from the Word of God. False theories, which were received as truth because they came from the lips of rabbis, were exalted above the words of God. Christ said to these teachers: "Ye are both ignorant of the Scriptures and of the power of God."

Thus it is in our day. Darkness hath covered the earth, and gross darkness the people. Students have left our schools with a deficient education. Some think that they know all that is worth knowing, and that they are qualified to manage institutions. But they have much to unlearn and much to learn. They must know more of God. They must realize their deficiency. They must know what constitutes Christianity.

Nothing can elevate man, nothing can make him pure, and keep him pure, but believing in and practicing the truth. He must eat the flesh and drink the blood of the Son of God. This is the lesson all should learn. They should see that to be sanctified means more than to have a theoretical knowledge of the truth. They must have living faith. They must do more than denounce wrongs in others; they must fight it in themselves. They must be whole-souled Christians, possessing the earnestness and living energy derived from Christ.

The youth should be taught to look upon physiology as one of the essential studies. They should not be satisfied with mere theory; they should practice the knowledge obtained from books on this subject. This matter has not yet been patiently and perseveringly worked out. Those who neglect this branch of study, which comprehends so much, will make haphazard work in attempting to teach the youth. They are not qualified to direct in our schools, because the way of the Lord must be learned in order to be practiced.

Many go from our schools with some knowledge, but without that all-round harmonious character that would enable them to be teachers of principle.

The principles of true education, that will fit students to be practical business men, have been very poorly carried out. This class of education is needed in all our missionary enterprises: and if the teachers in our schools did their duty, according to the "It is written," they would send forth from school men of moral worth men who would know how to take hold of the work in a new field, and use their brain, bone, and muscle in making it a harmonious whole.

Many who have been educated in our schools are headless. They do a little somewhere else, but they show they have not been educated for practical work. Students should remember that the first thing they must do is to make themselves practical, all-round useful men and women, who in an emergency can do the work necessary to be done. When students are given this kind of education, it will not be necessary to spend money to transport men thousands of miles to plan schools, meeting-houses, and colleges. Students should be encouraged to combine mental and physical labor. The physical powers should be developed in proportion to the mental faculties. This is essential to form an all-round education. They will then be at home in any place. They should be prepared to teach others how to build, how to cultivate the soil. A man may have a brilliant mind, he may be quick to catch ideas: but this is of little value to him and to others if he has no knowledge of practical work, if he does not know how to put his ideas into execution. Such a one is only half educated.

A teacher who has an intelligent knowledge of the best methods and who can not only teach the theory, but can show by example how things should be done, will never be a drug on the market. Young men should not always be as servants, who must be told what to do, and who when one job is done have no perception to look around and see what more needs to be done. They should look the situation squarely in the face, saying this will not do. Unless I learn how to work, how to manage difficult problems, how to wrestle with difficult problems, I will be of no practical value. I must and will rise. I will mount from the lowest to the highest round of the ladder. He who manifests this determination will make a trustworthy worker; for his aim is to advance in knowledge and increase in understanding. He can be depended on as a thoughtful caretaker.

There are those who are quick to see and grasp ideas in advance, but who do not weigh every point and apply their ideas in a way that produces the best results. They are heedless; they do not work in opinions, lest they should be obliged to retrace their steps. If they are not careful, their course will be uneven and uncertain. They will fail to make straight paths for their feet, lest the lame be turned out of the way. They will surely lead away those who admire their flashes and brilliancy, unless they determine to know why they know the things they claim to know. They should be careful how they order their steps. They should pray much, fearing to make mistakes. Unless they walk guardedly, they will be losers.

God's holy Word gives us the principles that form the standard of correct management in temporal as well as spiritual things. God's will is to be made the will of the human agent, and this will is to be kept prominent. Men are not to act as though there were one rule for the master and another for the servant. Christ was a servant. He lived not to please Himself, and by His life of service He has exalted all service.

E. G. White

Chapter 16—True Education

Education, as it is conducted in the schools of today, is one-sided, and therefore a mistake. As the purchase of the Son of God, we are His property, and every one should have an education in the schools of Christ. Wise teachers should be chosen for our schools. Teachers have to deal with human minds, and they are responsible to God to impress upon those minds the necessity of knowing Christ as a personal Saviour. But no one can truly educate God's purchased possession unless he himself has learned in the school of Christ how to teach.

I must tell you from the light given me by God, I know that much time and money are spent by students in acquiring a knowledge that is as chaff to them; for it does not enable them to help their fellow-men to form characters that will fit them to unite with saints and angels in the higher school. In the place of crowding youthful minds with a mass of things that are distasteful, and that in many cases will never be of any use to them, a practical education should be given. Time and money is spent in gaining useless knowledge. The mind should be carefully and wisely taught to dwell upon Bible truth. The main object of education should be to gain a knowledge of how we can glorify God, whose we are by creation and by redemption.

The earth is corrupt and dark and idolatrous; but amid the darkness and corruption a pure, divine light, the Word of God, is shining. But although we have known the truth for many years, little advancement has been made by those who have been given light. Whose plan was it to produce that class of books that have been patronized in our schools? It was the plan largely of men who had not the experience of Moses and Joshua and Daniel, and the other prophets and apostle, who endured the seeing of Him who is invisible. Seeing God by faith given a conception of the divine character, the perfection of heaven. But to place in our schools the books that have been placed there as standard books, is an offense to God. In this age, as never before, when the two great forces of the Prince of Heaven and the prince of hell have met in decided conflict, our youth need instruction in Bible principles. Like the branches of the True Vine, the Word of God presents unity in diversity. There is in it a perfect, superhuman, mysterious unity. It contains divine wisdom that is the foundation of all true education; but this book has been treated indifferently.

Now, as never before, we need to understand the true science of education. If we fail to understand this, we shall never have a place in the kingdom of God. "This is life eternal, that they might know thee the only true God, and Jesus Christ whom thou has sent." If this is the price of heaven, shall not our education be given on these lines? Christ must be everything to us. "Unto us a child is born, unto us a son is given; and the government shall be upon his shoulders and his name shall be called Wonderful, Counsellor, The mighty God, The everlasting Father, the Prince of peace.' What foundation is here laid for the faith of those who shall live in all ages! When Christ ascended to heaven, he ascended as our Advocate. We always have a Friend at court. And from on high Christ sends his representative to every nation, kindred, tongue, and people. The Holy Spirit gives the divine anointing to all who receive Christ.

This is the great subject that underlies all true, sanctified education. When this is made the theme of our conversation, no idle common talk will fall from our lips. Jesting and joking are heard because the soul-temple is unsanctified and unholy.

God, the everlasting Father, gave His only begotten Son to the world, that all who come to him might have everlasting life. And in this gift he opened to us a channel of the richest and most inexhaustible treasures. This sacred theme should be the food of our minds. With this bread of life we should satisfy our soul-hunger. If we do this, we can not hunger for worldly excitement or grandeur. Our religious experience is of exactly the same quality as the food we give our minds.

The Lord's anointing was upon Christ. "The Spirit of the Lord God is upon me," he declared, "because the Lord hath anointed me to preach good tidings unto the meek; he hath sent me to bind up the broken-hearted, to proclaim liberty to the captives, and the opening of the prison to them that are bound; to proclaim the acceptable year of the Lord, and the day of vengeance of our God: to comfort all that mourn; to appoint unto them that mourn in Zion, to give unto them beauty for ashes, the oil of joy for mourning, the garment of praise for the spirit of heaviness; that they might be called trees of righteousness, the planting of the Lord, that he might be glorified."

"And they shall build the old wastes, they shall raise up the former desolations, and they shall repair the waste cities, the desolations of many generations." This work is given to all who return to their loyalty by keeping God's commandments. "For I the Lord love judgment, I hate robbery for burnt offering; and I will direct their works in truth; and I will make an everlasting covenant with them. And their seed shall be known among the Gentiles, and their offering among the people: all that see them shall acknowledge them, that they are the seed which the Lord hath blessed. I will greatly rejoice in the Lord, my soul shall be joyful in my God; for He hath clothed me with the garments of salvation, He hath covered me with the robe of righteousness, as a bridegroom decketh himself with ornaments, and as a bride adorneth herself with jewels. For as the earth bringeth forth her bud, and as the garden causeth the things that are sown in it to spring forth; so the Lord God will cause righteousness and praise to spring forth before all the nations."

These words of Inspiration present before those who claim to believe present truth the work that should now be done in educational lines. This work should be of the same character as Christ's work: for "we are laborers together with God." Christ worked in a way altogether different from that of any other teacher.

The truths contained in the Scriptures are grand, elevating, uplifting, ennobling. If the lost image of God is restored in this world, these truths must be cherished. They are graced with such simplicity that they could not possibly have originated in any human mind. A sower from a higher world went forth to sow in the world with seed. This higher phase of education only is able to prepare students for the higher school, where Christ and God will be the teachers, and where throughout eternity, we shall learn how best to magnify and glorify God's name.

Men that are not burdened to learn Greek and Latin may yet possess a most earnest zeal to prepare in this life to receive life eternal, and enter the higher school, taking with them the result of their studies in this world. When they reach the heavenly school their education will have advanced just in proportion as in this world they strove to obtain a knowledge of God and the world's Redeemer. And just in proportion to the advancement they have made in seeking God and His righteousness will they be rewarded in the future immortal life.

The scheme of redemption is not a common study. Had it been, so many souls would not have been disloyal to God. Commencing with the apostasy and the gospel presented to Adam and Eve in Eden, and tracing down prophetic history, the Word of God unfolds the plan of redemption, gathering fresh and increased evidence, until the fulness of time came, and then Christ made His advent into the world. In Christ the Deity was represented. He was the great instructor in divine philosophy. He came without display, having no outward glory to stimulate mere admiration, and possessing no earthly riches.

When Christ came to this earth, the traditions that had been handed down from generation to generation, and the human interpretation of the Scriptures, hid from men the truth as it is in Jesus. The truth was buried beneath a mass of tradition. The spiritual import of the sacred volumes was lost; for in their unbelief men locked the door of the heavenly treasure. Darkness covered the earth, and gross darkness the people. Truth looked down from heaven to earth; but nowhere was revealed the divine impress. A gloom like the pall of death overspread the earth.

But the Lion of the tribe of Judah prevailed. He opened the seal that closed the book of divine instruction. The world was permitted to gaze upon pure, unadulterated truth. Truth itself descended to roll back the darkness and counteract error. A Teacher was sent from heaven with the light that was to light every man that comes into the world. There were men and women who were eagerly seeking for knowledge, the sure word of prophecy, and when it came, it was as a light shining in a dark place.

As a golden treasure, truth was entrusted to the Jewish Nation. The Jewish economy, bearing the signature of heaven, was instituted by the great teacher, Jesus Christ. In types and shadows important truths and mysteries that needed an interpreter, were veiled. The shadow pointed to the substance; and when Jesus came to our world, it was to let spiritual light shine forth. Hear, O heavens! and be astonished O earth! The appointed Instructor was no less a personage than the only begotten Son of God. God was revealed in Christ. He made plain the treasures of truth. He displaced the rubbish that had been piled on the Sabbath of the fourth commandment, declaring himself the Lord of the Sabbath. He who made the world and made man made also the Sabbath, and gave it to man to keep holy.

"The Lord spake unto Moses. saying, Speak thou also unto the children of Israel, saying, Verily my Sabbaths ye shall keep; for it is a sign between me and you throughout your generations; that ye may know that I am the Lord that doth sanctify you? Ye shall keep the Sabbath therefore; for it is holy unto you: everyone that defileth it shall surely be put to death: for whosoever doeth any work therein, that soul shall be cut off from among his people. Six days may work be done; but in the seventh is the Sabbath of rest, holy to the Lord: whosoever does any work on the Sabbath Day, he shall surely be put to death. Wherefore the children of Israel shall keep the Sabbath, to observe the Sabbath throughout their generations, for a perpetual covenant. It is a sign between me and the children of Israel forever: for in six days the Lord made heaven and earth, and on the seventh day he rested, and was refreshed."

God's standard of character is his law. Satan said, I will tear down this standard, and will plant my own standard in its place. This he has tried and is still trying to do, that God's standard may be eclipsed or seen through a glass darkly. The Jews did not see it, and that is why they crucified Christ. The Christian world do not see it; and that is why they refuse to acknowledge the law of God. In so doing they make themselves accountable for the sins that destroyed the inhabitants of the old world by a flood, that brought fire and brimstone upon Sodom, and that destroyed the Jewish nation. Shall those to whom God has given wonderful opportunities and great light follow in the tread of those who rejected light, to their ruin? Shall those to whom God has entrusted wonderful truth remain on the low level of the teachers of this generation?

Mrs. E. G. White

Copied July 8, 1897.

Chapter 17—Controlling Brethren

"Sunnyside," Cooranbong, N. W. W., Mar. 12, 1897.

Dear Brethren Daniells, Palmer, and Colcord:--

I have been deeply moved. In the night season, as we were in a meeting where several were assembled, we were setting forth the present situation, and how few there were to do the work so important and essential to be done. One of commanding appearance, who had been listening to the description of the condition of things, arose, and said, "Will you please to look carefully, and see if you are accepting the men that are waiting to do service for the Master? Have you not mistaken your callings, and what it comprehends, in the positions you occupy toward one who has moved to another field of labor? What if this move was not according to your ideas of order, or according to your human wisdom? Have you, in your experience, been faultless? Have you not made mismoves and blunders? He has his strong traits of character, and you have yours. All these imperfections God sees. He sees that some have made independent moves, even without the counsel of God.

"All ye are brethren." To no one has the Lord given permission to rule over a brother. All need their hearts refined, and cleansed from weakness, from natural and hereditary traits of character. All are amenable to God. If a brother errs in his ministerial work, remember that you have all erred, and shown great want of faith in the Lord. Yet, God has not discarded you, and given you no place to work. Had he done this, his action would have been just as sensible as your action in this case.

Be careful what power you take into your finite hands. Be careful how you denounce those whom you should only pity, and comfort, and help. The Lord does not see the works of men with the same vision that men see them. He has many kinds of men to deal with, and he knows just how to deal with all. But let every man, whatever his position, remember that he is not to rule any man's conscience, or sit on the judgment seat against any man. The Lord does not pronounce as just the judgment you have formed.

Satan is a masterly worker, and he will lose no opportunity to make the most of his chances to work for those who are left in a very disagreeable situation. There are those who make grave mistakes, but they seldom see the aggravated character of their own faults, or their more disagreeable results. But if another passes over the ground, and does no worse, and perhaps not nearly as bad, how easy for the brother who first sinned to tear down his brother with an unsparing hand. There are men who are severely tempted and tried who meet their temptations, at times feeling desperately, because they know not what to do in an emergency. Jesus pities them. He sees them meeting their temptations with a noble purpose, and wrestling with the devil foot to foot, breast to breast, and he says to them, as he said to Peter, "Get thee behind me, Satan. Let me come close to my tempted one. Satan hath desired thee, that he might sift thee as wheat, but I have prayed for thee that thy faith fail not."

Speak gently to ministers who are seeking, fully as earnestly as your own self, to do their duty under difficulties. They are but men, with all the clamoring of Satan to discourage them. "Wherefore lift up the hands which hang down, and the feeble knees." Be careful to make straight paths for your feet, lest that which is lame be turned out of the way; but rather let it be healed. "Follow peace with all men, and holiness, without which no man shall see the Lord: Looking diligently lest any man fail of the grace of God; lest any root of bitterness springing up trouble you, and thereby many be defiled.

The Lord has accepted men, and borne with them, when their brethren have treated them indifferently. They have allowed their masterly spirit to come in, to rule, and in thus doing, they have counterworked the work of God. You have managed this case, from first to last, in evidently a faithless manner. He is in God's service. He is God's property. You have no right to handicap him, as you have done. You should deal with him just as you would choose to be dealt with under like circumstances. By going to another field to work, without consulting his brethren do not understand just how God will bring about the accomplishment of the work he would have done. This very moving to another part of the field may be wholly in the Lord's order. Let men be delicate, and exercise their caution when it will tell for God's glory in the end.

But this brother was not so much to be censured in his action; for your own course of action revealed movements that did not encourage confidence in your faith or in your judgment. He was willing to submit to the judgment of others, altogether too much so. The Lord is not pleased when men go to men, and yield up their own will and judgment to follow their counsel. When the one giving it has not more wisdom and faith than themselves, it is all a mistake. Erratic movements will be made, according to present appearance, and not according to the mind and will of God. All must stand in God. If there was not another person on the globe but ourselves, we should be Christians, for our own individual present and eternal good. Life can be pure only when it is under God's control. No man is to rule his fellow men.

The brethren in the portion of the field to which this brother has gone should not have looked to Elder Daniells to know their duty, but to God. They should have set him at work, because he is in service, under bonds to God. He is not to be a canvasser, only as it shall be connected with his ministerial work. He is to present the Word. He has many things to learn, as well as have all who have given themselves to the ministry. Many rush into matters in a hurry, and make mistakes. Some forget that they are only human, with the deficiencies of humanity upon them and they give expression to principles that are not Christian. Thus they set an example that leads others astray.

Ignoble, egotistic, weak criticizing has become a false science, which must be cut out of the life experience. It is no marvel that many, having sensitive natures, who thought Christian work the noblest, and longing for some word of direction, or some counsel of encouragement, have been driven aside by wrong management, and turned church foes.

The Lord's workers need the melting love of Jesus in their hearts. Let every minister live a man among men. Let him in well-regulated methods go from house to house, bearing ever the censer of heaven's fragrant atmosphere of love. Anticipate the sorrows, the difficulties, the troubles of others. Enter into the joys and cares of both high and low, rich and poor.

Let not the shepherds of God's pasture treat coolly their fellow-laborers. "All ye are brethren." The Lord Jesus died to save sinners, and he longs to see men with hearts tender and full of compassion, not full of self-dignity. This must be laid in the dust. Ministers must touch lovingly and tenderly their brother minister who is battling with difficulties that appear stubborn and unyielding. But in your decision in regard to this case, you have shown much more of self and earthliness than of kindness, meekness, gentleness, or love.

All are to gather the precious treasures of love, not merely for every soul who has his hand and heart in the work of the ministry; for all who do this work are the Lord's. Through them he works. Learn lessons of love from the life of Jesus. Let men be careful how they speak to their fellow-men. There is to be no egotism no lording it over God's heritage. A bitter answer should not rise in any mind or heart. No tinge of scorn be heard in the voice. Speak a word of your own, take an indifferent attitude, show suspicion, prejudice, jealousy -- and by mismanagement the work may be done for a soul.

Ministers are but men; and God has said that one man's mind and judgment is not to control another man's mind. Let the graces of our Elder Brother be copied. With heart and spirit, and all the power that piety and art can bestow, do true, faithful work. Show thyself an example by working earnestly for the Master, drawing all men to Christ. Thy work is but to proclaim; God's work is to convert the barren hearts of men.

When the work seems to go hard, dip the words and spirit into the oil of God's love; and then, under the working of the Holy Spirit, thou canst pray with all earnestness, and preach with all power. And God giveth the increase.

Allow not your hearts to grow cool and unimpressible. Your religious life may be praiseworthy as is represented by the church at Ephesus, but deficient in love to God and to your neighbors. Suffer not a Pharisaical harshness to come in and hurt your brother. "Unto the angel of the church at Ephesus write; These things saith he that holdeth the seven stars in his right hand, who walketh in the midst of the seven golden candlesticks, I know thy works, and thy labor, and thou hast tried them which say they are apostles, and are not, and hast found them liars: and hast borne, and hast patience, and for my name's sake hast labored and hast not fainted. Nevertheless I have somewhat against thee, because thou hast left thy first love. Remember therefore from whence thou art fallen, and repent, and do thy first works; or else I will come unto thee quickly, and will remove the candlestick out of his place, except thou repent."

"And unto the angel of the church of Sardis write: These things saith he that hath the seven spirits of God, and the seven stars: I know thy works, that thou hast a name that thou livest, and art dead. Be watchful, and strengthen the things which remain, that are ready to die; for I have not found thy works perfect before God. Remember therefore how thou hast received and heard, and hold fast, and repent. If therefore thou shalt not watch, I will come on thee as a thief, and thou shalt not know what hour I will come on thee. Thou hast a few names even in Sardis which have not defiled their garments; and they shall walk with me in white: for they are worthy."

Cry unto God the Lord, Pardon our infirmities, and their infirmities: but give not up one hour of service. Keep all at work in their own line, and handicap none of God's servants because they did not come to you for counsel, and do according to your bidding. You have bidden and directed too much. God's ministers should look to him for their directions. Your plans were not God's plans. Had your brother come to you for instruction, you would have discouraged or misdirected him. No man whom God has chosen to do his work is to be under the control of any other man's mind. Men may converse as equal men, but when it comes to laying down the rules and commands, leave that for the Lord to do. This is not the line in which you are called to work.

The Lord has been working to bring certain things around for his own name's glory. Had your brother done just as you think he should have done, he would have become discouraged by the way you would have handled his care. God would have you work with your fellow men with this idea in view, that they are human like yourself, subject to temptations; and you are to meet them on equal ground. Treat them respectfully as men who are chosen of God. They may not always have been wise or perfect in their judgment; but humanity must meet humanity just where it is, remembering that all are of value with God. Your brethren are as precious in God's sight as your individual selves. Under stress of circumstances, because you did not exercise faith, and reveal trust in God, you have made grave blunders. If men err in the same lines in which you have erred, if they move hastily by looking at appearances, do not do with them as you have done in the case of the one who has been laboring for the Master. You can not bind him to your heart or influence for good by the course of action you have pursued. Come into union and agreement without delay. Act your part nobly; for you have erred. You have dealt with him as no minister should deal with a fellow-laborer. The Lord will not sanction any such example for your fellow workers to follow.

A man who could have been at work in New Zealand; has not been permitted to work. His fellow-laborers in New Zealand have echoed your sentiments, which they thought they must carry out. They have made themselves, in connection with you, answerable to God for all that man could have done and did not do. The Lord could have used him to speak and to pray, to help souls that are in suffering need of help.

Men have become feeble by looking to men; and trusting in men. They go when men say go. They ought to look to God, and trust to him for wisdom. ...

I ask you, my brethren in Melbourne, who have allowed your impressions and circumstances to quench your love for your brother, to consider the circumstances connected with his labor. He has shifted from place to place, and was sent into the canvassing field because there did not seem to be any place for him, or money to sustain him. If he felt urged by duty to go to New Zealand, the right way would have been for him to go to you, my brethren, tell his difficulties and ask for counsel. But he was in debt, mortified and strengthless. His heart-courage was gone.

When he went to New Zealand, because Brother Daniells expressed the opinion that his course had been wrong, he was left with nothing to do. But ought men's opinions to be regarded as infallible? Must men follow the expressed opinion of a fellow-laborer who has shown devotions to the work? Did his brethren kneel down and seek the Lord in his behalf, making his case their own? There are souls to be saved everywhere, but he did not have courage to work, because he had fallen into debt. He needed a brother, with the Elder Brother's heart of sympathy and humanity, to touch his heart of humanity. Were you afraid, Brother Crowthers, Brother Farnsworth, and Brother Steed, to take this brother by the hand, and say "We all have our trials, Brother Hickox, and we will help you all we can by our sympathy and prayers. If you have made a mistake, it is what we all do. Brace up like a man, and go to work. Do not feel that you are outside the ring. Be true to principle, and we will help you. The Lord needs one hundred laborers where there is one now. It may be that the Lord has sent you here, to engage with us in the work."

Never say it is time to make an example of this brother, even though he may have erred. Wait till you can say, "It is time to make an example of me by the withdrawal of your confidence and favor, because I have not moved wisely." But there are so many who, though willing to make out a recipe, that others may take the bitter medicine, would not be pleased to take it themselves. With many it makes every difference whether it is I or my brother. Well did the apostle say, "You have many teachers, but few fathers." It is spiritual fathers that we need in our gospel work.

I have not received a line from Brother Hickox or from his wife. All that I have heard is from these whom I know are not moving in the counsel of God. I think that it would be best for us to humble our hearts before God, and obtain bowels of mercy, and the incense of sanctified love, and see if this will not change the recipe given to Brother Hickox. I do not speak of him as a perfect man; for he is the same as his brethren. He has the same liability to err, and the same need of a teachable spirit. But if you think that the course pursued toward him will enable you to obtain his confidence, and lead him to rely on his brethren, believing that if he makes a mistake, they will have wisdom to help him, you have made a wrong calculation.

We all need to sow a crop of patience, compassion, and love. We shall reap the harvest we are sowing, Our characters are now being formed for eternity. Here on earth we are being trained for heaven. We owe everything to grace., free grace, sovereign grace. Grace in the covenant ordained our adoption as sons of God. Grace in the Saviour effected our redemption, our regeneration, and our adoption to heirship with Jesus Christ. Let this grace be revealed to others.

From the light which has been given me in the past and at the present, I do not see the spirit which Christ possessed in his life, revealed in your dealings with Brother Hickox. If I were where I could see him, I should urge him to respect all in positions of trust and not to make flesh his arm, but always in everything to make Christ his strength and efficiency. I would converse with him as one who, if he had sinned, had not sinned willfully. If he has sinned, there is a God of pity, who is forbearing and tender and longsuffering, ready to pardon and forgive.

I am so wearied and tired out with the heartless manner in which human, erring man treats his brother, who may be just as much beloved of God as he himself is. Little love is expressed in attitudes and words when one is supposed to have moved not in accordance with the will of men. How do you know but that the Lord has brought this about in order to set Brother Hickox and his wife where they could be laborers together with God where he could stand in earnest labor, presenting the truth to those in darkness? Who is responsible for all the good that might have been done by these two workers in opening the Scriptures to others, in union with their brethren? There is no excuse for this manner of dealing, and in the name of the Lord I protest against it.

I wish that occasionally the curtain could be rolled back and all could see the manner of the Lord's working, and the wonderful activity in the courts above. The Lord often works in a manner which is not in accordance with the ideas of the men who are in responsible positions. The speculations and calculations of human minds are not always in wisdom of God. Some move altogether too slowly, and their caution is a defective spoke in the wheel, keeping it from rolling. Again, others may devise and plan how this one and that one shall work, when the Lord has other work for these men to do, other places where he wants them to till in as his agents. His plans are not built on any foundation that is laid by man, but as the high and lofty one that inhabiteth eternity, he lays the foundation, and erects the structure, in lofty independence through those who will be worked by him. The Lord Jesus takes those that he finds will be molded and uses them for his own name's glory, to meet his own spiritual conception. He sees material that others would pass by, and works all who will be worked. Through very simple means a door is opened in heaven, and the simplicity of the human agent is used by God to reveal God to man.

The Lord Jesus never attempts to prove his teachings or vindicate himself. He speaks as one having authority, as the Source from which all wisdom flows. His word is spoken out, and the Holy Spirit's work is to find a place for that word. He is the light of the world. His own ideas are light. He simply shines, and men are to be enlightened. His work upon human hearts is not to be interfered with by men. All men must keep their place, and let God work upon hearts and minds, and enlighten the understanding. He does not want men to walk in darkness. He has given ability and talents to men, in order that they may use them and improve them.

Men are not left in absolute darkness. As the light of the world, Christ addresses the world. His light is not at all mingled with darkness. It is clearer, brighter, and far more penetrating than any other light. His light shineth in darkness, but the darkness comprehendeth it not. "But as many as received him, to them gave he power to become the sons of God, even to them that believeth on his name." He is waiting and watching, taking the imperfect ideas of men, not extinguishing them but correcting their errors, supplying their defective ideas with correct ideas, and putting his own truth in the place of their erroneous principles.

Christ is the light of the world. O how condescendingly he takes out of the mind the traditions, the false theories, and the maxims, authority, and commandments of men, which are working counter to the commandments of God. But the enemy strives to hinder God's working in human minds.

I am pained to see the little value placed upon men whom the Lord has used, and whom he will use. God forbid that men's minds shall follow in the channel of another man's mind. One man's mind may be by some, exalted as being in every degree superior but every mind has its own peculiar weakness, and its peculiar strength. One man's mind will supply another man's deficiency. But if all work in the one harness, and are given encouragement to look, not to men to know their duty, but to God, they will develop under the Holy Spirit's guidance, and will work in unity with their brethren. One will supply another's lack.

We need young, strong workers, such as Brother Hickox and his wife. The Lord will use both of them if they will walk humbly with God. The time they have spent doing little has not been so spent because the Lord refused to use them, but because of the Pharisaism manifested by the men who need the converting power of Christ, the light of the world, to shine into their confused human minds, teaching them that they are not gods, and that they must leave God to deal with his workmen. There is only one true method by which any man can work. He must learn of Him who is meek and lowly in heart. We must go more earnestly and humbly, with more contrition of soul, and ask of God wisdom, as he has appointed. For the same reasons that Brother Hickox is not received and supported by his brethren in his work, other ministers might be regarded as unfit for labor. I want to put this matter before you in the light in which it has been placed before me. The Lord has high claims upon Brother and Sister Hickox. They have much to learn, as have all who are connected with the great work of the Master; but I entreat the men who should be helpers of those who in an emergency need help, not to prove hindrances and stumbling blocks in their way.

It is a desirable thing to do God service; but it is not always an easy thing. The world is against us. At times, the way seems to be hedged up, and Satan seems to get hold of the mind. And, too often, when the brethren of the tempted one should be wise, the human side of their characters is manifested instead of the godly side, It is lamentable. If these tempted ones had not, by a course of teaching, been educated to look to men, they would turn their face toward God, and trust in God. They need greater strength than human power, greater strength than their own.

When men have to swim against the stream, there is a weight of waves driving them back. Let a hand then be held out, as was the Elder Brother's hand to a sinking Peter and let hopeful advice be given that will establish confidence and awaken love. You can not tell how such a work is registered in the heavenly books. Let the one who is supposed to have moved wrong be given no occasion by his brother to become discouraged, but let him feel the strong clasp of a sympathizing hand; let him hear the whisper, "Let us pray." The Holy Spirit will give a rich experience to both. It is prayer that unites hearts. It is prayer to the Great Physician to heal the soul that will bring the blessing of God. Prayer unites us with one another and with God. Prayer brings Jesus to our side, and gives new strength and fresh grace to the fainting, perplexed soul to overcome the world, the flesh and the devil. Prayer turns aside the attacks of Satan.

O remember that we are his offspring, children of one family, "All ye are brethren." His tender mercies are over all his works. Ever bear in mind that money is of little value compared with souls. Many, if left to impulse, represent God as stern, watching to denounce and condemn, who would not receive the soul in error as long as he had a legal excuse of not helping him. This is not God who is thus represented; for he is full of goodness and mercy and truth. Christ came to remove all such feelings, and thoughts of God. He wants every erring soul to "look and live." He would have them feel that God's yearning, fatherly love is toward them. He has revealed that which is not apprehended. If men would eat of Christ's flesh and drink his blood, which means to be doers of his word, they would manifest the attributes of Christ. He was a man of sorrows and acquainted with grief. He was wounded for our transgressions, and bruised for our iniquities.

The chastisement of our peace was upon him, and with his stripes we are healed. Wherein is our self-denial, and self-sacrifice, and patience, and mercy, and long-suffering, and love exercised to bring back the erring to repentance and to fellowship with God? If this were done, what a reformation would be wrought in individual souls, and in families, and in the church, under the transforming grace of the Holy Spirit! Why do we not act as Christians, as shown in the lessons Christ has given?

God is the one who orders all things. Have you not had any idea that this movement made by Brother Hickox was under the ordering of God? Did not the Lord see that you might not deal with his servant wisely? Did he not see that he needed to do service in some other part of his vineyard, just where he is? He who is the orderer of all things, he who numbers the hairs of our head, worked through his Spirit to transfer him to a field where he could do greater good, just as the careful, tender, earthly father would do in the interests of his children; only our God is infinitely more watchful over the interests of his sons and his daughters. He is too wise to err, and too good to do them harm. He has a wise love, a great and unbounded love. "Are ye not of more value than many sparrows? and yet your heavenly Father feedeth them."

The Lord will by his own methods, break up this indifference of man toward his fellow-man. He will educate and train and discipline his children, O how kindly and lovingly, for their greater consecration and usefulness is his work, and fit them for a higher life. It is by his Word that he instructs, and by experience that he develops virtues and powers, making those in his service meet for the inheritance of the saints in light. If they will surrender to God, and not look to man, or depend on the finite in the place of the Infinite, he will work out for them a far more exceeding and eternal weight of glory. Darkness and mysteries compass the path of some who have (not) permitted the Lord to carry forward his work in their hearts, who have not brought their thoughts into captivity to him. If these poor souls who now rise before my mind, had only learned of Jesus, and had not taken counsel of their own unconverted, unsubdued souls, they would now be in the path of obedience, co-workers with Jesus Christ. But they put themselves in their own hands, and did not trust the Lord; and they are not enjoying his blessing, or the faith that works by love and purifies the soul.

O that everyone would realize the great love, the self-sacrifice, the benevolence, and the kindness of our heavenly Father, in giving his Son to die for us that we might, if we believe and do his commandments, have a sweet peace, the Father's joy, the Father's love, and unite with him, heart, soul, mind, and strength, to maintain righteousness and to draw in even lines with Christ. It is not the sacrifice of Christ only; it is the Father's sacrifice also. The Father, in union and loving sympathy, with his Son, subjected himself to suffer with his Son. He spared not his only begotten Son but freely delivered him up for us all. This gift of Christ is the crowning truth of God's love, and this Fatherhood, through all time and through eternity. Here is the love of God in his Fatherhood. Let us drink in this love, that we may know by experience what a real, tender, joyful, experience there is in a realization of the Fatherhood of God. Let brotherly love continue. By bearing one another's burdens, we are fulfilling the law of Christ. "All the paths of the Lord are mercy and truth unto such as keep his testimonies." "The mercy of the Lord is from everlasting to everlasting upon them that fear him, and his righteousness unto children's children, to such as keep his covenant, and to those who remember his commandments to do them."

E. G. White.

Chapter 18—Exercise Versus Amusement

To the Teachers and Students of our College in Battle Creek, and in all our Educational Institutions:

Many prayers have been offered for the outpouring of the Holy Spirit, and recently there have been demonstrations of gladness of heart in those who have looked intently and undividedly to Jesus Christ, the Lamb slain from the foundation of the world. There has been in your midst repentance and confession of sin, with true remorse of soul. There was a sense of the all-sufficient sacrifice, and the realizing of the fulfillment of the promise in the pardon, in transferring the live coal from the altar of atonement and touching the lips, which was the pledge of forgiveness. Lips defiled with sin were expressing the loftiest praise. Hosannah! Blessed be he that cometh in the name of the Lord! Hosannah in the highest!. ...

But what returns have our young people made to the Lord? Has it been as it was with the people of Israel on that most solemn occasion described in Exodus? Moses had gone up into the Mount to receive instruction from the Lord, and the whole congregation should have been in humble attitude before God; but instead of that, they ate and drank and rose up to play. Has there been a similar experience in Battle Creek? Have not many lost their hold on God? Did the exercise in games of football bring the participants into more close relation to God?

In the night seasons messages have been given to me to give to you in Battle Creek, and to all our schools. While it is in the order of God that physical powers shall be trained as well as the mental, yet the physical exercises should in character be in complete harmony with the lessons given to the world and should be seen in the lives of Christians, so that in education and self-training the heavenly intelligences should not record in the books that students and the teachers in our schools are "Lovers of pleasure more than lovers of God." This is the record now being made of a large number, -- "Lovers of pleasure more than lovers of God." Thus Satan and his angels are laying their snares for your souls, and he is working in a certain way upon teachers and pupils to induce them to engage in certain exercises and amusements which become intensely absorbing, but which are of a character to strengthen the lower powers, and create appetites and passions that will take the lead and counteract most decidedly the operations and working of the Holy Spirit of God upon the human heart.

What saith the Holy Spirit to you? What was its power and influence upon your hearts during the General Conference and the conference in other states? Have you taken special heed to yourself? Have the teachers in the school felt that they must take heed? If God has appointed them as educators of the youth, they are also "overseers of the flock." They are not in the school work to invent plan for exercises and games to educate pupils; not there to bring down sacred things on a level with the common.

I was speaking to teachers in messages of reproof. All the teachers need exercise, a change of employment. God has pointed out what this should be -- useful, practical work; but you have turned away from God's plan to follow human inventions, and that to the detriment of the spiritual. Not a jot or a tittle of the after influence of an education in that line will fit you to meet the severe conflicts in the last days. What kind of education are our teachers and students receiving? Has God devised and planned this kind of exercise for you, or is it brought in by human inventions and human imaginations? How is the mind prepared for contemplation and meditation, and serious thoughts, and the earnest, contrite prayer, coming from hearts subdued by the Holy Spirit of God; "As it was in the days of Noah, so shall it be when the Son of Man is revealed." "And God saw that the wickedness of man was great in the earth, and that every imagination of the thoughts of his heart was only evil continually."

The Lord opened before me the necessity of establishing a school at Battle Creek that should not pattern after any school in existence. We were to have teachers who would keep their souls in the love and fear of God. Teachers were to educate in spiritual things, to prepare a people to stand in the trying crisis before us; but there has been a departure from God's plan in many ways. The amusements are doing more to counteract the working of the Holy Spirit than anything else, and the Lord is grieved. ...

I am alarmed for you at Battle Creek. Teachers are very exact in visiting with denunciations and punishments those students who violate the slightest rules, not from any vicious purpose, but heedlessly; or circumstances occur which make it no sin for them to deviate from rules which have been made, and which should not be held with inflexibility if transgressed, and yet the person in fault is treated as if he had grievously sinned. Now I want you to consider, teachers, where you stand, and deal with yourselves, and pronounce judgment against yourselves; for you have not only infringed the rules, you have been so sharp, so severe upon students; but more than this, there is a controversy between you and God. You have not made straight paths for your feet lest the lame be turned out of the way. You have departed from safe paths. I say, Teachers -- I do not specify names. The Lord God of Israel has wrought in your midst again and again. You have had great evidences of the stately steppings of the Most High. But a period of great light, of the wonderful revealing of the Spirit and power of God is a period of great peril, lest the light shall not be improved. Will you consider Jer. 17: 5-10; 18: 12-15: for you are most surely coming under the rebuke of God. Light has been shining in clear and steady rays upon you. What has this light done for you? Christ, the chief Shepherd, is looking upon you with displeasure, and is inquiring, "Where is the flock that was given thee, thy beautiful flock?" "Wherefore I take you to record this day, that I am pure from the blood of all men; for I have not shunned to declare unto you all the counsels of God. Take heed therefore, unto yourselves, and to all the flock over which the Holy Ghost hath made you overseers, to feed the church of God which he hath purchased with his own blood." Acts 20: 26-30. "Feed the flock of God which is among you, taking the oversight thereof not by constraint, but willingly; not for filthy lucre, but of a ready mind."

These teachers who have not a progressive religious experience, who are not learning daily lessons in the school of Christ that they may be ensamples to the flock but who accept their wages as the main thing, are not fit for the solemn, awfully solemn position they occupy. For this Scripture is appropriate to all our schools established as God designs they should be, after the order of example of the schools of the prophets, imparting a higher class of knowledge, mingling not dross with the silver, and wine with water, which is a representation of precious principles. False ideas and unsound practices are leavening the pure and corrupting that which should be ever kept pure and looked upon by the world, by angels, and by men as the Lord's institution, schools where the education to love and fear God is made first. "And this is life eternal, that they might know thee, the only true God, and Jesus Christ whom thou hast sent." "Neither be ye lords over God's heritage, but be ye ensamples to the flock."

Let the teachers who claim to be Christians be learning daily in the school of Christ his lessons. "Take my yoke upon you, and learn of me, for I am meek and lowly in heart, and ye shall find rest unto your souls." I ask you, Is every educator in the school wearing the yoke of Christ, or manufacturing yokes of his own to place upon the necks of others, yokes which they themselves will not wear, sharp, severe, exacting; and this, too, while they are carrying themselves very loosely toward God, offending every day in little and larger matters, and making it evident in words, in spirit, and in actions, that they are not a proper example for the students, and are not having a sense that they are under discipline to the greatest Teacher the world ever knew. There needs to be a higher, holier mold on the school in Battle Creek, and in other schools which have taken their mold from it. The customs and practices of the Battle Creek school go forth to all the churches, and the pulse heart-beats of that school are felt throughout the body of believers.

It is not in God's order that thousands of dollars shall be expended in enlargements and additions in institutions in Battle Creek. There is altogether too much there now. Take that extra means and establish the work in suffering portions of other fields to give character to the work. I have spoken the word of God upon this point. There are reasons many do not see, that I have no liberty to open before you now; but I tell you in the name of the Lord you will make a mistake in your adding building to building; for there are being entered in Battle Creek responsibilities that are altogether too much for one location.

(Note: Private by order of Sister White) In some respects students would come out with better education, and full as true to principle, in some schools that are not of our faith.

There are too many lords in the school who love to rule over God's heritage. There is altogether too little of Christ and too much of self. But those who are under the dictation of the Spirit of God, who are under rule to Christ, are examples to the flock; and when the chief Shepherd shall appear, they shall receive a crown of glory that fadeth not away.

"Likewise, ye younger, submit yourselves unto the elder, Yes, all of you be subject one to another, and be clothed with humility; for God resisteth the proud, and giveth grace to the humble. Humble yourselves, therefore, under the mighty hand of God that he may exalt you in due time." All your self-uplifting works out the natural result, and makes you in character such as God will not for a moment approve. "Without me," says Christ, "ye can do nothing." Work and teach, work in Christ's lines, and then you will never work in your own weak ability, but will have the cooperation of the divine combined with the God-given human ability. "Casting all your care upon Him; for he careth for you. Be sober, be vigilant." (Not in kicking football, and in educating in the objectionable games which ought to make every Christian blush with mortification at the after-thoughts) be sober, be vigilant, because your adversary, the devil, as a roaring lion, walketh about seeking whom he may devour."

Yes, he is on your playground watching your amusements, catching every soul that he finds off his guard, sowing his seeds in human minds and controlling the human intellect. For Christ's sake call a halt at the Battle Creek College and consider the after-workings upon the heart and character and principles, of these amusements copied after the fashion of other schools. You have been steadily progressing in the the ways of the Gentiles, and not after the example of Jesus Christ. Satan is on the school ground, he is present in every exercise in the school-rooms. The students that have had their minds deeply excited in their games are not in the best condition to receive the instruction, the counsel, the reproof most essential for them in this life, and in the future immortal life.

Of Daniel and his fellows the Scripture states: "As for these four children, God gave them knowledge and skill in learning and wisdom, and Daniel had understanding in all visions and dreams." In what manner are you fitting yourselves to cooperate with God. "Draw nigh to God, and he will draw nigh to you; resist the devil, and he will flee from you." Let the diet be carefully studied; it is not healthful. The various little dishes connected for desserts are injurious instead of helpful and healthful, and from the light given me there should be a decided change in the preparation of food. There should be a skillful, thorough cook, that will give ample supplies to the hungry students of substantial dishes. The education in this line of table supplies is not correct or healthful and satisfying, and there is a decided reform essential. These students are God's inheritance, and the most sound and healthful principles are to be brought into the boarding school in regard to diet. The dishes of soft foods, the soups and liquid foods, or the free use of meat, are not the best to give healthful muscles, sound digestive organs, or clean brains. Oh, how slow we are to learn! And of all institutions in our world the school is the most important. Here the diet question is to be studied; no one person's appetite, or tastes, or fancy, or notion is to be followed, but there is need of great reform: for life-long injury will surely be the result of the present manner of cooking. Of all the positions of importance in that college is the one who is employed to direct the dishes to be prepared to place before the hungry students; for if this be neglected, the mind will not be prepared to do its work, because the stomach has been treated unwisely and can not do its work properly. Strong minds are needed. The human intellect must gain expansion and vigor and acuteness and activity. It must be taxed to do hard work, or it will become weak and inefficient. The brain power is required to think most earnestly: it must be put to the stretch to solve hard problems and master them, else the mind decreases in power and aptitude to think. The mind must invent work, and wrestle, in order to give hardness and vigor to the intellect; and, if the physical organs are not kept in the most healthful condition by substantial, nourishing food, the brain does not receive its portion of nutrition to work. Daniel understood this, and he brought himself to a plain, simple, nutritious diet, and refused the luxuries of the king's table. The desserts which take so much time to prepare are, many of them, detrimental to health. Solid foods requiring mastication will be far better than mush or liquid foods. I dwell upon this as essential. I send my warning to the College at Battle Creek, to go from there to all our institutions of learning. Study up on these subjects, and let the students obtain a proper education in the preparation of wholesome, appetizing, solid foods that nourish the system. They do not and have not had the right kind of training and education as to the most healthful food to make healthful sinews and muscle and give nourishment to the brain and nerve powers.

The intellect is to be kept thoroughly awake with new, earnest, whole-hearted work. How is it to be done? The power of the Holy Spirit must purify the thoughts and cleanse the soul of its moral defilement. Defiling habits not only abase the soul, but debase the intellect. Memory suffers, laid on the altar of base, hurtful practices, "He that soweth to the flesh shall of the flesh reap corruption; he that soweth to the spirit shall of the spirit reap life everlasting." When teachers and learners shall consecrate soul, body, and spirit to God, purify their thought by obedience to the laws of God, they will continually receive a new endowment of physical and mental power. Then will there be heart yearnings after God, and earnest prayer for clear perceptions to discern. The office and work of the Holy Spirit is not for them to use it, as many suppose, but for the Holy Spirit to use them, molding fashioning, and sanctifying every power. The giving of the faculties to lustful practices disorders the brain and nerve power, and though professing religion they are not and never will be agents whom God can use; for He despises the practices of impurity in lessening physical vigor and mental capabilities, so that everything like mental taxation will after a short time become irksome. Memory is fitful, and oh, what a loathsome offering is thus presented to God.

Then when I look upon the scenes presented before me, when I consider the schools established in different places, and see them falling so far below anything like the schools of the prophets, I am distressed beyond measure. The physical exercise marked out by the God of Wisdom, (is that) some hours each day should be devoted to useful education in lines of work that would help students in learning duties in practical life, which are essential for all our youth. But this has been dropped out, and amusements introduced, which simply give exercise without being any special blessing in doing good and righteous actions, which is the education and training essential.

The students every one need a most thorough education in practical duties. The time employed in physical exercise which step by step leads on to excess, to intensity in the games and the exercise of the facilities, ought to be used in Christ's lines, and the blessings of God would rest upon them in so doing. Everyone should go forth from the schools with educated efficiency so that when thrown upon their own resources they would have a knowledge they could use which is essential to practical life. The seeking out of many inventions to employ the God-given faculties most earnestly in doing nothing good, nothing you can take with you to future life, no record of good deeds, or merciful actions, stands registered in the books of heaven, "Weighed in the balance and found wanting."

Diligent study is essential, and diligent hard work. Play is not essential. The influence has been growing in their devotion to amusements to a fascinating, bewitching power, to the counteracting of the influence of the truth upon the human mind and character. A well balanced mind is not usually obtained in the devotion of the physical powers to amusements. Physical discipline in practical life, sweetened always by the reflection that it is qualifying and educating the mind and body better to perform the work God designs men shall do in various lines. The more perfectly youth understand how to perform the duties of practical life, the more keen, the more useful and the more helpful will be their enjoyment day by day in being of use to others.

The mind thus educated to enjoy physical taxation in practical life becomes enlarged, and through culture and training well disciplined and richly furnished for usefulness; and a knowledge essential to be a help and blessing to themselves and to others. Let every student consider, and be able to say, I study, I work, for eternity. They can learn to be patiently industrious and persevering in their combined efforts of physical and mental labor. What force of powers are put into your games of football and your other inventions after the way of the Gentiles, exercises that bless no one. Just put the same powers into exercise in doing useful labor, and would not your record be more pleasing to meet in the great day of God? Whatever is done under the sanctified stimulus of Christian obligation, because you are stewards in trust of talents to use to be a blessing to yourself and to others, gives you substantial satisfaction, for all is done to the glory of God.

I can not find an instance in the life of Christ where he devoted time to play and amusement. He was the great Educator for the present and future life. I have not been able to find one instance where he educated his disciples to engage in amusement of football or pugilistic games to obtain physical exercise, or in theatrical performances; and yet, Christ was our pattern in all things. Christ, the world's Redeemer, gave to every man his work, and bade them, "Occupy till I come." And doing his work, the heart warms to such an enterprise, and all the powers of the soul are enlisted in a work assigned of the Lord and Master. It is a high and important work. The Christian teacher and student is enabled to become steward of the grace of Christ and be always in earnest.

All they can do for Jesus is to be in earnest, having a burning desire to show their gratitude to God in the most diligent discharge of every obligation that is laid upon them, that by their fidelity to God they may respond to the great and wonderful gift of the only begotten Son of God, that through faith in Him they should not perish, but have everlasting life.

There is need of each one in every school and in every institution to be as was Daniel -- in such close connection with the Source of all wisdom that his powers will enable him to reach the highest standard of his duties in every line, that he may be able to fulfill his scholastic requirements, not only under able teachers, but also under the supervision of heavenly intelligences, knowing that the all-seeing, the ever sleepless Eye is upon him. The four Hebrew children would not allow selfish motives and love of amusements to occupy the golden moments of this life. They worked with willing heart and ready mind. This is no higher standard than every Christian may attain. God requires of every Christian scholar more than they have given him. "Ye are a spectacle to the world, to angels, and to men."

Ellen G. White

Chapter 18.1—Behavior of Students

"Sunnyside," Cooranbong, N. S. W., July 7, 1897.

I have a burden that I must communicate to the teachers and students in our school. The Lord has presented your case before me. . . . . The principal and teachers of our school have withheld reproof. They have felt very anxious that every student should feel his own responsibility to God, and overcome the sin of foolish talking and foolish acting. ...cv

In their rooms, students are apt to speak words that are frivolous. A great deal of this is done. Foolish talking, jesting, and joking are indulged in. Cheap remarks are made, which create a spirit of careless disregard for order. This cheap nonsense shows that the heart contains no treasure that is good. Thus minds are turned from the important subjects that have been presented before them. This cheap stuff, wood, hay, stubble, some choose to put into their character building. The Lord Jesus gave his life to save these precious souls, and he has given them ability to learn, and power to obey his requirements. Students are not given the privilege of making wise improvement of their time. The truth is able to make them wise unto salvation.

While special pains may be taken to make the school what it should be, two or three students, who act like larrikins, may make it very hard for those who are trying to maintain order. The students who want to do right, who want to think soberly, are greatly hindered by the association of those who are doing cheap miserable work. "In the multitude of word there wanteth not sin." A few may be able to separate from such company, and retire to some place where they can ask the Lord Jesus to guard them from all defilement by keeping their minds stayed upon him. But the trial to which they are subjected by their associates is not at all necessary.

Nothing is to be tolerated in the school that will counterwork the very object for which the school was established. In believing and receiving the truth, we may be doers of the words of Christ. Thus day by day we receive grace sufficient for the duties and trials of the day. But no students should be allowed to remain connected with the school who allow their own mischievous, cheap, common practices to control their whole minds. They themselves receive no good, and others are hindered from receiving good. Satan takes possession of them, and works through them to bring not only their own souls into captivity, but the souls of other youth who have not moral power sufficient to say, We have had enough of this malarious atmosphere which poisons our thought. By their words, students can confess or deny Christ.

The older students must remember that they have the power of educating the younger ones in their habits and practices. Do not watch to find something at which to grumble, but make the best of the situation. Improve your opportunities for grasping all you can, and then fasten it in your memory. Listen to nothing it is not right for you to know.

Those who have been in the habit of telling everything they see and hear need to be converted on this point. If those connected with the home see any change made, they are not required to think that the Lord has made them daily bulletins. Do not think it your duty to carry everything you see and hear to others. They will take it to their homes, and comment upon it, and then pass the dish to someone else. If, after consultation with the other teachers, the matron makes some changes in the home plans, these changes are told by those who feel it no harm to pour forth everything that they think they know. Children that are educated to relate everything they see, which takes place at the table and in the classes, will forfeit the confidence of their teachers, by communicating to others their parcel of nonsense.

In these matters silence is eloquence. You are at the school to keep your observations to yourself, unless they are of such a character that they should be immortalized by being communicated. Let fathers and mothers realize that this class of education should not be perpetuated. Let them decide that they have had enough of this: -- "Report....and we will report it." Let students and teachers keep their own counsel. Already I meet here and there little incidents and transactions that have taken place at the school.

Students, understand that you have not been appointed by the Lord to be an informer. Your work is to study your Bible and the other branches of education, as for your life. Do not make it your business to be a talebearer. As matters are reported, each one makes the report a little more pronounced or varied, and thus painful discrepancies cause many to form wrong conclusions. Therefore guard well your words; put a bridle on your tongue. If you allow yourself to become a talebearer, you will not be welcome in any family, because of your propensity to report every transaction that may occur. I have decided that it is unsafe for me to visit, not because I am guilty of any known wrong, but because something will be said or inferred that will be misrepresented; and therefore I prefer to remain at home.

Mrs. E. G. White

Chapter 19—Words to the Young

Shall we see persons pursuing a wrong course to their own detriment and to the injury of others, and yet have nothing to say? Do we love souls, and still let them pass on in evil, flattering themselves that they are all right, and never tell them that the work they are doing will never stand the test of the judgment?

Shall the faithful servant of God keep silent when there is under his notice those who make it evident by the way they perform their daily duties, that unless their evil habits are changed, he will work at a great disadvantage? There are some young men and women who have no method of doing their work. Though they are always busy, they can present but little results. They have erroneous ideas of work, and think they are working hard, when if they had practiced method in their work, and applied themselves much more in a shorter time. By dallying over the less important matters, they find themselves hurried, perplexed, and confused when they are called upon to do those duties that are more essential. They are always doing, and they think, working very hard; and yet there is little to show for their efforts. Under circumstances like these, where young men and women are making such mistakes in their life discipline, it would be sinful not to speak words of advice and counsel.

It is an extremely delicate thing to tell people of their faults. The reprover is likely to find in those reproved, pride and stubbornness to assert themselves, and the will is arrayed in defiance and opposition. But for all this, advice should be given, and faults should be laid bare. Let the young cultivate a teachable spirit that they may be benefitted by the efforts of those who seek to help them. You may feel that you are doing your best, and that you have been reproved for very trifling matters, and you may be impatient that any one should feel that it is his duty to reprove you for such small matters; but this is the injunction given by the Apostle: "Obey them that have rule over you, and submit yourselves; for they watch for our souls, as they that must give account, that they may do it with joy, and not with grief; for this is unprofitable for you." These specific directions would not have been given, unless there were those who needed reproof and counsel.

There are persons who will never receive reproof, who build themselves up in their own way, and insist on clinging to their own evil habits and practices. When reproved they say, "Why do you tell me these things? I can not be any different." But they deceive themselves in saying this. They could make changes if they would; but they prefer to have their own way, rather than to make a determined effort to seek a better and more perfect way, by which their usefulness might be greatly increased, and their ability developed to fill positions of trust.

Those who will never admit that they are wrong, feel injured when reproved, and bring forth reasons as numerous as vain, to justify themselves. They always think that they are right, and so continue to practice their wrong habits, thus making it more and more improbable that they will reform. They are too indolent to put forth a determined effort to make reformation. Cautions, counsels, prayers, entreaties, result in making little change in their course of action. They do not see that they are defective, and are satisfied with their own erroneous way of doing, and think that every one else should be a satisfied with them as they are with themselves. They see no necessity for reproof and counsel. The Word of God describes such cases in this language: "Seest thou a man wise in his own conceit? There is more hope of a fool than of him."

There are young men and young women who are very much opposed to order and discipline. Let them purpose in their hearts that they will bring themselves under discipline, and practice orderly rules. God is a God of order, and it is the duty of the youth to observe strict rules; for such practices will work to their advantage.

As far as possible, it is well to consider what is to be accomplished through the day. Make a memorandum of the different duties that await your attention, and set apart a certain time for the doing of each duty. Let everything be done with thoroughness, neatness, and dispatch. If it falls to your lot to do chamber work, then see that the rooms are well aired, and that the bed clothing is exposed to the sunlight. Give yourself a number of minutes to do the work, and do not stop to read papers and books that take your eye, but say to yourself, "No, I have just so many minutes in which to do my work, and I must accomplish my task in a given time." If the room is decorated with little ornaments, and you would have an eye single to the glory of God, let these little idols be stored away; but if this can not be done and these ornaments must be exposed to your admiration, then handle them expeditiously. Do not take them up, one after another, as you dust them, dream over each one, and hesitate and admire, keeping it in your hand as though you were loath to replace it. Let those who are naturally slow of movement, seek to become active, quick energetic, remembering the words of the Apostle, "Not slothful in business; fervent in spirit; serving the Lord."

If it falls your lot to prepare the meals, make careful calculations, and give yourself all the time necessary to prepare the food, and set it on the table in good order, and on exact time. To have the meal ready five minutes earlier than the time you have set is more commendable than to have it five minutes later. But if you are under the control of slow, dilatory movements, if your habits are of a lazy order, you will make a long job out of a short one; and it is the duty of those who are slow, to reform, and become more expeditious. If they will, they can overcome their fussy, lingering habits. In washing dishes, they may be careful, and at the same time do quick work. Exercise the will to this end, and the hands will move with dispatch.

Another defect which has caused me much uneasiness and trouble, is the habit some girls have of letting their tongues run, wasting precious time in talking of worthless things. While girls give their attention to talk, their work drags behind. These matters have been looked upon as little things, unworthy of notice. Many are deceived as to what constitutes a little thing. Little things have an important relation to the great world. God does not disregard the infinitely little things that have to do with the welfare of the human family. He is the owner of the whole man. Soul, body, and spirit are his. God gave his only begotten Son for the body as well as the soul, and our entire life belongs to God, to be consecrated to his service, that through the exercise of every faculty he has given, we may glorify him.

Let no one say, "I can not overcome my defects of character;" for if this is your decision, then you can not have eternal life. The impossibility is all in your will. If you will not, that constitutes the can not. The real difficulty is the corruption of an unsanctified heart, and an unwillingness to submit to the will of God. When there is a determined purpose born in your heart to overcome, you will have a disposition to overcome, and will cultivate those traits of character that are desirable, and will engage in conflict with steady, persevering effort. You will exercise a ceaseless watchfulness over defects of character, and will cultivate right practices in little things. The difficulty of overcoming will be lessened in proportion as the heart is sanctified by the grace of Christ. Earnest, persevering effort will place you on the vantage-ground of victory: for he who strives to overcome, in and through the grace of Christ, will have divine enlightenment, and will understand how great truths can be brought into little things, and religion can be carried in the little, as well as in the large concerns of life.

Ellen G. White.

Youth's Instructor. Aug. 31 and September 7, 1893.

Chapter 20—Hearing and Doing

By eating to excess the stomach is made to do double work, and the mind is affected and unfit to take in and comprehend eternal realities. Those who indulge the appetite to the expense of the brain and nerve power will not, and can not, take the messages the Lord gives, the spiritual bread from heaven, which is the word of God. There are thousands upon thousands who are intemperate in eating, and the result is that the lust of the flesh is warring against the Spirit, and the Spirit against the flesh.

These are persons who have had great privileges and great light, and they have supposed that they would in time enter the ministry. I told them that we would just as soon send wolves among the sheep; for their consciences were seared as with a hot iron. The process that has been made thus, has been a disregard in little things, a deviation in character from right principles in little things. These dealings with these two human agents has greatly alarmed me. They fail to hear and retain the words I speak to them. And the words which they do not hear, are the words which require a reformation in life practice, to do these things which they consider will humiliate self, and they will deny that these words were spoken to them.

I have been shown that all who love indulgence in sin, are the ones who do not hear, do not perceive the words spoken. Why? Because evil angels have so long led them and controlled their powers, that the words, spoken to awaken conviction, are changed by Satan to mean something else. This is evidencing the power of Satan over human ears to hear things all crooked and strange; and the very things which the Lord would have them hear, they do not understand. They say that you never spoke to them the words that you know you did speak. But Satan interrupted the words so that they did not hear them.

Meat-Eating

I have never felt that it was my duty to say that no one should ever taste of meat under any circumstances. To say this when people have been educated to live on flesh to so great an extent, would be to carry matters to extremes. I have never felt that it was my duty to make sweeping assertions. What I have said, I have said under a sense of duty, but I have been guarded in my statements, because I did not want to give occasion for any one to be a conscience for another.

Sister Davis has just called my attention to an article printed in the Youth's Instructor of May 31, 1894. The question asked is, Did I design to have this sentence just as it appeared in the Instructor? I am surprised to see it just as it appears -- "A meat diet is not the most wholesome of diets, and yet I would take the position that meat should not be discarded by everyone." I can not explain why this appears just as it does. Since the campmeeting at Brighton I have absolutely banished meat from my table. It is an understood thing that whether I am at home or abroad, nothing of this kind is to be used by my family, or come upon my table. I have had some representations before my mind in the night season on this subject that I feel that I have done right in banishing meat from my table. I would desire that the sentence should be modified by changing the "not" -- "Yet I would not take the position that meat be wholly discarded by everyone."-- for instance, by those dying of consumption.

In California there is an abundance for the table, in the shape of fresh fruit, vegetables, and grapes, and there is no necessity that meat be used.

There may be consumptives who demand meat, but let them have it in their own rooms, and do not tempt the already perverted appetite of those who should not eat it.

Hot biscuit and flesh meats are entirely out of harmony with health reform principles.

You may think you can not work without meat; I thought so too, but I know that in His original plan, God did not provide for the flesh of dead animals to compose the diet for man. It is a gross, perverted taste that will accept such food. To think of dead flesh rotting in the stomach is revolting.

Make fruit the article of diet to be placed on your table, which shall constitute the bill of fare. The juices of it mingled with bread will be highly enjoyed. Good, ripe, undecayed fruit is a thing we should thank the Lord for, because it is beneficial to health. Try it. To educate your children to subsist on a meat diet is harmful to them. It is much easier not to create an unnatural appetite than to correct it and reform the taste after it has become second nature. Our Sanitariums should never be conducted after the manner of a hotel. I am sorry it is such a difficult matter for you to deny your appetites and reform your habits of eating and drinking. A meat diet changes the disposition, and strengthens animalism. We are composed of what we eat, and eating much flesh will diminish intellectual activity. Students would accomplish much more in their studies if they never tasted meat. When the animal part of the human nature is strengthened by meat-eating, the intellectual powers diminish proportionately.

Physicians' Charges

There are occupations in which it is impossible to work reform; for they are thoroughly bad, and all that can be said to those persons who persist in engaging in them is, "Depart ye, ye thieves." But the profession of medicine is an elevated, noble calling, and there is a remedy for all the evils which have become attached to this branch of work. Christ may be represented in the character and action of every physician, and all who claim to expect to become physicians should expect to work unselfishly, as He worked, requiring a fair price for their services, and exacting no more, although they see that they could obtain more by following the selfish customs of the world. It is just as consistent for the minister of the gospel to demand an excessive salary for visiting the sick, comforting the desponding, bringing peace and joy to the oppressed, as for the physician to make large charges for his professional visits.

The work of the Christian physician is to bear on its face the nature of self-denial, and not have even the appearance of fraud and extortion. It has become general among physicians who have not the fear of God before them, to hide that which is plain and simple in the guise of mystery. When dealing with humanity, Jesus made every dark thing plain to the understanding of men, and promised at His ascension to send the Comforter, whose office was to reveal truth.

The character and destiny of a man is determined by the principles which control his actions. Selfishness is an attribute of Satan, and, if this governs his life, it will be manifested in any profession or occupation, however humble and philanthropic it might be represented to be. A multitude of sins have been covered under the profession of medicine, although there has been a witness to every unholy action, a just verdict rendered in the decision of every case. Many things that are thought lawful in this profession are unlawful, and need the small cords in the hand of Christ that they may be driven out. Many good and merciful acts have been done by practicing physicians, for they have a broad field in which to work, but I was shown that as a general thing the medical profession as a body has become a den of thieves. In connection with the cause of God the profession of medicine is to be beautified by the presence of Christ, for he would cooperate with the physician who professes His name, but when men become extortioners, all he can do is drive them from His courts.

Those who enter the medical profession should be educated from a higher point of view than that found in the popular schools of the land.

Luxuries

I dreamed I was visiting those who believe the truth; and I saw in their houses trinkets and ornaments. But while I felt like weeping like a little child, over the future prospects -- on account of lack of means -- in regard to advancing the cause of Present Truth, the Spirit of the Lord came upon me, and I said, "In this house are many idols." If these things that can do your souls no good were sold, and the money put in the Lord's treasury, there would not be the deprivation of any of your comforts, and the means would help advance the cause of God." I went from house to house and pointed out the needless things that the Lord's money entrusted to his stewards had bought. That very means could have been a great blessing to help build our school buildings in the land, also our meetinghouses, that as churches are raised up we must hire. There are many campmeetings to be held in new places, and how to obtain the means is a problem.

If household ornaments could be disposed of and money invested in the work and cause of God, they would be as rivulets to swell into a large stream to carry forward the work of God. My heart aches to see the work advance so tardily, the little done and the great work to be done.

I implore all who have ornaments or trinkets that they could exchange into money or even into useful articles, to do so in order to help us here and to help the needy cause in America as well as in foreign countries. Let all church members individually consider what each can do now while mercy's voice is pleading, now, while the four winds are being held, now while heaven's opened door is ready to receive every repentant soul.

We are educating the people here who are not inclined to put brain, bone and muscle into their work, that it must become a fixed conviction in their souls that religion merely handed down from our fathers will not withstand the temptations of Satan. We are trying to demonstrate to them that while there is no panoply but truth for us in order to be saved, diligence in business is essential to guard us against temptation. Indolence and idleness, games and parties and holiday picnics are opening many avenues to temptation. Doing away with these abundant pleasure gatherings and making precious time tell in doing something useful in the service of Christ, will be a greater educating force to make all-sided students than loading down the mind with studies of authors usually studied in our schools. It is not toil in trades nor in cultivation of the soil, that degrades any man; it is not hard taxing labor that weakens the brain power, and creates sickness and disease; it is the little use made of the living machinery that enfeebles and causes disease and premature death. Disease of the organs that God has given to the living human agent is the cause of disease and feebleness of all powers, the intellect included. Adam was created in innocence, yet God gave him employment, to tend the garden. This did not degrade him. Here was his book of study -- God in nature. He was to study God and obey Him. Paul had to work laboring with his hands, and felt no dishonor in it. All who would resist temptations that assail them from without and within must make sure that they are on the Lord's side, that His truth is in their hearts; that it keep a sentinel watch in their souls, ready to sound an alarm and summon them to action warring against evil. All knowledge that deserves the name of science is found in the higher education, in the Word of God and should be acquired by all human agents.

True education strengthens the moral powers, expands the mind, and should be cultivated. But the grand educating book found in nature, which hears and sees God, has been greatly neglected. God help us to teach correctly what constitutes an all-sided education.

Counsellors

Some men have insight into matters, having ability to counsel. It is a gift of God, and in moments in which the cause of God is in need of words, sound and solemn and solid, they can speak words which will lead minds perplexed and in darkness, to see as a quick flash of sunlight the course for them to pursue, which has filled them with perplexity and baffled their minds in study for weeks and months. There is an unravelling, a clearing up of the path before them and the Lord has let his sunlight in, and they see that prayers are answered, their way is made clear.

Divine wisdom has his hand hold of the living machinery in human agencies; men are selected as fitting instruments to do a given work; and O! what a precious ability is given of God to man to know his fellow men, so that he can use, through the grace of God, the human agencies and organize a working company to do the best work, according to their recognized ability. This is a sanctified gift, genius; it is a wise generalship that can make use of man according to his ability.

Let there be much praying done and even with fasting, that not one shall move in darkness, but move in the light as God is in the light. We may look for anything to break forth outside and within our ranks, and there are minds undisciplined by the grace of the Holy Spirit, that have not practiced the words of Christ, and who do not understand the movings of the Spirit of God, and will follow a wrong course of action, because they do not follow Jesus closely. They follow impulse and their own imagination. Let there be nothing done in a disorderly manner, that there shall be a great loss or sacrifice made upon property because of ardent, impulsive speeches which stir up an enthusiasm which is not after the order of God, that a victory that was essential to be gained shall, for lack of level-headed moderation and proper contemplation of sound principles and purposes be turned into defeat. Let there be wise generalship in this matter, and all move under the guidance of a wise, unseen counsellor, which is God. Elements that are human will struggle for the mastery, and there may be a work done that does not bear the signature of God.

We can not have a weak faith now; we can not be safe in a listless, indolent, slothful attitude. Every joy or ability is to be used, and sharp, calm, deep thinking is to be done. The wisdom of any human agent is not sufficient for the planning and devising in this time. Spread every plan before God with fasting, with humbling of the soul before the

Lord Jesus, and commit thy ways unto the Lord; the sure promise is, He will direct thy path. He is infinite in resources. The Holy One of Israel, who calls the host of heaven by name, and holds the stars of Heaven in position, has you individually in His keeping.

Temperance Movement

To exalt these reforms as though they were in advance of us who, had we followed the light God has given, might have been marching steadily forward in reform for many years, is a sad mistake. If the others choose to take steps in reform hold out your hand to them; but do not step down from your own high standpoint of reform, among them, to work for theirs. It is a shame to those who have had great light and truth upon temperance, that they have not received and practiced it more thoroughly. Had they cherished and lived up to the light they have had, they would be far in advance of what they are now. Some are far behind worldlings upon the point of temperance in many things.

Ease-loving men and women do not wish to be stirred up and obliged to change their habits and customs. They love their own way and opinions. They do not want their aspirations and ambitions broken in upon. They love self-indulgence in eating, drinking, and in display and lust for worldly gain. Time is not changing things for the better in this respect, but for the worse. Genuine reforms are always attended with loss, sacrifice and peril; opposition is provoked, calumny and hatred are called out, and the better rejected for the worse.

We can not attach our names to a pledge presented by a society which indulges the use of the body-and-soul destroying narcotic, tobacco. How can we unite with this class, how work with them, how form a society with them? How is it possible to work successfully in their way and after their order?

As far as the temperance cause advances, we would sanction it, but ever keep aloft the higher standard. No one who views reforms from a Christian standpoint should discourage any advance in this direction from unbelievers.

The question for us to settle is whether we will be identified with certain movements and organizations which claim to be adopted to benefit society. If these parties are what they claim to be, they deserve the sympathy and support of all Christians. If, on the other hand, they have no foundation in principle, no actuating spirit of beneficence which characterizes reform, we need not mistake our duty. The Word of God is the infallible guide.

The temperance question is to be respected by every true Christian, and especially should it receive the sanction of all who profess to be reformers. But there will be those in the church who will not show wisdom in their disrespect to any reforms arising from any other people besides those of their own faith; in this they err by being too exclusive. Others will eagerly grasp every new thing which makes a pretense of temperance, having every other interest swallowed up on this one point. The peculiar, holy character of our faith is ignored, the views of others upon temperance are embraced, and an alliance formed between God's commandment-keeping people and all classes of persons.

Years ago light was given on health reform and temperance in all things. Temperance societies and clubs have been formed among those who make no profession of truth, while our people, although far ahead of every other denomination in the land of principle and practical temperance, have been slow to organize into temperance societies, and thus have failed to exert the influence they otherwise might have done.

The Great Science

Much of the talk about science I know is a snare; men have erroneous views about science. They should be searching diligently to see if they are accepting Christ as their personal Saviour.

Talk less, exalt science less; let your Redeemer be the One exalted. The melody of heaven is praise to God and the Lamb: it sounds forth from the voices of ten thousand times ten thousands of thousands. Why does not praise flow from our lips? Why are we so dumb? The Lord is ready to disclose to His church more and more of His wonderful power, and to open new lines of thought in regard to the great plan of redemption, the love, the matchless love, that moved him to give his only begotten Son, that whosoever believeth in Him should not perish but have everlasting live.

Let me tell you, it is not safe for us to employ as instructors in our institutions those who are not believers in the Present Truth. They advance ideas and theories that take hold of the mind with a bewitching power, that absorb the thoughts, making the world of an atom and an atom of the world. If we had less to say in regard to microbes and more to say in regard to the matchless love and power of God, we would honor God far more. These things are dwelt upon too much, and the things we ought to know, which concern our eternal interest, receive altogether too little attention. Throw a veil over the poor decaying earth, which is corrupted on account of the wickedness of its inhabitants, and point to the heavenly world. There is need of far more teaching in regard to having in this life a vital connection with God through Christ, that we may be fitted to enjoy heaven and dwell forever with our Lord. If we would attain to a pure and elevated ideal of character, we must lift up Jesus, the perfect example; the exalting of science will never accomplish the work.

Every drop of rain or flake of snow, every spire of grass, every leaf and flower and shrub, testifies of God. These little things so common around us teach the lesson that nothing is beneath the notice of the infinite God, nothing too small for his attention.

God is to be acknowledged for what he does not reveal of himself than from that which is open to our limited comprehension. If men could comprehend the unsearchable wisdom of God, and could explain that which he has done or could do, they would no longer give him reverence or fear his power. In divine revelation God has given to men mysteries that are incomprehensible, to command their faith. This must be so. If the ways and works of God could be explained by finite minds, he would not stand as supreme.

E. G. White.

Chapter 21—Unity in Work and in Counsel

To the Workers in our Institutions:

The Spirit of the Lord has presented to me things which I now present to you. There needs to be a deeper work of grace among God's workers. Their minds, their spirit, and their characters need to be molded and fashioned after the similitude of his divine character before he can work in and through them. Less of self and more of Jesus Christ must be seen in their lives. Close and trying tests are coming to all and the religion of the Bible must be interwoven with all that we do and say. All business transactions are to become a fragrance as from God, because of the presence of God, which is to be mingled with every action.

Individually, you should realize that you are in the presence of the unseen Watcher. Your methods and your temperaments need to be fashioned after the divine pattern. Constantly you should cherish the thought, I am in the presence of the One whom I love and fear and reverence. I must think no thought and do no action in my own spirit or after my own inclination. Unless I have the mind and the spirit of God, I can not be safely entrusted with sacred responsibilities. My own mind, my own judgment, must not rule. It is the mind and judgment of the great I AM that must bear rule.

If we would obtain an all-round experience, we must plow deep for truth and wisdom. We must cultivate faith in the Word of God. The alpha and omega of our experience must be "Thus saith the Lord." As brethren, located where you must be more or less connected in your work, you must draw closer together, in your counsels, in your associations, in spirit, and in all your work. Each one among you is to stand nobly in his lot and place, doing the work which God has committed to him. Every individual among you must do for these last days a work that is great and sacred and grand. Every one must bear his weight of responsibility before God. The Lord is preparing each one to do his appointed work, and each one is to be honored and respected as a brother chosen of God and precious in his sight. No one man among you is to be made the counsellor for all. One man is not to be selected as the one to whom all plans and methods shall be referred, while others are not consulted. If this is done, errors will appear, wrong moves will be made, and harm rather than good will be done. No one should be afraid of the other, lest he shall have highest place. Each is to be treated without partiality and without hypocrisy.

The same line of work is not to be committed to each one, and therefore you need to counsel together in that freedom and confidence that should exist among the Lord's workmen. All need to have less confidence in self, and far greater confidence in the One who is mighty in counsel, who knows the end from the beginning.

As you cultivate respect for one another, you will learn to respect Jesus Christ. You are to show no preference, for the Lord does not show preferences to his chosen ones. He says, "I call you not servants, but friends; for the servant knoweth not what his Lord doeth; but I have called you friends; for all things that I have heard of my Father I have made known unto you." This is the confidence that the Lord would have you cherish toward one another. Unless you do this more than you have in the past, you will not walk and work under the dictation of the Spirit of God. God would have you united in pleasant cords of companionship. As the Lord's workmen, you are to open your plans to one another. These plans must be carefully and prayerfully considered, because those who do not do this the Lord will leave to stumble in their own supposed wisdom and superior greatness.

"Ye have not chosen me, but I have chosen you, and ordained you, that ye should go and bring forth fruit, and that your fruit should remain; that whatsoever ye shall ask the Father in my name, he may give it you. These things I command you, that ye love one another." No one must suppose that his wisdom will secure him from making any mistakes. God desires that the greatest should choose that humility that will lead him to be the servant of all, if duty demands it.

But while you are to love as brethren, and think mind to mind, soul to soul, heart to heart, life to life, you are individually to lean your whole weight upon God. He will be your support. He is not pleased when you depend on one another for light and wisdom and direction. The Lord must be our wisdom. We must know individually that he is our sanctification and redemption. To him we may look, in him we may trust. He will be to us a present help in every time of need.

Whatever your duties may be in the various lines of work, always remember that God is the General over us all. You must not withdraw from him to make flesh your arm. We are too much inclined to measure ourselves among ourselves, and compare ourselves one with another, placing our own estimate upon the importance of our work. But these comparisons may fall wide of the mark. The Lord does not estimate by position or rank. He looks to see how much of the Spirit of Christ you possess, and how much of his likeness your life reveals. He who loves the Lord most, listens most earnestly and intently for the Voice of God, and as he loves most, he is most beloved by the Father.

"Learn of me," says the greatest Teacher the world ever knew, "for I am meek and lowly in heart, and ye shall find rest unto your souls."

There is need for this prayer to be offered: "O my best Friend, my Maker, my Lord, shape and mold me into thy divine likeness. Make me entirely like thyself. Refine, purify, quicken me, that I may represent the character of God." We must not think that religion and business are two separate things; they are one. All who trust in the Lord implicitly will be tested and tried; then the superscription of God will be placed upon them.

There is important work before us. And we must prepare for this work by preparing our own hearts. Heaven must be cherished in our hearts, and the rubbish of selfishness excluded that Christ may change us into his image. As this work goes on, by beholding Christ, we are changed from glory to glory, and from character to character. His strength is made perfect in our weakness.

We must humble self, today, tomorrow, and constantly. With a willing, sanctified heart, we must cooperate with God. We are living in the time when Satan has come down in great power. He is walking about like a roaring lion, seeking whom he may devour. But the Lord is ready to take away the sin that hinders us from yoking up with Christ. If we wear the yoke of Christ, he will be our Immanuel, - "God with us" supplying every weakness with his strength, every inefficiency with his power and success. But if we take glory to ourselves, he removes his excellency from us, and we no longer ride prosperously.

Take up the stones, remove the rubbish from your hearts. Behold the Lamb of God, which taketh away the sin of the world. God's servants need constantly to lay hold with one hand of souls ready to perish, while with the hand of faith they lay hold of the throne of God. Souls possessed with evil spirits will present themselves before us. We must cultivate the spirit of earnest prayer, mingled with genuine faith to save them from ruin, and this will confirm our faith.

God designs that the sick, the unfortunate, those possessed with evil spirits, shall hear his voice through us. Through his human agents he desires to be a comforter such as the world has never before seen. His words are to be voiced by his followers: "Let not your heart be troubled, neither let it be afraid. Ye believe in God, believe also in me."

The Lord will work through every soul that will give himself up to be worked, not only to preach, but to minister to the despairing, and to inspire hope in the hearts of the hopeless. We are to act our part in relieving and softening the miseries of this life. The miseries and mysteries of this life are as dark and cloudy as they were thousands of years ago. There is something for us to do: "Arise, shine, for thy light is come, and the glory of the Lord is risen upon thee." There are needy close by us; the suffering are in our very borders. We must try to help them. By the grace of Christ, the sealed fountains of earnest, Christ-like work are to be unsealed. In the strength of Him who has all strength, we are to work as we have never worked before. The time of need and necessity makes plain our great need of a present, all-powerful God, in whom is everlasting strength and in whose power we may work.

The secret of success is not in learning, not in our position, not in our numbers, nor the greatness of our talents; it is not in the will of man. The Lord God of Israel is our strength. The willing and obedient will gain victory after victory. The Lord's workers must feel their inefficiency, must contemplate Christ, and conquer through Him who is the thought of all thought, the strength of all strength. Grasp the hand of Christ, and say, I will not let thee go except thou bless me. He will respond, keep near to me; I will hold your hand. My grasp shall never relax. Possess your souls in patience, in meekness, in humbleness of mind, and yet, "Arise, shine, for thy light is come, and the glory of the Lord is risen upon thee."

Day by day God must be with us, preparing us to learn of Him, that he may teach us perfect obedience, that we may be ever with Him.

E. G. White.

Chapter 22—Dress Reform

"Sunnyside", Cooranbong, N. S. W., July 4, 1897.

My Brother:

Your letter has been received and read, and this is the first mail that could bear an answer to you.

The subject that has been placed before me for counsel is one to be carefully considered. Our sisters whose minds are agitated upon the subject of again resuming the reform dress should go prayerfully cautious in every move they make. We have now the most solemn, important test given to us from the Word of God for this special period of time. His test is for the whole world. The Lord does not require that any tests of human invention shall be brought in to divert the minds of the people or create controversy in some line. It may be that some are thirsting for distinction in some way. If they are thirsting for a battle with satanic agencies, let them be sure that they first have on every piece of the armor of God. If they have not, they will surely be worsted, and make for themselves grievous trials and disappointments which they are not prepared to meet. Let all seek the Lord most earnestly for the deep and rich experience that is to be found in the subject of heart preparedness to follow Christ where he will lead the way. "If any man will come after me," he says, "let him deny himself and take up his cross, and follow me." These words are to be weighed well. The man who wishes to follow Christ, who chooses to walk in his footsteps, shall find self-denial and the cross in that path. All who follow Christ will understand what this involves.

God's tests are now to stand out plain and unmistakable. There are storms before us, conflicts of which few dream. There is no need now for any special alteration in our dress. The plain, simple style of dress now worn, made in the most healthful way, demands no hoops and no long trails, and is presentable anywhere; and these things should not come in to divert our minds from the grand test which is to decide the eternal destiny of the world,--the commandments of God and the faith of Jesus.

We are nearing the close of this world's history. A plain, direct testimony is now needed, as given in the Word of God, in regard to the plainness of dress. This should be our burden. But it is too late to become enthusiastic in making a test of this matter. The desire to follow Christ in all humility of mind, preparing the heart, purifying the character, is by no means an easy work. Our ministers may be assured that the Lord has not inspired them to make a test of that which was once given as a blessing, but which by many was hated and despised as a curse.

The reform dress which was once advocated, proved a battle at every step. Members of the church, refusing to adopt this healthful style of dress, caused dissension and discord. With some there was no uniformity and taste in the preparation of the dress as it had been plainly set before them. This was food for talk. The result was that the objectionable feature, the pants, was left off. The burden of advocating the reform dress was removed because that which was given as a blessing was turned into a curse. There were some things which made the reform dress a decided blessing. With it the ridiculous hoops which were then the fashion could not possibly be worn. The long dress skirts trailing on the ground and sweeping up the filth of the streets, could not be patronized. But the more sensible style of dress now being adopted does not embrace the objectionable features. The fashionable part may be discarded, and should be by all who will read the Word of God. The time spent in advocating the dress reform should be devoted to the study of the Word of God.

The dress of our people should be made most simple. The skirt and sack I have mentioned may be used. -- not that just that pattern and nothing else should be established, but a simple style as was represented in that dress. Some have supposed that the very pattern given was the pattern that all should adopt. This is not so. But something as simple as this would be the best we could adopt under the circumstances. No one precise style has been given me as the exact rule to guide in their dress. But this I know, that the very same objections, only much stronger, exist today as when the short dress was discarded. The Lord has not indicated that it is the duty of our sisters to go back to the reform dress. Simple dresses should be worn. Try your talents, my sister, in this essential reform.

The people of God will have all the test that they can bear. The Sabbath question is a test that will come to the whole world. We need nothing to come in now to make a test for God's people that shall make more severe for them the test than they already have. The enemy would be pleased to get up issues now to divert the minds of the people, and to get them into a controversy over this subject of dress. Let our sisters dress plainly, as many do, in having the dress of good material, durable, modest, appropriate for this age, and let not the dress question fill the mind. ...

The Lord has not moved upon any of our sisters to adopt the reform dress. The difficulties that we once had to meet are not to be brought in again. There was so much resistance among our people that it was removed from them. It would then have proved a blessing. But there must be no new branching out into singular forms of dress.

There have been plenty of strange doings in Battle Creek with the bicycle craze, which has greatly displeased the Lord and greatly dishonored the cause of present truth. God holds those responsible who have expended money in this direction. They have greatly injured the influence of the work and cause of God. Let there be no tests manufactured now to absorb time and minds, to bring in new reforms. We have now to face tremendous issues, and all the time and power of our thought are to be called to the living issues before us. I know that the voice raised to create something new in the matter of dress now should be quenched. Put all there is of you into working to get as close as possible to perishing souls. See if you can not by consistent, harmonious, all-round character, by the presentation of truth to individuals who are out of Christ, save some souls from ruin.

I beg of our people to walk carefully and circumspectly before God. Follow the custom of dress in health reform, but do not again introduce the short dress and pants unless you have the Word of the Lord for it. Each of my brethren and sisters has a safer guide than any human agent. Let them understand that there is an individual duty for them to perform. This is but feebly understood by a large number of the members of the churches. There is far greater need in this day of deception and false claims of heeding the proclamation of John "Behold the Lamb of God, that taketh away the sin of the world."

There are those who with all the light of the Word of God will not obey his directions. They follow their own tastes and do as they please. These give the wrong example to the youth, and to those who have newly come to the truth, who have made it a practice to copy every new style of dress in trimmings that take time and money, and there is little difference between their apparel and that of the worldling. Let our sisters conscientiously heed the Word of God for themselves. Do not begin the work of reform for others until you do; for you will have no success; you can not possibly change the heart. The working of the spirit of God inwardly will show a change of dress outwardly. Those who venture to disobey the plainest statements of inspiration will not hear and receive, and no human efforts made will avail to bring these idolaters to a plain, unadorned, simple, neat proper dress, that does not in any way make them odd or singular. They will continue to expose themselves by hanging out their colors to the world. To get up a different style of dress will not change the heart. The difficulty is that the church needs converting daily. There are many things that will come to try and test these poor, deluded, world-loving souls; they will have deep trials. Let there be no human-made test; for God has prepared to prove them and to try them.

E. G. White.

Chapter 23—Study for Time and Eternity

The school located in Avondale is to be conducted in accordance with the mind and will of God. Every student should work from principle, his motto being, I study for time and for eternity. I use my muscles to do the very things that some one must do. Students should perform physical labor in the early morning and in the cool of the day, using the hours during the heat of the day for study. The limbs and muscles are God's gift just as verily as are riches and intellect. Every part of the human machinery must be used proportionately, or else some parts will be clogged and enfeebled. ...

It is just as essential to do the will of God when erecting a building as when bearing a testimony in meeting. In every building raised, if the workers have brought the right principles into their character-building, if they work with an eye single to the glory of God, striving in all ways to do their best, they will grow in grace and knowledge. This will require true diligence; it may often be hard work; but it will pay. In everything you do, do your best. ...

Negligent, slothful work is not so great an offense against men as against God. By doing it, you are forming your character for unfaithfulness. The only right way to do is to do all to the glory of God. Take no human being as your criterion. Let no human voice lay down the limit of your duty. One human being may have a lawful authority over another, and may rightly inspect his work. But every worker is to look beyond to the divine, to Him who rules in the heavens, whose eyes behold all the works of our hands. The Lord has called us to be his servants in all things, and no unfaithful work will bear the signature of "Well done."

While we are in this world, we must secure by the sweat of our brow the bread that we eat. Many are inclined to divorce temporal business from spiritual service. Many think that the time devoted to temporal things is lost. They think that if they could devote their time wholly to religious duties, they would be much more fervent and earnest in religious things. But Christ has left us no such example. He was a true worker, in temporal as well as spiritual things; and into all he did, he brought a determination to do his Father's will. It is not God's intention that the business of life shall stand still, that all duties shall be regarded as unimportant but the ministry, and the lines of work embraced by the ministry. To every man God has given his work, according to his several ability. ...

As wise teachers, parents should labor earnestly for their children, leading them to cooperate with God. They should study carefully and prayerfully how to manifest kindness, courtesy, and love, but not blind affection. True Christian parents are teachers in the home. Said Christ, "I sanctify myself, that they also might be sanctified through the word." God-fearing parents will pray with unfeigned lips that they may be more deeply impressed by the exceeding great and precious promises of God's word, and through Christ perfect holiness in his fear.

Parents, as teachers of your loved ones, the truth should have a controlling power over your conscience and your understanding, presiding over word and deed. Be as faithful in your home life as you are in the worship of God. Give a right character to all within the home. Angels of God are present, noting how younger members of the Lord's family are treated. The religion of the home will surely be brought into the church.

The greatest and most responsible of all work is to mold and fashion children to proper habits of speech. The education of children should begin in the home; but parents can not properly fulfill their responsibilities unless they take the Word of God as the rule of their life, unless they realize that they are to so educate and fashion the character of each dear human treasure that it may at last lay hold of eternal life.

It is a parent's duty to speak right words. Children should be taught to speak respectfully and lovingly to their parents. Day by day parents should learn in the school of Christ lessons from One that loves them. Then the story of God's everlasting love will be repeated in the home school of the tender flock. Thus, before reason is fully developed, children may catch a right spirit from their parents.

Parents must learn the lesson of implicit obedience to God's voice, which speaks to them out of his Word; and as they learn this lesson, they can teach their children respect and obedience in word and action. This is the work that should be carried on in the home. Those who do it will reach upward themselves, realizing that they must elevate their children. This education means much more than mere instruction.

How startling is the proverb, "As the twig is bent, the tree is inclined." This is to be applied to the training of our children. Parents, will you remember that the education of your children from their earliest years is committed to you as a sacred trust? These young trees are to be tenderly trained, that they may be transplanted to the garden of the Lord. Home education is not by any means to be neglected. Those who neglect it neglect a religious duty.

Mrs. E. G. White

(Copied July 30, 1897)

Chapter 24—Short Work in School

Dear Brother George A. Irwin:

Your letter written from the campground, Oakland, Calif., June 6, 1897, was received July 20, 1897.

You mention the school. I pray the Lord that he will stand at the head of the school as principal, and that all may work under His divine guidance. If the Lord's will is done, students will not be encouraged to remain in the school for years. This is the devising of man, not the plan of God. Those who come to this school, if they put their minds into studying the Book of all books, will, through prayer and close, deep research, obtain in a much shorter period of time a knowledge of Bible education. They will learn of Jesus in the school of Christ. The years of study of those books which should not be made study books, unfits students for the work to be done in this important period of this earth's history. One young man, after five years' study, has come from the school unfitted to teach or preach. He has to unlearn and unload a mass of rubbish which will disqualify him for efficiency in any line of the work to be done for this time.

It makes my heart ache when I consider how many would be glad of the privileges of a short period in the school, where they can be brought up on some points of study. There are those who would consider it an inestimable privilege to have the Scriptures opened to them in its pure, unadulterated simplicity, to be taught how they can keep out of the argumentative, debating methods, and come close to hearts, how in simple, direct, straightforward lines they might learn how to teach the truth so that it shall be clearly discerned. These years of study are cultivating many habits and methods in the students that will cripple their usefulness. They need to go through another process of education, and unlearn many things that they have acquired. The proper methods have been presented to me. Let students with their mental studies call into exercise the physical and moral powers. Let them work the living machinery proportionately. The constant working of the brain is a mistake. I wish I could express in words just that which would express the matter. The constant working of the brain causes a diseased imagination. It leads to dissipation. The education of five years in this one line is not of much value as an all-round education of one year.

Let the students take up the work of using the knowledge they have obtained. Let them impart to others the benefits they have received. The Bible studies are to be diligently kept up. If the students will humbly seek him, the Lord of heaven will open their understanding. They will take time to review their studies in book knowledge: they will critically examine the advancement they have made in the school-room, and will combine with their studies physical exercise, which is the most important in obtaining an all-round education. If your men and women would grow up into the full stature of Jesus Christ, they must treat themselves intelligently. Conscientiousness in methods of education is just as essential as in the consideration of the doctrines of our faith.

The student should place himself in school, if he can through his own exertions pay his way as he goes. He should study one year, and then work for himself the problem of what constitutes true education. There is no dividing line. "Whether ye eat or drink or whatsoever ye do, do all to the glory of God." The learning heaped up by years of continued study is deleterious to the spiritual interests. Let teachers be prepared to give good counsel to the students who shall enter the schools. Let them not advise students to give years of study to books. Let them learn, and then give to others that which they have received and appreciated. Let the student set himself to work at manual labor, thus acquiring an education that will enable him to come out with solid principles, an all-round man.

E. G. White

"Sunnyside", Cooranbong, N. S. W., July 22, 1897.

Chapter 25—Rational Education

"Sunnyside", Cooranbong, N. S. W., July 23, 1897.

Prof. E. A. Sutherland

Battle Creek

Dear Brother:

I am more and more burdened as I see young men coming from the school at Battle Creek deficient in the education they should have. It pains me as I realize how many who should be instructed have not the privilege. From the light given me from the Lord, I know that four or five successive years of application to book study is a mistake. Those who encourage this close application to books, working the brain, and neglecting the education they should gain by using the muscles proportionately with the brain, are simply incapable of retaining the lessons they endeavor to learn. If one-third of the time now occupied in the study of books, using the mental machinery, were occupied in learning lessons in regard to the right use of one's own physical powers, it would be much more after the Lord's order, and would elevate the labor question, placing it where idleness would be regarded as a departure from the word and plans of God. The right use of one's self includes the whole circle of human obligations to one's self, to the world, and to God. Then use the physical power proportionately with the mental powers.

While studying authors and lesson books part of the time, students would study with the same application the human machinery and at the same time demonstrate the fact by using physical organs in manual labor. Thus they answer the purpose of their Creator. They become self-made men and women.

Had teachers been learning the lessons the Lord would have them learn, there would be a class of students whose bills must be settled by some one, or else they leave the college with a heavy debt hanging over them. Educators are not doing half their work when they know a young man to be devoting years of close application to the study of books, not seeking to earn means to pay his own way, and yet do nothing in the matter. Every case should be investigated; every youth kindly and interestedly inquired after, and his financial situation ascertained. One of the studies put before him as most valuable should be the exercise of his God-given reason in harmony with his physical powers, head, body, hand, and feet. The right use of one's self is the most valuable lesson that can be learned. We are not to do brain work and stop there, or make physical exertions and stop there; but we are to make the very best use of the various parts composing the human machinery, brain, bone and muscle; body, head and heart. No man is fit for the ministry who does not understand how to do this.

The study of Latin and Greek is of far less consequence to ourselves, to the world, and to God, than the thorough study and use of the whole human machinery. It is a sin to study books to the neglect of how to become familiar with the various branches of usefulness in practical life. With some, close application to books is a dissipation. The physical machinery being untaxed leads to a great amount of activity in the brain. This becomes the devil's workshop. Never can that life that is ignorant of the house we live in be an all-round life. The schools are not half awake. The neglect of some parts of the living machinery, while other parts are put to the tax, and wearied and overworked, makes many youth too weak to resist evil practices. They have little power of self-control. The blood is called too liberally to the brain, and the nervous system is overworked. Exercise should be taken, not in play and amusement merely to please self, but exercise in the science of doing good. There is a science in the use of the hand. In the cultivation of the soil, in building houses, in studying and planning various methods of labor, the brain must be exercised; and students can apply themselves to study to much better purpose when a portion of their time is adopted to physical taxation, wearying the muscles. Nature will then give repose and sweet rest.

The hand was made to do all kinds of work, and students who think that education consists only in book study never make a right use of the fingers and hands. Students should be thoroughly taught to do this very work that thousands of hands are never educated to do. The powers thus developed and cultivated can be most usefully employed.

Students who apply themselves wholly to brain labor in the school-room injure the whole living machinery by confinement. The brain is wearied, and Satan brings in a whole list of temptations, enticing them to engage in forbidden indulgences to have a change, to let off steam. Yielding to these temptations, they do wrong things which injure themselves and do mischief to others. This may be done in sport. The brain is active and they desire to play some pranks.

Teach the students that their life is a talent to be highly appreciated, and to be dedicated to the Lord. Teach them that they are to work in Christ's lines. Students, your life is God's property. He has entrusted it to you that you may carefully study how you can best honor and glorify him. You are really the Lord's; for he created you. You are his by redemption; for he gave his life for you. Who was it that paid the price of the ransom for your deliverance from Satan? It was the only begotten Son of God. He was the Majesty of heaven, and for His sake you should appreciate every power, every organ, every sinew and muscle. Preserve every portion of the living machinery, that you may use it for God. Preserve it for Him.

Your health depends upon the right use of your physical organism. Do not misuse or abuse any portion of your God-given powers, physical, mental, or moral. All your habits are to be brought under the control of a mind that is itself under the control of God. Unhealthful habits of every order, late habits of night, late hours in bed in the morning rapid eating, are to be overcome. The digestion begins in the mouth. Masticate your food thoroughly. Let there be no hurried eating. Have your room well ventilated, and perform useful physical labor. To young ladies I would say, tightlacing is a sin, and will bring its sure results. The lungs, the liver, the heart, need all the room the Lord has provided for them. Your Creator understood how much room the heart and liver require in order to set their vital parts in the human organism. Let not Satan tempt you to crowd the delicate organs, so that they shall be trammeled in their work. Do not, because the fashions of this degenerate world are taken up as desirable, so crowd the life forces that they have no freedom. Satan suggested all such fashions, that the human family might suffer the sure results of abusing God's handiwork.

The giving way to violent emotions endangers life. Many die under a burst of rage and passions. Many educate themselves to have spasms. These they can prevent if they will; but it requires will power to overcome a wrong course of action. All this must be a part of the education received in the school; for we are God's property. The sacred temple of the body must be kept pure and uncontaminated, that God's Holy Spirit may dwell therein.

We need to guard faithfully the Lord's property; for any abuse of our powers shortens the time that our lives can be used for the glory of God. Bear in mind that we must consecrate all, soul, body, and spirit to God. It is His purchased possession, and must be used intelligently, to the end that we may prolong and preserve the talent of life itself. By properly using our powers and talents to the fullest extent in the most useful employment by keeping every organ in health to do the best and most useful service to God, by preserving every organ that body and mind, sinew and muscles, may work harmoniously, we may do the best and most precious service for God. There are invalids in our world born with feeble constitutions. They suffer from no fault of their own. Let these study patient endurance. In so doing they can glorify God.

Students, study for time and for eternity. Bring good, hard, earnest labor into your scholastic life. Do not feel that you must take a classical course before you enter the ministry. The Lord has given light that the largest number who have done this have, through the protracted study of books, disqualified themselves for the labor which was essential for them to do. What is Paul's charge to Timothy? "Therefore, I endure all things for the elect's sakes, that they also may obtain the salvation which is in Jesus Christ with eternal glory. It is a faithful saying: For if we be dead with him, we shall also live with him; if we suffer, we shall also reign with him; if we deny him he also will deny us; if we believe not, yet he abideth faithful: he can not deny himself. Of these things put them in remembrance, charging them before the Lord that they strive not about words to no profit, but to the subverting of the hearers. Study to show thyself approved unto God, a workman that needeth not to be ashamed, rightly dividing the word of truth."

Mrs. E. G. White

Chapter 26—Training an Army of Missionaries

"Sunnyside", Cooranbong, N. S. W., December 15, 1897.

Prof. E. A. Sutherland,

Dear Brother:

In your letter you ask me serious questions, and lay out propositions which are sensible and right. There should be schools established wherever there is a church or company of believers. Teachers should be employed to educate the children of Sabbath-keepers. This would close the door to a large number who are drifting into Battle Creek,--the very place where the Lord has warned them not to go. In the light that has been given me, I have been pointed to the churches that are scattered in different localities, and I have been shown that the strength of these churches depends upon their growth in usefulness and efficiency.

A large amount of the responsibility piled up in Battle Creek is not in accordance with the principles that the Lord has set before us. There should be fewer buildings erected in Battle Creek to call the crowds of people there. All these large buildings should not be crowded together as they are. They should have been placed in different localities, and not in the very midst of one city. The various cities should have representative of the truth in their midst. I can not go contrary to the will of God, and say, erect more buildings in Battle Creek; but I would say, build in other localities. There should be fewer interests centered at Battle Creek, and far more in other places where there is nothing to give character to the work of God.

In all our churches there should be schools, and teachers in those schools who are missionaries. It is essential that teachers be educated to act their important part in educating the children of Sabbath-keepers, not only in the sciences, but in the Scriptures, These schools established in different localities, and conducted by God-fearing men and women, as the case demands, should be built upon the same principles as were the schools of the prophets.

Special talent should be given to the education of the youth. The children are to be trained to become missionaries: and but a few understand distinctly what they must do to be saved. Few have the instruction in religious lines that is essential. If the instructors have a religious experience themselves, they will be able to communicate to their students the knowledge of the love of God they have received. These lessons can only be given from those who are themselves truly converted; and this is the noblest missionary work that any man or woman can undertake.

Children should be educated to read, to write, to understand figures, to keep their own accounts, when very young. They may go forward, advancing step by step in this knowledge. But before everything else they should be taught that the fear of the Lord is the beginning of wisdom. They may be educated line upon line, precept upon precept, here a little, and there a little; but the one aim ever before the teacher should be to educate the children to know God, and Jesus Christ whom he has sent.

Teach the youth that sin in any line is defined in the Scriptures as "transgression of the law." Sin originated with the first great apostate. He was a disobedient subject. He led the family of heaven into disobedience, and he and all who were united with him were cast out of the paradise of God. Teach the children in simple language that they must be obedient to their parents, and give their hearts to God. Jesus Christ is waiting to accept them and bless them, if they will only come to him and ask him to pardon all their transgressions and take away their sins. And when they ask him to pardon all their transgressions they must believe that he will do it.

God wants every child of tender age to be his child, to be adopted into his family. Young though they may be, the youth may be members of the household of faith, and have a most precious experience. They may have hearts that are tender and ready to receive impressions that will be lasting. They may have their hearts drawn out in confidence and love of Jesus, and live for the Saviour. Christ will make them little missionaries. The whole current of their thought may be changed, so that sin will not appear a thing to be enjoyed, but to be hated and shunned.

Small as well as older children will be benefitted by this instruction; and in this simplifying the plan of salvation, the teachers will receive as great blessings as those who are taught. The Holy Spirit of God will impress the lessons upon the receptive minds of the children, that they may grasp the ideas of Bible truth in their simplicity. And the Lord will give an experience to these children in missionary lines; He will suggest to them lines of thought which the teachers themselves did not have.

The children who are properly instructed will be witnesses for the truth. Teachers who are nervous and easily irritated should not be placed over the youth. They must love the children because they are the younger members of the Lord's family. The Lord will inquire of them as of the parents. "What have you done with my flock, my beautiful flock?"

It is surprising to see how little is done by many parents to save their own children. Every family in the home life should be a church, a beautiful symbol of the church of God in heaven. If parents realized their responsibilities to their children, they would not under any circumstances scold and fret at them. This is not the kind of education any child should have. Many, many children have learned to be fault-finding, fretful, scolding passionate children, because they were allowed to be passionate at home. Parents are to consider that they are in the place of God to their children, to encourage every right principle, and repress every wrong thought.

If in their own homes children are allowed to be disrespectful, disobedient, unthankful, and peevish, their sins lie at the door of the parents. It is the special work of fathers and mothers to teach their children with kindliness and affection. They are to show that as parents they are the ones to hold the lines, to govern, and not to be governed by their children. They are to teach that obedience is required of them, and thus they educate them to submit to the authority of God.

In educating children and youth, teachers should never allow one passionate word or gesture to mar their works for in so doing they imbue the students with the same spirit that they themselves possess. The Lord would have our primary as well as our more advanced schools, of that character that angels of God can walk through the room, and behold in the order and principles of government, the order and government of heaven. This is thought by many to be impossible; but every school should begin with this, and should work most earnestly to preserve the spirit of Christ in temper, in communications, in instruction, the teachers placing themselves in the channel of light where the Lord can use them as his agents, to reflect his own likeness of character upon the students. They may know that as God-fearing instructors they have helpers every hour to impress upon the hearts of the children the valuable lessons given.

The Lord works with every consecrated teacher; and it is for his own interest to realize this. Instructors who are under the discipline of God do not manufacture anything themselves. They receive grace and truth and light through the Holy Spirit to communicate to the children. They are under the greatest Teacher the world has ever known, and how unbecoming it would be for them to have an unkind spirit, a sharp harsh voice, full of irritation. In this they would perpetuate their own defects in their children.

Offer a clear perception of what we might accomplish if we would learn of Jesus. The springs of heavenly peace and joy, unsealed in the soul of the teacher by the magic words of inspiration, will become a mighty river of influence, to bless all who connect with him. Do not think that the Bible will become a tiresome book to the children. Under a wise instructor the Word will become more and more desirable. It will be to them as the bread of life, and will never grow old. There is in it a freshness and a beauty that attract and charm the children and youth. It is like the sun shining upon the earth, giving its brightness and warmth, yet never exhausted. By lessons from Bible history and doctrine, the children and youth can learn that all other books are inferior to this. They can find here a fountain of mercy and of love.

God's holy, educating spirit is in his Word. A light, new and precious light, shines forth upon every page. Truth is there revealed and words and sentences are made bright and appropriate for the occasion, as the voice of God speaking to them.

We need to recognize the Holy Spirit as our enlightener. That spirit loves to address the children, and discover to them the treasures and beauties of the Word of God. The promises spoken by the great Teacher will captivate the senses and animate the soul of the child with a spiritual power that is divine. There will grow in the fruitful mind a familiarity with divine things which will be as a barricade against the temptations of the enemy.

The work of teachers is an important one. They should make the Words of God their meditation. God will communicate by his own Spirit to the soul. Pray as you study, "Lord, open thou mine eyes, that I may behold wondrous things out of thy law." When the teacher will rely upon God in prayer, the Spirit fills the mind and heart with pure thoughts, and God will work through him by the Holy Spirit upon the mind of the students. The Holy Spirit fills the mind and heart with sweet hope, and courage, and Bible imagery, and this will be communicated to the students. The words of truth will grow in importance and assume a breadth and fullness of meaning of which you never dreamed. The beauty and riches of the Word of God have a transforming influence upon mind and character; the sparks of heavenly love will fall upon the hearts of the children as an inspiration. We may bring hundreds and thousands of children to Christ if we will work for them.

Let all to whom these words may come be melted and subdued, Let us in our educational work embrace far more than we have done of the children and youth, and there will be a whole army of missionaries raised up to work for God. I say again, establish schools for the children where there are churches, let there be schools. Work as if you were working for your life to save children from being drowned in the polluting, corrupting influences of this life.

Too much is centered in Battle Creek. I need not advise that the sound of ax and hammer be heard in Battle Creek in erecting new buildings. There are places where our schools should have been in operation years ago. Let these now be started under wise directors. The youth should be educated in their own churches. In America you can build three school houses cheaper than we can build one in this country. It is a grievous offense to God that there has been so great neglect to make provision for the improvement of the children and youth when Providence has so abundantly supplied us with facilities with which to work.

Can we wonder that children and youth drift into temptation, and become educated in wrong lines by their association with other neglected children. These children are not wisely educated to use their active minds and limbs to do helpful work. Our schools should teach the children all kinds of simple labor. Can we wonder, neglected as they have been, that their energies become devoted to amusements that do them no good, that their religious aspirations are chilled and their spiritual life darkened? "It is so much trouble," says the mother, "I would rather do these things myself, it is such a trouble; you bother me."

Does not mother remember that she herself had to learn in jots and tittles before she could be helpful? It is a wrong to children to refuse to teach them little by little. Keep these children with you. Let them ask questions, and in patience answer them. Give your little children something to do, and let them have the happiness of supposing they help you. There must be no repulsing of your children when trying to do proper things. If they make mistakes, if accidents happen, and things break, do not blame. Their whole future life depends upon their educations you give them in their childhood years. Teach them all their faculties of body and mind were given them to use, and that all are the Lord's, pledged to his service. To some of these children the Lord gives an early intimation of his will. Parents and teachers, begin early to teach the children to cultivate their God-given faculties.

My brother, I feel deeply over the mistake of locating so many important interests at Battle Creek. There is a world to receive the light of truth. Had interests been located in cities where nothing is being done, the warning message would be given to other cities. You have asked me in regard to the schools being opened in our churches. I have tried to answer you. That light which has centered in Battle Creek should have been shining in other localities. Schools should have been opened in places where they are so much needed. This will provide for the children and youth who are drifting in to Battle Creek. Let the church carry a burden for the lambs of the flock in its locality, and see how many can be educated and trained to do service for God.

E. G. White

Chapter 27—To Teachers

I was a few nights since in my dreams in conversation with the teachers in the school or chapel room. I was speaking to the teachers and said, "I have a message for you." and in substance I presented that which I now write. I was speaking to the teachers in regard to their responsibility of being at all times under the control of the Spirit of God. I repeated these words, "Abide in me, and I in you." "As the branch can not bear fruit of itself, except it abide in the vine; no more can ye, except ye abide in me." "I am the vine, ye are the branches; he that abideth in me, and I in him, the same bringeth forth much fruit: for without me ye can do nothing."

The Lord Jesus is our example in all things. There are those who are acting in the capacity of teachers at___who will do lasting harm to the children who are brought into connection with them because they are not learning daily in the school of Christ. They indeed need that one to teach them, that unless the love of Christ is an abiding principle in the soul temple, it will be defiled with impatience, with fitful, impulsive actions, just because the feelings which control them tend to those results. But every one who has to do with educating the younger class of students should consider that these children are affected by, and feel the impressions of, the atmosphere, whether it be pleasant or unpleasant.

If the teacher is connected with God, if he has Christ abiding in his heart, the spirit that is cherished by him is felt by the children. When a teacher manifests impatience or fretfulness toward a child, the fault may be not in the child one-half as much as it is in the teacher, who himself needs to be disciplined and trained, and observe a heavier punishment than he puts upon the child, for he is old enough to know better. Teachers become tired with their work, then something the children say or do does not accord with their feelings; but will they let Satan's spirit enter into them and lead them to create feelings in the children very unpleasant and disagreeable, through their own lack of tact and wisdom from God? There should not be a teacher employed, unless you have evidence by test and trial, that he loves and fears to offend God. If teachers are taught of God, if their lessons are daily learned in the school of Christ, they will work in Christ's lines. They will win and draw with Christ, for every child and youth is precious.

Every teacher needs Christ abiding in his heart by faith; he needs to possess a true, self-denying, self-sacrificing spirit for Christ's sake. One may have sufficient education and knowledge in science to instruct but has it been ascertained that he has tact and wisdom to deal with human minds? If instructors have not the love of Christ abiding in the heart, they are not fit to be brought into connection with children, and to bear the grave responsibilities placed upon them, of educating these children and youth. They lack the higher education and training in themselves, and they know not how to deal with human minds. There is the spirit of their own insubordinate, natural hearts that is striving for the control; and to subject the plastic minds and characters of children under such a discipline is to leave scars and bruises upon the mind that will never be effaced. This matter has been presented to me in such a variety of ways, tracing from cause to effect, and while the matter is again brought before me and urged upon me by the Spirit of the Lord, I dare not forbear to trace with my pen the evils.

If a teacher can not be made to feel the responsibility and the carefulness he should ever reveal in dealing with human minds, his education has in some cases been very defective, in the home life the training has been harmful to the character, and it is a sad thing to reproduce this defective character and management in the children brought under his control. We are standing before God on test and trial to see if we can individually be trusted to be of the number of the family who shall compose the redeemed in heaven. "And I saw the dead, small and great, stand before God; and the books were opened: and another book was opened, which is the book of life; and the dead were judged out of those things which were written in the books, according to their works."

Here are represented the great white throne and him that sat on it, from whose face the earth and heaven fled away. Let every teacher consider that he is doing his work in the sight of the universe of heaven. Every child with whom the teacher is brought in contact has been purchased by the blood of God's only begotten Son, and he who has died for these children would have them treated as his property. Be sure that your contact, teachers, with every one of these children shall be of that character that will not make you ashamed when you meet them in that great day when every word and action are brought in review before God, and with its burden of results laid open before you individually. "Bought with a price." O what a price eternity alone will reveal! The Lord Jesus Christ hath infinite tenderness for those whom he has purchased at the cost of his own suffering in the flesh, that they should not perish with the devil and his angels, but that he can claim them as his chosen ones. They are the claim of his love, his own property, and he looks upon them with unutterable affection; and the fragrance of his own righteousness he gives to his loved ones who believe in him. It requires tact and wisdom and human love, and sanctified affection for the precious lambs of the flock, to lead them to see and appreciate their privilege in yielding themselves up to the tender guidance of the faithful shepherds. The children of God will exercise the gentleness of Jesus Christ.

Teachers, Jesus is in your school every day. His great heart of infinite love is drawn out not only for the best behaved children, who have the most favorable surroundings, but for children who have by inheritance objectionable traits of character. Even parents have not understood how much they are responsible for the traits of character developed in their children, and have not had the tenderness and wisdom to deal with these poor children, whom they have made what they are. They fail to trace back the cause of these discouraging developments, which are a trial to them. But Jesus looks upon these children with pity and with love, for he sees, he understands from cause to effect.

The teacher may bind these children to his or her heart by the love of Christ abiding in the soul temple as a sweet fragrance, a savor of life unto life. The teachers may, through the grace of Christ imparted to them, be the living human agency to be laborers together with God to enlighten, lift up, and encourage, and help to purify the soul from its moral defilement, and the image of God shall be revealed in the soul of the child, and the character become transformed by the grace of Christ.

The gospel is the power and wisdom of God, if it is correctly represented by those who claim to be Christians. Christ crucified for our sins should humble every soul before God in his own estimation. Christ risen from the dead, ascended on high, our living intercessor in the presence of God, is the science of salvation which we need to learn and teach to children and youth. Said Christ, "I sanctify myself, that they also may be sanctified." This is the work that ever devolves upon every teacher. There must not be any haphazard work in this matter, for even the work of educating the children in the day schools requires very much of the grace of Christ and the subduing of self. Those who naturally are fretful, easily provoked, and who have cherished the habit of criticism, of thinking evil, should find some other kind of work that will not reproduce any of their unlovely traits of character in the children and youth; for they have cost too much. Heaven sees in the child the undeveloped man or woman, with capabilities and powers that, if correctly guided and with heavenly wisdom developed, will become the human agencies through whom the divine influences can cooperate to be laborers together with God. Sharp words, and continual censure bewilder the child, but never reform him. Keep back that pettish word. Keep under discipline to Jesus Christ your own spirit; then will you learn how to pity and sympathize with those brought under your influence. Do not exhibit impatience and harshness, for, if these children did not need educating, they would not need the advantages of the school. They are to be patiently, kindly, and in love brought up the ladder of progress, climbing step by step in obtaining knowledge.

It is a daily working agency that is to be brought into exercise, a faith that works by love, and purifies the soul of the educator. Is the revealed will of God placed as your highest authority? If Christ is formed within, the hope of glory, then the truth of God will so act upon your natural temperament that its transforming agency will be revealed in a changed character, and you will not by your influence through the revealings of an unsanctified heart and temper, turn the truth of God before any of your pupils into a lie, nor in your presentation of a selfish, impatient, unchristlike temper in dealing with any human mind, reveal that the grace of Christ is not sufficient for you at all times and in all places. Thus you will show that the authority of God over you is not merely in name but in reality and truth. There must be a separation from all that is objectionable or unchristlike, however difficult it may be to the true believer.

Inquire, teachers, you who are doing your work not only for time but eternity. Does the love of Christ constrain your heart and your soul, in dealing with the precious souls for whom Jesus has given his own life? Under his constraining discipline do old traits of character, that are not in conformity to the will of God, pass away and the opposite take their place? "A new heart will I give thee." Have all things become new through your conversion to the Lord Jesus Christ? In words and by painstaking effort are you sowing such seed in these young hearts that you can ask the Lord to water it, that it shall, with his imputed righteousness, ripen into a rich harvest? Ask yourself, Am I by my own unsanctified words and impatience and want of that wisdom that is from above, confirming these youth in their perverse spirit because they see that their teacher has a spirit unlike Christ? If they should die in their sins, shall I not be accountable for their souls? The soul who loves Jesus, who appreciates the saving power of his grace will feel such a drawing near to Christ, that he will desire to work in his lines. He can not, dare not, let Satan control his spirit and a poisonous miasma surround his soul. Everything will be placed one side that will corrupt his influence, because it opposes the will of God and endangers the souls of the precious sheep and lambs, and he is required to watch for souls as they that must give an account. Wherever God has, in providence, placed us, he will keep us; as our day, our strength shall be.

Whoever shall give way to his natural feelings and impulses makes himself weak and untrustworthy, for he is a channel through which Satan can communicate, to taint and corrupt many souls, and these unholy fits that control the person swerve his (principle) aside, and shame and confusion are the sure results. The Spirit of Jesus Christ ever has a renewing, restoring power upon the soul that has felt its own weakness and fled to the unchanging One who can give grace and power to resist evil. Our Redeemer had a broad, comprehensive humanity. His heart was ever touched with the known helplessness of the little child that is subject to rough usage, and he loved children. The feeblest cry of human suffering never reaches his ear in vain. And every one who assumes the responsibility of instructing the youth will meet obdurate hearts, perverse dispositions, and his work is to cooperate with God in restoring the moral image of God in every child. Jesus, precious Jesus, a whole fountain of love was in his soul. Those who instruct the children should be men and women of principle. The religious life of a large number who profess to be Christians is such as to show that they are not Christians. They are constantly misrepresenting Christ, falsifying his character. They do not feel the importance of this transformation of character, and that they must be conformed to his divine likeness, and at times they will exhibit a false phase of Christianity to the world which will work ruin to the souls of those who are brought into association with them, for the very reason that they are, while professing to be Christians, not under the control of Jesus Christ. Their own hereditary and cultivated traits of character are indulged as precious qualifications, when they are death-leading in their influence over other minds. In plain, simple words, they walk in the sparks of their own kindling. They have a religion subject to, and controlled by, circumstances. If everything happens to move in a way that pleases them, and there are no irritating circumstances that call to the surface their unsubdued, unchristlike natures, they are condescending and pleasant, and will be very attractive. If when things occur in the family or in their association with others which ruffles their peace and provokes their tempers, they lay every circumstance before God, and continue their request, supplicating his grace before they shall engage in their daily work as teachers, and know for themselves the power and grace and love of Christ abiding in their own hearts before entering upon their labors, angels of God brought with them into the schoolroom. But if they go in a provoked, irritated spirit to the schoolroom, the moral atmosphere surrounding their souls is leaving its impression upon the children who are under their care, and in the place of being fitted to instruct the children, they need one to teach them the lessons of Jesus Christ. They need to learn in the day's work that on such a day they were destitute of the abiding presence of Christ, and that they should have been corrected and punished in place of the children for their perversity, for they merely caught the spirit of the teacher -- the Satanic spirit surrounding their own souls works upon the children, and the children reflect back these influences.

Let every teacher who accepts the responsibility to educate the children and youth examine himself, and study critically from cause to effect. Has the truth of God taken possession of my soul? Has the wisdom which cometh from Jesus Christ, which is "first pure, then peaceable, gentle, and easy to be entreated, full of mercy and good fruits, without hypocrisy and without partiality" been brought into my character? While I stand in the responsible position of an educator do I cherish the principle that "the fruit of righteousness is sown in peace of them that make peace?" The truth is not to be kept to be practiced when we feel just like it, but at all times and in all places.

Well balanced minds and symmetrical characters are required of teachers in every line. Give not this work into the hands of young women and young men who know not how to deal with human minds. This has been a mistake, and it has brought evil upon the children and youth under their charge. They know so little of the controlling power of grace upon their own hearts and characters that they have to unlearn, and learn entirely new lessons in Christian experience. They have never learned to keep their own soul and character under discipline to Jesus Christ, and bring even the thoughts into captivity to Jesus Christ. Oh if you all who have any voice and influence in these important decisions of selecting teachers, would be more God-fearing, and would be more certain that you are making wise choices for the good of the children and the glory of God, there would be an improved condition of things in every way. There are all kinds of characters to deal with in the children and youth. Their minds are impressible. Anything like a hasty, passionate exhibition on the part of the teacher may cut off her influence for good over the students whom she is having the name of educating. And will this education be for the present and future eternal good of the children and youth? There is the correct influence to be exerted upon them for their spiritual good. Instruction is to be constantly given to encourage the children in the formation of correct habits in speech, in voice, in deportment.

Many of these children have not had proper training at home. They have been sadly neglected. Some have been left to do as they pleased; others have been found fault with and discouraged. But little pleasantness and cheerfulness have been shown toward them, and but few words of approval have been spoken to them. The defective characters of the parents have been inherited, and the discipline given by these defective characters have been objectionable in the formation of characters. Solid timbers have not been brought into the character-building. There is no more important work that can be done than the educating and training of these youth and children. The teachers who work in this part of the Lord's vineyard need to learn first how to be self-possessed, keeping their own temper and feelings under control, in subjection to the Holy Spirit of God. They should give evidence of having not a one-sided experience, but a well balanced mind, a symmetrical character, so that they can be trusted because they are conscientious Christians themselves, under the chief Teacher, who has said, "Learn of me, for I am meek and lowly of heart and ye shall find rest unto your souls." Then learning in Christ's school daily, they can educate children and youth.

Self-cultured, self-controlled, under discipline in the school of Christ, having a living connection with the great Teacher, they will have an intelligent knowledge of practical religion, and keeping their own souls in the love of God, they will know how to exercise the grace of patience and Christlike forbearance. The patience, love, long forbearance, and tender sympathies are called into activity. They will discern that they have a most important field in the Lord's vineyard to cultivate. They must lift up their hearts unto God in sincere prayer. Be thou my pattern, and then by beholding Jesus they will do the works of Jesus Christ. Jesus said, the Son can do nothing of himself, but what he seeth the Father do. So with the sons and daughters of God: they steadfastly and teachably look to Jesus, doing nothing in their own way, and after their own will and pleasure; but that which they have in the lessons of Christ seen him, their pattern, do--they do also. Thus they represent to the students under their instruction at all times and upon all occasions the character of Jesus Christ. They catch the bright rays of the Sun of righteousness and reflect these precious beams upon the children and youth whom they are educating. The formation of correct habits is to leave its impress upon the mind and characters of the children, that they may practice the right way. It means much to bring these children under the direct influence of the Spirit of God, training and disciplining them in the nurture and admonition of the Lord. The formation of correct habits, the exhibition of a right spirit, will call for earnest efforts in the name and strength of Jesus. The instructor must persevere, giving line upon line, precept upon precept, here a little and there a little, in all longsuffering and patience, sympathy and love, binding these children to his heart by the love of Christ revealed in himself.

This truth can in the highest sense be acted, and exemplified before the children. "Who can have compassion on the ignorant, and on them that are out of the way; for that he himself also is compassed with infirmity. And by reason hereof he ought, as for the people, so also for himself, to offer for sins." Heb. 5:2-3. Let teachers bear this in mind, and never lose sight of it when they are inclined to have their feelings stirred against the children and youth for misbehaviour. Let them remember that the angels of God are looking upon them sorrowfully; for if the children do err and misbehave, then it is all the more essential that those who are placed over them as teachers should be able to teach them by precept and example. In no case are they to lose self-control, to manifest impatience, and harshness and want of sympathy and love, for these children are the property of Jesus Christ, and teachers must be very careful and God-fearing in regard to the spirit they cherish and the words they utter, for the children will catch the spirit manifest, be it good or evil. It is a heavy and a sacred responsibility.

There need to be teachers who are thoughtful, considerate of their own weakness and infirmities and sins, and who will not be oppressive and discourage the children and youth. There needs to be much praying, much faith, much forbearance and courage which the Lord is ready to bestow. For God sees every trial, and a wonderful influence can be exerted by teachers, if they will practice the lessons which Christ has given them. But will these teachers consider their own wayward course, that they make very feeble efforts to learn in the school of Christ and practice Christ-like meekness and lowliness of heart? The teachers should be themselves in obedience to Jesus Christ, and ever practicing his words, that they may exemplify the character of Jesus Christ to the students. Let your light shine in good works, in faithful watching and caring for the lambs of the flock, with patience, with tenderness, and the love of Jesus in your own hearts. Never, never educate them to speak impatiently and passionately, because their teacher does these things. Never educate them by giving publicity to the errors and misdoings of any scholar, for they will consider it a virtue in them to expose the wrongs of another. Never humiliate a scholar by presenting his grievances, and mistakes, and sins before the school. You can not do a work more effectual to harden their hearts and confirm them in evil than in doing this. Talk and pray with them alone, and show the same tenderness Christ has evidenced to you who are teachers. Never encourage any one student to criticise and talk of the faults of others; hide a multitude of sins in every way possible by pursuing Christ's way to cure them. This kind of educating will be a blessing, made to tell in this life and stretching into the future immortal life.

To place young men and young women in such a field who have not developed a deep, earnest, love for God and the souls for whom Christ has died, is making a mistake which will result in the loss of many precious souls. The teacher needs to be susceptible to the influences of the Spirit of God. Not one who will become impatient and irritated, should be an educator. Teachers must consider that they are dealing with children, not men and women. They are children who have everything to learn, and it is much more difficult for some to learn than others. The dull scholar needs much more encouragement than he receives. If teachers are placed over these varied minds who naturally love to order and dictate and magnify themselves in their authority, who will deal with partiality, having favorites to whom they will show preferences, while others are treated with exactitude and severity, it will create a state of confusion and insubordination. Teachers who have not been blessed with a pleasant and well balanced experience may be placed to take charge of children and youth, but a great wrong is done to those whom they instruct. Those who accept such persons as teachers are responsible for the evil resulting from their course of teaching, and in giving a wrong mold to young human minds. It may be compared to a field untilled, and when tares are sowed with the wheat, a crop of thistles and weeds and briars is the result of this defective education.

A neglected field represents the neglected mind. Parents must come to view this matter in a different light. They must feel it their duty to cooperate with the teacher, to encourage wise discipline, and to pray much for the one who is teaching their children. You will not help the children by fretting, nor by censuring and discouraging them; neither will you act a good part to help them to rebel and to be disobedient and unkind and unlovable, because of the spirit you develop. If you are Christians indeed, you will have an abiding Christ and the spirit of him who gave life for sinners, and the wisdom of God will teach you in every emergency the course to pursue. Christ identifies his interests with every class and phase of humanity who are wrestling with temptations. You are not to countenance wrongdoing in any case, and you are not to make statements of wrongdoing which shall expel even the perverse doer. Never chastise in a way that increases stubbornness (unless you wish to bring upon your soul the same treatment from Jesus), and confirms the student in his evil course. Children are in need of having a steady, firm, living principle of righteousness exercised over them and enacted before them. Be sure to let the true light shine before your pupils. It is heaven's light that is wanted. Never let the world have the impression that your spirit and taste and longings are of no higher and purer an order than the worldling's. If you in your action leave this impression upon them, you let a false, deceptive light lead them to ruin. The trumpet must give a certain sound. There is a broad, clear, and deep line drawn by the eternal God between the righteous and unrighteous, the godly and ungodly; between those who are obedient to God's commandments and those who are disobedient.

The ladder which Jacob saw in the night vision, the base of it resting upon the earth, and the topmost round reaching unto the highest heavens, God himself above the ladder, and his glory shining upon every round, angels ascending and descending upon this ladder of shining brightness, is a symbol of constant communication kept up between this world and heavenly places. God accomplishes his will through the instrumentality of heavenly angels in continual intercourse with humanity. This ladder reveals a direct and important channel of communication with the inhabitants of this earth. The ladder represented to Jacob was the world's Redeemer who links earth and heaven together. Every one who has seen the evidence and light of truth and accepts the truth, professing his faith in Jesus Christ, is a missionary in the highest sense of the word. He is the receiver of heavenly treasures, and it is his duty to impart them, to diffuse that which he has received.

Then to those who are accepted as teachers in our schools is opened a field for labor and cultivation, for the sowing of the seed and for the harvesting of the ripening grain. What can give greater satisfaction than to be laborers together with God in educating and training the children and youth to love God and keep his commandments? Lead the children whom you are instructing in the day school and the Sabbath school to Jesus. What can give you greater joy than to see children and youth following Christ, the great Shepherd, who calls and the sheep and lambs hear his voice and follow him? What can spread more sunshine through the soul of the interested, devoted worker, than to show that his persevering, patient labor is not in vain in the Lord, and to see his pupils have the sunshine of joy in their souls because Christ has forgiven their sins. What can be more satisfying to the worker together with God than to see children and youth receiving the impressions of the spirit of God in true nobility of character and in the restoration of the moral image of God? The children seeking the peace coming from the Prince of Peace! The truth a bondage? Yes, in one sense it binds the willing souls in captivity to Jesus Christ, bowing their hearts to the gentleness of Jesus Christ. Oh, it means so much more than finite minds can comprehend to present in every missionary effort Jesus Christ and him crucified. But he was wounded for our transgressions. He was bruised for our iniquities, the chastisement of our peace was upon him, and with his stripes we are healed. For he made him to be sin for us who knew no sin, that we might be made the righteousness of God in him. This is to be the burden of our work. If any one thinks he is capable of teaching in the Sabbath school or in the day school the science of education, needs first to learn the fear of the Lord which is the beginning wisdom, that he may teach this the highest of all sciences.

Oh, I so much wish that the Lord of heaven would open many eyes that are now blind, that they might see themselves as God sees them, and give to them a sense of the work to be done in the fields of labor. But I have no hope that all the appeals I make will avail, unless the Lord speaks to the soul and writes his requirements upon the tablets of the heart. Can not every living human agent have a high and elevated sense of what it means to have a large and important field of home missionary work appointed to him, without the necessity of going to far-off lands? And while some must proclaim the message to them that are far off, there are many who have to proclaim the message to those who are nigh. Our schools are to be educating schools to qualify youth to become missionaries both by precept and example. Let the one who is acting in the capacity of teacher ever bear in mind that these children and youth are the purchase of the blood of the Son of God. They must be led to believe in God as their personal Saviour. The name of each separate believer is graven on the palms of his hands. The chief Shepherd is looking down from the heavenly sanctuary upon the sheep of his pasture. He calleth his own sheep by name and leadeth them out. "If any man sin, we have an advocate with the Father, even Jesus Christ, the righteous." O precious, blessed; truth! He does not treat one case with indifference.

His impressive parable of the good shepherd represents the responsibility of every minister and of every Christian who has accepted the position as teacher of children and youth and the teacher of old and young in opening to them the Scriptures. If one strays from the fold, he is not allowed with harsh words and with a whip, but with winning invitations to return. The ninety-and-nine that have not strayed do not call for the sympathy and tender pitying love of the shepherd. But the shepherd follows the sheep and lambs that have caused him the greatest anxiety and have engrossed his sympathies. The disinterested, faithful shepherd leaves all the rest of the sheep, and his whole heart and soul and energy are taxed to seek the one that is lost. And then the figure--praise God!--the shepherd returns with the sheep, carrying him in his arms, rejoicing at every step. He says, "Rejoice with me, I have found my sheep that was lost." I am so thankful we have in the parable the sheep found. And this is the very lesson the shepherd is to learn - success in bringing the sheep and lambs back.

There is no picture presented before our imagination of a sorrowful shepherd returning without the sheep. And the Lord Jesus declares the pleasure of the shepherd, and his joy in finding the sheep causes pleasure and rejoicing in heaven among the angels. Then when the children and youth stray from the fold, do not give them up, do not expel them from school. Do not show that you want to humiliate them; but with tender voice and yearning love seek them, knowing that all heaven is enlisted with you in the work of bringing them back to the fold. The Lord has presented these lessons for you who are educators. He has such a living interest for each separate child of his redeemed that he has not left them to be exposed and perish in the wilderness of temptation, because you drove them there for Satan to work his cruel will upon them. The wisdom of God, his power and his love, are without a parallel. It is the divine guarantee that not one even of the straying sheep and lambs is overlooked, and not one left unsuccored. A golden chain, the mercy and compassion of divine power, is passed around every one of these imperiled souls. Then shall not the human agent cooperate with God. Shall he be sinful, failing, defective in character himself, regardless of the soul ready to perish? Christ has linked him to his eternal throne by offering his own life.

Bear in mind, every teacher who takes the responsibility of dealing with human minds, that every soul who is inclined to err and is easily tempted, is the special object for whom Christ is solicitor. They that are whole need not a physician, but those that are sick. The compassionate intercessor is pleading, and will sinful, finite men and women repulse a single soul?

Shall any man or woman be indifferent to the very souls for whom Christ is pleading in the courts of heaven? Shall you in your course of action imitate the Pharisees, who were merciless, and Satan, who would accuse and destroy? Oh, will you individually humble your own souls before God, and let that stern nerve and iron will be subdued and broken?

Step away from the sound of Satan's voice and from acting his will, and stand by the side of Jesus, possessing his attributes, the possessor of keen tender sensibilities, who can make the cause of the afflicted suffering one his own. The man who has had much forgiven will love much. Jesus is a compassionate Intercessor, a merciful and faithful high priest. He, the Majesty of Heaven! The King of glory can look upon finite man, subject to the temptations of Satan, knowing that he has felt the power of Satan's wiles. "Wherefore in all things it behoved him to be made like unto his brethren (clothing his divinity with humanity), that he might be a merciful and faithful high priest in things pertaining to God, to make reconciliation for the sins of the people. For in that he himself hath suffered being tempted, he is able to succor them that are tempted.

Then I call upon you, my brethren, to practice working in the lines that Christ worked. You must never put on the cloak of severity and condemn and denounce and drive away from the fold the poor tempted mortals. But as laborers together with God, heal the spiritually diseased. This you will do if you have the mind of Christ. "For we have not an high priest which can not be touched with the feeling of our infirmities; but was in all points tempted like as we are, yet without sin." (Hebrews 4:15)

E. G. White

Chapter 28—Adopting Infant Children

From time to time persons have asked my counsel in regard to the advisability of adopting infant children. Among these several wives of ministers. Before answering these questions, I have tried, as far as possible, to learn all the circumstances of the case. And I have not dared to give counsel unless I knew that the Lord was leading me.

There are persons who have no little ones of their own, who may do good by adopting children. Those who have not the sacred responsibility of proclaiming the Word, and laboring directly for the salvation of souls, have duties in other lines of work. If they are consecrated to God, and are qualified to mold and fashion human minds, the Lord will bless them in caring for the children of others. But let the children of believers have our first consideration. There are among Sabbath-keepers very many large families of children that are not properly cared for. Many parents give evidence that they have not learned of Christ the lessons that would make them safe guardians of children. Their children do not receive the proper training. And there are among us many children whom death has deprived of a parent's care. There are those who might take some of these children and seek to mold and fashion their characters according to Bible principles. ...

But I dare not counsel our ministers and missionaries who are continually moving from place to place, to encumber themselves by adopting children, especially helpless infants. Those who have children of their own must share the responsibility of training them to do service for God. It is the wife's duty to care for the children and husband. The Lord will give her strength to do this work if she will put her trust in Him and obey the laws of life and health. The husband and wife are to unite in the work of bringing up the children in the love and fear of God. A well ordered and well disciplined family will have a powerful influence for good. But if you have no children of your own, it may be that the Lord has a wise purpose in withholding from you this blessing. It should not be taken as evidence that it is your duty to adopt a child. In some cases this might be advisable. When the Lord bids you take an infant to bring up, then the duty is too plain to be misunderstood. But, as a rule, it is not God's will for a minister's wife to encumber herself with such a responsibility.

The work of God demands most earnest labor, and the Lord would have ministers and their wives closely united in this work. The husband and wife can so blend their labor that the wife shall be the complement of the husband. The Lord desires them unitedly to watch for his voice, to draw closer and still closer to Him, feeding upon his Word, and receiving light and blessing to impart to others. They should be as free as possible to attend camp-meetings and other general gatherings. And the wife may continually be a great help to her husband in visiting, and other personal labor.

If the companion of a minister is united with her husband in the work of saving souls, it is the highest work she can do. But the care of a little child would absorb her attention, so that she could not attend the meetings and labor successfully in the visiting and personal effort. Even if she accompanies her husband, the child is too often the burden of thought and conversation, and the visits are made of no effect. Those whom God has called to be colaborers with him, are to have no idols to absorb their thought and affection which he would have directed in other lines. ...

We need carefully to search our hearts and study our motives. Selfishness may prompt the desire to do what appears to be an unselfish and praiseworthy act. The reason that many urge for desiring to adopt a child - the longing for something on which to center our affections - reveals the fact that the heart is not centered upon Christ: it is not absorbed in his work. When I have heard a wife mourning that her husband did not show her all the affection that she thought he should, I have sent a silent petition to God, that this soul might be refreshed with the Word. From the light that God has given me, I knew that she needed to drink the deep, cool waters of Lebanon, instead of the turbid streams of the valley. When women will feed upon the Water of Life, they will have far less sentimentalism, and far greater spirituality. They will purify their souls by obeying the truth. If a woman's life is connected with one whom God has chosen, to be a laborer together with God, let her consider that she can make his heart tired, and his soul sad, by her unconsecrated course of action. If self clamors for attention, and unless great devotion is shown her, she becomes unhappy, and she may greatly hinder him in his work. She needs to learn of Christ, who lived not to please himself. He is our example in all things.

If the wife is a colaborer with Christ in the work of saving souls, she will keep abreast with her husband in cultivating mind and heart. She will endeavor to stand equal with him in knowledge of the Word of God, and in obedience to all of His requirements. She will keep her own soul refreshed by eating the Word and drinking the waters from the wellspring of life. Then the words she speaks will not be prompted by envy or jealousy. They will proceed from a sanctified heart, that has been daily learning lessons at the feet of Jesus. Thus, instead of making herself a helpless burden, to be the object of her husband's solicitude, and to demand a large share of his attention, the wife may strengthen her husband to do the highest service for God.

The light which God has given me in regard to ministers' wives is, if their lives are kept in close consecration to God, as is the duty of all who are laborers together with Him, they will find so many souls to minister unto, that they will have no opportunity to be lonesome or to cultivate selfishness in any line. Jesus says, "Take my yoke upon you, and learn of me; for I am meek and lowly in heart, and ye shall find rest for your souls." Those who heed this invitation will have no thought of repining, no thought of loneliness. Their work is to do the will of Christ. As they do this, they will have sweet peace and rest of soul.

The question of adopting a child, especially an infant, involves a most serious responsibility. It should not be lightly regarded. One who has herself taken a baby to bring up, may feel that unless other ministers' wives shall follow her example, they are remiss in their duty. But this is an error. Our duty is not decided by what others may plan for us. The question for each to settle is, in doing this, shall I be merely gratifying my own wishes, or is it a duty the Lord has appointed me? Is this His way, or the way of my own choosing? All are to be workers for God. Not one is excused. Your talents are not your own, to employ as you may fancy. Inquire, what would the Lord have me do with the entrusted talents? Shall I labor for the salvation of souls? Shall I follow the directions of (Isaiah 58:6-11)?

There are deep, earnest lessons for us to learn, else self will be our center, the controlling power of our lives. The duty is of the present, vigilant, working, and earnest, solemn waiting in view of the solemn event of our Lord's appearing. Workings, watchings, praying,--these constitute the ideal Christian duty and responsibility, making the perfect man in Christ Jesus. Our life is not to be all waiting, not all bustle and activity and excitement, to the neglect of personal piety. The door of the heart must always be open to Jesus, that we may always hear his voice and invitation, "Behold, I stand at the door and knock; if any man hear my voice and open the door, I will come into him, and will sup with him, and he with me." We are to be "not slothful in business, fervent in spirit, serving the Lord." There is always a danger of taking upon ourselves a work the Lord has not placed in our hands, and neglecting that which he has given us to do, and which would better honor his name; that which to human eyes may appear praiseworthy, may be the very thing the Lord has not placed in our hands. Then let us individually consider the many branches of the work. There are various kinds of work to do. Consider prayerfully what would best tell for the cause of God. If there is a humble, unselfish heart, and a contrite spirit, in seeking to know the Lord's will, he will lead each of us in the path where he would have us walk.

Let no one feel condemned because she does not take a child to care for. The Lord may have a greater work for you to do in teaching those who know not God to do his will. Thus saith the Lord: "Neither let the son of the stranger, that hath joined himself unto the Lord, speak saying, The Lord hath utterly separated me from his people; neither let the eunuch say, I am a dry tree. For thus saith the Lord to the eunuchs that keep my Sabbaths, and choose the things that please me, and take hold of my covenant: even unto them will I give in mine house a place and a name better than of sons and daughters: I will give them an everlasting name, that shall not be cut off."

I have written these things that Satan may not allure any of my brother ministers or their companions into positions where they would be prevented from doing the very work that the Lord has assigned them. We must watch, we must pray, and when the Lord says, Whom shall I send to do this errand for me, we should be ready to say, "Here am I, send me." Serious work is to be done. It has been waiting for unselfish, consecrated workers. Brethren and sisters, open your hearts to the Spirit of God, and devote your God-given abilities to working as for your lives to pull some soul out of the fire. Keep in the channel of light, for there is to be more direct communication from heaven to earth. We have not a moment to lose. There is a heaven to win, and a hell to shun.

I call upon my brethren to come to the help of the Lord against the mighty. I call upon my sisters to stand by their side, and help them in the work. "Ye are not your own, for ye are brought with a price: therefore glorify God in your body, and in your spirit, which are God's.

Mrs. E. G. White

Chapter 29—Principles of Finance

Stanmore, Sydney, N.S.W., April 21, 1898.

Dear Brn. Evans, Smith, and Jones:

I received your letter, and will write a few lines now.

There are ministers' wives, Sisters Starr, Haskell, Wilson and Robinson, who have been devoted, earnest, whole-souled workers, giving Bible readings and praying with families, helping along by personal efforts just as successfully as their husbands. These women give their whole time, and are told that they receive nothing for their labors because their husbands receive their wages. I tell them to go forward and all such decisions shall be reversed. The Word says, "The laborer is worthy of his hire." When any such decision as this is made, I will in the name of the Lord, protest. I will feel it in my duty to create a fund from my tithe money, to pay these women who are accomplishing just as essential work as the ministers are doing, and this tithe I will reserve for work in the same line as that of the ministers, hunting for souls, fishing for souls. I know that the faithful women should be paid wages proportionate to the pay received by ministers. They carry the burden of souls, and should not be treated unjustly. These sisters are giving their time to educating those newly come to the faith, and hire their own work done, and pay those who work for them. All these things must be adjusted and set in order, and justice be done to all. Proof-readers in the office receive their wages, two dollars and a half and three dollars a week. This I have had to pay, and others have to pay. But ministers' wives, who carry a tremendous responsibility, devoting their entire time, have nothing for their labor. This will give you an idea of how matters are in this conference. There are seventy-five souls organized into a church, who are paying their tithe into the conference, and as a saving plan it has been deemed essential to let these poor souls labor for nothing! But this does not trouble me, for I will not allow it to go thus. In regard to the school's running in debt. The tuition has been altogether too low in America.

Can not those who conduct the schools in America understand that this is the only way out? Why do they keep the price so low? An increase in price of educational advantages would stop that increasing debt. The students are to be fed, and they need good, nourishing food. They should not be stinted in the wholesome fruit and vegetarian diet; but cut off everything like the desserts. Let abundance of fruit be eaten with the meals, but custards and pastries are of no manner of use--all unnecessary. Now when the wise heads officiating in our schools study to run the school upon a sum wholly insufficient, year after year, they are engaged in a work that will bring debts; it can not be prevented. They have begun this policy in Cooranbong, but the very same results will follow. There is no justice, or requirement of God, for them to make such loose calculations. They make it necessary to practice the closest economy, and it is not always wise to bring down the diet as a means of avoiding debt. Economy must be practiced in every line to keep afloat, and not be drowned with debts: but there is to be an increase in the sum paid for tuition. This was presented to me while in Europe, and has been presented since to you and our schools; and the problem, "How shall our schools keep out of debt?" will always remain a problem until there are wiser calculations. Charge higher rates for students' educational advantages, and then let persons have the management in cooking who know how to save and economize. Let the best talent be secured, even if good, reasonable wages have to be paid. The binding about the edges is essential. When these precautions are attended to, you will not have increasing debts in your schools. Let the teachers be health reformers; let them teach the Bible as the foundation study; let them practice the Word themselves. Let infidel books be laid aside, and the Word of God find its place in every school. Some will say, "We shall have fewer students." This may be; but those that you do have will appreciate their time, and see the necessity of diligent work to qualify them for the positions they fill. If the Lord is kept ever before the students as the one to whom they should look for counsel, like Daniel, they will receive of him knowledge and wisdom. All will then become channels of light. Lay the matter before the students themselves. Inquire who of them will practice self-denial and make sacrifice to cancel the debt already incurred. With some students only the willing mind is needed. God help the managers of our schools never to allow the outgoes to exceed the incomes, if the school has to be closed. There has not been the talent that is needed in the management of our schools financially. These things God will require of the managers. Every needless, expensive habit is to be laid aside, every unnecessary indulgence cut away. When the principles so manifestly indicated by the Word of God to all schools are taken hold of as earnestly as they should be, the debts will not accumulate.

Whatever may be the amount of means coming in, strictest economy is to be studied. Economy and care must be exercised in expending funds, not to please fancy, but to study the limited means. Care must be used, economy practiced from the very highest motives, linking all expenditures with God himself, for it is God's money we are handling, and we can limit the supply by our want of foresight. It is not best to purchase the cheapest things, but the most serviceable and enduring. They may be more expensive at the time, but if they are treated carefully they will not be the dearest in the end. Those who realize that all money is the Lord's, will get into the habit of asking the Lord how it shall be used, as to what they shall purchase in the little things as well as in the large. This is the right principle to work upon. ...

A word more. Everyone connected with the cause and work of God must keep his talent of wits in captivation, or we shall make grave blunders. This means to set the Lord ever before us. May the Lord help us, is my prayer. Heartless, improvements of talents and thoroughness, are to be cultivated, that no haphazard work shall be done.

God help you, strengthen and comfort you, is my prayer. Look up always. Jesus is a risen Saviour. He is not in Joseph's tomb with a great stone rolled before the door. We have a living, risen Christ, who stands at the head of his church. I hope our people will hang their helpless souls upon God. He can bear your weight; he can carry all your burdens. In much sympathy with all your perplexities, I will close this long letter.

Ellen G. White

Chapter 30—The Need of Harmonious Action Among Teachers

Cooranbong, April 27, 1898.

(Some of the statements in this Testimony are contained in Volume VI, "Hindrances to Reform" p. 141, ff., and Volume IX, "The Spirit of Independence," p. 257, ff.)

Teachers and students, you are associated together in school capacity, and you are to bear in mind that newly established schools are to be of an altogether different order from our older schools or colleges. In our schools generally there has been a patterning after the popular schools and seminaries; but the Lord in his providence has arranged that schools should be established, upon which the example of those already molded by wrong principles, shall have no influence.

In America the Bible has been brought in to some extent, but teachers and students have depended too much upon the books of authors whose ideas and sentiments are misleading. When the light of truth for these last days came to the world in the proclamation of the first, second, and third angel's messages, we were shown that a different order of things must be brought into school work; but it has taken much time to come to an understanding of the changes that should be made in the lines of study and the manner of teaching. It is the most difficult to follow right principles after being so long accustomed to the practices of the world; but reforms must be entered into with heart, and soul, and will. Altogether too long have the old habits and customs been followed.

The Word of God is to be made our study book. But how can this be done is the question asked again and again by the teachers in our long established schools. Attempts to do this have been made; but there have been so many questions asked, so many council meetings held, so much effort that every difficulty be discerned, that the reformers have been handicapped, and some have ceased to urge the reforms. They have been unable to stem the current of inquiry and criticism. But if teachers had advanced step by step in the right way as light shone upon their pathway, following the great Leader, the difficulties would have vanished. The approval of God would have made them hopeful. Ministering angels would have co-operated with the human agents, and they would have received light, and grace, and courage, and gladness.

There is work which God requires of human agents that has not been done. The first attempts to change the old customs have brought severe trials upon those who endeavored to walk in the way which God had pointed out; but teachers should understand that a soldier's life is one of aggressive warfare, of perseverance, and endurance. It is a real warfare in which we are engaged. Says the apostle; "Finally, my brethren, be strong in the Lord, and in the power of his might. Put on the whole armor of God, that ye may be able to stand against the wiles of the devil. For we wrestle not against flesh and blood, but against principalities, against powers, against the rulers of the darkness of this world, against spiritual wickedness in high places."

This is no make-believe conflict. We have to meet powerful adversaries, and for this work we are to find our strength just where the early disciples found their strength. "They were all with one accord in one place," and as they "continued with one accord in prayer and supplication," "suddenly there came a sound from heaven as of a rushing mighty wind, and it filled all the house where they were sitting. And there appeared unto them cloven tongues like as of fire, and it sat upon each of them. And they were all filled with the Holy Ghost, and began to speak with other tongues, as the spirit gave them utterance."

On another occasion, we read, "when they had prayed, the place was shaken where they were assembled together; and they were all filled with the Holy Ghost, and they spoke the word of God with boldness. And the multitude of them that believed, were of one heart and of one soul." This is the work that is needed in our schools. When self is merged in Christ, there will be a display of his power such as will melt and subdue hearts. The earnest prayer of contrite souls will ascend to the throne of God.

Those who enlist in the army of Christ are expected to do difficult work, to endure trials for Christ's sake; and they should now obtain an experience that will center their whole faith and hope and confidence in Christ. Then they will have nothing to fear when conflicts come that tear the soul asunder. They will have a refuge. Their energies may be taxed to the uttermost, but they will have the assurance of Christ, "Lo, I am with you alway, even unto the end of the world."

An army in battle would become confused and weakened unless all worked in concert. If the soldiers should act out their own impulsive ideas, without reference to each other's positions and work, they would be a collection of independent atoms; they could not do the work of an organized body. So the soldiers of Christ must act in harmony. They alone must not be cherished. If they do this, the Lord's people in the place of being in perfect harmony, of one mind, one purpose, and consecrated to one grand object, will find efforts fruitless, their time and capabilities wasted. Union is strength. A few converted souls acting in harmony, acting for one grand purpose, under one head, will achieve victories at every encounter.

Some may say, "I love the Lord, but I can not love my brother as I should." The brother may have ways that are very trying, he may do things that are unwise; but if his brethren who have had longer experience and a more even, well-balanced judgment, shall refuse to connect with the one who grieves and tries their souls, they reveal that they are not followers of Christ. They make manifest that they do not follow the example of Him who clothes his divinity with humanity that by laying aside his glory and his kingly honor, he might reach humanity. Christ might have remained in heaven, and retained all his outward glory and majesty; but he did not do this. In order to bless humanity with his presence and his example, he came to earth as a man, He came that he might call humanity to unite with him in his work, to become members of the firm in the great plan of salvation. In this work there is no such things as every man's being independent. The stars of heaven are all under law, each influencing the other to do the will of God, yielding their common obedience to the law which controls their action. And, in order that the Lord's work may advance healthfully and solidly, his people must draw together.

The spasmodic, fitful movements of some who claim to be Christians are well represented by the work of a span of strong but untrained horses. When one pulls forward, an other pulls back, and at the voice of their master one plunges ahead, and the other stands immovable. If men will not move in concert in the great and grand work for this time, there will be confusion. It is not a good sign when men will not unite with their brethren, but prefer to act alone, when they will not take their brethren into their confidence, because they do not just exactly meet their mind. If man will wear the yoke of Christ, they can not pull apart. They will draw with Christ.

Some workers pull with all the power that God has given them, but they do not sense that they must not pull alone. They must not isolate themselves, but draw with their fellow-laborers. Unless they do this, their activity will work at the wrong time and in the wrong way, they will often work counter to that which God would have done, and thus their work is worse than wasted.

Jesus came to a world all seared and marred by the curse, and, at an immense sacrifice to himself, took fallen man with all his mistakes, and invited him to wear his yoke. He gives the words of invitation to all, and all who will yoke up with him will cooperate with Christ, and be one in the great plan of redemption. All who believe the great truths for this time, if sanctified through the truth, will wear the yoke of Christ. They will lift the burdens of responsibility. No man can be a wise and good soldier, unless he wears the yoke of Christ. If from self-will or a too high estimate of his own wisdom and his own methods and plans, he wants to work in his own lines, he can not be a good soldier of Christ. The Christian soldier must act in concert, step in concert, with those who are connected with him. He must not take offense if every other mind does not run in the same channel with his own. Self-restraint is always needed in order to maintain concerted action. God is not the author of confusion, but of peace. ...

If we are in fellowship with Christ, we shall be in fellowship with our brethren, and shall learn to keep that harmony that should ever exist between the believers. Love must be cherished for one another, for the strengthening of the church, and that we may give to the world the very best impressions of our faith: "A new commandment I give unto you," said Christ, "that ye love one another; as I have loved you, that ye also love one another. By this shall men know that ye are my disciples, if ye have love one for another."

Ellen G. White.

Chapter 31—Life in Medical Missionary Work

"Sunnyside" Cooranbong, May 19, 1898.

Dear Brother Irwin:

I hope that now, as never before, you will all, ministers and church-members, come up to the help of the Lord, to the help of the Lord against the mighty powers of darkness. But I have written so much matter that I need not write largely to you. I will inquire why some of our ministerial brethren are so far behind in proclaiming the exalted theme of temperance? Why is it that greater interest is not shown in health reform? There are many who nourish and keep alive a constant prejudice against Dr. Kellogg. He is doing a large work. Why do they not fill their places in the ministry as well and as zealously as he is filling his place? Why do not the ministers of our churches do the very work that ought to have been done years ago? I am glad that someone has taken up the work which has been so neglected.

The complaint comes, Dr. Kellogg has gathered up all the young men he can get, and therefore we have no workers. But this is the very best thing that could be done for the young men and the work. To you, as President of the General Conference, and to Brother Evans, as President of the General Conference Association, and to Brother Durland, as President of the Michigan Conference, I would say, continue to work with tact and ability. Get some of these young men and young women to work in the churches. Combine medical missionary work with the proclamation of the third angel's message. Make regular, organized efforts to lift the churches out of the dead level in which they have been for years. Send out into the churches workers who will set the principles of health reform, connected with the third angel's message, before every church in Michigan. See if the breath of life will not then come into these churches.

There are too many today who are merely human moralists. A new element needs to be brought into the work, God's people must receive the warning, and work for souls right where they are; for people do not realize their great need and peril. Christ sought the people where they were, and placed before them the great truths in regard to his kingdom. As he went from place to place, he blessed and comforted the suffering, and healed the sick. This is our work. God would have us relieve the necessities of the destitute. The reason that the Lord does not manifest his power more decidedly is because there is so little spirituality among those who claim to believe the truth.

There are in our world many Christian workers who have not yet heard the grand and wonderful truths that have come to us. These are doing a good work, in accordance with the light they have, and many of them are more advanced in knowledge and practical work, than are those who have had great light, great opportunities.

The indifference among our ministers in regard to health reform and medical missionary work, is surprising. Even those who do not profess to be Christians treat the subject with greater reverence than do some of our own people, and they are going in advance of us. The word given to me for you is, "Go forward." "All power is given unto me in heaven and in earth. Go ye therefore, and teach all nations, baptizing them in the name of the Father, and of the Son, and of the Holy Ghost, teaching them to observe all things whatsoever I commanded you, and lo, I am with you always, even unto the end of the world."

The message has been given to those in Battle Creek to move into places where they could do this work, in connection with their temporal business. Had they moved out by faith, they would have obtained a rich experience in the things of God. But they thought they would find things a little less taxing in Battle Creek than elsewhere. Many crowd into Battle Creek who get no good there, because they do not make use of the knowledge they receive. They do no good in Battle Creek, and are only swelling the number who need conversion. They have no spirit of sacrifice. They have a great deal of self and a little bit of Christ, a little faith, and a few good works, and they think that they have religion. But it all amounts to nothing.

What do we read in the seventeenth chapter of John? "I have given unto them the words which thou gavest me; and they have received them, and have known surely (by experimental knowledge) that I came out from thee, and they have believed that thou didst send me." Please read this chapter; for it is full of richness. "As thou hast sent me into the world," Christ continued, "even so have I also sent them into the world. And for their sakes I sanctify myself, that they also might be sanctified through the truth. Neither pray I for these alone, but for them also which shall believe on me through their word." Are we voicing the words of Christ? Are we sanctifying ourselves through obedience to the truth?

"Neither pray I for these alone, but for them also which shall believe on me through their word; that they all may be one, as thou Father, art in me, and I in thee, that they also may be one in me; that the world may believe that thou hast sent me. And the glory which thou gavest me I have given them; that they may be one, even as we are one: I in them, and thou in me, that they may be made perfect in one; and that the world may know that thou hast sent me, and hast loved them, as thou hast loved me."

Apply these words to the members of our churches, and see if they are teaching the plan of salvation as Christ has appointed. Are they seeking for that perfect oneness that Christ prayed they should have? Have they indeed kept the words of the living oracle of God? I tell you, my brother, that there is a work to do beside preaching,--the work of ministering, which has been strangely neglected.

When any one in Battle Creek or in any place shall speak words which depreciate the medical work, ask them what they are doing to perform the work of God has given them to do. Let them take up the work just where they are, and cease this criticizing.

Brother Irwin, take hold of the work of health reform. If any of the ministers have the idea that the medical missionary work is gaining undue preponderance, let them take the men who have been working in these lines with them into their fields of labor, two here and two there. Let the ministers receive these medical missionaries as they would receive Christ, and see what work they can do. See if, in this way, you can not bring some of heaven's vital current into the churches. See if there is not a class who will grasp the education they need so much, see if they will not hear the testimony, "But God, who is rich in mercy, for his love wherewith he loved us, even when we were dead in sins, hath quickened us together with Christ (not aside from Christ), (by grace are ye saved): and hath raised us up together, and made us sit together in heavenly places (not in independent atoms) in Christ Jesus.". ...

Mrs. E. G. White

Chapter 32—Practical Missionary Work a Branch of Education

(A part of this Testimony is contained in "Counsels to Teachers," Page 545 ff.)

Bible study is to lie at the foundation of all true education: but more, far more than a mere theoretical knowledge of Bible truth is required. It is not enough to fill minds of the students with precious lessons of the deepest importance, and then leave lesson after lesson unused. Missionary work should be done by suitable ones, that they may learn to impart that which they have received. Those to whom light has been given are not to seal up the precious ointment, but are to break the bottle and let the fragrance be shared by all around. There are those among the students who have precious talents. Our counsellor says, "Let the talents be put out to usury."

It is necessary to the best education that we give the students time to do missionary work, time to become acquainted with the families among whom they live. They should not be loaded down with all the studies they can carry, but should be given time to use the knowledge they have acquired. They should be encouraged to do faithful missionary work, by becoming interested in those in the darkness of error, taking to them the truth where they are. With all humility of heart seeking knowledge from Christ, praying, and watching unto prayer, they may make known to others the truth that is placed them day by day.

Those who do this work will find many, both old and young, who are full of hereditary prejudice, who hate the truth because of a misconception of its character. As these become acquainted with those who know and practice the truth, they will see their own errors, and while wrath and spiteful passions may appear to be cherished, friendly intercourse will change these feelings. A thick veil of prejudice blinds many minds. They need love and pity and the holiness of truth.

The teachers and students in our school need the divine touch. God can do more for them than he has done, but in the past his way has been restricted. If a missionary spirit were encouraged, even though it took some hours from the program of study, if there were more faith and spiritual zeal, more of a realization of what God will do, much of heaven's blessing would be given them. There are holy chords yet to be touched. Teachers as well as students need to show greater teachableness. Just in proportion to the true missionary spirit there is brought into the education and training of the youth, will be the blessing bestowed. Students should begin to work in missionary lines, they should learn to take hold of Christ, while connected with persons of broad experience, with whom they may counsel and advise. As they do this, they will not only advance in knowledge and intellectual power, but will learn how to work, so that when the school term is ended, and they are separated from teachers and experienced advisers, they will be prepared to engage in earnest missionary labor, working under the direction of the greatest teacher the world has ever known. It is as essential that they should know how to communicate as that they should receive a knowledge of the truth. The practice of telling others about Christ, of reading and explaining his word, will stamp that Word in the mind, and make the truth their own.

"Thou shalt love the Lord thy God with all thy heart..... and thy neighbor as thyself." This is God's command. Jesus has given an additional requirement: "A new commandment I give unto you, that ye love one another; as I have loved you, that ye also love one another." Man never knew the strength of that love until Christ came to this earth and gave his life for sinners. "Greater love hath no man than this, That a man lay down his life for his friends." We are not merely to love our neighbor as ourselves; we are to love one another as Christ has loved us. "As the Father hath loved me, so have I loved you," he declared, "continue ye in my love. If ye keep my commandments, ye shall abide in my love, even as I have kept my Father's commandments, and abide in his love. These things have I spoken to you, that my joy might remain in you, and that your joy might be full. This is my commandment, that ye love one another as I have loved you."

The students and also the teachers in our school need to take time to become acquainted with the members of the community in which they live. The love that Christ has manifested toward us, we must cultivate for others. The truth will not long remain in the heart unless it works by love to save souls that are ready to perish.

God does not want our schools to be conducted on stereotyped human plans, as many are now being conducted. He would have us beware of human precision, of making a line on which every one must tread. A different element must be brought into our schools. Wrong maxims and methods of teaching, which have been looked upon as wholly essential, have been followed. Those who are connected with our schools must penetrate deeper than their own habits or opinions, which have been esteemed as good authority. There must not be so many studies and duties placed on the students that they will neglect to talk with the Great Teacher, the Lord Jesus Christ, and let into their hearts the softening, subduing influence that dwelt in him. It is essential that students be taught how to do missionary work, not only by pen and voice, but by working with them in various missionary lines. All about us there are persons who need to be taught how to cook and how to treat the sick. By engaging in these lines of work we practice the truth as it is in Jesus. Teachers and students need to study how to engage in this work. The teachers should take students to places where help is needed, giving them practical instruction in how to care for the sick.

The teachers must draw from the deep, central source of all moral and intellectual power, asking the Lord to give them the mind that was in Christ Jesus, that every case calling for sympathy and help, in physical as well as spiritual lines, may receive their attention. Teach the students to make a practical application of the lessons they have received. As they witness human woe, and the deep poverty of those whom they are trying to help, they will be stirred with compassion. Their hearts will be softened and subdued by the deep, holy principles of the Word of God.

The great Physician cooperates with every effort made in the behalf of suffering humanity, to give light to the body, and life and restoration to the soul. And why is this? Satan came into our world, and led men into temptation. With sin came sickness and suffering, for we reap that which we sow. Satan afterward caused man to charge upon God the suffering which is but the sure result of transgression of physical law. God is thus falsely accused, and his character misrepresented. He is charged with doing that which Satan himself has done. God would have his people expose this falsehood of the enemy. To them he has given the light of the gospel of health, and as his representative they are to give the light to others. As they work to relieve suffering humanity, they are to point out the origin of all suffering, and direct the mind to Jesus, the great Healer of both soul and body. His heart of sympathy goes out to all earth's sufferers, and with every one who works for their relief he cooperates. As with his blessing health returns, the character of God will be vindicated, and the lie thrust back upon Satan, its originator.

We must give the Lord a chance to do his work, his great work for the soul. Christ is our sufficiency. Each one of us must understand that it means to have the Word of God fulfilled in us. As Christ was in this world, so we are to be. If in this life we are like him in character, we shall in heaven have his likeness. If there is no likeness between Christ and us in this world, there can be no fellowship between us when he shall come in his glory and all the holy angels with him. As religious teachers we are under obligation to teach our students how to engage in medical missionary work. Those who do this work have many opportunities to sow the seed of truth in a way that will be successful. A heart full of gratitude to God can pray, "Teach me thy way, O God, lead me in a plain path because of mine enemies, or rather because of mine observers."

There is a work to be done all about our schools. If we are light-bearers to the world, we are pledged to teach the students how to communicate light, and to give them an opportunity to work. We are to give the invitation to the supper, for it is glad tidings for all people. Let all who are qualifying themselves for this work spend much time in prayer. Let them contemplate their duty in the light of the Word of God. We must now see what can be done to educate the students in practical missionary work, so that they can impart to others that which they have received. Who will devote a portion of his time to this work? Remember, Christ is the price of life, the rightful sovereign of all the byways and hedges, and he knows what they need.

God has placed on us a burden of responsibility that we do not recognize. We must learn deeper lessons in the school of Christ. We can do much in his strength. He would have us teach the students how to take up the work he has left them to do, that they may not lose the spirit of the work by too close an appreciation of the theory of the truth. It is an intelligent knowledge made perfect by practice that makes an efficient worker.

"This gospel of the kingdom must be preached in all the world for a witness to all nations: and then shall the end come." "All power is given unto me in heaven and in earth," Christ declares. This power he is ready to transfer to those who will cooperate with him in self-denial and self-sacrifice. We must without delay open a way that this branch of education may be developed. The students must be given special opportunities to do missionary work, that they may place themselves in the channel to receive and impart light. They must make known the truth that has made the Children of God.

If we believe the Word of God, our greatest aim and object should be to educate and train young men and women to go forth and do missionary work. Thus they can use the truth that has been so faithfully presented to them. As they visit families, the precious truths they have heard, the drill they have had on Bible themes, will be brought to their minds. As they read and explain the Word, "the Comforter, which is the Holy Ghost, whom the Father will send in my name, he shall teach you all things and bring all things to your remembrance, whatsoever I have said unto you." In this way not only will those who know not the truth be encouraged, but those who are telling the preciousness of Christ will be greatly blessed.

Mrs. E. G. White.

Chapter 34—Financial, Social, and Spiritual Education

Low Tuition

We do not want a dark cloud to gather over us in the form of a debt. We do not want our debt to accumulate. In our schools in America, the price of tuition for students has been set too low, and the managers of the schools have become convinced that even with proper economy, they could not continue these low prices. After one or two terms of school, a careful investigation has revealed to them that the sum set was not sufficient to cover expenses, that the tuition should be increased, thus avoiding a discouraging debt. Far better let all the students share in the expense, than allow the school to bear the whole weight; for this throws upon the managers of the institution on a continual suspicion of miscalculation, want of economy, and wrong planning. These debts are very discouraging to teachers.

The price of tuition should be used to pay the teachers their salary. Teachers should have some margin above their actual needs, that they may make donations when pledges are called for. It is a great satisfaction to them to have something with which to help in an emergency. Their wages should not be placed at the lowest; therefore, the sum for tuition, should at least be sufficient to pay the teachers and supply the table with abundant, healthful food. Debts must not be allowed to accumulate term after term.

During the vacation sufficient funds should come in to prepare for the opening of the school the following term. Through the summer school should be held several hours every day for the benefit of those students who because of the expense of traveling do not desire to leave Cooranbong. All those who have pleaded for low tuition should, before expressing their decision, weigh matters on all sides, and then after estimating the cost of table fare, teachers' wages, and the furnishing of rooms, bring in their figures.

Light has been given me that we are not to pattern after any school that has been run in America. There is to be a more durable education gained. It is the knowledge of the Word. And with every arrangement made, economy must be kept in view. The teachers must cooperate in requiring from the students sufficient funds to cover the running expenses or they must themselves agree to do their work for lower wages. The estimate of the school expenses must be considered, and if there is no way to keep free from debt, all are at liberty to arrange among themselves to donate a certain amount of their wages. It may be best to raise the tuition; then the teachers will have the privilege of using their means to help where they see that help is most needed. When a call is made for means, where it is a pleasure to assist, the teachers should have something in their own earnings to use as they shall see fit.

Those who have the truth in their hearts are always open hearted, helping where it is necessary. They lead out, and others imitate their example. If there are those who would have the benefits of the school, but who can not pay full price for their tuition, let the churches in our conferences show their liberality by helping them. This is an important subject, and calls, not for a narrow calculation, but for a thorough investigation. The counsel of the Lord is needed. The school should have a sufficient income to be able to furnish some things to students during the term of school, which it is essential for them to have in their work.

The School to be a Home

The school in Avondale is to be conducted upon no selfish plan. It is to be a home rather than a school like other schools. The teachers are to act as fathers and mothers. Let the teachers show an interest in the students one and all, such as fathers and mothers show in their children. The students are not to be educated to think that they are independent atoms, but that each one is a thread which is to unite with other threads in the web composing the fabric.

The students are here for special training, to become acquainted with all lines of work, that should they go out as missionaries, they could in one sense be morally independent, and able to furnish themselves with conveniences because they have educated ability. Whether men or women, they should learn to mend, wash, and keep their own clothes in order. They should be able to cook their own meals. They should learn to act always from principles, and to pursue a course of Christian consistency.

Many find this difficult, it may be because they did not receive their education at home. They did not sufficiently realize that they were a part of the family firm. They did not think it was their duty to bring all the help possible into the family, just as did our Saviour. They were not taught the importance of making the life of Christ their life, and the character of Christ their character. In many cases the natural inclination of the children has been left to flow at liberty. They have been allowed to neglect the little things which they should do without being told. They have not been taught to bear burdens and to contradict natural inclinations.

It is not a mark of a lady or gentleman to disdain restraint, either in the home or in the school. Bear in mind that if you are children of God, you should be under subjection, whether it is at home or school authority. Christ will give grace in all things. Religion can only bless the life it influences. All who exclude its influence shut out also the blessing that ever follows well-doing. If we exclude the sunshine from our rooms, and then complain of darkness, who is to blame? If you long for joy and gladness, open the door of your heart to the sunbeams of the Sun of Righteousness. Happiness is yours if you will have it; for happiness is composed of little things, as well as of large.

This school is to be a family school. Tenderness, sympathy, unity, and love are to be cherished. The teachers are to have a care for the health and happiness of the students, and seek to advance them in every essential branch of knowledge. Special care is to be shown for the souls of the students. The students should in no case be allowed to take so many studies that they will be prevented from assembling for prayer and religious exercise. This school is to be a training school, a school where every student will receive special help from his teachers, as a family should receive help in the home. If the number of studies forbids this special education in these lines, have fewer studies, and work by careful drawing, to bring students into the school of Christ, where they may learn of the great Teacher.

The Lord has means for us in the hands of his stewards. We call upon all to consider the advance work that has been done since we came to Australia. We have not done the work, but the Lord has called upon us to be colaborers with Him, and this is what we desire to be. In this school, if all will act a part in sustaining it, a missionary work will be done, the far-reaching influence of which few can realize. I think we should all consider gratefully what the Lord has done. We have seen a good work done in Melbourne, and if the church members who have been long in the truth will wake up to their God-given responsibilities, and be converted and consecrated anew, God will make them a blessing to those newly come to the faith.

The Bible is our Counsellor. We are educating students in the Scriptures. Every day we are seeking the Lord for wisdom. Debts must not be allowed to accumulate. We must have help with which to carry on our school. It will be so much better to make donations now, to lessen the principal, thus lessening the interest to be paid. A great work is to be done to give these precious souls, God's heritage, a true education, that they may reach the higher grade, and the heavenly family in the paradise of God, sons and daughters of the King. We are making the Word of God our study. We can not depend upon lesson books that breathe the breath of infidelity. Oh, how much we have lost by making the Word of the living God secondary! The writings of human inventions, human authors, whose sentiments are opposed to God, are as tares sown among wheat.

Students are to be taught to understand that Book which should ever be represented as the book to study. The assertion that there are dark, mysterious, and incomprehensible things in the Word, things hard to understand, perplexing and uncertain, is a false one. Please read the first, second, and third chapters of Ephesians. ...

God will (not?) hold men responsible for that which they can not understand. The Scriptures were given to all men for the purpose of making them wise unto salvation. There is nothing left in obscurity, or hard to be understood. The lessons we are to learn involve the happiness, the holiness, the unselfishness of man, that he may be complete in Jesus Christ. The mystery referred to by the great apostle as hard to be understood is the existence of God. "Who by searching can find out God?"

Much of that which is revealed is dark to human minds, because the jewels of truth are not searched for as for hidden treasure. The truth lies hidden beneath the rubbish of human systems, human wisdom and philosophy. Infinite, eternal truth, the revelation of God, is explained in the light of human conjectures. God's Word, they assert, is modified, remodeled to suit the changing times, to suit their own mind and ideas. They have been educated from wrong books, and have left a plain "Thus saith the Lord" which involves eternal interests, to adjust itself. Spiritual things can only be discerned by the Holy Spirit's power.

The Lord has signified that a reform must be made by those who have placed man's human wisdom in the place of the living oracles. Human wisdom is foolishness; for it misses the whole of God's providence, which looks into eternity. "After that in the Wisdom of God the world by wisdom knew not God, it pleased God by the foolishness of preaching to save them that believe." The Word must be searched, yea, eaten, in order to purify and prepare men to become members of the royal family, children of the heavenly King. From the first, the schools that are conducted by Seventh-day Adventists should take the Word of God as their lesson book, and in doing this, the teachers and students will find the higher education. In opening the Word of God and searching pages, they will find the hidden treasures.

E. G. White

Chapter 35—School Finance

Dear Brother: Your letters have been received. Your last in reference to the College came this morning. I was not aware that our College was in debt twenty thousand dollars. This must make it a necessity to call for donations.

The evils to centering so many responsibilities in Battle Creek have not been small. The dangers are great. There are unconsecrated elements waiting only for circumstances to put all their influences on the side of wrong. I can never feel exactly safe in regard to Battle Creek or Battle Creek College. I can not at this time state all my reasons. That which led me to write as I did was the great need of business managers, godly devoted men to take hold of the work and push it in a God-fearing manner.

Whatever may have been the object of placing the tuition of students at so low figures, the fact that the College has been running behind so heavily is sufficient reason for changing the price, so that this shall not be the showing in the future. The low price is not in its favor, even if at higher rates the College is not so largely patronized. Those who really want the advantage to be obtained at Battle Creek will make extra exertions to receive those advantages, and a large class who would be induced to come because of the low tuition would be of no benefit to other students or to the church. The larger the number, the more tact, skill, and vigilance are required to keep them in order, and from becoming demoralized.

Some provision should be made to have a fund raised to loan to worthy poor students who desire to give themselves to the missionary work, and in some cases they should even receive donations. Then these youth should have it plainly set before them that they must work their way as far as possible and partly defray their expense.

The churches in different localities should feel that a solemn responsibility rests upon them to train youth and educate talent to engage in missionary efforts. When they see any in the church who give promise of making useful workers, but who are not able to educate themselves, they should lift that responsibility and send them to College to be instructed, and developed, with the object in view of becoming workers in the cause of God. There is material that needs to be worked up, and that would be of good service in the Lord's vineyard, but they are too poor to obtain the advantages of the College. The church should feel it a privilege to take the responsibility of defraying their expenses.

The tuition should be placed higher, and if there are some who need help, let them be helped as above stated. When the College was first started there was a fund placed in the Review and Herald Office for the benefit of those who wish to obtain an education, but who had not the means. This was used by several students until they could get a good start, and earn enough to replace that which they had drawn so that others could be benefited by it. That which cost little will be appreciated little, but that which costs something near its real value will be estimated accordingly.

If there were fewer students, and they were of a hopeful character, it would be a blessing to Battle Creek. If there are men as teachers in the College, and associated with it, who are well balanced, and have a strong moral influence, who know how to deal with minds, and possess the true missionary spirit; then if the College was crowded so as to necessitate the building of another equally as large, that would be the best missionary field in the world. It is this ability that is greatly needed in the College.

If these superior qualities were found in the men connected with the Office at Battle Creek, the outlook would be more encouraging. Great and important interests are in danger of being misshaped, and of coming forth defective from their hands. If some felt their ignorance more and would depend less on self, be less self-sufficient, they might learn of the Great Teacher meekness and lowliness of heart.

In regard to the College I would say, Raise the price of tuition and have a better class of students. But provision should be made to do the very best for those who come: to secure for them every healthful, intellectual, and moral advantage. I see the need of still another boarding house, and there may be the need of another building for the students. I can not see how you could do better than you have in calling for means while this debt is against the College. It ought not to be there, and if there had been the right kind of planning it would not exist; that is, if those especially employed in the College were all enterprising men, of broader ideas. They would constantly be exercising ingenuity and tact, and devising means whereby the College should not become burdened by debt.

If we only had devoted, spiritual-minded workers connected with our important institutions, who relied upon more than themselves, we might certainly look for far greater prosperity than we have had hitherto. But where there is a decided want of humble trust, and of an entire dependence upon God, we are sure of nothing. Our great need today is men who are baptized with the Holy Spirit of God, men who walk with God as did Enoch, men who are not so narrow in their outlook that they will bind about the work in place of enlarging it, men who will not say "business is business, religion is religion." We need men who can take in the situation, men who are far-seeing, men who can reason from cause to effect. ...

I will here give some extracts from a letter written November 8, 1880: "The interest of every part of the cause is as dear to me as my life. Every branch of the work is important. I was shown that there was great danger now of making the tract and missionary work so absorbing that it will become perplexing and absorb every other interest. It was brought before me that there was too much machinery in the tract and missionary and in the Sabbath School work. There was form and arrangement, but little of Christ-like simplicity felt or practiced by the workers. We want less machinery and mechanical arrangement, and more heart work, more real piety and true holiness, especially in the missionary work everywhere. There needs to be piety, purity and wise generalship, and then for greater and much better work would be done with less expenditure of means.

There is a broad field to be covered, and a getting above the simplicity of the work. Now is the time to work, and to work in the wise counsel of God. If you connect unconsecrated persons with the mission fields and with the Sabbath Schools, our work will take on a formal mold and be without Christ. The workers must study carefully, prayerfully in every part of the field, how to work with the simplicity of Christ, and in an economical manner, to plan and devise the most successful manner of reaching hearts.

We are in danger of spreading over more territory and starting more enterprises when we can possibly attend to properly. There is danger of our overdoing some branches of the work, and leaving some important parts of it to be neglected. To undertake a large amount of work and do nothing perfectly, would be a bad plan. We are to move forward, but must not be so far above the simplicity of the work that it will be impossible to look after the enterprise entered into without sacrificing our best helpers to keep things in order. Life and health must be regarded. While we should ever be ready to follow the opening providence of God, we should lay no larger plans, nor occupy more ground than there are help and means to bind off and work well, keep up and increase the interest already started. While there are broader plans and fields constantly opening for the laborers, our ideas and views must broaden in regard to the workers who are to labor to bring souls into the truth."

E. G. White

Chapter 36—The Education Our Schools Should Bring

As we are about to establish our facilities for the manufacture of health foods, the question has come up: How shall we treat this matter? Where shall we locate the work so important to ourselves and to the school established in Cooranbong? Shall this branch of business be established in Cooranbong, and thus open ways and means whereby many more students may obtain an all-round education?

From the light given me in regard to the location and building up of our school interests, I know that it is the purpose of God that this institution be established at a distance from the city that is so full of temptations and snares, of amusements and holidays, which are not conducive to purity and piety and religious devotion. He designs that we shall connect manual labor with the improvement of the mental powers. I have been shown that study in agricultural lines should be the A B and C of the educational work of our schools. This institution must not depend upon imported produce,--for the fruits so essential to healthfulness, and for their grains and vegetables. This is the very first work that must be entered upon. Then as we shall advance and add to our facilities, advance studies and object lessons should come in. We are not to subtract from that which has already been taken hold of as a branch of education.

From the light given me there is to be opened to our youth means whereby they, while attending school, may learn how to use tools. Buildings should be erected on the school grounds by the students themselves. Under the guidance of experienced workmen, carpenters who are apt to teach, patient, kind, the youth are to learn how to build economically. Then it is essential that our printing should be done where our principal school is established, and we should have a printing press and fonts of type where another class of students may be trained to manage everything connected with typesetting and press work.

Again, our youth, both men and women, should be taught how to cook savingly, and to dispense with everything in the line of flesh foods. This is a very serious matter to the world. Thousands of human beings who subsist upon the flesh of dead animals, are suffering and dying from causes of which they are ignorant. By painstaking effort they can be taught to discriminate between a proper healthful diet and the use of flesh meats. No encouragement should be given in the training of our youth to prepare dishes which are composed in any degree of flesh meats; for this is pointing to the darkness and ignorance of Egypt rather than to the purity of health reform. Teach the students to prepare healthful drinks from grains suitably prepared to take the place of tea. This drink is unhealthful in its purest preparation, and it is so adulterated, mixed with other ingredients that resemble tea, that is has become a dangerous beverage.

All the arts are to come into the education of the students. Even in the school at Avondale there are too many studies taken by the students. The youth should not be left to take all the studies they shall choose, for many will be inclined to take more than they can carry, and if they do this, they can not possibly come from the school with a thorough knowledge of each study. There should be less study of books, and greater painstaking effort made to obtain that knowledge which is essential for practical life. The youth are to learn how to work interestedly and intelligently, that, wherever they are, they may be respected because they have a knowledge of those arts which are so essential for practical life. In the place of being day laborers under an overseer, they are to strive to be masters of their trades, to place themselves where they can command wages as good carpenters, printers, or as educators in agricultural work.

If the brain is overtaxed by taking too many studies, the student is robbed of physical health. This can only be secured to him by the exercise of the muscles. The human machine must be taxed proportionately, or health and vigor can not be maintained. When brain and muscle work proportionately, the youth can bring to the study of the Word of God healthy perceptions and well-balanced nerves. They can have wholesome, healthful thought and can retain the precious things that are brought from the Word. They will digest its truths, and as a result will have brain power to discern what is truth. Then, as occasion demands, they can give to every man that asketh a reason of the hope that is in them with meekness and fear.

The question has been asked me, Have you any light for us? If so give it to us. From time to time many things have been opened before me, and often has come just before difficulties have arisen. Thus it was when I was at Stanmore a few weeks ago. All through the night, in my dreams, we were making changes. Some were packing up, and moving to other localities. When examination was made of the purposes of each, there was much said. Some said they were on the way to Cooranbong, where they intended to locate in connection with the school. They said they purposed to work as work should be provided for them in any line whatever. If they could not take all the studies they would take what they could, and learn how to work. This, they said, would fit them for practical life and for the work to be done in the missionary field. They said they could see that great changes must be wrought in their own minds in the living policy before they could be prepared to enlighten other minds.

Good ideas were brought out in regard to temperance in eating and drinking. Said he, We must first learn ourselves; then, as we shall go out to do missionary work for others, we can give them our own experience. In Cooranbong, we shall have the most favorable opportunities, not only to obtain a practical knowledge of how to work, but we shall also learn to read and study our Bibles. Then we shall know in our own experience the words of David in the 119th Psalm: "Wherewithal shall a young man cleanse his way? By taking heed thereto according to thy word. With my whole heart have I sought thee: O let me not wander from thy commandments. Thy words have I hid in mine heart, that I might not sin against thee."

Quite a number, both of men and women, were awakened to a purpose. Then questions were asked as to the advisability of educating others to supply the place of meat and tea and coffee with a more healthful diet. Should we make known our methods; and thus cut off from ourselves the benefits we might receive in establishing the trade in the colonies? Should we give away the science of how to make these healthful foods? Should we teach the poor people how they can live without using the flesh of dead animals. Should we teach the poor people who come into the truth how to plant and raise nuts, how to produce for themselves those things which would cost too much if they bought them prepared by other hands? Should we teach them how to prepare these foods for themselves?

These seemed to be important questions, and hard to solve, Then the voice of wisdom was heard: the subject of health reform is a great subject, and important subject, and this missionary work is to be carried into the highways and byways of life. The third angel's message is present truth for 1898, and the health question is as closely connected with that message as the arm is to the body. Therefore light must be given to the best methods of introducing health reform. Meat is the greatest disease breeder that can be introduced into the human system. But you can not touch health reform unless you present the most inexpensive methods of living. The enemy must have no advantage in any line. The Lord can only bless those who are keeping every precept he has given in relation to this life.

Many physicians in our world are of no benefit to the human family. The drug science has been exalted, but if every bottle that comes from every such institution were done away with, there would be fewer invalids in the world today. Drug medication should never have been introduced into our institutions. There was no need of this being so, and for this very reason the lord would have us establish an institution where he can come in and where his grace and power can be revealed. "I am the resurrection and the life," he declares.

The true method for healing the sick is to tell them of the herbs that grow for the benefit of man. Scientists have attached large names to these simplest preparations, but true education will lead us to teach the sick that they need not call in a doctor any more than they would call in a lawyer. They can themselves administer the simple herbs if necessary. To educate the human family that the doctor alone knows all the ills of infants and persons of every age, is false teaching, and the sooner we as a people stand on the principles of health reform, the greater will be the blessing that will come to those who would do true medical work. There is a work to be done in treating the sick with water and teaching them to make the most of sunshine and physical exercise. Thus in simple language we may teach the people how to preserve health, how to avoid sickness. This is the work our sanitariums are called upon to do. This is true science.

We are laborers together with God. Believest thou this? The knowledge, the capabilities, the powers, God has given us are not to be hoarded as men hoard riches. We are not to do as the selfish money-loving men of this age are doing. The passion to accumulate their possessions and retain their power has grown upon the men of the world. In their selfishness they buy up wheat and goods so that others in their need will have to buy them; then they charge whatever prices they desire. This is the spirit that is prevailing in the world, and is making the money-hoarder Satan's co-partner in robbing the poor. This is keenly felt by the poorer classes, and the devil leads them to do his will in stubbornly resisting the things they can not help. Thus selfishness and violence are exercised by man over his fellowman. The ones who are robbed and injured become exasperated, and violence and wickedness and cruelty are created in the world.

The greed of the moneyed man increases as it is indulged, and this spirit will rule the church unless its members are followers of Christ. "Pure and undefiled religion before God and the Father is this: that ye visit the fatherless and the widow in their affliction and keep yourselves unspotted from the world."

This worldly policy has wrestled for the victory among Seventh-day Adventists, and the principles which should have been kept pure and unadulterated have been overcome, and selfishness has come into the very courts of the Lord. The Lord has permitted those who did not love the light, who departed from a plain "Thus saith the Lord," to walk in the sparks of the fire of their own kindling; but he says, "They shall lie down in sorrow."

This condition of things has been created in our conference and churches under a religious cloak which existed in the world. Confederacies have been formed to make their showing stand out as superior, and they have gained the name of having done a large work in their responsible positions of trust. They flatter themselves that they were doing God service when they were establishing principles of robbery. They were depriving their brethren of their rights in gathering everything in the book line under their control, and making their own laws and rules,--rules that were not after God's order at all, but which revealed the very attributes of Satan.

It was this spirit that was manifested by the priests and temple officials in their gatherings for the Passover. Cattle were bought by the dignitaries, the moneyed men, who oppressed them of whom they purchased. The representation was made that these animals were to be offered as a sacrifice to God at the Passover, and thus urged the owners sold them at a cheap price. Then these scheming men brought their purchases to the temple,--purchases which meant double robbery-robbery of the men of whom they had purchased, and robbery of those who wished to sacrifice, to whom they were sold again at exorbitant prices.

They used the courts of the temple as though the animals brought there made them of the highest value. Oh, what deceit, what hypocrisy was practiced. Twice Christ's displeasure was evidenced against them. Divinity flashed through humanity, and he drove out the buyers and sellers from the temple courts, saying, "Take these things hence: it is written, My Father's house shall be a house of prayer, but ye have made it a den of thieves. He overturned the tables of the money changers, and priests and people fled before that one man as though an army of soldiers with drawn sword were pursuing them.

This work has been carried on at Battle Creek. The publishing office was turned from the original design; men made terms with authors; councils were formed; schemes were entered into. While one author was engaged in the services of a meeting at a distance, the expenses of one man were paid to go and see this brother and induce him to put the lowest figures on his books. They urged that they wished to get this important matter before as many people as possible, and that the book would have a very much larger sale if it were sold at cheap price.

The royalty was placed at the lowest figure. Then this confederacy held this example up as a rule for others. Warnings were given me that all this was the working out of a system of oppression and robbery, and that the whole institution was leavened throughout with corrupt principles, that the light of God was fast departing from all who were engaged in this confederacy. God sanctioned none of this spirit. He could not place his signature upon this devising. He would forsake those men, remove his spirit from those who entered upon this course, and the glory of his presence would depart from them.

The cause of God is not to be advanced by such policy; for it is born of Satan, and can only have his inspiration. All who do not repent and seek to set things right, God will leave to stumble on in darkness. They have not discerned unrighteousness in practice. They have secured books, and diverted them from their original design to make up the sum which they wished to secure. But every page of that dark history is written in the books of heaven to react upon every soul who has engaged in these schemes, unless they shall repent with that repentance that needeth not be repented of. The Lord can not tolerate any such transactions as those that have been professedly done in his name. He abhors all such Satanic principles.

What shall be done in the future? Lest you offend God, place no responsibility upon any man who has become leavened by connection with this work, unless he shows that he has sense of the evil practice, and separates from the institution, unless he condemns all that savors of injustice, overbearing, or lording it over God's heritage. There has been a betrayal of sacred trusts. The work of God has been abused, and covered up with man's unsanctified attributes, and God says, Shall I not judge for these things?

It is for such workings as these that Christ says, "I come not to send peace, but a sword.' May God grant that never again shall this policy exist in our institutions, that no events or combination of events shall lead men to repeat the past.

There is a work to be done that has not yet been done. The temple courts are not yet cleansed as they must be before the work which Christ did after the cleansing of the temple can be done. Then all the sick were brought to him, and he laid his hands upon them, and healed them all. Here was revealed true godliness, true righteousness, a true use of the temple for a practical purpose which brought no defilement.

That faith which works by love and purifies the soul is to be revealed among God's people. The Lord has no commendation for those who were lording it over God's heritage. He sets his face against every such work. He blows upon all pharisaical forms and prayers and ceremonies. Religion, what is it unless the experimental elements of piety are revealed in deep heart service because of the indwelling of the Holy Spirit. "Pure and undefiled religion before God and the Father is this: that ye visit the fatherless and the widow in their affliction, and keep yourselves unspotted from the world."

I see a work to be done that may appear to be working against our own interests financially. This is to give to others that information which we would have others give us. Teach those whom we wish to restore to correct principles of health reform, how to prepare for themselves the simple nut foods. They are too poor to obtain them if they do not work them up for themselves.

There is a work to be done by our churches that few have any idea of. "I was an hungered," Christ says, "and ye gave me meat; I was thirsty, and ye gave me drink; I was a stranger, and ye took me in; naked, and ye clothed me: I was sick, and ye visited me; I was in prison, and ye come unto me." We shall have to give of our means to support laborers in the harvest field, and we shall rejoice in the sheaves gathered in. But while this is right, there is a work as yet untouched that must be done. The mission of Christ was to heal the sick, encourage the hopeless, bind up the broken-hearted. This work of restoration is to be carried on among the needy suffering ones of humility. God calls not only for your benevolence, but your cheerful countenance, your hopeful works, the grasp of your hand. Relieve some of God's afflicted ones. Some are sick and hope has departed. Bring back the sunlight to them. There are souls who have lost their courage; speak to them, pray for them. There are those who need the bread of life. Read to them from the Word of God. There is a soul sickness no balm can reach, no medicine heal. Pray for them, and bring them to Jesus Christ. And in all your work, Christ will be present to make impressions upon the human hearts.

This is the kind of medical missionary work to be done. Bring the sunshine of the Sun of Righteousness into the room of the sick and suffering. Teach the inmates of poor homes how to cook. "He shall feed his flock like a shepherd, "with temporal and spiritual food. Christ invites you. "Take my yoke upon you and learn me, for I am meek and lowly of heart, and ye shall find rest unto your souls. For my yoke is easy and my burden is light."

E. G. White

Chapter 37—A Satanic Program

If the written word of the most high God is obeyed, it will educate the believer to cooperate with God in bringing up to a high level the debased and fallen. Then the ignorant will learn that the enactment of God means peace and goodness, mercy and love. Satan [does not want this presentation to be made of God. He desires] selfishness to prevail, the love of money to become the relying element in the heart. He wants that fraud, crime, and injustice prevail in the world. He desires to see the poor suffer from hunger, and for want of food and clothing, and the world today become as full of violence as was the world before the flood. Then he can bring about his ends, charging all the misery upon God.

To a large extent Satan has carried out his plans. The Lord's property is embezzled; God is robbed. The means that has been lent to man to relieve the necessities of the poor and to uplift and sustain the fallen in righteousness and truth, is used to please and glorify self. From the beginning to the end the crime of tobacco-using, of opium and drug medication, has its origin in perverted knowledge. It is through plucking and eating of poisonous fruit, through the intricacies of names that the common people do not understand, that thousands and ten thousands of lives are lost. This great knowledge, supposed by man to be so wonderful, God did not mean that man should have. They are using the poisonous productions that Satan himself has planted to take the place of the tree of life, whose leaves are for the healing of the nations. Men are dealing in liquors and narcotics that are destroying the human family. Deathly mixtures are used, that make men mad, and murder and violence are prevailing everywhere.

The time is near when all these wicked inventions will come to an end. At the last the passion for obtaining means by fraud will increase. Theft and robbery will become prevalent. The fruit of the tree of knowledge will be greedily eaten. Satan will come down with great power, working with all deceivableness of unrighteousness in them that perish. Amusements of every kind will increase, and money, God's money, will be abused and misapplied while thousands are perishing for food in all our cities. The dead will be honored with costly sepulchers and expensive monuments, and attention will be called to those things as something worthy of laudation. The householders will turn away from the real wants of human beings, and glorify Satan in embellishing the tombs of the dead.

The cries of humanity from India, from Africa, from China and from many places, are going up to God. Misery and anguish and physical suffering are coming up before him, and the Lord will soon sweep the earth of its moral corruption,--not by a sea of water as in Noah's day, but by a sea of fire that can not be quenched by any human devising. Admonitions are given to the inhabitants of the earth who are corrupting their ways before God, who are plucking of the tree of the knowledge of evil to the ruin of human beings. God will avenge his own elect which cry unto him day and night. Yes, he will avenge them speedily.

Mrs. E. G. White

Chapter 38—Bible Teaching in our Schools

September 22, 1898.

A revival in Bible study is needed throughout the world. Attention is to be called, not to the assertions of men, but to the Word of God. As this is done, a mighty work will be wrought. When God declared that his word should not return unto him, void, he meant all that he said. The gospel is to be preached to all nations. The Bible is to be opened to the people. A knowledge of God is the highest education, and it will cover the earth with its wonderful truth as the waters cover the sea.

The Bible is to be the great text-book of education; for it carries in every page the evidence of the truth. The study of God's Word is to take the place of the study of books that have led minds away from the truth.

In every school that God has established there will be, as never before, a demand for Bible instruction. Our students are to be educated to become Bible workers, and Bible teachers can do a most wonderful work if they will themselves learn from the great Teacher.

God's Word is true philosophy, true science. Human opinions and sensational preaching amount to very little. These who are imbued with the Word of God can teach it in the same simple way in which Christ taught it. Too much depends upon the opening of the Scriptures to those in darkness, for us to use one word that can not be readily understood. With all their learning many of those who claim to teach the higher education do not know what they are talking about. The highest education is that which he made so plain as to be understood by the common people. The greatest Teacher the world ever knew used the simplest language and the plainest symbols.

The Lord calls upon his shepherds to feed the flock of God with pure provender. He would have us present the truth in the simplicity line upon line, precept upon precept, here is a little and there a little. When this work is done faithfully many will be convicted and converted by the Holy Spirit. There is need of workers who will come close to unbelievers, not waiting for unbelievers to come close to them, workers who will search for the lost sheep, who will do personal labor, and who will give clear, definite instruction.

It should be the aim of our schools to provide the best instruction and training for the Bible workers. Our Conference should see that the schools are provided with teachers who are thorough Bible teachers and who have a deep Christian experience. The best ministerial talent should be brought into our schools, and the salaries of these teachers should be paid from the tithe.

At the same time the churches have a part to act. They should see that those who ought to receive the benefits, should attend the school. They should assist worthy persons who have not the means to obtain an education.

If our church members were awake, they would multiply their resources; they would send men and women to our schools, not to go through a long course of study, but to learn quickly, and go out into the field. Through a vital connection with God, men and women may quickly gain a knowledge of that great text-book, the Word of God, and go forth to impart what they have received.

Let workers enter the field without going through many preliminaries. Teach them that they are to walk humbly with God, and to begin labor just where they see it is needed. Thus our working force may be greatly increased.

A great work is being done in medical missionary lines, and its necessities are constantly making themselves felt; but this work need not absorb the funds required in other lines. The medical missionary work, if rightly managed, may be made largely self-sustaining. Let our conferences and our churches see that our youth are educated in the Scriptures: for the gospel is the power of God unto salvation.

E. G. White

Chapter 39—Dealing with Delinquent Students

One thing I wish you to understand, that I have not been in harmony with the expelling of students from the school, unless human depravity and gross licentiousness make it necessary, that others shall not be corrupted. There has been an error in sending students from the school, as in the case of Connecticut, and other cases, which has been a great evil. Souls thus treated have opened before them a course of action that has secured them in the ranks of the enemy as armed and equipped enemies.

Again, as to making public to the school the errors of students I have been brought in to see and hear some of these exposures, and then have been shown the after influence. It has been harmful in every respect, and has no beneficial influence upon the school. Had those who had acted a part in these things had the spirit and wisdom of Christ, they would have seen a way to remedy the existing difficulties more after the likeness of Jesus Christ. It never helps a student to be humiliated before the whole school. It creates a wound that mortifies. It heals nothing, cures nothing.

There are students who are suspended from school. They are in this action thrust upon Satan's battle-ground to cope with principalities and powers without armor or defense, to become an easy prey to Satan's devices. Let me speak a word to you in the name of the Lord. When there is a proper course taken, in cases where students seem so easily led astray, there will be found no necessity for suspension or expulsion. There is a right way, and the Spirit of the Lord must move the human agent or else there will be grave mistakes made. It is the nicest work that was ever entered upon by the human agent, the dealing with human minds. Teachers are to consider that they are not dealing with angels, but with human beings who have like passions as they themselves have. Characters are not formed in one mold. Every phase of character is received by (different) children as an inheritance. The defects and the virtues in traits of character are thus revealed. Let every instructor take this into consideration. Hereditary and cultivated deformity of human character, as also beauty of character, will have to be met, and much grace cultivated in the instructor as to know how to deal with the erring for their present and eternal good. Impulse, impatience, pride, selfishness, and esteem, if cherished will do a great amount of evil which may thrust the soul upon Satan's battle-ground without the wisdom to navigate his bark, but he will be in danger of being tossed about at the sport of Satan's temptations until shipwrecked.

Every teacher has his own particular traits of character to watch, lest Satan should use him as his agent to destroy souls, by his own unconsecrated traits of character. The only safety for teachers is to learn daily in the school of Christ, his meekness, his lowliness of heart; then self will be hid in Christ, and he will meekly wear the yoke of Christ, and consider that he is dealing with his heritage. I must state to you that I have been shown that the best methods have not always been practiced in dealing with the errors and mistakes of students, and the result has been that souls have been imperilled and some have been lost. Evil tempers in the teachers, unwise movements, self-dignity, all have done a bad work. There is no form of vice, worldliness or drunkenness, that will do a more baleful work upon the character, imbittering the soul, and setting in train evils that overbear good, than human passions not under the control of the Spirit of God. Anger, getting touched, stirred up, will never pay. How many prodigals are kept out of the kingdom of God by the unlovely character of those who claim to be Christians. Jealousy, envy, pride, and uncharitable feelings, self-righteousness easily provoked, thinking evil, harshness, coldness, lack of sympathy, these are the attributes of Satan. Teachers will meet with these things in the students' characters. It is a terrible thing to have these things to deal with; but in seeking to cast out these evils, the worker has in many instances developed similar attributes which have marred the soul of the one with whom he is dealing.

We live in a hard, unfeeling, uncharitable world. Satan and his confederacy are plying every art to seduce the souls for whom Christ has given his precious life. Every one who loves God in sincerity and truth, will love the souls for whom Christ has died. If we wish to do good to souls, our success with these souls will be in proportion to their belief in our confidence in them and appreciation of them. Respect shown to the struggling human soul is the sure means through Christ Jesus of the restoration of the self-respect the man has lost. Our advancing ideas of what he may become is a help we can not ourselves fully appreciate. We have need of the rich grace of God every hour, then we will have a rich, practical experience, for God is love. He that dwelleth in love, dwelleth in God. Give love to them that need it most. The most unfortunate, those who have the most disagreeable temperaments, need our love, our tenderness, our compassion. Those who try our patience need most love. We pass through the world only once; any good thing we can do, we should do most earnestly, untiringly, with the same spirit as is stated of Christ in his work. He will not fail nor be discouraged. The rough, stubborn, sullen dispositions are the ones who need help the most. How can they be helped? Only by that love practiced in dealing with them which Christ revealed to fallen men. Treat them, you say, as they deserve? What if Christ had treated us thus? He, the undeserving, was treated as we deserve. Still we are treated by Christ with grace and love as we did not deserve, but as he deserved. Treat some characters as you think they richly deserve, and you will cut off from them the last thread of hope, spoil your influence, and ruin the soul. Will it pay? No, I say no, a hundred times no. Bind these souls who need all the help it is possible for you to give them close to a loving, sympathizing, pitying heart, overflowing with Christ-like love, and you will save a soul from death and hide a multitude of sins. Had we not better try the love process?

Be careful what you do in the line of suspending students. This is a solemn business. It should be a very grave fault which requires this discipline. Then there should be a careful consideration of all the circumstances connected with the case. Students sent from home a short distance or a long distance, thousands and thousands of miles, are away from and deprived of the advantages of home, and if expelled are refused the privileges of school. All their expenses have to be met by some one who had had hope and confidence in these subjects that their money would not be invested in vain. The student enters into, or falls into, temptation, and he is to be disciplined for his wrong. He feels keenly that his record is marred, and he disappoints those who have trusted him to develop a character under the influence of his training in his scholastic life which would pay all that has been invested in his behalf. But he is suspended for his foolish course of action. What will he do? Courage is at the lowest ebb, courage and even manliness are not cherished. He is an expense, and precious time is lost. Who is tender and kind, and feels the burden of these souls? What wonder that Satan takes advantage of the circumstances? They are thrust on Satan's battleground, and the very worst feelings of the human heart are called into exercise, are strengthened, and become confirmed.

I put the case as it has been presented to me. I wish all could view this as it has in all its bearings been shown me. I think there would be radical changes made in many rules and methods of dealing with human minds. There would be more physicians to heal human souls, who understand how to deal with human minds. There would be far more forgiveness and sympathy and love practiced, and far less discouraging, tearing-down influences exercised.

Supposing that Christ should deal with all his sons and daughters who learn of him, as the human agent, as teachers deal with those under their charge; that when the law of the Lord, his rules, his injunctions, have been disregarded by us, the guilty were expelled or suspended, turning the erring away from his saving, uplifting, educating influences, leaving him to pick and choose his own way and course of action without Christ's divine assistance; what would become of our souls? Christ's constant, forgiving love is binding up our souls' interest with himself. O the mightiness of the love of Jesus overwhelms me as I consider it. The yoke of Christ is easy, and his burden is light. When we enter more entirely into the love of Jesus by practice, we shall see far different results in our own advancement as Christians, and in the molding of the characters of those brought into relationship with us. The most difficult business for individuals is the giving up of that which one thinks is his right. Love seeketh not her own. Heaven-born love strikes deeper then the surface. Love vaunteth not itself, is not puffed up. Fortified with the grace of Christ, love doth not behave itself unseemly. He that dwelleth in love dwelleth in God. God is love. We all need love, gentleness, tenderness, compassion, forbearance. Expel from the soul every vestige of selfishness of human dignity.

When all hope was excluded from Adam and Eve, in consequence of transgression and sin, when justice demanded the death of the sinner, Christ gave himself to be a sacrifice for the sin of the world. The world was under condemnation. Christ became substitute and surety for man. He would give his life for the world, which is represented as the one lost sheep that had strayed from the fold, whose guilt as well as helplessness was charged against it in the way, hindering its return. Herein is love, not that we loved God, but that he loved us and sent his Son to be a propitiation for our sins. All we like sheep have gone astray; we have turned every one to his own way; and the Lord hath laid on him the iniquity of us all. Every son and daughter of God, if they have an abiding Saviour, will act our Christ. Every soul that has not an abiding Saviour will reveal in unChristlikeness of character. Love is not cherished and put into exercise. "Lift him up, the risen Saviour," in our words, in our conversation, in our dealing with the erring.

I know by the burden which is rolled upon me, that many who are officiating in our schools need themselves to learn in the school of Christ his meekness, his tender dealing with the erring, his compassion and love. Until they are melted over and the dross separated from the character, they will work at cross purposes. I am deeply grieved in my heart, for serious results in unwise dealings have followed, more serious then many are willing to admit to their own conscience or to God. Self is so large in many, ever striving for the mastery. There are those who profess to be followers of Jesus Christ who have never died to self. They have never fallen on the Rock and been broken, Until this shall be, they will live unto self, and if they die as they are, it is forever too late for their wrongs to be righted. I love their souls. Jesus loves their souls, and he will do a good work for them, if they will humble themselves under his mighty hand, repent and be converted, surrender every day to God. It must be a constant daily surrender. We must be minute men and women, ever on guard over self, and watching to improve every opportunity to do good and only good for the souls for whom Christ has given his life to make them his own. When the human agents deal with these souls in a hard spirit, they grieve the heart of Christ, and put him to open shame, for they misrepresent in their own character the character of Christ, Said one, "thy gentleness hath made me great." I pray to our heavenly Father that all connected with our schools may be in Christ as the branch is united to the living vine.

Chapter 40—The Review and Herald and the College Debt

June 6, 1899.

I read in the G. C. Bulletin proposals that the Review and Herald forgive the indebtedness of the Battle Creek College. That night instruction was given me from the Lord, that there were debts upon the Review and Herald, which would make it unjust for the R. & H. Pub. Co. to do this. The General Conference and the Review and Herald are acting for the whole of the people in the Sabbath-keeping ranks. They take the people's money that is there invested, and use it to relieve the school debt. If the word of the Lord had been heeded, these debts would not now exist. The light the Lord gave years ago was that the school building last proposed should not be erected. But unwise advisers turned from the counsels of God. There should be no more necessities made, no more inducements offered to bring people to Battle Creek.

Over and over the word of the Lord has come to us that plants both of churches and schools should be made in other localities. Get the people out of the cities, and establish interests in other places. So many students need not come to Battle Creek if there were other schools in different places. There were too many weighty responsibilities in one place. This was the instruction given. But the additional building was erected just the same. That building should have been located in some favorable situation outside the cities, in some place where there was plenty of land to be cultivated. Thus the standard would have been lifted in a new place. Had two-thirds of the students been taken out of Battle Creek, and a division been made, the money expended on the extra building would have abundantly provided for two new plants in other localities, and there would have been the growing of the tree and the bearing of the fruit that has not been because men choose to follow their own wisdom. The gathering together of so many students in one school is not wise. If two-thirds of the people in Battle Creek would become plants of the Lord in other localities, they would have chance to grow. The time and energy bestowed upon the large school in Battle Creek to make a growth would be far more favorable for the growth of the Lord's plants in other localities. Where there is room for agricultural pursuits to be carried on as a part of the education. If there had been a willingness to follow the Lord's ways and his plans, there would have been light shining in other places. The great expense incurred to add new buildings where there was all there should be, called for additional expense in furnishings, and the tuition was placed too low, for students must be secured to fill the building. When a school is found to be constantly increasing its debts, let the faculty come together and study how the school can be made self-sustaining. This should be done in every school that shall be established. Let teachers lessen their wages by making some personal sacrifice. Let the price of tuition be raised. It is far better to let a whole school share the expense than to run in debt.

The debt for the additional building has been hanging over the school as a discouragement, and thus it will ever be until there shall be a deeper consecration and self-sacrifice all through our churches. Every true character, and no other, will be qualified to cope with difficulties in following a "Thus said the Lord." Men are not prepared to understand their obligation to God until they have learned in Christ's school to wear his yoke of restraint and obedience. Sacrifice was the very beginning of our work in advancing the truth and in establishing institutions. Sacrifice must become habitual in all our building in this life, if we would have a building of God not made with hands, eternal in the heavens.

There are lessons to learn daily in regard to offering praise and thanksgiving to God. To praise God and glorify him in the fulness and sincerity of heart is as much the duty of those who love God as is prayer. We are to show to all the heavenly intelligences that we appreciate their ministrations, and that we are expecting and waiting for the goodness and mercy and large blessings of God. Never should we lose sight of his wondrous love for the fallen human family. We are under obligations to God to offer thanksgiving. Whoso offereth praise glorifieth God. After a special outpouring of his Holy Spirit, our cheerfulness, our helpfulness, our joy in the Lord will be increased by recounting his goodness and his wonderful works to the children of men. This will make the Christian courageous and yet simple and trustful as a little child. Read Matt. 18: 1-6. True humility will be evidenced by recounting the mercies of God. Think of his goodness and praise his name. The more we see and tell of the love and goodness and compassion of God, the more will gratitude spring up in our hearts. This will put a stop to grumbling. Distrust, censuring, jealousy, and evil surmising are never cherished in a heart that is thankful because of the mercies of God. True Christian life is that of higher and still higher education. Christian must grow up to the full stature of men and women in Christ Jesus. This is the character we must form if we have the wisdom of the Lord with us.

But I am almost forgetting my subject. The Lord does not require the General Conference or the Review and Herald, that is now under a burden of debt, to bear the burden of the College debt. That would be doing injustice to the general necessities of the cause in new fields and in foreign lands. Methods must be devised to stop this continued accumulation of debt. The whole cause must not be made to suffer because of these debts. which will never be lifted unless there is an entire change and the work is carried forward on some different basis. Under the present embarrassment, I could not advise that the interest of the money due from the College to the Review and Herald should be remitted. It can not be done as though the Review and Herald were a person dealing with another person, or even as though it were handling its own goods. Those who are bearing responsibilities in the Review and Herald Office or in any of the interests relating to the General Conference, are dealing with capital which is not their own, which has been brought in by the people; and they have no right to handle these goods as they have been doing. The means should not be grasped as it has been by selfish men, who have not helped to build up the work, but whose selfish hearts, knowing little of sacrifice, have grasped all the wages they could obtain. God has been dishonored by those men who have worked as worldlings work. The means which is in the hands of responsible men should be carefully and faithfully handled.

The publishing institution was built up by sacrifice, but by the example men in responsible places have given to the people, this spirit has been lost. The Lord has not stirred hearts to give for the advancement of the cause, and selfishness has leavened the churches. Unfaithful stewardship has been revealed in the payment of large wages to men who have made God's work and cause a matter of merchandise by which to enrich themselves. Those at the very heart of the work have displeased the Lord, and he has turned away from his people. Temptations came to the people, and back sliding was the result. If they had called together the men of the conference and demanded an investigation of matters - which it was their right to do - decisive measures would have been taken to stop the existing evil. But this was not done. Had they changed the order of things, and brought in the same principles which were revealed in the work when the first buildings were erected, the spirit of self-sacrifice would have been retained, and the work have moved onward and upward. God's people would have understood that the way and work of the Lord can not prosper when his people are unwilling to sacrifice self. Heavenly intelligences would have helped them to climb to higher levels, to understand by experimental knowledge that they were to be laborers together with God. God desires that his people shall be conquerors, moving bravely through all difficulties. God is faithful. He will make his people complete in him.

There has been a mistake all round; and it is a great work to come back from every wrong path and choose the right. The Lord has honored men by allowing them to unite with his work; but to manifest sympathy for the tempted, to encourage them in an evil course by showing confidence in them will not help the wrong-doer or enrich the experience of those who by their course become partakers of their evil deeds. Those men who should have stood firm as a rock to principle, spoiled their influence by succumbing to temptation when brought into a strait place. The saving power of Christ was not with them. Christ's sympathy was not impaired by his sinlessness. It was his steadfast adherence to righteousness and truth that made him a power of grace to redeem. All emergencies will call the faithful ones to action. All combinations of difficulties which arouse us to seek God's help are really working together for good to those who love God, and who will maintain their integrity at all hazards. When emergencies force men to a decision, and the ones who act their part unselfishly, bravely, are called to resist the working of evil men, they are obtaining a clearer self-knowledge. They see the necessity of standing steadfast to pure, unadulterated principles, if they would save the souls ready to perish. Such a sympathy Christ had when he rebuked wrong.

When men were bringing in wrong principles, and were criticizing those who would not vindicate their course of selfishness, if those entrusted with holy interests had refused every approach to selfishness, refused to cover selfishness in any one connected with the work, they would have become followers of Christ, strong in uplifting faith, determined to press close to the side of Christ. They would have realized the ideal of his Sonship, which God has revealed in and through Christ.

These thoughts I can not possibly express in the few moments I have to write. I will say, The College has no right to draw from the General Conference or the Review and Herald to pay its indebtedness. Let all who have acted a part in allowing this cloud of debt to cover them now feel it their duty to do what they can to lessen it. Lessen expenses, and raise the fee for tuition.

Training of Students

Brother Sutherland, be careful not to go to opposite extremes. We very much dislike to present wrongs to be corrected, lest the opposite extreme shall be taken. You must not let the students suppose that their education is to be loose and haphazard. Let the students, the young especially, study books that are free from infidelity. As fast as possible let the youth perfect their knowledge of the common branches. Bring in the Word of God and its principles as the foundation of a solid education. Not all the youth are to receive a medical education in order to be fitted for labor. Young boys and girls need to go through the proper period of discipline in the study of the common branches and Bible lessons. But let them have no encouragement that they can engage in medical missionary work, unless they give evidence of thorough conversion.

When men and women are sent to our schools to learn how to work for the Master, do not teach them that they must have a five years' drill in Latin and Greek. Many who take this course come from the school deficient in a knowledge of the Bible. They know scarcely anything of the reasons of our faith. Teach the students solidly. Teach them how to learn and how to keep learning. Let them become as efficient as possible, that they in their own turn may be educators, ministers and those who have been fitting themselves for missionary work should not spend years in medical missionary classes. Little boys and girls need thorough discipline in study, but there are those who need only a short time at school.

It seems to be unnecessary to go into all these particulars, but I fear lest some may go to extremes that will weaken in the place of strengthening the work of God. May the Lord give sanctified understanding, is my prayer.

E.G. White.

Chapter 41—School Diet

Toowoomba, Queensland, Oct. 21, 1899.

Dear Brother Magan:

W. C. White has sent me a copy of his answer to your letter. I think he has answered you wisely.

I am much troubled in regard to writing cautions to my brethren in regard to the management of the work and in regard to bringing in reforms; for they mingle their own ideas with the light given. Will my brethren not cease to make appear as one the instruction given and the inferences which they draw from this instruction?

The carrying of the indebtedness of the school in Battle Creek by the General Conference is plainly stated to be wrong. The Conference has no funds with which to do this, and the missions in foreign lands help which they do not receive. This is the game Satan has been playing to bind about the work of God. Through a disregard of the positive directions given by the Lord in various lines, he has sought to bring in his own methods. By human suppositions men have made the instruction given of God of none effect. They have interpreted the plain words of the Lord to mean something after man's wisdom and not after the wisdom of God. Then they have gone straight forward with their own suppositions and plans.

Light has been plainly given that those who minister in our schools, teaching the word of God, explaining the Scriptures, educating the students in the things of God, should be supported by the tithe money. This instruction was given long ago, and more recently it has been repeated again and again. Only a few months ago it was plainly defined. Will my brethren use that which has been given them by the Lord just as it is, or will they mislead minds by following their own human devising, making it still harder for those who have been reproved by the Lord, when it is hard enough for them to receive correction?

Light was given in regard to the unfair dealing which had been shown in the matter of royalties. This matter could have been arranged in quietude, without giving publicity to the evils corrected. But great publicity was given to the matter, and this brought in claims for royalty which were born entirely of selfishness. People came forward to press claims who were grasping for a chance to secure that which was not really theirs, while the real wrongs, which should have been made right years ago, were entirely neglected, because of a spirit of bitterness and prejudice of which the actors should have been ashamed.

When those who had been misused and deprived of their just dues were advised to pass the sponge over the account, it was for them to say they would do it. It was for them to say they would forgive the wrong done them, leaving the matter with the Lord. It was not left for those in authority to take the sponge and erase the figures. I was shown that this also was a test which would reveal hearts.

As has been stated before, wrong actions were taken in regard to "The Gospel Primer." Certain selfish men in positions of responsibility took a decided course in the wrong direction, and Elder Olsen allowed them to follow this course. Thus was done a work which demanded restitution. This work robbed the Southern field of the means which God designed should go to it; and this money, both principal and interest, should be refunded. Not one penny of the money used in the publication of "The Gospel Primer" should have been charged against it. This should have been given as a donation. And the other books that shall be prepared for the Southern field should be published gratuitously.

Other dishonest, intriguing actions were done in a secret, artful manner, People were turned away from their rights. Some of these things have never been adjusted. Men were inspired by the suggestions of the great adversary of souls to turn aside the counsels of God for human inventions. God declares, "Neither will I be with you any more until you put away all these unholy things from you."

At the last General Conference a work was started which God desired to have carried to every Seventh-day Adventist church in America. But Satan came in with the sons of God, and the very work that ought to have been carried forward by those who ought to have been worked by the Spirit of God, failed of completion. The high expectations were without proper results. The influence which began to work at the Conference was genuine, but the enemy interposed himself and spoiled the work by the deception he had prepared. The faith of many was dead, being alone. There was a large work to be done in cleansing the temple and the court thereof, but this work was not done. The life and power of God can not be manifested until there is seen that faith which works by love and sanctifies the soul. As far as the work went, it was done with earnestness, fervor, and true zeal. And so far God's blessing was given. But in the case of a large number, especially those in responsible positions in our institutions, the work of the Spirit was quenched by a deception of the enemy. There was a reaping of that which had been sown. These things need to be studied.

In regard to the school work, God does not want it to die, but live. But actions directly contrary to a plain "Thus saith the Lord" have been taken. The indebtedness of the school work has been increased by the erection of buildings in places where there were already buildings enough. The reason given for the erection of these buildings were not sound. The money thus used should have been invested in the erection of schools in new localities, thus distributing the light and gathering in a class of students who would not otherwise be reached. The knowledge of the truth should have been extended to places where there are no memorials to tell what truth is.

God would have his Word and his wisdom demonstrated. Truth has been so covered with the rubbish of error that it can not shine forth in its native purity and brightness to illuminate the surrounding darkness. God would have his directions followed to the letter, that truth may be rescued from the companionship of error. He calls for all the talents with which he has endowed men. He calls upon his servants to receive from the Holy Spirit his sanctifying power, that the light may shine forth in clear, distinct rays, amid the constantly increasing moral darkness, which is becoming as black as sackcloth of hair over our world. ...

As regard the debt on the Battle Creek College, I think that W.C. White has written wisely. It is your privilege to present the case to the churches, and ask them to help to lessen this debt. Then devise methods by which the school may be made self-supporting. This could have been accomplished in past years by increasing the rates of tuition. Here at Avondale the tuitions at first were too low. Embarrassment was brought upon the school.

We need to move solemnly and intelligently, under the sanctification of the Holy Spirit. God has not forsaken his people; but his people have not followed the light given them. Had they obeyed his instruction, the sure result of obedience would have been seen; for heavenly agencies would have cooperated with human instrumentalities.

The work would have extended and enlarged, and God would have been glorified. Our people are asleep, upon the very borders of the eternal world. In our publishing houses, the increasing expense of book-making is consuming means which should be used to produce and impart solid instruction, and to multiply the agencies for the extension of truth to places where there are now no memorials of His truth.

E. G. White.

Chapter 41.1—W.C. White to P.T. Magan (1899)

Text unavailable.

Chapter 41.2—W.C. White to G.A. Erwin (1899)

Text unavailable.

Chapter 42—Help to be Given to our Schools

January 22, 1900.

I have not been able to sleep since one o'clock. I am troubled in regard to the debt on the Battle Creek College. I now ask the Review and Herald what it will do to relieve the situation.

In the night season, I seemed to see several looking over the account books of the Review and Herald. In these books were recorded the interest on the money loaned to the school.

Notwithstanding the light given by God, ten thousand dollars were called for, and double that amount was used, in building an addition to the school. The managers of the Review and Herald had much to do in this matter. These things must be considered. The Review and Herald is not required to pay the College debt; for if this were done, calls would be made for other schools to be helped in the same way. But the interest on this debt should be made as low as possible. Interest should not be charged upon interest. Neither should those who have loaned money charge a higher rate of interest than they themselves pay. One institution should have the tenderest and most kindly feelings for its sister institution. The work done in one is as much the Lord's work as the work done in the other.

The time has come when the Lord would have all the powers of his people brought into exercise to relieve the situation of our schools. In order to help in this cause, I have proposed giving my book on the parables. I feel very anxious that the General Conference shall act unselfishly in regard to this book, which is to be published to help the schools. This is a time when the Conference should stand before the people in a better light than it has hitherto done. We shall call upon the people to help to the utmost of their ability just now. We shall call upon them to do a work which will be pleasing to God in purchasing the book. We shall ask that every available means be used to help to circulate this book. We shall ask that the whole field be supplied with canvassers. We shall call upon our ministers, as they visit the churches, to encourage men and women to go out as canvassers, to make a decided forward movement in the path of self-denial by giving part of their earnings to help our schools to get out of debt. Surely they can do this much to help the Master.

A general movement is needed, but this must begin with individual movements. Let each member in each family in each church make determined efforts to deny self. Let us have the whole-hearted cooperation on all in our ranks. Let us all move forward willingly and intelligently to do what we can to relieve those of our schools that are struggling under a pressure of debt. Let the officers of each church find out who among them has been sent to school and helped by the school. Then let the church refund the tuition money. Let those who have had success in canvassing come up to help of the Lord. As they handle this book, let them in the name of the Lord work in faith.

The movement I have suggested will result in reconciliation. It will unify the churches. If all will help to lift the debts in our schools, the publishing house in Battle Creek will be strengthened to do its part. Therefore it is for the interest of the school in Battle Creek to act a full part in helping to pay back the money that has been so long bound up in it.

The school must be helped. Let all lift harmoniously, and help as much as they possibly can. Great blessings will come to those who will take hold of this matter just now. Let no discouragement be offered by our ministers, as though it were not a proper thing to do. They should take hold of this work. If they do it aright--cheerfully, hopefully--they will find in it a great blessing. The Lord does not force any man to work, but to those who will place themselves decidedly on his side he will give a willing mind. He will bless the one who works out the spirit which he works in. God will make the movement for the help of our schools a success if it is made in a free, willing spirit, as to the Lord. Only in this way can be rolled back the reproach that has come upon our schools all over the land. If all will take hold of this work in the spirit, of self-sacrifice, for Christ's sake and for the truth's sake, it will not be long before the jubilee song of freedom can be sung throughout our borders. ...

Mrs. E. G. White.

Chapter 43—Kingly Power

(Verbatim report of remarks by Mrs. E. G. White, at a meeting held in Battle Creek College library, April 1, at the General Conference of 1901.)

I would prefer not to speak today, but still not because I have nothing to say, because I have; I have something to say. And the state of things as has existed in our conference and the leading responsibilities are not nearly understood in their influence by themselves or by those that are taking responsibilities in the work. The work has been increasing; it has been growing; and from the light that I have had for some time, and has been expressed, has been expressed over and over again, not to all there are here, but has been expressed to individuals, and the plans that God would have all to work from, that never should one mind or two minds or three minds nor four minds, or a few minds I should say, be considered of sufficient wisdom and power to control and mark out plans and let it rest upon the minds of one or two or three in regard to this broad, broad field that we have; that we are not coming up to reach that high standard with the great and important truths that we are handling, that God expects us to reach. There are minds which must be brought into altogether more lively action than they are at the present time. And in reference to our conference, it is repeated o'er and o'er and o'er again, that it is the voice of God, and therefore everything must be referred to the Conference and have the conference voice in regard to permission or restriction or what shall be and what shall not be done in the various fields.

Now from the light that I have, as it was presented to me in figures: There was a narrow compass here; there within that narrow is a king-like, kingly ruling power. Here the outlets are blocked. And the work all over our field demands an entirely different course of action than we have had. We have heard enough, abundance, about that "everything must go around in the regular way." When we see the regular lines are altered and purified and refined, and the God of the heavens mold is upon the regular lines, then it is our business to establish the regular lines. But when we see message after message that God has given has been accepted, but no change, just the same as it was before, then it is evident that new blood must be brought into the regular lines. The leaders of the regular lines, they must have and entire change, an entire new organization, and to have a committee that shall take in not merely half a dozen, that is to be a ruling and controlling power, but it is to have representatives of those that are placed in responsibility in our educational interests, in our Sanitariums, that are working, and the life in them, constantly at work, constantly adding, constantly giving to the field the talent that has come from it.

And then the comparison that has been presented to me, where the fields are that have been opened; Where are the fields that have been opened here, the new fields in America? Where is it in California? Where is it here at the great heart of the work? And here are the two great centers - where is the wrestling to get new fields, whether it costs or whether it does not cost, whatever way it shall be? God has his treasures that he had given to the work. He has his treasures in the hills; he has his treasures in every place and in every country, and in all these countries, far and near, he wants to be an arousing, broadening, enlarging power. And a management which is getting confused in itself, not that anyone is wrong or means to be wrong, but the principle is wrong, and the principles have become so mixed and so fallen from what God's principles are, and the message has been coming constantly in regard to the principles, sacred, holy elevating, ennobling, in every institution, in the publishing houses, and in all the interests of the denomination, everything that concerns the handling of the work, it requires minds that are worked by the Holy Spirit of God; and unless that evidence is given, unless there is a power that shows that they are accepted by God to impart to the responsibilities that have to be handled, then there should be a renovation without any delay. To have this conference pass on and close up as the conferences have done, with the same manipulating, with the very same tone, and the same order,--God forbid! (Voices, "Amen") God forbid, brethren. (Voices, "Amen".) He wants every living soul that has a knowledge of the truth to come to their senses. He wants every living power to arouse; and we are just about the same thing as dead men. And it is time that we should arise and shine because our light has come, and the glory of the Lord has arisen upon us, and until this shall come we might just as well close up the conference today as any other day.

But what we must have is the taking in of other minds. Where there are minds that have been at work, minds that have been at work in the same tone and in the same channel, they have become discouraged, and they have become confused. Well, now, we can not trust to such as that in such tremendous responsibilities as are going to be handled here. Why, from the light that God has given me, everything about this conference should be the most sacred. Why? Why, because it is to put ideas and plans and work upon its proper basis. And this thing has been continued and renewed for the last fifteen years of more, and God calls for a change. God wants that men of capabilities and of mind should understand there is a ladder for them to climb, round after round, and if they climb this ladder, round after round, why they will step off finally into the kingdom of our Lord and Saviour Jesus Christ. We want our course heavenward. And we want that all the selfishness, every thread of it, that has been woven into the pattern, that every thread of this selfishness is to be got out, and here is a work that, from the light that God has given me, it should stand, yes, a hundred per cent, higher than it stands today.

Here are our enemies. Here are those Satanic agencies that are at work. There is a waking up on the part of every working agency. Let me tell you that the enemy is getting the victory all the time. God wants us to arouse. God wants us to take hold of this work, every human agency, and he wants us to work for time and for eternity. And treading over and over just the same ground - here are our churches, our large churches, and they ought to be turning out men, educating them and training, and disciplining, and there ought to be those that should connect with them here, bearing responsibilities that should go on into the fields to carry the message into the barren places - that have been, oh, so barren, especially the Southern field that is scarcely touched, notwithstanding the message has come from God for the last -- I might say -- well, I do not know how many years; it is quite a number of years. But those things have been told, and this standstill has got to come to an end. But yet every conference has woven after the same pattern. It is the very same loom that carries it, and finally, why, it will come to naught.

Now God wants a change, and it is high time, it is high time that here was ability that should connect with the conference, with the General Conference, right here in this city; not wait until it is done, and then find, - not wait till it is all done and over with, and then gather up the forces and see what can be done. We want to know what can be done right here; we want to know what can be done right now, and what power and intellect that there is that shall be brought into this work, and that they shall unite their powers and take hold of it intelligently, and that God can work with them.

Now this is what they want and you want, they every institution that bears a responsibility, bears a voice in the working of this cause. They have a decided interest in it, and God wants that we shall, every one, come into a position where that we shall work: that we will not lay off the burden upon two or three men, and let them carry it all. Brother Irwin will soon be where he can not work at all. He wants supporters, and he has been in this work of wrestling and discouragement until he should have a change. He should have some one come in his place, or he is going to give all out. It can not be. We must have responsible men, and we want men that shall stand just as true as the compass to the pole, and God will test these men, and unless they can show a better idea of what principle is, what sanctified and living and Christ-like principle is, then they will have to be changed and try another.

But God is going to have a change. He wants us to know what it means to work on the principles of heaven. He wants that all of us should know what it means to stand in their lot, and stand in their place, and every soul that has had a responsibility, that they should have been workers, that they should have had these principles, that they should have had patience, just as it is reported "Add to your faith virtue; and to virtue knowledge; and to knowledge temperance; and to temperance patience; and to patience godliness; and to godliness brotherly kindness; and to brotherly kindness charity." 2 Peter 1:5. Brethren, we all need these letters written and hung in the chambers of the mind, and to him that doeth these things,--if you live on this principle you will never fail; "For so an entrance shall be ministered unto you abundantly into the everlasting kingdom of our Lord and Saviour Jesus Christ."

Now God is in earnest with us, and he says he calls,--oh, I can not tell how it is. It is contemptible in the sight of God - contemptible. They pause for fear they are not going to get all that they ought to have, and it leaves a man where he can not - if he considers that as the principles of heaven, why, it leaves the man where he will never get to heaven. He can not get in there. The nobility, the generosity, the tenderness, the compassion, the love of Christ - why, they are as destituted of it as the hills of Gilboa, that had not dew nor rain - just as destitute of it, and we can not rouse them from it. Enough has been said, over and over and over again, but it did not make any difference. The light shone upon them, just the same, professedly accepting it, but they did not make any change. That is what frightens me. It frightens me because that I saw unless there was more tenderness, more compassion, more of the love of God - the Lord knew what he was talking about when he was talking to the church at Ephesus, "Ye have lost your first love," and tells them to repent speedily or he will remove the candlestick out of its place. What we want is to study all through John and see what is said about the love of God and the love that we should express, and that love has not been cultivated, and if it is not being cultivated the opposite attribute is being cultivated. Now it has not been cultivated in our institutions of publication, and when by every little sharpness that can be exercised by them, by which they think that they are going to gain a little something, they lose four-fold, yes, ten-fold in that little transaction, until the light will soon be moved out of its place. They don't know when it is for the interests of the institution, but God knoweth. Every one God knoweth, and should come right up to the help of the Lord, and to have a new creation of sentiment. Now God never will acquit us until that is there, until this is taught in our institutions, every one of them and God means what he says, "I want a change here." Will it be the same thing, going over and over the same ideas, the same committees--and here is the little throne: the king is in there, and these others are all secondary, those minds that are so much sharper because they have not been working on this narrow, conceited plane.

I feel intensely in this matter. I do not want to talk here but I dare not hold my peace. I feel this condition. I think we should hold for the tenderness of God and break your hearts before him, and if you get where you can see these things clearly, you will see that God hates selfishness, and when we bring it into his cause, oh, it makes the crime a hundred fold greater. And when we bring that selfishness in, as though we were going to benefit the cause, we do not benefit it at all: it makes God ashamed of you.

We are to be representatives of Jesus Christ; we are to be representatives of his character. We are so to do that we are carrying out the living principles in every line of action everywhere, in every country, everywhere, and in every place that there is anything to do with God's service. He will not accept common fire. He wants you to take sacred fire that he kindles on the divine altar, and he wants you to work, and that fire to consume all your commonness, all your intemperance, all your selfishness, all your cheap ideas, all your licentiousness, all this lust. He wants it taken away from a people that are trying to fashion a people to stand in the last great conflict, which is just before us. Self must be hid in God, and when self is hid in God, then will the Lord God appear, and not self. He will appear as the great worker, and when you think to improve upon God's plans by your narrowness, by your conceited ideas, and by your planning and grasping and thinking you are going to gain something,--and if you have not learned better than that now, you will have to learn. God wants that these committees that have been handling things for so long should be relieved of their command and have a chance for their life, and see if they can not get out of this rut that they are in,--which I have no hope of their getting out of, because the Spirit of God has been working, and working, and yet the king is there still.

Now the Lord wants his Spirit to come in. He wants the Holy Ghost king. He wants everything of the sharpness, that it shall not be exercised toward outsiders, it shall not be exercised toward one that is trying to serve God and trying to exercise all his power to serve him, that is bringing his tithes here to sustain the ministry. He has a treasury, and that treasury is to be sustained by the tithe, and that tithe is to be a sacred tithe, and it is to be God's tithe, and that tithe is to be so liberal that it will sustain the work largely; each one to act in their capacity in such a way that the confidence of the whole people will be established in them, and that they will not be afraid, but see everything just as light as day until they are in connection with the work of God and the people. I know my husband used to work in that way. He would sit down with this man that he thought had good judgment, and with that man, and with the other man, and with another man - that was when the cause was young. He did not feel that he was capable of carrying the conference when it was very young. But he had these men, these committees, that were brought in from places all around. It was not just in Battle Creek, but it was in different places, that those that felt a responsibility for the work would go home and feel a larger responsibility for the work. To carry it on in right lines, in heaven's lines, in purity, in holiness, in uplifting, in solidity, to the glory of God, should be that which would make every one of us to be joyful and proud that God has given us the privilege to be co-workers with Jesus Christ.

Now there is all that power that was pledged to us when we pledged ourselves to God. That power that all the provision was made in heaven, all the facilities, all the riches of the grace of God was to be imparted to every worker that was connected with the cause; and every one of these are wholly dependent upon God, and when we leave God out of the question, and leave Jesus Christ out of the question, and allow hereditary and cultivated traits of character to come, let me tell you, we are on very slippery grounds. We are making, not straight paths for our feet, but crooked paths that the lame shall be turned out of the way - and we can not afford it. It has cost too much to heaven to give us Jesus; it has cost too much to heaven for Christ to lay aside his royal robe, to lay aside his royal crown, and to step down from his high command, the Prince of Life and Glory, in order that he might make himself in humanity, and in order that he might the better combine the human with the divine, as the stepping-stone for man to step on. It was not humanity, but humanity and divinity combined, and that man could step on that stepping-stone, and that he would be on vantage ground with God, because of the perfume - because of the holy sanctified character of God imbues the life of every soul that eats of the Bread of Life and drinks of the water of salvation. And every one that eats of Christ, that takes his word and practices it, should have eternal life. It is in him, because it is in Christ, and Christ is in him. Now here is the way the matter is presented. But when there is a, "I don't care; I am going right contrary to the law that God has given in his Word, I don't ask him to take my word, I don't ask him to do it,"--

Lay Sister White right to one side: lay her to one side. Don't you never quote my words again as long as you live, until you can obey the Bible. When you take the Bible and make that your food, and your meat, and your drink, and make that the elements of your character, when you can do that you will know better how to receive some counsel from God. But here is the Word, the precious Word, exalted before you today. And don't you give a rap any more what "Sister White said"-- "Sister White said this," and "Sister White said that," and "Sister White said the other thing." But say, "Thus saith the Lord God of Israel," and then you do just what the Lord God of Israel does, and what he says,

Christ says, "I do the works of my Father. The works that I saw him do, I do." Now the works and the sentiments and the principles that we have seen, that God has manifest in dealing with one another, the the purchase of the blood of Christ - only think of it. Here we are, the purchase of the blood of our Lord and Saviour Jesus Christ. You just think of it. It cost his life. He was crucified for us, and yet here is the very instrumentality that God would have stand next to heaven, that God would have stand where the light of His glory can shine upon them in unmistakable rays, and they know that the light of heaven is with them. It is no emotion, but it is a living faith that is founded on a living Word and a living God, and the Saviour, who proclaimed over the sepulcher of Joseph. "I am the resurrection and the life."

He wants you to eat his principles: to live his principles; - but those that are there now never will appreciate it. They have had their test, they have had their trial, they have had their warnings, and now there must be a change. Give them an opportunity to go out and see what it means to wrestle in the grace of God as some of his workmen have. Let them see what it means to build up. Let them go into the waste places of earth; let them begin to see what it means to establish things out of nothing. When they do this, they will understand that God hath his servants, his church, established in the earth, composed of many members, but of one body; that in every part of the work one part must work as connected with another part, and that with another part, and with another part, and these are joined together by the golden links of heaven, and there is to be no kings here in their midst at all. There is to be no man that has the right to put his hand out and say, No, you can not go there; we won't support you if you go there. Why, what have you to do with supporting? Did they create the means? The means come from the people, and those who are destitute fields. The voice of God has told me to instruct them to go the people and to tell them their necessities, and to draw all the people to work just where they can find a place to work, to build up the work in every place they can.

There is a work to be done. And we want to know if you have been doing the work, with your committees. Here are the committees: where are the monuments? As we look over the cities, where are the monuments? Where, I ask you, are the churches that are left to glorify God? There are the workers. I thank God that there is a work going on, and I thank God for the medical missionary work, and every soul that shall obtain that education in connection with the gospel of the Lord Jesus Christ, God will call for you. God has a place for you. And those that are laboring for the youth in any line in our schools, in the sanitariums, and wherever they are at work, don't you put one stone in their way! The Lord has revealed that he will work with those who work.

Ye are laborers together with God. Where are the churches? My heart ached when I was in California. There are young men traveling around and around in the churches, but where is the power, where is the power to open the fields for them, and to say, Here we are, not to stay with the people that know the truth, here is a field that knows nothing about it, and this field is to be converted and educated, as far as they will yield to the truth. But the seeds of the truth must be sown. Lift up your heads, for the fields are all ripe with the harvest. But he wanted them to look at it; and he wanted them to see; and he wants everyone of you to see it and to fill your hands full. But these who travel from place to place, and from place to place, to to look after the churches, God help you by giving you the spirit of the message, that your souls shall yearn after other souls, and you will not let go until they are converted. This is the work we want to see done, and until that spirit comes in and takes hold of every mind in every conference that they are conducting, that they are elevating the very light that should be elevated,--health reform - that they are elevating by their self-denial and self-sacrifice.

Oh my soul, how it has hurt me to have the blocks thrown in the way in regard to myself. They will tell you that Sister White did this, or Sister White did that,--for instance, "Sister White ate cheese, and so we are all at liberty to eat cheese." Who told them that I ate cheese? I never have cheese on my table. There was one time when I was at Minneapolis, one or two times I tasted it, but that is a different thing from making it a diet, entirely a different thing. I have tasted of very bitter herbs on special occasions, but I would not make a diet of them. But there was a special occasion in Minneapolis where I could get nothing else, and there were some small bits of cheese on the table, and my brethren were there, and one of them had told me that if I would eat a little of that it would change my condition, and I did. I took a bit of that cheese, and I do not think I touched it again the second time.

Another says, "Sister White drinks tea, and we can drink tea." Who of my brethren has made that statement? Who has ever heard it of me? I never have tea in my home or set it before anyone. Now I have not eaten any meat for years and years.

Now for instance some one may tell you that Sister White don't eat meat. "Now I want you not to eat it, because Sister White doesn't eat it." Well, I wouldn't care a farthing for anything like that. If you haven't got a better conviction, that you won't eat meat just because Sister White don't eat it, I would not give one farthing for your health reform. But I want that every one of you shall stand on your individual dignity, in your individual consecration to God, that the soul temple shall be dedicated to God. Whosoever defileth the temple of God, him will God destroy. Now I want you to see these things, and not to make any human being your criterion.

What you want is this: You have got a body here, wonderfully made, and you want that that body should be, oh, so carefully dealt with. I have seen, it has been represented to me, the finest machinery was in this body - and a good thing we can carry too far, like inhaling too much and swelling out. God did not make these precious organs to be swelled like a balloon. He never made them for that, and he wants every living soul to deal with this machinery as God's machinery, that they must keep in perfect order to keep the brain power all right. The brain must work, and every burden you put upon your stomach which should not be in your stomach will just becloud the brain. You go into a conference like this - you sit down and eat hearty meals and neglect to exercise, and then come into the conference meeting, and you are all sleepy; your ideas are not good for anything, and you really do not know what you are consenting to,

Now God wants every soul here to sharpen up. He wants every soul here should have his converting power. You need not refer, not once, to Sister White; I don't ask you to do it. God has told me that my testimony must be borne straight to this conference, and I am not to try to make a soul believe; that my work is to leave the truth with human minds, and those having found the truth in the Word of God will appreciate it, and will appreciate every day the ray of light that God has given for poor lame souls, that they should not be turned out of the way, and I want you to make straight the paths for your feet, lest the lame be turned out of the way.

Now we want that in the Conference we shall have the ability that God has given unto Dr. Kellogg - I don't suppose he is here - I don't know that he is, at any rate-

(Voice: "Yes, he is here.")

I can't see without my congregational glasses - but I want to say the Lord wants you to make the most of the capabilities that he is using in every part of the work. He does not mean the medical missionary work separated from the gospel work, nor the gospel work separated from the medical missionary work. He wants them to blend together, and he wants that this educating power of the medical missionary work shall be considered as the pioneer work, the breaking-up plow, for the breaking down of the prejudices that have existed and that nothing will break down like it; and God wants every soul to stand shoulder to shoulder with Dr. Kellogg. He has become all but desperate, and came nearly - almost losing his life because of the positions that have been taken, and everyone throwing a stone right before the car so that it should not advance. Now God wants the health and missionary work to advance. He wants God's work to be carried on.

Really, when I came here I did not know what to do. Courteously Dr. Kellogg had asked me to come to his house and let them give me treatment a week or two before the conference, that I should be able to attend the conference. Then came up the question, Here, what about this? They will say that Dr. Kellogg has manipulated you. Let them say it if they want to; they have said it enough when there was not a particle of ground for it. But I was going to take all the difficulty out of the way: so I sent word, "Find me a place." Dr. Kellogg has kindly opened his place to me, but to remove all occasion for talk I decided that I would not go there. Now find me a place. On Friday night I was knelt in prayer, saying, "O Lord, tell me where to go and what to do." There I had been sick, and was still sick - and, why, I didn't choose to come to Battle Creek to the conference was, that I knew it would be a terrible trial for me. This is the third winter I am passing through. I passed through one in Australia, one in California, and I am passing the third here. And now you can judge that all this tells upon my system. Then the heated houses, where there was no more need for having it heated than there was in California; but they were heated, and so brought me down into a terrible condition of malaria, and I have had it here ever since Christmas, and then the very crisis came when I was at Los Angeles, and there I knew nothing - after I had been speaking on Sunday I didn't know anything more until two o'clock the next morning, when I found them all working over me - and I didn't know anything about it, or about what had been done, or anything about it; and then it was that the fullness that I had had in my head passed through the whole channel of the body. And that brought on the bloody flux, and I have been traveling all this time up to the time I came here, with that terrible disorder, the bloody flux. I couldn't sit up at all, only lie down all the time - and yet I have not disappointed a single place but one since leaving Los Angeles. I got up, stood on my feet, and the strength of God helped me up. At Vicksburg I spoke twice, at Nashville I spoke twice, at Memphis I spoke once, and at Chicago I spoke twice and God helped me to speak, and then I came here, and I have been speaking ever since I came here.

Now you see I was afraid of all this, and I didn't want to sacrifice my life, and so I said that I couldn't come here. I couldn't come across the plains. I was afraid. I nearly melted the tendons during the cold weather when I was traveling, because of a heated coil running right under where I was lying on the way across from Australia. So I said I couldn't come. Then they said they would have the conference in Oakland. But in the night season I was talking to you just as I am here today. I was bearing a message night after night and night after night, and then I would get up and write it out, and I would get up at 12 o'clock, and 2 o'clock, and write out the message that I had. And it was then, while I was considering these things, that there came messages from London, that they had hoped they could see me and meet me, but now they couldn't come so far, and it cost so much and I heard it would cost from five to eight thousand dollars more, and then I said, "We have got no such money to spare, and if I sacrifice my life, I will try it, anyway."

Well, Dr. Kellogg never persuaded me at all to come here. When I spoke of the particulars, the cold weather, "Why," he said, "would it make any difference if," - the only words he spoke to me - would it make any difference if the conference could be changed to a few weeks later?" I said, "It would". Then I began to think on that plan, after he had gone. Well, we knelt down to pray, and I was asking the Lord where I should go and what I should do. I was backing out and not going. Sarah says, "You are not fit to go anywhere, you are not fit to go anywhere.

Well, while I was praying and was sending up my petition there was, as at other times - I saw a light circling right around in the room, and a fragrance like the fragrance of flowers, and the beautiful scent of flowers, and then the voice seemed to speak gently, and said that I was to "accept the invitation of my servant, John Kellogg, and make his house my home." Then the word was, "I have appointed him as my physician. You can be an encouragement to him." That is why I am here, and that is why I am at his home.

Now I want in every way possible, If I can, to treat Dr. Kellogg as God appointed me his physician, and I am going to do it. And I want that my brethren, that they should unite. "They say, they say, they say." You just put the "They says" right away from you. Watch, saith the Lord, to hear what He will say. You look to the Lord, and don't you look to any human power and get their mind, for they are nothing but human, they are nothing but evil; but you just look to the Lord God of Israel, and He will give you understanding, and He will give you knowledge. But you are not to lean your helpless soul on any other human being. You have got a character to form for your own individual self, and that character God has given every encouragement should be after God's order.

Now in addition to this that I tell you, the next night - that night I slept happy, very happy. The whole family was melted and broken down. They knew nothing of what I had in my mind at all, nothing at all that I had seen, but the Spirit of God was there. They were all weeping and broken, and the blessing of God had taken hold upon us, and Sister Druillard was praising God, and we all there had an outpouring of the Spirit of God. Such things are more precious to me than the gold of Ophir.

Now I want to say, for Christ's sake, let's unify. Let us put away - we can not reform our selves by putting our fingers on somebody else's wrongs and think that is going to cover our own. God says we must love one another. God says, "I hate your false weights and your false measures. But he tells us that he knows us, in every testimony that he has given in other cases. It is the Lord who wants us to come into the closest connection with Him. You know He told Cornelius all about where Peter was. He knew just where to look, and he told him all about these things - how he was with one who was a tanner - and here it was all worked out. The Angel of God could have told Cornelius all about this message, but no, God's church must connect together, and the law that God imparted to Peter was to be imparted to Cornelius and all his family. Now that is what God wants, and he speaks to every one of us to come to him, and while we are as weak as we are, because we are crippling over somebody else. Now let the Lord God of Israel come into our place. Give him room. Give him place, and let us begin to exercise the love of God in our hearts instead of hatred. Just as soon as you begin to build up yourself, you begin to hate others. God help us to come into right positions and I believe he is here today. If I didn't believe he was here, I would not be saying the things I have said. But I believe you can take these things home to your hearts.

And there must be a heart work done here. Not doing nothing, but work right out on Christ's principles, and when you work on the principles of heaven you see the salvation of God revealed, and God wants you to stand ready to strike. He wants you to open the windows heavenward and close them earthward. He wants the salvation of God to be revealed. He wants the medical missionary work and the gospel combined and bound up together just as fast together that they will be inseparable. And he wants that this work shall blend, and that there should be a united whole with this people. He wants the talent that is in Dr. Kellogg; he wants the talent that is in the school; he wants that which is in every institution to be connected with the management of his work and his churches. He does not want two or three minds to set themselves as kings and the rest of them to be managed by these two or three minds. He wants that there shall be committees that are holding a part in every part of his work. And then the medical missionary work you understand will be wrought upon a higher grade than it has ever been wrought before. God wants it wrought. I have seen people ready to. "Why," some say, "why, they have had more than their proportion, more than others have had in Australia." We have had none too much, only we ought to have had ten times what we had to begin with, that we could establish something that would be an entrance, something that would be a pioneer to the work. That will take everywhere. There is no use to shut it down, it will take everywhere. There is not a place but what medical missionary work will take, and it will open the way for the gospel. Now God has not blessed us as He would have blessed us had there been an appreciation of the work that he is carrying on. I thank God that Dr. Kellogg has not sunk into despondency and infidelity. I have been afraid of it, and I have written some very straight things to him, and it may be, Dr. Kellogg (if he is here), that I have written too strong, for I felt as though I must get hold of you and hold you by the power of all the might I had.

But I have seen the work, I have seen the work that has been carried on, and how can anybody see it and not see that God is at work? That is the mystery to me. I can not understand it. I can not explain it. That those that shall have any knowledge of the work wrought here, should be the men that should represent it, that they should stand to give character to the work, and to the higher classes, that they may be reached. And every soul of you ought to feel honored before God that he has given you instrumentalities that the higher classes may be reached, and that the wealthy classes should be reached. You should feel to thank God for the honor that He has bestowed. And I want to say that I want to take hold to the utmost of my ability. Well, I have done the very best that I could in the medical missionary line. We have helped - But I won't tell you. I won't say anything about it more, but I want to tell you we have found poverty that we have had to relieve clear up to the last moment when we left Australia. It has been poverty, poverty, poverty all the way through that we have met with everywhere. But I thank God that His blessing has accomplished it.

And now I think that for the present time I have said enough. But God's ministers must come into altogether a different position. They must be evangelists. They must be medical missionaries. They must take hold of the work intelligently. They must press the work into far-off places - and it is of no use to think they are doing it if God has given us a work in connection with the gospel, and they drop that work and take up the gospel, then you need not expect that you are going to be filled with intensity because you have not more than one-half of the facilities that God wants you to have.

But the Lord loves you yet. Now let us praise God for that. Now let us take hold of the work in a new way. Let us take hold of the work with heart and mind and soul. Do not pick flaws any more. If I see a lot of buzzards, and I see a lot of vultures that are watching and waiting for dead bodies,--and we don't want anything of that. We want no picking of flaws in others. Attend to No. 1, and you got all that you can do. If you attend to No. 1, and if you purify your souls by obeying the truth, you will have something to impart. You will have a power to give to others. God help you; I beseech of him to help you, every one of you, and to help me. I want help; I want strength.

But don't you quote Sister White. I don't want you ever to quote Sister White until you get your vantage ground where you know where you are. Quote the Bible. Talk the Bible. It is full of meat, full of fatness. Carry it right out in your life, and you will know more Bible than you know now. You will have fresh matter - O, you will have precious matter; you won't be going over and over the same ground, and you will see a world saved. You will see souls for whom Christ has died. And I ask you to put on the armor, every piece of it, and be sure that your feet are shod with the preparation of the gospel.

Chapter 44—The Regular Lines

June 28, 1901.

Dear Brother Daniells:--

I am sending you some things which I wrote some time ago, but have not before had the strength to search for.

Pharisaism in the Christian world today is not extinct. The Lord desires to break up the course of precision which has become so firmly established, which has hindered instead of advancing his work. He desires his people to remember that there is a large space over which the light of present truth is to be shed. Divine wisdom must have abundant room in which to work. It is to advance without asking permission or support from those who have taken to themselves a kingly power. In the past one set of men have tried to keep in their own hands the control of all the means coming from the churches, and have used this means in a most disproportionate manner, erecting expensive buildings where such large buildings were unnecessary and uncalled for, and leaving needy places without help or encouragement. They have taken upon themselves the grave responsibility of retarding the work where the work should have been advanced. It has been left to a few supposed kindly minds to say what fields should be worked and what fields should be left unworked. A few men have kept the truth in circumscribed channels, because to open new fields would call for money. Only in those places in which they were interested have they been willing to invest means. And at the same time, in a few places, five times as much money as was necessary has been invested in buildings. The same amount of money used in establishing plants in places where the truth has never been introduced would have brought many souls to a saving knowledge of Christ.

For years the same routine, the same "regular way" of working has been followed, and God's work has been greatly hindered. The narrow plans that have been followed by those who did not have clear, sanctified judgment has resulted in a showing that is not approved by God.

God calls for a revival and a reformation. The "regular lines" have not done the work which God desires to see accomplished. Let revival reformation make constant changes. Something has been done in this line, but let not the work stop here. No! Let every yoke be broken. Let men awaken to the realization that they have an individual responsibility.

The present showing is sufficient to prove to all who have the true missionary spirit that the "regular lines" may prove a failure and a snare. God helping his people, the circle of kings who dared to take such great responsibilities shall never again exercise their unsanctified power in the so-called "regular lines". Too much power has been invested in unrevived, unreformed human agencies. Let not selfishness and covetousness be allowed to outline the work which must be done to fulfill the grand, noble commission which Christ has given to every disciple. He, our Lord and Master, has given us an example, in his life, of self-sacrifice, of the way in which we must work to advance the kingdom of God.

God does not call upon his missionaries to show their devotion to him by burying themselves in monasteries, or by going on long, painful pilgrimages. It is not necessary to do this to show a willingness to deny self. It is by working for those for whom Christ died that we show true love. By humiliation, suffering, and rejection Christ purchased the salvation of the human race. By his death he made it possible for man to enjoy a home in his eternal kingdom. Those who love the Lord will look at Calvary, and will think of how the Lord of life and glory laid aside his royal robes and kingly crown, and clothing his divinity with humanity, came to a world all seared and marred with the curse, to stand at the head of the fallen race, becoming their example in all things, bearing all the trials they have to bear and enduring all the temptations they have to endure. He lived the life of the poorest, and suffered often with hunger. "The foxes have holes, and the birds of the air have nests," he said, "But the Son of Man hath not where to lay his head."

As a man beholds this divine love, this wonderful sacrifice, he is filled with a desire to spend his life in the service of the Redeemer,

As the sinner convicted and converted, Jesus says to him, "Follow me, and you shall not walk in darkness." To each human being God has assigned an individuality and a distinct work. Abraham was called to go into new territory. He was to be a light-bearer to the heathen. Those who believe in the Lord are not to live to please themselves. The soul of every sinner is precious in the sight of God, and demands the care of those whose names are on the church books.

Christ's commission is, "Go ye into all the world, and preach the gospel to every creature." Those who are impressed to take up the work in the home field or in regions beyond are to go forward in the name of the Lord. They will succeed if they give evidence that they depend upon God for grace and strength. At the beginning, their work may be very small, but it will enlarge if they follow the Lord's plan. God lives, and he will work for the unselfish, self-sacrificing laborer, wherever and whoever he may be.

We look to see whether new fields have been worked whether the barren portions of the Lord's vineyard have received attention. We see that most of those who have sought to begin work in new regions, as Brother Shireman has done, have been discouraged by those at the heart of the work, for fear that they would need money from the treasury. Yet from that same treasury money has been used to erect imposing and unnecessarily expensive buildings. If men had received the wisdom of God, they would have exercised justice and equity in regard to the outlay of means. All parts of the Lord's vineyard would have received a just proportion of help.

There are many who, with proper encouragement, would begin in out-of-the-way places to make efforts to seek and to save that which is lost. The Lord blesses those self-sacrificing ones, who have such a hunger for souls that they are willing to go anywhere to work. But, in the past, how much encouragement has been given to such workers by their brethren? Many of them have waited for something to do, but no attention has been given to them.

If the ministers had given help and encouragement to these men and women, they would have been doing the work appointed them by the Lord. They have been the spiritual poverty of unworked fields, and have longed to do something to help. But it has taken so long for encouragement to come to them that many have gone into other lines of work.

Shall the "regular lines", which say that every mind shall be controlled by two or three minds at Battle Creek, continue to bear sway? The Macedonian cry is coming from every quarter. Shall men go to the "regular lines" to see whether they will be permitted to labor, or shall they go out and work as best they can, depending on their own abilities and on the help of the Lord, beginning in a humble way and creating an interest in the truth in places in which nothing has been done to give the warning message?

The Lord has encouraged those who have started out on their own responsibility to work for him, their hearts filled with love for souls ready to perish. A true missionary spirit will be imparted to those who seek earnestly to know God and Jesus Christ, whom he hath sent. The Lord lives and reigns. Young men, go forth into the places to which you are directed by the Spirit of the Lord. Work with your hands, that you may be self-supporting, and as you have opportunity, proclaim the message of warning.

The Lord has blessed the work that J.E. White has tried to do in The South. God grant that the voices which have been so quickly raised to say that all the money invested in the work must go through the appointed channel at Battle Creek, shall not be heard. The people to whom God has given his means are amenable to him alone. It is their privilege to give direct aid and assistance to missions. It is because of the misappropriation of means that the Southern field has no better showing than it has today.

I do not consider it the duty of the Southern branch of our work, in the publication and handling of books, to be under the dictation of our established publishing houses. And if means can be devised to reduce the expense of publishing and circulating books, let this be done.

I have to say, my brother, that I have no desire to see the work in the South moving forward in the old, regular lines. When I see how strongly the idea prevails that the methods of handling our books in the past shall be retained, because what has been must be, I have no heart to advise that former customs shall continue. Let those who are laboring in Nashville do the will of God in all humility. I sincerely hope that the changes will be made that the necessities of the case demand.

I have more to write, but have no time now.

Ellen G. White.

Chapter 45—Neglect of the Southern Field

Oakland, Ca., July 8, 1901.

Dear Brother Evans:--

I can not sleep past one o'clock. I awake with an aching heart, for I have been in conversation with you, presenting before you the necessities of the Southern field. I was in a council meeting. The Spirit of the Lord came upon me, and I addressed you, my brother, saying, "What more can be said to impress you with the necessities of the cause of God? Why do you feel inclined to do so little for the Southern field? Where do you suppose its help is coming from?

At the different places at which I stopped on my way from Battle Creek, I tried to create an interest in the work in the South, but received only a little money; I think one thousand dollars would be all that was given. What does this mean? Our people have means, and the work at Nashville has been taken up with the commendation of God. He approves the work that has been done by J.E. White and his helpers. What further evidence can my brethren want that it is their duty to help? The fact that the field has been wronged, the very fact that the matter has been presented, should be sufficient to lead the people of God to do all in their power to help.

Light has been given me by God that unless something more is done in behalf of the Southern field than has yet been done, those who ought to see the condition of the field, and to realize its need, will be held responsible for the means they have diverted from the object for which it was raised. The failure to do that which should have been done to place the work where it should be, shows that the past unfaithfulness is unhealed. Something has been done to help, but it falls far short of what ought to be done.

The position taken by the workers in Nashville in regard to the planning of the work there is approved by God. The Lord is not in the unfavorable propositions which have been presented. God's purposes are contrary to the supposition of men. I have been watching with intense interest the movements made in the South. The rebuke of God is upon these who in the past have brought forward propositions that have caused the work in the South to be greatly hindered, so that it is far behind where it should be. This work would have been far in advance if the men in sacred office had been controlled by the Holy Spirit.

I am now instructed to say, Do your long neglected duty. There is to be no questioning in this matter. Justice, mercy, and the love of God have been so long excluded from the managing force at the heart of the work, that eyes have become blinded and spiritual perceptions perverted. Let not those now on trial in positions of responsibility be unfaithful to the duty which has been made known. His rebuke has come to his people because of their neglect. It is his desire that something shall be done, and done at once. Let not those who are now in positions of trust work contrary to his purpose. Let them take up their work, and help where help is needed. Decide what should be done, and then do it. Let the good work begin at the late Conference, where the Lord was present, teaching line upon line and precept upon precept, be carried forward to a glorious completion.

I am instructed to keep the Southern field before you, that for your own good you may make ample restitution to this field. False representations have been made regarding the work done in the South. Men have not had sufficient interest in the work to go to the field and make a disinterested examination. Think of the prevarication which has been shown, the schemes which have been entered upon, to get control of that which the Lord created to help the Southern field. The past course has been crooked. Wrong methods have been followed. But the errors of the past are unconfessed and unrepented of. Men have in their own minds justified the course that was then taken. They have viewed things, from beginning to end, in an altogether false light; and from the present, showing, the same course will be followed in the future.

The Lord will accept no excuse for the past neglect of the Southern field. Restitution has not yet been made in full to this field. The reproach is not yet wiped out. Christ has been wronged in the person of his saints. God has been robbed of the revenue with which he desired to open the work in the South. And this miserable selfish work will be repeated, as surely as it has been done in the past, unless it is seen in a true light.

Edson White and others have been crowded in most disagreeable positions. They have been forced to the wall. God has seen this unjust dealing. Wherein did those who took part in this unrighteousness love God supremely and their neighbor as themselves? "If therefore ye have not been faithful in the unrighteous mammon, if ye have not shown wisdom in using what was another's, who shall give you that which is your own?" This strikes to the very root of the matter. Unjust, unholy actions have brought the frown of God upon the Review and Herald Office. Evil work has brought the cause of God into disrepute, and has kept the backsliders from obeying his holy law.

I thought that I should never be called up on to write on this subject again; but I dare not keep silence when these things are presented before me. Last night is the second time that this matter has been brought before me.

When my brethren wrote to me about erecting another building in Battle Creek, saying that money could be obtained with which to do this, my heart was pained, and I have not been free from the pain since. The work in the South should be given the attention which it should have had long ago. It has been robbed of its just dues. And yet those who have done so little for this new field now propose to put up another building in Battle Creek, for the purpose of gaining greater room and conveniences. What would be the influence of such an action, after the light that God has given on this subject? Take the four thousand dollars that would be needed for the erection of this building, and place it where it belongs, that it may bear fruit to the glory of God.

Nashville is to be made a center from which the light of truth is to shine forth. Place the money in the work there. Make restitution to the Southern field. Learn constantly in the school of Christ. Keep your principles pure and holy. It would be wrong to add another building to the buildings already erected in Battle Creek.

I have words of encouragement for the workers in the South. Self-denial and self-sacrifice have been shown by them in their work. God will strengthen them in every effort they make to advance his kingdom, if they will walk in His way, and do His will. He will give them true happiness. The Lord is their helper. He will prepare the way before them. Misrepresentation and falsehood have done their baleful work, but the Lord declares if his workers will walk humbly with him, he will go before them, and will enable them to do a true work, a work that will ensure their happiness, honor, and usefulness. Hitherto the Lord has helped them. They are under His guidance. They are to put their trust in God, regulating their expenditures according to His directions. Whether they eat or drink, or whatsoever they do, they are to do all to the glory of God.

The angels of God will prepare their way as far as financial matters are concerned; but the Lord desires to give those who have done him great wrong by hindering the work in the South, an opportunity to repent and make restitution.

The question comes, "Shall Edson White's name be placed on the little paper published at Nashville, "The Gospel Herald?" I answer, "Yes, indeed. Edson White has done nothing to debar him from placing his name where by right it should be."

Let the Lord have opportunity to magnify his name. Talents, hitherto unused, are to be set in operation. They will develop by use. There is great need for the education of talent. This education must go forward in the church, and must reach from the church to regions beyond. Falsehoods are not changed into truth by being circulated for many years. In spite of their age, they are still falsehoods.

The Lord calls upon his people to help the Southern field. This call brings with it a solemn, sacred responsibility, which can not be evaded. The field speaks for itself. Neglected, down-trodden, oppressed, ignorant, who need our help more than the colored people of the South? Let this field be helped, without waiting until every other call for help is answered. God calls for a right appropriation of his means, that the work may enlarge and extend, where such extension will help other barren and forsaken parts of the vineyard.

Everything is to be done that can be done to enlarge the sphere of Christian influence. Christ's church members are to work earnestly for those who are perishing in their sins. Let the church prayer meetings be a source of spiritual life, a place where the members of the church may learn to work in spiritual lines. Let all enter upon the Lord's work with sanctified earnestness. Let those who in the past have been merely consumers, now become producers. Let the Lord's people bring their gifts and offerings for the furtherance of his work. Thus the kingdom of God will be greatly extended.

Let everyone work on the principles of self-sacrifice. Work while the day lasts; for the night cometh, in which no man can work. As God's people work humbly, earnestly, self-sacrificingly, they will gain the rich rewards of which Job speaks, "When the ear heard me, then it blessed me; the blessings of him that was ready to perish came upon me, and I caused the widow's heart to sing for joy." Christ will be acknowledged as the Creator and Redeemer. Those who are laborers together with God will be recognized and appreciated. The recognition of the faithful servants of God detracts not one iota from the gratitude and praise we offer to God and to the Lamb.

When the redeemed stand around the throne of God, those who have been saved from sin and degradation will come to those who worked for them with the words of greeting, "I was without God and without a home in the world. I was perishing in corruption and sin. I was starving for physical and spiritual food. You came to me in love and pity, and fed and clothed me. You pointed me to the Lamb of God, who taketh away the sin of the world.". ...

Ellen G. White.

Chapter 46—The Work of COL & the Barrien Springs School

St. Helena, Cal., July 12, 1901.

To the Managers of the Review and Herald Office

Dear Brethren:--

I have something to write in regard to the school interest. "Christ's Object Lessons," in accordance with the Lord's instructions, was donated to our schools for the special purpose of releasing them from debt. And this gave the Review and Herald opportunity to do a generous work in behalf of the Battle Creek School. If the work of selling "Christ's Object Lessons" had not been taken up, there would scarcely have been a hope that the debt of the Battle Creek College to the Review Office would ever have been paid. From the light given me by the Lord, I know that he will be displeased if the Review and Herald is in any way exacting in dealing with those who are trying to release our schools from debt. As those in the Review and Herald see their brethren struggling to free the schools debt, they are to cooperate with them. Those who have charge of this work have carried a heavy burden. Nothing could have been done without earnest effort and determined vigilance. And nothing else could have done that which "Christ's Object Lessons" have done to bring relief to the schools.

Let men show their appreciation of God's gracious design, and be laborers together with him in making the most of his blessing. Nothing could displease the Lord more than for the Review and Herald to show narrow-mindedness and make exacting demands upon the school, putting out a hand of power to do work similar to the work which has been done in the past, to the shame of some in the service of God. < God has wrought in a wonderful manner through "Christ's Object Lessons". Let not selfishness reach out the hand to spoil the pattern. The Review and Herald have profited by the work which has been done to raise the debt on the Battle Creek School. Let those in the Review and Herald remember that their brethren, who have labored so earnestly in behalf of the schools, deserve the favors God designs them to have as they seek to establish the school in a more favorable locality. Let not those in the Review and Herald Office think that they will do God Service by binding about the school interests.

God saw that his servants were sacrificing and trying to raise money to free the schools debt. Then the still, small voice spoke to God's humble servant, telling me to make known that God had heard the prayers and witnessed the tears of his people, and that he had a plan for the relief of the schools, a plan by which many would be helped, but which was especially to relieve the schools from their pressure of debt. This plan was carried forward. Faith and works combined brought success. And God will continue to make the work on "Christ's Object Lesson" a means of great good.

Let not one thread of selfishness be woven into the work of the Lord. Those in responsible positions are on test and trial. God calls for more mercy, more tenderness, more pity, more courtesy, than has been shown. There should be a reformation among the workers, Those who handle the work of the Lord should show themselves to be men of broad minds, men who appreciate what has been done for the relief of the schools. Let not that which was designed to relieve the schools be made no relief because of the grasping spirit of selfishness.

All our institutions, sanitariums, schools and publishing houses are to stand shoulder to shoulder, to help and bless one another. The coming of the Lord is right upon us. Those connected with God's service are not to seek to grasp the largest benefits for their line of work, irrespective of circumstances. The Lord has devised a plan whereby the Battle Creek School may be released from debt and established in a more favorable location. Is the school, through the selfishness of men, to be left where it will, in some respect, be worse off than before any effort was made for it?

The Lord would have his word received. He desires men to appreciate the work he has been doing to unify his people. He calls upon those connected with his institutions to be soundly converted. It is Christ's desire that men shall receive him, and work in perfect harmony, serving God with heart and soul and strength, not only for a hope of heaven, but that in unselfishness, purity, and holiness they may be a blessing to others. We are not merely to be trees of righteousness. Christ said, "It is my Father's good pleasure that ye bear much fruit."

I hear that there is some thought of locating the school at Berrien Springs, in the southwest of Michigan. I am much pleased with the description of this place. The one hundred and twelve acres of unimproved land will be a great blessing to the school in many ways; also the forty acres of woodland. It will be a great blessing to have cheap water transportation. And the offer of buildings is of great value. The good hand of the Lord appears to be in this opening, and I hope and pray that if this is the place for the school, no hand will be stretched out to prevent the matter from reaching a successful issue. In such a place as Berrien Springs, the school can be made an object lesson, and I hope that no one will interpose to prevent the carrying forward of this work.

The Review and Herald and the Sanitarium should help in this matter. I appeal to these institutions to do all in their power to help to secure this favorable opening. Let the school be established in such a place, and name of the Lord will be magnified. I hope to see that which we ought now to behold - the establishment of important interests outside of Battle Creek. I hope that there will be a revival and a reformation among our people, bringing back to hearts the first love of the gospel.

Ellen G. White.

Chapter 47—The Church School

Instruction to Teachers and Parents

The establishment and location of church schools is a matter of the utmost importance, and should receive careful attention. Only after the most wise, judicious plans have been laid, should such a school be established. Mistakes may be made by being in too great haste to locate and establish church schools.

Very much of the success of a church school depends on the teacher chosen. Church school teachers, should not be children, who have not come to maturity, who are able to do only a cheap class of work. The one placed in charge of a church school should be of suitable age; and where the number of students is sufficient, assistants should be selected from the students. Thus the students can gain an experience of great value.

Church school teachers should be men and women who have a humble estimate of themselves, who are not full of vain conceit. They should be humble, faithful workers, filled with the true missionary spirit, workers who have learned to put their trust in God and to do their work in his name. They should possess the attributes of Christ's character - patience, kindness, mercy, and love; and into the daily experience they should bring the Saviour's righteousness and peace and grace. Then, working with fragrant influence, they will give evidence of what grace can do through the weakness of the human agents who make God their dependance and their trust.

The Lord has shown me what can be done for the younger children of our people, if they are educated in the fear and love of God. Let every church school established be conducted with such order that Christ can honor the schoolroom with his presence. There is much work to do for the Master. He will accept no cheap, shoddy service. Let teachers be learners, putting the whole mind to the task of learning how to do service for the Master. "The fear of the Lord is the beginning of wisdom." Let the one who is preparing to labor as a church school teacher learn to work on correct principles.

"Precept must be upon precept, precept upon precept; line upon line, line upon line, here a little, and there a little." Thus the children attending a church school are to be educated. Let teachers show sympathy and tenderness in dealing with human minds. Let them reveal the love of God. Let the words they speak be kindly and encouraging. Then as they work for their students, what a transformation will be wrought in the rough characters of those who have not been properly educated in the home. The grace of God, revealed in words and works, will touch hearts.

Teachers should not aspire to do wonderful things in their own strength. In all their service they must reveal the love of Jesus. True self-respect must be mingled with all their work. The Lord can make even youthful teachers channels for the revealing of his grace.

Teachers are not to allow themselves to be quick-tempered. They should not manifest temper. They should not punish harshly the children that are in need of reform. Let the teachers first know and understand that self must be kept in subjection. Think of the boundless love Christ has bestowed on human beings. Never forget that over you there is a divine Teacher, whose subject you are, and under whose control you are ever to be. Humble the heart before God. It will be softened and subdued by the thought of the riches God has bestowed on his children. You will realize something of the meaning of the words, "You, that were sometimes alienated and enemies in your mind by wicked works, yet now hath he reconciled in the body of his flesh through death, to present you holy and unblameable and unreproveable in his sight."

Sometimes it is found that the school has been established in a church where the disorderly element among the children make the work very hard. The children who have not received proper training in the home will cause much trouble in the school, and by their perversity will make the heart of the teacher sad. But let not the teacher become discouraged. Test and trial bring experience. If the children and disobedient and unruly, there is all the more need of strenuous effort. The fact that there are children with such characters is one of the reasons why church schools should be established. The children that parents have neglected to educate and discipline aright must be saved.

Never give up the school work in a place where a church school has been established, unless God plainly directs that this should be done. With God's help, the teacher may do a grand, saving work in changing the order of things. If the teacher works patiently, earnestly, perseveringly, in Christ's lines, the reformatory work done in the school will extend to the homes of the children, creating a purer, more refined, more Christlike atmosphere. This is indeed missionary work of the highest order. Teachers who do this work are doing God service for this life and for the life eternal.

Parents also have a part to act in this work. Let parents remember that much more will be accomplished by the work of the school, if they themselves realize the advantages their children will obtain in such a school. Let them understand that there must be a change in the management of their children, before they and their children reveal the peace and love which comes with God's converting grace.

If parents will only realize that their neglect of duty is a grave sin, which should be repented of, if they will only unite with the teacher who is working for the salvation of their children, a most wonderful work can be done for the children. By prayer, by patience, by forbearance, parents can undo much of the wrong caused by their impatience and unwise indulgence. Let the church school be a place where parents as well as children shall be educated. Let parents and teachers take hold of the work together. Parents, remember that you yourselves will be benefited by the presence of an earnest, God-fearing church school teacher.

The Lord desires the churches in every place to take hold more diligently of the church school work, giving liberally to sustain the teachers. The question has been asked, "Could not the second tithe be used for the support of the church school work?" It could be used for no better purpose.

Parents should devise ways and means for keeping their children usefully busy. Let the children be given little pieces of land to cultivate, that they may have something to give as a freewill offering. Parents must never forget that they must work earnestly for themselves and their little ones, if they with them are gathered into the ark of safety. We are still in the enemy's country. Let parents strive to reach a higher standard, and to carry their children with them. Let them cast off the works of darkness and put on the armor of light.

Prove your willingness to make every effort in your power to place your children in the most favorable situation for forming the character that God requires his servants to form. Exercise every spiritual sinew and muscle to save your little flock. The powers of hell will conspire for your destruction. Pray much more than you do. Lovingly, tenderly teach your children to come to God as a heavenly Father. By your example in the management of the home, teach them self-control. Teach them to be helpful in the home. Tell them that Christ lived not to please himself. The Holy Spirit will fill your mind with the most precious thoughts as you work for your own salvation and the salvation of your Children.

Parents, gather the rays of divine light which are shining upon your pathway. Walk in the light as Christ is in the light. As you take up the work of saving your children and maintaining your position on the highway of holiness, the most provoking trials will come. But do not lose your hold. Cling to Jesus. He says, "Let him take hold of my strength, that he may make peace with me, and he shall make peace with me." Difficulties will arise. You will meet with obstacles. Look constantly to Jesus. When an emergency arises, ask, "Lord, what shall I do now?" If you refuse to storm or fret or scold, the Lord will show you the way through. He will help you to use the talent of speech in such a

Christlike way that the precious attributes of patience, comfort, and love will be brought into the home.

Parents, you have not all obtained victory in the use of talent of speech, May the Lord save you from lowering yourselves in the estimation of your children by speaking indiscreet, passionate words. Do all in your power to stand on vantage ground before your children. By following a Christlike course of action, holding firmly to the promises of God, you may be evangelists in the home, ministers of grace to your children.

Learn the lesson which Christ gave after the miracle of feeding the five thousand. "Gather up the fragments that remain, that nothing be lost." The Lord is constantly exercising his miracle-working power in helping parents as they strive to lead their children to him.

Fathers and mothers, tell your children about the miracle-working power of God. Take them into the garden, and explain to them how he causes the seed sown to grow. As the children study the great lesson book of nature, God will impress their minds. The farmer plows his land and sows his seed, but he can not make the seed grow. He must depend upon God to do that which no human power can do. The Lord puts his own vital spirit into the seed, causing it to spring forth into life. Under his care the germ of life breaks through the hard crust encasing it, and springs up to bear fruit. First appears the blade, then the ear, then the full corn in the ear. As children are told of the work that God does for the seed, they learn the secret of growth in grace.

Nature is full of lessons of the love of God. Rightly understood, these lessons lead to the Creator. They point from nature to nature's God, teaching these simple, holy truths which cleanse the mind, bringing it into close touch with God. These lessons emphasize the truth that science and religion can not be divorced.

Christ came to this earth to teach men the mysteries of the kingdom of God. But men could not by human reasoning understand his lessons. Man's wisdom can not originate the science which is divine.

The Great Teacher came from heaven to plant in this world trees of light. He calls on nature to reflect to human minds the light that floods the threshold of heaven, that men and women may obey his word. And nature does the bidding of the Creator. To the heart softened by the grace of God, the sun, the moon, the stars, the lofty trees, the flowers of the field, utter their words of counsel and advice. The sowing of the seed carries the mind to spiritual seed-sowing. The tree stands forth declaring that a good tree can not bear evil fruit, neither can an evil tree bear good fruit. "Ye shall know them by their fruits."

Even the tares have a lesson to teach. They are of Satan's sowing, and if left unchecked, spoil the wheat by their rank growth.

When man is reconciled to God, nature speaks to him in words of heavenly wisdom, bearing testimony to the eternal truth of God's Word. As Christ tells us the meaning of the things in nature, the science of true religion flashes forth, explaining the relation of the law of God to the natural and the spiritual world.

It seems cruel to establish our schools in the cities, where the students are prevented from learning the precious lessons taught by nature. It is a mistake to call families into the city, where children and youth breathe an atmosphere of corruption and crime, sin and violence, intemperance and ungodliness. Oh, it is a terrible mistake to allow children to come in contact with that which makes such a fearful impression on their senses. Children and youth can not be too fully guarded from familiarity with the pictures of iniquity as common as in all large cities.

Years ago schools should have been established on large tracts of land, where children could have been educated largely from the book of nature. Had this been done, what a different condition of things there would now be in our churches. We are in need of being uplifted, cleansed, purified. In our conversation we are altogether too cheap and common. There are tares growing among the wheat, and too often the tares overtop the wheat.

I rejoiced when I heard that the Battle Creek School was to be established in a farming district. I know that there will be less temptation there for the students than there would be in the cities that are fast becoming as Sodom and Gomorrah, preparing for destruction by fire. The popular sentiment is that cities should be chosen as locations for our schools. But God desires us to leave the sin-polluted atmosphere of the cities. It is his design that our schools shall be established where the atmosphere is purer.

Ellen G. White.

Chapter 48—Lines Regular and Irregular

(In connection with the two following Testimonies, see Testimony of September 12, 1908.)

St. Helena, Cal, July 27, 1901.

Dear Brother Johnston:

A few weeks ago I sent a letter to Elder Shireman. He was presented before me as worried and suffering in mind. I was given instruction regarding the course you are pursuing toward him, a course which is not dictated by the counsels of God. You are causing Brother Shireman suffering. It is not your work to go into another man's field of labor and take up a work which by much labor and sacrifice he has established. There are plenty of fields as barren and as needy as was this one when Brother Shireman first entered it. Why should you not go to these fields, and there give evidence of your capability, tact, and ingenuity? Do not, I beg of you, act the part of a usurper, or an accuser of the brethren; for the Lord will not justify any such course of action. This is not the work you are appointed by the Conference to do.

What has led you, my brother, to locate in a place where another man, by patient labor and hard wrestling, and with great self-denial and self-sacrifice, has established a good work? The Lord is not pleased with you for stepping into another man's field, after he has done all the pioneering, to criticize and condemn, leaving the impression upon other minds that the work has not been done right. It is not the work of a minister of Christ to go to another man's field of labor and ignore the worker, showing no appreciation of his work. How much nobler to go to some unworked part of the vineyard and show there what can be done to make a beginning.

From the light the Lord has been pleased to give me, there are many openings just as promising as was the place where Brother Shireman began his work. And you have the advantage of possessing physical strength. Seek a hard place, and go to work. Labor with humility and earnestness, as Brother Shireman has done. Learn how he has accomplished his work, and then begin as he began, showing your zeal by making earnest efforts to establish something. Cultivate a part of the Lord's vineyard where nothing has been done. Thus you can consistently show what capabilities you possess. Thus you can show that your work is genuine.

Brother Shireman has taxed his energies for many years in a way that many of our younger ministers would shrink from doing. He has opened the Scriptures to the people and erected buildings, and the Lord has blessed him and gone before him. To some his work may appear crude, not elegant enough to suit their taste, but he has worked according to the ability given him by the Lord. God will bless any man who does this. You should be careful not to dishonor God in the person of his saints. Let the aged minister of God work in the place where he has accomplished so much, till the Lord by his Holy Spirit moves upon him to work in another place.

The Conference should understand that it has no right to send a man to take the work out of the hands of one who has done the hard labor, gaining his way little by little, by hard strokes, the Lord working with him, and giving him his hire in souls for his labor.

Study the action of Christ, as recorded in John 4:1-3. In regard to the property which Brother Shireman has built up, let no selfish greed force him to make it over to the Conference. There may be other places where he should work, and he should have something with which to operate. If he were called away suddenly, he could make this property over to some one he could trust. He should be allowed to control his own property, the results of his hard labor, and never feel himself destitute.

Brother Shireman will always need helpers, but not men who will seek to set him aside and supersede him. His helpers should be men of fine perceptions and delicacy of feeling, who will give credit where credit is due, who will not ignore the one used by God to do the hard, pioneer labor.

How dare any one minister or lay member, bar the way of God's servants by unjust, unfeeling speeches? But this has been done, and thereby some laborers have been discouraged and many souls lost who might have been saved. Those who do this work are not prompted by the Spirit of God, but by another Spirit. Scornful criticisms and discourteous remarks are from Satan. Abraham was a courteous man. If teachers, ministers, and people would practice Bible courtesy, they would find hearts open to receive the truth that are now closed, and the Lord would be glorified.

He who comes into another man's field of labor to scoff at his work, is not fitted for ministerial labor. He might better, far better, use his power in some other work. Those who search for something with which to find fault have taken the enemy's side of the question. Can Christ say of them, "Well done, good and faithful servant?" Are they giving the trumpet a certain sound? Are they proclaiming to a perishing world the last message of mercy?

For years the Lord has shown me that he uses many gifts in the work of saving souls. All who can, should do personal labor. As they go from house to house explaining the Scriptures to the people in a clear, simple manner, God makes the truth powerful to save. The Saviour blesses those who do this work.

For many years Brother Shireman has done a good and unselfish work. While others have sought rest and comfort, he has toiled in poverty, earning means to carry forward God's work. He is now working with labor, and God desires him to be sustained, not discouraged. He should lay off some of his burdens, but the cause of God needs his experience. It needs his words, which have a comforting, soothing influence on sinsick souls.

Brother Shireman should not allow his spirit to be grieved by the course which others pursue toward him. He should not allow a combative spirit to take possession of him. He should not feel called upon to defend himself. He has no need for self-justification. His works speak for him. Those with whom God works are not to be at all intimidated by the criticisms of men who need to understand what it means to build up an interest in a new and barren field, who might far better use the talent of speech in warning those who know not the truth than in criticizing those who are doing their best.

Treat Brother Shireman with the tenderness with which you would wish to be treated were you in his place. Remember that workmen for God will spring up in many places. He who forsakes all that he has in order to advance the work of God, is doing that which must be done. Every weight, every besetting sin, must be laid aside. God's watchmen are to lift up the voice, saying, The morning cometh, and also the night. "Come out from among them, and be ye separate ... and touch not the unclean thing." "Be ye clean that bear the vessels of the Lord."

The church can not measure herself by the world, not by the opinions of men, nor yet by what she once was. Her position in this world is to be compared with what it would have been had she continually pressed onward and upward, from victory to victory.

Ellen G. White.

Chapter 48.1—St. Helena, Aug 6, 1901

Brother Johnston:

I am greatly troubled in behalf of Brother Shireman, whom I know the Lord loves. God will be his friend and helper and his exceeding great reward.

The Lord presented the situation before me. I was shown Brother Shireman in great sorrow, suffering from criticisms of those who had done nothing to build up his work. I immediately wrote a letter of encouragement to Brother Shireman, and I wrote a letter to you also, and thought I had sent it, but I find that I did not. I will now write a little more to send with it.

The Lord is no respecter of persons. He who wounds the feelings of an aged brother, needs the converting power of God. How ashamed he ought to be, with his young strength, to slight one who has grown gray in serving God. How different his course would be could he see how highly Christ estimates the humble, earnest worker.

Christ accepts and communes with the most lowly, He does not accept men because of their capabilities or eloquence, but because they seek His face, desiring His help. His spirit moving upon the heart arouses every faculty to vigorous action. In these unpretentious ones the Lord sees the most precious material, which will stand storm and tempest, heat and pressure. God sees not as man sees. He judges not from appearance. He searches the heart and judges righteously.

God is displeased with the spirit you have manifested. Your insinuations and criticisms are most unbecoming. When you ought to be a teacher, you have need that one teach you. Do you know that you are criticizing the work of a man who has been visited by the angels of the Lord? Who has sent you to a field where a good work is in progress, to show your zeal by tearing it in pieces? If this is working in the "Regular lines", it is high time that we worked in irregular lines.

No minister should dishonor his position as a Christian worker by being severe, critical, and overbearing, riding roughshod over men who God is using, men whom He loves because they appreciate His grace and do not abuse His mercies. Those who desire to be dealt with in mercy and compassion, must show mercy and compassion when dealing with their brethren.

It is acting the part of a thief and a robber to step into another man's field of labor and destroy his harvest. Paul the greatest preacher among believers, did not desire to go upon another man's ground. His desire was to preach the gospel to those who had never heard it. He writes, "Yea, so have I striven to preach the gospel, not where Christ was named, lest I should build upon another man's foundation; but as it is written, To whom He was not spoken of, they shall see; and they that have not heard shall understand." And of Christ, it is written, "So shall he sprinkle many nations; the kings shall shut their mouths at him; for that which had not been told them they shall see, and that which they had not heard shall they consider."

There is true honor among those who have the love of God in their hearts. Our object in working for the Master should be that His name may be glorified in the conversion of sinners. Those who labor to gain applause are not approved by God. The Lord expects His servants to work from a different motive.

There are many who will spend and be spent to win souls to Christ. In obedience to the great commission, they will go forth to work for the Master. Under the ministration of angels ordinary men will be moved by the Spirit of God to warn people in the highways and byways. Humble men, who do not trust in their gifts, but who work in simplicity, trusting always in God, will share in the joy of the Saviour as their persevering prayers being souls to the cross. We would say to them, Go forth, brethren; do your best humbly and sincerely, and God will work with you. They should be strengthened and encouraged, and as fast as possible fitted for labor, that success may crown their efforts. They harmonize with unseen, heavenly instrumentalities. They are workers together with God, and their brethren should bid them Godspeed, and pray for them as they labor in Christ's name. No one is authorized to hinder such workers. They should be treated with great respect. No one should speak a disparaging word of them as in the rough places of the earth they sow the gospel seed.

Christ will be with these humble workers. The angels of heaven will cooperate with them in their self-sacrificing efforts. By the power of the Holy Spirit Jesus will move upon hearts. God will work miracles in the conversion of sinners. Men and women will be gathered into church fellowship. Meeting houses will be built, and institutions of learning established.

These workers are trees of the Lord's planting. In a peculiar sense they bear fruit equal to the fruit borne by the apostles. They receive a reward in this life, and a glorious reward awaits them in the future life.

It is time that church members understood that everywhere there is a work to be done in the Lord's vineyard. No one is to wait for a regular process before they make any efforts. They should take up the work right where they are. There should be many at work in what are "irregular lines." If one hundred laborers would step out of the "regular lines," and take up self-sacrificing work, such as Brother Shireman has done, souls would be won to the Lord. And the workers would understand by experience what it means to be laborers together with God.

Can it be that our brethren think that their criticisms are the productions of the Holy Spirit? It will be found that those who are criticized have more to show for their efforts than those who criticize. The names of the humble are stamped on the books of heaven, with the words, "Well done, good and faithful servant; enter thou into the joy of the Lord." But opposite the name of the critics stand the words, "Thou are weighed in the balances, and found wanting."

You have had educational advantages. But God has not imparted His gifts to you to be used in disparaging another man's work. The Lord has not told you to enter into another man's field, to rob him of the influence God has given him, to show how wise you are as contrasted with him. I pray that you may be converted. Unless you are changed in disposition and spirit, the gates of heaven will be closed against you.

Life's best things-simplicity, honesty, truthfulness, purity, unsullied integrity - are not to be bought or sold; they are as free to the illiterate as to the educated, to the white man as to the black man, to the poor as well as the king upon his throne.

Read and study the first chapter of First Corinthians, and see if you can not get back into right lines of work.

God is leading out a people preparing them for translation. Are we who are acting a part in this work standing as sentinels for God. Are we seeking to labor unitedly? Are we will to be servants to all? Are we following in the footsteps of Jesus, our great exemplar?

In the field of life we are all sowing seeds. As we sow, so shall we reap. Those who sow self-love, bitterness, jealousy, will reap a like harvest. Those who sow unselfish love, kindness, tender thoughtfulness for the feelings of others, will reap a precious harvest.

Ellen G. White.

Chapter 49—Student Teachers

St. Helena, Cal., Oct. 16, 1901.

Dear Brother Sutherland:

We are thankful to our heavenly Father that Brother Magan is being restored to health. I know that many are praying for him. ...

I hope that the Lord will give Elder Brunson clear light in regard to his post of duty. It is a man's privilege to know for himself whether he is in the right place, without depending on any other man's preferences or decisions as to where he shall devote his energies.

Everything is to be carefully considered. Brother Brunson should take the matter to the Lord, and then decide for himself what the Lord says to his servant. Because Brother Brunson can fill a place at Berrien Springs, this is no evidence that he is not needed more in some other place.

The way that the Lord has presented the matter to me is that it is not the best thing for the school to have a long list of salaried instructors. It is to be as the schools of the prophets. It is to have a sufficient number of teachers, but not too many. An extra teacher at the school might be very much needed in some other place, where his special talent could be used to great advantage.

It is not wise general ship for our brethren at Berrien Springs to reach out and draw men from work just as important as the work of the school, work where their talents are greatly needed. We need to offer most earnest prayer to God, that the right men may be placed in the right places. Let the Lord's will be done. Man may propose but God must do the disposing. ...

The teacher is to feel entire dependence on Christ. As capable a teacher as can be secured should be provided to take charge of the Bible studies.

There are those who are learners who are fully capable of taking some part in the work of instruction. If the teachers will employ the help thus provided, much care and labor will be spared them. There are students who can be asked to spend part of their time in teaching. Students are not to be like those represented in the Word of God as ever learning and never able to come to a knowledge of the truth. They are to receive to impart.

The student should not think that because he is asked to conduct a class in reading or spelling or some other study, he is being deprived of any of the time he desires for instruction. He should not feel that he is losing time, because he is not. In imparting to others what he has received, he is preparing his mind to receive more. He may remember, as he strived to do his best, that the angels sent forth to minister to those who shall be heirs of salvation, understand the situation, and will lead his mind, quickening his understanding and bringing to him thoughts that shed light on the subject under consideration, making it plain and clear.

The youthful teacher who fears God will be instructed while instructing. And as thoughts of real value flash into his mind, let him offer thanksgiving to God, praising Him as the One from whom all blessings flow, recognizing and acknowledging Him as the source of all true, noble thoughts. ...

There is such a thing as leaning heavily on men and lightly on God. Those in charge of our schools should put into active service every talent possessed by the students that can be used for the help of the school. When this is done as it should be, it will be found that students will not hanker for football, tennis, and other amusements. What the students need to be taught is how to make themselves as useful as possible wherever they may be placed. They should learn how to adapt themselves to the work in hand. Christ says, "I pray not that thou shouldest take them out of the world, but that thou shouldest keep them from the evil.". ...

You know that I have a deep interest in the school at Berrien Springs. It is the Lord's school, and I will send you his ideas to consider. May he help and strengthen and bless you. Look and live. He will prepare the way before you. Only have faith. God is our helper, our defense. Let us act in accordance with the Scriptures. We are exhorted to be found "praying always with all prayer and supplication." Again we read, "Be ye therefore sober, and watch unto prayer." We are to feel it our privilege to pray, to seek wisdom from God, looking to him for encouragement and spiritual strength. If we were permitted to know one half of the dangers that surround us, we would pray more .

Ellen G. White.

Chapter 50—The School at Berrien Springs

St. Helena, Cal., November 5, 1901.

Dear Brother Magan and Brother Sutherland:

I was very sorry, Brother Magan, to hear of your indisposition and serious illness. We thank the Lord that he has heard our many prayers in your behalf.

I shall probably see you soon, for after a week of conviction I have decided to leave for the East. By my former decision not to leave home I came to a crisis in my experience, and I will leave for New York City tomorrow morning, if the Lord will. And this seems to me to be His will.

I am surprised that there should be talk of separating Brother and Sister Salisbury from the faculty of the Berrien Springs school. Did not the Lord discern what should be done in reference to this school question, when He so graciously instructed you not to allow your school faculty to be broken up?

The question was asked, if brother and sister Salisbury are not especially needed in the school, and are needed elsewhere, should not they be permitted to go? I told them that circumstances might alter cases; but all the light given me is that a mistake is being made in planning for members of your faculty to go to Europe to engage in the school work.

The Lord desires to have the same faculty, if they are disposed to put their whole being into the work, taking hold in faith and with good courage. If they rely upon the Lord, He will be their strength and their efficiency. But they must keep advancing in the upward way, gaining victory after victory in their onward progress. Because of opposite theories they need not be faint-hearted. Have we not had to breast opposition from the beginning in any forward, upward movement?

Go forward, brethren, saying, I will not fail nor be discouraged. Brother Magan, say to Brother Sutherland, Talk faith, pray faith and go forward. Those who have ever been walking in unbelief will throw their past experience and knowledge as stumbling-blocks in your way. But in the words, "It is written," you have the staff that you should take.

Draw from God, hoping, praying, believing. Always be fragrant in spirit. Speak pleasantly. When I see others so disagreeable in the expression of their feelings, I dislike the spiritual atmosphere so much that I feel like opening the windows heavenward and letting the fragrance of the presence of the Lord shine in, thus scattering the disagreeable fog.

Do not be in haste to reveal the spirit of unbelief. Close the windows earthward, and then sing the songs of Zion. Perfect confidence in God is essential. Be not faithless, but believing. Thus far the Lord has certainly helped you. Although His overworked servant has been afflicted, in His great mercy the Lord has spared his life. Then rejoice in the Lord always; and again I say, Have faith in God, and rejoice.

There is much to be done. You no need to educate, educate, educate. Let no one take away your needed facilities. Have you a printing outfit? This you must have, if you do not have it; for you will want to do much of your own printing, issuing the books and other publications which you need in your work. You need the very best educator to teach typesetting and presswork to the students, giving them the education essential for this class of work.

You also need the very best and most experienced bookkeeper that you can secure. Let bookkeeping be one of the regular studies. Make it a specialty.

Voice Culture should be taught in your school. Do not lightly pass over this matter; for if the expression is defective, all the knowledge that shall be obtained will be of but very little use. The cultivation of the voice is of the greatest importance, in order that grace and dignity may be brought into the impartation of truth.

By learning correctly to use the voice in speaking, many who are weak-chested may save their lives. Make the student stand erect, throwing back his shoulders. The ladies especially need to cultivate the voice.

In every reading exercise, require the students to speak the words distinctly, clearly pronouncing even the last syllable. Teach the students not to let their voice die away at the end of the sentence. Require a full, clear, round tone of voice to the very close, including the last syllable.

Many who use their vocal organs in so careless a way that they can scarcely be called vocal organs, if allowed to continue speaking defectively, will die of consumption. For want of exercise the lungs will close their healthful action. In the respiration there is not a full inhalation of pure, vital air to give nourishment to the lungs, consequently they become diseased.

Educate all to speak slowly. Do not allow any hurried reading or rapid delivery. Teach the student to inhale the God-given, vital air, and then in the exhalation clearly express their words. Thus the vital properties of the air are utilized.

Never allow an indistinct utterance to pass unnoticed. Let the speech be as perfect as possible. Accept nothing else. By cultivating the voice a grand work will be done, not only in learning how to breathe, inhaling the pure, life-giving air and exhaling by speaking in loud, clear tones, but also in the preservation of life.

In speaking there need be no strain put upon the throat or the lungs. The abdomen is the powerful engine from which the organs of speech are to receive the power which keeps them in perfect tone and expression. There needs to be an economizing of nervous strength, in order that the voice may be perfected, thus enabling laborers to speak in such a way that the truth will lose none of its force and beauty by being bunglingly presented.

This subject of voice needs special attention. May the Lord help you as teachers to see the bearing on which this subject sustains to the communication of the truth. Workers should know how to use the voice in such a way that in speaking they will properly represent the grand subjects of present truth. If the mind and the will are set to make progress and advancement, there will be improvement in the forcible presentation of the Scriptures.

You should endeavor to train the very best class of workers, who as teachers and ministers of the gospel will be able to educate others. I think that if it is possible you should have Elder Prescott connected with your faculty during the first term. This first term must be a success. The Lord desires our Brother Prescott to learn many things in educational lines. His ideas of education are to be different from what they once were. And I thank the Lord that He has been giving him the light that is so much needed by the students who shall go forth as teachers.

All who now are connected with the work of education must not follow the same, same old methods. Our schools should be more after the order of the schools of the prophets.

Be of good courage in the Lord. Do not talk unbelief. Brethren, look not on the dark side. The Lord has a work for you to do. You need more faith, more hope. Commit the soul to God, as unto a faithful Creator.

If for the time being Brother Magan should go to Nashville, Los Angeles, or St. Helena, the entire change would be a blessing to him. For a time he needs to be carefully and tenderly handled, and located wherever his mind will be most at rest.

Do not at present let Brother and Sister Salisbury leave you. Hold them until you know that it is duty for them to go.

In much love, Ellen G. White.

Chapter 51—Faith Under Discouragements

South Lancaster, Mass., Dec. 7, 1901.

P. T. Magan, c/o Dr. F. B. Moran,

315 West Third Street

Los Angeles, California

Dear Brother Magan:

Your letter from Chicago received yesterday. I am very sorry that circumstances have taken the shape that they have, but why are you so faithless? Thank the Lord that you have few students, because you are not prepared for a large number. Brother Sutherland and yourself have done bravely and well, and why will you worry yourself out of the arms of your precious Saviour? Has the bank of heaven failed? Have you overdrawn the resources? Is Christ, the Light of the World, in Joseph's new tomb? Do we not read, "Wherefore He is able also to save them to the uttermost that come to God by Him, seeing that He ever liveth to make intercession for them?

Now look away from every discouraging presentation, because we have a living Christ, to save them to the uttermost that come unto God by Him. The bank of heaven has not failed, you have not overdrawn: "For such an high priest became us, who is holy, harmless, undefiled, separate from sinners, and made higher than the heavens." "Who needeth not daily, as those high priests, to offer up sacrifices, first for his own sins and then for the people's, for this he did once when he offered himself, for the law maketh men high priests which have infirmity, but the Word of the oath, which was since the Law, maketh the Son, who is consecrated forevermore." Heb. 10:14. "For by one offering He hath perfected forever them that are sanctified. Whereof the Holy Ghost also is a witness to us; for after that he had said before, This is the covenant that I will make with them after those days, saith the Lord, I will put my laws in their hearts, and in their minds will I write them, and their sins and their iniquities will I remember no more." Heb. 10: 19-24; 6:17-20. Let your faith be strong in God. Look not upon appearances at this time. Chap. 2:16-18. Brethren Sutherland and Magan, God is testing your faith, but let not your faith fail. Cling to the promises, with full faith, in the One back of the promise.

I have been having a severe test of my faith. Overdoing is not profitable. I have been shorn of my strength, quite feeble, nearly voiceless, too weak to see or converse with any one except it was positively essential. I have not dared to go from the rooms assigned me in the sanitarium, dared not go home to California, which I so much desired to do in my weakness. Many prayers have been offered to God in my behalf. I have had every attention given me in solid treatment. Yesterday was the first day of recovery, and though sorely perplexed as to what I should do in regard to traveling, I have not become discouraged....

My brethren, have faith in a living all pitiful, and loving Saviour. I have words given me for you and Brother Sutherland, "Fear thou not, for I am with thee, be not dismayed, for I am thy God: with the right hand of my righteousness. Behold, all they that were incensed against thee shall be ashamed and confounded, they shall be nothing, and they that strive with thee shall perish. Thou shalt seek them, and thou shalt not find them, even them that contend with thee: they that war with thee shall be as nothing, and as a thing of nought. For the Lord will hold thy right hand, saying unto thee, Fear not, I will help thee: fear not, thou worm Jacob, and ye men of Israel, saith the Lord, and thy Redeemer, the Holy One of Israel."

Your business now is simply to trust in the Lord. In your intense earnestness your efforts to make a success in a good work have been too much for your human frame, but you put your trust in the Lord, my Brother, fear not....

Now in regard to the school, you seem to think that the plant is to be put forth full bloom, lilies, roses, and pinks, before the root is fully set deep to do this grand work. You must begin small, and not think that you can show all strength in establishing a school after an advanced order, taking in higher studies, and do not worry about leading teachers or under teachers before you have sufficient students to warrant the steps you take. Let not human pride hurt your record. Do not you suppose the Lord sees, and is acquainted with the favorable and unfavorable presentations? Has not the Lord an oversight over his own work? You may suppose, my brethren, that you have to do all the devising, all the strengthening, and all the organizing: and I ask you, Is it not best to show that you have confidence in God? You must not be anxious to develop too fast. The hand of providence is holding the machinery. When that hand starts the wheel, then all things will begin to move.

How can finite man carry the burdens of responsibility for this time? His people have been far behind. Human agencies under the divine planning may recover something of what is lost because the people who had great light did not have corresponding piety, sanctification, and zeal in working out God's specified plans. They have lost to their own disadvantage what they might have gained to the advancement of the truth if they had carried out the plans and will of God. Man can not possibly stretch over that gulf that has been made by the workers who have not been following the divine Leader. We may have to remain here in this world because of insubordination many more years, as did the children of Israel, but for Christ's sake, His people should not add sin to sin by charging God with the consequence of their own wrong course of action. Now, have men who claim to believe the Word of God learned their lesson that obedience is better than sacrifice? "He hath showed thee (this rebellious people) O man, what is good, and what doth the Lord require of thee but to do justly, and to love mercy, and to walk humbly with thy God"?

Now the Lord will not be pleased with those men, whom He hath appointed to do a certain work, who take on many lines of work and carry them until they become so wearisome that it breaks their strength. You, nor any other agency, can not heal the hurt that has come to God's people by neglect to lift up His standard, and occupy new territory. The churches should now be acting in their strength, with capabilities, talents, and means, carrying the work, reaching higher and broader in capacity to stand before the world in the power of invincible truth. But if all now would only see and confess and repent of their own course of action in departing from the truth of God, and following human devising, then the Lord would pardon. Warnings have been coming, but they have been unheeded, but a few who may now seek to bridge the gulf that stands so offensively before God must haste slowly, else the standard bearers will fail, and who will take their place?

Now, my brother, I am deeply sorry for you and your family. I reproach thee not for thy zeal, for if others had shared the burdens as they should have done, the work would have been far advanced, but not, just now, you must come apart and rest awhile. Be not concerned in regard to your wages. God will not leave you without some help and comfort for yourself, your wife, and little ones. Be of good courage in the Lord. Trust Him fully. Let the Lord carry the burden of the school. You are not to become loaded down with burdens that will accomplish only the work that finite man can do. When you put your trust wholly in God, then you will see in every passage of your experience One going before you preparing the way. I cannot tell you what you should do, but I can tell you what not to do; do not worry, be not unbelieving, and do not think that you can blossom into a perfect school in its very planting on new soil. You must remember that it takes time to plant, and to perfect that plant. You just hold fast every inch you have. Broad daylight now - I have been writing since half past three. Much love to your family; be of good courage.

Ellen G. White.

Chapter 52—Help for Berrien Springs

Nashville, Tenn., Dec. 27, 1901.

To the Ministers and other Friends of the Berrien Springs School:

There are times when things do not look as bright and cheerful as we could wish, because difficulties stand in the way of rapid advancement; but we hope, by brethren and sisters, that you will be encouraged to take a thorough interest in the establishment of the school at Berrien Springs, and aid it by the sale of "Christ's Object Lessons" and in other ways. Let the sale of "Christ's Object Lessons" be taken hold of interestedly in our large cities and in the smaller settlements. Brethren, wake up. The good hand of the Lord has been with our people in the selection of a good place to locate the school. This place corresponds to the representations given me as to where the school would be located. It is away from the cities, and there is an abundance of land for agricultural purposes, and room so that the houses will not need to be built one close to another. There is plenty of ground where students shall be educated to educate the land. "Ye and God's husbandry: ye are God's building."

We would have all to understand when canvassing for "Object Lessons", that they are doing a work that is essential to be done for the school which should now be going on. The Lord will help each one who will pray and work, and work and pray. The light which I have tried to present before our people is that we must arouse ourselves from sleep, and feel an interest in the school that is to be built up at Berrien Springs. Do not let this matter of erecting suitable buildings fade away from your interest. It is for this purpose that the sale of "Object Lessons" should be vigorously carried forward. Let our prompt action enable the interested ones to make successful that work of moving our school out of Battle Creek.

The land has been secured, and now the work of preparing suitable buildings is to be entered without delay. Let all plans be laid, and the fitting place be now selected. Let those who have been faithful workers take right hold and do their best. Let not this work fail. Let the students take right hold of this matter in earnest. Let not managers, teachers, or helpers swing back in their old customary ways of letting their influence negative the very plans the Lord has presented as the best plan for the physical, mental, and moral education of our youth.

The Lord calls for steps in advance. Because the teachers may never have been trained to physical, manual labor, they are not easily persuaded in regard to the very best methods to secure for the youth an all-round education, and even the very ones who have been most reluctant to come into line in this matter, had they been given in their youth the physical, mental, and moral education combined, might have saved themselves several attacks of illness, and their brain, bone, and muscle would at this time be in a more healthy condition because all of the Lord's machine would be proportionately taxed. Precious lessons from the best instructors should be secured in spiritual lines, in agricultural employments, and also in carpenter's trade and in the printing business. The Lord would have these mechanical industries brought in and taught by competent men.

Whoever shall take up the work of selling "Christ's Object Lessons" should have the help and encouragement of their brethren.

Ellen G. White.

Chapter 53—The Necessity of a Close Walk with God

Sunnyside, Cooranbong, N.S.W., August 11, 1898.

The work before God's stewards demands faith and courage and hopefulness. We have to pass through moral dangers, and in Christ is our only hope. He will not fail any one of his workers. There is need for every soul to be gathering strength and spiritual experience. The Lord will work for his people when they will answer the prayer of Christ.

Great dishonor is shown to God in the lack of faith and respect that is manifested for one another. Christ's likeness must be cherished. God can not use to his name's glory those who are self-satisfied. We must advance but it must be done with great consideration. God's work must not bear the imperfections of man. We must move solidly and healthfully, doing a work that will not need to be raveled out because of dropped stitches.

In this work, God's word will be found a sure and profitable guide. Poverty may bind about the work, because we abide by God's simple truth; but there must be a firm adherence to the truth still. You may have to drop men, but not one thread of truth must be conceded. Said the great teacher, "Man shall not live by bread alone, but by every word that proceedeth out of the mouth of God." Truth, eternal truth, is to be lived in the daily life. The maxims that the Author of our salvation has given must be strictly adhered to. The living principles are as the leaves of the tree of life, for the healing of human woes.

In a "Thus saith the Lord" is eternal wisdom. Notwithstanding God's word is so little practiced, this is the only remedy for the healing of individual and national woes. Man can not bow upon his knees in the streets and in the market place to offer up his prayers to God, but never forget, wherever you may be, that there is a God upon whom you may call for wisdom. The Lord declared to John: "Behold, I have set before thee an open door, and no man can shut it: for thou hast a little strength, and hast kept my word, and hast not denied my name."

Enoch walked with the unseen God. In the busiest places of the earth, his Companion was with him. Let all who are keeping the truth in simplicity and love, bear in mind. The men who have the most to do have the greatest need of keeping God ever before them. When Satan presses his suggestions upon their mind, they may, if they cherish a "Thus saith the Lord", be drawn into the secret pavilion of the Most High. His promises will be their safeguard. Amid all the confusion and rush of business, they will find a quiet resting place. If they will place their trust in God, he will be their resting place.

Take God with you in every place. The door is open for every son and daughter of God. The Lord is not far from the soul who seeks him. The reason why so many are left to themselves in places of temptation is because they do not set the Lord before them. It is in the places where God is least thought of that you need to carry the lamp of life. If God be left out of sight, if our faith and communion with Him is broken, the soul is in positive danger. Integrity will not be maintained.

The Lord is our helper, our defense. God has provided that no soul that trusts in him shall be overcome by the enemy. Christ is just as much with his believing ones when they are compelled to be associated in any sense with the world, as when they meet in his house to worship him. Think of these words: "Thou has a few names even in Sardis who have not defiled their garments; they shall walk with me in white; for they are worthy. He that overcometh, the same shall be clothed in white raiment; and I will not blot out his name out of the book of life, but I will confess his name before my Father, and before his angels."

These words are given for the people while they are in connection with the world, subject to temptations and influences which are deceiving and deluding. While they stay their mind upon Him who is their sun and their shield, the blackness and darkness that surround them will not leave one spot or stain upon their garments. They will walk with Christ. They will pray and believe and work to save the souls that are ready to perish. These are trying to break the bands that Satan has fastened upon them, and they will not be put to shame if, by faith they will make Christ their companion. Temptations and deceptions will be constantly brought up by the great deceiver to spoil the work of the human agent, but if he trusts in God, if he is humble and meek and lowly of heart, keeping the way of the Lord, heaven will rejoice, for he will gain the victory. God says, "He shall walk with me in white (with unsullied garments), for he is worthy."

The Lord of Israel is the only hope and refuge of his people. The people of God who will make use of his word, who will have faith in his promises, shall see of his salvation. Because so little faith is exercised, there is little deep, earnest, abiding experience. There is a need of constant dependence upon God, as well as constant faith and earnest fervency of spirit. All heaven is interested in those who have received Christ, in whatever position in life they are placed.

Some who are numbered among merchant princes will take their position to obey the truth. God's eye has been upon such as have acted according to the light they have had, maintaining their integrity. Cornelius, a man of high position, maintained his religious experience, strictly walking in accordance with the light he had received. God had his eye upon him, and he sent his angel with a message to him. The heavenly messenger passed by the self-righteous ones, and came to Cornelius and called him by name. And he said, "What is it, Lord?" And he said unto him, Thy prayers and thine alms are come up for a memorial before God. Then instruction was given to him as to what he should do to receive greater knowledge. He was to become acquainted with the disciples of Christ.

This record is made for the special benefit of those who are living in these last days. Many who have had great light have not appreciated and improved it as it was their privilege to do. They have not practiced the truth. And because of this the Lord will bring in those who have lived up to all the light they have had. Those who have been privileged with opportunities to understand the truth, and who have not obeyed its principles, will be swayed by Satan's temptations for self-advancement. They will deny the principles of truth in practice and bring reproach upon the cause of God. Christ declares that he will spue these out of his mouth, and leave them to follow their own course of action to distinguish themselves. This course of action does indeed make them prominent as men that are unfaithful householders. The Lord will give his message to those who have walked in accordance with the light they have had, and will recognize them as true and faithful, according to the measurement of God. These men will take the place of those who, having light and knowledge, have walked not in the way of the Lord, but in the imagination of their own unsanctified hearts.

We are now living in the last days, when the truth must be spoken: when in reproof and warning it must be given to the world, irrespective of consequences. If there are some who will become offended and turn from the truth, we must bear in mind that there were those who did the same in Christ's day. When the greatest Teacher the world has ever known spoke the truth, many of his disciples became offended and walked no more with him.

But truth will bear away victory. Those who will maintain the truth, irrespective of consequences, will offend some whose hearts are not in harmony with the truth as it is in Jesus. These persons cherish theories of their own, which are not the truth. The truth does not harmonize with their sentiments; and rather than give up their own ideas, they walk away from those who obey the truth. But there are men who will receive the truth, and these will take the place made vacant by those who become offended and leave the truth.

Christ declared, "They went out from us, but they were not of us." Men of true Christian principles will take their places, and will become faithful, trustworthy householders, to advocate the word of God in its true bearings, and in its simplicity. The Lord will work so that the disaffected ones will be separated from the true and loyal ones. Those who, like Cornelius, will fear God and glorify him, will take their places. The ranks will not be diminished. Those who are firm and true will close up the vacancies that are made by those who become offended and apostatize.

By the wonderful works of God, Cornelius was led to bring his energetic, faithful life into connection with the disciples of Christ. Thus shall it be in the last days. Many will prize the wisdom of God above any earthly advantage, and will obey the word of God as the supreme standard. These will be led to great light. These will come to the knowledge of the truth, and will seek to get this light of truth before those of their acquaintance, who, like themselves, are anxious for the truth. Thus they become conscientious light-bearers to the world. Themselves constrained by the love of God, they will constrain others, and will improve every opportunity to invite and urge others to come and see the beauty of the truth, and to give their abilities to advance the work of God.

There is a work of a superior order to be done. A clear understanding of business matters will qualify men to conduct business for the work and the cause of God, to keep it upon a high and holy basis. The missionary work, in all its branches, needs wise, careful, judicious men, who have ability and experience to act in the capacity of treasurers - men who will prove trustworthy in bringing the truth before the men in the highways, and who will bring all the advantages of their experience, their soundness of principle, their unbending integrity and uprightness into the work to which they are appointed. Faith unfeigned in its largeness and fullness is wanted just now.

E. G. White.

Chapter 54—Results of Indulgence in Meat-Eating

From MS. 1, '88 (P).

Shall meat become the staple article of food because those who are in responsible positions have been educating themselves to enjoy a meat diet? Shall the physicians be free to indulge their own perverted habits, to gratify appetites as they choose, and thus mold the sentiments of the institution? Shall those who have had great light, and who are professedly seeking to walk in that light, and to reflect the light, see their efforts counterworked by both precept and example in our sanitariums? In the name of the Lord I am charged to testify that those who plead for indulgence of appetite in meat-eating are the very ones who need to reform, and bring themselves into line. They will not give directions for the patients to eat the flesh of dead animals, because their own appetites crave meat. When the habits and tastes are brought into correct lines, it will be seen that light and truth are guiding the ones who are acting as guides to poor, weak, self-indulgent, intemperate souls.

The physicians should educate the patients so as to lead them away from the use of hurtful things, and should point out safe paths for the feet to walk in. If the minds of patients are left to their own direction, many will, of course, choose the gross diet of flesh, rather than the fruits of the ground and of the trees. When those who act as physicians lead away from health principles, God is not honored. When this is the case, whatever may be the religious instruction, there is a dead fly in the ointment.

How can you plead that you are conscientious in the work? Know ye not that there is a good conscience and a bad conscience? Which is pure and elevating and ennobling? When one takes a course that is in harmony with his own perverted, hereditary and cultivated taste, in indulgence of appetite, shall his claims of conscientiousness be respected as of heavenly birth? Is it safe for him to follow his own human impulses? Shall he become a law unto himself, and by precept and example encourage others in the indulgence of appetite, entirely contrary to the light which God in his mercy has been pleased to give? The development of evil in this age of the world is largely due to and strengthened by that which is placed in the stomach for food. We are built up from that which we eat. Physicians should study from cause to effect. The animal propensities should not be educated and strengthened to rule the whole being.

"What? Know ye not that your body is the temple of the Holy Ghost which is in you, which ye have of God, and ye are not your own? For ye are bought with a price: therefore glorify God in your body, and in your spirit, which are God's." This expression, "bought with a price" means everything to us. In consideration of the price paid for us, shall we not yield our bodies and souls up to Him who has bought us with His blood? Shall not that which He has redeemed be kept in as wholesome and pure and holy a condition as possible? Christ has redeemed us; our very flesh He has saved at an infinite cost, giving His own flesh for the life of the world. The lower passions have their seat in the body, and work through it. The words, "flesh", or "Fleshly lusts" or "Carnal lusts", embrace the lower, corrupt nature: the flesh of itself cannot act contrary to the will of God. We are commanded to crucify the flesh, with the affections and lusts. How shall we do it? Shall we inflict pain on the body? No; but put to death the temptation to sin. The corrupt thought is to be expelled. Every thought is to be brought into captivity to Jesus Christ. All animal propensities are to be subjected to the higher powers of the the soul. The love of God must reign supreme; Christ must occupy an undivided throne. Our bodies are to be regarded as Christ's purchased possession. The members of the body are to become the instruments of righteousness.

What is the result of giving loose rein to the lower passions? The delicate organs of women are worn out. ... Loathsome practices lead to loathsome diseases. That which God has given as a blessing is made a curse. ... The most terrible diseases are the sure result of incontinence that is pursued. And the animal propensities are inflamed by gross living, practices, especially by a flesh diet...

What is the special work that we are called upon to do in our health institutions? Instead of giving, by precept and example, an education in the indulgence of perverted appetite, educate away from these things. Life up the standard of reform in every line. The Apostle Paul lifts up his voice, "I beseech you, therefore, brethren, by the mercies of God, that ye present your bodies a living sacrifice, holy, and acceptable unto God, which is your reasonable service. And be not conformed to this world: but be ye transformed by the renewing of your mind, that ye may prove what is that good, and acceptable, and perfect will of God.

Our health institutions are established to present the living principles of a clean, pure, healthful diet. Knowledge must be imparted in regard to self-denial, self-control. Jesus who made man, who redeemed man, is to be held up before all who shall come to our institutions. The knowledge of the way of life, peace, health, and sanctification of the soul and body, must be given line upon line, precept upon precept, that men and women may see the need of reform. They must be led to renounce the debasing customs and practices which existed in Sodom and in the antediluvian world, whom God destroyed because of their iniquity. Said Christ, "But as the days of Noe were, so shall also the coming of the Son of Man be. For as in the days that were before the flood they were eating and drinking, marrying and giving in marriage, until the day that Noe entered the Ark, and knew not until the flood came, and took them all away; so shall also the coming of the Son of man be."

All who shall visit our health institutions are to be educated. The plan of redemption should be brought before all, high and low, rich and poor. Carefully prepared instruction is to be given, that indulgence in fashionable intemperance in eating and drinking may be seen as the cause of disease and suffering, and of evil practices that follow as a result.

Shall those things go on, and the victims be uninformed, unwarned? Are the youth to follow in the footsteps of the lovers of pleasure more than lovers of God? Shall the cleansing fountain be shown to all? Shall the last message of mercy be given to the world? Are there to be no faithful sentinels who will work, with all their God-given powers, to reform those who are debased, and restore the moral image of God in man? In Battle Creek some are doing a good work, but not half what they might do. Faithful workers need to be multiplied. Missionaries in every line are needed to reach the hearts and consciences of all that shall come in contact with those who have had the light, who know that the end of all things is at hand. Let all who fill important positions of trust know that God has placed a solemn work upon them to let their light shine in clear, strong ways to a world perishing in their sins.

Chapter 55—Meat Diet and Life in Cities

From MS. 133, '02 (P).

When will those who know the truth, take their stand on the side of right principles for time and for eternity? When will they be true to the principles of health reform? When will they learn that it is dangerous to use flesh-meat? I am instructed to say that if ever meat eating were safe, it is not safe now. Diseased animals are taken to the large cities, and to the villages, and sold for food. Many of these poor creatures would have died of disease in a very short time, if they had not been slaughtered; yet the carcasses of these diseased animals are prepared for the market, and people eat freely of this poisonous food. Such a diet contaminates the blood and stimulates the lower passions.

Many parents act as if they were bereft of reason. They are in a state of lethargy, palsied by the indulgence of perverted appetite and debasing passion. Our ministers, who know the truth, should arouse the people from their paralyzed condition and lead them to put away those things that create an appetite for flesh-meat. If they neglect to reform, they will lose spiritual power, and become more and more debased by sinful indulgence. Habits that disgust the heavenly universe, habits that degrade human beings lower than the beasts are practiced in many homes. Let all those who know the truth say, "Flee fleshly lusts that war against the soul."

Let not any of our ministers set an evil example in the eating of flesh-meat. Let them and their families live up to the light of health reform. Let not our ministers animalize their own nature and the nature of their children. Children whose desires have not been restrained, are tempted not only to indulge in the common habits of intemperance, but to give loose rein to their lower passions, and to disregard purity and virtue. These are led on by Satan not only to corrupt their bodies, but to whisper their evil communications to others. If parents are blinded by sin, they will often fail of discerning these things.

To parents who are living in the cities, the Lord is sending the warning cry, Gather your children into your own houses; gather them away from those who are disregarding the commandments of God, who are teaching and practicing evil. Get out of the cities as fast as possible.

Parents can secure small homes in the country, with land for cultivation, where they can have orchards and where they can raise vegetables and small fruits to take the place of flesh-meat, which is so corrupting to the lifeblood coursing through the veins. On such places the children will not be surrounded with the corrupting influences of city life. God will help his people to find such homes outside of the cities.

Chapter 56—Selection of Sanitarium Workers

From K. 200, 02 (P).

In regard to your statement that Dr. _____ would come to help you in the Wahroonga Sanitarium, on certain conditions, including the privilege of serving whatever food he might desire to serve at the table, I would say that you had better not accept the services of those who will come only on condition that such terms shall be made; for the terms on which they would come are evidence that you do not want them. They would be a perplexity to you rather than a help. Any one who makes propositions of this kind would, I fear, cause you more anxiety and trouble than you could afford...

If Dr. _____ were connected with the Wahroonga Sanitarium, his influence would be exerted to launch out in such a way that you would not know how you stood financially, until embarrassments came upon you from which you could not relieve yourselves. His education and training are of such a nature that extravagance is as natural to him as is the act of breathing. His tendency is to take matters into his own hands; and I fear you could not prevent him from doing this. There would be many difficulties to surmount as the result of extravagance, which would make of none effect the principles that Christ has given us in His life of self-denial and in his teachings.

Let us not have connected with the institution any one who would be a burden to your soul. Wait on the Lord. Not until you have sure evidence that Dr. _____ is converted will the time come for you to make terms with him.

As regards the flesh-meat question, I know that if such men as Dr. _____ should connect with the institution, you could not deal with this question without great worry and perplexity.

I have been instructed that there was a time when the Lord looked with great tenderness upon Dr. _____: but your brother desired to carry out his own plans, and this made it difficult for him to work in harmony with the Lord's way. I think that if he were sanctified and humble before God, he has qualifications that would make him a blessing. When he is converted, when he is willing to learn of Jesus and to take counsel with God, he wi-l be able to strengthen his brethren, and to connect with the great enterprise which we have undertaken, without bringing deterioration into it.

My brother and sister, you are to labor in a judicious manner, that those with whom you are brought in contact in the sanitarium will recognize that a sanctified spiritual atmosphere surrounds your soul. This can be, and should be. It is truth that is needed -- truth that can not be bound. The greatest necessity of your patrons is a heart willing to receive the truth. Some will decide to come to the Sanitarium as the prodigal son determined to return to his father. These souls can be judiciously labored for and saved. Truth, brought into the life-experience, is a saving power.

If connected with the institution there were some one whose principles and words did not have a saving influence, he would testify against the sanctifying power of the truth. If a work were done by the holy Spirit in the heart of such an one, he would rise to a higher, holier standard, where he could have a transforming influence upon the unbelieving patrons.

Until Dr. ____ is converted, he would, if connected with your medical institution, undo the very work that the Lord desires to have done. In the Sanitarium there must be a judicious ministration of the Word. Dr. ____'s influence would counteract this religious influence. God forbids this. I should be so glad if Dr. ____'s heart, mind, and character, could, by his own consent, be brought into pleasing captivity to the will of Christ Jesus. ...

Please read and study the third chapter of Colossians. It states plainly what we must do in order to leave on the minds of unbelievers an impression favorable to the truth.

A few words more in regard to what you ought to do toward securing physicians and other helpers for the new Sanitarium. Go to the Lord and to His written word. Do not connect with any one who will prove to be a hindrance in spiritual things. I have earnestly longed and prayed that Dr. ____ would be enlightened by the Holy Spirit, that he may see wherein he is not a laborer together with God.

I had hoped that Brother and Sister ____ would have seen before this time that they are not obeying the Word of the Lord. It has been presented to me that were they to connect with the Sanitarium as they now are, their influence would not leave a right impression on the minds of those with whom they would be brought in contact. Their ideas regarding Christian deportment are not correct. They would not honor the Lord. They both need to be united with Christ. Until this union is formed, they could not be other than a great burden if brought into the Sanitarium. It will never do for them to be placed in connection with other workers unless they see and understand what it means to be chosen of God.

I write you this because I dare not withhold it. I believe that you will understand me. I love these souls, but I know that until they are prepared properly to represent health reform, to set a right example, they should not be connected with the Sanitarium; for they would be a drawback to the success of its work. When they are prepared to meet the requirements of God, you will know it. They need a re-conversion.

We are living in a solemn and important time. The effort to build the sanitarium has been a tremendous one, and we can not afford to bring into connection with it those who would prove a hindrance to its work and an injury to its reputation.

In regard to flesh-meat, do not bring it into the Sanitarium. Neither tea nor coffee should be served. Caramel-cereal, made as nicely as possible, should be served in the place of these health-destroying beverages. In regard to the third meal, do not make eating but two meals compulsory. Some do best healthwise when eating three light meals, and when they are restricted to two, they feel the change severely.

Chapter 57—Systematic Giving

From "A Test of Gratitude and Loyalty", Review and Herald, February 4, 1902.

The duty and privilege of systematic giving to the cause of God is a matter that should by no means be neglected by our ministers. God has called them to watch for souls as they that must give an account. He has commissioned them to bear His message to the churches. They should see that none are left in ignorance concerning this subject. They should seek to impress the people with a sense of their entire dependence upon God, and their accountability to Him for all His benefits.

God has given special direction as to the use to which the tithe should be devoted. He does not design that His work shall be crippled for want of means. That there may be no haphazard work and no error, He has made our duty on all these points very plain. The portion that God has reserved for himself is not to be diverted to any other purpose than that which he has specified. Let none feel at liberty to retain their tithe, to use according to their own judgment, They are not to use it for themselves in an emergency, nor to apply it as they see fit, even in what they may regard as the Lord's work. God has shown honor to men in taking them into partnership with himself in the great work of redemption. He expects His agents to labor not against Him, but in unison with Him, that His treasury may be supplied.

The minister, should by precept and example, teach the people to regard the tithe as sacred. He should not feel that he can retain it and apply it to his own judgment, because he is a minister. It is not his. He is not at liberty to devote to himself whatever he thinks is his due. Let him not give his influence to any plans for diverting from their legitimate use the tithes and offerings dedicated to God. Let them be placed in the Lord's treasury, and held sacred for his service as He has appointed.

Ellen G. White.

Chapter 58—The Use of the Tithe

Mountain View, Calif., Jan. 22, 1905.

Elder Watson:

My brother, I wish to say to you, Be careful how you move. You are not moving wisely. The least you have to speak about the tithe that has been appropriated to the most needy and the most discouraging field in the world, the more sensible you will be.

It has been presented to me for years that my tithe was to be appropriated by myself to aid the white and colored ministers who were neglected and did not receive sufficient properly to support their families. When my attention was called to aged ministers, white or black, it was my special duty to investigate into their necessities and supply their needs. This was to be my special work, and I have done this in a number of cases. No man should give notoriety to the fact that in special cases the tithe is used in that way.

In regard to the colored work in the South, that field has been and is still being robbed of the means that should come to the workers of that field. If there has been cases where our sisters have appropriated their tithe to the support of the ministers working for the colored people in the South, let every man, if he is wise, hold his peace.

I have myself appropriated my tithe to the most needy cases brought to my notice. I have been instructed to do this; and as the money is not withheld from the Lord's treasury, it is not a matter that should be commented upon; for it will necessitate my making known these matters, which I do not desire to do, because it is not best.

Some cases have been kept before me for years, and I have supplied their needs from the tithe, as God has instructed me to do. And if any person shall say to me, Sister White, will you appropriate my tithe where you know it is most needed, I shall say, Yes, I will; and I have done so. I commend those sisters who have placed their tithe where it is most needed to help to do a work that is being left undone; and if this matter is given publicity, it will create knowledge which would better be left as it is. I do not care to give publicity to this work which the Lord has appointed me to do, and others to do.

I send this matter to you so that you shall not make a mistake. Circumstances alter cases. I would not advise that any should make a practice of gathering up tithe money. But for years there have now and then been persons who have lost confidence in the appropriation of the tithe who have placed their tithe in my hands, and said that if I did not take it they would themselves appropriate it to the families of the most needy minister they could find. I have taken the money, given a receipt for it, and told them how it was appropriated.

I write this to you so that you shall keep cool and not become stirred up and give publicity to this matter, lest many more shall follow their example.

Ellen G. White.

Chapter 59—The Work in Nashville

St. Helena, Cal., May, 1902.

From the light given me, I know that the Lord used Edson White and W. O. Palmer to do missionary work in the South. This field has been presented to me as a field sinfully neglected by those who believe in the truth. God's people have not done the work that ought to be done there. The Lord accepted those two souls, brought from darkness to light, and put it into their hearts to do a work in the Southern field. The history of these workers has revealed much that can not be repeated here. But the Lord has shown me that He has accepted Edson White's work, and has several times preserved his life when in perilous places. He has put His spirit upon him, and has opened the way before him, and given him success.

The establishment of the work in Nashville was in God's order. In and around Nashville there are large colleges built for the education of the colored people. These grand buildings stand as representatives of a great and good work that is being done for this race. The Lord has favored and blessed those who have given themselves to this work. It was in the order of God that Seventh-day Adventists should enter Nashville. I was instructed that memorials for God were to be established in this place, not only right in the city, but at a little distance from it. Efforts were to be made to reach both the white and colored people. The medical missionary work was to be established there; for it is the right hand of the gospel. But the work would have to move slowly; for there was not much means with which to carry it on. The work was not to be carried forward as a private business, but as a conference enterprise.

A deep interest should be shown in the building up of the work in and around Nashville. A sanitarium should be established. If possible, a building already erected should be secured, if a suitable one can be found in a favorable locality. As soon as possible, steps should be taken to advance this work. When this institution is established, it will have great influence among the people. Let us ask the Lord to open the way for this work, and to lead us in its advancement. We have a God who hears and answers prayer.

In this work, one man's mind is not to control. The work is to be done in the fear of the Lord. All the brethren are to have a voice in the final decision.

The Lord in his providence will work upon minds as he has worked in the past, leading men to favor our people by offering them property at low prices.

Mistakes have been made in the work in Nashville, but let not those who have acted no part in the work give expression to unkind criticism. If the brethren consider their own mistakes and errors, they will refuse to be the first to cast a stone.

Investments have been made in the work in Nashville that might better not have been made until there was a better showing there. Some of the money spent in buildings should have been kept until actually needed for printing materials.

The work of expending means required a man who had not so many and so varied responsibilities as were resting upon Edson White. He should sit with the leading men in Council; for he has been chosen and accepted by God to do a work in the Southern field; but he should have given the financial management of affairs into the hands of a man wise in management, who had not so many burdens resting upon him. While other men are to stand in their place as leaders in their lines of work, he is to occupy his position as leader in his specific line of work.

All these men who act as leaders are to be subject one to another. The voice of no one of them is to be heard above all the rest in settling important questions.

I have much to say, but not now, in regard to the way in which the work should be carried forward. I have felt very desirous that Edson should carry forward the work that the Lord has said he should do in the ministry of the Word. If he will give himself to this work, if he will humble his heart as the heart of a little child, if he will depend upon his heavenly Father, God will bless and strengthen him.

He is to unite with his brethren, some of whom have already been his associates in labor. Elder Butler is president of the Southern Union Conference, and I believe that this is right. The men who have been placed in office are to carry forward their appointed work. By walking humbly with God, they are to learn how to bring their different lines to perfection. There is to be perfect unity among the workers. They are to respect and uphold one another, each esteeming the other better than himself, each standing steadfastly at his post of duty.

Brother Palmer is very much worn and exhausted. He can not continue to carry the responsibilities that he has been carrying. He must lay off some of his burdens. Edson White is not to have the deciding voice in framing and carrying out financial plans for the work in the South for these matters mean very much. The work must be carried forward in straight lines. Edson and Brother Palmer are not to be laid aside, but connected with them are to be other men, men of wisdom and intelligent understanding.

To Edson White I am instructed to say, Cut down your work to that which you understand best. You have carried so many responsibilities that you are nearly bankrupt in mental and physical strength. Do not try to rush things as you have been doing. You can not afford to sacrifice your needed rest and sleep in order to drive forward your work. You are wearing out altogether too fast. With overtaxed nerves, aching head and sleepless nights, you have been losing ground physically, mentally, and spiritually.

The Lord would have you make straight paths for your feet, lest that which is lame be turned out of the way, He desires both you and Brother Palmer to stand with all the armor on, prepared by sanctified experience to show yourselves strong men. He wants you to be successful in your work. There are those who will misrepresent your motives, as they have misrepresented them over and over again. Therefore, move with moderation and great caution.

You have felt your trials pressing you sorely. But has not Christ borne all that you are called on to bear? He can make you rich even amidst the humiliation of the deepest poverty. You may feel that you are accused wrongfully. Was not this the daily experience of your Master? Bear patiently all that comes. In the last great day those who have been so ready to judge will be greatly surprised by Christ's estimate of character. To those who in sincerity have followed righteous principles, will be given a great reward. Nothing has ever been thought or said or done that has escaped the Lord's notice. He knows the motives that prompt men to action. Therefore have courage in Him.

The work in Nashville demands our first attention. I was a little surprised at first to know that five hundred dollars from the funds of the Southern Union Conference had been apportioned to the work in Graysville, while there was such need of means in Nashville. But the light given me was that this was the right thing to do. Brother Kilgore has helped the work in mission fields. He has not been wanting in liberality; and now, if means has been sent to Graysville to help the work there in an emergency, let no one question the matter. All the workers should be filled with a noble spirit of helpfulness and of willingness to use the Lord's money where it is needed most. Graysville needed the money at the time that the five hundred dollars was sent there; and when the work there is firmly established, and the time comes for a school and sanitarium to be built at a little distance from Nashville, the workers can with confidence call for help from Graysville.

We are in this world to help one another. In Christ's work there were no territorial lines, and those who attempt to make such lines in Christ's work today might better pray, "Lord, give me a new heart." When they have the mind of Christ, they will see the many parts of the Lord's vineyard that are still unworked. Never will they say, "Our means is needed to carry forward the interests we have in hand. It is of no use to call for means from us."

For their usefulness and success, the Lord's servants are dependent on Christ. He reads their hearts. He knows their motives and purposes, and He calls upon them to separate themselves from everything that would prove a hindrance to their success in presenting the truth for this time. This is the work that is to be made first of all. As they give themselves to it, success will surely crown their efforts. Angels of God will impress hearts, and many will be brought into the light of the truth.

"I therefore the prisoner of the Lord, beseech you that ye walk worthy of the vocation wherewith ye are called, with all lowliness and meekness, with longsuffering, forbearing one another in love; endeavoring to keep the unity of the Spirit in the bonds of peace. There is one body and one Spirit, even as ye are called in one hope of your calling; one Lord, one faith, one baptism, one God and Father of all, who is above all, and through all, and in you all. But unto every one of us is given grace according to the measure of the gift of Christ."

We are to learn from past experience how to avoid our failures. We pray to our heavenly Father, "Lead us not into temptation," and then, too often, we fail to guard our feet against leading us into temptation. We are to keep away from the temptation by which we are easily overcome. Our success is brought out by ourselves through the grace of Christ. We are to roll out of the way the stone of stumbling that has caused us and others so much sadness.

Listening to the words of Christ, we are safe. Whatever your calling, whatever your hope, listen: "If any man will come after Me," he says, "Let him deny himself, and take up his cross, and follow me." Obeying these words, in entire dependence on the Saviour, go forth to give to the world an example of what it means to be a Christian. Yoke up with Christ. This is the only bond of the gospel. Learn daily how to carry out more acceptable the instruction Christ has given. Live as becomes the subjects of His kingdom. To carry out the words, "Thy will be done on earth, as it is done in heaven," - this is our lifework.

Ellen G. White.

Chapter 60—Instruction Regarding the Southern Work

Elmshaven, May 28, 1902.

During the night season I have received instruction regarding the work in the South. Some days ago things were presented to me that I could scarcely understand, and that I could not explain by pen or voice. Again, on another day, the same things were presented to me. I had been feeling deeply distressed. My mind had been much troubled in regard to the light that had been given me concerning the work of my son, J. E. White, in the Southern field.

Last night it seemed that important matters were being discussed in a company of select men gathered together for counsel. The business part of the work in the Southern field had been brought up for consideration. Changes were being made in the committees having charge of the various parts of the work. The perplexities connected with the financial side of the work were presented. The brethren were trying to adjust matters of a most perplexing nature. Some changes had been made in the business arrangements.

One of the company arose, and going to the last seat in the room, placed his arm around J. E. White, and led him to the front. He then rehearsed the facts concerning his labor in the South. He spoke of the efforts that had been made when he and Brother Palmer first went there. He went into the history, from point to point, of the publication of the little book, "Gospel Primer". This book - the only hope that seemed to present itself for the relief of the Southern field - was coveted by men who had no burden for that field. The author, driven to extremities, felt that he was forced to sell the plates and copyrights of his book.

The Speaker referred to the continued efforts made by Edson White, and to the counter efforts made to frustrate the work, among these the calling of Brother Palmer from the work, the real purpose of which was to discourage Edson White, and to weaken his hands, so that he would be compelled to leave the field.

It was the steadfast purpose of Edson White to do a work for the Lord in the Southern field. And from time to time the Lord gave him words of encouragement, and put into his mind plans and ways of managing so that he and his fellow workers would not, for lack of means, be forced to leave this, the hardest of all fields.

The Lord has looked with sadness upon the most pitiable of sights - the colored race in slavery. In our work for them, He desires us to remember their providential deliverance from slavery, their common relationship to us by creation and by redemption, and their right to the privileges of freedom.

The Lord has accepted all who have put forth unselfish effort for the uplifting of these, the most needy of his creatures. God desires men and women to labor for the colored people, keeping in view their essential good. He does not favor the most favored, to the neglect of the colored and white people who are of a lower grade. He does not leave those in need of assistance without help or notice.

The cross of Calvary should make the distinctions of society fade away and become contemptible. If the Lord is so gracious as to accept sinners from the white race, and forgive their sins, holding out to them the assurance of the higher life, the hope of a place in the redeemed family when he comes in the clouds of heaven, and the righteous dead rise from their grave to meet Him, will he not accept sinners from the black race, and will He not forgive their sins? Does He not hold out to them the same hope that He holds out to the white race? Will He not, if they believe on him, receive them as his sons and daughters? Will He not raise them from ignorance and degradation by the working out of His plan? Does He not, through the instrumentality of the more favored white race, who claim to be children of the same Father, wish to uplift and ennoble them?

All people, of whatever nationality, are amenable to the same law. All will be judged according to their deeds. All, both white and black, have the same offer of salvation. God has given to all the promise of the same heaven on the same terms. What right have we, then, to pass the colored people by without doing our best to save them?

And when God inspires in men and women the desire to help these poor, neglected, ignorant ones, to educate them to establish schools, to teach them to be self-supporting, should we not encourage these workers? Should we not do all in our power to help those who work for the people of the South, both white and black, striving to instruct them, to lead them to have faith in Jesus?

Seventh-day Adventists have done something in this field. The work has been carried forward in hardship and difficulty, against the stress of poverty.

I can not now write all that was said. The Speaker put his arm round Edson White, and said, "The Lord laid upon this man the burden to work for the people in the Southern States of America; and he accepted the charge. For years he struggled against innumerable difficulties and discouragements, in trying to do this work. He carried on the work by means of a small steamer, on which meetings were held. Thus many heard the truth in its simplicity. He met the people where they were, and the Lord was with him. He was the Lord's mission worker, and some of those who worked with him in managing the boat were converted, and in their turn became missionaries, uniting with him in holding meetings. If one soul is worth more than the whole world, what then must those souls be worth?

"Edson White was taken by the Lord Jesus Christ and bidden to go forward in his work. His sins were pardoned, and then his work began. It began in deep poverty. Several had begun the work among the colored people in the Southern field, and becoming discouraged, had left the field for a more promising one.

"From time to time the Lord sent Edson White word, "You're not to fail nor to become discouraged. You are preparing the way of the Lord. You are learning how to meet difficulties and how to carry the work forward."

"The work was not always pleasant, or the way smooth. The efforts put forth have been made under the most discouraging circumstances because many who ought to have assisted, stood back, and did next to nothing. The struggle was hard and trying as the workers went from place to place endeavoring to arouse and interest in the truth. But God was guiding and directing, and much good has been accomplished, though the work has been carried forward amidst great discouragement.

"And now the work has begun at Nashville. This is in order of the Lord. Nashville is the place for a beginning to be made in the publishing work. In this place there were buildings that could be secured at much less than the original cost. A building suitable for the work was purchased at a very low rate, and the work of publishing was commenced. The Lord provided excellent helpers. Some of these came of their own accord and gave themselves to the work. Who moved them to do this?--The Lord Jesus Christ. He inspired them with a desire to engage in the work, and prepared them for it.

"Thus workers have labored with an unflagging determination for the advancement of the work, and the results achieved have been wonderful. The growth of the work has been rapid. The labors of J.E. White and his associates have been unremitting. They have planned and devised and wrestled. The result is seen in the work accomplished. God has blessed the almost superhuman efforts made to advance the work.

"But through unforeseen circumstances, trials have come that have brought about a condition of things not easily described. The present showing of a publishing work in Nashville is not as favorable as it should have been and might have been. It was taken up with worthy aspirations and noble ambitions. The laborers have put the whole energies of body, mind, and soul into its upbuilding. But a murmuring, questioning, selfish spirit has been manifested by some in other places. This has made the work very hard, and because of it less progress has been made than otherwise would have been made. ..." The words were spoken: "God knows the objectionable features in the character of every one here assembled, and the Lord Jesus covers His servants with the mantle of his righteousness. God judges righteously the motives of the workers he chooses. Man can not read the heart of man; therefore many are misjudged. But in the end men will be valued as they stand in the sight of God, not as they appear to their fellowmen.

"This man has labored most earnestly to advance the work among the colored people. In this work he has pushed the triumphs of the cross more decidedly than any other of the laborers in this field. He is not a fraud. He has not selfishly, willfully, knowingly done wrong. The Lord is very zealous for those who have united with this his servant, and when occasion requires He will work mightily for them. Mistakes have been made: but the Lord, the Creator, has in charge those who are striving to do the work that needs to be done. They are not shielded for their wrongs, but in His pity and kindness and love, and the Lord has mercy on them. He knows all about everyone of them. They have had to pass through the fire of affliction. They have exhausted their life energy in doing the breaking-up, pioneer work, that others would not do. They are as gold tried in the fire. God will be glorified in those who have been laborers together with Him in breaking up the ground in fields that have never before been worked.

"The Lord throws his royal banner of love about this His servant. He has not divorced him from His work. Even when he let go the only hand that could sustain him, God would not allow him to pass into the hands of Satan. He would not allow the enemy to triumph. He snatched the brand from the fire; for He would use it as a light to shine amid the moral darkness. This man is a brand years ago plucked from the fire by a miracle of grace."

Turning to Edson White, the Speaker said, "Stand among your brethren as one who can give counsel and receive counsel. Unite with them in the bonds of Christian fellowship, and by hard labor bind up the work." "Thus said the Lord of hosts, If thou wilt walk in my ways, and if thou wilt keep my charge; then thou shalt also judge my house, and thou shalt also keep my courts, and I will give thee places to walk among these that stand by."

Ellen G. White.

Chapter 61—The Use of Talents

Petaluma, Cal., June 12, 1902.

My dear Son Edson:

I wish you and Emma to visit us at our home near St. Helena, Since the General Conference you and Brother Palmer have worked excessively to establish more firmly the work in Nashville. You have endeavored to make this work as presentable as possible, in order to show those who knew scarcely anything about your work, what has been accomplished in so short a time, and with so small an outlay of means. You wished all to see that needless calls for means had not been made, and that the money received had not been used in vain. You desired the work done in Nashville to be a sample of what could be done in other cities.

But you found that you had expended more than you intended to expend. In trying to do the things that you wanted to see done, you taxed yourself greatly, wearing out your strength. When the general meeting for the Southern workers was appointed to be held in Graysville, you thought it would be best to have it held in Nashville. The change was made, but the time was limited in which to prepare for the accommodation of the brethren. You worked far beyond your strength, spending anxious days and sleepless nights in planning and working to complete the building that you were erecting.

You have not yet recovered from the effects of the strain under which you were laboring at that time; but do not think, my son, that if you have erred in building this addition, you have reason for being discouraged. Others know little of the earnest, almost superhuman efforts you have made to complete this building. Your zeal has led you beyond your strength, causing you to injure yourself. In my letters to you, I have written much in regard to the work to be done in Nashville; and as the work has in the past been largely under your own jurisdiction, you were led to move independently in lines that led you beyond your depth. But even if you have spent more money than is at your command, you may make this, through its lessons of caution, a much greater blessing to you than would be an abundant inflow of means.

My son, you will find that you can not please all men. You will offend some even when you do your best. But be very careful and guarded not to give occasion for your good to be evil spoken of. You can not know how anxious I am to have you stand on vantage ground; for there are those who for years have covered their own neglect to take up work in the South, by finding fault with the active labors in that field. Instead of showing their tact and ability by doing their best to start the work in new places, they have stood to one side, criticizing what Edson White and his co-workers have been doing. Those who have not "put off the old man with his deeds." are standing as accusers of the brethren. Before angels and men Satan is zealously accusing the laborers who take up the work of God in new places. The men who do not take upon themselves the burden of God's work will be kept very busy by the enemy in accusing and picking flaws with those who are determined to advance the work in missionary fields.

I see no reason why you should not be on the committee of the Southern Union Conference as a counsellor; for you know more about how the work in the South should be carried forward than do some who have had less experience. And if your voice and your experience should be regarded by the committee as of much value, you must be careful not to think that your opinions are to be accepted as supreme, above the judgment of those with whom you are associated in labor. Remember that counsellors are to be connected with the various branches of our work. All are to pray and watch unto prayer, cherishing the wisdom that cometh from above.

It is well that something has been done to help Brother Shireman. He was in danger of making mistakes, and, for the time being, the best thing was done that could be done. If after due consideration, it should not be found best for you to lay down the responsibilities you are carrying in connection with the Hildebran School, let others take charge of this enterprise.

Brother and Sister Shireman have yielded to great temptations that the enemy has brought to bear upon them. They imagine that advantage has been taken of them. This has cost them the loss of peace with God and of faith and confidence in their brethren.

Edson, place yourself where Brother Shireman can have no cause for imagining that you mean to injure him. Arrange matters so that no suspicion shall rest upon you that you have been taking advantage of him. I know that you have been his true, disinterested, benevolent, tender-hearted friend and brother. Not one advantage would you knowingly take of him; but he imagines otherwise. I am sorry, so sorry that his soul and the soul of his wife are afflicted.

Brother and Sister Shireman have their appointed work. While they can do an excellent work in opening new fields and preparing the way for the kingdom of God to be established, they have not the ability to do regular school work. So far they have the ability, they can do good work in opening new schools; but others must come to their help in carry the school work forward on a higher plane of disciplinary and educational training than they could.

God has been pleased with the work that Brother Shireman has done in arousing an interest in educational work and in erecting church and school buildings in Hildebran. The Lord has accepted his efforts to trade upon his talents. As he has built his plain, unpretentious buildings, heavenly angels have been his helpers. It is this kind of work that make a good impression on the minds of unbelievers in regard to our brother's abilities. "Let your light so shine before men," the Saviour says, "that they may see your good works, and glorify your Father which is in heaven."

Brother Shireman has solicited testimonials from men of influence - from ministers and men in high official position - in praise of his work. Allowing his mind to dwell upon these things, he has hurt his soul by coming to think that he has talent for places that he could never fill. I do not want Brother and Sister Shireman to hurt their influence for good; but they will, I fear, unless they learn to recognize the necessity of connecting with the school work persons of varied talents.

God loves Brother Shireman, and will be with him, unless he draws away from the Source of his strength. Let our brother listen to the counsel of his brethren, and be as true as steel to principle. The enemy has tempted him sorely, and has nearly succeeded in spoiling his record. He has tempted him to do some strange things that God can not approve. But the Lord Jesus lives and reigns, and will deliver His servant from temptation.

In speaking of talented men, we usually think of those who have remarkable gifts, which enable them to do large things. Too often we think that only a favored few- men of superior genius and intellectual capabilities - can be called talented. But in Christ's parable of the talents are included all responsible human agents, from the humblest and poorest in this world's goods to those who are entrusted with talents of means and of intellect. Even those who faithfully use the least will hear from the Saviour's lips the words of commendation, "Well done, good and faithful servant." The value that God places on the least of talents is shown by the reward he gives for its right use --eternal life. To every faithful steward He will say, "enter thou into the joy of thy Lord."

The Lord gives talents proportionate to the several capabilities of His children. To every man is given his work. Those who do their duty to the best of their ability, using their talent aright, are doing a much-needed work, a work that hundreds of others could do if they only would.

Through faithful performance of his duty, trading on the farthings entrusted to him, Brother Shireman secured the recognition of heaven. He who diligently uses his talent aright in doing the work that needs to be done, as Brother Shireman has used his, need never feel that in order to be appreciated, he must do a higher work, for which he is not so well fitted.

The church of God is made up of many vessels, both large and small. The Lord works through the men who are willing to be used. He will bless our Brother Shireman in doing the work that has brought blessing to him in the past - the work of seeking to save souls ready to perish.

In all the Lord's arrangements, there is nothing more beautiful than His plan of giving to men and women a diversity of gifts. The church is His garden, adorned with a variety of trees, plants, and flowers. He does not expect the hyssop to assume the proportions of the cedar, nor the olive to reach the height of the stately palm. Many have received but a limited religious and intellectual training, but God has a work for this class to do, if they will labor in humility, trusting in Him.

The Lord has graciously fitted Brother Shireman to do a certain work. Not all men can do the work that he by his Christian experience is able to do. He can do excellent work in opening new fields, beginning in a humble way, and meeting the people where they are, coarse and rough though they may be. Working with Christ, he can adapt himself to the situation, winning the hearts of many. He is able to reach after souls and to draw them into the field. In many places he can find opportunity to read and comment upon the Bible to children and to older people. He and his wife can labor together for the conversion of souls. The Lord desires Brother Shireman to present the important points of truth to the people, in object lessons, line upon line, precept upon precept, here a little and there a little. He is to remember that the Lord Jesus is the one who moves upon the heart. If he walks humbly with God, the Lord will continue to use him, giving him health and strength to do his appointed work.

Our brother is to prepare the way in new fields for others to work. His brethren are not to expect him to do as he has done, working to obtain means for institutions, and afterward assisting to build them up. This is too hard a work for one man to do. But he should be given every possible encouragement to go forward and in his humble way reveal his loyalty to principle and his integrity to God. Let the truth fall from his lips in simple prayers and talks. In his unpretentious way he can reach a class that ministers generally can not touch.

Brother and Sister Shireman's danger is in supposing that their talents are sufficient to enable them to do all that must be done in one of our schools. They should not suppose that they can do the work that is essential in educating the youth. This work must be done by those whose talents and training fit them to be educators, enabling them to give the students a complete education. In stead of consenting to carry responsibilities that the Lord has not fitted them to carry, they should go out to other places to arouse an interest and to begin a work similar to the work begun at Hildebran. Taking with them some young helpers to cooperate with them, they could use the breaking-up plow, preparing the soil in new fields and sowing the seed. God will give the increase.

Individual, constant, united efforts will bring the reward of success. Those who desire to do a great deal of good in our world must be willing to do it in God's way by doing little things. He who wishes to reach the loftiest heights of achievement by doing something great and wonderful, will fail of doing anything.

Steady progress in a good work, the frequent repetition of one kind of faithful service, is of more value in God's sight than the doing of one great work and wins for his children a good report, giving character to their efforts. Those who are true and faithful to their divinely-appointed duties, are not fitful, but steadfast in purpose, pressing their way through evil, as well as good, reports. They are instant in season and out of season.

Brother Shireman is not to think that he has ability to do the most difficult work, the greatest service. Let him do a small work, and see it grow under his hand. In the past, the Lord has blessed him in doing his God-given work, and He will still bless him, if he continues to work in the same line. Let him keep at the work by which, through faithfulness, he has attained success.

Let no man despise the humblest of employments. Christ, the Majesty of heaven, assumed the nature of humanity, and for many years worked at the carpenter's trade with Joseph. I presume that while working on the buildings at Hildebran, Brother Shireman has often realized that he was cooperating with the great Master Builder, and has tried to do his work in the best way that he knew how to do it, knowing that this is all that Christ requires. The Lord Jesus is an Educator, and He will constantly help our Brother and Sister Shireman to become better and still better fitted for their work.

Tell Brother Shireman to put his trust in God alone, who will give him victory after victory. Angels of God will go before him, if he will do his appointed work, using the talent given him. Let him encourage others to unite with him in pioneer work, planning with them to open new fields successfully and to erect humble church and school buildings. In teaching others to do what he has done, he will be engaged in an educational work of the highest character.

Every one connected with the Southern Publishing House needs to have his eyes anointed with the heavenly eyesalve, in order that he may see things clearly. Let those in God's service who must meet the difficulties that are always connected with the working of new fields, draw nigh to God, and He will draw nigh to them. He is our Heavenly Father, "with whom is no variableness, neither shadow of turning."

The chief burden of every human being is to be the salvation of body, soul and spirit. Every Christian strives to accumulate true riches; for in this there is safety and consolation. In the place of lavishly investing means in uncertain enterprises, he yearly lays up treasure in the Bank of Heaven, his home. He keeps in circulation in the work of God upon the earth every talent entrusted to him, increasing his gifts by trading upon them. He knows that he can not become rich in heavenly treasure by binding up his talents, be they few or many, in anything against which God has warned him. He does not hide his gifts in worldly enterprises and uncertain projects. He invests his Lord's money in the cause, trading upon it to help the Saviour to secure his purchased possession. He realizes that he is entrusted with means to use for the advancement and glory of Christ's kingdom by saving the souls for whom the Saviour died.

Ellen G. White.

Chapter 62—The Trees of the Lord

"Elmshaven" Sanitarium, Cal., June 26, 1902.

Dear Brethren Kilgore and Jacobs:

The Lord has been giving me light in regard to many things. He has shown me that our Sanitarium should be erected on as high an elevation as is necessary to secure the best results, and that they are to be surrounded by extensive tracts of land, beautified by flowers and ornamental trees.

In a certain place, preparations were being made to clear the land for the erection of a sanitarium. Light was given that there is health in the fragrance of the pine, the cedar, and the fir. And there are several other kinds of trees that have medicinal properties that are health promoting. Let not such trees be ruthlessly cut down. Better change the site of the building than cut down these evergreen trees. There are lessons for us in these trees. God's Word declares, "The righteous shall flourish like the palm tree; he shall grow like a cedar in Lebanon." David says, "I am like a green olive tree in the house of the Lord; I trust in the mercy of God forever and ever."

The Christian is likened to the cedar of Lebanon. I have read that this tree does more than send down a few short roots into the yielding loam. It sends strong roots deep down into the earth, and strikes down further and still further in search of a still stronger hold. And in the fierce blast of the tempest, it stands firm, held by its network of cables beneath.

So the Christian strikes root deep into Christ. He has faith in his Redeemer. He knows in whom he believes. He is fully persuaded that Jesus is the Son of God and the Saviour of sinners. The goodly sound of the gospel is received without conflicting doubts. The roots of faith strike deep down, Genuine Christians, like the cedar of Lebanon, do not grow in the soft surface soil, but are rooted in God, riveted in the clefts of the mountain rocks.

Study these lessons from the trees. I could dwell long on this subject, but I must not just now. I ask you not to cut away your pine trees. They will be a blessing to many. Let them live.

I want to say to you, my brethren, that you have my prayers and my sympathy in your work. Remember that you are trees in the garden of the Lord, and that the divine protection is round about you; The more visible the line of demarcation between the flowers of God and the briar and thorn of Satan's planting, the more the Lord is glorified.

Our sanitariums should be surrounded with choice flowers, that by their growth and beauty they may reveal advantages of culture. They teach us that it is our privilege to improve. God desires us to bring fragrance into our life work. We are to be the plants of the Lord, serving Him in whatever way he wills. Let us do all in our power to beautify our characters.

The Lord has entrusted His garden to skilled tenders whose work it is to care for His beautiful plants. Tender care must be given to the delicate plants. The useless off-shoots must be taken away. The bruised parts must be carefully bound up. So those who are weak in the faith must have fostering care. We are to bind to our strong purposes the weaklings in the Lord's garden, giving them support.

From the endless variety of plants and flowers, we may learn an important lesson. All blossoms are not the same in form or color. Some possess healing virtues. Some are always fragrant. There are professing Christians who think it their duty to make every other Christian like themselves. This is man's plan, not the plan of God. In the church of God there is room for characters as varied as are the flowers in the garden. In His spiritual garden there are many varieties of flowers.

Brother Kilgore, when you have difficulty in locating new buildings and planning for their erection, pray, and believe that the Lord will impress your mind and the minds of your brethren as to just where the building should be. The Lord will certainly bring harmony among you if you ask Him with full purpose of heart. Counsel together. This is necessary in an enterprise such as the one in which you are engaged.

Attention to the Word of God will lead us to live by every word that proceedeth out of the mouth of God. Then we shall respect all his commandments.

Do that which presents itself in its time, demanding the first attention. Do not pass by the first duty to do the second. One duty accomplished prepares the way for the Lord's blessing. And the second duty is more easy if the first has been faithfully performed. The burden is off the soul. The heart is filled with the peace and gladness of Christ.

In your letter to W. C. White, you speak of selling some of the land you have recently purchased. Do not part with a foot of it.

Be of good courage in the Lord.

Ellen G. White

Chapter 63—The Mantle of Christ

Elmshaven, Sanitarium, June 27, 1902.

Elder G. I. Butler, My dear Brother:

Today I was writing a letter to Brother Palmer, when a scene passed before me, which I will try to describe as briefly as possible. I had written several pages of the letter when the scene passed before me. It was just before dinner.

I seemed to be looking upon a company assembled together, in which the question of whether Brother Stone should take the position of treasurer of the Southern Publishing Association was being discussed. Some seemed to be in favor of his taking this position, while others were troubled and distressed.

One of authority came forward, and placing one hand on Brother Palmer's shoulder, and the other on Edson White's shoulder, he said to the brethren, speaking with clearness and decision: "You are not prepared for a change in the workers in the office. Leave these men where they are at present. To make a change now would not be just to them, nor would it improve the condition of things. It would not be wise to make a change now. This would not lessen the difficulties that exist.

"In every age, the call of the hour is answered by the coming of the man. The Lord is gracious. He understands the situation. His will today is that for the present time the lamb-like kindness of Elisha shall exceed the severity of Elijah.

"The man that can build up, and create a fragrant, grateful atmosphere, is not yet presented by God. Whether the present work be to break down or to build up, to reinstate the old or to give place to the new, to enforce the demands of equity and judgment or to encourage hope and courage, and faith, the Lord knows what is needed. He is looking on. He, the great Master worker, is sure to have the very man for the place ready to do the work, when those connected with the work are ready for the change.

"Let the faith that works by love and purifies the soul be cherished. Hasty moves will not help the situation, but will bring in a host of difficulties that will not be for the glory of God.

"Let Edson White and Brother Palmer stand on their feet, not in their own strength, but in the strength of the Lord God of Israel, prepared to breast every difficulty that shall arise. Edson White is to stand with William Palmer, and William Palmer is to stand with

Edson White. Let them take hold of the work with renewed consecration and prove themselves men prepared to meet the demands of the hour with all the talents that God has given them. Encourage faith. Persevere. Work with all humility. The future is in the hands of God.

"The Word of God is to be taught. The life of a man upon whom is laid the work of teaching the Word of the Lord is to be an illustration of the power and righteousness of the principles that he offers to others. He who masters the art of educating others will himself prove a success by succeeding.

"He who wears the mantle, not of Elijah, but of Christ, will give evidence that he keeps his eye fixed on the Saviour. Imbued with Christ's Spirit, he is fitted to teach. He is constantly under the influences of the high and holy impressions made by God.

"Elisha received a double portion of the spirit that had rested on Elijah. In him the power of Elijah's spirit was united with the gentleness, mercy, and tender compassion of the spirit of Christ.

Edson White and Brother Palmer are to unite, and are to be instruments in God's hands of reaching the higher classes, and at the same time of lifting up the oppressed, relieving the needy, and helping the poor to help themselves. If, in their generosity and hopefulness they have made mistakes, let the spirit of forgiveness prevail.

My brethren, you can not be too earnest, too devoted to the will of the Lord. Pray constantly, "Hold up my goings in thy path; let not my feet slip." The Lord sees your dangers. Every natural and cultivated inclination of the heart rises up against true humiliation of self.

It can not be otherwise than that uneasiness will exist in regard to Brother W. O. Palmer or J. E. White handling the means given and loaned by our people for the work in the South. Should they do their very best, any mistake made would be most severely criticized. Brethren, you have both been too free in the expenditures of means. To meet the pressure of circumstances you have incurred obligations, hoping that means would come in, and sometimes you have been disappointed. Your only safety is in God. If you place your dependence wholly upon Him, there will be more safety in your management. But there is much that will have to be out away from your characters before there can be perfect safety in either of you occupying a position on which so much depends.

From the presentation today given me regarding this matter, I am certain that Elder Stone is not the one whom God has selected for the work of treasurer and financier of the Southern Publishing Association. In some things he might do well, but in other lines there is danger of great mistakes. It will never answer to figure too closely in our dealing with believers or unbelievers.

Since the Lord has given me the instruction I have written out in this letter, I feel very much relieved in regard to the situation at Nashville. Let us plead with the Lord to guide his people in His own way. Let him have opportunity to carry out his will. Then his name will be honored and glorified.

Ellen G. White.

Chapter 64—Counsels In Reform

July 10, 1902.

For years a lack of wisdom has been shown in dealing with men who take up and carry forward the Lord's work in difficult places. Often these men labor far beyond their strength. They have little money to invest for the advancement of the work, and they are obliged to sacrifice in order to carry the work forward. They work for small wages, and practice the strictest economy.

They make appeals to the people for means, and they set an example of liberality. They give God the praise for what is done, realizing that He is the author and the finisher of their faith, and that it is by His power that they are enabled to progress.

Sometimes, after these workers have borne the burden and the heat of the day, and by patient, persevering effort have established a school or a sanitarium, or some other interest for the advancement of the work, the decision is made by their brethren that some other man might do better, and therefore that he is to take charge of the work they have been doing. In some cases, the decision is made without giving due consideration and credit to those who have born the disagreeable part of the work, who have labored, and prayed, and striven, putting into their labor all their strength and energy, and have not failed nor become discouraged.

God is not pleased with this way of dealing with His workers. He calls upon his people to hold up the hands of those who build up the work in new, difficult places, speaking to them words of cheer and encouragement.

In their ardor, their zeal for the advancement of the cause, these workers may make mistakes. They may, in their desire to get means for the support of needy enterprises, enter into projects that are not for the best good of the work. The Lord, seeing that these projects would divert them from what He desires them to do, permits disappointment to come upon them, crushing their fond hopes. Money is sacrificed, and this is a great grief to those who had fondly hoped to gain means for the support of the cause.

While the workers were straining every nerve to raise means to help them over an emergency, some of their brethren were standing by, criticizing and surmising evil, put into a prejudicial construction on the motives of the heavily burdened laborers, and making their work more difficult. Blinded by selfishness, these fault-finders did not discern that their brethren are sufficiently afflicted without the censure of the men who have not borne the heavy burdens and responsibilities. Disappointment is a great trial, but Christian love can turn the defeat to victory. Reverses will teach caution. We learn by the things we suffer. Thus we gain our experience.

Let care and wisdom be shown in dealing with workers who, though they have made mistakes, have manifested an earnest, self-sacrificing interest in the work. Let their brethren say, "We will not make matters worse by putting another in your place without giving you opportunity to retrieve your mistake and stand on vantage ground, free from the burden of unjust criticism. Let them be given time to adjust themselves, to overcome the difficulties surrounding them, and to stand before angels and men as worthy workers. Some have made mistakes, but would those who have questioned and criticized have done any better? To the accusing Pharisees Christ said, "He that is without sin among you, let him first cast a stone."

There are those who are premature in their desire to reform things that to them appear to be faulty. They think that they should be chosen to take the place of those who have made mistakes. They undervalue what these workers have done while others were looking on and criticizing. By their actions they say, "I can do great things. I can carry the work forward successfully." To those who think they know so well how to avoid mistakes, I am instructed to say, "Judge not, that ye be not judged. You might avoid mistakes on one point, but in other things you would make grave blunders, which would be very difficult to remedy, and which would bring confusion into the work. These mistakes might do more harm than the mistakes your brethren have made."

The instruction given me is that the men who lay the foundation of a work, and who, in the face of prejudice, fight their way forward, are not to be placed in an unfavorable light in order that others may take their place. There are earnest workers who in spite of the criticisms of some of their brethren, have moved forward in the work that God said should be done. Should they now be removed from their position of responsibility, an impression would be made that would be most unjust to them, and unfavorable to the work, because the changes made would be looked upon as a justification of the unjust criticisms made and the prejudice existing. The Lord desires that no move shall be made which would do injustice to those who have labored long and earnestly to build up the work given them.

Chapter 65—Unwise Changes

Many changes are made that might better never be made. Often, when workers become discontented, instead of being encouraged to stay where they are, and make a success of their work, they are sent to another place. But they take with them the same traits of character that have marred their work in the past. They will manifest the same unchristlike spirit; for they have not learned the lesson of patient, humble service. Thus our working force has often been weakened.

I plead for a different order of things. Changes must be made in the groups of workers in our conferences and institutions. Men of efficiency and consecration must be sought for diligently and encouraged to connect with the burden-bearers as helpers and colaborers. Let there be a harmonious union of the new and the old, in the spirit of brotherly love. But let not changes of management be made abruptly, in such a way as to bring discouragement to those who have labored earnestly and successfully to bring the work to its present stage of progress. God will not sanction anything done to discourage His faithful servants. Let the principles of justice be followed by those whose duty it is to secure the most efficient management for our publishing houses, our sanitariums, and our schools.

Chapter 66—The Work at Berrien Springs

There are those who with the Bible as their standard have been working in the fear of God to carry out the principles of true education. They are not old men, but they are, nevertheless, men whom the Lord desires to place on vantage ground. They have sought to bring into their teachings the principles that would lead the students to become Bible workers. They have walked humbly with God. They have wrestled with difficulties in different places. In their work there have been hard places to pass through, and many obstacles to surmount. There have been stern conflicts and fierce battles. These men are to have opportunity to prove themselves thoroughly trustworthy men.

But as they have tried, to carry forward the work, their efforts have been criticized, and the question has been raised, Should not older teachers be brought in to take the burden of this work? It is thought by some that older teachers would do a more complete work. But would they? Is it not those who have been connected with a work from the beginning who know how to help beginners? Does not their experience in carrying the work forward from its first stages adapt them to meet the needs of learners?

The Lord encouraged these brethren, giving them victories that taught them valuable lessons and strengthened their confidence. It is not according to His plan for some other worker to come in and take the burden of this work upon his shoulders, supposing that he can do a much better and larger work. This is not right. Let no one lay his hand upon another, forbidding him to go forward in his work, or asking him to step into a position of less responsibility, while another more learned and more experienced takes his place.

The high and holy work set before God's workers is to love their fellow-workers, who are just as honest and righteous as they themselves, although they may be tried with fire. He requires them to put self out of sight, and with pure hearts and clean hands work earnestly to help those who are working in hard places, and who are worthy of help. This is the Christian service appointed us. And by doing it, we show to the world, which knows not the truth, the riches of God's goodness and mercy.

The great Teacher wants these men, who have been gaining an experience in their work, to continue to carry it forward under his guidance. They possess traits of character that will enable them, if they trust in God, to go forward with success.

The Lord sent them the message that propositions would be made to divide their working force, sending one to one place and one to another; but that unless providence indicated that some of their number were needed to take charge of schools in other important places, they were to keep their company united, and carry forward their work in complete harmony. Their force must not be weakened; their strength must be added to rather than diminished. They must stand together in unity, showing that nothing is so successful as success.

The words of criticism that have been spoken have at times had a very discouraging effect. But again and again in their necessity, the Lord sent them the word to go straight ahead, to follow their leader. I have been instructed to lift up the hands that hang down and to strengthen the feeble knees, to encourage the faithful laborers with words from the Lord.

In the most trying times they took their stand firmly determined to breast every difficulty, and to free Battle Creek College from debt; also, if it were possible, to move the school from Battle Creek. I had been instructed by the Lord that the College should not remain in Battle Creek, because in that place there are many influences that are a temptation both to teachers and students. Just before the General Conference, there seemed to be a favorable opportunity to sell the school buildings. But the word of the Lord came to me for the brethren. "You are in too great a hurry. Follow on as God shall open the way. He will guide you. Work up the Sale of Christ's Object Lessons. Interest the people in the work that you are trying to do. You will find that believers and unbelievers will help you."

During the General Conference, the way opened for the school to be moved from Battle Creek with the full approval of our people.

Cautions were given to Brother Magan and Brother Sutherland against carrying their teaching so far above the spiritual line of education to which the students had been accustomed. They were told that the people were not prepared at once to understand and act intelligently upon the advanced light in regard to the Bible in education. I was instructed that they must advance steadily and solidly, and that they must guard against going to extremes in any line and against expressing their ideas in language that would confuse minds. Plain, simple language, must be used. Instruction must be given line upon line, precept upon precept, here a little and there a little, leading the mind up slowly and intelligently. Every idea that they expressed must be clearly defined.

They were told that unless they heeded this instruction, their teaching would result in a harvest of fanciful believers, who would not make straight paths for their feet, and who would look upon themselves as far ahead of all other Christians. In their teaching of truth, they were not to go so far in advance that it would be impossible for their students to follow them. Christ said to his disciples, "I have many things to say unto you, but ye can not bear them now."

I thank the Lord that the brethren heeded the instruction given them, and that they carried forward His work in simplicity and meekness, and yet intelligently. The Lord is qualifying them to teach the lessons He has given in His word, by object lessons from nature. This is the grandest, the most helpful, all-round education that the youth can have. Cultivating the soil, planting and caring for trees, sowing seed and watching its growth,-- this work teaches precious lessons. Nature is an expositor of the word of the living God. But only through Christ does creation answer the highest purposes of the Creator. The Saviour has wonderful revelations for all who will walk humbly with God. Under the discipline and training of the higher teachings, they will behold wondrous things out of His law.

In establishing schools, enough land should be secured to give the students opportunity to gain a knowledge of agriculture. If it is necessary to curtail the expense anywhere, let it be on the buildings. There should be no failure to secure land; for from the cultivation of the soil, the students are to learn lessons illustrating the truths of the Word of God, truths that will help them to understand the work of the Creator.

Those who have charge of the school at Berrien Springs have been learners in the school of Christ, and He has been working with them, preparing them to be acceptable teachers. It is right that they carry on the work they have begun. If they will watch unto prayer, and plead earnestly with God to supply them with His grace, they will increase in wisdom and knowledge.

It has been a tremendous struggle for them to advance in the face of great financial embarrassment. They planned and contrived and devised in every way, with self-denial and self-sacrifice, to bring the school through, and to free it from its burden of debt. Now they begin to see that the way pointed out was the way of the Lord's leading. This is the lesson that the Lord desires many more to learn.

It is not the Lord's will that at this time, other men, whatever their age or experience, shall take the place of these brethren. It would not be pleasing to Him for us to set them aside by calling others to fill their places. He will continue to work out His will through them if they will walk humbly before him. The fear of the Lord is the beginning of wisdom. As they labor in humility, they will have the assurance that growth in grace is sown by increased ability to grasp the great truths of the gospel, and to teach these truths. When men place themselves in a position where they can work out God's purposes, He stands at their right hand, to open ways of advance for them.

Chapter 67—A Call to Service

A Call to Service God calls for workers. The cause needs men who are self-made, who, placing themselves in the hands of God, as humble learners have proved themselves workers together with Him. These are the men that are needed in the ministry and in the school work. Let those who have shown themselves to be men, move out and do what they can in the Master's service. Let them step into the ranks of the workers, and by patient, continuous effort prove their worth. It is in the water, not on the land, that we learn to swim. Let them fill with fidelity the place to which they are called, that they may be qualified for still higher responsibilities. God gives all opportunity to perfect themselves in His service.

He who puts on the armor to war a good warfare will gain greater and still greater ability as he strives to perfect his knowledge of God, working in harmony with the plan God has laid down for the perfect development of the physical, mental, and spiritual powers.

Young men and young women, gather a stock of knowledge. Do not wait until some human examination pronounces you competent to work, but go out into the highways and hedges, and begin to work for God. Use wisely the knowledge you have. Exercise your ability with faithfulness, generously imparting the light that God gives you. Study how best to give to others peace, and light and truth, and the many other rich blessings of heaven. Constantly improve. Keep reaching higher and still higher. It is the ability to put to the tax the powers of mind and body, ever keeping eternal realities in view, that is of value now. Seek the Lord most earnestly, that you may become more and more refined, more spiritually cultured. Then you will have the very best diploma that any one can have - the endorsement of God.

However large, however small, your talents, remember that what you have is yours only in trust. Thus God is testing and trying you, giving you opportunity to prove yourself true. To Him you are indebted for all your capabilities. To Him belong your powers of body, mind and soul, and for Him these powers are to be used. Your time, your influence, your capabilities, your skill all must be accounted for to Him who gives all. He uses his gifts best who seeks by earnest endeavor to carry out the Lord's great plan for the uplifting of humanity, remembering always that he must be a learner as well as a teacher.

As young men go out into this work, and in spite of many difficulties, make a success, let not propositions be made that they take up another work, and that the work they have started be given into the charge of men who are older and more experienced. This is not the way to encourage our young men. As they struggle with difficulties, they may make mistakes, but if they press forward perseveringly, their defeats will be turned into victories.

My fellow-workers, persevere in the work that you have begun. Keep at it until you gain victory after victory, remembering that only by succeeding can you demonstrate the genuineness of your success. Educate yourself for a purpose. Keep in view the highest standard, that you may accomplish greater and still greater good, thus reflecting the glory to God.

Ellen G. White.

Chapter 68—The School of the Home

Talk, by Mrs. E. G. White, in the St. Helena (Cal.) Sanitarium Chapel, 6 a.m., July 14, 1902.

I promised that I would speak this morning in regard to the necessity of withdrawing our children from the public schools and of providing suitable places where they can be educated right. I have felt surprised at the apparently indifferent attitude of some, notwithstanding the oft-repeated warnings given the parents must provide for their families not merely with reference to their present interests, but especially with reference to their future, eternal interests. The characters that we form in this life are to decide our destiny. If we choose, we may live a life that measures with the life of God.

Every Christian family is a church in itself. The members of the family are to be Christ-like in every action. The father is to sustain so a close relation to God that he realizes his duty to make provision for the members of his family to receive an education and training that will fit them for the future, immortal life. His children are to be taught the principles of heaven. He is the priest of the household, accountable to God for the influence that he exerts over every member of his family. He is to place his family under the most favorable circumstances possible, so that they shall not be tempted to conform to the habits and customs, the evil practices and lax principles, that they would find in the world.

Setting a right example in the home, parents are able to exert a good influence in the church. They will not carry into the church the hasty spirit that causes dissension, making it almost impossible for two members to agree, unless the one come to the other's ideas and ways. Church-members should remember that no two leaves on a tree are exactly alike. They should recognize the fact that while as brethren and sisters in Christ Jesus they are connected with one another and with Christ as the leaves of a tree are connected with its branches and trunk, yet they are not all cut after the same pattern. Every parent has an individuality, a personality, of his own. He has just as much right to his personal independence as any ruler has; for he is to rule his own household in the fear of God. Into the home there must be brought the heavenly rule. This will fit us for church relationship as laborers together with God, and will make us examples to the world.

The Lord desires us to understand that we must place our children in right relation to the world, the church, and the family. Their relation to the family is the first point to be considered. Let us teach them to be polite to one another, and polite to God; "What do you mean," you may inquire, "by saying that we should teach them to be polite to God?" I mean that they are to be taught to reverence our heavenly Father, and to appreciate the great and infinite sacrifice that Christ has made in our behalf. Christ placed himself at the head of humanity, in order that he might exemplify what humanity could be in connection with divinity. Teach them that together, as children and parents, it is your privilege to be members of the church of God - living stones in His beautiful temple. Parents and children are to sustain so close a relation to God that the heavenly angels can communicate with them. These messengers are shut out from many a home where iniquity and impoliteness to God abound. Let us catch from His Word the spirit of heaven, and bring it into our life here below.

Some may say, "If we believe the Bible, why does not the Lord work miracles for us?" He will, if we will let Him. When a human mind is allowed to come under the control of God, that mind will reveal the miracle-working power of God; the power of the mind in action is like the miracle-working power of God.

In our prayers we are to hold on by faith to the children in our home; and we are to do faithfully the duties that belong to us. From the light that God has given me, I know that the husband and the wife are to be, in the home, minister, physician, nurse, and teacher, binding their children to themselves and to God, training them to avoid every habit that will in any way militate against God's work in the body, and teaching them to care for every part of the living organism. Parents are under a most solemn responsibility to keep themselves in physical soundness and in spiritual health, that the light of heaven may shine into the chambers of the mind and illuminate the soul-temple. Such parents are able to give their children instruction from babyhood as to what God wants them to do. Taking His Word as their counsellor, they bring them up in the nurture and admonition of the Lord.

Many parents allow their children to drift, as it were, hither and thither. But this is not right. Parents are held accountable to God for the salvation of their children. They are also held accountable for their physical health. In every way possible they should help them to grow up with a sound constitution. They should teach them not to indulge appetite or to imperil their physical and mental capabilities by wrong habits; for God desires to use all their powers.

Every word spoken by fathers and mothers has its influence over the children, for good or for evil. If the parents speak passionately, if they show the spirit shown by the children of this world, God counts them as the children of this world, not as His sons and daughters.

Parents, from the moment that we are born again into the kingdom of heaven, we are in God's service. Our lives are to be such that He can approve. The principles of heaven are to be brought into the government of the home. Every child is to be taught to be polite, compassionate, loving, pitiful, courteous, tender-hearted. Peter speaks of these characteristics of a Christian, and also instructs us how to rid ourselves of all evil by living on the plan of addition. "Giving all diligence," he says, "Add to your faith virtue, and to virtue knowledge, and to knowledge temperance, and to temperance patience, and to patience godliness, and to godliness brotherly kindness, and to brotherly kindness charity (love)."

We want the knowledge of our Saviour. It is not best for every one of us to begin to teach our children to be polite in the home and polite to God? Is not this the work that as "laborers together with God" it is our bounden duty to do?

From the light that God has given me for years, I know that the households of His people are in great need of purification. The end is nearer than when we first believed. As fathers and mothers, we are to purify ourselves, even as Christ is pure; that is, we are to be perfect in our sphere, even as God is perfect in His sphere. Instead of backsliding, we should now be informed to the will of heaven, the heavenliness of heaven. Let us put away the spirit of murmuring and complaining, remembering that by cherishing such a spirit we are disrespectful to God. We are living in his dwelling-place; we are members of His family - His by creation and by redemption. Every one is to cherish feelings of respect and tenderness for those with who he associates. In our relations with one another we should be careful never to mar and scar the life and the spirit of others. When in life and character we show the miracle-working power of God, the world will take knowledge of us, that we have been with Jesus and learned of Him.

I feel burdened over these matters. Last night I could not sleep past two o'clock. Early this morning I have been writing on this subject, trying to present it so that it shall be understood. We are not to feel that we have reached perfection. We need to be melted over, that we may be purified from all dross. We are in need of the rich blessings that Heaven is so ready to bestow, the blessings promised to every believer.

The Lord withholds from us no good thing. He declares, "Ask what ye will, and it shall be done unto you." He does not tell us to restrict our asking to certain things, but assures us that He will bless us according to the riches of His grace. He is more willing to give the Holy Spirit to those who ask Him, than parents are to give good gifts to their children. To show His willingness, He refers to the tender relationship that a father sustains to his son. "What man is there of you," He says, "whom if His son ask bread, will he give him a stone? or if he ask a fish, will he give him a serpent? If ye then, being evil, know how to give good gifts unto your children, how much more shall your Father which is in heaven give good gifts to them that ask him?"

Parents can learn this lesson in all its significance. Children who ask for something that is not for their best good are not to be rebuffed, but kindly told, "That would not be for your good. You can not have it, because it would injure you. But although we can not give it to you, we will try in every way possible to make you happy."

The father should always feel kindly disposed toward his children. How sad it is that the father's disposition is not always that which it should be! The father of boys is to come in to close connection with his sons, giving them the benefit of his larger experience, and talking with them in such simplicity and tenderness that he binds them to his heart. He is to let them see that he has their best interest, their happiness, in view all the time.

Parents, let us constantly keep before our children the relation that we sustain to our heavenly Father. Let us tell them that we are His children, and that we desire to treat them as He treats us. He does not indulge us in injurious things. He gives us only the things that are for our best good. He says, "Ask, and it shall be given you; seek, and ye shall find; knock, and it shall be opened unto you: for every one that asketh receiveth; and he that seeketh findeth; and to him that knocketh it shall be opened."

We are all amenable to God. When we take into consideration our accountability to Him for every action, when we remember that we are "a spectacle unto the world, and to angels, and to men", we will desire to be purged from our fretfulness and harshness, our lack of sympathy and tenderness for one another. These evils are as tares amid the wheat, and must be destroyed.

Children to be Shielded from Contaminating Influences

Upon fathers and mothers devolves the responsibility of giving a Christian education to the children entrusted to them. They are never to neglect their children. In no case are they to let any line of business so absorb mind and time and talents that their children, who should be led into harmony with God, are allowed to drift until they are separated far from Him. They are not to allow their children to slip out of their grasp into the hands of unbelievers. They are to do all in their power to keep them from imbibing the spirit of the world. They are to train them to become helpers together with God. They are God's human hand, fitting themselves and their children for an endless life in the heavenly home.

The education of our children begins in the home. The mother is their first teacher. When they become old enough to attend school, shall we permit them to enter the public school?

Many years ago, in Oakland, my husband and I conversed with a public-school teacher in regard to the public schools in the city. He said to us: If parents knew of the iniquity that is to our certain knowledge practised in these schools, there would be a furor raised in regard to these schools such as neither you nor I can imagine. The young people are rotten; and what kind of homes they have is more than our teachers can tell."

This statement was made over twenty years ago. Have the conditions in our public schools improved since that time?

Some fathers and mothers are so indifferent, so careless, that they think it makes no difference whether their children attend a church school or a public school. "We are in the world" they say, "and we can not get out of it." But, parents, we can get a good way out of the world, if we choose to do so, we can avoid seeing many of the evils that are multiplying so fast in these last day. We can avoid hearing about much of the wickedness and crime that exist.

Everything that can be done should be done to place ourselves and our children where we shall not see the iniquity that is practiced in the world. We should carefully guard the sight of our eyes and the hearing of our ears, so that these awful things shall not enter our minds. When the daily newspaper comes into the house, I feel as if I wanted to hide it, that the ridiculous, sensational things in it may not be seen. It seems as if the enemy is at the foundation of the publishing of many things that appear in the newspapers. Every sinful thing that can be found is uncovered and laid bare before the world.

The line of demarcation between those who serve God and those who serve him not, is ever to remain distinct. The difference between believers and unbelievers should be as great as the difference between light and darkness. When God's people take the position that they are the temple of the Holy Ghost, Christ Himself abiding within, they will so clearly reveal Him in spirit, words, and actions, that there will be an unmistakable distinction between them and Satan's followers.

Some may inquire, "If we are to remain a distinct people, why do we have sanitariums to which we invite every one?" I answer, In bringing men and women of other denominations into our institutions, do we tell them that we are undenominational? If we do, we deny God's law. We are denominational; but we open the doors wide and seek to have all come in who possibly can come. "Let your light so shine before men," the Saviour said, "that they may see your good works, and glorify your Father which is in heaven." We are to seek to restore to physical health the diseased and the suffering. Many men and women have been improperly educated in habits of living. Many children are sick because they have never been taught the laws of the human mechanism - the mechanism that let David to exclaim, "I am fearfully and wonderfully made!"

A Lesson from Israel

While the judgments of God were falling upon the land of Egypt, the Lord directed the Israelites not only to keep their children within their houses, but to bring in even their cattle from the fields. Before the first-born were slain, the Lord, through Moses, said to His people; "Draw out and take you a lamb according to your families, and kill the passover. And ye shall take a bunch of hyssop, and dip it in the blood that is in the basin, and strike the lintel and the two side-posts with the blood that is in the basin; and none of you shall go out at the door of this house until the morning. For the Lord will pass through to smite the Egyptians; and when He seeth the blood upon the lintel, and on the two side-posts, the Lord will pass over the door, and will not suffer the destroyer to come in unto your houses to smite you."

As the Israelites kept their children within their houses during the time when the judgments of God were in the land of Egypt, so in this time of peril we are to keep our children separate and distinct from the world. We are to teach them that the commandments of God mean much more than we realize. Those who keep them will not imitate the practises of the transgressors of God's law.

Parents must regard God's Word with respect, obeying its teachings. To the parents in this day, as well as to the Israelites, God declares: "These words....shall be in thine heart: and thou shalt teach them diligently unto thy children, and shalt talk of them when thou sittest in thine house, and when thou risest up. And thou shalt bind them for a sign upon thine hand, and they shall be as frontlets between thine eyes. And thou shalt write them upon the posts of thy house, and on thy gates.

Notwithstanding this plain instruction, some of God's people permit their children to attend the public schools, where they mingle with those who are corrupt in morals. In these schools their children can neither study the Bible nor learn its principles. Christian parents, you must make provision for your children to be educated in Bible principles. And do not rest satisfied merely with having them study the Word in the church school. Teach the Scriptures to your children yourselves when you sit down, when you go out, when you come in, and when you walk by the way. Walk with your children much oftener than you do. Talk with them. Set their minds running in a right channel. As you do this, you will find that the light and glory of God will come into your homes. But how can you expect His blessing when you do not teach your children aright?

I am merely touching upon a few points on a number of subjects relating to the training and education of children. Sometime I hope to treat upon these points more fully; for I have been thoroughly aroused to realize that these matters must be presented before our people. Seventh-day Adventists must move in a way altogether different from the way in which they have been moving, if they expect the approval of God to rest upon them in their homes.

Every faithful parent will hear from the lips of the Master the words, "Well done, good and faithful servant. . . enter thou into the joy of the Lord." May the Lord help us to be good and faithful servants in our dealings with one another. He tells us to "consider one another to provoke unto love and to good works," helping and strengthening one another.

The Need of a Church School at Crystal Springs

We are almost home. We are standing on the borders of the eternal world. Those who prove worthy will soon be introduced into the kingdom of God. We have no time to lose. We should establish the work in right lines here at Crystal Springs. Here are our children. Shall we allow them to be contaminated by the world, by its iniquity, its disregard of God's commandments? I ask those who are planning to send their children to the public school, where they are liable to be contaminated, How can you take such a risk?

We desire to erect a church school building for our children. Because of the many calls made for means, it seems a difficult matter to secure sufficient money or to arouse an interest great enough to build a small, convenient schoolhouse. I have told the school committee that I will lease them some land for as long a time as they care to use if for school purposes. I hope that interest enough will be aroused to enable us to erect a building where our children can be taught the Word of God, which is the life-blood and the flesh of the Son of God. "Whoso eateth my flesh" He declares, "and drinketh My blood, hath eternal life. . . It is the Spirit that quickeneth; the flesh profiteth nothing: the words that I speak unto you, they are spirit, and they are life." We are to eat and drink the Word of life, carrying out its instruction much more closely than we have ever done before.

Will you not take an interest in the erection of this school building in which the Word of God is to be taught? One man, when asked how much he was willing to give to the school in labor, said that if we would give him three dollars a day and his board and lodging, he would help us. But we do not want offers of this kind. Help will come to us. We expect to have a school building, in which the Bible can be taught, in which prayers can be offered to God, and in which the children can be instructed in Bible principles. We expect that every one who can take hold with us will want to have a share in erecting this building. We expect to train a little army of workers on this hillside.

We know that all are interested in the success of this enterprise. Let those who have spare time, give a few days in helping to build this schoolhouse. Not enough money has been subscribed yet to pay merely for the necessary material. We are glad for what has been given, and we now ask every one to take hold of this matter interestedly, so that we shall soon have a place where our children can study the Bible, which is the foundations of all true education. The fear of the Lord - the very first lesson to be taught - is the beginning of wisdom.

There is no reason why this matter should drag. Let every one take hold to help, persevering with unflagging interest until the building is completed. Let every one do something. Some may have to get up as early as four o'clock in the morning, in order to help. Usually I begin my work before that time. As soon as it is daylight, some could begin work on the building, putting in an hour or two before breakfast. Others could not do this, perhaps, but all can do something to show their interest in making it possible for the children to be educated in a school where they can be disciplined and trained for God's service. His blessing will surely rest upon every such effort.

When we built our meetinghouse in Cooranbong, Sister McEnterfer and I went through the district where the carpenters lived, asking them how much they would charge to work for us by the day. Many of them promised to work for much less than the ordinary wage. A few promised to give some time; others with families to support, being too poor to work for nothing, offered to work for six shillings - a dollar and a half - a day. The meeting-house was built, and stands today as a monument for God, a miracle wrought by his power. Many of the believers had just begun to keep the Sabbath. Some of them were very poor, and at first we had to help them. Now they are all self-supporting. They keep up the church expenses, and pay a faithful tithe. This is the way we worked to build our meeting-houses in many places in Australia.

Brethren, and sisters, what will you do to help to build a church school? We believe that every one will regard it as a privilege and a blessing to have this school building. Let us catch the spirit of the work, saying, We will arise and build. If all will take hold of the work unitedly, we shall soon have a schoolhouse in which from day to day our children will be taught the way of the Lord. As we do our best, the blessing of God will rest upon us. Shall we not arise and build?

Ellen G. White.

Chapter 69—Consolidation and Control

Elmshaven, Sanitarium, Cal., September 2, 1902.

Day by day I am impressed by the Holy Spirit that the very last messages of warning are now to be given to our people.

There is much to be said in regard to establishing what I shall designate as small sanitariums. In no place should a mammoth sanitarium be built up; for a great work is to be done in many places. In planning for new sanitariums, our brethren should reason soundly and solidly, and restrain the desire to surprise the world by building up something large in one or two places.

In all our great cities there will be a binding up in bundles by the confederacies and unions formed. Men will rule other men and demand much of them. The lives of those who refuse to unite with these unions, will be in peril. Everything is being prepared for the last great work to be done by the One mighty to save and mighty to destroy.

Some who have had great light have had an almost uncontrollable desire to bind all our medical institutions under the supervision of one power. I am instructed to say that this desire is prompted by the same spirit that in the world manifests itself in the efforts of the unions to become a controlling power. The work that God has given His people to do is to bind up the testimony and to seal the law among His disciples.

In all our sanitariums there is much, very much, that needs to be reformed. Justice, mercy, and the love of God are to prevail. The work in our sanitariums has been carried on more or less according to circumstances. Let none say, "You must bind yourselves by specified agreements to do thus and so, or else you can not be endorsed by us." The signing of such agreements must cease. The day for work of this kind is past. It has already wrought much mischief. The Lord is our Guide and our Ruler. Let us bind ourselves up with Him. God does not desire men to be under binding agreements; for He is to move in His own way. Every yoke is now to be broken. The truth as it is in Jesus is of sufficient binding force to hold every mind, control every impulse, and direct every movement. Those whom God would control if they would submit to Him, but who do not choose to walk humbly with Him, are not to make terms for others. Let every man look to God, not to men. The Lord God of heaven rules.

These words I have been instructed to write out plainly. The condition of things before the flood has been presented to me. The same binding up in unions that exists today existed in Noah's day. But never before have such transactions taken place as are now carried on in the selection of officers to govern the people. Those who occupy the highest positions in governments reveal how little confidence God can place in their rulership.

This is a wonderful age in which we are living. God is beholding the deplorable state of society. He requires those who believe His gospel to come out from the world. "Be ye separate, saith the Lord, and touch not the unclean thing."

Human, kingly power among God's people in any branch of His cause, is represented by the documents prepared for men to sign, is not ordained of God. Let those who believe the Bible study the principles that are to govern them in dealing with human minds. God is not the author of confusion, but of peace. The selfishness that exalts one man to rule the minds of his fellow men is not inspired of God; for the Lord works in and through those who will be worked by Him, and who in every line of Christian service will act in accordance with divine enlightenment.

God is the author of all that is good. He blesses the children of men with prosperity, and gives abundantly to them by causing the earth to yield her treasures. But what does He behold among the few educated and trained men of talent? - Not many are working after the divine order. Yielding to temptation, they rule the markets and control the merchandise in accordance with Satan's principles. They have the money which belong to the people, the money which would give them a fair chance. God's poor are left to suffer and perish, while man's cupidity grasps every advantage.

Chapter 70—September 3

Last night I slept well. I know the Lord is hearing my prayers. I desire to draw nigh to Him; for the Word declares, "Draw nigh to God, and He will draw nigh to you." This promise I value. I have proved it.

I am instructed to call attention to some matters. There has been need of reforms in regard to the way in which the workers in our sanitariums, the men and women who bear wearing burdens in caring for the sick, are dealt with. This is an especially delicate question. Those who stand as educators need to be close students themselves of the lessons of the greatest Medical Missionary that ever walked and worked in our world, lest they lose their connection with God and bind themselves as a supreme whole.

It is not the empty cup that we have trouble in carrying; it is the cup full to the brim that must be carefully balanced. Affliction and adversity may cause much inconvenience and may bring great depression; but it is prosperity that is dangerous to spiritual life. Unless the human subject is in constant submission to the will of God, unless he is sanctified by the truth and has the faith that works by love and purifies the soul, prosperity will surely arouse the natural inclination to presumption.

Often prayers are solicited for the believing souls in adversity and sickness. But those who are suffering reverses are represented by the bush, which, though burning, was not consumed. As Moses was keeping the flock of Jethro in the land of Midian, "The angel of the Lord appeared unto him in a flame of fire out of the midst of a bush, and he looked, and, behold, the bush burned with fire, and the bush was not consumed." Moses draws near to see a strange thing. The fire in the bush does not consume the bush. He learns that the Lord is in the midst of the bush. So it is in life. It is not deprivation and affliction that is to be most dreaded; for the Lord is in it all, helping and sustaining. Our prayers need most to be offered for the men in high places. They need the prayers of the whole church, because they are entrusted with prosperity and influence.

In the valley of humiliation, where men depend on God to teach them and to guide their every step, there is comparative safety. But let every one who has a living connection with God pray for the men in positions of responsibility - those who are standing on a lofty pinnacle and who, because of their exalted position, are supposed to have much wisdom. Unless such men feel their need of an Arm stronger than the arm of flesh to lean upon, unless they make God their dependence, their view of things will come distorted, and they will fall.

The Lord has instructed me to urge every one to realize that man is human. The church of Christ is in need of close communion with the Lord Jesus. Those who feel most their dependence upon God are usually those who have the least amount of earthly treasure on which to depend.

Of all the trees, the Scotch fir-tree is one of the best from which Christians may draw inspiring lessons. The Scotch fir requires less soil for its roots than any other tree. In a dry soil and amidst barren rocks it finds sufficient nourishment to keep it as green in the winter as in the summer. With the least amount of earth about its roots, it towers above all the other trees of the wood, reaching the highest toward heaven. It would be well for us to plant and cultivate the Scotch fir; for this tree is an object lesson, bring to the minds of all what a Christian should be.

I would that I could present the meaning of this symbol as it has been presented me. The church members who are standing in their lot and place are trees of righteous, the planting of the Lord. Although their surrounding circumstances may be adverse, yet, like the fir-tree with little soil about its roots, they constantly reach heavenward, drawing nourishment from above. Like the fragrant boughs of the fir-tree, they impart grace for grace received. The hidden nourishment that comes from God is returned to Him in purest service.

Every soul in this world is bought with a price. To every man is given his work. "Ministers," this term includes all who do their appointed work, giving God honest service. No one is to apologize for recognizing his personal accountability to God by standing in his lot and in his place. God calls for every man's best energies. No man can find in any human being the strength that will enable him to serve God with all his powers. He must be a partaker of the divine nature. There is now a great work to be done in a short time, and it is essential for the men and women in God's service to look unto Jesus every moment. Brethren and sisters, break every yoke that man would fasten upon you. Take upon you the yoke of Christ. Learn of him who is meek and lowly in heart.

There are but two classes in the world demanding of us our deepest interest and consideration in connection with the medical missionary work that Christ in His life has taught us to do - those are sinners, in need of a Saviour, yet not realizing their need, and those who in every line of God's service are reaching forward. Whatever their rank, their capabilities, their entrusted talents, this latter class are "laborers together with God." Regenerated by the grace of Christ, they are God's faithful workers, by their influence regenerating others through the grace given them.

When this is duly appreciated, there will be no attempt to exercise authority. God's workers will be at unity in love, and will not bind themselves up in confederacies by contracts. I am instructed to say, Shun the signing of contracts that have been originated because of a failure to understand the meaning of true sanctification.

Chapter 71—The Influence of Diet on Council-Meetings

From "Pacific Recorder". Oct. 9, 1902.

Before our brethren come together in council or board meetings, each one should present himself before God, carefully searching the heart and critically examining the motives. Pray that the Lord may reveal self to you, so that you may not unwisely criticize or condemn propositions.

At bountiful tables men often eat much more than can be easily digested. The overburdened stomach can not do its work properly. The result is a disagreeable feeling of dullness in the brain. The mind does not act quickly. And when several kinds of food are eaten at the same meal, indigestion is often the result. Some foods do not agree with other foods. A disturbance is created by improper combinations of food, fermentation sets in, the blood is contaminated, and the brain is confused.

The habit of overeating, or of eating too many kinds of food at one meal, is frequently the cause of dyspepsia. Serious injury is done to the delicate digestive organs. In vain the stomach protests and appeals to the brain to reason from cause to effect. The excessive amount of food eaten, or the improper combination, does its injurious work. In vain do disagreeable premonitions give warning. Suffering is the consequence. Disease takes the places of health.

Some may ask, What has this to do with board meetings? - Very much. The effects of wrong eating are brought into Council and board meetings? The brain is affected by the condition of the stomach. A disordered stomach is productive of a disordered, uncertain state of mind. A diseased stomach produces a diseased condition of the brain, and often makes a man obstinate in maintaining erroneous opinions. The supposed wisdom of such a man is foolishness with God.

I present this state of affairs as the cause of the situation in many councils and board meetings, where questions demanding careful study are given but little consideration, and decisions of the greatest importance are hurriedly made. Often when there should have been unanimity of sentiment in the affirmative, decided negatives have entirely changed the atmosphere pervading a meeting. These results have been presented to me again and again.

I present these matters now, because I am instructed to say to my brethren in the gospel ministry; By intemperance in eating you disqualify yourselves for seeing clearly the difference between the sacred and common fire. And by this intemperance you also reveal your disregard for all the warnings that the Lord has given you. His word to you is: "Who is among you that feareth the Lord, that obeyeth the voice of His servant, that walketh in darkness, and hath no light? let him trust in the name of the Lord, and stay upon His God. Behold, all ye that kindle a fire, that compass yourselves about with sparks; walk in the light of your fire, and in the sparks that ye have kindled. This shall ye have of mine hand; ye shall lie down in sorrow."

Shall we not draw near to the Lord, that He may save us from all intemperance in eating and drinking, all unholy, lustful passions, all wickedness? Shall we not humble ourselves before God, putting away everything that corrupts the flesh and the spirit, that in the fear of the Lord we may perfect holiness of character?

"Whether therefore ye eat, or drink or whatsoever ye do, do all to the glory of God." All are now being tested and proved. Many to whom precious light has been given desire to return to the flesh-pots of Egypt. Many who are supported by the tithe from God's storehouse are by self-indulgence poisoning the life-giving current flowing through their veins. Disregarding the light and the warnings that God has given during the past twenty-five or thirty years, some continue to gratify their desire for flesh-meat.

We are not to make the use of flesh-meat a test. But we may and should consider the influence that professed believers who use flesh-meat have over other churches. Those who use flesh-meat disregard all the warnings that God has given concerning this question. They have no evidence that they are walking in safe paths. They have not the slightest excuse for eating the flesh of dead animals. God's curse is resting upon the animal creation. Many times when meat is eaten it decays in the stomach, and creates disease. Cancers, tumors, and pulmonary diseases are largely caused by meat-eating.

As God's messengers shall we not bear a decided testimony against the indulgence of perverted appetite? Will those who claim to be ministers of the gospel, proclaiming the most solemn truth ever given to mortals, make the stomach a cesspool? God has provided an abundance of fruits and grains, which may be healthfully prepared and used in proper quantities. Why, then, do men continue to choose flesh-meats? Can we possibly have confidence in ministers who at tables where flesh is served join with others in eating it?

The parents who know the truth in regard to the indulgences of appetite should not permit their children to eat to excess, or to eat flesh-meat or other foods that excite the passions. Man is built up from what he eats. The use of flesh-meat strengthens the lower propensities, and excites them to increased activity. Parents should discard everything that endangers the moral and physical health of their children. They should not place flesh-meat on the table. And if they allow their children to eat meat freely, use butter and eggs, disease in some form will surely result, impairing the health of mind and body. Thus spirituality is weakened and often destroyed.

Fathers and mothers, watch unto prayer. Guard strictly against intemperance in every form. Teach your child the principles of true health reform. Already the wrath of God has begun to be visited on the children of disobedience. What crimes, what sins, what iniquitous practices are now being revealed on every hand! As a people we are to exercise great care in guarding our children against depraved associates.

If we could know what abominable iniquities are practised by the members of many families who claim to be Christians, we should be more deeply concerned in regard to the spiritual atmosphere surrounding our children, not only in the public schools - even in Seventh-day Adventist church schools. If the children of Sabbath-keepers are not carefully instructed line upon line, precept upon precept; if they are not kept from associating with corrupt children, they are in danger of being corrupted.

In order to be purified and to remain pure, Seventh-day Adventists must have the Holy Spirit in their hearts and in their homes. The Lord has given me light that when the Israel of today humble themselves before Him, and cleanse the soul-temple from all defilement, He will hear their prayers in behalf of the sick, and will bless in the use of His remedies for disease. When in faith the human agent does all that he can to combat disease, using the simple methods of treatment that God has provided, his efforts will be effectual. "The heavens are Thine, the earth also is Thine," and they that dwell therein."

If, after so much light has been given, God's people still cherish wrong habits, indulging in self and refusing to reform, they will suffer the sure consequence of transgression. If they are determined to gratify perverted appetite at any cost, God will not work miracle after miracle to save them. They shall lie down in sorrow.

"My brethren, be not many masters, knowing that we shall receive the greater condemnation. For in many things we offend all. If any man offend not in word, the same is a perfect man, and able also to bridle the whole body. Behold, we put bits in the horses's mouths, that they may obey us; and we turn about their whole body. Behold also the ships, which though they be so great, are driven of fierce winds, yet are they turned about with a very small helm, whithersoever the governor listeth. Even so the tongue is a little member, and boasteth great things. Behold, how great a matter a little fire kindleth! And the tongue is a fire, a world of iniquity; so is the tongue among our members, that it defileth the whole body, and setteth on fire the course of nature; and it is set on fire of hell. For every kind of beasts, and of birds, and of serpents, and of things in the sea, is tamed; and hath been tamed of mankind; but the tongue can no man tame;

it is an unruly evil, full of deadly poison. Therewith bless we God, even the Father; and therewith curse we men, which are made after the similitude of God. Out of the same mouth proceedeth blessing and cursing. My brethren, these things ought not so to be."

"Ye shall diligently keep the commandments of the Lord your God! Every one who transgresses the laws of health will surely be visited with God's displeasure. Oh, how much of the Holy Spirit we might have day by day, if we would walk circumspectly, denying self, and practicing the virtues of Christ's character!

"And now, Israel, what doth the Lord thy God require of thee, but to fear the Lord thy God, to walk in all His ways, and to love Him, and serve the Lord thy God with all thy heart and with all thy would, to keep the commandments of the Lord, and His, statutes, which I command thee this day for thy good."

Ellen G. White.

Chapter 72—Establishing Schools in the South

November 16, 1902.

I am glad that "Christ's Object Lessons" has been a help to the work in the Southern Field. Let its sale go forward, that there may be money for the establishment of schools in this field. I can call upon the officers of the Southern Union Conference and of the Southern Missionary Society to be quick and earnest to take advantage of the present opportunities offered in the gift of "Christ's Object Lessons" to the educational work.

Small schools for the colored people should be established in many places in the South. Let the proceeds from the sale of "Christ's Object Lessons" in the Southern field be used for this purpose also. Let this means act its part also in defraying the expenses of the schools already established. The children are to be taught something more than merely how to read. Industrial lines of work are to be carried forward. The children and youth are to be provided with facilities for learning trades that will enable them to support themselves.

This work will require talent, and above everything else, the grace of God. The colored youth will be far more difficult to manage than the white youth, because they have not been taught from their childhood to make the best use of their time. There are very many of them who have had no opportunity to learn how to take care of themselves. Those who for years have been working to help the colored people, know their needs; and they are best fitted to start schools for them.

As far as possible, these schools should be established outside of the cities. But in the cities there are many children who could not attend school away from the cities; and for the benefit of these, schools should be started in the cities as well as outside the cities.

My brethren and sisters in the South, move forward in earnest with the work of selling "Christ's Object Lessons", that means may be furnished for the establishment of schools. No line of work will be of such telling advantage to the Southern field as the establishment of schools. Let our people in the South wake up to the importance of this matter. There has been too much hovering over the churches, and too little aggressive work done.

A school should be established near Nashville. If every way of advance for the work in Nashville is closed up, will God be glorified? Has not enough of this been done in the past? Shall we have a second edition of what has been? Let the work of selling "Christ's

Object Lessons" be taken up in this city. Endeavor to interest the merchants in what you are trying to do. Tell them that the proceeds from the sale of the book you are selling are used for missionary purposes. Go to the large schools in and near Nashville, and tell the teachers about the work you are trying to do. Tell them that the book you are selling contains truth that they need in their schools.

By these efforts two objects will be gained, - the truth will be brought before those who need to hear it, and means will raised for the establishment of schools.

We are not to hold ourselves apart from these institutions of learning. There are those who are specially fitted to work for the teachers in these schools. Let such ones visit these schools, and speak words of commendation regarding that which is being done for the colored race. Let them watch for opportunities to introduce our literature, and to tell of the work that you are trying to do. And let them not forget the instruction that Christ gave His disciples when He sent them forth: "Be ye wise as serpents and harmless as doves."

To my brethren and sisters in the churches throughout America, I would say: I feel very thankful to my heavenly Father for the interest you have taken in the sale of "Christ's Object Lessons". This book contains precious truth. It shows how Christ used the objects of nature to illustrate immortal truth."

Will you not, from now till the close of the year, make a special effort to sell "Christ's Object Lessons"? Study the instruction contained in this book. This will help you to live the truths that it contains. Then take it to your friends and neighbors, and in a humble, gentle manner tell them of the object for which the book is being sold, and ask them to buy a copy. Believe that you will not be repulsed. Let the love that fills the heart be expressed in the countenance. If the grace of Christ is cherished in your heart, it will shine forth. Commit sentences of the book to memory, and repeat them as opportunity offers.

In taking up this work, you will be doing good service for the Master. You will sow seeds that will spring up and bear fruit to the glory of God. As you go forward in the work, you will gain an experience that will enable you to sell our larger books, and the Lord will bless you. The larger books, indited by the Lord, and full of precious instruction, should be sold, and can be sold, The Lord will open the way for the people to receive the precious light that these books contain.

As you go out to sell "Christ's Object Lessons", will you not take the prospectuses for "Desire of Ages" and "Great Controversy", and call the attention of the people to them? Many of these books are lying on the shelves of our publishing houses in America. The

Lord desires the people to have the light that they contain. In canvassing for these books, you will take light to the people, and you will help me to produce other books. I greatly desire that these books shall be circulated; for they contain knowledge given me by the Lord for the people. Let this work be carried forward zealously.

"Christ's Object Lessons" was given as much for the advancement of the educational work in the South as for any other part of the world. My brethren and sisters, do you not want to help the work in the South by selling this book? Let all do what they can to help the work now in need of help in the Southern field. Schools are needed there. The small schools that have been established for the colored people are in need of help. Let every one bring to the treasury something that will place the schools on vantage-ground.

My soul longs to see the work built up in the South that the Lord has outlined. The great necessities for schools in the cities and out of the cities demand that we do everything that we possibly can. This barren field is sending up to heaven its pitiful appeal for help. Where can you find a field where the need is so great?

The Lord has designated Nashville as the center for the present. The interests there are to be built up until they stand as memorials of His truth. The workers in the publishing house at Nashville must submit to the divine will. Then their hearts will be melted and subdued. Then will they be filled with invincible faith. They will press together and will work for one another's interests.

This world is a training school for the higher school, this life a preparation for the life to come. Here we are to be prepared for entrance into the courts above, where no sin can ever come. Here the truth is to be received and believed and practised, until we are made ready for a home with the saints in light.

True religion is an imitation of Christ. The true Christian is a follower of Christ. Following implies obedience. No soldier can follow his commander without obeying his orders. Our leader says to us, "Follow me."

The best citizens of this great republic are those who have learned the lessons that Christ came to teach, those who love and to obey the higher law that God has written in His Word. Abiding in Christ, their example is a power in favor of the truth. Let every Christian show his high birth by his circumspect conversation and modest bearing. Let God's workers be witnesses for Him, in every word and act testifying that they are citizens of heaven. Let not one careless word or unkind action mar their work for God. As high as the heavens are above the earth, should the ways and work of the Christian be above the ways and works of the worldling.

Keep the truth of God in your hearts. Let the law of kindness be ever on your lips. Thus you do true missionary work. By a holy and consistent life, honor and glorify God. Pray much, and watch unto prayer. God will bless all who walk carefully before Him.

I leave these words with you. I urge you to do your utmost for the good work before you. Let the means from the sale of "Christ's Object Lessons" be used to carry forward the school work in that field.

I am instructed by the great teacher to say to those in the Southern field who are now passing through trial: Watch and pray and believe. Do your best. The present discouraging aspect will change when you change in word and spirit and action, becoming one with Christ. Try it. Then with joy you will bear witness that Christ's yoke is easy and His burden light.

Ellen G. White.

Chapter 73—Instruction in Regard to Sanitariums

From MC. 115, 1903 (P).

Regarding Long Courses of Study

Questions have arisen in regard to the management of sanitariums, and in regard to the plans to be followed in the education of physicians and nurses. We are asked whether few or many should take a five years' course.

All are to be left perfectly free to follow the dictates of an enlightened conscience. There are those who with a few months' instruction would be prepared to go out and do acceptable medical missionary work. Some can not feel that it is their duty to give years to one line of study. ...

Practical Instruction to be Given

Great care should be exercised in the training of young people for the medical missionary work; for the mind is molded by that which it receives and retains. To much incomplete work has been done in the education given. The most useful education is that found in practical work.

Our institutions are not to be so overgrown that the most important points in education do not receive the proper consideration. Instruction should be given in medical missionary work. The teaching given in medical lines should be blended with a study of the Bible. And the physical training should not be neglected.

Great care should be exercised in regard to the influences that prevail in the institution. The influences under which the nurses are placed will mold their character for eternity. ...

The youth in their waywardness and inexperience need to associate with teachers who feel an intense interest in the work of educating and training the members of the Lord's family. The teachers are to have no favorites among their students. They are not to give the most attention to the bright, quick students.

First impressions are not to be trusted. It is those who apparently are the most unpromising, who need the most tact and kindly words that will bind their hearts to the heart of the teacher. Angels of God come to every schoolroom. If their presence is welcomed, they will keep the minds of the students fresh with the love of God. And they will help the teacher to preserve order and discipline.

Students who at first may seem to be dull and slow may in the end make greater progress than those who are naturally quicker. If they are thorough and systematic in their work, they will gain much that others will fail to gain. Those who form habits of patient, persevering industry will accomplish more than those of quick, vivacious, brilliant minds, who, though grasping a point quickly, lose it just as readily. The patient ones, though slower to learn, will stand ahead of those who learn so quickly that they do not need to study.

Sanitariums to be in the Country

I have received much instruction regarding the location of sanitariums. They should be a few miles distant from the large cities, and land should be secured in connection with them. Fruit and vegetables should be cultivated, and the patients should be encouraged to take up out-door work. Many who are suffering from pulmonary disease might be cured if they would live in a climate where they could be out of doors most of the year. Many who have died of consumption might have lived if they had breathed more pure air. Fresh out-door air is as healing as medicine, and leaves no injurious after-effects.

To the young and strong the bustle of the city are sometimes more agreeable than the quiet of the country, but the sick long for the quiet of the country.

As these things are presented before me, and as I think of how much is lost by an indoor life, I can scarcely endure the thought of our sanitariums being situated where the patients must endure the rigor of cold winters, where during the winter months they must remain inside most of the time, the rooms heated with steam coils, and the air impure. In every place there are in winter time some things that are disadvantageous to the sick, but some places have fewer disadvantages than others. There are localities where all the year round fruit-bearing trees may be seen, and where but little fire is needed for purposes of warmth. In sanitariums established in such places the patients can have the advantages of the out-door air at all seasons of the year. When fire are required, there should, if possible, be open fireplaces in which wood can be burned.

Why do not our physicians see and understand that patients should be treated out of and away from the cities? And not the patients only, but physicians and nurses need a cheerful, sunshiny atmosphere. Is it surprising that under gloomy surroundings, workers should be down-hearted and depressed, leading unbelievers to think that their religion makes them gloomy? Let there be light and love and cheerful song in the place of gloom, and what a change would take place? ...

Simplicity in Diet and Treatments

It would have been better if, from the first, all drugs had been kept out of our sanitariums, and use had been made of such simple remedies as are found in pure water, pure air, sunlight, and some of the simple herbs growing in the field. These would be just as efficacious as the drugs used under mysterious names, and concocted by human science. And they would leave no injurious effects in the system.

Thousands who are afflicted might recover their health if, instead of depending upon the drug-store for their life, they would discard all drugs, and live simply, without using tea, coffee, liquor, or spices, which irritate the stomach and leave it weak, unable to digest even simple food without stimulation. The Lord is willing to let his light shine forth in clear, distinct rays to all who are weak and feeble.

Vegetables, fruits and grains should compose our diets. Not an ounce of flesh-meat should enter our stomachs. The eating of flesh is unnatural. We are to return to God's original purpose in the creation of man. ... There is blessing in the association of old and young. The young may bring sunshine into the hearts and minds of the aged. Those of hoary heads need the vitality and action of the young. And the young need the wisdom and mature experience of older persons. There is to be a blending of the two. Wisdom and patience will do a great work for the weak and sickly. ...

The Lord has a controversy with the inhabitants of the earth. They are no longer of benefit to the world in advancing truth and righteousness. They are about to be gathered in bundles, ready to be burned. They are as faggots ready to be cast into the fire.

Ellen G. White.

Chapter 74—Strong Minds and Weak Stomachs

From B. 44, 1903 (P).

It is well for Brother and Sister A and Brother and Sister B to have strong minds. Each is to maintain his individuality. Each is to preserve an individuality that will not be submerged in the individuality of another. No human being is to be the shadow of another human being. But God's servants are to labor together in a unity that blends mind with mind. Do you think that this unity can exist among the workers in the sanitarium unless you all take a judicious, sanctified position?

"The glory which Thou gavest Me I have given them; that they may be one, even as we are one." Are you willing to make sacrifices to answer this prayer? Or will you, because there is a difference of opinion regarding certain articles of food that one or the other thinks should not or should not be set on the table, or regarding the hours for meals, will you say that you can not work together? Is this Bible sanctification? ...

My brother, a firm will is a good thing when it is sanctified. But I know, from the light God has given me, that you and your wife need to yoke up with Christ, and to learn that in some respects your ideas and plans and methods would be improved if modified.

The Sanitarium has been established that all classes may be reached with the truth. I ask you and Brother and Sister B to do all in your power to bring into the sanitariums the unity for which Christ prayed.

Reveal His love. Let the truth rule in the heart, and you will be one with Christ in God.

You say that you are dyspeptics. Is it not possible that your plan of eating may not be the best? I am instructed to say that you need to change in some things, else you will injure your digestive powers. I do not say what you shall or shall not eat. But if, while eating the things you choose, you have dyspepsia, I think you ought to make a decided change. ...

If I were a dyspeptic, I should make changes in my diet until I knew for a certainty that I was eating the food that my stomach could best care for. A craving for certain things may need to be brought into subjection. Self is rebellious, and must be strictly disciplined.

Be regular in your habits of eating, and be sure not to overburden the stomach by eating too many kinds of food at one time. Stop eating before you feel entirely satisfied.

The stomach is the most abused organ of the whole body. It is often wearied by the effort to take care of food that should not be eaten at the same time. A disturbance is created by the kinds of food brought together. Soon there is an all-gone feeling, and many think that this is hunger. But it is not. The trouble is that the stomach has too much to do. Let it be given less to do, and it will recover its healthy tone. The simpler the food eaten, and the fewer the kinds, the easier is the stomach's work.

The same rule of eating can not be made for all. I make it a rule never to eat custards; for when I eat them, they always make a disturbance in my stomach. But there are those in my family who suffer no inconvenience from eating custards, and because I can not eat them, I do not say that they ought not to eat them. We must each experiment and know for ourselves what is best for us to eat. We may have to abstain from many things that others can eat without inconvenience. ...

Half-hearted Christians are worse than infidels; for their deceptive words and non-committal position may lead many astray. The infidel shows his colors. The luke-warm Christian deceives both parties. He is neither a good worldling nor a good Christian. Satan uses him to do a work that no one else can do.

Chapter 75—Counsels on Health and the Southern Field

From B. 200, 1903 (P).

If things were as they should be in the households that make up our churches, we might do double service for the Lord. The light given me is that a most decided message must be borne in regard to health reform. Those who use flesh meat strengthen the lower propensities and prepare the way for disease to fasten upon them. There are those among Seventh-day Adventists who will not heed the light given them in regard to this matter. They make flesh meat a part of their diet. Disease comes upon them. Sick and suffering as a result of their own wrong course, they ask for the prayers of the servants of God. But how can the Lord work in their behalf when they are not willing to do His will, when they refuse to heed His instruction in regard to health reform?

For thirty years the light on health reform has been coming to the people of God, but many have made it a subject of jest. They have continued to use tea, coffee, spices, and flesh meat. Their bodies are full of disease. How can we, I ask, present such ones to the Lord for healing? ...

Brother B. keep your heart stayed upon the Lord. He lives and reigns. He is our general. Look not to man. Believe not every report that comes to you. Be as a man who has ears, but hears not, and eyes, but sees not. David says, "I, as a deaf man, heard not; and I was as a dumb man that openeth not his mouth. Thus was I as a man that heareth not, and in whose mouth are no reproofs. "Let the watchman of God keep their own counsels. They will be troubled as they bear their message, but the Lord will help them.

Satan will do that which will close the Southern field against the truth, if the Lord does not interpose. And the trade unions will be one of the agencies that will bring upon this earth a time of trouble such as has not been since the world began. ...

I have not much confidence in doing a large amount of work for those who already know the truth. Nothing will stir the South like taking hold of the work in new places. The cities are to be entered. But to try to bring those who know the truth, yet do not do their best, up to where they ought to be, is, I must say, almost labor lost, and greatly hinders aggressive work. Let the workers press into the cities still in ignorance. Let men and women be trained to conduct schools and sanitariums for white people. Let colored workers be educated to labor for their own people. And let the workers all remember that no raid is to be made on slavery and cruel task-masters.

God does not expect His workers to attend to trifling matters. They are to preach the gospel. They will find that short discourses are the most effective. In every place in which the work is begun, the standard is to be raised higher and still higher. The truth of Christ's soon coming is to be proclaimed. And all the workers, whether they speak from the pulpit or give Bible readings are to be taught to speak in a clear, expressive manner."

Chapter 76—Points in Diet

From B 62, 1903 (P).

Be very careful that unhealthful rich preparations of food are not presented as a sample of health reform cooking.

You have said that you are a dyspeptic. I see no reason why you should be thus, if your preparations of food are wholesome, and if you eat at the right hours. I ask you to look carefully into these matters. I appreciate you most highly, my dear brother and sister. But I must tell you that you have lessons to learn in regard to your eating that you have not yet learned. I advise you to study closely into these things, and then give the stomach the best of care.

For thirty-five years I have made it a practice to eat only two meals a day. Occasionally when traveling, I have eaten irregular meals when I have been thrown out of line by not being able to get my meals at the regular time. I am seventy-five years old; but I do as much writing as I ever did. My digestion is good, and my brain is clear.

Our fare is simple and wholesome. We have on our table, no butter, no meat, no cheese, no greasy mixture of food.

Chapter 77—The Work of Our Fernando School

Remarks by Mrs. E. G. White, at the Los Angeles Campmeeting, Sept. 17, 1902.

I read from the second epistle of Peter: "Simon Peter, a servant and an apostle of Jesus Christ, to them that have obtained like precious faith with us through the righteousness of God and our Saviour Jesus Christ; grace and peace be multiplied unto you through the knowledge of God, and of Jesus our Lord, according to His divine power hath given unto us all things that pertain unto Life and Godliness, through the Knowledge of Him that hath called us to glory and virtue: where by are given unto use exceeding great and precious promises: that by these ye might be partakers of the divine nature, having escaped the corruption that is in the world through lust."

This scripture is full of instruction for those who are engaged in educational work for our youth. Our brethren in positions of responsibility should give special study to the management of matters in connection with the establishment of new schools for the training of our children, in order that the youth may be surrounded by circumstances the most favorable for the formation of a character strong enough to withstand the evils of this world.

A Lesson from Israel

After the descendants of Abraham has spent many years in Egyptian servitude, God raised up Moses to deliver them from their oppressors. In order to induce the Egyptians to heed the message given to them through Moses, God brought upon them many plagues. But they continued to harden their hearts. Because of their stubborn resistance, Moses was at last directed to say to Pharaoh, "Thus saith the Lord, Israel is My son, even My firstborn; and I say unto thee, Let My son go, that he may serve Me. And if thou refuse to let him go, behold, I will slay thy son, even thy firstborn."

Before Egypt was visited by this terrible judgment, the word of the Lord came to the fathers and mothers among the Israelites, directing them to gather their children with them into the house, there to remain until the destroying angel had passed over the land. "Moses called for all the elders of Israel, and said unto them, Draw out and take you a lamb according to your families, and kill the passover. And ye shall take a bunch of hyssop, and dip it in the blood that is in the bason, and strike the lintel and the two sideposts with the blood that is in the bason; and none of you shall go out at the door of his house until the morning. For the Lord will pass through to smite the Egyptians, and when He seeth the blood upon the lintel, and on the two side-posts, the Lord will pass over the door, and will not suffer the destroyer to come in unto your house to smite you."

"The children of Israel, ... did as the Lord had commanded Moses and Aaron."

"It came to pass, that at midnight the Lord smote all the firstborn in the land of Egypt, from the firstborn of Pharaoh that sat on his throne unto the firstborn of the captive that was in the dungeon; and all the firstborn of cattle." God passed over the homes of the Israelites. Upon the children of the parents who were faithful in gathering their little ones within the circle of the home, no judgment fell.

This experience of the Israelites is a wonderful lesson for us today. In this time of peril, God-fearing parents, like the fathers and mothers of ancient Israel, should understand the will of the Lord concerning themselves and their children. In planning for the education of their children outside the home, they should realize that it is not safe now to send them to public schools. Parents should endeavor to send their children to schools where they can obtain an education based on a scriptural foundation ... and education to be gained gradually, line upon line, precept upon precept, here a little, and there a little.

The Establishment of Christian Schools

Some may ask, "How are such schools to be established?" We are not a rich people, but if we pray in faith, and let the Lord work in our behalf, he will open ways before us to establish small schools in retired places for the education of our youth not only in the Scriptures and in book-learning, but in many lines of manual labor.

The necessity for establishing such schools is urged upon me very strongly because of the cruel neglect of many parents properly to educate their children in the home school. Multitudes of fathers and mothers have seemed to think that if the lines of control were put into the hands of their children, they would develop into useful young men and young women, but the Lord has instructed me in regard to this matter. In the visions of the night I saw standing by the side of these neglected children the one who was cast out of the heavenly courts because he originated sin. He, the enemy of souls, was standing by, watching for opportunities to gain control of the mind of every child whose parents had not given faithful instruction in regard to Satan's snares.

The Home School

Upon every Christian parent there rests the solemn obligation of giving to his children an education that will lead them to gain a knowledge of the Lord, and to become partakers of the divine nature through obedience to God's will and way. A child's first school should be his home. His first instructors should be his father and his mother. His first lessons should be the lessons of respect, obedience, reverence and self-control. If he is not instructed aright by his parent, Satan will instruct him in evil through agencies that are most objectionable. How important, then, is the school in the home! Here the character is first shaped. Here the destiny of souls is often largely influenced. Even the parents who are endeavoring to do their best, have not a hundredth part of the realization they should have of the value of a human soul.

The school is the home that should be a place where children are taught that the eye of God is upon them, observing all that they do. If this thought were deeply impressed upon the mind, the work of governing children would be made much easier. In the home school our boys and girls are being prepared to attend a church when they reach a proper age to associate more intimately with other children. Constantly parents should keep this in view, realizing that their children are God's purchased little ones, to be trained for lives of usefulness in the Master's service and for a home in the future, eternal world. The father and the mother, as teachers in the home school, should consecrate hands, tongue, brain, and every power of the being to God, in order that they may fulfill their high and holy mission.

To shield their children from contaminating influence, parents should instruct them in principles of purity. Those who form the habit of obedience and self-control in the home life will have but little difficulty in school life, and, if surrounded by Christian influences, will escape many temptations that usually beset the youth. Let us train our children so that they will remain true to God under all circumstances and in all places. In their tender years let us surround them with influences that will tend to strengthen character.

The Fernando School

Parents who give their children proper instruction at home, will train them to obey their teachers at school. And, unless surrounded by unusual circumstances, they will, in time, see the necessity of sending their children to some school outside the home. This school may be simply a church school, or it may be an intermediate school or a large training school. I am pleased to learn that here in Southern California you have established a school at Fernando, and that it will be opened in about a week. I am glad that the Lord has wrought for you in providing a place for the education of your children.

A few days ago I had the privilege of seeing the building and the surroundings of the Fernando school. My time was very limited, but I was thankful for the opportunity of visiting the school grounds. I am glad that you are several miles away from the city of Los Angeles. You have good buildings, and are in a favorable place for school work. I greatly desire that you shall make a right beginning. In planning for the erection of cottages for our brethren and sisters who may move there, be careful not to allow buildings to be put up too near the school property. Try to secure the land lying near the school, so that it will be impossible for houses to be built close to the campus. The land may be used for agricultural purposes. Later on, you may find it advisable to introduce various trades for the employment and training of the students; but at present about all that you can do is to teach them how to cultivate the land, so that it shall yield its fruit.

The Subjects to be Taught

The question has been asked, "What shall we teach in the Fernando school?" Teach the very simplest lessons. You should not make a great parade before the world, showing what you expect to do, as if you were planning to do something wonderful. No, indeed. Take hold of this school with meekness. Tell your brethren and friends that you are planning to conduct an industrial school, a school in which practical instruction in agriculture and various trades will be connected with instruction in book-learning. Boast neither of the branches of study you expect to teach nor of the industrial work you hope to do; but tell every one who inquires that you intend to do the best you can to give your students a physical, mental, and spiritual training that will fit them for usefulness in this life, and prepare them for the future, immortal life.

What influence do you think it would have, to publish in your announcement of the school, that you would endeavor to give to the students a training that would prepare them for the future, immortal life, because you desire to see them live throughout the ceaseless ages of eternity? I believe such a statement would have a far greater influence upon the brethren and sisters of this conference, and upon the community in the midst of which the school is located, than would the display of any number of courses of study in ancient and modern languages and other higher branches of learning.

Let the school prove itself. Then the patrons will not be disappointed, and the students will not claim that they were promised instruction in certain studies which, after entering the school, they were not permitted to take up. Let it be understood at the beginning that the Bible likes at the foundation of all education.

An earnest study of God's Word, resulting in transformation of character and in a fitness for service, will make the Fernando school a power for good. My brethren who are to be connected with this school, your strength lies not in the number of languages you may teach, or in telling how large a "college" you have. Keep silent on these points. Silence in regard to the great things you plan to do, will help you more than all the positive assertions and the promises that you might publish in your announcements. You need to publish nothing of the kind. By faithfulness in the school, you should demonstrate that you are working on foundation-principles, principles that will prepare the students for entrance through the pearly gates into the heavenly city. The saving of souls is worth far more than mere intellectual training. A pretentious display of human learning, the manifestation of pride of personal appearance, is worthless. The Lord values obedience to His will; for only by walking humbly and obediently before Him, can man glorify God.

In giving us the privilege of studying His Word, the Lord has set before us a rich banquet. Many are the benefits derived from feasting on His Word, which is represented by Him as being His flesh and blood--His spirit and life. By partaking of this Word, our spiritual strength is increased; we grow in grace and in a knowledge of the truth; habits of self-control are formed and strengthened; the infirmities of childhood - fretfulness, wilfulness, selfishness, hasty words, passionate acts - disappear, and in their place are developed the graces of Christian manhood and womanhood.

If your students, besides studying God's Word, learn no more than how to use correctly the English language in reading, writing, spelling, and speaking, a great work for humanity will have been accomplished. Those who are trained for service in the Lord's work should be taught how to talk properly in ordinary conversation and before congregations. Many a laborer's usefulness is marred by his ignorance in regard to correct breathing and clear, forcible speaking. Many have not learned to give the right emphasis to the words they read and speak. Often the enunciation is indistinct. A thorough training in the use of the English language, is of far more value to a youth than is a superficial study of foreign languages, to the neglect of his mother tongue.

Let the Fernando school be conducted along the lines of the ancient schools of the prophets, the Word of God lying at the foundation of all. Let not the students attempt to grasp the higher rounds of the ladder first. There are those who have attended other schools, thinking that they could obtain an advanced education; but they have been so intent on reaching the higher rounds of the ladder, that they have never been humble enough to learn of Christ. Had they placed their feet on the lower rounds first, they could have made progress, learning more and still more of the Great Teacher.

The instructors will find it greatly to their advantage to take hold interestedly with the students in manual labor, showing them how to work, By cooperating with the youth in this practical way, the teachers can bind the hearts of the students to themselves by the cords of sympathy and brotherly love. Christian kindness and sociability are powerful factors in the winning of the affections of the youth.

Teachers, take hold of the school work with diligence and patience. Realize that your's is not a common work. You are laboring for time and for eternity, molding the minds of the students for entrance into the higher school, the school above. Every right principle, every truth, learned in an earthly school will advance us just as much in the heavenly school. As Christ walked and talked with His disciples during His ministry on this earth, so He will teach us in the school above, leading us by the side of the river of living waters, and revealing to us the truths that in this life must remain hidden mysteries because of the limitations of the human mind, so marred by sin. In the heavenly school we shall have opportunity to attain, step by step, to the greatest heights of learning. There, as children of the heavenly King, we shall ever dwell with the members of the royal family; there we shall see the King in his Beauty, and behold his matchless charms.

The Training of Missionaries

It is important that we should have such schools as the one soon to be opened at Fernando. To us has been committed a great work--the work of proclaiming the third angel's message to every nation, kindred, tongue, and people. We have but few missionaries. From home and abroad are coming many urgent calls for workers. Young men and young women, the middle-ages, and, in fact, all who are able to engage in the Master's service, should be putting their minds to the stretch in an effort to prepare to meet these calls. From the light God has given me, I know we do not use the faculties of the mind half as diligently as we should in an effort to fit ourselves for greater usefulness. If we consecrate mind and body to God's service, obeying His law, He will give us sanctified moral power for every undertaking.

Every man and every woman in our ranks, whether a parent or not, ought to be intensely interested in the work of educating our youth for active service in the Lord's vineyard. We can not afford to allow our children to drift away into the world and to fall under the control of the enemy. Let us come up to the help of the Lord, to the help of the Lord against the mighty. Let us do all in our power to make the Fernando school a blessing to our youth. Teachers and students, you can do much to bring this about, by wearing the yoke of Christ, daily learning of Him, His meekness and lowliness. Those who are not directly connected with the school, can help to make it a blessing, by giving it their hearty support. Thus we shall all be "laborers together with God", and receive the reward of the faithful, even an entrance into the school above.

Chapter 78—Professionalism Versus Simplicity

"Elmshaven", St. Helena, Cal, Oct. 20, 1902.

Surgery

Dear Brethren:

Last night I seemed to be in the operating room of a large hospital, to which people were being brought, and instruments were being prepared to cut off their limbs in a big hurry. One came in who seemed to have authority, and said to the physician, "Is it necessary to bring these people into this room?" Looking pityingly at the sufferers, he said, "Never amputate a limb until everything possible has been done to restore it." Examining the limbs which the physicians had been preparing to cut off, he said, "They may be saved. The first work is to use every available means to restore these limbs. What a fearful mistake it would be to amputate a limb that could be saved by patient care. Your conclusions have been too hastily drawn. Put these patients in the best room in the hospital, and give them the very best of care and treatment. Use every means in your power to save them from going through life in a crippled condition, their usefulness damaged for life."

The sufferers were removed to a pleasant room, and faithful helpers cared for them under the speaker's direction; and not a limb had to be sacrificed.

Publishing in the South

Other scenes passed before me. I was in a room where a number were assembled in Council. Brother E. R. Palmer was presenting the idea that small, local presses were not needful, and were run at great expense. He said that he thought that all our book-making should be done at one publishing house, at one place, and thus save expense.

There was present One of authority, and after making some inquires He said, "These smaller printing offices can be managed in a way that will make them a help to the work of God, if sufficient attention is given to them. In the past, great lack of principle has been brought into the management of our book work, and this experience will be repeated unless men's hearts are thoroughly converted, thoroughly changed. There are some who have been converted, but the work that God desires to see done on hearts is not yet all done. Those who frame yokes for the necks of their fellow beings will, unless they repent, be brought to the place where they will understand how these yokes bind and gall the neck of the wearer.

Let the Southern field have its own home published books. Selected books from the Old and New Testaments can be published in separate volumes, with simple explanations and inexpensive illustration. In addition to these books, there can also be published some illustrated books suitable for school children. These books will be a great help in the work in the South. The publication of these books can be done acceptably in the Nashville office. The work of this institution is not to be limited to the publication of the "Gospel Herald", and a few children's books. But let not the workers try to embrace too much.

The books especially designed for the Southern field are not to be pushed in the North unless there is a real demand for them.

There is a need of better understanding of the work to be done in heart, mind, and character for the workers in our institutions in the North as well as in the South. Let those in our Northern institutions lay aside their prejudices, and let these in the South humble their hearts before God, and then there will be a sitting in heavenly places in Christ Jesus.

The workers need to wear the yoke of Christ and to blend together in love and unity. The Lord will bless and strengthen them as they do this. His people are to depend on Him alone, walking before Him in all humility of mind.

There is need in the Southern field of a publishing house for the publication of the truth for this time. But this work can not be done with divided minds and divided interests. In order for the publishing house at Nashville to be made a success, the workers must have a constant sense of the supervision of God, and they must be subject to one another. The converting power of God is needed. "Humble yourselves therefore under the mighty hand of God."

Be very careful how you treat the Lord's heritage. Each worker is to be drawn to the other by the cords of Christ's love. There is no need of their being estranged from one another. They are all embraced in Christ's prayer that the disciples might be one with Him as He is one with the Father.

"Neither pray I for these alone," Christ said, "But for them also which shall believe on me through their word; that they all may be one; as thou, Father, art in Me and I in thee, that they also may be one in us; that the world may believe that thou has sent Me. And the glory which thou gavest Me; I in them, and thou in Me, that they may be made perfect in one; and that the world may know that thou hast sent Me, and hast loved them, as thou hast loved Me."

Will you do all in your power, my brethren, to answer this prayer? In the work at Nashville there has been a departure from avowed principles and plans of work. Great evils have resulted. The Lord would have saved from all this if the workers had prayed more and had walked humbly with God. It will never answer for these mistakes to be repeated. They must stand as warnings against deviations from the plain path marked out for us by God. And how shall we treat those who have erred? Let those who have had experience, and who have passed over the ground, show sympathy for those who have done this unadvised thing.

Chapter 79—The Work in the South

"Elmshaven", Sanitarium, Cal., November 7, 1902.

I can not sleep after one o'clock. My mind is now clear in regard to matters about which I have been uncertain. I have been asking my heavenly Father to pardon me for looking to men, supposing that they must be wise. The Lord have me warnings, which at first were presented to me in figures, but are now clearly opened before me. God has instructed me in regard to the work to be done in Nashville.

In the past I have received much instruction regarding the work in the Southern field, and for years I have followed the work and workers with intense interest. This field, as it now is, stands as a reproach against those who claim to be fulfilling the commission that Christ gave His disciples just before His ascension.

Recently the question was asked me by the Lord: "Will you do that which many of your ministering brethren would be only too pleased to see you doing? Will your voice no longer be heard presenting clearly and distinctly the needs of this long-neglected field? If so, you yourself will bear the reproach that rests on the minister and people who have not done for the Southern field the work He has given them to do, who have passed by on the other side those who are their neighbors, treating them indifferently and with cruel neglect.

Oh, that the presidents of our Conferences would encourage the church members to take an active interest in the work in the South, and to do all in their power to wipe out the reproach resting upon Seventh-day Adventists because of the condition of this field. Our people are believers in the Bible, but they are pursuing a course that is bringing reproach upon themselves and upon the cause of God.

There are ministers who have stood on Satan's side of this question, as men who do not desire to become interested in the work for the South. To those who were inclined to send help to the work in Nashville, they have talked their own unbelief so discouragingly that this place, which God has said plainly should have special advantages, has not received the help that it should have received. Over and over again, money that has been given to this field has been diverted into other channels. Thus is being repeated the mistake in the past in regard to the misappropriation of means. There are those who, instead of strengthening and sustaining the work in Nashville, have tried to tear it down by unjust criticism and evil surmisings. They have placed a mole close to the eye, and it has become to them a mountain. Nothing but it can they see. If they would remove this mole, as they could if they so desired, they would see the glory beyond. But will they do this, which would be an act of such mercy to themselves? They can not see the way in which the Lord regards their present attitude. They are picking at straws. They need not be as they are. Their condition depends on themselves. But they must submit to the will of God. Until they do this, the words spoken of Moab are applicable to them: "Moab. . . hath not been emptied from vessel to vessel; therefore his taste remained in him, and his scent is not changed."

There are many who have engaged in the work of gathering up titbits of evil, many who have made mountains out of molehills. Christ has told them plainly how He regards work of this kind. But they do not heed his holy instruction. Why? Because they do not will to do the will of God. They want to carry forward just the lines of work in which they themselves are interested, and they think that the means in hand should be used in these lines of work.

The question was asked: "What influence are you bringing into the Lord's work by following such a course? You use time and money to impede the work already started. Might not this time and money be better employed? If you had striven to fulfill the commission given by Christ, if you had acted like sensible men, as Christ would have acted in their place, lines of work that would have glorified God might have been started and advanced in many places. But you have turned from the instruction given Christ.

It is the Saviour's desire that unity and love and Christian fellowship shall prevail among His followers. The lesson that He gave his disciples in the fifth chapter of Matthew is the lesson that his disciples today are to spend their time in learning. Condemnation must follow a failure to learn this lesson. God can not cooperate with those who do not obey His teaching, who look upon their own way as better than His. The example of such ones is directly contrary to the lessons that God has given to aid His people in the formation of Christlike characters.

Those who receive Christ as a personal Saviour, doing His work, and following His way, become members of the royal family. But there are many who, with the clearest evidence before them, are walking directly contrary to His instruction, following in the way of sinners. They do the very same work of accusation that open sinners are doing. In the place of being laborers together with God, washing their robes of character and making them white in the blood of the Lamb, that they may be representatives of the Saviour, setting in word and deed a Christlike example, they employ their faculties and powers in a way that the followers of Satan employ their faculties and powers. They think and speak evil. They spend time and money gathering together jot and titles of evil, and the mouth that ought to be employed in offering thanksgiving to God, is employed in reporting this evil. Many are engaged in Satan's work -- worrying, finding fault, and accusing those who are trying to do the very work that they themselves ought to be doing. The talent of speech is used to destroy the confidence of believers in their brethren. And many Seventh-day Adventists stand before the world as fractious and fault-finding, instead of bound together by oneness with Christ.

Unity Among Believers

"A new commandment I give unto you", Christ said, "That ye love one another; as I have loved you, that ye also love one another. By this shall all men know that ye are My disciples, if ye have love one to another."

"Verily, verily, I say unto you, he that believeth on Me, the works that I do shall he do also; and greater works than these shall he do, because I go to my Father. And whatsoever ye shall ask in My name, that will I do, that the Father may be glorified in the Son. If ye shall ask anything in My name, I will do it. If ye love Me, keep My commandments. And I will pray the Father, and He shall give you another Comforter, that He may abide with you forever, even the Spirit of Truth, whom the world can not receive, because it seeth Him not, neither knoweth Him; but ye see Him; for he dwelleth with you, and shall be in you. I will not leave you comfortless; I will come to you."

Will our faith take hold of this promise? Can we not see how great is the advantage offered us in the assurance of such a Comforter?

"He that hath my commandments, and keepeth them, it is he that loveth me; and he that loveth Me shall be loved of My Father, and I will love him, and will manifest Myself to him. . . If a man love Me, he will keep my words; and my Father will love Him, and we will come unto Him, and make our abode with Him. He that loveth me not keepeth not my sayings; and the word which ye hear is not mine, but the Father's which sent me."

Thus saith the Lord: "Will my people hear the message from my servant, when they will not keep my word? Disobedience, a failure to practice my teachings, is the reason that there are so many voices and so much variance among my people. While they follow the impulses of their stubborn, rebellious hearts, they have no inclination to do my will. They set up their own will and choose their own way, and their way is not my way, neither are their thoughts my thoughts. "As the heavens are higher than the earth, so are my ways higher than your ways and my thoughts than your thoughts!"

Love for Christ leads to obedience. Those who disregard the word of Christ have not Christ's wisdom, or his peace, or his light. Whatever their qualifications, however firmly they may trust in their own wisdom, their plans will result in foolishness, while they themselves will become inflated with ideas of their own greatness. They do not obey Christ; they have not his love in their hearts; and therefore they have not the mind of Christ. Their human nature refuses to be conformed to his will and way.

The success of every worker depends on having the mind of Christ. Unquestioning faith in the Father and the Son is the great safeguard against annoyance and trouble. Those who have this faith realize that the all-sufficient support is ever underneath them.

We have not studied and obeyed the words of Christ as we should. Christ likens His words to his flesh and blood. Speaking of this on one occasion, He said, "Ye seek me not because of the miracles, but because ye did eat of the loaves, and were filled. Labor not for the meat which perisheth, but for the meat which endureth unto everlasting life, which the Son of Man shall give unto you; for him hath God the Father sealed."

"Then said they unto him, What shall we do, that we might work the works of God? Jesus answered unto them, This is the work of God, that ye believe on Him whom He hath sent.

"What sign showest thou then," they said, "that we may see and believe thee? What dost thou work? Our fathers did eat manna in the wilderness, as it is written, He gave them bread from heaven to eat."

They were urging Him to work a miracle similar to that which had been worked for the children of Israel in the wilderness.

"Then said Jesus unto them, Verily, verily I say unto you, Moses gave you not that bread from heaven; but my Father giveth you the true bread from heaven. For the bread of God is He which cometh down from heaven, and giveth life unto the world. Then said they unto Him, Lord, evermore give us this bread. And Jesus said unto them, I am the bread of life; he which cometh to Me shall never hunger, and he that believeth on Me shall never thirst. But I said unto you, That ye also have seen Me, and believe not."

This is the position taken by many today who claim to be the children of God. They do not understand what it means to receive Christ as a personal Saviour. They have never crucified self.

I am instructed to say to those who minister in word and doctrine, My brethren, you need a practical knowledge of genuine faith in God. There is a fearful lack of this faith among our people. Doubt and unbelief are gaining such power that the Lord can have no influence over our willful, stubborn hearts. The infinite, eternal, omniscient One can not move the hard hearts because men and women refuse to cast self out. Shall this want of faith, this lack of love and unity, continue to strengthen, until those in holy service become unholy and unsanctified, unkindly and miserable? Shall not the breath of life from Christ revive the spark of love for God and man? Unbelief is cruel. Evil thinking and evil speaking are the fruit of an evil tree. Love and faith and trust develop gentleness. Let the heart break before God in longing for true holiness.

So much of self is cherished that the life of Christ in the soul is quenched. The truth that is presented tastes of the dish. The vessels need to be purified. There needs to be deeper ploughing in the heart, that the seeds of the eternal word of Christ may take root and spring up to bear fruit to the glory of God. The faith of many must be shallow, valueless in the sight of God, else the fruit would be of a different quality. There is need of deep heart-searching.

Read Christ's prayer for His disciples, offered just before His crucifixion: "Neither pray I for these alone, but for them also which shall believe on me through their word; that they all may be one; as thou, Father, art in Me, and I in thee, that they also may be one in us; that the world may believe that thou hast sent me."

By their love and unity the disciples were to bear witness to Christ's power. Thus the world was to be led to see that God had indeed sent His Son to save sinners. Since this is so, should we not do all in our power to bring about such a glorious result? Should we not cultivate the attributes that will enable us to answer Christ's prayer for us? The blessing of God will rest upon all who respect and honor Christ by revealing love for one another, by striving for the unity that he prayed might exist.

How can the professed people of God be content to be at variance with one another? Surely they see in the world enough of the sad result of alienation and strife. Satan strives to bring disunion into the ranks of God's followers, that Christ's heart may be pained. Let those who are serving the Lord make sure that their service is not a pretence. This is what it is when they talk against one another, giving way to a spirit of envy and fault-finding.

"And the glory which Thou gavest me I have given them; that they may be one, even as we are one; I in them, and thou in me, that they may be made perfect in one; and that the world may know that thou hast sent me, and hast loved them as thou hast loved me. Father, I will that they also whom thou hast given me, be with me where I am; that they may behold my glory, which thou hast given me; for thou lovedst me before the foundation of the world. O righteous Father, the world has not known thee; but I have known thee, and these have known that thou hast sent me. And I have declared unto them thy name, and will declare it; that the love wherewith thou hast loved me may be in them, and I in them."

Mrs. E. G. White.

Chapter 80—Our Attitude Toward the Work and Workers in the Southern Field

(Diary)

November 17, 1902.

While attending the campmeeting at Fresno, Calif., held October 1-10, in the visions of the night I was in a certain meeting. I was desirous of learning the object of this meeting, but was in darkness. I sat in a place that seemed to be separated from the room where the people had assembled. Somewhere I have written in regard to this meeting, and I think the manuscript has been copied.

The brethren in this meeting were counselling in regard to the work in Nashville. Matters were presented in a strong light. Some of the brethren present had gathered up the testimonies of those who were unfavorably inclined toward the Nashville publishing house. If actions had been taken based upon these misrepresentations, great injustice would have been done to the Southern work. Decisions would have been made that would have had a most discouraging effect, and that would have seemingly upheld as right all that the Lord has condemned in regard to the Southern field.

The course that Brethren E. R. Palmer and A. G. Daniells have desired to outline would work an injustice, and would result in an incorrect showing. Acting upon false impressions, the brethren would bring about something that the Lord could not in any way endorse. These brethren must remember that money has not been given freely to establish the work in Nashville. Had they been connected with this work, had they carried the anxieties and burdens that others have carried, had they made the decisions and one the many, many deeds that called for self-sacrifice, would they have succeeded any better under these difficulties than have the men who have been connected with this work from the beginning? I have felt distressed beyond measure over these matters.

November 5, 1902. I have been carrying upon my soul a most grievous burden. I ought never to have thought that it was my duty to keep my lips close, withdraw my influence, and allow the brethren who have been taking burdens upon themselves carry out their preconceived ideas in regard to the supposed necessity of showing James Edson White his proper place and of reorganizing the whole work in the Southern field.

When the brethren came to me for counsel, I told them that I would not stand in the way of their carrying out their plan of reorganization that they had regarded as essential. But afterward, in the night season, I was in a meeting where this was being done; and the manner in which the work was carried on was so objectionable that I could not keep silent. Then I was moved by the Spirit of God to say that three times had the messenger of the Lord given me instruction that this pressure against Edson White is unreasonable, and that he is given an inferior place. The heavenly Messenger put his arm around Edson, and led him forward, to stand not at the foot, but in the very midst.

November 7, 1902. Again matters at Nashville have been opened before me, and I am encouraged.

The Lord has given me cautions to give both to Elder Daniells and to Brother E. R. Palmer. God has not inspired their decision that a wonderful overturning will have to take place in the South. By no means has the Lord left Nashville. Many things there will in time work and adjust themselves.

When first the Lord presented before me a certain meeting where the Southern work was being considered, I could not discern the speakers. Later the Lord removed the heavy, heavy burden from my mind by instructing me that in every place where a center is to be made, there will be encountered difficulties that require more than mortal wisdom to overcome. The dependence of the workers must be in God. In every movement they are to be actuated by pure, clean, high principles. But let not the men who have not been in the press of the battle, act as if they had all knowledge in regard to the aftersight, when they have had nothing to do with the foresight.

It would be most strange if no mistakes have been made. There are things in the history of the work the meaning of which it is impossible for human minds to fathom. Let not men, when dealing with those who have made mistakes, work on the supposition that under similar circumstances they would have done much better. Let them not have too much self-esteem; for every one will be tested and tried. Let them not do as many are doing - magnifying errors, and carrying reports that have no foundation in truth. If they think that they would have avoided the perplexity and the burdens that always come to those engaged in aggressive warfare, let them try to do the same kind of work, opening new fields in the South, before condemning others. Let them go into cities and establish the advantages that have to be built up from the foundation in every place selected as a working center. It is wrong for those who have had no part in bearing the inconveniences, the burdens, and the many embarrassments connected with establishing new enterprises, to criticise those who are struggling under these multiplied difficulties.

Over and over again the Lord has presented before me the pioneer work that must be done in new fields. In past years I have shared with others the burden of establishing His work in important centers. For years we have suffered from false reports and the pressure of opposition, and have struggled to overcome the obstacles placed before us by our brethren. We have always gone forward, plowing our way through prejudice. From the first, every effort has been made to find and to make public the mistakes of God's servants placed in trying positions, --mistakes greatly magnified, that many have taken up and used to discourage the workers and to retard the progress of the cause, when they should have interestedly put their shoulder to the wheel to help lift the load.

Should our dear Brethren Palmer and Daniells follow their own judgment and carry out the ideas they now hold in regard to the cause in the Southern field, they would do a work that bears not the approbation of God. Seeming success would be short-lived. Brethren, the Lord does not bid you to encourage your brethren to cultivate a spirit of accusation and condemnation by listening to their distorted reports. Listen not to those who are annoyed because they can not manage everything in accordance with their own will and way.

My brethren, you are not to thrust blindly in the dark; for you know not which will prosper, this or that. Restrain the tendency to judge motives. You do not know or understand in regard to the presentation that has been given me. I can not help being intensely interested in every movement made in the Southern field. I know much about that work; for I have kept pace with it and with the planning and devising of the workers, I have known of the struggles and makeshifts, the self-denial and self-sacrifice, that have been bravely borne. I have helped the workers as much as I could, sharing their work and encouraging them by sending them gifts of money and of books. And I know something in regard to what these books have already done and will continue to do.

While in Australia, I kept track of the work done in the South and of the little encouragement given the work among the colored people by their ministering brethren. Encouragement was withheld by the brethren in the North because they knew that encouragement would sooner or later mean the raising of means to support the workers in this new fields. I called for means for the Southern work before there was much of a showing in this field. I knew that unless means were sent, new territory could not be added.

The work that has been begun in Nashville is established in the right place. Because some men complain and criticise, shall the workers there become discouraged? I answer, No, no!

We had no ordinary experience in Australia. It was no easy matter to obtain means to work this new field. The soil had to be broken up, the ground prepared, and the seeds of truth sown. Ours was an aggressive work, carried forward, too, while grumblers were constantly trying to discourage us. But notwithstanding the voices of opposition, the message I received from the Lord was, "Add new territory; use the breaking-up plow in new soil."

And this is the message that I sent across the waters to my son, Edson White, who was working among the colored people in the South. "God says to you," I wrote to him, "Do not fail nor be discouraged."

My son wrote to me saying, "What shall I do? Colored men are accepting the truth but they have no decent clothing to wear when attending meetings." I myself was living in a missionary field, where poverty abounded, and I needed every penny to help the destitute there, and to advance various lines of work in that field; but I requested the office of publication to send to my son some money that was coming to me, and to charge the same to my account; which money was to be used to supply destitute colored people with clothing, in order that they might be presentable in appearance when gathered together to worship God. Whose work was it to relieve the situation?

Had our brethren and sisters in America been awakened by the appeals that long ago were made to them to do something for the colored people in the Southern states, years would not have passed into eternity with so little done. What do you see now? Among other things, we see a work begun in Nashville. But in the visions of the night the Southern field has passed in review before me, and it is still destitute. Our brethren in positions of trust are not to neglect this field, and send to foreign fields nearly all the money raised for advance work. The Southern field requires constant labor.

Although some mistakes have been made, the light given me is that instead of criticising and condemning, all should learn how to avoid such mistakes in the future. Who makes as his own the message of truth for this time. The Prince of Life offered Himself, a willing sacrifice, to save sinners living in the Southern states, as well as to save sinners living in remote parts of the earth. Workers must be called to this field as well as to distant lands. And the very least that these new laborers can say of the mistakes made, the better it will be for their own souls and for the future prosperity of the work. God views matters correctly. The infinite One alone is wise enough to pronounce correct judgment upon the work done. The Lord Jesus calls for workers, and he is the only Agency who can work through human minds and hands for the full development of the interests of his cause in this field.

How little do we enter into sympathy with God on the point that should be the strongest bond of union between us and Him, --compassion for depraved, guilty, suffering souls, dead in trespasses and sins!

If men shared the sympathies of Christ, they would have constant sorrow of heart over the condition of the Southern field, so destitute of workers. The needs of this field call for hundreds of medical missionaries.

Jesus wept over Jerusalem, because of the guilt and obstinacy of his chosen people. He weeps also over the hard-heartedness of those who, professing to be co-workers with him, are content to do nothing. Are those who appreciate the value of souls carrying, with Christ, a burden of heaviness and constant sorrow mingled with tears for the wicked cities of the earth? The destruction of these cities, almost wholly given up to idolatry, is impending. We ask if those who professedly know the truth for this time are content to do nothing in the cities of the South. In the great day of final reckoning what answer can be given for neglecting to enter these cities now?

The entering of Nashville by our workers was providential. When I visited this place, I was instructed that it was to become a center for the Southern work. Graysville and Huntsville are so near by that the institutions there can be helping hands to sustain the institutions in Nashville. Some of our brethren desired to begin the publishing work elsewhere, within their own borders; but this was not God's plan. There are to be memorials for God erected in cities. His work is not to be done in a corner, or simply at one or two points, like Graysville and Huntsville, but in many places and in a variety of ways.

Our brethren in the South now have opportunity to reveal the strength of their faith, whether or not they have faith sufficient to begin to make centers of influence in various places. If they continue to cherish a spirit of disunion, envy, and accusation against every one who will do advanced work, they will fail of meeting the test.

I had hoped that our brethren in the South would recognize the Lord's hand in leading our brethren to begin work in Nashville, making this a center. In this city buildings offered at a low price were purchased, and fitted up for use. Advantages were taken of circumstances favorable for a beginning. An excellent company of workers was brought together to labor in the publishing house. The Lord God looked upon the lovingly and approvingly. Had the brethren in the South appreciated the situation and been converted by the Holy Spirit of God, their influence would have been a saver of life unto life. If they had done more praying, and less talking with one another, each deferring, this company of workers in the office of publication would have had peace and contentment and rest of soul. But the clashing of words has brought evil. This is one of the reasons that so little has been done in the South. The Lord calls upon his people to be converted, and instead of hindering the work, to help it, so that it shall advance.

Ellen G. White.

Chapter 81—Principles for the Guidance of Men in Positions of Responsibility

While at Fresno, I passed through a peculiar experience. I seemed to be in an assembly where a number of brethren were in council. There seemed to be a cloud over the company. I could not discern faces, but I could hear voices. I thought that in one speaker I recognized the voice of Elder Daniells, but his manner of speech and his words seemed to be Brother E.R. Palmer's. At first I could not understand the things that were said by this speaker. Afterward I heard something said in regard to the way in which he thought the publishing work should be carried on. The assertion was made that this work should be placed on a more sure and elevated basis.

When I heard these words, I thought to myself, What do these statements mean? I have been instructed that the arbitrary authority exercised at one time in Battle Creek to control all our publishing houses was never again to have sway. To make such propositions was more like going back to Egypt than on to Canaan.

From the light given me, I know that such a charge as was proposed by this speaker would bring into the publishing work a ruling power claiming jurisdiction over the entire field. This is not God's plan. No man's intelligence is to become such a controlling power that one man will have kingly authority in Battle Creek or in any other place. In no line of work is any one man to have power to turn the wheel. God forbids.

Many more things were said, and I became more and more heavily burdened, because I knew that the great changes proposed would take us back to where we would have to wrestle with the same difficulties with which we wrestled in past years. I knew that those who advanced these ideas were blind as to the results.

Among the things said was the statement that great changes were to be made,--that the plans which in past years our brethren formulated to advance the publishing work, would have to be remodeled.

Then One of authority stepped forward and said: "The plans that have been made are not to be torn to pieces. Instead of doing this, the men who are handling sacred things are to cease looking to men for wisdom, and begin looking to the One from whom alone any man, great or small, learned or unlearned, can receive wisdom. A change must take place in the hearts of all who have any connection with God's work. At this stage of the publishing work no man is required to come in and so arrange matters that any one human being shall become a voice for the whole, a ruling power, having kingly authority.

In the past, the Lord's work has been carried on altogether too much in accordance with the dictation of human agencies. The propositions made in this meeting were originated in blindness, and throw no light on the situation. A time of great perplexity and distress is not the time to be in a hurry to cut the knot of difficulty. In such a time are needed men of God-given ingenuity, tact, and patience. They are to work in such a way that they will "hurt" not the oil and the wine".

"Too heavy responsibilities are not to be placed on any one man. In the direction of the canvassing work, the Lord will exercise His power and grace through various men in all parts of His vineyard. He will use men of Christian experience, men who are daily growing in grace and in a knowledge of the truth, men who are capable because they are yoked up with Christ.

"Let those in positions of responsibility accept the Saviour's invitation to wear His yoke. "Come Unto Me," He pleads, "all ye that labor and are heavy burden, and I will give you rest. Take my yoke upon you, and learn of me; for I am meek and lowly in heart; and ye shall find rest unto your souls. For my yoke is easy, and my burden is light!"

"The advice that was given to Moses when he was overburdened with cares and perplexities, is of the highest value today to those who are in positions of responsibility in God's cause. The counsel given him should be carefully studied by those entrusted with the management of the work in the Lord's vineyard. No one man or set of men is to have supreme authority to shape and to control the policy of the workers in the entire field, even with respect to the canvassing work; for every section of the country, especially the Southern field, which has been so long neglected, has its peculiar features, and must be worked accordingly. Let men be willing to understand these features and in their work for these fields prepare themselves by putting on every piece of the Christian armor, not forgetting to wear the gospel shoes." The apostle says: -- (Quoted, Ephesians 6:11-18.)

My brethren, these are the directions given you by God. Let no man complicate or mystify the plain directions by the highest Authority. Preach the Word: speak according to a "Thus said the Lord." with all the earnestness of the Holy Spirit. Never remove from your feet the gospel shoes. Be sure to keep them on. Your feet are always to be "shod with the preparation of the gospel of peace."

Observing carefully every direction that the Lord has specified in regard to the Christian armor, you will walk before him softly, and will work discreetly. You will not carry with you any yokes to bind men to your plans, nor will you attempt to make the Lord's workers amenable to any finite mind. The maxims and precepts of men are not to control His laborers. Let no man be placed in a position where he can lord it over God's heritage; for this imperils alike the soul of him who rules and the souls of those who are under his rule.

No man is so high in power and authority but that Satan will assail him with temptation. And the more responsible the position a man occupies the fiercer and more determined are the assaults of the enemy. Let God's servants in every place study his Word, looking constantly to Jesus that they may be changed into his image. The inexhaustible fullness and the all-sufficiency of Christ are at our command, if we walk before God in humility and contrition.

Christ has laid the only foundation on which we can safely build. "Other foundation can no man lay than that is laid, which is Jesus Christ." Build on this foundation. On doing this depends your present peace and happiness, and your future well-being. Be careful how you build. Do not bring to the foundation material represented in the Word of God as wood, hay, and stubble. Do not bring your own inventions into your character-building. These are perishable, and will be consumed. Do not put human wisdom in the place of Him who is the Light of the World the Sun of righteousness, our peace and assurance forever.

Among the Lord's servants there is to be no commanding. No yokes are to be placed on the necks of God's blood-bought heritage. Every yoke is to be broken. Men and women are more precious in the sight of God than the human mind can estimate. Christ understands their value; for he sacrificed Himself for their redemption. We are his property, the purchase of his life-blood. Sign not away your allegiance to any human jurisdiction or power. "You are not your own; for ye are bought with a price; therefore glorify God in your body, and in your spirit, which are God's."

Take unto you the whole armor of God, and never forget the gospel shoes of peace. Go not to any man with a heavy tread or with anger in your voice. Let all God's servants, from those occupying the highest positions to those in the lowest service, walk humbly before Him.

Learn of Christ, and the peace that passes all understanding will come into your hearts. In Him there is an unfailing supply of Grace. Daily eat of the bread of heaven, and daily drink of the water of life. Carefully and prayerfully study the Saviour's words, and you will grow strong in his strength. Make the Scriptures the man of your gospel. Worship God, not man. Christ is your hope and your crown of rejoicing: bring into the daily life His meekness and lowliness. This will make your experience of value. Thus you will gain a preparedness for service.

Just before His crucifixion, Christ said to His disciples, "A new commandment I give unto you, that ye love one another: as I have loved you, that ye also love one another."

To the disciples this commandment was new; for they had not loved one another as Christ had loved them. He saw that new ideas and impulses must control them, that new principles must be practiced by them; through His life and death they were to receive a new conception of love. The command to love one another had a new meaning in the light of his sacrifice. During every hour of Christ's sojourn on earth, the love of God was flowing from him in irrepressible streams. All who are imbued with his spirit will love as he loved. The very principles that actuated Christ will actuate them in all their dealings with one another.

"By this shall all men know that ye are my disciples, if ye have love one to another. "Christ declared. Let us follow the Saviour's example. Let none take upon himself the grave responsibility of ruling the conscience of his fellow men. This God forbids. We are all God's little children. No kingly power is to be exercised.

Ellen G. White.

Chapter 82—The Work in the Southern Field

December 26, 1902.

To My Brethren in Positions of Responsibility:

During the night following our interview in my house and out on the lawn under the trees, October 19, 1902, in regard to the work in the Southern field, the Lord instructed me that I had taken a wrong position.

In our morning council-meeting statements were made that I need not repeat, statements showing why a successful work could not be done in Nashville, because Edson White would be sustained by his mother. This was the tenor of the remarks made. Strong representations were made in regard to the terrible condition of things existing in the institutions at Nashville. It was stated that if I would sustain Edson White in his methods of working, nothing could be done to change the situation. The brethren put questions to me, and I spoke words in reply that gave them liberty to do in Nashville all that they would, under similar circumstances, do elsewhere. I was cut to the heart. I thought to myself, "Why should not I give them this liberty? If wrongs exist, as the brethren represent, most thorough work should be done to make these wrongs right."

But after I went to my room I passed through an experience. For three nights in succession I was instructed by the Lord that I had spoken unadvisedly; that matters had not been correctly represented to me, some of the particulars not being given; and that I should not consent merely because Edson White is my son, to allow him to be condemned, or to allow his God-given work to be hindered and wronged, as it certainly had been, and would continue to be, unless the light that the Lord had given me in regard to the work in the southern field were used in a way altogether different from the way in which the brethren planned to use it. I was instructed that the understanding of these men had been perverted by the words of those who, prompted by a perverse spirit, understood not what they were saying. If these men had passed through the same experience that the brethren in Nashville have, not one of them would have accomplished as much as the workers there have. They would have given up, discouraged.

In connection with the Southern work, transactions have taken place that never should have been permitted. Money that was called for to use in breaking up the ground in places that have never been worked, was appropriated to places where work has been carried forward for some time. It was wrong not to allow the means given for opening new fields, to be used where the people supposed it would be. Every facility, every advantage, should be given to the men whom the Lord has appointed and fitted to enter new territory. Men who by past experience know how to plan and devise methods for doing a work similar to the work that has already been done in several places. Every hand should be outstretched to encourage the workers and to prepare the way before them. Liberal gifts should be made in response to the calls for means to advance the great work that must be one in this field, a field where the greatest difficulties must be met and overcome.

Nashville to be Made a Center

Years ago the Spirit of the Lord moved upon the hearts of men to establish in Nashville institutions of learning to educate the colored people of the South. The Lord now desires his people to establish institutions in this center, where a good work has already been done. In this place prejudice is not so easily aroused; buildings that can be utilized to advantage may be secured in which to make a beginning; workers for the colored race are protected, so that they can labor in safety; and the buildings in which they carry forward their work are not so liable to be destroyed.

Some of our brethren saw these advantages, and decided to make this city a center for the work in the Southern states. The Lord approved of this step. But not a few of the brethren were dissatisfied. Their ideas were not met by the decision to establish the publishing house in this city, and they selfishly endeavored to divert to other places the means that our brethren in the North had given in response to appeals, means that the donors supposed was being used in Nashville. Obstacles were thrown before the workers by our own people, making every step of the way hard and trying. O how much less difficult this work would have been, if men to whom God had given such great light had not brought in their own ideas to hinder the work.

Notwithstanding this opposition, the Lord wrought, and the work began. A building suitable for a printing office was secured for much less than its real value, and equipped. By the time the institution was ready to be opened, an excellent class of workers had been gathered together. The Lord revealed to me that some of these needed to be carefully looked after and held by the hand of faith, lest under adverse influences they might become discouraged.

Soon the leaven of criticism and accusation was introduced among the helpers in the office. This was enough to sadden and discourage those who had made a beginning, but still they went forward. Those who have spoken disparagingly of the work that these pioneer accomplished, have not spoken in accordance with God's will; for from the light given me, I know that He who reads beneath the surface, sees that those who have gathered up reports against this work, could not have done so well, with so small an outlay of means, as have those who began by utilizing buildings already erected.

Notwithstanding the voices that were raised in favor of establishing the publishing work in some other place, the Lord gave light and encouragement to the brethren to begin in Nashville. These voices that have so often been heard on the negative side of questions, were on this occasion silenced by the reproof of the Lord; for His hand was in the work in this place from the beginning. However, these adverse influences have by no means been checked completely by the light that the Lord has been pleased to give. Some of the brethren have been as men convinced against their will, and are of the same opinion still.

God has wrought in the southern field; yet if these who have received light had walked in the light, how much more might have been accomplished. How much farther advanced the work would have been, if they had used their supposedly superior capabilities, and shown what they could to in working a field that had never been worked before. I have much more to say in regard to the way matters have been treated in this field. In time, these things will all be seen as they are, and those who do not now understand them will then be able to reason from cause to effect.

The Lord is not pleased with the movements made by those who have opposed the work that centers in Nashville. He reads the heart of every man. Those who have opposed the clear light he gave in regard to making this place a center, should have awakened to a realization of their duty to establish centers of influence by erecting memorials for God. If they had manifested a desire to do their best to help, the work would not have been so hard and trying for the laborers, some of whom, constantly criticized and accused, have nearly lost their lives on account of overwork and anxiety.

The Spirit Manifested During The First Union Conference Held in Nashville

A mistake was made in trying to finish one of the buildings in time to accommodate those who attended the Southern Union Conference held in Nashville about a year ago. In the effort to have everything convenient For those who came, those in charge labored for a time under heavy pressure, greatly taxing their physical and mental strength, and thus endangering their lives. They thought that if the buildings could be completed, the visiting brethren would be so favorable impressed by the good beginning made, that their fault-finding would be changed to commendation.

For one of the office-rooms, a carpet was purchased, costing seventy-five cents a yard. Some office furniture, too, was secured. The purchase of these things might have been delayed, but should not be regarded as a sin. Nevertheless, small transactions of this nature were seized upon by some of the delegates, and condemned. Their minds were open to receive wrong impressions, they were imbued with a spirit of criticism, and they dishonored the Lord. Blinded by prejudice, they could not see that the motive was good which prompted the laborers to make these purchases. The workers in Nashville had borne the burden of much extra labor and wearing night work in order to make it possible for the meeting to be held there. They hoped that their work would be approved. They did everything that they could to accommodate and make comfortable the guests who came. But what was seen by him who seeth in secret? A little group of men here, another of women there, communicating to one another the leaven of criticism. If they had had the Spirit of Christ, they would have commended instead of criticizing.

It gave me much pleasure to see in the building where I had a room, some of the articles of furniture that had once been in my own home in Battle Creek. I saw a sofa and a chair that formerly belonged to my husband, Also some sets of furniture and other conveniences that I had given to be used where most needed. But many of these who were cared for at the meeting, dishonored God by their criticisms. They gave but little encouragement to the men who had worked almost beyond human endurance in order to make them comfortable. I was on the ground. I speak the things I know. The Lord has not pronounced the judgment, that those so forward to condemn have pronounced. He was not pleased with the spirit of accusation, and of imagining evil where no evil existed.

Contemplated Changes

In general meetings that have been held since that time, decisions were made that should never have been made. The men who had borne the burden in the heat of the day became disappointed and confused. Changes were made that did not improve matters in the sight of him who sees the end from the beginning.

It was thought best by some to place the management of the publishing house in the hands of new men. If at this time the Lord had not spoken and presented matters in a different light, everything would have been in the utmost confusion. As these things have been written out, I know that the thoughts of the Lord are of good, and not of evil. Not all has been done that should have been done, and that would have been done if more of the brethren in the Southern field had been moved by the Spirit of God, and had worked in willing cooperation with Him, filling their place by building up the work in the city which God specified should be made a center. But a good work has been done, Not one of the fault-finders could have done better.

It would have been best not to work on borrowed capital; and the brethren would not have needed to do this, if all the believers had worked unitedly to one end. Just at this time the showing presented as the result of working on borrowed capital, gives the enemy an advantage. Notwithstanding this every square foot of room in the building erected is needed, and will be utilized either now or in the near future. The present financial embarrassment has been magnified in such a way as to make the work hard and to leave wrong impressions on minds. It would not be surprising if souls were lost beyond recovery, on account of these impressions. O what can not evil surmisings and jealousies do? They are as cruel as the grave. The false reports spread by the enemy result in disunion and in efforts to tear down. The Lord desires his workers to labor in harmony, building up the interests of his cause.

In connection with our institutions in various places, there are sometimes, among a few of the brethren, one-sides secret conversations. Misunderstandings arise and multiply. Misrepresentations are made, and words are spoken in regard to dishonest work being done, until finally what is at first merely a supposition or a report seems to be so fully substantiated that men are led to believe a lie, and to think that they must do quick work to remedy the supposed evil. The Lord Jesus sees it all. He himself interposes, and changes the plans that have been proposed to cure these imagined evils.

Thus it was in Nashville. God forbade the brethren in responsibility to take the hasty steps that they had decided to take. He said that they were in no case to be allowed to follow such a course; for at that time they would be unable to remove the wrong impressions that would be left on the minds of the people. If changes had been made in the publishing house when the brethren anticipated making them, if those who had worked faithfully had been tried, judged, and condemned according to man's wisdom, a deep and lasting injustice would have been done to the ones misjudged.

Too many mismoves have already been made. Men are not gods. Our brethren so desirous of making changes should have remembered the instruction given to the children of Israel through the prophet of Zachariah: "The hands of Zerubbabel have laid the foundation of this house; his hands shall also finish it; and thou shalt know that the Lord of hosts hath sent me unto you. For who hath despised the day of small things? for they shall rejoice, and shall see the plummet in the hand of Zerubbabel with those seven; they are the eyes of the Lord, which run to and fro through the whole earth."

In the visions of the night I was in a meeting of the brethren in the Southern field. J. E. White was sitting far back in the room. In that company there was one of heaven's appointment, who placed his hand on Edson's shoulder, and led him to the front ranks, saying, "This is your place. In influence you are to stand with your brethren. You are to have a voice in their council-meetings. You are deserving of all the approval that is given to one who has carried heavy burdens in the heat of the day." Addressing the company, the Messenger continued: "In his effort to advance the work in the South, he has made many sacrifices, and has nearly lost his life. Now he is deserving of the full confidence of all in this assembly. Not that he had made no mistakes, but those who judge and condemn would, under similar circumstances, have done no better. "He that is without sin among you, let him first cast a stone."

Although J. E. White resigned his position of trust, this was not because he was convicted of unfaithfulness. Some, it is true, made it appear that this was why he offered to withdraw from official responsibility. He resigned because of the Spirit, the words and the deportment of others. There were men who were more than willing to take his place, but they would have proved that they were not fitted for carrying such responsibilities.

The matters that have been so perplexing will be adjusted by the Lord. My brethren, you are not to turn out of office the ones whose work God has accepted, even if in your judgment they have made some mistakes. Meddle not with matters that you do not comprehend because you have not passed over the ground. Some of you have a wrong conception of many things. Do you not see that you are ceasing to follow in the way of the Lord? You are deviating from the path of duty appointed you. Guard well your own souls. Do the work that God had given you. Leave His appointed workers with Him. Your unconsecrated movements have been placed upon others very heavy burdens, and have made necessary the expenditure of much time and money in order to settle matters that would have adjusted themselves if meddlesome minds had not placed the worst possible construction upon the transactions that they could make appear in a false light.

Men do not understand how serious are the issues connected with their relation to God's cause. When men do things crookedly, the Lord calls upon them to make them straight. My brethren, keep straight ahead. If you neglect your own work to criticize and condemn the work given someone else, much time and effort will be required to recover what you have lost. Thus trials are created that need never exist. We are simply to follow our leader. To turn from the pathway of duty brings trial. No one can leave his place without suffering the ensuing confusion.

Opposition Against Making Nashville a Center

In a meeting presented before me for three successive nights while I was in Fresno, I saw that there was a confederacy, as it were, of men in Nashville who were united in sentiment, and who were sustained by some of the brethren in Graysville. The wicked work of this confederacy was laid open before me. There are several who have never been reconciled to the plan of making Nashville a center. I could mention names, but will not do so now. The Lord knows their names, and he can not endorse their works.

There were no good or justifiable grounds on which to work this confederacy against the establishment of the work in Nashville. The Lord bids me stand at my post against this movement. Not one of those men in opposition know what they are doing. They have had very little experience in pioneer work in the South. They might have entered new fields years ago. They would thus have gained an experience that they do not now have. The Lord bids them stand aside, if with humbled hearts they will not come into line and acknowledge the wickedness of the raid they have tried so hard to make against the work centering in Nashville. Who could have the courage to stand as targets for the words of criticism and condemnation hurled by those whose minds are leavened with the misrepresentations of the ones who choose to stand in opposition to God's work in this city? If those who have confederated against the work in Nashville refuse to repent, the sooner they separate from the work in the South the better it will be for this field. The Lord has marked every impulse that has led from cause to effect. None could have done a better work than have the laborers in Nashville.

It is truly amazing to see what gross misrepresentations can be conjured up, and what the results of these misrepresentations are. To cherish feelings of bitterness and hatred because certain suggestions and plans have not been adopted, is not in accordance with the principles of sound reason or Christianity. How foolish it is to try to hedge about a work that God had bidden us to carry forward and sustain. These false statements have done their evil work. Those who have used the talent of speech to tear down a work that God commends, have revealed that they can not be trusted to establish missionary centers.

The assailing element is strong, but it can not prevail. If it were to prevail, the result would be the worst chapter in the experience of our people. Notwithstanding this opposition, Nashville is being made a center. How much this effort has cost the ones whom God appointed to do this work, I can not tell. The record is in the books of heaven, and words traced by angels can not be perverted into a lie.

A Call to Repentance

What is the real strength of a church? - Not its members; not those who are supposed to have knowledge and experience. A cultured intellect, unsanctified, is as nothing. Why should not the truth prevail in Nashville? Shall the truth be powerless because unsanctified hearts are seeking for the supremacy? Because unconsecrated tongues have given false representations? God calls for workers who will wear Christ's yoke. "Take my yoke upon you." the Saviour says, "and learn of me; for I am meek and lowly in heart, and ye shall find rest unto your souls. For my yoke is easy, and my burden is light."

I have a message for the laborers in the Southern field. Selfishness is seeking recognition and support. Other centers besides Nashville shall be created; but make this center your rallying point now. Take not the forthcoming council meeting in Graysville, but come right to the center of action. Then if all will humble their hearts in repentance and confession before God He will pardon.

Those who engage in the work of uprooting things in Nashville are not led by the Spirit of God, but by another Spirit.

Let the opposition develop; for such things will be seen in these last days. Amidst it all, God's work will move forward, leaving behind the elements that would block the way; for truth is truth, falsehood is falsehood. A lie is not the truth. Many misrepresentations have been in circulation, but why should the truth be blanketed? Remove the blanket. Why should not the truth prevail? Can we doubt God's word? What has He ever said that He has not done? Is it not written, My Word.... shall not return unto me void, but it shall accomplish that which I please, and it shall prosper in the thing whereto I send it."

Time is too short, our work too important, for any one to engage in an effort to tear down the work of another man whom God has appointed to service. My brethren, the schemes that seem so plausible to you, are not of God's devising. Satan will instigate all that he possibly can to discourage, to draw men of talent from the work of preaching the Word, publishing the truth, and circulating our publications in the highways and byways. You have not time to aid the enemy in his effort to drive God's workers out of the Southern field. This is not the work that God has given you.

In the name of the Lord I say to the men who desire to do some great thing, Please, for the sake of your spiritual life, keep your hands off the ark of God. There is One who is ever working. He will take care of his holy work.

Wherein lies the strength of the church? In unity, in humility, in perfect adherence to the Word of the Lord. In selfish superiority, men would take the throne, as if there was no God to direct and to give power to His workers. Let those connected with our publishing houses, our schools, and our medical institutions be men and women chosen of God and regenerated through His Holy Spirit. Let them seek for truth as for hidden treasure.

My brethren, many of you have left your first love. "Remember therefore from whence thou art fallen, and repent, and do the first works." To those who do not repent, Christ declares, "I will come unto thee quickly, and will remove thy candlestick out of his place, except thou repent." Put away the devisings and theories of men. No longer follow in the light of the sparks of your own kindling. Remember the words, "Except thou repent." "I will come unto thee quickly, and will remove thy candlestick out of his place."

The Lord bids me say to those who are opposing the work centering in Nashville; Discern your spiritual condition. Return to the first love that you have left. Satan is seeking to entice all to leave their first love, and to devote their God-given talents to the enemy's service, tearing down that which the Lord desires to build up. I ask those at Nashville and at Graysville whose names I have not mentioned, to seek the Lord while He may be found. "Call ye upon Him while He is near: let the wicked forsake his way, and the unrighteous man his thought! Let him return unto the Lord, and He will have mercy upon him; and to our God; for he will abundantly pardon. For My thoughts are not your thoughts, neither are your ways My ways, saith the Lord. For as the heavens are higher than the earth, so are My ways higher than your ways, and my thoughts than your thoughts."

My brethren, read the seventeenth chapter of John, and see if you can not understand that you have left your first love. Christ prayed that his disciples might be one, as he was one with the Father. "As thou hast sent me into the world," he declared to the Father, "even so have I also sent them into the world. And for their sakes I sanctify myself, that they also might be sanctified through the truth. Neither pray I for these alone, but for them also which shall believe on Me through their word: that they all may be one; as thou, Father, are in Me, and I in Thee, that they also may be one in us; that the world may believe that thou hast sent me. And the glory which thou gavest me I have given them, that they may be one, even as we are one: I in them, and thou in me, that they may be made perfect in one: and that the world may know that thou has sent me, and hast loved them, as thou hast loved me. Father, I will that they also, whom thou hast given me, be with me where I am, that they may behold my glory, which thou hast given me; for thou lovedst me before the foundation of the world. O righteous Father, the world hath not known thee, but I have known thee, and these have known that thou has sent me. And I have declared unto them thy name, and will declare it, that the love wherewith thou hast loved me may be in them, and I in them."

Light to Shine Forth

Light will shine upon the workers in Nashville. From this center of light will shine forth in the ministry of the Word, in the publication of books large and small. We have as yet merely touched the Southern Field with the tips of our fingers. "The earth shall be filled with the knowledge of the glory of the Lord, as the waters cover the sea." The same

Voice that at the beginning said, "Let there be light," in these last days declares that a knowledge of God's Word shall not be confined merely to a few places.

The laborers who have the missionary spirit will go forth as heralds of the morning. Christ, Heaven's Conqueror, is in the midst of you. From the experiences you are now passing through in the South, all may learn lessons. Truth and righteousness live, and will continue to shine amidst the darkness of this degenerate age.

My brethren in Nashville, when any attempt is made to divert your minds from the work that the Lord has appointed you to do, let your voices ring out in accents clear and distinct. With unmistakable determination say: "I am doing a great work, and can not come down. Why should this work cease, as it would if I were to leave it and come down to you?" Never, never although surrounded by those who desire to quench the last spark of life that God is keeping alive, should you consent to such proposal.

Those whom the truth makes free are free indeed. We are not to be under bondage to any man or confederacy of men. We need the guidance of the Holy Spirit. We have followed man's wisdom long enough. And we can avoid the consequences of following this wisdom, if we choose to follow the Lord now, just now. We need a wisdom greater than the wisdom of man to strengthen the things that remain, that are ready to die.

Words of Encouragement

To Brother W. O. Palmer I would say: Be not discouraged. When your fellow workers manifest the spirit of the enemy by saying and doing things that hurt, keep silent; for this is your strength. When you are misjudged and tantalized, remember that you are not the only one who is wounded. Christ, in the person of his saints, receives the insults that are intended for us. Look to Jesus; behold his hands and his feet pierced for your sake; say within your heart, He was wounded for my transgressions. He was bruised for my iniquities, the chastisement of my peace was upon him, and with his stripes I am healed.

There are seasons of trouble when you can see nothing to calm and reassure, seasons when you feel helpless under the pressure of implied guilt. In the confusion, you know not which way to turn. Neither you nor Edson White should ever speak words of retaliation. Pray together. Remember the storm on the sea of Galilee. The disciples did all they could to save themselves and the ship, but their strength and skill availed them nothing. Helpless in the grasp of the tempest, they looked into one another's faces, and could read only discouragement and despair. Their boat was filling.

Absorbed in their efforts to save themselves, they had forgotten that Jesus was on board. Suddenly they came to their senses. They remembered at whose command they had set out to cross the sea. In Jesus was their only hope. "Master, Master!" they cried.

There was no response to their call. Again they called; again no response. Suddenly a flash of lightning revealed him sleeping. Arousing him, they exclaimed, "Lord, save us, we perish! And he saith unto them, Why are ye fearful, O ye of little faith? Then he arose, and rebuked the winds and the sea; and there was a great calm. But the men marveled, saying, What manner of man is this, that even the winds and the sea obey him?"

There seasons of trouble when no human being on the earth can help us. To such a time the disciples had come, when they remembered that Jesus was on board their vessel.

Could our eyes be opened, we should behold Satan watching for an opportunity to stir up the human passions, to prompt men and women to speak words that cause the tempted one to lose vantage ground with God and to stand on the enemy's ground, where he will be overcome by Satan's wiles. Thus the confidence of the brethren in one another is hurt and destroyed. Let every one look unto Jesus, and keep the tongue from uttering any words but those that Jesus uttered when he was tempted in all points like as we are. He always met the tempter with the words, "It is written." This we can do in all safety. When the feelings are stirred, not one word should be uttered, even in answer to a provoking question.

There are times when those who claim to be God's children can be very exasperating: for, inspired by Satan, they manifest a perverse, stubborn spirit, making it very hard for others who desire to do right. But let every tried and tempted one remember that the Majesty of heaven has been tempted in all points like as the members of the human family are tempted, and he knows how to succor those who are beset by the powers of darkness.

Paul, in his epistle to the Hebrews, writes: "Every high priest taken from among men is ordained for men in things pertaining to God, that he may offer both gifts and sacrifices for sins: who can have compassion on the ignorant, and on them that are out of the way; for that he himself also is compassed with infirmity. And by reason hereof he ought, as for the people, so also for himself, to offer for sins. And no man taketh this honor unto himself, but he that is called of God, as was Aaron. So also Christ glorified not himself to be made an high priest; but he that said unto him, Thou art my Son, today have I begotten thee. As he saith also in another place, Thou art a priest forever after the order of Melchisedec. Who in the days of his flesh, when he had offered up prayers and supplications with strong crying and tears unto Him that was able to save him from death, and was heard in that he feared; though he were a Son, yet learned he obedience by the things which he suffered; and being made perfect, he became the author of eternal salvation unto all them that obey him."

"Seeing then that we have a great high priest, that is passed into the heavens, Jesus the Son of God, let us hold fast our profession. For we have not an high priest which can not be touched with the feeling of our infirmities; but was in all points tempted like as we are, yet without sin. Let us therefore come boldly to the throne of grace, that we may obtain mercy, and find grace to help in time of need."

My brethren, you need to bear in mind that you are in the presence of One who has compassion on the ignorant, and on them that are out of the way; for that he himself also is compassed with infirmity." Let all our workers in every place keep this in mind. He who puts his trust in Christ can never be severed from him by any man. "Draw nigh to God, and he will draw nigh to you." Will you believe this, even when sorely tempted by Satan to speak unadvisedly? Not a word can be spoken to arouse in another man's mind feelings that will unbalance Him, but that Christ himself is hurt in the person of one of the members of his family.

How subtly Satan works to create disaffection and strife among brethren! Those who are so ready to criticize and condemn should study their Bibles. Christ says, "Whoso eateth my flesh, and drinketh my blood, hath eternal life.... It is the Spirit that quickeneth; the flesh profiteth nothing! the words that I speak unto you, they are spirit and they are life."

I am instructed to send words of warning to the workers at Nashville: Look to Jesus, and not to men. We must realize that nothingness of man's wisdom. Christ is saying to you personally: Your case is in my keeping. So long as you cooperate with Me, you are entirely safe. Your comfort, your peace, lie not in human agencies or in the confederacies you may form. Those who are willing to wear my yoke and learn of me my meekness and lowliness, shall find rest, because they make me their trust, their dependence. "Cease ye from man, whose breath is in his nostrils; for wherein is he to be accounted of?" Your comfort and peace lie not in seeking for the mastery or in striving for selfish advantage.

There are workers who are under the leadership of Him who is above all principalities and powers. These have peace and rest in Christ Jesus. They are not watching for defects in their fellow workers. They do not stand on Satan's side of the controversy as accusers of their brethren, weakening and destroying the influence of God's children.

The work to be done is the Lord's, and He has entrusted this work to man. Our call to ministry is received from no human being. To every man God has given his work. How careful every one should be not to neglect his God-given work by devoting his mind, his tongue, his influence, to discourage another laborer of God's appointment, and to try to break up a good work. To do this is to fight against God.

When the light of Christ's countenance is revealed in the faces of his workers, when Christlikeness characterizes their spirit and disposition, this will be so unmistakably plain that none can help seeing that they have been with Jesus and have learned of Him.

Ellen G. White.

Chapter 83—To the Teachers of the Fernando School

St. Helena, Cal, May 17, 1903.

I have something to say in regard to the school in Fernando. Last night I was in earnest conversation with the school faculty. I was bearing them a decided message.

We are very grateful to God that there have been conversions in the school. But the school is not in all things reading the high standard to which it may attain. A mistake was made in choosing the name adopted, and in the announcement of studies that it was said would be taught. It is not wise for a new school to lift its banner and promise a high grade of work, before it has proved that it is fully able to do preparatory work as it should be done. It should be the great aim in every intermediate school to do most thorough work in the common branches.

In every school that is established among us, the teachers should begin humbly, not grasping the higher rounds of the ladder before they have climbed the lower ones. They are to climb round after round, beginning at the bottom. They are to be learners, even as they teach

the common branches. When they have come down to the simplicity of true education, they will better understand how to prepare students for advanced studies. Teachers are to learn as they teach. Advancement is to be made, and by advancement experience is to be gained.

Our teachers are not to think that their work ends with giving instruction from books. They should devote several hours each day to working with the students in some line of manual training. This should in no case be neglected.

In every school there should be those who have a store of patience and disciplinary talent. It should be the part of these to see that every line of work is kept up to the highest standard. Lessons in neatness, order, and thoroughness are to be given to the students. They are to be taught to keep everything in the school and about the grounds in perfect order.

A teacher should learn to control himself before he attempts to deal with the youth. If he is not a constant learner in the school of Christ, if he has not the discernment and discrimination that enable him to employ wise methods in his work, if he can not control those in his charge with firmness, yet pleasantly and kindly, how can he be successful in his teaching? The teacher who is not under the control of God needs to heed the invitation, "Take my yoke upon you, and learn of me; for I am meek and lowly in heart, and ye shall find rest unto your souls. For my yoke is easy, and my burden is light."

Every one acting in the capacity of a teacher should learn daily of Jesus, wearing his yoke of restraint, sitting in his school as a student, obeying the rules of Christian principle. The teacher who is not under the guidance of the great Teacher will not be able to meet successfully the different developments that will arise as the result of the perversity of the children and youth with whom he is dealing.

Let the teacher bring love and peace and cheerfulness into this work. Let him not allow himself to become angry or provoked. The Lord is looking upon him with intense interest, to see if he is being educated by the great Teacher. The child who loses his self-control is far more excusable than the teacher who allows himself to become angry and impatient. When a teacher has a reproof to give, let him give it in a soft, gentle voice. Let him be careful not to make the child stubborn by speaking to him harshly. Let him follow every correction with drops of the oil of kindness. His heart should be softened by love and kindness. He should never forget that he is dealing with Christ in the person of one of Christ's little children.

Let it be a settled maxim that in all school discipline faithfulness and love are to reign. When a student is corrected in such a way that he can not get the idea that the teacher desires to humiliate him, love for the teacher springs up in his heart.

Ellen G. White.

Chapter 84—To Those in Charge of the Fernando School

St. Helena, Cal, May 17, 1903.

My dear Brethren:

I have received a letter from Brother Santee regarding the work of the Fernando school. He says, "God has blessed our Fernando school in many ways, and there is prospect of a much larger attendance in the next school year." "We have labored for the students faithfully, and nearly all have given themselves to the Lord."

For this encouraging report I am very thankful. It is for this that we have hoped, and for this that we have prayed. Every student attending our schools should put on Christ, that by and by he may sit with the angels in heavenly places with Christ.

The light given me is that the educational branch of our work will be of great importance. What is it that will make our schools a power? It is not the size of the buildings. It is not the number of advanced studies taught. It is the faithful work done by teachers and students, as they begin at the lower rounds of the ladder of progress, and climb diligently round by round.

Intermediate schools are highly essential. There are many parents who do not know how to train their children to be workers together with God. They have not in all things outgrown their childishness, and therefore they know not now to care properly for the church in their homes. Fathers and mothers have become indifferent to their obligations to God and unmindful of their duty to their children. Therefore we must establish schools that will be as the schools of the prophets.

Recently it has been clearly presented to me that by the continued sale of the book, "Christ's Object Lessons", we may obtain means to help in establishing these schools, and in freeing from indebtedness those already in operation.

The word of God is to lie at the foundation of all the work done in these schools. And the students are to be taught the true dignity of labor. They are to be shown that God is a constant worker. Let every teacher take hold heartily with a group of students, working with them, and teaching them how to work. As the teachers do this, they will gain a valuable experience. Their hearts will be bound up with the hearts of the students, and this will open the way for successful teaching.

Thorough work must be done in these schools; for many students will go from them directly into the great harvest field. They will go forth to use what they have learned, as canvassers, and as helpers in various lines of evangelistic work. Many workers, after studying for a time in the field, will feel the need for further study, and with the experience gained in the field will be prepared to value school privileges and to make rapid advancement. Some will desire an education in the higher branches of study. For these our colleges have been established.

It would be a sad mistake for us to fail to consider thoroughly the purpose for which each of our schools is established. This is a matter that should be faithfully considered by our responsible men in each union conference. All the different educational interests should be given careful consideration, and then each school should place its work on a proper basis.

I fear that my brethren have misunderstood my words regarding the Fernando school. I did not suppose that they would call it a college, or undertake to do college work. I was pleased with the number of students present at the opening, and with their appearance, and I wished to encourage them to reach the highest standard of excellence and usefulness. But I knew quite well that the school was not prepared to do the work done at Healdsburg College in advanced studies, or to give instruction that would entitle it to the appellation of college.

It is a mistake for our schools to get out flowery notices of what they intend to do. It would have been well if at the very start you had counselled more freely with your brethren of the union conference, who have had experience in educational work.

Some may think that at Fernando we should undertake to do the same work as at Healdsburg College. But we must remember that Healdsburg College was designed to do advanced work for our students in many conferences, and that it took years for Healdsburg College to reach its present advancement. In order for it to do this, a solid foundation had to be laid. Never did I entertain the thought that the present faculty of the Fernando school could do the work done in Healdsburg.

Ellen G. White.

Chapter 85—To the Students of the Fernando School

St. Helena, Cal., May 17, 1903.

I am very much pleased to know that during the first term of the school souls have been converted. I hope that you will always remember that it is for your eternal interest to make the most of your capabilities and opportunities. Remember that in your school life here below you can, if you choose, fit yourself for entrance into the school above.

Those who are indeed Christians will reveal in their lives a fragrance of character that will win others to Christ. While you are in school, help your teachers all you can. Do not grieve and perplex them. They are human, like yourselves, and they need the grace of Christ as verily as you need it. Make the way as pleasant as possible for them. Be pleasant and agreeable. Be careful in regard to your words and actions. Do not make it necessary for your teachers to correct you again and again in regard to your personal habits.

Correct all that is lax or careless in your speech or your habits. Do not pass this over as a matter of little consequence. Wherever you are, keep your room clean and tidy. Let no dirt or rubbish accumulate, "lest the Lord pass by and see your uncleanness." Christ is pure and holy and undefiled. Do not grieve the heavenly angels by cherishing untidy, shiftless habits. It rests with yourselves to decide whether you will be accepted by the Lord as vessels unto honor, fit for his use.

The Lord desires to see in you a daily improvement. Your parents sent you to school with the hope that you would obtain an education that would make you more helpful in the home, more obedient, more kind, more thoughtful, The school term is about to close, and as you return to your homes, let your parents see that the school has accomplished much for you, making you a blessing in the home and in the Lord's work.

Ellen G. White.

Chapter 86—Right Principles of Management

St. Helena, Ca., April 15, 1903.

To the Physicians and Managers of our Medical Work:

I address you as men upon whom the Lord has bestowed great blessings. I must tell you that some of your business transactions are not pleasing to God. Some of your ways of working He can not endorse. In order to secure advantages for certain lines of work, unsanctified, ambitious projects have been resorted to. But the carrying out of these projects will bring a heavy retribution to those responsible for them.

The Lord calls upon you to work in holy, upright lines, in every transaction following the pure, elevated principles given in the Word of God. No business that will misrepresent God and harm his people will bring a particle of honor to you or to the cause which you love. The less you have to do with plans and documents drawn up in accordance with the policy of lawyers, the better it will be for you.

In business transactions you have complied with the customs of the lawyers whom you have employed, arranging matters in a way that you think will guard the work in which you are engaged against the possibilities and probabilities that might occur. Ought you to be surprised, then, that the Watchmen that God has placed on the walls of Zion should also endeavor to fulfill their God-given responsibility, seeking to make all pertaining to our institutions perfectly secure? The Word was spoken by my Instructor: "God's watchmen, who should have been wide awake, who should have understood the condition of our institutions, have been blind as to how things were being carried on by our medical missionary workers in responsible places.

God calls upon our pastors and teachers to be wide awake and not stand as blind watchmen. Let them obtain from Christ the eyesalve that will enable them to see all things clearly. Then let them examine the foundation timbers of our institutions. Not all pertaining to our work is being carried forward in an elevated, upright way. God wants his people to have a clear understanding of all the important transactions pertaining to his cause, that they may know that they are following a course he can approve.

Business transactions should not be veiled with so many technicalities that the real bearing of the agreement is not clearly understood. For years one thing after another has been brought into the Medical Missionary Association--business propositions that are received as fair and just, but which are not. These propositions may prove to be a pit of disappointment for certain ones who did not know that there was the least danger.

There certainly must be a careful investigation of the foundation of our institutions, especially of the Sanitarium, We must not stand by any unfair propositions or allow advantages to be taken of the ones whose money is received in our institutions. Better by far would it be to suffer disappointment in our plans, than to have means to use as we please, and lose the crown of the overcomer. Better far the cross and shattered hopes than to sit with princes and forfeit heaven. "What shall it profit a man if he gain the whole world, and lose his own soul? or what shall a man give in exchange for his soul?"

We seemed to be assembled in a meeting. Our Instructor looked upon the doctors present, and said, You are not all faithful stewards, else there would have been brought into the medical missionary work only that which will build up its reputation, only that which is in harmony with its high title. Those who have the living truth in their hearts, will not accept some of the documents which you have approved. Long documents, filled with blind specifications and technical conditions, may serve to place men where, if they wish to take unfair advantage, they can do a work that God can not approve. These papers may be worded so as to be difficult of understanding, and the common people may be deceived. It may appear that provisions have been made to secure from less those of whom means are solicited, while at the same time the means may be bound up in such a way that it can not be obtained without great difficulty.

You have been very particular to have things securely bound about, so that no undue advantage should be taken of the institution. Is it not right that those who in good faith place their means in the institution, should have just as good security on their side, that no unfair advantage can be taken of them?

The word of the Lord is our guide under all circumstances. It points out of duty to God and to our fellow men. It is the standard for all.

It is perfectly adapted to our necessities. It is the light placed in our hands to guide us to the heavenly home. It tells us that in order to be heirs of God and joint heirs with Christ, we must obey the commands that God has given. Any group of men, whatever their standing or position, however high their profession of godliness, who follow practices that God disallows, can not be approved of heaven. The Lord can not accept the service of those who are grasping and selfish in their dealings, like men of the world, who have no acquaintance with the things of God.

The Lord's people are not to follow the customs of worldly men, taking advantage of circumstances to gain advantage for themselves or for the work which they represent.

Neither are they to follow an unfair course of action. Christ said: "Woe unto you also, ye lawyers! for ye lade men with burdens grievous to be borne, and ye yourselves touch not the burdens with one of your fingers.... "Woe unto you, lawyers! for ye have taken away the key of knowledge; ye entered not in yourselves, and them that were entering in ye hindered."

God says to every minister of the gospel, to every medical missionary worker, to every other worker in his cause, Take your stand on the elevated platform of truth and justice. God will not serve with any man who draws threads of selfishness and unfairness into the web, by his example leading others astray. Our ministers and doctors are to put on the garment of Christ's righteousness. They are to wash their robes of character and make them white in the blood of the lamb.

He who has lost his sensitiveness of character is in danger of losing his soul, and with it an eternity of joy. God will not be trifled with. He will not sanction the least approach to underhand dealing to secure advantage for any branch of his work. The actions of our medical missionaries are to be as clear as the day. These workers are to do all in their power to proclaim the gospel message. They are not, by following a misleading, scheming course, to assure the worldly man that under certain circumstances his course of unjust dealing is justifiable and advisable. Compliance with customs founded on a false basis is to be shunned by every medical missionary.

We are preparing for a life that measures with the life of God. Never should a Seventh-day Adventist medical missionary do anything that will dishonor the name that he bears. Every medical missionary is to show to the world, to lawyers, to doctors, to the church, and to the gospel ministry, that he is a Christian, bound by a solemn covenant to be upright in word and action, to follow a course free from all deception and subterfuge. His life is to be holy. He is to respect his God-given talents, using them in a way that will honor the One who gave his life to redeem humanity from all iniquity, and to purify unto himself a peculiar people, zealous of good works. There must be in his life no taint of dishonesty, no perversion of the holy principles of truth.

In the world men are tried by the standard of wealth and position. Men worship men who meet this standard. But is this the true standard of character? No, no. It is riches, but purity of heart and life, that will gain for human beings entrance into the city of God.

To all our medical missionary workers the Lord says, Lift up the standard of truth higher and still higher. Hold fast to your integrity. Let your lives bear a good report regarding your Saviour's keeping power. Keep no position at the expense of conscience. Smile not at falsehood. Consent not to any dishonest practice. Say to the tempter, Get thee behind me, Satan; and say it with so much meaning, so much decision, that he will see that you have emptied your soul of every falsehood. Do not rest satisfied until you are a partaker of the divine nature, having escaped the corruption that is in the world through lust. Go to the word of God to find out your duty as medical missionaries, else you are not worthy of the name. You are to be "not slothful in business, fervent in spirit, serving the Lord." Those who combine these three essentials are on safe ground.

Let every minister, every doctor, every medical missionary worker, remember that he is not to put his conscience to the rack to favor any business transaction that is not straight-forward, on the part of any man. Whatever his calling or profession, a man is not a Christian unless he follow the example of Christ, by His grace holding fast to his integrity, humility, not of boasting and parade. His life is to show that he has accepted the invitation, "Come unto Me, all ye that labor and are heavy-laden, and I will give you rest. Take my yoke upon you, and learn of me; for I am meek and lowly in heart, and ye shall find rest unto your souls. For my yoke is easy and my burden is light."

One is our Master, even Christ. We have pledged ourselves to live to His name's glory. God grant that the veil that separates us from Him may be drawn aside, and that we may accept him as our Companion and Teacher. We are not to look upon ourselves as gods, able to carry out our own will, our own devising. We are to remember that in order to be successful in our work, we must be sustained by God, we must have the power that Christ gives to all who believe in Him--the power to become the sons of God. We are faithfully to discharge the duties enjoined on us in the Word of God, shunning everything that would make us in character like the arch-deceiver.

Ellen G. White.

Chapter 87—To Those in Council at Battle Creek

"Elmshaven", Sanitarium, Cal., April 16, 1903.

Dear Brethren:

The members of the Medical Missionary and Benevolent Association, and the responsible men of the General Conference, are now to act in concert in regard to the work to be carried on. All must now awake and seek the Lord, lest the powers of the enemy shall obtain the victory. There are much greater depths of spiritual truth to be reached by experience. Christ will lead us to higher and still higher planes, where spiritual perception and spiritual action shall enter into unquestionable discoveries, and where the sacred truths of the gospel shall be understood in all their bearings.

As God's Word is received as food for the soul, the character in spiritual lines will correspond to the truths of the gospel that have been eaten and digested. Thus our spiritual strength will be refreshed as we become partakers of the divine nature, having overcome the corruption that is in the world through lust. The nutritious properties of the heavenly food may be compared with the strength-restoring properties of the leaves of the tree of life, which are for the healing of the nations. Seek for unity, and seek it in faith. Faith we must have, in order that we may walk by faith.

My mind is deeply impressed by the Spirit of God. Instruction is given to me in clear lines. Our work is not left in the hands of finite men. God rules, and he will turn and overturn. He will not allow his work to be carried forward as it had been. His medical missionary work is not to be ruled, controlled, and molded by one man, as for some years it certainly has been. The exercise of such a power, if continued, will mar the work, and will be the certain ruin of the man exercising control. God will work with the men entrusted with large responsibility, if they will take the Lord's way as humble obedient servants, waiting wholly upon him. But if any man sets himself up as being above God, and takes the work under his finite supervision, the watchmen standing on the walls of Zion must discern the danger and take heroic action to save the man and the cause.

Yesterday I read the following incident: "A notable painter was adorning the frescoes in the dome of a cathedral. When a certain portion of his work was done, he stepped backward upon the small scaffold of planks on which he stood, to admire the effect of his skillful craft. Suddenly a comrade who was with him rushed forward to the picture, and with the brush in his hand smeared and spoiled the delicate work so painfully accomplished. Rushing forward, the artist cried angrily, "What is that for?" "Look", said his companion, "one more step backward, and you would have fallen, bruised and mangled on the pavement below." The artist was thankful that his life was saved. Will our brethren in peril consent to be saved from the dangers they are in?

In no case does God require His servants to bear burdens that He has not given them. He does not require them to gather to themselves more responsibilities than they can patiently and successfully carry. Those professing Christians who do this, dishonor the name they bear, and lower the standard of Christianity.

By the managers of the Sanitarium, and the leaders in the medical missionary work, there has been a binding up with the world, which has led to entanglement, There has been much working upon a wrong policy. One man has embraced so many responsibilities that it is impossible for him to give to each proper thought that a careful performance of the Lord's work requires. Men who will carry forward in right lines the work for this time, should rally around the leaders in the work, sharing the responsibilities that they are now carrying, bringing all their plans before their brethren for consideration. Whenever one man devises plans, and seeks to carry them out in a manner so determined that his work savors of oppression, there is need of bringing into connection with him other minds that will keep uplifted the high standard suggested by the name we bear.

Many plans have been devised that God has not ordained. The root from which these plans have sprung, is the mind of finite man. God's watchmen have been blind. They should have been wide awake to see that no man's mind, one man's judgement, was becoming a power that God could not and would not endorse. To invest one man or a few men with so much power and responsibility, is not in accordance with God's way of working.

There must be reorganization. Supreme power must not be vested in a group of men connected with a few large institutions. At the General Conference of 1901 the light was given, Divide the General Conference into union conferences. Let there be fewer responsibilities centered on one place. Let the work of printing our publications be divided.

The principles that apply to the publishing work apply also to the sanitarium work. Students should not be crowded in Battle Creek to receive an education in medical missionary lines. It is not best to encourage the gathering together in one institution of so large a company of people as have been gathered in Battle Creek Sanitarium. Let medical missionary plants be made in many places.

The youth who desire to become missionaries should not be brought in large numbers to Battle Creek. Provision should be made that they may receive an education out of and away from Battle Creek, in places where there is a different religious atmosphere. By fire the Lord removed the great argument in favor of gathering many students to Battle Creek. He swept away the Sanitarium to prevent the carrying out of the idea that Battle Creek was to be the great center for the training of medical students. To carry out this idea would be out of harmony with the work for these last days, and with the plan of the Lord.

God works by means of instruments or second causes. He uses the gospel ministry, medical missionary work, and the publications containing present truth, to impress hearts. All are made effectual by means of faith. As the truth is heard or read, the Holy Spirit send it home to those who hear and read with an earnest desire to know what is right. The gospel ministry, medical missionary work, and our publications are God's agencies. One is not to supersede the other. But you have sought to make the medical missionary work the whole body, instead of the arm and hand.

Let the living gospel be taught in our schools. Let students be educated in its principles, that they may be prepared to impart the truth to others. Let them learn to minister to the spiritual and physical needs of those whom they will meet in their work. By the ministry of the word, the gospel is preached: by medical missionary work the gospel is practiced. The gospel is bound up with medical missionary work. Neither is to stand alone, bound up in itself. The workers in each are to labor unselfishly and unitedly, striving to save sinners.

Ellen G. White.

Chapter 88—To Our Brethren in Council at Battle Creek

St. Helena, Cal., April 17, 1903.

Some way must be devised in which our medical institutions shall be helped. According to the light given me, the Lord will institute ways and means by which the Battle Creek Sanitarium can be helped. When our watchmen shall recover from their blindness, and reason from cause to effect, God will help them to devise ways and means for the relief of our medical institutions.

If we put our trust in the Lord, if we walk in his ways, the Battle Creek Sanitarium can be placed on vantage ground. When the Sanitarium is placed on its proper foundation, when our people can see that it stands as when first established, when they can understand that the institution belongs to the work of the Lord, and can see that no one man is to have control of everything in it, then God will help them all to take hold with courage to build it up.

Our leading brethren, the leading positions, are to examine the standing of the Battle Creek Sanitarium, to see whether the God of heaven can take control of it. When, by faithful guardians, it is placed in a position where he can control it, let me tell you that God will see that it is sustained.

God wants his people to place their feet on the eternal Rock. The money that we have is the Lord's money: and the buildings that we erect with this money, for his work, are to stand as his property. He calls upon those who have received the truth not to quarrel with their brethren, but to stand shoulder to shoulder, to build up, not to destroy.

The light that God has given me is that there are proper ways that the Conference shall devise to help the Sanitarium in Battle Creek. I wish that a portion of the work of this institution had been taken elsewhere. But the Sanitarium has been erected in Battle Creek, and it must be helped. God will institute ways and means by which it can be helped. But he does not wish his people to invest their money in bonds.

One night it seemed to me that we were assembled in council with the leaders of the medical work at Battle Creek. One of authority arose, and holding up a long paper read from it many things that perplexed me. Neither I nor many others could discern the meaning of that which he read. Then He who read from this paper said, "These are men who have allowed the paper to pass as a legal piece of business, as a security for the issuing of bonds to secure money. That long list of conditions is not necessary, but they show unsafety for those who invest their means."

This is not the kind of work that should be placed before those who have the utmost confidence in the men bearing responsibility, supposing them to be faithful, intelligent guardians of the people. Many things will be managed after this same order unless a reorganization shall take place.

There are those who will have nothing to do with the bonds issued, but there are many who will accept them without criticism because they have confidence in the Medical Missionary Association as being loyal to the high principles that it advocates. They will not question the things that they can not understand because they have faith in the original Seventh-day Adventist Medical Missionary Association

No document should be a accepted which is so worded as to make it possible for the medical missionary workers in office so to manage affairs that injustice will be done to those putting confidence in the medical missionary association. These matters must be carefully examined into by the men in position of responsibility in the Medical Missionary Association and the General Conference. There is a snare in these documents, and I am to say, Watch and pray, lest ye enter into temptation. The standing of the Sanitarium and its relation to the cause of God is to ascertained. Everything regarding its organization is to be closely examined, that Seventh-day Adventists may know that true standing of the institution.

Ellen G. White.

Chapter 89—Be Strong, and of Good Courage

"Elmshaven," Sanitarium, Cal., July 27, 1903.

Dear Brother Magan:

I received your letter two or three days ago. I have also received letters from several others, among them one from a Brother Howard of Washington, in regard to the color line. I have been kept very busy answering these letters.

When you see W. C. W. and talk with him, you will understand we have not changed the plans that we made with you. We feel that to change these plans would be to make a great mistake.

My dear brother, be of good courage in the Lord. Have faith in regard to your wife. We are praying for her. We shall have to wrestle with principalities and powers and spiritual wickedness in high places. And we shall have to contend with enemies in the form of our fellow-beings, men who are spiritually blind, and who know not at what they stumble. I see that you are in the struggle. You and Brother Sutherland know what it means to struggle with the calamities of life. Is not the spiritual conflict far greater, when we meet with the disguised powers of darkness, who seem determined to destroy us?

One thing is certain: those Seventh-day Adventists who take their stand under Satan's banner will first give up their faith in the warnings and reproofs contained in the Testimonies of God's spirit.

The call to greater consecration and holier service is being made, and will continue to be made. Some who are now voicing Satan's suggestions will come to their senses. There are those in important positions of trust who do not understand the truth for this time. To them the message must be given. If they receive it, Christ will accept them, and will make them workers together with him. But if they refuse to hear the message, they will take their stand under the black banner of the Prince of Darkness.

I am instructed to say that the precious truth for this time is open more and more clearly to human minds. In a special sense men and women are to eat of Christ's flesh and drink of his blood. There will be a development of the understanding, for the truth is capable of constant expansion. The divine originator of truth will come into closer and still closer communion with those who follow on to know him. As God's people receive his word as the bread of heaven, they will know that his goings forth are prepared as the morning. They will receive spiritual strength, as the body receives physical strength when food is eaten.

We do not half understand the Lord's plan in taking the children of Israel from Egyptian bondage, and leading them through the wilderness into Canaan.

As we gather up the divine rays shining from the gospel, we shall have a clearer insight into the Jewish economy, and a deeper appreciation of its important truths. Our exploration of truth is yet incomplete. We have gathered up only a few rays of light. Those who are not daily students of the Word will not solve the problems of the Jewish economy. They will not understand the truths taught by the temple service. The work of God is hindered by a worldly understanding of his great plan. The future life will unfold the meaning of the laws that Christ, enshrouded in the pillar of cloud, gave to his people.

We do not comprehend the deep things of God. Oh, if we did, faith would grasp the promises, and your wife would be healed. It is not the Lord, but the power of Darkness, that keeps her where she is. Go to the Saviour, my brother, and in faith ask Him to cast Satan out. Believe, only believe. In your wife's behalf lay hold of the merciful Healer.

Be strong, and of good courage. In order to fight successfully, a soldier must have courage, and strength. Of ourselves, we are weak and feeble. But we have the promise, "They that wait upon the Lord shall renew their strength, they shall mount up with wings as eagles; they shall run and not be weary, they shall walk and not faint."

May the Lord bless you, and give you strength and grace, and may he send his healing powers to your wife, is my prayer.

Ellen G. White.

Chapter 90—The Reopening of Battle Creek College and the Fault of Large Institutions

St. Helena, Cal., August 3, 1903.

Brethren Daniells, Prescott, and W. C. White:

... I am very sorry to hear that there is a plan to reopen Battle Creek College. To establish a college in Battle Creek, after such plain warnings have been given against doing this, would be to make a great mistake.

I can assure you that the large number of patients at the Sanitarium is no evidence that the institution is where it should be, or that it is conducted after God's order. Christ's plan for teaching truth can not be carried out in so large an institution as the Battle Creek Sanitarium, where so large a number of patients of all classes are gathered together. There may be some conversions at the Sanitarium at Battle Creek, among those who go there for treatment, but these will meet with greater difficulty than in almost any other place. Because of the large number of patients, this sanitarium is necessarily conducted as a large hotel. Worldlings of all classes are of course entertained there, and the helpers are constantly brought into connection with an influence that tends to draw them away from Christ. Oh, why can not those who know the truth follow the instruction that God has given? Why do they not make plants in places that have never yet heard the truth? Let us pray to God for help to do His work as in his very presence.

The enemy works untiringly to deceive human beings, and lead them away from God. He and his angels will in the future assume the shape of human beings, and work to make the truth of God of no effect. ...

Those who know the truth, but who walk contrary to the truth, may never place their foot in the path that Christ followed.

We are to "stand fast in the liberty wherewith Christ hath made us free, and be not entangled again with the yoke of bondage." No man or woman is to bind himself or herself to serve for a certain number of years under the control of a medical association. This is not God's plan, but a plan of human devising. Human beings belong to the Lord, body, soul, and spirit, and they are to be guided and controlled by him. He has bought us. We are under obligation to be laborers together with him. No one should bind himself to serve for a certain number of years in any institution.

I know that some have thought it advisable for the workers in our sanitariums to sign certain contracts. But I know also that it is not in accordance with God's plan for the workers to sign these contracts. They are pledged to God, and if he moves upon them to take the message to a certain place, shall they be bound by a pledge that hinders them from going? Never, never, We are not contracts to do this or that. We are to work under our Master, Christ Jesus, looking to him for directions. We are to pray and work and believe, following always the course that he marks out.

There are among professing believers many who know little of what is comprehended in the third angel's message. They have not followed the straight pathway of truth. They have not purified their souls by obeying the word. They are unconverted. They need to "seek the Lord while he may be found, and to call upon Him while he is near." "Let the wicked forsake his way, and the unrighteous man his thoughts, and let him return unto the Lord, and he will have mercy upon him, and to our God, for he will abundantly pardon."

Our ministers need this message. There are among them those whose feet are standing in slippery places. They slip first one way and then another, and continue to slip and slide. May God help them to place their feet in the footprints of Jesus.

Our churches are in the condition described in the message to the Laodicean church. They are neither cold nor hot. They need a fresh, new experience. God calls upon them to prepare for his coming; for it is near at hand.

Ellen G. White.

Chapter 91—Bound Not to Men But to God

"Elmshaven," Sanitarium, Cal., August 4, 1903.

Elder A. G. Daniells:

My dear Brother:

Yesterday I sent you the letter containing the warning that has been given again and again: The workers in our sanitariums are not to sign contracts binding themselves to an association or an institution for a certain number of years. They are to be bound, not to men, but to God.

No man is to treat those who learn under him as if he owned them, body, soul, and spirit. The Lord wants no such binding up with human beings, even if these human beings are without blame. There are those who are not holding the beginning of their confidence firm to the end. The gospel ministry and medical missionary work are to be united.

I have recently been instructed that no one should be advised to pledge himself to spend two, three, four, five, or six years under any man's tuition. Brethren, we have no time for this. Time is short. We are to hold out urgent inducements to the men who ought now to be engaged in missionary work for the Master. The highways and byways are yet unworked. The Lord calls for young men to labor as canvassers and evangelists, to do house-to-house work in places that have not yet heard the truth. God speaks to our young men, saying, "Ye are not your own; for ye are bought with a price; therefore, glorify God in your body, and in your spirit, which are God's.

The Lord must be given an opportunity to show men their duty and to work upon their minds. No one is to bind himself to serve under the direction of any human being; for the Lord himself will call men, as of old he called the humble fishermen, and will himself give them the education he desires them to have. He will call men from the plow and from other occupations, to give the last note of warning to perishing souls. There are many ways in which to work for the Master, and the great Teacher will open the understanding of these workers, enabling them to see wondrous things in his word.

The signs that show Christ's coming is near are fast fulfilling. The Lord calls for canvassers and evangelists. Those who will go forth to this work under his direction will be wonderfully blessed.

Let our churches be guarded. Let our people work intelligently, not under the rule of any man, but under the rule of God. Let them stand where they can follow the will of God. Their service belongs to Him. Their capabilities and talents are to be refined, purified, ennobled. In this lower school--the school of earth,--they are to be prepared for translation into the school of heaven, where their education will be continued under the personal supervision of Christ, the great Teacher, who will lead them beside the living waters, and open to them the mysteries of the kingdom of God.

Those who in this life do their best will obtain a fitness for the future immortal life.

The Lord calls for volunteers who will take their stand firmly on his side, and will pledge themselves to unite with Jesus of Nazareth in doing the very work that needs to be done now, just now.

There are many young men and young women among us who, if inducements are held out, would naturally be inclined to take several years' course of study at Battle Creek. But will it pay? Has not the Lord some practical work to do in missionary lines? Manly young men will be needed to enter the printing office when it is established in Washington, to learn the printer's trade. Our publications are to be prepared to go forth to the world. Canvassers are to be educated to take up the work of circulating these publications. Our books and papers are to go to places that are still in the darkness of error.

The Lord calls upon young men to enter our schools. Schools are to be established in which our youth can receive and education that will prepare them to go forth to do evangelical work and medical missionary work. Let schools be established out of the cities.

I call upon all to fasten themselves to Christ. He invites them, "Come unto me." "Take my yoke upon you, and learn of me; for I am meek and lowly in heart, and ye shall find rest unto your souls. For my yoke is easy, and my burden is light."

Let us not be in any way deceived. Let us realize the weakness of humanity, and see where man fails in his self-sufficiency. We shall then be filled with a desire to be just what God desires us to be, pure, noble, sanctified. We shall hunger and thirst after the righteousness of Christ. To be like God will be the one desire of the soul.

This is the desire that filled Enoch's heart. And we read that he walked with God. He studied the character of God to a purpose. He did not mark out his own course, or set up his own will, as if he thought himself fully qualified to manage matters. He strove to conform himself to the divine likeness.

A school such as has been planned for, should be in some place where the students would not be closely associated with the large numbers who are expected to patronize the sanitarium at Battle Creek. It is not wise to plan to maintain such a school in a place where a worldly element prevails to so great an extent as to counterwork that which the Lord has outlined should be done for our youth in our educational institutions. So many youths should not be brought together in Battle Creek.

The Lord presented to us the reasons for removing the College from Battle Creek. This instruction should now be searched out and studied by those who are planning to organize another educational institution there. Let the light already given, shine forth in its purity and beauty, that God's name may be glorified.

E. G. White.

Chapter 92—To the Leaders in Our Medical Work

St. Helena, Cal., August 4, 1903.

Dear Brethren:

I have a message for you. I am instructed to say that all the arrangements connected with the management of the medical missionary work are not to originate in Battle Creek. It is the deceptive power of the enemy of all righteousness that leads to the repeated attempts to bring all our medical institutions under the control of one organization. Certainly such efforts are not inspired by the Lord. The medical missionary work is God's work, and in every conference and church we are to take a decided stand against allowing it to be controlled by men.

After I received word in regard to the excellent meeting of confession and unity that had been held in Battle Creek, I was writing in my diary, and was about to record the thankfulness I felt because a change had come, when my hand was arrested, and there came to me the words: "Write it not. No change for the better has taken place. The Doctor is ensnared in a net of specious deception. He is presenting as of great worth things that are turning souls from the truth into by-and-forbidden paths,--things that lead human agents to act in harmony with their own inclinations, and to work out their unsanctified purposes; things that result in destroying the dignity and power of God's people, obscuring the light that would otherwise come to them from God through his appointed agencies.

The leaders in our medical work at Battle Creek have endeavored to bind our medical institutions fast, in accordance with their plans, notwithstanding the many warnings given that this should not be done. Who has authorized them to lay these plans, and to try in many ways to bring about their purposes? Our sanitariums do not belong to them; and yet they desire to tie up these institutions some way so that all our medical work will be under their control.

In the past I have written much upon this subject; and now I must repeat the admonitions given, because it seems difficult for my brethren to understand their perilous position.

"The Lord forbids that every sanitarium and bath-house established should be brought under one control, bound up with the medical institution at Battle Creek. The managers of the Battle Creek Sanitarium have their hands full now. They should devote their strength to the work of making this sanitarium what it should be.

"The light given me of God is that Dr. Kellogg is assuming too much responsibility in these matters. He is not to think that he can be conscience for every one of our medical workers; for men are to look to the Lord God of heaven alone for wisdom and guidance.

"In establishing and developing medical institutions, our brethren must not be asked to work in accordance with the plans of a ruling, kingly power. A change must be brought about. Dr. Kellogg must see and understand this, and bind about his desires to fasten every medical institution to the central organization at Battle Creek. The Lord forbids.

"For years I have been instructed that there is danger, constant danger, that our brethren will look to their fellow men for permission to do this or that, instead of looking to God. Thus they become weaklings, and permit themselves to be bound about with man-made restrictions disapproved by God. The Lord can impress minds and conscience to do his work under bonds to God, and in a spirit of fraternity that will be in accordance with his law. ...

"God knows the future. He is the One to whom we are to look for guidance. Let us trust him to direct us in the development of the various branches of his work. Let none attempt to labor in accordance with unsanctified impulses. ...

"The division of the General Conference into district union conferences was God's arrangement. In the work of the Lord in these last days there should be no Jerusalem centers, no kingly power. And the work in the different countries is not to be tied up by contracts to the work centering in Battle Creek, for this is not God's plan. Brethren are to counsel together; for we are just as much under the control of God in one part of the vineyard as in another. Brethren are to be one in heart and soul, even as Christ and the Father are one. Teach this, practice this, that we may be one with Christ in God, all working to build up one another.

"The kingly power formerly revealed in the General Conference at Battle Creek is not to be perpetuated. The publishing institution is not to be a kingdom of itself. It is essential that the principles that govern in General Conference affairs should be maintained in the management of the publishing work and the sanitarium work. No one is to think that the branch of work with which he is connected is of vastly more importance than other branches.

"There must be educational work in every sanitarium that shall be established. It is not the duty of Dr. Kellogg to carry so many responsibilities. God has control of the work, and no human agency is to feel that everything done in the sanitariums established must first be submitted to Dr. Kellogg. This course God forbids. The same God who instructed Dr. Kellogg will instruct the men and women who are called to do service for the Master in various parts of his vineyard.

"Human laws and arrangements are being framed that are not acceptable to God. They will not prove a savor of life unto life. I am under the necessity of lifting the danger-signal. The managers of every one of our institutions need to become more and still more intelligent regarding their individual work, not by depending upon another institution, but, while preserving the identity of their work, by looking to God as their Instructor, and by revealing their faith in him through whole-hearted service. Then they will develop talents and capabilities."

Every man needs now to take his position on the old-time foundation of obedience to God. Let no one allow the propositions of any group of men to lead him, through a spirit of compromise, to accept wrong plans and principles. I have been instructed that history will be repeated, and the specious working of Satan will be revealed by human agents. We must work discreetly and determinedly to adjust matters. The recent effort to induce God's people to accept binding propositions, is the last that should be passed by without a decided protest. Let us not take another step toward the acceptance of such propositions, lest we be ensnared.

Brethren, let us firmly take our position now. In justice to our churches, we must now decide this matter; for we have a great work to do. We must now determine that every medical institution shall stand in its own individual right. Let every cord now be broken. Let our medical institutions refuse to be tied up with the Medical Association in Michigan.

I shall now be prepared to say to our brethren, Cut loose, cut loose! After taking your position firmly, wisely, cautiously, make not one concession on any point concerning which God has plainly spoken. Be as calm as a summer evening, but as fixed as the everlasting hills. By conceding, you would be selling our whole cause away. We must now take hold of these matters decidedly. I have many things to say that I have not wanted to say in the past, but now my mind is clear to speak and act.

I am sorry to be compelled to take the position that I am forced to take in behalf of God's people. In taking this position, I am placed under the necessity of bearing the heavy burden of showing the evil of the plans that I know are not born of heaven. This is the burden that many times in the past the Lord has laid upon me, in order that his work might be advanced along right lines. How much care and anxiety, how much mental anguish and wearing physical labor, might be saved me in my old age! But still I am under the necessity of going into the battle, and of discharging in the presence of important assemblies the duty that the Lord has laid upon me,--the duty of correcting the wrong course of men who claim to be Christians but who are doing a work that will have to be undone at a great loss, both financially and in the shaking of the confidence of the people.

If I act conscientiously, I must meet the crisis; for I believe that the precepts which the Lord has given concerning his work in the past and at the present time point out the right way. And his plans, his thought, are as much higher than man's plans, man's thoughts, as the heavens are higher than the earth. God's voice is to be heard; his wisdom is to guide us. We must not be broken up by any human wisdom of devising. God has outlined his plan in his Word and in the Testimonies he has sent to his people.

Oh, how sad it is that men allow themselves to be so wrought upon by the enemy that they dare venture to exalt their finite judgment in opposition to God's plans and purposes! Man's authority bears the signature of man. We are not to permit the rank and file of our people to come under the generalship of the weak, confused sentiments of man. God's authority is to stand supreme. And I must call upon his people to recognize his authority, which bears the evidence of its divine origin. [Every believer is called upon to unite inseparably with God's authority.

The foundation on which the truth has always been based is sure, and upon this foundation all are to stand who are doing the Lord's work. God's word reveals his design; and that work only which is carried on in accordance with the principles of the word will stand fast forever, approved both by the heavenly host and the adopted family living on the earth during the remnant of time remaining before the close of this earth's history.

Finite man, yielding to Satan's devising, can easily lose sight of the Lord's purpose concerning him; for by yielding to temptation man loses his power of discernment. Every Christian is to strive to be a laborer together with God.

Christ calls for service altogether different from that which is given him. Men in positions of responsibility should, through the power of the Holy Spirit, reveal the Redeemer much more clearly to the world than they have revealed him. The Infinite God so loved the world that he gave his only begotten Son as a sacrifice for us, in order that, receiving him by faith and practicing his virtues, we should not perish, but have everlasting life. My brethren, how do you suppose he regards the great lack of spiritual enthusiasm manifested over the record of the great sacrificial offering made for our individual salvation?

All human ambition, all boasting, is to be laid in the dust. Self, sinful self, is to be abased, not exalted. By holiness to God in the daily life here below, we are to manifest the Christ-life. The corrupt nature is to become pure and undefiled; subdued, not exalted. We are to be humble, faithful men and women. Never are we to sit upon the judgment-seat. God demands that his representatives shall be pure vessels, revealing the beauty of sanctified character. The channel is always to remain unobstructed, that the Holy Spirit may have free course; otherwise, spiritual leaders will gloss over the work that must be done in the natural heart in order to perfect Christian character; and they will present their own imperfections in such a way that they make of none effect God's truth, which is as steadfast as the eternal throne. And while God calls upon all his watchmen to lift the danger-signal, at the same time he presents before them the life character of the Saviour as an example of what they must be and do in order to be saved. Concerning his disciples, Christ prayed, "Sanctify them through thy truth; thy word is truth." A pleasant, self-satisfied feeling is not an evidence of sanctification. A faithful record is kept of all the acts of the children of men. Nothing can be concealed from the eye of the high and holy One, who inhabiteth eternity. Some make Christ ashamed by their course of devising, planning, scheming, God does not approve of their conduct; for the Lord Jesus is not honored by their spirit of their works. They forget the words of the apostle, "We are made a spectacle unto the world, and to angels, and to men."

In consequence of the unfaithful lives of men who adorn not the doctrine of Christ our Saviour, Bible truth is blasphemed. My soul is grieved night after night, and day after day, as I view the present situation.

Ellen G. White.

Chapter 93—Be Not Weary in Well-Doing

St. Helena, Cal., Aug. 9, 1903.

My brethren and sisters, why is so little being done to sell "Christ's Object Lessons"? Have you become weary in well doing? Let this work advance; for there is great need that it be carried steadily forward. The school at Berrien Springs needs the money that the sale of these books will bring. This school is making advancement as fast as possible, but it is in need of funds with which to erect buildings. The Lord is pleased with the way in which the school has been conducted, and with the education that is being given to the students gathered there. Will you not remember that in doing your best to bring in means for the advancement of this school, you are cooperating with Him? There is much that needs to be done before the winter sets in. Buildings must be erected, and other lines of work carried forward.

Brother Magan and Brother Sutherland have worked with heart and soul to bring this school to its present stage of advancement, and the blessing of the Lord has attended their labors in a marked manner. I wish to say that my confidence in these men has not at all lessened. The Lord is not unmindful of the self-sacrifice and their labors of love. I have feared that they were in danger from trying to do more than they could do. I saw that they were in danger of over-taxing their strength in the effort to advance the work and to economize in the use of means.

The lives of these men are precious in the sight of the Lord. He does not want them to overwork, and thus sacrifice their strength; for in the end this would mean great loss.

My brethren and sisters, I ask you, in the name of the Lord, to do all that you can to advance the work of the Berrien Springs school. I hope and pray that you will not become weary in well-doing. In carrying forward the work of selling "Christ's Object Lessons", you will receive a most precious blessing. As you show, this book to your friends and neighbors, telling them of the instruction that it contains and why you are trying to sell it, you will gain an experience that will enable you to do more successful work for the Master. As you take up this pleasing work--for such it will prove to all who take it up with faith and prayer--the peace of Christ will come into your hearts. The thought that you are doing a good work will fill you with joy and courage.

At one time the suggestion was made to me that it might be best, when the Relief of the Schools Campaign was finished, to make "Christ's Object Lessons" a regular subscription book. It was said that this book would have as ready a sale as any that could produced.

As I heard this suggestion, the thought came to me, "Here is an opportunity for me to get out of debt. Is not this the right thing for me to do?" I said that it might be right to do as the letter had suggested. Then I sent to heaven the prayer, "Lord, teach me to speak right words." Quickly the answer came, In an instant the light given at the first regarding "Object Lessons" flashed into my mind, and the instruction then given was repeated. I seemed to hear the words, "God signified that this book should be given to our schools, to be to them a continual blessing. Would you exchange his plan for human devising? This book is to be treated as a sacred offering, made to God and His plan regarding it is unselfishly carried out, the result will be wholly satisfactory."

I immediately said that I would not make any change in the handling of "Object Lessons", unless God gave me plain instruction that this should be one. As I said this, I felt the blessing of God resting upon me.

My brethren and sisters, as you go out to sell this book, the Lord Jesus and His angels will open the way before you. Success has attended the effort to sell the book in the past, because God's people have worked in cooperation with heavenly agencies; and success will attend the effort in the future, if our people will still carry forward the work. All, will receive grace for grace as they give what they can, in time and influence, to the circulation of "Christ's Object Lessons".

I leave these words with you, praying that the blessing of God may rest on the self-sacrificing workers at Berrien Springs, and upon all who continue in the work of canvassing for "Object Lessons". Time is short, and there is much to be done. Let all who can, old and young, men, women, and children, take up this work. As they go forth, the Lord will open the way before them. The words that they speak will be as seeds sown in good ground. Many souls will be saved as a result of their willing service. And at last, when we join the royal family in the courts above, the Lord will open before us the good that has been accomplished by "Christ's Object Lessons".

Chapter 94—The Training of Medical Missionaries

"Elmshaven", Sanitarium, Cal., August 27, 1903.

Dear Brother Daniells:

During the past few days I have been writing some things that were urged upon my mind. I have not had all the matter copied; but when it is copied, I will read it, and then I hope that other things will come to my mind to add to these manuscripts.

I can not keep matters from coming before the people. I have not changed my mind at all. I have had some very plain talks with Elder A. T. Jones. I told him that I could not and would not consent to his coming to the Pacific Coast to present to the brethren and sisters here the situation at Battle Creek, and to call upon them for gifts and pledges to meet the needs of the work there. As we consider the work that must be done in Washington City, and the varied lines of work that should be taken up in the Southern field and in the cities of our land, it is becoming more and more manifest that it is unwise to allow our conferences to be stripped of means that they can not assist in establishing memorials in fields where God has instructed us to do a special work.

In the places where labor is to be put forth, advantages should be provided for the training of men and women, as well as the youth, to work in the Master's vineyard. All that can possibly be done with native help in the Southern field, should be done. A large amount of most hopeful evangelistic work can be carried on to good advantage, and thus much of the vineyard be worked, in order that fruit shall be borne. It is fruit that we want. Christ wants fruit to satisfy his hunger. The leaves may appear ever so inviting, but they are not satisfying. His divine soul hungers for fruit.

We have a work to do in securing the best talent, and in placing these workers in positions where they can educate other workers. Then when our sanitariums call for physicians, we shall have young men who, through their experience gained by practical work, have become fitted to bear responsibilities. We have failed, decidedly failed, in allowing so much to be done in one place. Everything is not to be brought under the control of one institution. Such an effort, carried out, results in placing an open door of temptation before the man at the head of the principal institutions.

Much more educational work needs to be done than has been done. The Berrien Springs School can do more, and should have the best talent obtainable to carry on the work of training young men for the gospel ministry. Encourage those who are well balanced in mind and attend this school, and to make an earnest effort to understand the truth, in order that they may impart it to others.

All who desire to enter the medical missionary work, and who are worthy, should be given an opportunity to learn. We could with profit drop much of the dispensary work that is done. Giving the common treatments to the sick will accomplish much more, and will give opportunity to those who administer these hygienic treatments to labor with earnestness for the spiritual recovery of their patients. Let the hearts of all who are working along these lines, be softened and subdued. Let the workers learn to consult the Great Physician in prayer much more than they have done. Pray, watch, wait, and believe.

In training workers to care for the sick, let the minds of the students be impressed with the thought that their highest aim should always be to look after the spiritual welfare of their patients. To this end they should learn to repeat the promises of God's Word, and to offer fervent prayers, daily, while preparing for service. Let them realize that they are always to keep the sweetening, sanctifying influence of the great Medical Missionary before their patients. If those who are suffering can be impressed with the fact that Christ is their sympathizing, compassionate Saviour, they will have rest of mind which is so essential to recovery of health.

In new places where schools are being set in operation, arrange to have a treatment-room or rooms connected with the school. Let this place be outside the main school building, so that the sick will be where it is quiet. Let those who are qualified to teach, give lessons on treating the sick. Soon much permanent fruit will be gathered, in physical improvement and in spiritual advancement, which, combined, will be of great advantage.

Over the medical missionary department, as well as over every other department of the school, there should be a head instructor to teach those under him. The beginning may be small. There may be only a few patients; but as the head instructor gives treatments, to these, quite a number of students can look on to see how he does this work, and they can help him in many ways. Thus they will learn to do this kind of work themselves.

We must certainly arouse from our passive position along these lines. Much may be learned by visiting the hospitals. In these hospitals not a few of our young people should be learning to be successful medical missionaries in caring for the sick intelligently. Observation, and the practice of that which has been learned, will result in consecrated youth becoming active, efficient medical missionary workers. Many who could not otherwise secure a training in these lines of work, can thus prepare themselves for usefulness. But the surgical work must be done by faithful, skilful physicians.

May God help us to develop plans so that our youth can become genuine medical missionaries. We can not afford to allow our very best and most promising young men and young women to drift to Battle Creek, when we have before us the work of establishing a smaller medical institution near Washington at once. No time is to be lost. Call for the best talent, and make arrangements for conducting a nurses' training school. All that can be done should be done to make a deep impression in favor of the truth for this time. Place at the head of this institution one who can be trusted. Obtain facilities for giving treatments, and secure God-fearing youth as your helpers.

We have lost time; but the gospel medical missionary work will yet open the way for the conversion of souls. We need to encourage our young men and young women not merely to carry the "Life Boat" but publications on present truth, as they go out to distribute literature. We must take up the matters that will bring us to the attention of the public. We must help our young people to understand the important truths which make us a peculiar people, denominated by God. Those who work faithfully will gather most precious, enduring fruit.

We should reveal to the world that we are not beggars; that we are glad to do medical missionary work without price for those who can not pay. Here in California we shall need all the means that we can raise, to open up various lines of work in this state. We must be ready to help the sick whenever and wherever they need help. Medical missionary work is to be bound up with the gospel ministry. Thus it was in Christ's day. It is His helping hand, in healing, that will make the deepest impression on the minds of the people to whom we desire to proclaim the third angel's message.

Ellen G. White

Chapter 95—The Development of the Medical Missionary Work

St. Helena, Cal. Sept. 21, 1903.

To the Teachers in Emmanuel Missionary College:

... Medical missionary work is yet in its infancy. The meaning of genuine medical missionary work is known by but few. Why? Because the Saviour's plan of work has not been followed. God's money has been misapplied. In many places practical evangelistic medical missionary work is being done; but many of the workers who should go forth as did the disciples are being collected together and held in a few places, as they have been in the past, notwithstanding the Lord's warning that this should not be.

Many of the men and women who should be out in the field, working as medical missionary evangelists, helping those engaged in the gospel ministry, are collected in Battle Creek, acting over the same program that has been acted over in the past, confining the forces, binding them up in one place. God has spoken against this by sending His judgments upon the institutions in Battle Creek; but notwithstanding this, every movement on the part of those striving to heed the warnings by laboring to change the order of things, has been made very hard because of the misconception of some regarding the way in which the medical missionary work should be carried forward.

God has not given us the work of erecting immense sanitariums, to be used as health resorts for all who may come. Neither is it his purpose that medical missionary workers shall spend a long term of years in college before they enter the field. To build up a school in Battle Creek, as some of our people there desire, would tend to counterwork the influence that God has declared should be exerted on his people in these last days of this earth's history.

The interests that the Lord has declared should not remain in Battle Creek are not now to be brought back and re-established there. Much of the force that would be needed to carry forward there, amidst many disadvantages, the work of these interests, should be used in doing gospel medical missionary work in the large cities still unworked.

"Break up the large centers," has been the word of the Lord, "Carry the light to many places." Those who are desirous of receiving a training for effective medical missionary work, should understand that large sanitariums will be conducted so much like institutions of the world, that students laboring in such sanitariums can not obtain a symmetrical training for Christian medical missionary work.

The proclamation of the truth in all parts of the world calls for small sanitariums in many places, not in the heart of cities, but in places where city influences will be as little felt as possible.

I am obliged to say that the making of so large a plant in Battle Creek, and the calling together of those who should be engaged in medical missionary work in many places, is doing just what God has specified should not be done.

The fact that many patients are coming to the new sanitarium at Battle Creek is not to be read as a sign that the planning for so large a work there was for the best. To this large institution will come many men and women who are not really sick. Workers will be required to wait on them; our nurses will become the servants of worldly men and women who are not inclined to piety or religion. But this is not the work that God has given to his medical missionaries. Our charge has been given us by the greatest Medical Missionary that this world has ever seen. Standing but a step from His Father's throne, Christ said to his disciples:

"All power is given unto me in heaven and in earth. Go ye therefore, and teach all nations, baptizing them in the name of the Father, and of the Son, and of the Holy Ghost." "Go ye into all the world," He said, "and preach the gospel to every creature," "Teaching them to observe all things whatsoever I have commanded you; and, lo, I am with you alway, even unto the end of the world."

Let our ministers who have gained an experience in preaching the Word, learn how to give simple treatments, and then labor intelligently as medical missionary evangelists.

Workers - gospel medical missionaries - are needed now. We can not afford to spend years in preparation. Soon doors now open to the truth will be forever closed. Carry the message now. Do not wait, allowing the enemy to take possession of fields now open before you. Let little companies go forth to do the work to which Christ appointed his disciples. Let them labor as evangelists, scattering our publications, and talking of the truth to those they meet. Let them pray for the sick, ministering to their necessities not with drugs, but with nature's remedies, and teaching them how to regain health and avoid disease.

Let the workers remember always that they are dependent on God. Let them not trust in human wisdom, but in the wisdom of the One who declares. "All power is given unto me in heaven and in earth. . . Lo, I am with you always, even unto the end of the world." Let them go forth two and two, depending on God, not on man, for wisdom and success.

Let them search the Scriptures, and then present the truths of God's word to others. Let them be guided by the principles that Christ has laid down.

Ellen G. White.

Chapter 96—Teach the Word

St. Helena, Cal., Sept. 22, 1903.

To the Teachers in Emmanuel Missionary College:

I have some things to say to our teachers in reference to the new book, "The Living Temple". Be careful how you sustain the sentiments of this book regarding the personality of God. As the Lord represents matters to me, these sentiments do not bear the endorsement of God. They are a snare that the enemy has prepared for these last days. I thought that this would surely be discerned, and that it would not be necessary for me to say anything about it. But since the claim has been made that the teachings of this book can be sustained by statements from my writings, I am compelled to speak in denial of this claim. There may be in this book expressions and sentiments that are in harmony with my writings. And there may be in my writings many statements which when taken from their connection, and interpreted according to the mind of the writer of "Living Temple" would seem to be in harmony with the teachings of this book. This may give apparent support to the assertion that the sentiments in "Living Temple" are in harmony with my writings. But God forbid that this opinion should prevail.

We need not the mysticism that is in this book. Those who entertain these sophistries will soon find themselves in a position where the enemy can talk with them, and lead them away from God. It is represented to me that the writer of this book is on a false track. He has lost sight of the distinguishing truths for this time. He knows not whither his steps are tending. The track of truth lies close beside the track of error, and both minds may seem to be one to minds which are not worked by the Holy Spirit, and which, therefore, are not quick to discern the difference between truth and error.

In regard to the faith to be cherished and preserved in these last day, very little light is given in "Living Temple," and this light is so uncertain that it would not help God's people at this stage of their work.

In the visions of the night this matter was clearly presented to me, before a large number. One of authority was speaking, and He said, "If the suppositions and statements found in this book were essential, if these statements were pure provender, thoroughly winnowed from the chaff, there would be some decided mention of them in the revelation given by Christ to John to give to the churches. To John the Lord Jesus opened the subjects that He saw would be needed by his people in the last days. The instruction that He gave is found in the book of Revelation. Those who would be co-workers with our Lord and Saviour Jesus Christ will show a deep interest in the truths found in the book of Revelation. With pen and voice they will strive to make plain the wonderful things that Christ came from heaven to reveal."

The first chapter of the book of Revelation was then read, with great solemnity.

"The Revelation of Jesus Christ, which God gave unto Him, to show unto His servants things which must shortly come to past; and he sent and signified it by his angel unto his servant John, who bare record of the word of God, and of the testimony of Jesus Christ, and of all things that he saw. Blessed is he that readeth, and they that hear the words of this prophecy, and keep these things which are written therein; for the time is at hand."

Our Instructor presented the solemn messages that have been given in their order in Revelation, and that are to occupy the first place in the minds of God's people.

All through the book, "The Living Temple," passages of scripture are used, but in many instances these passages are used in such a way that the right interpretation is not given them. The message for this time is not, "The temple of the Lord, the temple of the Lord, the temple of the Lord are we." Whom does the Lord receive as vessels unto honor? Those who cooperate with Christ, those who believe the truth, who live the truth, who proclaim the truth in all its bearings.

There are those whose minds will be taken up with smooth words and fair speeches, put into language that they can not understand or interpret. Precious time is rapidly passing, and many will be robbed of the time that should be given to the proclamation of the messages that God has sent to a fallen world. Satan is pleased to see the diversion of minds that should be engaged in the study of the truths that have to do with eternal realities.

The testimony of Christ, a testimony of the most solemn character, is to be borne to the world. All through the book of Revelation there are the most precious, elevating promises, and there are also warnings of most fearfully solemn import. Will not those who profess to have a knowledge of the truth read the testimony given to John by Christ? Here is no guess-work, no scientific deception. Here are the truths that concern our present and future welfare. What is the chaff to the wheat?

Our Instructor passed on to the third chapter of Revelation, and read the following:

"Unto the angel of the church in Sardis write, There things saith He that hath the seven Spirits of God, and the seven stars: I know thy works, that thou hast a name that thou livest, and art dead. Be watchful, and strengthen the things which remain, that are ready to die; for I have not found thy works perfect before God. Remember therefore how thou hast received, and heard, and hold fast, and repent. If therefore thou shalt not watch, I will come on thee as a thief, and thou shalt not know what hour I will come upon thee."

These words were spoken with such strength and force that those present seemed to be afraid, and hid their faces in their hands, as if they were arraigned before the Judge of all the earth. Some seemed about to faint.

Then the subject changed. The Speaker read:

"Thou hast a few names even in Sardis which have not defiled their garments; and they shall walk with Me in white; for they are worthy. He that overcometh, the same shall be clothed with white raiment; and I will not blot out his name out of the book of life, but I will confess his name before my father, and before his angels. He that hath an ear, let him hear what the Spirit saith unto the churches.

"And unto the angel of the church in Philadelphia write: These things saith he that is holy, he that is true, he that hath the key of David, he that openeth and no man shutteth, and shutteth and no man openeth: I know thy works; behold, I have set before thee an open door, and no man can shut it; for thou hast a little strength, and hast kept my word; and hast not denied my name. Behold, I will make them of the synagogue of Satan, which say they are Jews, and are not; behold, I will make them to come and worship before thy feet, and to know that I have loved thee. Because thou hast kept the word of my patience, I also will keep thee from the hour of temptation, which will come upon all the world, to try them that dwell upon the earth. Behold, I come quickly; hold that fast which thou hast, that no man take thy crown. Him that overcometh will I make a pillar in the temple of my God, and he shall go no more out; and I will write upon him the name of my God, and the name of the city of my God, which is New Jerusalem, which cometh down out of heaven from my God; and I will write upon him my new name. He that hath an ear, let him hear what the Spirit saith unto the churches."

In these words there is no smooth saying.

The Speaker held up "Living Temple", saying, "In this book there are statements that the writer himself does not comprehend. Many things are stated in a vague, undefined way. Statements are made in such a way that nothing is sure. And this is not the only production of the kind that will be urged upon the people. Fanciful views will be presented by many minds. What we need to know at this time is, "What is the truth that will enable us to win the salvation of our souls?"

The sophistries regarding God and nature that are flooding the world with skepticism, are the inspiration of the fallen foe, who is himself a Bible student, who know the truth that it is essential for the people to receive, and whose study it is to divert minds from these great truths relating to the things that are soon coming upon the world. Let our teachers beware lest they echo the soothsaying of the enemy of God and man.

Pointing to some present, our Instructor said, "You are making a mistake. The word, the word revealed by God, this is to be the foundation of your faith. Study the commandments of God and the testimony that Jesus has borne to the truth. He is the faithful and true Witness."

Then was repeated the message to the Laodicean church. The whole of the third chapter of Revelation, from first to last, was read.

"Unto the angel of the church of the Laodiceans write, These things saith the Amen, the faithful and true witness, the beginning of the creation of God. I know thy works, that thou art neither cold or hot; I would thou wert cold or hot. So then because thou are lukewarm, and neither cold nor hot, I will spue thee out of my mouth. Because thou sayest, I am rich, and increased with goods, and have need of nothing; and knowest not that thou art wretched, and miserable, and poor, and blind, and naked; I counsel thee to buy of me gold tried in the fire, that thou mayest be rich; and white raiment, that thou mayest be clothed, and that the shame of thy nakedness do not appear; and anoint thine eyes with eyesalve, that thou mayest see.

"As many as I love, I rebuke and chasten; be zealous therefore, and repent. Behold, I stand at the door, and knock; if any man hear my voice, and open the door, I will come into him, and will sup with him, and he with me. To him that overcometh will I grant to sit with me in my throne, even as I also overcame, and am sat down with my Father in his throne. He that hath an ear, let him hear what the Spirit saith unto the churches."

The Lord is soon coming. The watchman on the walls of Zion are called upon to awake to their God-given responsibility. Many of them are in the stupor of insensibility. God calls for watchmen who in the power of the Spirit will give to the world a warning message; who will proclaim the time of night. He calls for watchmen who will arouse men and women from their lethargy, lest they sleep the sleep of death.

Ellen G. White.

Chapter 97—A Warning of Danger

St. Helena, Cal., Sept. 23, 1903.

To the Teachers in Emmanuel Missionary College:

... Perilous times are before us. Every one who has a knowledge of the truth should awake, and place himself, body, soul, and spirit, under the discipline of God. Wake up, brethren, wake up. The enemy is on our track. We must be wide awake, on our guard against him. We must put on the whole armor of God. We must follow the directions given in the spirit of prophecy. We must love and obey the truth for this time. This will save us from accepting strong delusions. God has spoken to us through his Word. He has spoken to us through the Testimonies to the church, and through the books that have helped to make plain our present duty and the position that we should now occupy. The warnings that have been given, line upon line, precept upon precept, should be heeded. If we disregard them, what excuse shall we offer?

The new theories in regard to God and Christ, as brought out in "The Living Temple", are not in harmony with the teaching of Christ. The Lord Jesus came to this world to represent the Father. He did not represent God as an essence pervading nature, but as a personal being. Christians should bear in mind that God has a personality as verily as has Christ.

Christ came to our world to restore in man the moral image of God. He came to bring fallen human beings power to obey God's commandments, that in them might be restored the divine character, that in their lives might be adorned with the holiness of God. Of those who are thus transformed in character it is said, "Now they desire a better country, that is, an heavenly, wherefore God is not ashamed to be called their God; for he hath prepared for them a city."

Christians are to represent Christ. They are to reveal his spirit and character. Those who are imbued with His Spirit will have an intense love for every one for whom he died, and will work earnestly to bring into the heavenly garner a harvest of souls. Filled with his Spirit, they will be animated with the same desire to save sinners that animated Christ in his lifework as a missionary sent of God.

The enemy of Christ is intensely active. He seeks to take possession of human minds, that he may bring in division, discord, and a party spirit. He seeks to create division among the people of God, that they may be weakened, and that their influence for good on the world may be lessened. He presents scientific propositions that are contrary to Christ's teaching, and contrary to the faith and the doctrines that have been outlined before us ever since the first proclamation of this message,--doctrines that are sustained by the Scriptures. Our message is to be definitely proclaimed. We are to exalt the truths that were given to John on the Isle of Patmos, showing that the end is near.

The pope claims authority over the practice of many who do not recognize Christ as our only Authority. He places himself in a position of God, and the weak and uninformed are kept from the knowledge that would reveal to them their privilege as children of God. We are to have no kings, no rulers, no popes among us. It is time for us diligently to heed the messages that have brought us out from the world.

Ellen G. White.

Chapter 98—The Battle Creek College Debt

October 8, 1903.

Brethren Magan and Sutherland and their associates have wrestled with many difficulties in connection with the educational work at Battle Creek and Berrien Springs. But few have understood how heavy has been the financial burdens and how great have been the perplexities brought to these brethren by the removal of the school from Battle Creek at Berrien Springs. Much was involved in the transfer, and in the constant effort made to build up an educational institution the work of which would be in accordance with the exalted principles underlying Christian education.

In harmony with the instructions given by the Lord, our brethren have devoted themselves to the task of beginning anew, and of introducing into their model school only those books and methods of teaching that they thought would help the students to form symmetrical characters and to become useful workers in the cause. They desired that their school should be approved by God for the excellence of its work and for the exalted standard that it maintained. Their effort was at first largely experimental--an attempt to answer the question, "How shall our training schools for Christian workers be established and carried on?"

In this pioneer effort our brethren advanced not inch by inch, but in sweeping strides, in the right direction. Some tried to discourage them; others criticized and condemned; but God blessed their efforts.

Not the least discouraging feature of this pioneer work was the question of finances. A heavy debt rested on the old Battle Creek College property. Those in charge of the institution at the time the school work was removed to Berrien Springs, were not responsible for incurring this debt. The buildings and grounds were worth considerable more than the debts, and if the property could have been sold for its full value, there would have remained, after the payment of all debts, a good sum to be used in providing the necessary facilities at Berrien Springs. Those who had conducted the affairs of the College in past years, and who were to some extent responsible for the debts on the institution, should at this time come forward, and nobly say: "We are responsible for these debts; and we will take upon ourselves a large part of the burden resting altogether upon those who are establishing the school in a place where the surroundings are more favorable for training our young people." By an effort to share the burden of these heavy obligations, those who had been largely responsible in creating them would have been acting in harmony with the first four as well as the last six commandments.

When the book, "Christ's Object Lessons", was given for the relief of the school, all who were connected with Battle Creek College worked very hard to carry out the Lord's plan for reducing the indebtedness of our educational institutions. They hoped that they might be able to lessen the debt on their own school, that they could feel free to leave Battle Creek, and to reopen the College in some place where they could follow out the Lord's instruction in regard to Christian education.

About the time of the General Conference in 1901, the way opened for the sale of the Battle Creek College property; and the understanding was that the buildings and grounds would be used for the American Medical Missionary College. Our brethren left Battle Creek, and established Emmanuel Missionary College at Berrien Springs. They secured a beautiful tract of land in the country, and began small. There they have labored untiringly for the upbuilding of an educational institution that would be an honor to God and his cause. They have striven to get things in order, so that they could receive and properly care for the students who came. Faithfully have they endeavored to train the youth to be laborers together with God, and to depend upon Him for wisdom and guidance. Through their efforts, many young men and young women have been imbued with a love for souls, and have been prepared to give to the world the message of warning that is to be proclaimed before Christ's second advent.

From the light given me by the Lord, I know that the teachers connected with the Berrien Springs school walked out by faith, depending wholly on God's promises. They have made mistakes, it is true, but they have not allowed these mistakes to stop their work; instead, they have turned their mistakes into victories, by learning wisdom from their errors, and by avoiding them there after. The Lord helped them, gave them courage, and increased their faith.

All this was not done without severe trials. The heavy debt on the Battle Creek College property has been a burden to Brethren Magan and Sutherland, and they have labored very hard to reduce this. The strength of both men has been severely taxed. At one time Brother Magan, worn by the burden he was carrying, suffered a severe attack of typhoid fever, and for a time his life was despaired of. He had given himself no periods of rest. This was not after the Lord's order; the life and health of his servants is precious in his sight.

While attending the General Conference at Oakland, the Lord instructed me that Brethren Sutherland and Magan should be relieved from some of the financial burdens they were carrying. They have used much of their time and strength in the effort to decrease and, if possible, wipe out the heavy indebtedness on the Battle Creek College,--a debt for the creating of which others were responsible. Those who were more directly responsible should labor to relieve their brethren at Berrien Springs of this burden. They should place themselves in the position of these pioneers who were under constant pressure to pay obligations they had not incurred,--pioneers who had by faith left Battle Creek, and who now are building up a school that God can approve. Too long the burden has rested on our brethren at Berrien Springs. They have kept their gracious intentions in view, devoting themselves to the task of clearing the old College property from debt. How pleasing to God it would be for all our people to share in lifting the obligations of the old Battle Creek College!

In the councils of our brethren, it was arranged that the Battle Creek College debt be paid from the proceeds of the Missionary Acre Fund. It was thought that our people throughout America who had land, could set apart a small portion of it for the Lord, and send the proceeds to the general treasure, to be applied in the payment of the College debts, and the clearing of the property for the use of the American Medical Missionary College. It was suggested that those who had no land to use might give of their earnings. Those who kept chickens could contribute from the profits received from this source. Our brethren felt sure that if our people everywhere would give liberally of the fruit of their toil, a large sum could be raised, and the debt be cancelled.

Recently some have questioned the propriety of sending means for the Missionary Acre Fund, and consequently scarcely anything is now being received for the payment of the College debt. This is not as it should be. Let all our brethren and sisters understand that the purchase of the Battle Creek College property, for the use of the Medical Missionary College, was approved of God, and that the Missionary Acre Fund plan of raising means for this purchase is a good enterprise. Those who will help in this way will be blessed.

Some have thought that the sale of "Object Lessons" should meet the demands; but it will not, in the purchase of this property for the medical college. Brethren Magan and Sutherland have worked with earnestness to carry out the Lord's plan to cancel the debts of our schools. At the Oakland Conference I tried to point out the fact that these brethren worked untiringly, and that the past must not be repeated. Brother Magan nearly lost his life in the struggle to free the schools from debt. Their talents are needed in the Lord's work. They should be provided with proper facilities at Berrien Springs. On account of the scarcity of funds, they have been obliged to move very slowly.

Ellen G. White.

Chapter 99—Giving Heed to Seducing Spirits

"Elmshaven", Sanitarium, Cal., October 9, 1903.

Dear Brethren Magan and Sutherland:

I am sure that the Lord will work to bring you upon higher ground, where you will not be so severely harassed or perplexed.

I wish to write you a few words in regard to the employment of Dr. E. J. Waggoner as a teacher in the Berrien Springs school. I have had much confidence in Brother Waggoner, but I know that just now he is in special danger. He is in danger, as many others are, of accepting incorrect views of God, as set forth in the new book, "Living Temple". Take him into the school at Berrien Springs. My counsel regarding his work is that you help him to place his feet on solid ground, even the Rock of Ages. I believe that he will recover his former clearness and power.

However favorably our physicians and others may view the theories regarding God that are presented in "The Living Temple", I must tell you that these theories are faulty, incorrect, false. All through the book passages of scripture are used, but many of these scriptures are used in such a way that they are misinterpreted. These scriptures, read in their connections and understood in their simplicity, do not sustain the theories that the writer is endeavoring to maintain.

Those who present such theories are lost in the woods. They know not the nature of the theories that they are handling. I know how dangerous these theories are. Before I was seventeen years old, I had to bear my testimony against them before large companies, and all through my experience for the last fifty years I have had to meet and oppose these delusive theories.

Soon after Dr. Kellogg first connected with the Sanitarium, I was shown that he was in danger of entertaining false views of God. I labored with him, telling him that his case had been presented to me, and that I had been shown just what the holding of such ideas would lead to.

Dr. Kellogg has not always been led by the Lord. Good seed has been sown in his heart, but he has not always responded to the Lord's call. While we were in Australia, I saw that the doctor would link up with ministers not in the truth. I heard conversations between him and these ministers, in which he told of the large things that he was planning to do in the cities.

I was instructed that there was danger of Dr. Kellogg becoming unsettled in regard to the truth, that he was not standing firm upon the true foundation. He has labored so hard to make the medical missionary work the whole body that he has lost sight of the spirit of the message. I was instructed that he was allowing his mind to depart from the faith, and was giving heed to seducing spirits, and that, unless he righted himself, all associated with him would be in danger of being led away by theories that greatly dishonored God. I was instructed that unless a change came, Dr. Kellogg would discard the testimonies of God's Spirit in order to establish theories of his own, and would bring upon himself the condemnation of the Lord.

I have ever done all that I could to save Dr. Kellogg's soul, but of late I have not written to him as frequently as in former years. I am greatly disappointed that so many of our medical missionary workers seem to be spiritually blind. I can not regard them as safe teachers. They are sowing tares among the wheat. Those who venture to speak of God as He is spoken of in "The Living Temple", are on very dangerous ground.

I say, and have ever said, that I will not engage in controversy with any one in regard to the nature and personality of God. Let those who try to describe God know that on such a subject silence is eloquence. Let the Scriptures be read in simple faith, and let each one form his conceptions of God from his inspired word.

No human mind can comprehend God. No man hath seen him at any time. We are as ignorant of God as little children. But as little children we may love and obey Him. Had this been understood, such sentiments as are in this book would never have been expressed.

There are men bearing large responsibilities who do not know God. They do not understand the reasons of our faith. They have lost their way. Should I keep these things to myself any longer, I should be afraid that I should be brought under condemnation for suffering our people to be deceived. The enemy has sown his seed in the mind of our leading physician, and he is sowing the same seed in other minds. I should not be clear before God did I keep silent any longer regarding these things. The leaders in the medical missionary work ought to understand in regard to them.

At this time, just before the close of this earth's history, we need in the cause of God spiritual-minded men, men who are earnest in principle, and who have a clear understanding of what is truth. Immortality is obtained only by eating the flesh and drinking the blood of the Son of God. "Verily", verily I say unto you," Christ declared, "He that believeth on me hath everlasting life....I am the living bread which came down from heaven; if any man eat of this bread, he shall live forever; and the bread that I will give is my flesh, which I will give for the life of the world. . . Whoso eateth my flesh, and drinketh my blood, hath eternal life; and I will raise him up at the last day. For my flesh is meat indeed, and my blood is drink indeed. He that eateth my flesh and drinketh my blood dwelleth in me, and I in him. . . It is the spirit that quickeneth; the flesh profiteth nothing: the words that I speak unto you, they are spirit, and they are life."

We all need to cling to the Lord Jesus Christ. In regard to the Father, we shall soon understand in regard to his personality. I am bidden to speak these words to our medical workers and to our church members. Be not deceived; God is not mocked. Let those who have need of being converted seek diligently for the truth, else the words spoken by Christ will be applicable to them: "Ye shall seek me, and shall not find me; and where I am, thither ye can not come.

Chapter 100—Proposed Plan for Book Education

St. Helena, Cal., October 14, 1903.

Elder Prescott and Daniells:

My dear Brethren:

I wish to say a few words to you in regard to the proposed special effort to sell a large number of copies of my new book, "Education". I do not know much about the arrangements that are proposed. One thing I do know: I desire to get out of debt, if it be possible for me to do so, without diverting means that would otherwise be used in some branch of the cause. If the circulation of this book could be wisely managed in such a way that the income from it would relieve me of the burden of debt, I should regard the effort made by our people to accomplish this, as a great favor.

With reference to "Christ's Object Lessons", I wish to tell you that I have not appropriated to myself one penny of the income derived from the sale of this book. The office in Oakland has furnished me with a few copies without cost; and these I have given away to the poor and to others who were glad to receive and read them. But I have not used many "Object Lessons" even in this way.

I desire to place my book affairs in the hands of W. C. White, J. E. White, and one other person to represent the General Conference, who shall work together, and share the responsibility of making appropriations from the means that the sale of my books shall bring in. I hope, also, to be able to do something soon to help the sanitarium.

Taking into consideration my age and labors, I am enjoying excellent health. For this I praise the Lord; because I wish to complete several more books.

The proposed plan to sell the book "Education", so as to lift my debts, did not originate with me. But I thank the Lord for the consideration manifested in this proposal. When these plans were devised, I was very busily engaged in writing out important instructions; and I am still busy.

When I have time, I must write to you about the publishing work at College View. I approve of an effort to have our German and Scandinavian publishing work located there. I hope you will devise plans for the encouragement of this work.

The whole burden of this work must not be left with our foreign brethren. Nor should our brethren throughout the field leave too heavy a load on the Conferences near College

View. The members of these conferences should lead out and do their best, and all should come to their assistance.

Again: I hope that Brethren Magan and Sutherland can be relieved of the strain under which they have been laboring. I trust that you will study what I have written concerning their work. I very much desire that Emmanuel Missionary College shall become what it should be. I hope that the teachers and students there will be provided with comfortable quarters in which to pass the winter. I wish I had more means; for I should be so glad to help our brethren at Berrien Springs in this their time of need. But I have barely enough with which to live and to pay my workers. The Lord knows all about this matter, and he will help us. I am not distrustful, but am full of faith and hope and courage. I present these matters before you, and leave them with you. I pray that you may be guided by the Lord.

Ellen G. White.

Chapter 101—Stepping Off the Platform

St. Helena, Cal., Oct. 14, 1903.

Dr. David Paulson,

My dear Brother:

It would be very gratifying to me to see you and have an opportunity of conversing with you. Before I went to the Oakland Conference, I realized that you were in peril. I was troubled over your great confidence in Dr. Kellogg; for I knew that if you continued to put such confidence in him or in any other man that lives, you would be in danger of deception. But, upon reflection, I said to myself, "Dr. Paulson is an earnest Christian. He will not permit himself to be deceived."

Since that time, however, I have not been at ease regarding your safety. With sorrow I have witnessed Dr. Kellogg's influence over you.

In a vision last night I saw you writing. One looked over your shoulder, and said: "You, my friend, are in danger. As God's messenger, I come to say, The less you have to do with the matter concerning which you are writing, the clearer will be your judgment. The scriptures teach you all you can learn regarding God, except that which you may learn through an experimental knowledge of Christ, your Teacher.

"The Lord saith, While your leaders promise you liberty, they themselves are the servants of sin, and have been for a long time. Place no man's yoke on your neck. You are this day working counter to God. From the teachings of God or of Jesus his son you have not received the sentiments that you now entertain. The garden of your heart is being sown with tares; your faith is being weakened. You have turned from the path of truth; but the steps that you have already taken can now be retraced, if you will realize that you have been turning aside into a false path."

You were much surprised at these words, and inquired concerning the One who was speaking to you. The angel replied:--

"You are conversing with a messenger from heaven. I am instructed to warn you that you are stepping off the platform of eternal truth. The ideas that some are presenting in regard to God are seductive and untrue. Those who teach these sentiments will be held accountable for greatly dishonoring God. You should understand clearly that Satanic agencies are clothing false theories in an attractive garb, even as Satan in the garden of

Eden concealed his identity from our first parents by speaking through the serpent. You are instilling into human minds that which to you seems to be a very beautiful truth, but which in reality is error. The hypnotic influence of Satan is upon you, and upon all others who turn from the plain word of God to pleasing fables.

"Dr. Kellogg, sustained as he is by his associates, walks proudly and boastingly, and feels confirmed in his own will and way, which for years the Lord has been warning him to avoid. His associate physicians may strengthen the faith of men and women in his supposed wonderful enlightenment; but the light emanating from him is not the light shining from the Holy of holies; it is a false light that allures to spiritual death."

The heavenly messenger continued: "I have come to warn you. You seem to be dazed. Before you can do a work acceptable to the Lord, you must first break this spell that is upon you. God would have you link up with your brethren. He would not have you defend Dr. Kellogg in the falsehoods that he is now presenting, and thus help to fasten him securely in Satan's snare; for God will send his judgments upon all who walk in the light of Satanic theories, the evil results of which are far-reaching. You now see only the beginning, but the influences exerted will continue to widen and deepen until the Lord shall by His judgments arrest the men who are deceived and deluded, and who, by false representations and deceptive statements are rapidly bringing in misunderstandings, strife, and dissension.

"Study your Bible, heed the testimonies that God has sent to you and be wise. Help your brethren to free themselves from the snare into which they have fallen. Instead of sustaining Dr. Kellogg in the deceptive errors he is advocating, and thus helping to destroy the man, try to save his soul.

"Break the spell that is upon you. Come into the light. If you continue to walk in the path in which you are no walking, you will spoil your Christian experience, sever your connection with God, and lose eternal life. Can you afford to do this?

Brother Paulson, I awoke at one o'clock, and have arisen to write out these words of instruction from the heavenly messenger. I plead with you for Christ's sake, to break the spell. Many of our people are now terribly deluded. And many of our medical workers are helping Satan in his work. God calls upon his people to be in unity with Him. He loves those who strive to do his will, and he acknowledges them as his colaborers.

My dear brother, you are making a great mistake. Redeem yourself as soon as possible. You are not now glorifying God. Specious theories have been introduced in a very subtle manner. Shall the cause of God be imperiled? Will you unite with Dr. Kellogg to make it appear that the Testimonies which God has given through his Holy Spirit, sustain these theories, which are being advanced only as a "feeler?" Unless a change of heart takes place, the errors already published will be followed by other misleading theories.

I am so sorry, my brother, that you have not heeded the caution that I gave you in Oakland. I was instructed to talk with you, and tell you some things that you should know. But while you admitted certain things, you did not see where you yourself were in danger. I have had great confidence in you; but I hear that you are trying to make it appear that the sentiments expressed in "Living Temple" in regard to God can be sustained by my writings; therefore I am obliged to make a statement of denial of this, that our people shall not be deceived.

The Lord has been very merciful to you, my brother, but you are in great danger. Your eyes are blinded; you are accepting as truth the specious sophistry of the enemy.

Let me tell you of a scene that I witnessed while in Oakland. Angels clothed with beautiful garments, like angels of light, were escorting Dr. Kellogg from place to place, and inspiring him to speak words of pompous boasting that were offensive to God.

All who sustain a brother in his boastful positions are held accountable by God for confirming him in a perilous delusion. You should have discernment to see the delusion which, before the General Conference of 1901, began to take possession of the Doctor's mind, and which ever since has been gradually gaining ground. At that time I hoped that he was coming out clear and straight on the side of obedience to the commandments of the Lord. He was given great encouragement. I labored earnestly to remove from the minds of our people the wrong impressions that they had received.

Before I went to the Conference, the Lord declared to me: "In going to Battle Creek, and bearing your testimony in clear, decided lines, all who hear the instruction given by you, the Lord's messenger, will be left without excuse. I will put my words in your lips." I went, and the Lord gave me a message to bear before the thousands assembled.

Afterward, I received letters from the Doctor, in which he stated that there was nothing now between him and our ministers and churches, and that he himself was a changed man. But notwithstanding all the light that the Lord gave him through the Spirit of Prophecy, he still continued in a wrong course. The evil of urging upon our people agreements that bound all our medical institutions to one central organization, had often been presented to him, and yet he still urged the adoption of these agreements. When his propositions were not accepted, he would work in one way, and then in another way, and then in still another way, to accomplish his purpose. Feelings were aroused because his brethren in the ministry could not sanction all his plans. He cherished and expressed the thought that the ministers were wronging him, when in fact he was wronging himself and his brethren by failing to act as a Christian and a gentleman should act.

At the time of the last General Conference, the Lord instructed me to have no interviews with Dr. Kellogg. I was warned that he would say things that were not true, in order to uphold his positions; and that he would misreport to his associates the words I might speak. I felt it my duty to declare to him, in the presence of the leading brethren, including his medical associates, many things that the Lord has presented to me. I felt a deep interest in him, and I believed that he would take a right position and save himself by breaking his heart before God.

Three times I went down to the meeting place to open before the brethren some things regarding him and the deceptions under which he was laboring; but oh, how my heart ached for him! I did not desire to disparage him in any way before the people if it could be avoided, while there was still opportunity for him to repent. And so I forbore.

I have feared to say to Dr. Kellogg the plain things given me for him, lest he should be led to take a course that would forever decide his case. Had I when in Oakland borne the message that I thought I should have to bear, it might have resulted in Dr. Kellogg's taking his position fully with the powers of darkness. This he has been about to do again and again, but has not fully done it.

The Lord still has thoughts of mercy toward John Kellogg, but the fallen angels are close by his side, communicating with him.

For many years I have tried to hold fast to Dr. Kellogg. But for some time he has been revealing what spirit has been controlling him. The Lord will take this matter in his own hands. I must bear the testimonies of warning that he gives me to bear, and then leave with Him the results. I must now present the matter in all its bearings; for the people of God must not be despoiled.

Soon after the Oakland conference, in the night season the Lord portrayed before me a scene, in which Satan, clothed in a most attractive disguise, was earnestly pressing close to the side of Dr. Kellogg. I saw and heard much. Night after night I was bowed down in agony of soul, as I saw this personage talking with our brother. I was instructed that notwithstanding the warnings, counsels, and reproofs given, he has followed his own way, when as a people we have been receiving instruction to advance in an opposite direction. In the place of cooperating with the angels of heaven, he has cooperated with evil angels.

The theories that Dr. Kellogg is now advocating are similar to the theories that Satan presented to the holy pair in Eden. I told Elder A. T. Jones that which the Lord has presented to me in regard to the source from which the Doctor was receiving his education in these seductive theories. I told him that our brother was under the influence of Satanic agencies, and that for so long a time had he been working away from the principles of truth and righteousness, that he had been entangled, and had in himself no power to escape from the snare of the enemy.

I wrote out many plain messages, but decided to withhold some of them for a time. Not all these have been delivered yet. After bearing Testimonies of warning to Dr. Kellogg, I would weep as if my heart would break. Night after night, upon awaking, I would pray for him, I hoped and prayed that he would come out into the clear light. Thus the burden of his soul rested upon me after I returned from the Oakland General Conference.

If a change does not take place during the council meeting now being held in Washington, it may be that I shall have to go to Battle Creek, and bear a decided testimony for God and for the truth in behalf of God's people. Things have been allowed to drift so far and so fast that I dare not hesitate now. If the Lord bids me to go, be assured that I shall be in Battle Creek this winter; and the things that I could have said at the conference in Oakland, but that I hoped I would never need to say, God will strengthen me to say. I will speak whatever may be the consequences. I can not stand by silent, and see God dishonored and his people divided and spoiled by Satan's workings. Were I to do so, I should be unfaithful to my trust. I will continue to stand for truth, for exalted principles.

If right principles had been followed, the relation existing between the physicians and their brethren would be exactly what the Lord designed it to be; but for years an effort has been put forth to make the medical missionary work the body. God designs that the medical missionary work shall be bound up with the gospel ministry.

God has chosen a people out of the world, and has instructed them to remain forever separate from the world. While living in the world, they are not to be of the world. Dr. Kellogg has bound up himself with worldlings by inviting them into his councils; and he has been dishonoring the sacredness of the truth by bringing worldly lawyers into connection with the work of God's people. The Lord has signified that it is His purpose to keep his people free from the contaminating influences of the world; but the leaders of the medical work at Battle Creek have been working in a way altogether different from the way marked out by the Lord. The first and the second chapters of First Peter are full of instruction in regard to the manner in which we should labor.

I would not now speak so plainly, were it not for the intense desire I feel that our medical workers shall be molded and fashioned after the similitude of Christ, in order that all their work and their relation to God's cause may be in harmony with his purpose. God calls upon every physician and every medical missionary worker to take his stand on the platform of truth, where he shall not be influenced by any man's false theories and wrong devising. The pure, living principles of the gospel are to be respected. God has a people in his church who are laboring just as disinterestedly to save sinners, as the medical missionary workers have been laboring. He calls upon His medical missionary workers to labor unitedly with his church, and not to allow any physician to control their efforts by his authority. The Lord now calls upon his people to unify. Let all our medical missionaries unite with our ministers in soul-saving work.

Nothing should be allowed to stand in the way of perfect, complete unity between the medical missionary workers, and the gospel ministry. God has not empowered Dr. Kellogg with spiritual grace to be lord over all our physicians and other medical missionaries. It is time that the teachings of the great Medical Missionary should be brought into the life-practice of our medical missionary workers. It is time that God's voice should be heard; for his words, spoken in truth, are spirit and life. He never makes a mistake.

If Dr. Kellogg would unite with his ministering brethren, and give them his confidence, believing that they will work as Christ works through them, then he himself could see that others should be granted the privilege of standing in their God-given lot and place, and that he should respect all whom God has called as gospel missionaries to work in his cause. Working as Christ worked, our brethren would not be divided at all. But so long as our brother determines to carry things in his own way, irrespective of the Lord's workers, as if he were the only man whom heaven could acknowledge as a leader, God is displeased. If he were to occupy his proper place, he would be respected; but never is he to be regarded as he has regarded himself,-- as chief of all the medical missionary workers, as one who has the privilege of consulting only those who exalt him, and of ignoring as not worthy of acting a part in the great medical missionary work, all the gospel ministers who disapprove of some of his ideas.

God has appointed His workers to stand true to him at their respective posts of duty. They are not to work in accordance with the plans of worldly-wise men, nor are they to take such men into their councils. Those who are true to their trust will not make lawyers the main support of the securities of our institutions.

I intended to say these things while I was at the Oakland General Conference. I felt an intense desire that Dr. Kellogg should be led to take a sound position in favor of the truth and of the last warning message of mercy that is to be given to the world.

The gospel is to be proclaimed as Christ has specified. Just before his ascension, Jesus spake unto his disciples, saying, "All power is given unto me in heaven and in earth. Go ye therefore, and teach all nations, baptizing them in the name of the Father, and of the Son, and of the Holy Ghost; teaching them to observe all things whatsoever I have commanded you; and, lo (while you are doing this), I am with you alway, even unto the end of the world."

Let Christ's words be repeated. He is to be regarded as the greatest medical missionary worker that ever trod this earth. Bring into the medical missionary work none of the sentiments and devisings of men.

Let not any man try to carry his ambitious projects without presenting them before his brethren and asking for counsel in regard to how the work shall be carried forward.

In Oakland, there was spread before me a long, lawyer-framed document, filled with technicalities, which document was a copy of the conditions under which the Sanitarium issued bonds. The provisions of this bond issue were such that money gathered in from all parts of the country is tied up in the medical institution at Battle Creek for a long period of time. Our people should never have been expected to tie up so great an amount of money as was needed to rebuild the large Sanitarium there. It was not right to endeavor to gather in means to make sure of a great work in one place, irrespective of other parts of the field. The Lord presented before me many places where small sanitariums were to be established. One is greatly needed near Nashville, at some point convenient to the large educational institutions in the suburbs of this Southern city. In many other places where medical missionary work has not yet been established, there is urgent need of small medical institutions.

After the last General Conference, there was presented before me the necessity of our establishing a sanitarium at Washington city. The interest of the mammoth institution at Battle Creek will require Dr. Kellogg's attention and labors there, and our brethren at Washington have been instructed to establish in their city a sanitarium, which shall not stand as a rival of any similar institution, but which shall be another agency for holding aloft the standard of health reform. Our people are not to be dependent upon the counsels of their fellow workers in Battle Creek regarding the management of the institution in Washington. And the Lord desires, too, that our sanitariums already in running order shall not depend so much upon the medical association at Battle Creek.

God has counseled us that if the sanitarium work shall be carried forward in the right way, it will be the means of doing great good. In no case are our medical institutions to be so conducted that they will be a means of leading our workers into worldly paths.

We have also been instructed that some would grasp selfishly for means with which to do a work that was not endorsed by the Lord; and that when in times of special need, God's servants would call for means with which to carry forward aggressive work in new fields, they would be met with the response, "Our money is tied up for several years in bonds we purchased from the Battle Creek Sanitarium, and we can not help in this crisis."

With respect to many matters, Dr. Kellogg's management is not after God's order. He will set in operation every device possible to gather in means for his line of work, without reference to the great necessities in every other part of the Lord's vineyard. I have been instructed that I should have to bear my testimony on this point, and not permit our people to be drawn into the matters that they can not correctly understand.

God was dishonored by the plans devised for issuing bonds as a means of obtaining money with which to complete the Battle Creek Sanitarium building; for the talent of means in the hands of our people is thus tied up where it can not be used for the proclamation of the third angel's message in fields still unentered. There is a world to be warned; and God's people must be cautioned against becoming so impoverished financially by tying up their means in great institutions that they will have little or nothing left with which to provide facilities in needy fields and with which to carry forward the Lord's work in all parts of the earth.

The work of the Creator as seen in nature reveals his power. But nature is not above God, nor is God in nature as some represent him to be. God made the world, but the world is not God; it is but the work of his hands. Nature reveals the work of a positive, personal God, showing that God is, and that he is a rewarder of those who diligently seek him.

Let us take the word of God as the man of our counsel. As we diligently study the Scriptures, we shall be able to serve the Lord more intelligently and more earnestly than ever before, and we shall be truer representatives of him; for we shall be imbued with his Spirit.

The warning messages given to the church in Sardis comes to us today:

"I know thy works, that thou hast a name that thou livest, and art dead. Be watchful, and strengthen the things which remain, that are ready to die; for I have not found thy works perfect before God. Remember therefore how thou hast received, and hold fast, and repent. If therefore thou shalt not watch, I will come on thee as a thief, and thou shalt not know what hour I will come upon thee."

My brother, read the third chapter of Second Peter. Truth, Bible truth, is alone worth living for. God and his glory are not to be diminished by any pleasing sophistry of human wisdom. The state of the world, with its abominations and crimes, in fulfillment of the prophecies concerning the wickedness that would prevail during the last days, is enough to lead true Christians to live lives of humility and prayer.

Ellen G. White.

Chapter 102—The Specious Working of Satan

"Elmshaven", Sanitarium, Cal., November 11, 1903.

Dear Brother Magan and Sutherland,

Brother Magan left with Willie's copy written for a circular, regarding the Berrien Springs School. In it there are some things that I think would be better left out. Let us not dwell on the dark chapters in the experiences of Seventh-day Adventists. They bring up a discouraging, depressing picture, and it would seem as if Christ, the Light of the world, had not been near to help. There was no need of the dearth of knowledge, as he ever will be, the way, the truth, and the life. He was ready to help, and no one need have made grave mistakes or errors.

The time to which you referred, a time dark, perplexing, and discouraging,--let it stay in the past. Do not talk of it unless forced to. To make reference to the worst features in the experience of those now in positions of trust in the work of God, does not benefit anyone. Let us not call up the dark shadows of the past. Let the past lie where it is, with all its objectionable features. Into the present we are to bring pleasantness, hope, and courage.

If there are those who are allowing the enemy to obtain an advantage over them, tempting him to tempt them, and carrying out his plans, let not this appear. And do not bring up the dark, unchristlike deeds of the past. The dear Saviour was all the time inviting those who did these deeds to cease to dishonor God, and to turn to him for help to do right.

At the present time we have plain evidence of the specious, artful working of Satan on human minds. We have to meet the working with determined effort. But let the dark pictures of the past be buried, and let them stay buried. Let us not cloud the mind of any one by bringing up these representations. Let us at this time bring in all the light possible.

Few realize the dangerous character of the sentiments that we are having to meet. I have been over the ground. I have been given plain words to speak concerning these specious, bewitching sentiments. If they are not most decidedly met and reproved, souls will be lost. We can not afford to be deceived. We must point our people to the old landmarks. We are to obtain strength and courage from on high, that we may obey the command given me, "Meet it."

"Ye are the children of the light and of the day. We are not of the night nor of darkness." Christ is the way, the truth, and the life. The trouble with us is that we do not press on in the way illuminated by the Sun of Righteousness. In order to walk in this way, we must receive strength from the Life-giver. As we move forward in obedience to Christ's commands, His light shines on our way, and his strength sustains us. Thus we go forward from strength to strength, from grace to grace, by obedience becoming more and more Christlike.

We are not to follow human leading. Christ is our leader. At all times and in all places, in every time of need, we shall find him a present help. Because there are those professing to be Christians who dishonor Christ in thought, word, and deed, we are to give plainer evidence than ever before of our completeness in him. We are to walk in the light of his countenance. We can each show that Christ is the light, and that in him is no darkness at all. If we will submit to his guidance, he will lead us from the low level on which sin has left us to the loftiest heights of grace.

We are not to darken our lives by talking of our own imperfections or of the imperfections of others. We are to be all light in the Lord.

From Christ all truth radiates. Apart from Christ, science is misleading, and philosophy is foolishness. Those who are separated from the Saviour will advance theories which originate with the wily foe. Christ's life stands out as the contrast of all false science, all erroneous theories, all misleading methods.

Pretenders will arise with theories that have not foundation in the word of God. We are to hold aloft the banner bearing the inscription, the Commandments of God and the faith of Jesus. We are to hold the beginning of our confidence firm unto the end. Let no one attempt to dilute truth with a mixture of sophistry. Let no one attempt to tear down the foundation of our faith, or to spoil the pattern by bringing into the web threads of human devising. Not one thread of pantheism is to be drawn into the web. Sensuality, ruinous to soul and body, is always the result of drawing these threads into the web.

"Let us who are of the day, be sober, putting on the breastplate of faith and love; and for an helmet the hope of salvation. For God hath not appointed us to wrath, but to obtain salvation by our Lord Jesus Christ, who died for us, that, whether we wake or sleep, we should live together with Him. Wherefore comfort yourselves together, and edify one another, even as also ye do.

"And we beseech you, brethren, to know them which labor among you, and are over you in the Lord, and admonish you; and to esteem them very highly in love for their work's sake. And be at peace among yourselves.

"We exhort you, brethren, comfort the feebleminded, support the weak, be patient toward all men. See that none render evil for evil unto any man, but ever follow that which is good, both among yourselves and to all men. Rejoice evermore. Pray without ceasing. In everything give thanks; for this is the will of God in Christ Jesus concerning you. Quench not the Spirit. Despise not prophesyings. Prove all things; hold fast that which is good. Abstain from all appearance of evil. And the very God of peace sanctify you wholly; and I pray God your whole spirit and soul and body be preserved blameless unto the coming of our Lord Jesus Christ. Faithful is he that calleth you, who also will do it.

Ellen G. White.

Chapter 103—A New Conversion Needed

Sanitarium, Cal., December, 1903.

Dr. J. H. Kellogg,

Sanitarium,

Battle Creek, Michigan. My dear Brother:

I praise the Lord for the letters that I have recently received from you. I greatly desire that you may now make a thorough work of repentance for time and for eternity. So long have you been retrograding toward union with the world, that it is difficult for you to see where you might now be standing, had you constantly advanced heavenward. You have lost many blessings because you have not felt your need of light.

If your faith in the word of God is strengthened, if you will fully accept the truths that have called us out of the world, and made us a people denominated by the Lord as his peculiar treasure, if you will unite with your brethren in standing by the old landmarks,--then there will be unity. But if you remain in unbelief, unsettled as to the true foundation of faith, there can be no more hope of unity in the future than there has been in the past.

I am instructed to say that you need to be taught the first principles of present truth. You have not believed the messages that God has given for this time. Think you that while you remain in doubt and unbelief, you can be fully united with those who have stood for the truth as it is in Jesus, and who have accepted the light that God has given to us as a people?

Ask yourself candidly whether you are bound in the faith. Do all in your power to come into unity with God and with your brethren. As a people, we can not receive the full measure of the blessing of God, while some who occupy leading positions are working against the truth that for years we have held sacred, and obedience to which has brought us what success we have had.

"Unto the angel of the church of Ephesus write: These things saith he that holdeth the seven stars in his right hand, who walketh in the midst of the seven golden candlesticks: I know thy works and thy labor, and thy patience, and how thou canst not bear them which are evil; and thou hast tried them which say they are apostles and are not, and hast found them liars; and hast borne, and hast patience, and for my name's sake hast labored, and hast not fainted. Nevertheless I have somewhat against thee, because thou hast left thy first love."

If you had kept the faith, you would not have left your first love, and you would not have brought yourself into the unsettled condition in which you have been for years.

"And unto the angel of the church in Sardis write: These things saith he that hath the seven spirits of God, and the seven stars: I know thy works, that thou hast a name that thou livest, and art dead. Be watchful, and strengthen the things which remain, that are ready to die; for I have not found thy works perfect before God.

These words point out your true spiritual condition. The warning comes: "Dr. Kellogg is not a converted man. Some of his associate physicians are so deceived by Satan that they are unable to distinguish between the true and the genuine, the false and the deceptive. They stand directly in his way, hindering him from making a thorough work of repentance."

You need an entire change of heart, before you can discern the error into which you have fallen. You have listened to the arch deceiver. You do not discern where the sophistries you have received will lead. Read carefully the fifth chapter of Hebrews. You have no time to lose. The angel of God calls, "Close up the ranks. John H. Kellogg, come into line."

A Bible institute should be held in some place where medical missionary workers and ministers may meet together to study the scriptures. Let the Bible explain its own statements. Accept it just as it reads, without twisting the words to suit human ideas, "What is the chaff to the wheat?"

Teach All Nations

The gospel commission as recorded in Matthew was given not only to the disciples of Christ who were then living, but to all who should afterward receive him. Upon every one who accepts him as personal Saviour is placed the burden of proclaiming the gospel message. Will the church today refuse to recognize its obligation to do the work so plainly outlined in the words; "Go ye therefore, and teach all nations; baptizing them in the name of the Father, and of the Son, and of the Holy Ghost, teaching them to observe all things whatsoever I have commanded you." Were it not for the promise of Christ's presence, we might well draw back. But he ways, "Lo, I am with you alway, even unto the end of the world."

This work is not to be confined to a few. The proclamation of the gospel is not to be limited to one city or one state. "Go ye therefore, and teach all nations."

God is in earnest with his people. He calls upon them to overcome the spirit of covetousness. We must be careful not to tie up the Lord's means by establishing institutions larger than is consistent with the plan of God. It is his purpose that facilities should be provided for the advancement of his work in all parts of the world. Large sums of money are not to be invested in one or two places. The erection of many buildings in one place reveals a selfish outlay of means. Thus the money brought into the treasury by the liberality of God's people is absorbed in one place by those having charge of the work in that place. When men are freed from selfishness, they will not make such earnest efforts to grasp all that they possibly can for the place in which they are most interested. They will be willing to sacrifice their ambitions in order that other places may receive a share of the means available for the advancement of God's work.

Christ Our Only Hope

As we see the condition of mankind today, the question arises in the minds of some, Is man by nature totally and wholly depraved? Is he hopelessly ruined?

Men have sold themselves to the enemy of all righteousness. They can not redeem themselves. Of themselves they can do no good thing. But there is always an escape. When man sinned, Christ offered to stand as his substitute and surety, in order to provide a way whereby the guilty race might return to loyalty. He took humanity, and passed over the ground where Adam stumbled and fell. Without swerving from his allegiance, he met the temptations wherewith man is beset. Only by accepting Christ as a personal Saviour, can human beings be uplifted. Beware of any theory that would lead men to look for salvation from any other source than that pointed out in the Word. Only through Christ can men sunken in sin and degradation be led to a higher life. Theories that do not recognize the atonement that has been made for sin, and the work that the Holy Spirit is to do in the hearts of human beings, are powerless to save.

Man's pride would lead him to seek for salvation in some other way than that devised by God. He is unwilling to be accounted as nothing, unwilling to recognize Christ as the only One who can save to the uttermost. To this pride Satan appealed in the temptation that he brought to our first parents. "Ye shall be as gods; ye shall not surely die," he said. And by belief of his words, they place themselves on his side. Of Christ it is written, "There is none other name under heaven given among men, whereby we must be saved." "In all things it behooved him to be made like unto his brethren, that he might be a merciful and faithful high priest in things pertaining to God, to make reconciliation for the sins of the people. For in that he himself hath suffered being tempted, he is able to succor them that are tempted."

Ellen. G. White.

Chapter 104—God Above All

Sanitarium, Cal., Jan. 2, 1904.

Dr. J. H. Kellogg,

Sanitarium, Battle Creek, Mich.

My dear Brother:

I have received your letter, and also a copy of a circular letter recently sent out by you. Thank you. I have ever had an intense desire to see you standing firm in God, working under the direction of the great head Physician.

My brother, I ask you to remember that Christ is our Leader. The beings that he has purchased with his blood are to study the life that he lived in this world, in order to learn what path they are to follow. His voice is heard, "If any man will come after me, let him deny himself, and take up his cross, and follow me." "So shall he be my disciple." He who supposes, like Nebuchadnezzar, that he can lift up or cast down, will find that he is reckoning without God.

I ask you to consider him, who though the Majesty of heaven, the King of Glory, took humanity upon him, and came to this world to show what those who serve him may become. God has given you precious knowledge regarding the treatment of the sick. But you have not appreciated this knowledge as a gift of God.

I am thankful that you see something of what has been lost by your consenting to take the heavy burden of business matters, and by your effort to control the general work. Again and again your devisings have hindered the advancement of the work of God. Time has been lost during which victories might have been gained if you had stood out of the way. Your vision has been narrow.

I am glad that you see the evil influence of division. Had you put yourself where you should have been, there would long ago been a united company, and medical missionary work, in connection with the gospel ministry, would have had a far-reaching influence for good. This I know: for the truth has been presented to me too clearly for me to turn away from it.

You have manifested altogether too much kingship in your work as physician. For the last twenty years warnings in regard to this have been presented to me. I have been instructed that had you acted your part in giving recognition to men who were deserving of recognition, we should today have had men doing as good a work as yourself in some things; physicians qualified to fill important positions of trust. But there is a dearth of workers at a time when we so much need men who show all-around efficiency, because they acknowledge God and Christ as supreme.

Christ is your example. If you fall short of following the example that he came to our world to give, God could not safely admit you into the heavenly courts.

Infinite possibilities are placed within the reach of every human being who in humility and contrition returns to his allegiance to God, as a little child acknowledging the authority of his law, and obeying its precepts. The Father and the Son have provided for man great things, broad and high and deep and inexpressible. This they have done that man, becoming one with Christ in God, might trade on his talents to advance the kingdom of heaven in this world. But man, choosing the kingship, will, in pursuance of his object, reveal what self will do by its devising, setting aside the only One to whom belongs the kingship, who is the alpha and omega of all things, besides whom there is none else.

God, the living, personal God, the author and ruler of nature, is above all science. He is acquainted with science that is inexplainable to the greatest minds in our world. In his sight the nations before him are as a drop in the bucket. He taketh up the isles as a very little thing. Lebanon is not sufficient to burn, or the beasts thereof for a burnt offering.

How few have any knowledge of God! How few understand the greatest and majesty of our God! Human language can not define Him. His ways are past finding out.

God sees that the world is in need of cleansing. In the very near future, this cleansing will come. It will at first be done in a limited degree, and then with greater and still greater power, till men will see that God means to bring them to repentance. ...

(There is then quoted Isaiah 24: 1--26:4.)

Ellen G. White.

Chapter 105—Work Misrepresented

Not the laws of the impulsive tongue or hand, but the loving pulsations of the converted heart, are from God. "God is love; and he that dwelleth in love dwelleth in God, and God in him." He sets forth love as a rule of life in still another way: "Be ye therefore merciful, as your Father also is merciful." (Luke 6:36)

God displayed his power and wisdom in the work of creation. He revealed his majesty in the giving of his law. And, finally, in the person of his Son, he came to the world to show his love and grace. The only begotten Son of God was nailed to the cross of Calvary, that he might bequeath to the fallen race a legacy of pardon.

Satan's work is directly opposed to the work of God. The enemy of all good, he stands as the general of the forces drawn up to hurt the souls of men. He looks on with fiendish triumph as he sees the professed followers of Christ biting and devouring one another. He stands ever ready to mar the lives of those who are trying to serve God. Heavenly angels marvel that men should aid Satanic agencies in their work, discouraging hearts, making God's people weak strengthless, faithless.

A clear revelation has been given me in regard to the need of our people assembling together, confessing their sins, repenting before God, and continuing in prayer until the Lord manifests himself to them with power. If ever a people needed to offer a prayer such as Daniel offered, it is our people. There is among them such self-confidence, such presumption! The Lord has been sending light to them, but the testimonies of his Spirit have not been heeded. There has been a departure from his expressed commands, a working contrary to the messages that for many years he has been giving relative to the different features of our work. There has been a selfish gathering of facilities to a few favored places, and a neglect of other parts of the field. Great neglect has been shown to the needs of the people in our large cities and in the Southern field. This need not be, and it will not be when those who claim to believe the truth practice the truth.

I have been enjoined by the Lord to gather together the testimonies given for the Southern field, and put them before the people. While attending the campmeeting at Fresno, Cal., I was, in the visions of the night, in a certain meeting. I could not call those present by name; for I could not see them. There seemed to be a cloud of darkness over the assembly. I sat in a place that seemed to be separated from the room where the people had assembled.

The brethren in this meeting were counseling in regard to the work at Nashville. One present was speaking in a very decided manner, expressing his views in regard to the publishing house in Nashville and the general management of the work there. Much was said, and it was all very discouraging. Matters were presented in a strong light. Some present had gathered up the testimonies of those who were unfavorably inclined toward the Nashville publishing house. If actions had been taken based upon these misrepresentations, great injustice would have been done to the Southern work. Decisions would have been made that would have had a most discouraging effect, apparently upholding that which the Lord condemns.

If the course outlined by the brethren present, who were connected with the work at Battle Creek, has been followed, it would have worked an injustice, and would have resulted in a wrong showing for the work in Nashville. Acting upon false impressions, the brethren would have brought about something that the Lord could not endorse.

One of authority arose, and said: "These matters are not being presented in righteousness and truth. The very ones who should have taken a Christlike interest in the Southern work have passed it by. Wrong impressions have been made on minds in regard to the work at Nashville, and these impressions will work as leaven among meal, preventing the suffering Southern field from receiving the help that it needs. Your representations have been false, your criticisms cruel. Your words have been as sharp arrows. How much glory will they bring to God? You are endeavoring to bring in plans and theories that will greatly retard the work. Let no more such hindrances be brought in. All difficulties are easily settled, all wrongs easily righted, when human beings are under the control of the Spirit of God.

"If there be therefore any consolation in Christ, if any comfort of love, if any fellowship of the Spirit, if any bowels and mercies, fulfill ye my joy, that ye be like minded, having the same love, being of one accord, of one mind. Let nothing be done through strife, or vainglory; but in lowliness of mind let each esteem other better than themselves. Look not every man on his own things, but every man also on the things of others! (Phil. 2:1-4)

"The Lord is grieved. The work can not possibly be adjusted and conducted to his glory unless the workers allow Him to be their helper. Show a loving, generous regard for those who, to advance the work, have taxed their powers of endurance to the utmost limit, laboring almost at the sacrifice of their lives. They have been sustained by the power of God. The Saviour of humanity recognizes the almost superhuman efforts made to press the work forward, while not a few were placing blocks before the wheels.

"If those who now view matters with perverted vision had talked constantly with God, pleading with him for grace and guidance, they would have followed a different course. They would have called to mind their own experience in a new field, and would have striven to establish more firmly that which had been established. As they learned Christ's lessons, they would have become meek and lowly and humble, and they would have been partakers of his loving-kindness and his unselfish regard for others. But without a kind, loving regard for those who have as deep an interest as themselves in the cause of God, who have at heart the needs of suffering humanity, how can men serve God acceptable? How can they adjust matters in a way that will glorify him? Those who are striving to obey the word, 'Be ye therefore perfect, even as your Father which is in heaven is perfect,' will not hurt the souls of Christ's purchased possession."

Humanity alone is a very poor combination of opposites. Naturally, human beings are self-centered and opinionated. But when they learn the lessons that Christ desires to teach them, they become partakers of the divine nature, and henceforth they live Christ's life. They regard all men as brethren, with similar aspirations, capabilities, temptations, and trials, needing tests and difficulties, craving sympathy and help.

Never feel that it is your prerogative to humiliate a fellow-worker. If mistakes have been made, learn about them, not from a desire to crush the one who has made them, but from a desire to help, that no one be separated from God's work. Help those who have erred, by telling them of your experiences, showing how, when you have made grave mistakes, patience and fellowship, kindness and helpfulness, on the part of your fellow-workers, gave you courage and hope. Harsh judgment is not becoming. Be afraid to condemn where God has not condemned. Remember that your brethren love God, and that they are striving to keep his commandments as verily as you are. You have been in the Battle, and you carry the scars of conflict. Will you not deal merciful with those who are fiercely assailed?

Mistakes have been made in the work in the South, but these are not such as to require the doing of the work that some have supposed to be necessary. There are those who, instead of strengthening and sustaining the work in Nashville, have tried to destroy it. They have given place to evil surmisings and unjust criticisms. They have placed a mote close to the eye, and it has obscured their vision. Nothing but it can they see. If they would remove this mote, as they could if they so desired, they would see the glory beyond.

Chapter 106—Unify

Berrien Springs, Mich., May 20, 1904.

Dear Brethren Daniells and Prescott:

Yesterday a very strong impression came upon me that now is our time to save Dr. Kellogg. We must now work with determined effort. We must not prescribe the precise steps which he must take, but we must lay hold of the man himself, and let him see that the spirit of God and the spirit of soul-saving are in us. Satan has worked to bind him up with himself, but shall we stand by and make no effort to pull him away from Satan? Shall we not in the name of the Lord call for Dr. Kellogg to come to this meeting, not that we may make accusations against him, but that we may help him and all of us draw with Christ.

Not one of us is above temptation. There is a work that Dr. Kellogg is educated to perform as no other man in our ranks can perform; and if he will draw nigh to God, God will draw nigh to him. We are to draw with all our power, not making accusations, not prescribing what he must do, but letting him see that we are not willing that any should perish, but that every man should have that which Christ died to present to him--eternal life.

Is it not worth the trial? Satan is drawing him, but last night I saw a hand reached out to clasp his hand, and the words were spoken: "Let him take hold of My strength, that he may make peace with Me. As he sees Me do, so must he do."

Here is a point! Leave the individuality of the man for God to work with at the present time. Every one needs to remember that Christ pardoned all transgression and all sin, because He came to seek and to save those who were lost!

To all-for there were many looking on--He said: "Look not on this man, but look on Me. I gave my life to save him unto eternal life. He has dishonored Me. It is my name that must be honored as a sin-pardoning Saviour. I will open blind eyes."

"Take heed, every soul, take heed to yourselves, lest at any time your hearts be overcharged with surfeiting and drunkenness, and the cares of this life, and so that day come on you unawares. For as a snare shall it come on all those that dwell on the face of the whole earth. Watch ye therefore, and pray always, that ye may be accounted worthy to escape all these things that shall come to pass, and to stand before the Son of man.

The day of the Lord so cometh as a thief in the night. For when they shall say, 'Peace and safety', then sudden destruction cometh upon them, as travail upon a woman with child; and they shall not escape."

Then the Saviour stretched out his hand, saying: "But ye, brethren, are not in darkness, that that day should overtake you as a thief. Ye are all the children of light and of the day. If ye be obedient to the knowledge ye have received from my word, then walk according to my word, ye are the children of the day. Ye are not of the night, nor of darkness, therefore ye are not to sleep as do others, but to watch and be sober. Walk as children of the day. You all need a more earnest hold upon heavenly things. All need the faith that works by love and purifies the soul. You have not already attained, neither are you now perfect. A work of purification should now be done in your souls, then your lives will demonstrate that you are pressing toward the mark of your high calling in Christ Jesus.

"Every man needs to walk humbly with God. Grow in grace and the knowledge of our Lord and Saviour Jesus Christ. By looking unto your Saviour, beholding with open face as in a glass the glory of the Lord, you will be changed into the same image, from glory to glory, even as by the Spirit of the Lord. As I work with you and you abide in Me, you will reveal perfection of character, you will be made perfect in one. John Kellogg, put on the Lord Jesus Christ, that you may see that of yourself you can do nothing. You can not possibly atone for your own sins. Through faith in Christ Jesus purify your soul from all dross, and reveal the righteousness of Christ, which is of God by faith. Christ has marked your desires when your spirit has striven with you."

Then John Kellogg exclaimed: "I am sinful, but He hath covered me with his own righteousness, and henceforth I will go in the strength of the Lord God. Henceforth, I will make mention of thy righteousness, even of Thine only."

Confessions were made, and the words were spoken by Christ: "Unless you walk in all humility of mind, Satan will obtain the victory."

Dr. Kellogg exclaimed: "He hath broken the bands of Satan; He hath covered me with the robe of righteousness. I will go in the strength of the Lord God. I will make mention of Thy righteousness."

A hand was laid upon the hand of Dr. Kellogg and upon the hand of Willie Kellogg, and the Saviour said: "I have not been unmindful of your struggles, but ye would not come unto Me that ye might have life. Take my yoke upon you, and unite with your brethren, all of whom need to wear my yoke. Learn of Me, for I am meek and lowly of heart, and ye shall find rest to your souls. For my yoke is easy and my burden is light. Ye were sometimes in darkness because ye did not wear my yoke. If you will wear my yoke, and learn of me, you will henceforth reveal my meekness and lowliness. You were sometimes darkness, but henceforth you are to be the children of light. If you will keep hold of my strength, you will all be light in the Lord. Have no fellowship with the unfruitful works of darkness, reprove them. All things that are reproved are made manifest by the light."

Christ took the hands of both John Kellogg and Willie Kellogg, and said: "Awake to your responsibilities, but take on yourselves fewer burdens than you have in the past. Awake, thou that sleepest, and arise from the dead, and Christ shall give you spiritual light. See that you both walk unitedly. I will be your sufficiency. Do you walk in your own strength, but with the sense that I am your helper. See, then, that ye walk circumspectly."

Then his hand was laid upon the hands of Elders Daniells and Prescott and W. C. White, and these words were spoken: "Let the words of the Lord dwell in you richly in all wisdom. The sword of the Spirit is the Word of God. The Word of God is quick and powerful, and sharper than any two-edged sword. The weapons of our warfare are not carnal, but mighty through God to the pulling down of the strongholds of the enemy, casting down imaginations and every high thing that exalteth itself against the knowledge of God, and bringeth into captivity every thought to the obedience of Christ."

Then he turned to the gospel medical missionaries, and said: "Ye strike too low. There is a broader work for you to do. Leave the smaller work for those who need the experience, but teach them all to be ever reaching a higher standard. Keep your souls in the love of God. Broaden your work. Teach those who know not the truth. The cities are to be worked. All the work to be done, God will open before those who are striving to save souls perishing in their sins. There are various lines of work: but unite, unite, unite, in perfect harmony. This is your safety and your wisdom and your strength."

Except a man be born again, he can not see the kingdom of God. If any man be in Christ, he is a new creature; old things are passed away; behold, all things are become new. A new heart also will I give you, and a new spirit will I put within you; I will take away the stony heart out of your flesh, and I will give you a new heart of flesh, Purge out therefore the old leaven, that ye may be a new lump, the new man which is created after God in righteousness and true holiness. Thou shalt be called by a new name which the mouth of the Lord shall name. The Lord your God proveth you to know whether you love Him with all your heart and with all your soul. He shall sit as a refiner and purifier and silver; and he shall purify the sons of Levi, and purge them as gold and silver, that they may offer unto the Lord an offering in righteousness. Every man's work shall be made manifest; for the day shall declare it, because it shall be revealed by fire, and the fire shall try every man's work, of what sort it is.

"Unify. Your unbelief and lack of unity have been a standing reproach to the people of God who have been given so much light. The pride of the human heart has dishonored the greatest work ever given to mortals. Unify, come into the sanctifying circle of truth. Draw together; walk humbly with God' and be subject one to another according to the light of the Word. Let no man seek to be the greatest. This has been an offense to God. Press together and heed every word that will create oneness. Avoid all fault finding and dissension, perplexing matters will adjust themselves if each one will walk circumspectly.

"As you seek to reach the highest standard, I will turn my hands upon thee and will purge away thy dross, and take away thy sin. I will melt and try them. Put off concerning the former conversation of the old man, which is corrupt according to the deceitful lusts, and be renewed in the spirit of your minds, and put on the new man, which after God is created in righteousness and true holiness. You are to be one. Strive no longer to be first. If ye then be risen with Christ, seek those things which are above, where Christ sitteth at the right hand of God. Read the first twelve verses of the second chapter of First Peter. God gave these words through his servant. Let all help their brethren to be one as Christ is one with the Father.

I can write no more now. I am bidden to present this to my brethren, for them to carry to others, who are not at this meeting. Work with all diligence in harmony with Christ. We have not a moment to spend in contention. Every soul is to be hidden with Christ in God. There is to be a time of trouble such as there has not been since there was a nation. Those who have any realization of this will not regard it as a virtue to make little differences a hindrance to their own spirituality and to the advancement of the work of God. Let the Lord's entrusted means be put in operation that new fields may be opened. Let lines of work be set in operation to warn the cities and villages as fast as possible; for the time will soon be upon us when the enemy will imbue all wicked men with his devising. The secret of the Lord is with them that fear Him, and he will show them his covenant. God calls upon his people to assist with their means, that in the places which he has specified should be worked, there may be wise men to carry the work forward.

Ellen G. White.

Chapter 106.1—Remarks Made at Berrien Springs

Berrien Springs, Mich., May 22, 1904.

by Mrs. E. G. White.

We may find valuable instruction in the words of Christ: "If thou bring thy gifts to the altar, and there rememberest that thy brother hath ought against thee, leave there thy gift before the altar, and go thy way; first be reconciled to thy brother, and then come and offer thy gift."

In moving the College from Battle Creek and establishing it in Berrien Springs, Brethren Magan and Sutherland have acted in harmony with the light that God gave. They have worked under great difficulties. Upon the school there was a heavy burden of debt that they had not created. They labored and toiled and sacrificed in their endeavor to carry out right lines of education. And God has been with them. He has approved of their efforts.

But who has appreciated the work that has been done in this place? Many have taken an attitude of opposition, and have spoken words that have caused sadness, and have made it hard to carry forward the work. Wicked prejudice and false accusations have been met. With some there has been a settled disposition to complain and to find fault with those who have striven with all their right to carry out the Lord's instruction.

Sister Magan worked with her husband, struggling with him, and praying that he might be sustained. She did not think of herself but of him. And God did sustain them, as they walked in the light. From her small store of money, Sister Magan gave five hundred dollars, to erect the Memorial Hall. She strove untiringly to maintain a perfect home government, teaching and educating her children in the fear of God. Twice she had to nurse her husband through an attack of fever.

But it seemed to her as if some of our brethren had not a heart of flesh. After the General Conference in Oakland, a report was circulated that Sister White has turned against Brother Magan. There was not a word of truth in this statement. But his poor wife, who had toiled and sacrificed and prayed with him, was informed that Sister White had taken a stand against her husband. O, why did ever anyone say such a thing? Sister White never turned against Brother Magan or against Brother Sutherland. But Sister Magan was so weighted down with sorrow that she lost her reason.

I ask, Who in the day of judgment will be held responsible for putting out the light of that mind that should be shining today? Who will be accountable in the day of God for the work that caused the distress which brought on this sickness? She suffered for months, and the husband suffered with her. And now the poor woman has gone, leaving two motherless children. All this, because of the work done by unsanctified tongues.

Her husband has the comfort of the promise, "Blessed are the dead which die in the Lord." Sister Magan was a Christian. She was one of Christ's followers, and He loved her. Her works do follow her.

You see the work that has been established here. You see that advancement has been made, and that the education has been carried forward in right lines, under very discouraging circumstances. This work of opposition and dissatisfaction has come from the enemy. It has cost the life of a wife and mother. But it has not taken away her crown of eternal life, nor hindered her from receiving the commendation,, "Well done, good and faithful servant. . . . enter thou into the joy of thy Lord."

I would say to Brethren Magan and Sutherland, God has looked with pleasure upon you as you have struggle through the difficulties you have had to meet here. Now the work has reached a point where you can go to labor elsewhere. You have written to me that you had a burden to work in the Southern field. There is plenty of room for you there. They are in need of more workers. They need school-teachers, they need managers. We have been looking and praying for men to take up the work there, and we are glad that God has opened the way for you to work in that field.

And to the brethren I can say, Brother Sutherland and Brother Magan do not go out from this place as men who have made a failure, but as men who have made a success. They have taught the students from the Bible, according to the light given through the Testimonies. The students that have been with them need not be ashamed of the education they have received.

To the students I would say, You are to let your teachers go willingly. They have had a hard battle here, but they have made a success, and as they leave, the Lord will go with them. His arms will be beneath them. If they will follow on to know the Lord, they shall know that His going forth is prepared as the morning. Let the teachers and students who remain take hold of the work in the name of the Lord. Do not be discouraged or depressed.

The burdens here have rested heavily upon Brother Magan. He has not yet fully recovered from the effect of the first long attack of fever. He should be allowed to rest for at least one year, that he may have opportunity to regain his strength.

Brethren and sisters, has there not been among us enough of this work of criticising and accusing? Think you that can carry this spirit with you to the heavenly courts? You might far better have been asking the Lord to bless these men. You might far better have been doing the work of the Lord, than trying to discourage those who were endeavoring to carry out the educational principles that God has presented before them. Now let there be a thorough examination of your past lives. And wherever you see that you have in any way taken advantage of one of your brethren, repeat of it, and make it right.

I speak the truth as God has presented it to me. Sister Magan died as a martyr, right among her own brethren. My brethren, this work of hurting one another does not pay. May God help you to cleanse your hearts from this evil thing. Ask pardon of God, and ask pardon of those whom you have wronged. Soon it will be too late for wrongs to be made right, and while we have a little opportunity granted us, let us, O let us right every wrong.

Everyone is to be judged in the courts of heaven according to the deeds that are done in the body. And this work of oppressing souls, of making the work doubly hard for those who are willing to make any sacrifice to advance the cause of God, will make every poor showing in the books of heaven. Shall we not cease this work? We need sanctified tongues, and we need our lips touched by a live coal from the altar. Our voices should give forth melody. When you speak to those who are in discouragement, let them know that they have your sympathy. How much better to speak kind and tender and loving words than words that will bruise and wound the soul. Will you remember that these souls are the purchase of the blood of Christ? He says, "As ye do these things unto one of the least of these, my brethren, ye do them unto me. They are Christ's property, and we want to lift them up, that they may be in health, in courage, in faith, in hope.

Let us seek the Lord. Let us make a covenant with Him by sacrifice. God longs to meet us here. He does not want us to go away as we are now. He wants every soul to melt into tenderness before Him, that He may bestow His rich blessing upon us. Will not you, who have been accusing your brethren, come off Satan's ground? It will not blister your tongue to speak words of tenderness and kindness. It will do you good. It will encourage in you the spirit that should dwell in you. Gather with Christ, but do not, by word or action, discourage those who are putting to the strain every nerve and muscle to carry out the work that God has directed to be done.

Let us humble ourselves before God, lest He shall punish us for our course of action in these things. We want to walk humbly with God, and let the spirit of kindness reign in our lives. Let affection, and love be cultivated. Let the sweet spirit of Christ come in and abide with us. When you sit together with Christ in heavenly places, let me tell you, you will reveal in your countenances the very light of heaven.

If Brethren Sutherland and Magan shall leave Berrien Springs-- and believe it is their duty to go,--I beg of you, for Christ's sake not to follow them with criticism and faultfinding. And take right hold to help and strengthen whoever comes in here to take their place.

Several times, even before they took up their work at Berrien Springs, Brethren Magan and Sutherland expressed to me their burden for the work in the South. Their hearts are there. Do not blame them for going. Do not put any impediments in their way. Let them go, and may God go with them, and may His blessing attend them. They will take with them from this place many pleasant memories of seasons of peace and joy. There have been time of sorrow, but they do not go because of this. They think that they can better glorify God by going to a more needy field. This is their own choice; I have not persuaded them. They did not know but what Sister White would stand in their way. When they laid the matter before me this morning, I told them that I would not hinder them for one moment. Any one who takes up work in the South has before him a hard battle. The work there should be far in advance of what it is now. We should encourage the men who go there, and hold them up by our faith, by our prayers, and with our means.

In the South also, our brethren have had to work under a spirit of faultfinding and accusing. I say these things to you now, that you may realize that you are not called by God to say depressing things, or to manifest a spirit of coldness and indifference to those who go to carry burdens in the South. We hope that you will remember these words, and that the terrible history of the past may not be repeated.

For over twenty years, the work of the Southern field has been held up before you, but you have not done for the work what should have been done. There is a large field there, and the burden of sustaining the laborers there belongs to the people of America.

If any of the students and workers here desire to go with Brother Sutherland and Brother Magan, let them go and help them to carry the light to those who have never heard the truth, to a class of people that has been suffering with neglect and poverty. I know that Brother Haskell and Brother Butler will be glad to have the help of Brethren Magan and Sutherland, and will unite with them in the work of God. They will have a hard time of it at the best, but if God is with them, they may know that He will sustain them.

Ellen G. White.

Chapter 106.2—Extracts from Talks at the Lake Union Conference

June 17-27, 1904.

By Mrs. E. G. White.

What we need to keep the bodily machinery in running order is the physical and mental taxation combined so that all parts will be taxed proportionately. You go and sit down and study, study, study. I have known it to lay many in the grave.

Every portion of the living machinery is to act its part. That is why in Berrien Springs they came out here to clear the land, that the youth may have a fair understanding of what true education is, and we want all to help this work.

To the school that shall be carried on at Berrien Springs, and to the students that shall be here, we want to say, Work diligently for yourselves and those around you. To the teachers, If you take hold of the mighty power of God you will realize his power. O, that we might have that faith that works by love and purifies the soul! Christ's arms are open to you.

God has been in the work at Berrien Springs, and from the light given me the work has been such as God has approved. But some felt that they could not have it so. They wanted to find something to complain of. These men have struggled with all their might to come right up to the mark that God has given, but there have been accusing and discouragements from men who have come to them, but they are pressing it through, pressing it through. At the conference in Oakland this kept coming in. God sustained these men, and kept giving them light. They were walking in the light.

You see what has been done here. You see what the students have done. You see what the education has been. The education is carried forward in the right lines, and all that dissatisfaction and irritation was of the devil, every particle of it.

I will say to Brethren Sutherland and Magan if they are here, There is a field that is open before you. God has looked with pleasure upon the manner in which you have borne the irritation that has been kept up, and that you have had so much difficulty with. Now the work has come to a point where you can go and enter upon a work elsewhere. We have been looking and looking to see who could go into the Southern field, and now God will open the way so that you can go in there and have the sympathy and tenderness of the brethren and sisters.

Brother Sutherland and Brother Magan do not go out from this work as those who have made a failure, but as men who have made a success. The students that go from this school they have not to be ashamed of at all. They have taken them right to the Bible and the light that God has given in the Testimonies.

Students, you must be willing to let your teachers go. They have had a hard battle to fight, but they have had success attending their work. As they go, let me tell you the Lord will go with them. They can go where their work will be appreciated, but here the sore has been so great that they have little hope that it will be cured. When they have been managing to the best of their ability, and no words of encouragement have been spoken to them, they feel little hope that they can remain here. They feel now that others can come in and fill their places. They go as those who have made a success, and may God bless them as they go to a field where they will find rest to their souls.

We hope that every one who is here today will remember not to repeat the history of the past. I know about it, and it has been a terrible history.

I want to say to the teachers and students that shall labor in this school, Take hold of the work in the name of the Lord, and do not be discouraged with words that shall come in. Do not let anything depress you.

If these brethren leave here, as I believe it is their duty to do, then I beg of you, for Christ's sake, not to follow them with criticism wherever they go. And whoever comes in here to take their places, lift them up and help them. There is a great work to be done here and in the South. These brethren feel that they can glorify God better by going South, I have not persuaded them. Their heart is there, Now, let them go, and do not blame them for going.

God has a large field in the South, and it belongs to all America to sustain the workers there. God wants you to consider that the field has been before you for twenty years. He told you what to do and you have not done it. If these brethren can take some of their student workers with them, let them go and carry the light to those who have never heard the truth.

I know that Brethren Haskell and Butler will unite with these brethren, and will be glad to have their help.

Now, I am very thankful that a work has been done here in Berrien Springs, and it might be done a hundred places where there is one if there will be those who have the moral courage to take the Word of God and to practice it.

The Lord was in this school's being established. The Lord helped these brethren as they progressed with their school, and as they were teaching the very principles that were taught in the schools of the prophets. Do you think in the schools of the prophets they went back to all those books that are brought into the school to give an education? Do you think they took the study books that were in the common schools? No, No! What were they taught? To have a knowledge of Jesus Christ. If they have a practical knowledge of Jesus Christ, let me tell you, they understand that they must be partakers of the divine nature in order to escape corruption that is in the world through lust, and come out of the cities. It is the very thing to do today. Get them out of the cities into the rural places, where they may be educated in agriculture and the various lines of business and trade. Do you suppose that when the times are growing worse and worse that you will all be left together here in one company? No, we shall be scattered. If those who are helping educate in this place shall give the right kind of education, these students will be qualified to go out into new places and begin with ABC work to educate others. As they commence, the Holy Spirit of God will stand by their side.

The less you have of the powers of darkness in your education, the more you have of Christ, and you will have an education that you can carry to every part of the world.

We want to say to the students here, You are just where the Lord wants you to be. You have been obtaining an education, and the Lord wants you to go on from grace to grace, from point to point, not to settle down here, but to obtain an education to go out, you know not where.

We want these students to feel while they are here obtaining an education, that the eye of the Lord is upon them. If you will cooperate with the angels of God and be strictly temperate in your diet (and I have no reason to think that you are not), and be careful of the brain power, God will cooperate with you. Do not read novels. Put them right away. What we want is the Bible Truth. It is to be our foundation and our lesson book. We do not want any of the fallacies that come through the popular books that are brought into other schools.

Now, it is of no use for the teacher to give you lesson after lesson and try to instruct you, unless you cooperate with that instruction. There will be those who have taught in the schools out of the books who will be right on hand to tell you that you are losing, that you should have a knowledge of this, that, and something else. Tell them we have not time. We are getting ready to be translated into the kingdom of our Lord and Saviour Jesus Christ. We want to know what we must do to inherit eternal life. That lies at the very foundation of all education, and the more you are instructed in the Word, and understand the Word, the sooner you are prepared to take right hold to use your education. You do not want your mind all rumpled up with the errors of the books used in the schools of today, but you do want an education that is free from all rubbish, that you can use. You want to learn that you may be able to teach others. That which you receive from Christ Jesus you must impart. You want to learn how to educate.

Students, I want to tell you, I thank God that you have advanced as you have in your studies, that there are those today who, as these brethren shall leave the school, can accompany them and carry on their education right where they shall go. How carry it on? By using the very education they have to the very best account, and be going into the houses as evangelists, Bible workers. When teaching the Scriptures, you will find that there is a knowledge that comes to you which you never thought of. Words will come, ideas will come, sentiments will come. You can begin to work for the ignorant, those who need your help, and you have an Educator right by your side; that is, the precious Jesus. The angels of God will help you in education. You remember how it was with Daniel. You know all about how he gave God the glory. He gave him glory for the work that he had done for him. He and his three companions were taken away from their country, from their parents, from their educators, at a very young age. They were so kind, respectful, and polite in all their manners, that the one who had charge of them fell in love with them.

I want you to understand that Christ said that you shall be brought before kings and rulers to answer for your faith. If it is so that you are to be brought in before kings and rulers you want a clear brain. You want to understand what is truth and practice it. We must prepare for what is coming upon us. We must have the truth in wrought in nerve, in brain, in soul, in body.

Our perceptive facilities must be educated to learn what is truth and what is error, and we must plant our feet upon the platform of eternal truth. This is what God requires of us and of everyone. Respect and help your teachers, and do not worry them, but help them to help you. If you keep where they can see that their efforts are responded to, then they have courage and can help you, and you can all work together as members of Christ's family here below, and then you will become members of Christ's family above.

May the blessing of God rest upon you all.

Chapter 107—The Huntsville School

Monday morning, July 20, 1904, I went from Graysville to Huntsville. We found the school situated in a beautiful country place. In the school farm there are more than three hundred acres of land, a large part of which is under cultivation.

Several years ago Brother S. M. Jacobs was in charge of the farm, and under his care it made great improvement. He set out a peach and plum orchard, and other fruit trees. Brother and Sister Jacobs left Huntsville about three years ago, and since then the farm has not been as well cared for. We see in the land promise of a much larger return than it now gives, were its managers given the help they need.

Brother Jacobs put forth most earnest, disinterested efforts, but he was not given the help that his strength demanded. Sister Jacobs also worked too hard, and when her health began to give way, they decided to leave Huntsville, and go to some place where the strain would not be so heavy. Had they then been furnished with efficient helpers, and with means to make the need improvements, the advancement made would have given courage to Brother Jacobs, to the students, and to our people everywhere. But the means that ought to have gone to Huntsville did not go, and we see the result in the present showing.

Recently the question was asked me, "Would it not be well to sell the school land at Huntsville, and buy a smaller place." Instruction was given me that this farm must not be sold, that the situation possesses many advantages for the carrying forward of a colored school. It would take years to build up in a new place the work that has been done at Huntsville. The Lord's money was invested in the Huntsville school farm, to provide a place for the education of colored students. The General Conference gave this land to the Southern work, and the Lord has shown me what this school may become, and what those may become who go there for instruction, if His plans are followed.

In order that the school may advance as it should, money is needed, and sound, intelligent generalship. Things are to be well kept up, and the school is to give evidence that Seventh-day Adventists mean to make a success of whatever they undertake.

The facilities necessary for the success of the school must be provided. At present the facilities are very meager. A small building should be put up, in which the students can be taught how to care for one another in times of sickness. There has been a nurse at the school to look after the students when they were sick, but no facilities have been provided. This has made the work very discouraging.

The students are to be given a training in these lines of work that will help them to be successful laborers for Christ. They are to be taught to be separate from the customs and practices of the world. They are to be taught how to present the truth for this time, and how to work with the hands and with the head to win their daily bread, that they may go forth to teach their own people. They are to be taught to appreciate the school as a place in which they are given the opportunity to obtain a training for service.

Wise plans are to be laid for the cultivation of the land. The students are to be given a practical educational in agriculture. This education will be of inestimable value to them in their future work. Thorough work is to be done in cultivating the land, and from this the students are to learn how necessary it is to do thorough work in cultivating the garden of the heart.

The man who takes charge of the Huntsville school should know how to govern himself and how to govern others. The Bible teacher should be a man who can teach the students how to present the truths of the Word of God in public, and how to do house to house work. The business affairs of the farm are to be wisely and carefully managed.

The teachers should constantly seek wisdom from on high, that they may be kept from making mistakes. They should give careful attention to their work, that each student may be prepared for the line of service to which he is best adapted. All are to be prepared to serve faithfully in some capacity. Teachers and students are to cooperate in doing their best. The constant effort of the teachers should be to make the students see the importance of constantly rising higher and still higher.

The leading, controlling influence in the school is to be faithfulness in that which is least. Thus the students will be prepared to be faithful in greater things. Each student is to take himself in hand, and with God's help overcome the faults that mar his character. And he is to show an earnest, unselfish interest in the welfare of the school. If he sees a loose board in a walk or a loose paling on the fence, let him at once get a hammer and nails, and make the needed repairs. Nothing in the house or about the premises is to be allowed to present a slack, dilapidated appearance. The wagons and harnesses should be properly cared for and frequently examined and repaired. When harnesses and wagons are sent out in dilapidated condition, human life is endangered.

These little things are of much more importance than many suppose in the education of students. Business men will notice the appearances of the wagons and harnesses, and will form their opinions accordingly. And more than this, if students are allowed to go through school with slack, shiftless habits, their education will not be worth half as much as it would be if they were taught to be faithful in all they do. "He that is faithful in that which is least is faithful also in much." Little things needing attention, yet left for days and weeks, until they become an unsightly neglect, teach the students lessons that will cling to them for a lifetime, greatly hindering them in their work. Such an example is demoralizing, and students whose education is after this order are not needed in the world.

Should not our God be served most faithfully? We are called upon as teachers to rise up with firm purpose of heart, and discipline ourselves with sternness and vigor to habits of order and thoroughness. All that our hands find to do is to be well done. We have been bought with a price, even the blood of the Son of God, and all that we do is to honor and glorify our Redeemer. We are to work in partnership with Christ, as verily as Christ works in partnership with the Father, We are to lay aside every weight, "and the sin that doth so easily beset", that we may follow our Lord with full purpose of heart.

The soul suffers a great loss when duties are not faithfully performed, when habits of negligence and carelessness are allowed to rule the life. Faithfulness and unselfishness are to control all that we do. When the soul is left uncleansed, when selfish aims are allowed to control, the enemy comes in, leading the mind to carry out unholy devices and to work for selfish advantages, regardless of results.

But he who makes Christ first and last and best in everything will not work for selfish purposes. Unselfishness will be revealed in every act. The peace of Christ can not abide in the heart of a man in whose life self is the mainspring of action. Such a one may hold the theories of truth, but unless he brings himself into harmony with the requirements of God's Word, giving up all his ambitions and desires for the will and way of Christ, he strives without purpose; for God can not bless him. He halts between two opinions, constantly vacillating between Christ and the world. It is like some one striving for the Master, yet cumbering himself by clinging to heavy weights.

Ellen G. White.

Chapter 108—The Necessity of Harmony

Takoma Park, July 23, 1904.

Dear Brethren Magan and Sutherland:

I have words of counsel for you. There must be harmony between you and the men in responsible positions in the General Conference. You catch at straws in matters concerning Elder Daniells and Elder Prescott. Why? Because they have not harmonized with you in all your plans, and have not given you the credit that you deserved. But when the Lord corrected errors, and spoke encouraging words concerning your efforts, why did you not thank Him, and show your gratitude by manifesting forgiveness, and showing an appreciation of the burdens borne by these fellow workers? Why did you cast imputations upon Elders Daniells and Prescott, or allow others to cast imputations upon them?

Your feelings in regard to Elder Daniells and Elder Prescott are not correct. If you expect them to harmonize with you, you must harmonize with them. The Lord has declared that He will harmonize with Elder Daniells and Elder Prescott. I know of what I am speaking; for these things have been represented to me.

I wish to ask you a question. Whom would you have selected for president of the General Conference? Will you please to name the man? At the time of the last General Conference, the situation was a most trying one, and there needed to be chosen as president a man who was in harmony with the work that God was trying to do through the Testimonies.

Elder Daniells and Elder Prescott have made some mistakes. But a grave mistake was made when you and Elder A. T. Jones set yourselves to the defense of the movement for the reopening of the Battle Creek College, the full results of which neither of you understand. The Lord did not inspire the words spoken in defense of that movement, and the criticisms which were made against the attitude of the men who felt it their duty to point out the dangers attending the effort to bring a large number of our youth to Battle Creek. Another counsellor had taken the place of the divine Counsellor.

In this perilous time the Lord has given us men of His choice to stand as the leaders of His people. If these men will keep humble and prayerful, ever making Christ their confident, listening to and obeying his words, the Lord will lead and strengthen them. God has chosen Elder Daniells to bear responsibilities and has promised to make him capable, by his grace, of doing the work entrusted to him. The responsibilities of the position he occupies are great, and the tax upon his strength and courage is severe; and the Lord calls upon his people to hold up Elder Daniells' hands, as he strives with all the powers of mind and body to advance the work. The Lord desires every church to offer prayer for him as he bears these heavy responsibilities. Our brethren and sisters should not stand ready to criticize and condemn those who are bearing heavy burdens. Let us refuse to listen to the words of censure spoken regarding the men upon whom rest such weighty responsibilities.

Elder Daniells is a man who has proved the testimonies to be true. And he has proved true to the Testimonies. When he has found that he has differed from them, he has been willing to acknowledge his errors, and come to the light. If all others had done the same, there would be no such state of things as now exists. The Lord has given Elder Daniells reproof when he has erred, and he has shown his determination to stand on the side of truth and righteousness, and to correct his mistakes.

My brethren, let us now do our best, not to discover wrong in Elder Daniells, but to help him. He has shown himself to be the man for the place. At this time there are needed men who dare to differ with those who are counterworking the plans of the Lord for his people. You have not discerned the true condition of the leaders of the medical missionary work at Battle Creek. You have not placed a correct estimate upon their actions. You have encouraged their ideas and plans altogether too much.

I know that Elder Daniells is the right man in the right place. He has stood nobly for the truth, and has striven earnestly to deal in a right way with the controversies arising regarding the relation of the medical work to the evangelical work.

If the men whom the Lord has chosen to stand in positions of responsibility will heed the testimonies that God has given and is giving, if they will keep close to His word, if they will separate from those who are binding up with worldly influences, they will be safe men for the times upon which we have entered.

The words and attitude of Brother E. A. Sutherland and Brother A. T. Jones at the Berrien Springs meeting struck an inharmonious note, --a note that was not inspired of God. It created a state of things which resulted in harm that they did not anticipate. It made the work of the meeting very much harder than it would otherwise have been. Had it not been for their injudicious course, the Berrien Springs Conference would have shown very different results.

My brethren, God is dishonored when you seek to throw a burden of censure upon your brethren, as you did at that meeting. You were not working in harmony with God;

for this is not the way in which He works. If you felt a duty to lay before your brethren matters reflecting upon the leaders in General Conference work, it was your duty first to call the most reliable men together, and modestly present to them your statements. You should not have thrown in your ideas without counsel, as you did. The impulsive disposition of Brother Jones has led him many times to make wrong movements, which have called for correction and reproof.

At the Fresno campmeeting, after I had borne a very plain testimony, Brother Jones acted the part of a man, doing thorough work in confession. He was working out his own salvation with fear and trembling. The blessing of the Lord came in, and the glory of God was revealed. Angels of heaven were in that meeting, and a great blessing was experienced by all who were present. And so it would have been in the meeting at Berrien Springs, if Dr. Kellogg had heartily accepted the message sent by the Lord, and had fully broken with the enemy. A spirit of humiliation would have filled every heart, and sincere confessions would have been made by all.

At the Berrien Springs meeting a special message of hope was given for Dr. Kellogg. He might have stood on vantage ground, accepting the Lord Jesus as his counsellor. In and through the power of the Saviour, he might then have broken the spell. But he did not.

For a long time Dr. Kellogg has not been humbly accepting Christ as his teacher, and, unknown to himself, has been taught by the master of sophistries. And the enemy has used him as a channel through which to exert a strong controlling influence upon the physicians associated with him. But the Lord will break the spell that is upon these men if they will allow the yoke that has been placed upon them to be broken.

Christ gives to all the invitation, "Come unto me, all ye that Labor and are heavy laden, and I will give you rest. Take my yoke upon you, and learn of Me; for I am meek and lowly in heart, and ye shall find rest unto your souls. For my yoke is easy and my burden is light." All who accept his invitation will bear testimony that his yoke is indeed easy and his burden light.

It means much to our physicians whether they are wearing the yoke of Christ or the yoke of some man. Those who are wearing a yoke that a man has placed on their necks must have this yoke taken away before they can act the part that God would have them act in proclaiming the truth. Those who receive and believe in Christ Jesus are not to wear any man's yoke; neither are they to be noncommittal in regard to where they stand. The conflict is raging between two powers,--the Prince of life and the prince of darkness. This conflict has a vital interest for the people of God.

Christ is the greatest teacher that this world has ever seen. Truth never languished upon His lips, never suffered in his hands. He declares, "He that is not with me is against me, and he that gathereth not with me scattereth abroad." God has given to every man his work. He expects every follower of his to exert an influence that will tell for the upbuilding of his kingdom. He who is not actively engaged in promoting unity and love and equity and sound principles, is exerting an influence that is contrary to Christ.

Those who are true to their divine Leader will put away the masterly sophistries that are coming in to deceive the people. Those who would be saved from the wily, deceptive influences of the foe must now break every yoke, and take their position for Christ and for truth, that they may be freed from the specious, fictitious sentiments that, if accepted, will surely spoil their faith and their experience. Unless they obtain this freedom, they will go on step by step in the downward path until they deny Him who has bought them with the price of his own blood.

The question that is asked us now is, Who will stand on the Lord's side, in the presence of good and evil men, in the presence of angels, in the presence of the Father, the Son, and the Holy Spirit? You can no longer remain neutral, and yet be Christ's followers, His faithful servants.

If those who profess to be medical missionaries had stood away from Dr. Kellogg's seductive sophistries, they would not now be where they are,--regarded by God as unfaithful stewards because they have harmonized with the doctor, who is certainly under the enemy's deceptive influence.

The cause of God is in great peril because the physicians in whose minds sophistry has prevailed against truth, are bracing themselves against the impressions of the Holy Spirit, and are placing themselves where the Lord can not use them as leaders of his people.

If Dr. Kellogg had heeded the light given him of God through the Testimonies of his Spirit; if he had made God his trust; if he had refused to give any attention to the scientific sophistries that he has been studying more or less for years; if he had followed his Guide, working with an eye single to the glory of God, he would have avoided the many, many crooked paths that he has followed. But in the place of heeding the warning given him, that evil angels were working with him, he has encouraged their presence by continuing to follow a course of transgression.

No one need be strengthless who is fighting in the army of the Lord, standing under his blood-stained banner. His true soldiers are partakers of the divine nature, having escaped the corruption that is in the world through lust. But those who choose their own way, and keep in correspondence with the great deceiver, are reckoned unworthy of eternal life.

Who will take his stand on the Lord's side? Let him step on to the platform of eternal truth, cutting loose from the seductive influences of the tempter. In the ranks of God's people there is to be seen a well-doing for Him, a zeal that is according to knowledge.

"Be strong in the Lord, and in the power of his might. Put on the whole armor of God, that ye may be able to stand against the wiles of the devil. For we wrestle not against flesh and blood, but against principalities, against powers, against the rulers of the darkness of this world, against spiritual wickedness in high places. Wherefore take unto you the whole armor of God, that ye may be able to withstand in the evil day, and having done all, to stand. Stand therefore, having your loins girt about with truth, and having on the breastplate of righteousness; and your feet shod with the preparation of the gospel of peace; above all, taking the shield of faith, wherewith ye shall be able to quench all the fiery darts of the enemy. And take the helmet of salvation, and the sword of the Spirit, which is the word of God". ...

Ellen G. White.

Chapter 109—The Signing of Agreements

(Not dated; but evidently some years before this time.)

To the managers of our sanitarium, and to our physicians, nurses, and medical missionary workers throughout the world, I am instructed to say that it is our duty highly to respect Dr. J. H. Kellogg and his associates in the medical missionary work at Battle Creek. We should feel profoundly thankful for the work that God has wrought through the labors of His faithful servants in the Battle Creek Sanitarium, and especially for Dr. Kellogg's steadfast adherence to and advocacy of the principles of hygienic reform.

The Lord has placed Dr. Kellogg in an important position, and his brethren are to honor and respect him, and to hold up his hands for the carrying forward of his God-given work. His influence will be a blessing as he works in connection with his brethren and in accordance with the plans of the great Master Worker.

But, while Dr. Kellogg is to be respected and honored, while we are to recognize the fact that God uses him as a channel through which to communicate great light to his people, we are in no case to place him where God should be, as our Wisdom, our Instructor, our infallible Guide.

The Lord has reproved those who claim to believe present truth for failing to cooperate with Dr. Kellogg and his faithful co-workers in walking in the light of health reform. Dr. Kellogg is to stand as God's physician, and is to do an exalted work. But if he is left to follow his own judgment in all things, he will make mistakes. He is laboring beyond his strength. He is doing three times as much as he should do. This is not God's will. By thus overworking, he is shortening his life. He is God's property, and he should keep himself hidden with Christ in God. Dr. Kellogg must not embrace so much as he has done in the past. And in some things his planning must be different.

To the leaders in the medical missionary work I must say that no one is to claim kingly power over God's heritage. God's people are to be under Him and Him alone. There is one Shepherd, and he has one flock. The Lord knows the future. He is the one to be looked to and trusted in to guide and guard and direct in the future development of the various branches of His work.

For several years I have been warned that there is danger, constant danger of men looking to men for permission to do this or that, instead of looking to God for themselves.

Thus they become weaklings, bound about with human ties that God has not ordained. The Lord can impress minds and consciences to do His work under bonds to him, and in a brotherly fraternity that will be in accordance with his law.

The Lord has not given wisdom regarding the medical missionary work only to the men associated in the work at Battle Creek. Humanity is not divinity. The most talented men in our ranks are not infallible. Not all of their methods are inspired of God. They make mistakes and they will continue to make mistakes if they do not walk in humble faith before God. The greatest temptations come to the men who bear the greatest responsibilities. Our only safety is in humbling the heart before God daily, and watching diligently lest any threads of selfishness are woven into the work. Let us so labor that it will be plainly seen that self is dead, and that our work bears the signature of heaven.

To every medical worker in connection with the cause of God are addressed the words spoken by Paul to Timothy: "Take heed to thyself and to the doctrine." We need to examine ourselves closely, and to renounce every plan or principle that will lead us to misrepresent the Lord. The past experience is to be closely reviewed. Every motive is to be critically examined. Every ambitious project that is contrary to the Word of God is to be put aside. We are to stand in preparedness before God. The word given to me to speak to you is, "I have not found thy works perfect before God." The Lord will not accept the most splendid service that means the putting of the least yoke upon his people. We are to frame no yokes for our fellow men. God's word to us is that we are to break every yoke.

A copy of the proposed agreement between the Medical Association and those establishing branch sanitariums, was read to me by Sister Druillard. A few day afterward I was praying, a scene passed before me representing the unfavorable results of the transactions that would follow the signing of this agreement. Other scenes also passed before me similar to those presented to me when I was at Summer Hill, a few weeks before our return to America. At that time representations of movements in America passed before me. I saw agreements drawn up for presentation to our people. In these agreements there were terms and conditions that should not be accepted. On no account should our brethren bind themselves by agreeing to such propositions. I was instructed that we know but little of what is before us, and that God forbids us to bind ourselves by contracts in order to secure means.

I was instructed to tell Brother Caro and Sharp that propositions would come to them containing conditions that they were not to accept or endorse. I saw a paper unrolled before these brethren, and one of dignity arose and said, "Put not your name to any writing that binds you to do or refrain from doing certain things in business lines. It is not God's plan that you should sign such agreements. This document is of man's production. That which will take place in the future you know not. God says, I will turn and overturn. For you to sign an agreement saying what you will do and what you will not do in the future is not in God's order. He who knows the end from the beginning understands what is in man's heart, and what are the dangers of the men to whom God has entrusted great responsibilities.

Man is not to assume more than God has given him. If he walks humbly with God, the good hand of the Lord will be with him. If he yields to his ambition to carry out a work of his own, according to his own plans, a work in which he is benevolent where he chooses to be benevolent, and selfish where he chooses to be selfish, a condition of things will be brought in that will dishonor God and his truth. Oppression will come in. Human power will be exercised in accordance with the terms of the agreements made and signed in the past, agreements deemed essential to protect the interest of the health food business and to give the sanitarium work financial security and support.

I have been instructed that rules and regulations are being brought in that God does not approve. The Lord forbids the signing of the agreements that have been prepared for our sanitariums in America and in other countries. It is not his will that every sanitarium and bath-house established by our people shall be brought under one control.

Those who seek to bind up the work in distant fields with the work at Battle Creek, by means of these agreements, are assuming too much responsibility. They must not take to themselves power that God has not given them. They must not place themselves where the people will look to them instead of looking to God.

Christ did not follow any human model. He says to his servants, Break every yoke that men may seek to bind upon you. Do not accept any yoke that will hinder your present or future movements in my service. Stand free. Take only my yoke. When you are yoked up with me, my words will make their impress upon your characters.

All of the plans formulated for our people will need to be thoroughly and carefully examined. No threads of human devising are to be drawn into the web. Unless we watch and pray diligently, the enemy will come into spoil the pattern. Ambition must not lead us to embrace too much in our plans.

Too much power is invested in humanity when matters are so arranged that one man or a small group of men have it in their power to rule or ruin the work of their fellow laborers. In the erection of medical institutions and the development of their work there is not to be a ruling kingly power as there has been in the past. The kingly power formerly exhibited in the General Conference is not to be perpetuated. The publishing work is not to be a kingdom of itself. It is essential that the principles that govern in the publishing work and the sanitarium work. No one is to think that the branch of work with which he is connected is of vastly more importance than other branches.

The division of the General Conference into district union conferences was God's arrangement. In the work of the Lord for these last days there are to be no Jerusalem centers, no kingly power; and the work in the different countries is not to be tied up by contracts to the work centering in Battle Creek; for this is not God's plan. Brethren are to counsel together; for we are just as much under the control of God in one part of his vineyard as in another. Brethren are to be one in heart and soul, even as Christ and the Father are one. Teach this, practice this, that we may be with Christ in God, all working to build up one another.

Educational work must be faithfully done in every sanitarium that is established. There is necessity for the managers of every institution to become more and more intelligent regarding their work. They need not depend on the managers of another institution for their work. They need not depend on the managers of another institution for guidance, but looking to God as their instructor they are to go forward in faithful, intelligent service, constantly developing greater talents and capabilities.

God calls upon men and women to look to him, that they may receive light and power and knowledge. He will not be glorified in our subscribing to rules and agreements and contracts binding one institution to follow the guidance of another institution thousands of miles away. It ought to have been foreseen that if we desire God to guide minds, these minds must not be bound by human regulations.

There is need of loyalty to principle. But a pledge from one who does not feel the need of obeying the word of the Lord is valueless. The placing of signatures to documents will not insure honesty, neither will it insure the exercise of justice, mercy, and the love of God.

The Lord would have the restraints broken that keep his work bound about by the wisdom of men. Those who unite with Christ are not to accept yokes which will prove a hindrance to them in their work with him. He says, "Come unto me. ... and I will give you rest. Take my yoke upon you and learn of me; for I am meek and lowly in heart, and ye shall find rest unto your souls. For my yoke is easy and my burden is light. The true and living God is to be exalted. All nations are to hear the proclamation of the gospel message.

Many convicted and converted will bow in humility before the Lord, making an unreserved consecration of themselves to Him. The message is to go to all parts of the world. "Look unto me and be ye saved, all the ends of the earth; for I am God, and there is none else. I have sworn by myself, the word is gone out of my mouth in righteousness, and shall not return, that unto me every knee shall bow, every tongue shall swear." The words inscribed on the Lord's temple harmonize with his unlimited invitation of mercy. "My house shall be called a house of prayer for all people." It shall proclaim that I am the living God, sit upon my throne as ruler, giving audience to the world. And what is the response?--"Let all the people praise thee, O God, let all the people praise thee, and let the whole earth be filled with thy glory."

The future is before us, and unforeseen events will surely take place, changing the present aspect of things in the world. Lust and greed are striving for the supremacy. Oppression and hatred will be exercised to destroy. Inspired by a power from beneath, Satan's instrumentalities will work with intensity to carry out his will. "The wicked shall do wickedly, and none of the wicked shall understand; but the wise shall understand." Every truly converted soul will put on the whole armor of God, and will bravely face the unseen for God's servants will realize the necessity of partaking of the divine nature.

I have been instructed to tell our people to read carefully the 34th chapter of Ezekiel and to guard against being deceived, and led to act the part of unfaithful servants.

With great solemnity the words were repeated: "Finally, my brethren, be strong in the Lord, and in the power of his might. Put on the whole armor of God, that ye may be able to stand against the wiles of the devil. For we wrestle not against flesh and blood, but against principalities, against powers, against the rulers of the darkness of this world, against spiritual wickedness in high places. Wherefore take unto you the whole armor of God, that ye may be able to withstand in the evil day, and having done all to stand. Stand therefore, having your loins girt about with truth, and having on the breastplate of righteousness; and your feet shod with the preparation of the gospel of peace; above all, taking the shield of faith, wherewith ye shall be able to quench all the fiery darts of the wicked. And take the helmet of salvation, and the sword of the Spirit, which is the Word of God, praying with all prayer and supplication in the spirit, and watching thereunto with all perseverance and supplication for all saints."

Now is our time of peril. Our only safety is in walking in the footsteps of Christ, and wearing his yoke. Troublous times are before us. In many instances, friends will become alienated. Without cause men will become our enemies. The motives of the people of God will be misinterpreted, not only by the world, but by their own brethren. The Lord's servants will be put in hard places. A mountain will be made of a molehill to justify men in pursuing a selfish, unrighteous course. The work that men have done faithfully will be disparaged and underrated, because apparent prosperity does not attend their efforts.

By misrepresentation these men will be clothed in dark vestments of dishonesty because circumstances beyond their control made their work perplexing. They will be pointed to as men that can not be trusted. And this will be done by members of the church. God's servants must arm themselves with the mind of Christ. They must not expect to escape insult and misjudgment. They will be called enthusiasts and fanatics. But let them not become discouraged. God's hands are on the wheel of his providence, guiding his work to the glory of his name.

God calls upon his people to be bright lights in the world, shining amid the darkness of sin. Living the life of the Life-giver brings its reward. He went about doing good. This every true follower of His will do, filled with a sacred sense of his loyalty to God and his duty to his fellow beings. Through the knowledge of the truth as it is in Jesus, Christians are to grow in grace, constantly drawing nearer perfection of character.

Ellen G. White.

Chapter 110—The Closing of the Southern Field

(The assertion has been widely made that the Testimonies state that our work will first be closed in the South. I think this is not true. No one whom I have requested to produce the reference has been able to find it. None of Sister White's helpers know of it. When I was at Sister White's home in 1913, I made a careful search of all the Testimonies on the Southern work, and failed to find this statement. Without saying who was first responsible for it, I think I am correct in ascribing the belief to a careless reading of a statement made by Sister White at the General Conference of 1901, in Battle Creek, Mich., a statement to be found on page 482 of the General Conference Bulletin of that year. I give here a passage containing this statement, which I have underscored. . A. W. S.)

I know not how to describe the way in which the Southern field has been presented to me. In this field thousands and thousands of people are living in wickedness and corruption, and they are right within the shadow of our doors. That field bears testimony to the neglect of a people who should have been wide awake to work for the Master, but who have done scarcely anything in this field. A little work has been done there, we have touched the field with the tip ends of our fingers, but not one-thousandth part of the work has been done that should be done. God calls upon his people to stand in a right position before him, to heed the light given ten or fifteen years ago--that the abused, down-trodden people of the South were to be labored for and helped. We have tried to lay this burden upon our people. But they need not carry it all themselves. There are many not of our faith who will willingly help a work for the uplifting of humanity.

The time is coming when the Southern field will be closed, locked up. But this is not yet the case. One place where the work was commenced was closed against the workers; and because of this the word went forth, the Southern field is closed; no more money will be needed for that work. But is this the way in which the Saviour worked? When one city was closed against him, did he say that his work on earth was done? Had he done this, what would have become of us? When he was driven from one place, he went to another, and he has left us the direction, "When they persecute you in this city, flee ye into another." When your life is in danger, go to another city, and when they persecute you there, go to yet another place: "For verily I say unto you, Ye shall not have gone over the cities of Israel, till the Son of Man be come." Shall we not take this advice?

Ellen G. White.

Chapter 111—The Work in the Southern States

From a talk at College View, Neb. Sept. 25, 1904.

I must speak in behalf of the work in the Southern field. The message of the soon coming of our Saviour must go to all its cities. We must wake up, and consider what this means to us individually in the matter of consecrated effort.

Some have been working and striving continually to learn how we should enter the various and important fields, and how the work can be done to the glory of God. But I can assure you that we have put none too much labor into this field. We have put none too much talent into it. We have given none too much money to it.

There are many present who have been much interested in missionary work in the South. To these I say, Rejoice, that the Southern field is being worked. Today I wish to leave this impression upon the mind of every one that is here, that the Southern field is to be thoroughly worked. This burden, as God has laid it upon us as a people, has been kept before us for many years. And the question for each individual is, What am I to do? To every man God has appointed his work. If we would only remember this, and seek humbly and perseveringly to know and to do our appointed work, guidance and grace would be given us to meet the trails and hardships of the way.

When the Jews asked Jesus, "What shall we do that we might work the works of God," he replied, "This is the work of God, that ye believe on Him whom he hath sent." His disciples are commissioned to "Go into all the world and preach the gospel to every creature."

You have neighbors. Will you give them the message? You may never have had the hands of ordination laid upon you, but you can humbly carry the message. You can testify that God has ordained that all for whom Christ died shall have everlasting life, if they believe on Him.

It is a great thing to believe on Jesus Christ. We have altogether too little faith. I am instructed to say to you that individually we each have our work to do. The Master has given to every man his work. And because others may not do just exactly the work you have to do, do not feel that you must criticize everything they do. No, indeed! No one ought to devote to faultfinding the time that he ought to spend in hunting for souls, fishing for souls, using every capability and power in his appointed work. When your powers are used in this way, you may know that the Lord God of heaven is right by your side, to strengthen and to guide.

There are many troublous questions about the work in the South, There are many destitute fields, many needy enterprises. And some have felt to say, This field is my field, and this location is under my direction; this branch of the work has been given to me. It is all the Lord's field, and one part is just as precious to Him as the other. What we want to study is how we can help one another to reach all the souls possible.

We shall become really the most successful workers when we learn to encourage one another, and then see that the work committed to us is done humbly and to God's acceptance. As we do that, we shall know what hard work is, and the more we know what hard work is, the more we shall have hearts of tender sympathy and compassion for every soul who works.

We would recommend to you all that you pray and work instead of talking and criticising. There has been a great deal of talking that was of no special account. Now let there be an awakening. Let everyone do his best.

Because some one goes to a city, and works at a great disadvantage, and can not at first make everything run smoothly, shall we put blocks in the way, or shall we work to clear the track and smooth the way? Now that is what we must do in the South.

That some mistakes are made is not to be wondered at. When men are laboring to the very best of their ability to gather up something with which they can advance the work, let us be considerate. Let those who would find fault with them go right out into a new place where the work is hard, and endeavor to give a presentation of a perfect work, as an encouragement to others.

Let us be kind and courteous, and let us be sure that we do not discourage at a time when we should cheer and lift up. God wants every soul to be encouraged that our brethren in Nashville have been striving to advance the work.

The work in the South will go forward. And I beg of you, Do not let any one here, whether he comes from the North or the South, listen to words of criticism and discouragement. When men's hearts are sanctified to God, and they see their brethren struggling with all their might and power to pull the heavy load up the hill, will they stand still and look on and tell the toilers what they should do? No, No; God will help us to draw.

While we were in Nashville, we had most precious meetings in the little chapel fitted up in the building of the Publishing Association. I thank God for that comfortable meeting place.

In the adjoining rooms through the week, the presses are running all the day and sometimes late into the night, printing the precious pages of truth to be circulated in all parts of the world.

In our meetings there the Spirit of God came in, and the light of heaven shone upon us. Elders Butler and Haskell were there, also Brethren Sutherland and Magan, and two or three of our workers from the Nashville Sanitarium. After talking a little while, I said, Let every one bear testimony today; and they responded heartily. One after another they bore their testimony promptly, four or five frequently being on their feet at one time.

Brethren, you may pray for them in the South as much as you please. But when you begin to find fault, let me tell you that the Spirit of the Lord is not with you.

Our brethren invited me to visit all the departments of the publishing house, that I might see the work now being done. At first I was too busy, and afterwards I was so sick that I could not go through the building as I had intended. But in the visions of the night I was led through every department of the building, and I saw the advancement that had been made since I first went there when they were beginning the work. I felt so grateful to God that I said to those present, "Let us pray." And as we knelt and prayed, the blessing of God came upon us. Then I distinctly heard a voice say, "Well done." "Thank the Lord," I said, "now I will not worry anymore about the work done in these buildings."

But why did the Lord give me this experience? Why were these things shown me, but that I might tell you that when you go into such a building, it is your privilege to believe that the ones entrusted with the work will be taught how to conduct it?

I want to say again, Let every one do his appointed work. And then let us all do all we can to encourage one another. When anyone becomes fearful that the workers in some institution are not doing just as they ought, let him go down on his knees before God, and ask him to give wisdom to those in charge, to carry on that work aright. Then let him pray for wisdom in his own work that he may set a right example.

For Christ's sake do not put on the cap of criticism, because it will hurt your mind. It will hurt your soul. You will be happier to leave it off. When we go from this place, the Lord would have us as living missionaries exert an influence in behalf of courage and faith. Let us all say, God help those who are trying to do their best.

There is a great work to be done. Some will ask, What can be done to work effectively in the city of Nashville? One way to success is to get a place a few miles out of Nashville, and there establish a school and a sanitarium, and from these institutions as a working center, being to work Nashville as we have not worked it yet.

It takes some planning to work without money. It is hard to make bricks without straw. But may God help us that we may make the most of everything we have, so that the blessing of God may rest upon it. Let us have the prayers of everyone of you for the Southern field; for if ever there was a field upon earth that needs to be helped; it is the Southern field. Why? Because the people have been educated wrong. They need to be helped. They need the light. They need the grace of God, and we want to help them to come to the light. May everyone of us settle it in our mind that we will look upon the best side. Let us determine to talk light and courage and hope.

E. G. W.

Chapter 112—Will You Help

From the Pacific Union Recorder, January 12, 1905.

I have a special message to give to our people regarding the necessities of the work in the Southern field, and especially regarding the necessities of the work in Nashville and Huntsville. A sanitarium near Nashville is greatly needed. Dr. Hayward and Brother Hansen have done and are doing a good work in Nashville, but they are in great need of better facilities. We had hoped the way would open for them to rent a roomy place near the city, but the way has not opened for them to do this. At present, they are working under great disadvantages, and they must have a building outside the city, with room enough to care for the patients who may come.

Brethren Sutherland and Magan and Sister Druillard, with other faithful helpers, have begun school work on a farm about nine miles from Nashville. There is on this farm abundant room for both a school and a sanitarium. The two institutions would be a help to each other in carrying out the purposes of God for them.

Brethren Sutherland and Magan have done a noble, self-sacrificing work at Berrien Springs. They might have remained there, but they felt impressed to go to the South, and work for the people there. They thought that perhaps they might begin their school work in some retired place, but we felt that they should unite with their brethren near Nashville.

It is with pleasure that I think of the farm which they have purchased, and on which they are beginning school work. The Lord will open ways before the humble, self-denying workers connected with this school, and will make them a great blessing. He will give them success in the unselfish missionary work that is to be done.

I ask our people to come up to the help of the Lord, acting their part in helping forward the establishment of this school. We see what has been done in Berrien Springs by the blessing of the Lord. He gave courage and strength to those who were struggling with inconvenience and difficulty, and helped them to make the school a success.

And now, as Brethren Sutherland and Magan, with other educators, have gone to a new hard field, to do pioneer work, (let us hold up their hands, and do all in our power to encourage them. Let us help them to make the school they are establishing a sample of the work that must be done in the South). ...

Many easier fields might have been chosen by those who have gone from Berrien Springs to Nashville. But these workers did not seek easy fields. They resolved to do what they could to help where help was most needed. And we ask our people not to leave them without assistance. (They have been given plain evidence that the farm which has been purchased is the place on which God would have them establish a school, and we call upon our people to help them in the great work that lies before them.)

As I looked at the large vineyards owned by our people in central and southern California, I thought, How I wish that those who own these vineyards could see and appreciate the needs of our workers in Nashville; for then they would surely help them by sending them gifts of fruit. My brethren and sisters, will you not see what you can do to help those who are just starting out in the establishment of a work that God has said must be done? Gifts of money or gifts of fruit would be greatly appreciated by the workers in these needy Southern schools. I have reason to know that they need your assistance. If you will take hold to help them, the Lord will certainly reward you liberally.

I have done what I could. I have given over two tons of prunes, to needy schools and missions. Who will join me in this work?

Ellen G. White.

Chapter 113—Unity Not Consolidation

Sanitarium, Cal., Sept. 12, 1908.

Dear Brother Shireman:

In the night season I was conversing with you, and speaking words of encouragement. The Lord our God is merciful. When his servants make mistakes, he sends them reproof. When the messages of reproof are received and accepted by those who have made mistakes, and changes are made in the life, the brethren should recognize the reformation, and they should encourage and seek to place on vantage ground those struggling to do right. I rejoice this is the way you feel towards Brother Johnson.

The Lord is now to be honored by the men who carry his work. Let there be a just recognition of the change in Brother Johnston. To neglect to do this, and to refuse to encourage and to build up the one who has been seeking to correct his course of action, is to refuse to carry out principles that Christ has clearly laid down in his word.

I am instructed to say to you that mistakes were made on both sides of this question. Brother and Sister Shireman did not view everything in a correct light. While brother Johnston did not take a right course, it is also true that others connected with him did not discern that their own spirit and words were also wrong.

Brother Johnston should now have encouragement. When a man of his temperament sees and acknowledges his wrong, and changes his course of action, there should be a disposition on the part of his brethren and sisters not only to forgive, but to do everything possible to restore confidence, and to strengthen his hands. The impression should never be left on a human mind, that the man who has done wrong, though he sees and corrects his wrong, should still be prevented from standing on vantage ground with his brethren. When such a course is pursued toward any erring soul, the Saviour is misrepresented. Those who recognize the reformation should show forgiveness, and treat the brother who has erred with confidence and special kindness.

This instruction has been given me during the night, and now, at one O'clock in the morning, I am writing to you the message I have received. We need to encourage the erring to confess their wrongs; we should forgive them freely, recognizing the instruction God has given in His Word.

We need to be very careful that we do not view in a wrong light matters connected with the work of God. We need to guard against the least injustice. Those who bear the burden of the work of winning souls to Christ are to be encouraged and helped.

The Lord requires that unity exist in every church, but the policy of consolidation must be guarded against. The workers in our institutions are to preserve their individuality; each is to sense the responsibility resting upon him, while he works under the divine leadership of the Lord Jesus. The workers are to counsel together, and to seek to bring in ideas that are in harmony with the teachings of truth, but never, as long as time shall last, is an arbitrary man-ruling power to come in to take the place and authority of God.

The Lord has been instructing us to move forward. Shall we go forward, or shall we stand still? Shall we not seek to increase in faith, that we may work and wait in assurance and confidence? The word of God is to be our guide under all circumstances. ...

Ellen G. White.

Chapter 114—Pioneers in the South

Sanitarium, Cal., July 19, 1905.

Elders I. H. Evans and J. W. Washburn.

Dear Brethren:

I am very grateful to God that the one-hundred-thousand-dollar fund has been made up, and that we have had the privilege of seeing the substantial and appropriate school buildings that have been erected at Takoma Park.

Near the close of the General Conference, in the night season many matters relative to the work in Washington and in Nashville, were opened before me. We seem to be in a council meeting. Elder Haskell, Elder Butler, and several others were talking together. Elder Haskell was telling of the opportunity that had come to them to purchase in Nashville a good church building in an excellent location. He said that five thousand dollars was asked for this church building and that the people in Nashville and the surrounding vicinity could not raise the money.

The Question was asked, "Has the full amount of the Washington Fund been raised?" The answer was "Yes, it has, and several thousand dollars' overflow has come in." A prayer and praise service was held. After the meeting, a piece of paper was placed in the hands of Elder Haskell. Unfolding it, he read, "This is to signify that we deem it to be the wise and Christian part to act toward our brethren in Nashville to place the first five thousand dollars' surplus that has come in to Washington, in the hands of these faithful servants of God, that they may secure the house of worship in Nashville, which they greatly need. We deem that it is but loving our neighbor as ourselves to make this transfer of means to a place where at this time there is so great a necessity."

After seeing this representation, I awoke, and I fully expected that the matter would take place as it had been presented to me. When Elder Haskell was telling me of the perplexity that they were in to carry forward the Southern work, I said, "Have faith in God. You will carry from this meeting the five thousand dollars needed for the purchase of the church."

I wrote a few lines to Elder Daniells, suggesting that this be done. But Willie did not see that the matter could be carried through thus, because Elder Daniells and others were at that time very much discouraged in regard to the condition of things in Battle Creek. So I told him that he need not deliver the note.

But I could not rest. I was disturbed, and could not find peace of mind. I was instructed that I had a message to bear to our leading brethren, to Elder Daniells, Elder Prescott, Elder Washburn, and Elder Evans. I was instructed that I must present before them the self-denying labors of Elders Haskell and Butler, and say, "Beware what impress you leave upon the minds of these tried servants of God, whose influence is of the highest value. They have known the truth from the earliest period of our work, and have ever sacrificed for the truth's sake."

Moreover, I was instructed that I must call attention to the history of our first work among the people, when these aged pioneers were men of earnest, enduring action. These men have their work to do, an important work. Even in their age their testimony and their endeavors to bear witness that the wheels of Providence are not constructed to stand still or to roll backward. In their labor is their happiness. It is not work that wears men out, but sadness, anxiety, and worry. If Elder Haskell and Elder Butler break down, it will be because of the heavy perplexity that has come upon them in trying without sufficient means or helpers to accomplish the urgent work before them in the Southern field.

The great Medical Missionary, who has purchased men with the price of his own blood, knows what it means to work under discouragement and perplexity. He carried many burdens, and his untiring labors made him very weary.

Christ was the mighty Healer. Of him we read, "And Jesus went about all Galilee, teaching in their synagogues and preaching the gospel of the kingdom, and healing all manner of sickness and all manner of disease among the people." His method of labor is an example of the way in which we are to work. Our missionary efforts are not to be confined to a few centers. In all the world we are to preach the gospel of the kingdom.

Elder Butler and Elder Haskell are to be given the assistance and advantages that will make their efforts successful. They are to be sustained in their labors. The Lord would have those of his people who are willing to give of their means for the advancement of his work, now turn their attention to the work in the South, and especially just now to Nashville. Twenty times as much could have been accomplished in the South as has been accomplished, had the sanitarium work been built up and had the necessary schools been established.

The Lord's tried servants in Nashville are becoming worn out with disappointment. Few realize the value of these staunch old soldiers. Sometimes they are not given the credit due them. These pioneers in the work are to bear the message given by John:--

"That which was from the beginning, which we have heard, which our hands have handled, of the Word of life (for the life was manifested, and we have seen it, and bear witness, and show unto you that eternal life, which was with the Father, and was manifested unto us): That which we have seen and heard declare we unto you, that ye also may have fellowship with us, and truly our fellowship is with the Father and with his Son Jesus Christ. And these things write we unto you, that your joy may be full."

"This then is the message which we have heard of him and declare unto you, that God is light, and in him is no darkness at all. If we say that we have fellowship with him, and walk in the light as he is in the light, we have fellowship one with another and the blood of Jesus Christ his Son cleanseth us from all sin. If we say that we have no sin, we deceive ourselves, and the truth is not in us. If we confess our sins, he is faithful and just to forgive us our sins, and to cleanse us from all unrighteousness. If we say that we have not sinned, we make him a liar, and his word is not in us."

These matters are fresh in my mind; for they have been revised and repeated since last Sabbath evening. In this letter I can only give a jot of the history of the self-denial and sacrifice with which the work was carried forward in the beginning and of how earnestly the laborers worked to meet emergencies. Brother Haskell has labored unselfishly and untiringly to raise money for the General Conference and for the Review and Herald, and other institutions. His persevering, self-sacrificing zeal carried him long distances through the heat of summer and in the cold of winter. On one occasion he drove a long distance in the winter in Minnesota. I think it was then that he froze his hands, causing himself great suffering; but he got the money that was needed. Though weary and worn, he had no thought of laying down the armor, but fought his way through every difficulty.

I want our brethren to read the first four verses of the first chapter of First Thessalonians, and to enter into the spirit of the writer: "We give thanks to God alway for you all, making mention of you in our prayers; remembering without ceasing your work of faith, and labor of love, and patience of hope in our Lord Jesus Christ, in the sight of God our Father; knowing, brethren beloved, your election of God."

Of Elder Haskell and Elder Butler, God says, "I will guide them. I will put my grace in their hearts. Because they have not been turned away from the truth to give heed to seducing spirits, but have stood firm, declaring the message given them, they are to be highly esteemed. They will not exchange the faith that they have boldly and fervently declared, for another doctrine, which is not true.

I am glad that these men are still able to do solid, substantial work. They must have greater encouragement in point of financial assistance in their work in the Southern field. Their efforts have brought many souls into the truth, and they must not be left to wear out their souls in discouragement. The Southern field is a very hard, needy field, and it must receive assistance. Chosen men should be appointed to receive the funds that will now be called for in behalf of the enterprises that must now come to the front in this most needy field.

Over and over again the light has been given that a special work is to be done in Huntsville. Men who are rooted and grounded in the truth in all its bearings are to be placed in charge of that work. A beginning has been made on an orphanage for colored children, but this work stands unfinished. On the beautiful farm of over three hundred acres, God purposes that an efficient missionary training school shall be conducted, which will develop many workers for the colored people.

A small sanitarium should also be established in connection with the Huntsville school. The sanitarium building should not be of shoddy character, neither should it be narrow and contracted. It should be built substantially, and there should be in it room for the physician and nurses to carry on the work of healing the sick, and giving patients and students an education in regard to the right principles of living.

I now make a call that means shall be sent direct to Nashville, that the fruit of the gospel in good works may appear. The work there is to be supervised by men who understand what needs to be done and who have learned how to economize.

The work in the South must now receive attention. It has stood in an unfinished condition long enough. I now expect that the necessities of this work will be seen and understood, and that our people everywhere will be encouraged to send donations great and small to Nashville. The workers there have waited patiently until the Washington Fund should be made up. This fund has been made up, and help should now be given to Nashville, to carry forward the work that must be accomplished.

Ellen G. White.

Chapter 115—The Conditions in Nashville

Sanitarium, Cal., July 20, 1905.

To the General Conference Committee:

Dear Brethren:

During the time that I was in Washington, the Lord was working upon my mind in the night season. Light was given me while I was there that the first five thousand dollars of the overflow about the one hundred thousand dollars sent in for the work in Washington, was due the Southern field, and that it ought to be appropriated to the present urgent needs of the work in Nashville. More than that amount which would otherwise have gone to Nashville, has gone to Washington, because of our appeals to give the Washington work our first attention.

I know that one thousand dollars was loaned to the brethren in Nashville to make the first payment on the church building. But I am instructed that the Lord would have been pleased had five thousand dollars been offered them, instead of one thousand. The workers in Nashville need encouragement that they have never received. The way in which the work there has been treated by some has made wounds that should now be healed. The Lord will not vindicate one vestige of selfishness. He calls upon men to act under his supervision.

The work in Washington is important and essential, and great efforts have been made to call the attention of our people to that field. But now the Lord would have us consider the work in the South.

These matters have been presented to me in such a way that I see my duty clearly. In the name of the Lord, I, as his messenger call upon the leaders of the people in his cause to do the works of righteousness. The souls of the people in Nashville are just as precious in the sight of the Lord as the souls of the people in Washington. The light of truth is to shine forth as brightly from Nashville as from Washington. The necessity at Nashville is at the present time far greater than it is at Washington.

Right is right. Justice must be shown to the Southern field. God sees a selfishness working for the mastery that must be overcome. Five thousand dollars should be appropriated to the work in Nashville. This question was asked, "Is it not just as essential that the work in Nashville shall make a proper showing, as the work in Washington?" I must be faithful to my work as God's messenger. Therefore I bear the message, Make up a fund of five thousand dollars, and send it to the brethren in Nashville. God is a God of love and equity.

If we expect the Lord to work with us and for us as his people, if we expect him to reveal his light and power to us in these last days, we must work in accordance with the mind and will, the mercy and compassion, of the Lord God of Israel, who so loved the world that he gave his only begotten Son, that whosoever believeth in him should not perish, but have everlasting life. The Lord calls upon those at the head of his work to send the first of the overflow that has come in on the Washington fund, to the work in Nashville; for the work there, which is as essential as the work in Washington, is in need of assistance. The Lord's servants who are laboring there should receive encouragement. I am bidden to say that selfishness and any form of injustice must not find a place in our work. Let our brethren repent before the Lord for any selfishness that has come in toward the work in the Southern states. This matter has been presented to me three times, and I was instructed that five thousand dollars ought to have been placed in Elder Haskell's hands before he left the Conference ground. ...

Over and over again I am bidden to urge upon your attention the necessities of the work in Nashville. The Lord has specified what should be done there. A grand work has been started, and it should by all means be sustained. It must not be hindered by neglect, but is to go forward in straight, clear lines. Brother Butler, Brother Haskell and his wife, and others, are laboring hard and earnestly, and are wrestling with many difficulties; and they must be given assistance. Souls in Nashville are as precious as souls in Washington. The conditions in Nashville make the work of the laborers doubly hard. If those in other parts of the field who have been highly favored by God do not awake to the true situation, the Lord will visit them for their indifference.

Brother Sutherland and Magan have been trying to advance in their school work, but while the means was flowing into Washington, they were exhorted to patience. They have made as much headway as possible. Recently a beautiful sanitarium site of thirty-five acres was chosen not far away from Nashville. On this site a sanitarium building must soon be put up. For a long time Dr. Hayward and his co-workers have been struggling on in the face of many difficulties. They must now be helped. I give this instruction to you as God has given it to me as his appointed messenger. Last Sabbath night I did not sleep at all through the entire night. So heavily were matters pressing upon my mind that I could only cry unto God, praying him to set this matter plainly in its true light before the men bearing responsibilities in Washington. ...

Ellen G. White.

Chapter 116—Judge Not

St. Helena, Cal., Jan. 12, 1906.

Dear Brethren and Sisters in Battle Creek:

I wish to write you a few lines. I understand how the enemy is working, and I wish to say to every soul, "Judge not, that ye be not judged. For with what judgment ye judge, ye shall be judged; and with what measure ye mete, it shall be measured to you again." There are times when we have to take a decided stand, but, in magnifying the Lord, be sure that you do not condemn and make charges against others. It would cause all the powers of hell to rejoice if our people were to become divided. The way has been preparing for contention and division. Some are in great danger of drifting into infidelity. Now, let your study be to save these imperilled souls. I have sorrow, great sorrow of heart, that they do not understand their bearings.

But whatever you may say to vindicate the truth in righteousness, be sure not to make a raid on the one who for many years has borne heavy burdens in connection with our medical missionary work. He has always personally treated me as respectfully as he would treat his mother. It is nothing he has done to me personally that has led me to speak as I have been compelled to. While it makes my heart ache, I must speak. God has given me a message to give to his people, that the sentiments contained in the book, "Living Temple," are mingled with fallacies that beguile the reader. It is the specious errors in that book that makes it a dangerous production. I can not hold my peace, and let the flock of God be misled. But I beseech you not to let a drive be made against our brother; for this would not be right.

Stand in defense of the truth; exalt the truth. God has given the erring one every encouragement to turn fully to him. Our brother has been following his perverted judgement, and his soul has been lifted up into vanity; but he should not be personally attacked, because it is not the right thing to do, to open those opposition charges before the world. Keep the affirmative of truth, as did Paul in his charge to Timothy: "Preach the Word; be instant in season, out of season; reprove, rebuke, exhort with all long suffering and doctrine. For the time will come when they will not endure sound doctrine; but after their own lusts, shall they heap to themselves teachers, having itching ears."

The truth of this I have experienced. In the early days of this message, I have passed through most trying ordeals in refuting false doctrines, and especially such doctrines as we are meeting now. We are passing over the same ground, and while we are to call error, error, and withstand delusive sentiments that will continue to come into our ranks to palsy the faith and assurance of the people of God, we are to make no tirade against men and women. We are to show the evil of the false sentiments that Christ himself has warned us not to receive; but let us consider that the power of the enemy is strong.

In the past, the one who has been recognized as our leading physician has, under the Spirit of God, done a grand work, and he has not received from some the encouragement that he should have received. There are ministers who have not accepted the principles of health reform, but have stood in opposition to them.

I have been carrying a great burden for the people in Battle Creek. Last night I was laboring most earnestly in prayer. The commission was given me by the Saviour, "It is not you they have rejected, but Me, their Saviour. You have nothing to retract of the messages that you presented during the General Conference held at Oakland and during the Berrien Springs meeting. You have a work to do of the same order. You have nothing to regret, in the words you have spoken and written, to the leading medical missionary workers. I have for you still more decided messages to bear. Those who have made light of the messages that I have given my messenger to bear have insulted the One who gave the messages." Our people need to humble their hearts, and confess their sins, and be converted. They need to fear and tremble lest God's Spirit be withdrawn from them, and they be left to hardness of heart and blindness of mind, because they have rejected the word God has given them. The messages that God has sent have been borne, line upon line, precept upon precept. The Lord is still working, and he gives the admonition, "Keep the people, the flock of my pasture, from being educated by physicians or teachers who reject the warnings I have given through my messenger. My Sabbath has been transgressed, and the light that would have shone forth has been quenched."

God would not have his people drawn into false paths, into a belief in sophistries and misleading scientific sentiments. For years the testimony has been given that Battle Creek has been and is, under an influence that is not spiritual. The message given is, "When the one who has borne responsibilities in the medical missionary work shall humble his heart in my sight, confessing his sins, I will speak peace to him. His associates who have helped him to walk in false paths, I will judge; for they have helped him to be deceived."

Since the Lord's will has not been done, since our enemies have had occasion to see a departing from the faith, as I know and am instructed that they have, will not the one who has been reproved now make a change? Will he not humble his heart as did Daniel, a man whom God calls "greatly beloved"? Will he not read the prayer offered by Daniel, and see what it means to humble himself before God?

Brethren, there is one thing you can do. You can see that you yourselves are in a condition of repentance. You hearts need to be converted. The end is near; the time is short. Plead with God, clear the King's highway, and lift up the trailing standard on which is inscribed, "The commandments of God and the faith of Jesus." As you advance, step by step, proclaim, "Here are they that keep the commandments of God and the faith of Jesus." Moses declared, "Behold, I have taught you statutes and judgments, even as the Lord my God commands me, that ye should do so in the land whither ye go to possess it. Keep therefore and do them; for this is your wisdom and your understanding in the sight of the nations, which shall hear all these statutes, and say, Surely this great nation is a wise and understanding people... Only take heed to thyself, and keep thy soul diligently, lest thou forget the things which thine eyes have seen, and lest they depart from thy heart all the days of thy life; but teach them thy sons and thy sons' sons."

Ellen G. White.

Chapter 117—The Madison Sanitarium

St. Helena Sanitarium, Cal., Feb. 10, 1906.

Dear Brother Magan,

I have this morning read your letter, and have much interest in that which I read. I am glad this matter has come to a head, and I am sure the time has come for a change in the atmosphere in Nashville. I am pleased that the exhibition of prejudice did not extinguish the exercise of mercy. The Lord is for us, and will be for us as long as we are for him. I think I will make an effort to raise some money. I will see what can be done. I found a long article in one of my diaries written some time ago in reference to the matters at Nashville,-- the location of the sanitarium. I am desirous that the work shall advance. I think we need not be discouraged in regard to the sanitarium in Nashville. Keep up good heart; have faith in God.

I am not backward to encourage sanitariums. I want to see them progressing every place where schools are established. I have been searching for a matter that I wanted very much in regard to the establishing of sanitariums wherever schools should be located, but if I should hunt just now I should lose my time to write this so important letter in response to your excellent letter. This must be prepared now as soon as finished.

I am troubled much in regard to Brother Will Palmer. It has seemed he was working in an objectionable way for a man that is preparing for the test of the judgment. I feel deeply. We must be much more with God in earnest prayer. We must make God our only trust. The Lord is our God, the strength of our soul. We must take hold upon the Lord. The Lord is pleased when we importune him for his grace and his favor, not only for ourselves but for those who are in need of help. O let us put implicit confidence in our Lord Jesus. Now pray, and believe, and pray, and the Lord will certainly hear us. I shall believe that you will begin work on that sanitarium very soon, and every stroke must be a stroke of faith. Press the battle to the gate; do not be discouraged. Move just as far as you can go. Make every preparation as if you know that building was going up. Mark out your ground, and get every jot and inch of advance possible. The Lord knows you need that sanitarium. Can not you make something with "Object Lessons?" We will hold up your hands, and prayer will reach the throne of grace. Trust in the Lord's power; trust, and lean your whole weight upon the Lord Jesus, and the salvation of God will be revealed.

We can move just as decidedly and fast as possible, for we have no time to lose. I wish to emphasize the importance of calling all who will be on the Lord's side to take this position. We will draw nigh to God ourselves. We will be in true earnest, for the end is nearer than when we first believed. I can scarcely take in the many things upon my mind to produce, but our prayers must ascend to God, and let our faith cling to Him who is might to save to the uttermost all who will come to him.

I am writing letters to Battle Creek. Will send you copies. We had a telegram that the man W. C. W., in the place of going to Portland, Oregon, was to go to Southern California, and that is all that came to us yesterday. When we shall see him now I do not imagine. I may be with him at Loma Linda before he hangs up his hat in his own home. I have not seen Loma Linda since it first opened. We are to do all we can, and then tell the Lord to open the way. I think the move we made for Loma Linda was in the right time, and they have had no embarrassment thus far in meeting their obligations. And I think the San Diego Sanitarium has no pressure except for furnishing, and they will be in this respect a little behind. They have an excellent school building in Fernando, and that school building is equal to any I have seen in this country, fully ahead of the school buildings in Battle Creek. Next, the Glendale Sanitarium: they say it is running over full all the time. We did not call for means for that sanitarium out of Southern California. And the Lord has favored us in the Loma Linda matter, by the hiring of money at five per cent interest and paying in the five thousand before it was due. Two hundred dollars was allowed them on the payments, and there is no reason why the whole can not be raised according to agreement. But I must be thankful for the advantages we have had; and we will be thankful for these three sanitariums; and the Fernando School is doing good work.

I have been so hurried I have not done much writing personally. I have had so little sleep because of the heavy burden that comes from rolling on from Battle Creek. Our only hope is in God. We trust no in man, nor make flesh our arm. Let us press together and walk humbly with God. I send you a copy of something I have written for Battle Creek. I wish I could be with you a little time, but my workers are right here. I know what matter should be sent here and there. I am sorry that Sister Druillard is suffering with poor health. I wish she were here for awhile and could remain here and get well.

Now I say, keep up good courage. I was up at two o'clock and slept not, night before last, after twelve o'clock. Am falling asleep while I write. I can not get this copied, so send it as it is. In much love to you all,

Ellen G. White.

Chapter 118—Harmonize As Christian Workers

Sanitarium, Cal., March 5, 1906.

To the Officers of the Southern Union Conference:

Dear Brethren:

I wish to write a few words to you, to accompany an article explaining why I am hoping that the Nashville Sanitarium shall be placed on the Madison School farm. If the school and the sanitarium will blend in their influence, this will prove to be a great advantage to both institutions. There are troublous times before us, and for years the plan of having a school and a sanitarium placed so that they can work in connection with each other, has been presented to me as the Lord's plan.

I have been instructed that our young physicians and teachers are in danger of becoming very set in carrying out their own plans and ideas, independent of the plans and views of their brethren. The Lord would have us all the subject to one another, and harmonize as Christian workers. This is the lesson that Dr. Hayward and his wife should seek to learn. They must work as true medical missionaries here below, if they would be prepared for the heavenly school in the mansions above.

God's family on the earth have many lessons to learn in order to answer the prayer of Christ,--his last prayer with his disciples before his humiliation. The seventeenth chapter of John, which contains this prayer, comprehends more than any other chapter in the New Testament.

Let every soul that shall assemble at Graysville, pray, "Lord, help me not to be self-centered, because no such thing can exist in heaven. Help me in this life to sanctify myself wholly to thy service. Help me to apply to myself the instruction given in Christ's prayer.

Ellen G. White.

Chapter 119—We Must Not Pull Apart

Sanitarium, Cal., April 2, 1906.

To the Brethren Assembled in Council at Washington:

We are living in an important period of the history of our cause, and the movements that we make now will have a decided bearing on the future of our cause. Recently I have been very much weighed down. I know that the enemy is working with intensity of effort to confuse the minds of those who have never before passed through such an experience as this. We must do all in our power to save the souls of those who are being tempted.

It has been presented to me that our ministers would be blessed in showing much more interest than they do in those who are in need of a helping hand. Those who are perplexed and confused should be worked for earnestly, in season and out of season. Satan is putting forth decided efforts to lead souls astray, and our brethren of influence everywhere must work with untiring earnestness to save souls.

I greatly desire that every move that is made shall be in accordance with Christ's prayer recorded in the seventeenth chapter of John. We must not pull apart; for this is not pleasing to God.

I was instructed to say to Brethren Magan and Sutherland, Do not lose your hold on God. The Lord has witnessed to the good work done by you at Berrien Springs, because you tried to follow out the instruction given you. The stand you took in Carroll House, Takoma Park, was witnessed by the angels of God. Your confessions covered the things that were brought to your mind, and the Lord blessed you. Since that time I have had increased confidence in you, and I want to say to you, "My brethren, do not fail or be discouraged. I have confidence in you both, and I feel sure that the Lord will bless your efforts."

Brethren Sutherland and Magan are not to be held in a position of uncertainty. This some are doing, but it is displeasing to the Lord. Will those who are so suspicious pray together and encourage faith in one another? We have not a man to spare. We need fifty workers where there is one. The Lord is coming in judgment to those who are not in the truth is--to go forth with the message.

I must urge our brethren not to appear indifferent, not to leave the tempted ones to become the sport of the enemy's temptations. We must watch for souls as they that must give an account. We must do all we can to prevent Satan from sowing his seeds in minds.

Let the leading men in the General Conference and the presidents of our state conferences go to those who have been under temptation, and try to help them. Talk with Brethren Paulson and Sadler, and help them to press the Battle to the gates. Talk with them alone, and do all in your power to disabuse their minds. We see with what determined effort Satan is working, and we are to labor with heart and mind and soul and strength to win others to Christ.

I wish you fully to appreciate the words that Christ spoke to help the indifferent and the deceived. Do not too readily give up your brethren and friends. "Watch therefore; for ye know not what hour your Lord doth come. But this know, that if the good-man of the house had known in what watch the thief would come, he would have watched, and would not have suffered his house to be broken up. Therefore be ye also ready; for in such an hour as ye think not the Son of man cometh."

I am instructed to seek for the sheep that are being destroyed by wolves. Let us not be over-sensitive regarding the representations of hatred made by others. Christ was mocked and insulted. Men for whom he was about to give his life, buffeted and smote him, saying, "Prophesy, who is it that smote thee?" Let us call to mind the scenes of Christ's suffering, and be prepared to suffer for his sake. And let no one of us give occasion for a brother to go over to the enemy's side. Let us make the kindest efforts to disabuse the minds of the tempted ones. Let it be our object to win souls to Christ, at the same time not compromising one point of truth. Let us stand on the affirmative, leaving others to do the accusing.

It has been decidedly presented to me that you are to seek to help Brethren Paulson, Sadler, Hayward, Morse, Reed, and Rile, and others associated with them, with your hearts softened and subdued by the grace of Christ. As you do this, the blessing of God will come to you.

Ellen G. White.

Chapter 120—Simplicity in Treatments

Elmshaven, Sanitarium, Calif., June 17, 1906.

Dear Brother Burden:

For several days, I have thought of writing to you, but could not because so many things demanding immediate attention have come in. I may have written to you regarding the equipment of your treatment rooms, but fearing that I have not, I will come straight to the point.

When we were at the Paradise Valley Sanitarium, we were conducted through the new treatment rooms. One room was elaborately fitted up with electrical appliances for giving the patients treatments. That night I was instructed that some connected with the institution were introducing things for the treatment of the sick that were not safe. The application of some of these electrical treatments would involve the patient in serious difficulties, imperiling life.

One was conversing with the doctors, and with great earnestness was saying, "Never, never carry out your wonderful plans. There have been various mechanical devices brought into the treatment rooms that are expensive, and the men who make a specialty of treating certain cases are liable to make grave mistakes."

There are men who make a specialty of treating the rectum, and some feel that they have been greatly benefitted. But I have been instructed that this treatment, as well as many surgical operations, leaves with many a serious weakness.

Several things were mentioned that have been brought into the Paradise Valley Sanitarium which were not necessary, and which should not have been purchased without consultation with other physicians. The amount of money which some of these machines cost, and the salary which must be paid to the one who operates them, should be taken into consideration. I felt impelled to talk with Brother Robinson in reference to these matters, although we were driving with a number of people, and it was not a favorable place to converse about such matters.

Now I am certain that great care should be taken in purchasing electrical instruments and costly mechanical fixtures. Move slowly, Brother Burden, and do not trust to men who suppose that they understand what is essential, and who launch out in spending money for many things that require experts to handle them.

Several times I have instructed that much of the elaborate, costly machinery used in giving treatments, did not help in the work as much as is supposed. With it we do not get so good results as with the simple appliances we used in our earlier experiences. The application of water in various simple ways is a great blessing.

I have been instructed that the X-ray is not the great blessing that some suppose it to be. If used unwisely, it may do much harm. The results of some of the electrical treatments are similar to the results of using stimulants. There is a weakness that follows. ...

Keep the patients out of doors as much as possible, and give them cheering, happy talks in the parlor, with simple reading and Bible lessons easy to be understood, which will be an encouragement to the soul. Talk on health reform, and do not you, my brother, become burden bearer in so many lines that you can not teach the simple lessons of health reform. Those who go from the Sanitarium should go so well instructed that they can teach others the methods of treating their families.

There is danger of spending far too much money on machinery and appliances which the patients can never use in their home lessons. They should rather be taught how to regulate the diet, so that the living machinery of the whole being will work in harmony. Let them become intelligent in regard to the importance of laying aside corsets and shortening their shirts. Such lessons will be to the women more valuable than they can estimate.

Chapter 121—Local Health Foods

Sanitarium, Cal., Sept. 27, 1906.

In many places, in different sections of the country, an effort should be made to utilize natural products for healthful foods. A good work along this line may be done at Loma Linda. Our brethren there should make a beginning soon, even if all the arrangements regarding this work can not be definitely decided upon at this time. As our brethren at Loma Linda study how to make the health food work a means of bringing the truth for this time before the minds of unbelievers, the Lord will add his blessing, and will make plain the course they should pursue in the conduct of the business.

A similar work is to be carried forward in the Southern states. Men and women who embrace the truth in the South will often need to be helped to find employment. Many will find opportunity to engage in evangelistic work; and these should learn, in connection with this work, to teach worldlings how to prepare simple, palatable food.

Outside the city of Nashville there are advantages that should be utilized in providing wholesome food for the people.

Chapter 122—The Work At Madison

Sanitarium, Cal., Oct. 10, 1906.

To the Brethren and Sisters in Nashville and in Madison:

Among brethren engaged in various lines of the Lord's work there should ever be seen a desire to encourage and strengthen one another. The Lord is not pleased with the course of those who make the way difficult for some who are doing a work appointed to them by the Master. If these critics were placed in the position of those whom they criticize, they would desire far different treatment from their brethren.

We are to respect the light that led Brethren Magan and Sutherland to purchase property, and to establish the school at Madison. Let no one speak words that would tend to demerit their work, or to divert students from the school. I do not charge anyone with an intention to do wrong, but from the light I have received I can say that there is danger that some will criticize unjustly the work of our brethren and sisters connected with the school at Madison. Let every encouragement possible be given to those who are engaged in an effort to give to children and youth an education in the knowledge of God and of his law.

To the workers in Madison I would say, Be of good courage. Do not lose faith. Your heavenly Father has not left you to achieve success by your own endeavors. Trust in Him and He will work in your behalf. It is your privilege to experience and to demonstrate the blessings that come through walking by faith and not by sight. Work with an eye single to the glory of God. Make the most of your capabilities, and you will increase in knowledge. Those who do the will of God may be permitted to pass through suffering, but the Lord will cause them to triumph at last.

The Lord has helped you in the selection of the location for the school, and as you continue to work under the guidance of the Holy Spirit, your efforts will be successful. The Lord will give you spirit and life, if you will not permit yourselves to become discouraged. We trust that from your brethren you may receive the help of harmonious action, of prayers, and of means. But let not one feeling of discouragement be cherished. The Lord has a work for you to do where you are, and those who are doing his work need never to be discouraged. ...

Those who criticize their fellow workers open a door through which the enemy will enter. What can be more sad than to see brother working against brother, expressing suspicion and doubts of the other's sincerity? There is room enough for all to use their God-given talents. All are laboring with the one object of inspiring belief in the words of inspiration. Then let everyone so order his speech and work that he may be in harmony with those who are laboring to the same end as he himself. ...

Let the gospel be presented as the word of God for life and salvation. Let not the ministers of Christ spoil the presentation of the gospel by the manifestation of a harsh spirit. The gospel will be commended by the revelation of a spirit that works by love. "How beautiful upon the mountains are the feet of him that bringeth good tidings, that publisheth peace."

I am glad that the school work has been begun at Madison. The Sanitarium and the school might have been a mutual help one to the other, had they been closely connected. But a solid work is to be carried forward in each of these institutions.

I am instructed that the Lord will give wisdom to minds to prepare simple health foods. It will not be necessary to pay large sums of money for the privilege of manufacturing some foods that have a large sale. Let the people be taught how to cook properly, making simple preparations of healthful food. In the school the products of the soil, the fruits, the grains, and the vegetables, may be used to advantage.

We remember you in our prayers. May the Lord guide you continually, and bless you in all your efforts. It is your privilege to stand undaunted, and through the help of the Lord to make a success of your work.

Ellen G. White.

Chapter 123—Silence is Eloquence

Sanitarium, Cal., Nov. 15, 1906.

To the Workers at the Madison School:

I write to you to be sure to bear in mind at this time that silence is eloquence. To open up all matters concerning the beginning of your work at Madison would not be wisdom. I have just received a letter regarding your work, but I can not now deal with it as I wish. I wish to say to you, Be as wise as serpents and as harmless as doves. Some will depart from the faith, giving heed to seducing spirits and doctrines of devils. It will not be well for you to open to everybody all things concerning the work in Nashville and in Madison. There are those who are associated with us, and who occupy positions of trust, who may not stand the test. It will not be safe to try to make all understand everything. Those things that are of a private character, you should not make public. Let them be kept within the knowledge of your special few.

I shall try to write more on this point, but can not now, as I must get things ready to go in the mail to Australia.

I have just found a sermon that I gave at the San Jose campmeeting more than a year ago. I shall send copies of this to you and to others in Nashville. I think you will find that it contains timely instruction.

Your sister in Christ,

Ellen G. White.

Chapter 124—Cautions to a Reformer

Sanitarium, Cal., November, 1906.

Elder J. A. Burden.

Dear Brother:

I have words to speak to you. The Lord has laid upon you responsibilities of no ordinary nature. At the time of the meeting held before you were settled at Loma Linda, when I was so sick, the Lord showed me what was to be your work as director of the sanitarium, and that if you would connect yourself with divine wisdom, you would be taught of God. You need a clear mind in order to settle wisely the many questions that come to you for decision. The Lord would have you taught of Him.

My brother, do not allow men of limited experience to come in, as Elder Reaser has done, and assume a controlling power. Brother Reaser has placed himself as teacher and adviser and ruler in may matters, and unless you work and watch carefully, such an influence will retard the work. Brother Reaser should learn that he is not qualified to do the work he supposes he is to do.

Brother Reaser supposes that if it were not for his watching of the finances, there would be serious losses; whereas if he had nothing to do and say in these matters, it would save many perplexities. He has taken upon himself burdens that the Lord has not laid upon him. He has learned some of his lessons of Elder Healey, who has done much to retard the work in the South. If he would attend to his work of ministry, and keep his hands off the work of directing, he would save himself and others many burdens. From the light that has been given me, I know that it is a mistake for him to be connected with our sanitarium; he should not be a manager.

In regard to the health food business, I would urge you to move slowly. Dr. Kellogg's proposition to sell the corn flake rights to our people for twenty years has just been considered by our brethren here; and I fear, if I had not been on the ground this matter would have been carried through to the loss of our food business. When a thing is exalted, as the corn flakes has been, it would be unwise for our people to have anything to do with it. It is not necessary that we make the corn flake an article of food.

I would advise you, my brother, to keep away from the influence of Dr. Kellogg's ingenious plans. Let us use our own ingenuity to invent the best kinds of food possible.

We are living in the closing days of this earth's history; souls are starving for a knowledge of the word of God and of healthful living. Let us seek to carry our work solidly, giving all possible instruction regarding the principles of health reform, praying with the sick, and teaching the people how to care for themselves in sickness and health.

The Lord has sent us valuable help in Dr. White, who is studying to know how to follow the way of the Lord. Let there be much earnest prayer on the part of the workers, each depending on the great Physician to carry the work according to His purposes. "For we are laborers together with God: ye are God's husbandry; ye are God's building." In our efforts to build up the cause of God in the earth, we are to make sure work for eternity.

Many workers who are bearing responsibilities are embracing too much authority; and they will certainly confuse the human judgement by their dictatorial authority. I must warn my brethren to be on their guard against this. The cause of God is imperiled when the workers become self-confident, and seek to embrace more than the Lord has laid upon them. Hindrance instead of advancement is the result of such a spirit.

Elder Burden, carry your work intelligently, even consulting the word of God; for this word is very precious to the worker in the cause. Study the messages that God has sent to his people for the last sixty years through the Spirit of Prophecy. Do not seek the counsel of men, but by earnest prayer seek the wisdom of God. A mistake has been made in the past by leaning upon the guidance of men. Seek to correct this mistake.

Chapter 125—Help the Workers

Sanitarium, Napa Co., Cal., January 19, 1907.

Elder A. G. Daniells,

Takoma Park Station, Washington, D. C.

Dear Brother:

Today I have been carrying a heavy burden on my heart. Last night some matters of special importance were opened up before me. I seemed to be passing through a severe conflict. I was addressing a company of men and women and presenting to them the dangers of our people. I spoke of our great need of being much with God in prayer. I had words of encouragement to give to different ones.

Words of instruction were given to me to speak to you and Elder Evans, and Elder Washburn. I said, You have a work to do to encourage the school work in Madison, Tenn. There are but few teachers among us who have had experience in carrying forward the work in hard places. The workers who have been striving to carry out the mind and will of God in Madison have not received the encouragement they should have had. Unless Brother Sutherland is relieved of some of the pressure that is upon him he will fall under the burden.

You may ask what is needed? I answer it is encouragement. Brethren Sutherland and Magan have had a severe lesson in the past. The Lord sent them correction and instruction, and they received the message from the Lord and made confession. It was a grievous mistake to plan to center so many interests in Battle Creek. Shall we be influenced by those who say that the men who made that mistake can not be trusted?

When I was in Washington I entreated Brethren Sutherland and Magan to believe that God had forgiven their mistakes, and I since tried by my help and encouragement to have them realize that the Lord had placed them on vantage ground.

It is your privilege, Brother Daniells, and the privilege of those who have wide influence in the work, to let these brethren understand that they have your confidence and encouragement in the work they are bravely doing. Brother Sutherland is in a precarious state of health. We can not afford to lose him. We need his experience in the school work. The brethren who have influence should do all in their power to hold up the hands of these workers by encouraging and supporting the work of the Madison school. Means should be appropriated to the needs of the work in Madison,---That the labor of the teachers may not be so hard in the future.

Our Individual Responsibility

Our churches are certainly in need of instructors. "Sanctify the Lord God of Hosts and let him be your fear and let him be your dread."

To every man is given his work. In the representation of the parable, the householder gave the talents to his servants "according to their several ability." All are not in possession of the same capabilities. Each has a special work to do, that there may be no schism in the body of Christ. Each is to take up his special place and turn with patience the race that is set before him.

We have moral and social obligations to meet. There is an abundance of work for all to do. Many are groping in darkness and following the paths of selfish gratification, while professing the name of Christ. They have not felt the responsibility developing upon them to grow up to the full stature of men and women in Christ Jesus. Such ones need the help of a kind heart, a helpful hand, to lead them back into the paths of righteousness. As Christians we have a special work before us which if we will do in humility of mind, God will honor with his blessing.

Ellen G. White.

Chapter 126—Awake! Awake! Awake!

January 24, 1907.

The times in which we live have a peculiar importance. Countries hitherto closed to the gospel are opening their doors, and are pleading for the word of God to be explained to them. Kings and princes will open their long-closed gates, inviting the heralds of the cross to enter. The harvest truly is great, but the laborers are few. Can the Christian, who has the world for his field, fold his hands in idleness, and leave the sheaves ungathered? Eternity alone will reveal the results of well directed efforts put forth now. Let every family who claims to believe the third angel's message put forth earnest, untiring efforts to proclaim the truth.

My sisters, do not spend your money needlessly for dress, but dress plainly. Fathers and mothers, educate your children to dress inexpensively; teach them to save their pennies for missionary work. Let every member of the family practice self-denial. Christ is our example. He was the Prince of Glory, but he had such an interest in our world that he left his riches, and came to this earth to live a life that should be an example to rich and poor alike. He taught that all should come together in love and unity, to work as he worked, to sacrifice as he sacrificed, and to love as children of God.

My brethren and sisters, you must be willing to be converted yourselves, in order to practice the self-denial of Christ. Dress plainly, but neatly. Spend as little as possible upon yourselves. Keep in your homes a self-denial box, into which you can put the money saved by little acts of self-denial. Day by day gain a clearer understanding of the word of God and improve every opportunity to impart the knowledge you have gained. Do not become weary in well-doing; for God is constantly imparting to you the great blessing of his Gift to the world. Cooperate with the Lord Jesus, and he will teach you the priceless lessons of his love. Time is short; in due season, when time shall be no longer, you will receive your reward. ...

From many places calls are coming for ministers, for teachers, for physicians to carry on the work in sanitarium, but we have not the trained workers to send. We have sanitariums, but we need more of these institutions in various places. We need schools that will be self-supporting and this can be, if teachers and students will be helpful, industrious, and economical. There is no need for debts to accumulate on our schools. And the old debts should be cleared away.

Sacrifices must be made on every hand; we must devise and plan, and labor to the utmost to be thrifty and economical.

Ellen G. White.

Chapter 127—Do Not Colonize

Sanitarium, Napa Co., Cal., February 11, 1907.

To our Brethren in Graysville, Tennessee:

I have a message for our people in Graysville. Christ sent forth his disciples to go to all countries and people and tongues. He is not pleased when many who are well instructed in the truth remain together in one place; for they are in danger of imbibing a spirit of criticizing and faultfinding. He desires them to engage in his work in new fields. He desires them to educate people who know not the truth. As they open the word of life to others, the Lord will move upon hearts to receive the truth, and new churches will be raised up.

Those who manifest pride by belittling the capabilities of others, and speaking contemptuously of them, need a personal experience in the service of God. Let them move out in humility and labor in new fields, under the supervision of God. To many of our people who are located in Graysville I am instructed to say, Go forth and labor in fields where the truth has never been proclaimed. The Holy Spirit will be your helper and teacher, and you will obtain a new and living experience.

I am bidden to say to our brethren in Graysville and in other centers, If the Lord has not called you definitely to a work where you are located, Go forth as missionaries sent by God. Labor as Christ did, preaching wherever you can obtain a hearing. Labor and pray. Christ will be with all who will do honest missionary work. New churches are to be built up, and in many places the word of life is to be proclaimed. Multitudes are to hear from inspired tongues the last message of mercy to a fallen world.

God will give to his messengers a knowledge of the truth of his word, and he will give them clear utterance. Souls will be converted, and they in turn will labor for others.

Let the members of the church in Graysville seek earnestly for the converting power of God upon their hearts. Let them seek to be brought under the softening, subduing influence of His Holy Spirit, to free them from the spirit of fault-finding, and to make them of one mind. When men are submissive to God, He can use them effectively in His great work.

"Christ being come an High Priest of good things to come, by a greater and more perfect tabernacle, not made with hands, that is to say, not of this building, neither by the blood of goats and calves, but by his own blood he entered in once into the holy place, having obtained eternal redemption. For if the blood of bulls and of goats, and the ashes of an heifer sprinkling the unclean, sanctifieth to the purifying of the flesh; how much more shall the blood of Christ, who through the eternal Spirit offered himself without spot to God, purge your conscience from dead works to serve the living God."

Ellen G. White.

Chapter 128—Helping the Madison School

Sanitarium, Napa Co., Cal., February 5, 1907.

Elder E. G. Hayes:

Dear Brother:

I write to ask you to interest yourself in the school at Madison. (Brethren Sutherland and Magan worked diligently, far beyond their strength, to open up the school work in this place, which is of the Lord's appointment. They have endeavored to establish a school that would fit young men and young women to act as missionaries in the Southern field.)

At the present time they should have five thousand dollars to enable them to provide suitable facilities for the work, and still more should be provided, in order that a small sanitarium may be connected with the school.

So far they have received very little help in this enterprise, compared with the needs and importance of the work. They have worked hard, and have laid plans for such an education as is essential to prepare workers to be able to teach the ignorant, and to explain the Scriptures. Besides the study of books, the students are taught to till the soil, to build houses, and to perform other useful labor.

The location of the Madison school is excellent, and possesses great advantages for the school work. But the leaders in this work are carrying too heavy a burden, and should be relieved from the great anxiety that has rested upon them, because of a lack of means with which to do what must be done to provide suitable conditions for a successful school.

Shall we allow these workers to be burdened beyond their strength, carrying forward almost alone a work in which they should receive the hearty co-operation of their brethren.

I appeal to our brethren in South Dakota to help in this emergency, and make a liberal gift to the Madison School, that they may erect a chapel and school building. Such a building should have been provided from them long ago. Let us not leave these men to work under present disadvantages, when time is too precious, and the need for trained workers in the South is so great.

The work in the south has been sadly neglected. It is high time that our churches were awakened to their duty to this needy field. The light must shine forth amid the moral darkness of ignorance and superstition. The truth in its simplicity must be brought to those who are in ignorance.

In the common schools some things are taught that are a hindrance rather than a blessing. We need schools where the work of God is made the basis of education. The Madison Training School for teachers should have the hearty support of God's people. Therefore I ask you and your associates on the conference committee to act liberally in helping our brethren in Madison in this important work.

Ellen G. White.

Chapter 129—Support to Be Given Madison

Sanitarium, Napa, Co. Cal., Feb. 24, 1907.

Southern Union Conference Committee:

... It is in harmony with the leadings of God's Spirit that Brethren Sutherland and Magan and their associates have begun a work at Madison. The Lord has guided them in the selection of a location for the school. Had a small sanitarium been established in connection with the school, this would have been in the order of God, and these two institutions would have been a mutual help. This has not yet been done, but our brethren in Madison need not be discouraged.

I would say to our brethren in the Southern field, Let there be no restrictions laid on the Madison School to limit its work in the field of its operation. If Brethren Sutherland and Magan have promised not to draw students to their school from the Southern states, they should be freed from any such restrictions. Such a promise should never have been asked nor granted. I am instructed to say that there should be no restrictions limiting their freedom to draw students from the Southern field. There is need of such an institution as has been established near Nashville, and let no one endeavor to hinder the attendance of those who can at that school best receive the training that will fit them to labor in the Southern states, and in other mission fields.

At Berrien Springs Brethren Sutherland and Magan carried on a work of self-sacrifice. They did not leave the North because they had lost their influence: They went to the South because they saw the needs of that field. In their work in Madison they should have encouragement from these whom they have come to help. Those who have in charge the disbursement of funds coming to the Southern field, should not fail to render proportionate help to the Madison School.

In the Madison school students are taught how to till the soil, how to build houses and perform other lines of useful labor. These are some of the lines of work that the Lord instructed us to introduce into our schools in Australia. With a practical training, students will be taught to fill useful positions in many places. Skill in the common arts is a gift from God. He provides both the gift and the wisdom to use the gift aright.

Chapter 130—Encourage the Workers

Sanitarium, Napa Co., Cal., March 4, 1907.

I have been instructed that encouragement should be given to the work in the South, and that special help should come to the work in Nashville, Madison, and Huntsville.

At the school in Madison it has been necessary to work with the strictest economy that the educational work undertaken there might be carried forward. Let our brethren who have means remember this school and its needs.

A good work was done by Brethren Magan and Sutherland at Berrien Springs, and in their labors in that place they labored beyond their strength, imperilling their health, and even their lives. In their work at Madison, they are working too hard, and amid many difficulties. These brethren need not only our confidence, but also our help, that they may place the Madison School where it can accomplish the work that God designs it to do. I pray that the Lord will sanctify the understanding of our people that these men will not be left to so work as to sacrifice their health in what they are trying to do. I pray that teachers and students may have wisdom and courage to act well their part, and that they may be especially blessed in making the school a success.

It is impossible to make the Madison School what it should be unless it is given a liberal share in the means that shall be appropriated for the work in the South. Will our brethren act their part in the Spirit of Christ?

The neglected South is to be especially favored now, because of the neglect of the past. The atonement for the failure of the past to meet the needs of this field, should be full and ample. The institutions in the South that for years should have stood on vantage ground are now to be especially favored. The Huntsville school must be encouraged to enlarge its work. Every possible advantage should be given to these schools, that they may show what can be done in making the earth to yield her treasures. The Madison and Huntsville Schools are to be an object lesson to the people in their vicinity.

I was shown that there is danger of these schools being circumscribed in their plans and limited in their advantages. This should not be. Everything possible should be done to encourage the students who need the class of instruction that can be given at those schools, that they may go forth properly instructed to do a work for others who need the same education and training that they have received. Fields are opening in every side to the work that such laborers could do.

At Huntsville a sanitarium is needed in connection with the school. I am interested to see a building on that school farm, equipped for the treatment of the sick.

Can not the students at Madison and Huntsville be trained to sell the books, "Christ's Object Lessons" and "Ministry of Healing"? And will not many of our people join them in this work?

For the sick in and about Nashville, we should do all we can to put it on a solid basis. The work should be conducted in a simple way, but in a way that will recommend the truth. There are many places in the South open to our work; but by all means begin the work in the important cities, and carry the message now. "For thus saith the Lord of hosts, Yet once, it is a little while, and I will shake the heavens and the earth, and the sea, and the dry land; and I will shake all nations, and the desire of all nations will come; and I will fill this house with glory, saith the Lord of hosts."

Ellen G. White.

Chapter 131—The Right Use of Means

Sanitarium, Napa Co., Cal., March 10, 1907.

To the Directors of the Nashville Sanitarium and the Southern Union Conference Committee.

Dear Brethren:

During the night some matters were brought before me, which I was charged to present to you. We seemed to be in a Council meeting, where certain questions were being considered. One of these questions was the necessary arrangements to be made for the prosecution of the work at Huntsville.

A mistake is being made in the use of means in some parts of the field. The workers need to sit down and count the cost of the tower they are building, to know if they are able to finish it.

In the past the work in the South has been carried on by earnest effort and with limited means. Now more money than is necessary is being invested in building the sanitarium at Nashville. This will not leave a correct influence on the workers in other parts of the field. At this time, when there is so great need of help in many lines of the work, any extravagance in fitting up the Nashville Sanitarium will leave an impression on the workers and on others that will not be healthful. There is great need of means to support the workers in the field, and the strictest economy should be practised with every advance step that is taken. The tendency to invest large sums of money in the Nashville Sanitarium must be guarded against. There must not be a large showing in one place while very little interest is manifested in other places of great importance.

There is a great work to be accomplished at Huntsville, and a large demand for means in order to erect appropriate buildings and carry on a successful work there for the colored people. Again, at Madison help is needed in order to continue the educational work that has been established there. It would be a great advantage to the school in Madison if a food factory were put into operation in connection with the work of the school.

The school at Madison has been established in the order of the Lord, and it requires its share of help. Brethren Sutherland and Magan, in their work at Berrien Springs, overtaxed their physical powers, and both need to be guarded against laboring beyond their strength, at Madison. Brother Sutherland needs to guard himself very carefully, and keep near to the great Healer. Both these workers are to be appreciated by their fellow workers.

The needs of the different parts of the field should be considered fairly, and proportionate help given to each. It is not right that those who have been laboring under burdens for years, and whose health has been broken by their arduous work, should be left to struggle along almost unaided under a great load of perplexity.

The use of means in the sanitarium at Nashville should be considered in a Bible light, not a selfish light. Christian benevolence will lead to a study of the needs of every branch of the work, and a determination that each shall have its proper part. The time is passing, and the work of God in the earth will soon be accomplished. Upon the men who act a leading part in the various branches of the work a large degree of the Holy Spirit must rest in order that the work may be carried to completion in the Lord's own way. The Lord lives and reigns, and he has promised to guide his people with judgment if they will walk humbly with him.

The workers in the printing office, in the school, in the food factory, and in the sanitarium, should blend their interests in every other branch. All should realize that every department of these various lines of work is to be conducted according to the principles of the word of God, and that the workers are to labor under the guidance of his precious counsel. Not one thread of selfishness must be woven into the web; for the Lord will not regard with favor anything of this sort. "All ye are brethren;" and the work is one. There is need of daily conversion on the part of the workers if they would feel a true concern for the work as a whole.

When you come together for worship and to seek the Lord, it should be your one aim to honor him whose requirements are all equal and just. His will, declared to you in his word, is to be carried out to the letter. The rule of righteousness revealed in the lives of his professing people is to make them conspicuous. We are to live with an eye single to the glory of God, ever seeking to be Christians in every sense of the word.

These words were spoken by our Instructor: "You are to be under the control of God. Learn how to harmonize. Love as brethren; be pitiful; be courteous. God's commandments are just and equal. All his workers are to be honored as laborers together with God.

The varied interests of the work are to be built up with care. From this time onward responsibilities will rapidly increase. God's will, the perfect rule of righteousness, is to be revealed in your work. Commune often everyday with your God, and listen to the voice that says to you, "Be still, and know that I am God." As your responsibilities increase with the advancement of the message, temptations will also increase. As the magnitude of the work presses itself upon the soul, humble your hearts before God. Act faithfully your part in the work, and stand faithfully in your individual accountability before God. God is not a respecter of persons. He that doeth righteousness is righteous. A mere profession is of no value, and knowledge is of worth only as it is used righteously.

"Murmur not; repine not; covet not; quarrel not," our Instructor continued. When you are afflicted, look to the great physician. You have need to rejoice, and to humble yourselves before the Lord. By indulging a selfish spirit, men become narrow and shortsighted; and then they fail to read from cause to effect. The word of the Lord is to be your guide in all things. "The Lord is in his holy temple; let all the earth keep silence before Him."

By the figure of the vine and the branches, Christ illustrated not only the relation that should exist between him and his followers, but also the union between every believer and his fellow believer. The branches of the vine are related to each other; but they are not alike. Each has its own individuality, which can not be merged into that of another, but all have a special connection with each other. The root that supplies nourishment to one branch supplies nourishment to every other branch. Each must depend alike on the vine for sustenance; all must be joined to the parent stalk. The life and growth and fruitfulness of each depend alike on the parent vine. In obedience to the laws of nature, their common hold of the true vine make them one; in their diversity there is unity.

The lesson of the vine and its branches holds a deep meaning for the workers in the cause of God. Every worker is to draw his strength from the same Source; and while the individuality of each is to be maintained, unity and harmony is to be preserved. When this spirit of oneness pervades the work, our institutions throughout the world will be united in their interests, while the individuality of any one of them will not be merged into that of any other one.

In the past it was urged by some that the interests of the cause would be furthered by a consolidation of our publishing institutions, bringing them all virtually under one management. This the Lord positively instructed us should not be. It is not the purpose of God to centralize in this way, bringing all the interests of one branch of the work under the management of a comparatively few men. In his great purpose of advancing the cause of truth in the earth, He designs that every part of his work shall blend with every other part. The workers are to draw together in the spirit of Christ. In their diversity, they are to preserve unity. One institution is not to be brought under the control of another, but all are to exercise their powers harmoniously. The work of direction is to be left with the great Manager, while obedience to the work of the Lord is to be the aim of all His workers.

In the different places where the work is established, it will often be small in its beginning. Then it will grow. This is represented by the prophet Ezekiel under the figure of water issuing from under the threshold of the house.

"Afterward he brought me again unto the door of the house, and, behold, waters issued out from under the threshold of the house eastward; for the forefront of the house stood toward the east, and the waters came down from under from the right side of the house, at the south side of the altar. Then brought he me out of the gate northward, and led me about the way without unto the outer gate by the way that looketh eastward; and, behold, there ran out waters on the right side."

These waters signify the gospel of Christ which went forth from Jerusalem and spread to all countries. The gifts and power of the Holy Spirit which accompanied the work caused it to yield great results.

"Then said he unto me, These waters issue out toward the east country, and go down into the desert, and go into the sea; which being brought forth into the sea, the waters shall be healed. And it shall come to pass that everything that liveth, which moveth, whithersoever the river shall come, shall live; and there shall be a very great multitude of fish, because these waters shall come higher; for they shall be healed; and everything shall live whither the river cometh. . . And by the river upon the bank thereof, one this side and on that, shall grow all trees for meat, whose leaf shall not fade, neither shall the fruit thereof be consume; it shall bring forth new fruit according to its months, because their waters they issued out of the sanctuary, and the fruit thereof shall be for meat, and the leaf thereof for medicine."

There is to be much more extensive work done in the future than has been done in the past. Had selfishness been entirely put away from the lives of the workers, we as a people would stand before God today in large numbers, ever one as true as steel to the principles of the word. The Lord now calls upon the men chosen for his work to stand as one man for the advancement of the cause of Christ. In their diversity of gifts and callings there is to be seen the unity represented by the figure of the vine and the branches.

Ellen G. White.

Chapter 132—A Broader Work

April 1, 1907.

"The sacrifices of God are a broken spirit; a broken and a contrite heart, O God, thou wilt not despise. Do good in Thy good pleasure unto Zion; build thou the walls of Jerusalem. Then shalt thou be pleased with the sacrifices of righteousness, with burnt offering and whole burnt offering; then shall they offer bullocks upon thine altar."

I have been shown that in the opening of new fields too much pride has often been manifested by our workers. In our work in the Southern field, we have kept too much to ourselves. Our efforts ought not to have been so closely confined to our own institutions. The light given me, and which I have given to our people, is that if workers of experience and wisdom would visit the colored schools established in Nashville and different places, and manifest an interest in their work, our workers would be invited to speak to the colored people in many places, and could thus impart to them precious truths that they do not understand. An excellent work has been done by these schools, and in drawing apart from them, we are not following the Lord's plan. An earnest sympathy should exist between our teachers and other teachers of colored schools in the South.

When the question of our establishing a printing plant in the Southern states was being considered, I was shown that the very existence of the large educational institutions for colored people in Nashville made it a favorable place for the opening of our work; for in these schools lay opportunities for building up the cause of present truth. In failing to manifest an interest in the work of the colored schools, and to become acquainted with the work they were doing, an advantage was lost that might have been used to remove much prejudice. A judicious effort to open up to the teachers in these large institutions the principles and plans of our educational work, would have been productive of much good. Young men of firm principles should be selected to attend these schools, and watch for opportunities to drop the seeds of truth into the hearts of the teachers. And our missionaries could learn much in these institutions.

I was also instructed that in the South a first class sanitarium should be erected where the colored people can be treated by hygienic methods, and where many youth can be trained to be skillful nurses and teachers of the gospel of Christ. Our people in the South must be quick in laying hold of advantages that are needed there. The true missionary spirit must be cherished in the hearts of all our workers. We have a school at Huntsville.

If we are wise, we will make very decided efforts that the work of this school may be strengthened, and conducted in no inferior way.

We need to be less diffident about making known our needs to those who can help us in carrying forward the work. The Lord will surely acknowledge determined efforts made to help the people who are in need of help. We should study carefully the second chapter of Nehemiah which records Nehemiah's request of the king, and the king's liberal response to his plea. The experiences of Nehemiah teach us that God does not prohibit his people from asking men in power for favors to advance the cause of God. Much more might be received for the advancement of the cause of God from men who have abundant resources, if the Lord's servants would lay their necessities before them. In the work of erecting sanitariums and school buildings in foreign countries God designs that the highest authorities shall be appealed to for assistance. This work should be done with prudence, taking care to present it as something that is being done for the benefit of the people, and as a work of God.

To those workers who are preparing to be teachers, I would say, Begin to work in a humble way as missionaries for God. Bear in mind the example of those who for the sake of the truth are subjecting themselves to all manner of inconveniences in foreign fields,-- to the hardships of an unsuitable climate and to the opposition of people of an idolatrous faith. God asks you to begin your mission work at home. Those who are seeking to be first, need to humble their hearts before God. Let each one take up the missionary work that lies neglected at his very door. The Lord calls for laborers for our cities. Every true believer has a message.

In visions of the night I seemed to be in a large congregation of our people in Nashville. One of authority stood before us. Reaching out His hand, he turned himself in every direction, saying, There is missionary work to be done in all the settlements about Nashville. There are among you those who should exercise their inventive faculties to devise plans for reaching the perishing souls whom you have neglected. When you take up the work that should be done in needy settlements right within your borders, the presence of the Lord will be with you, and angels will go before you. Your faculties will develop and your capabilities for work increase. And from Nashville you will pass to other cities to do the work that is waiting to be done. There is dearth of men and dearth of means; but when the missionary spirit shall be awakened, and you take hold of the work wherever you see souls hungering for the truth, then you will grow in grace and efficiency. There is work for all who want to work in the way Christ worked.

"Who among you," said the heavenly Messenger, "have tried to come into connection with the colored schools, that they might become acquainted with the teachers? How many have you converted to obedience to the truth?" The Lord is not pleased with the young men and the middle aged men who have felt no burden for the souls who are right around them. God desires that His servants shall explain the truths of his word in the darkest as well as in the most enlightened places. Consecration to God and prayer, earnest prayer, must be blended with the work.

So little genuine missionary work is being done, so little of the missionary spirit is being cultivated, that the Lord is displeased. The great cities of the South lie unworked. Those who feel no desire to educate themselves for missionary work need a new conversion.

Our young men and young women need a more pronounced experience in the work of God. Those who have learned the truths of the word must not be unwilling to place themselves in trying places in order to meet the people where they are. Work is waiting everywhere, and it is not all of the most pleasant kind. The Lord calls for young men who have cultivated a spirit of cheerfulness to go forth to convince others of the possibility of maintaining cheerfulness and refinement amid the most unfavorable circumstances. The message of truth must be given by means of practical missionary effort. Wake up, brethren, wake up. Watch and pray, and consecrate yourselves to the great work that is waiting to be done.

You who have educated yourselves in a love of criticism have lost the love of beauty and holiness out of your lives. Arouse, and rid yourselves of these hindrances to progress in the Christian life. When you feel disposed to criticize the work of some of your brethren, take hold yourselves of the hardest work you can find to be done, and do it in Christ's name. This you will find to be a most valuable education.

The children of God should never be rough and discourteous in their bearing toward one another. They should never blame and condemn. To those who want to give vent to a spirit of faultfinding, I would say, Go out among the rocks and stumps, and there relieve your mind of its evil thoughts; for these inanimate objects will not be harmed by your words. Only your own soul will suffer. After you have talked it all out, consider that it is written in the books of heaven what manner of spirit you are of. Then come to God with a broken heart and a contrite spirit, confess your need, and plead for his grace to make you one of his humble children. Let the ambition you have be exercised in a way that will bless needy souls.

There are some who need to give expression to their religion in a different way than they have done in the past. They need to be ashamed of their past course of action, their lack of consecration and love, and to be reconverted. Then they will take hold humbly of any part of the work that needs their help. They need to learn how to pray and work for souls. The truth for these last days is to be proclaimed by purified human lips. When the live coal from the altar shall touch the lips of the believers, and they have been refined and purified by the Holy Spirit of God, then God can entrust them with his solemn message, and use them to glorify his name. Then they can teach transgressors the way of the Lord, and sinners will be converted unto him.

Ellen G. White.

Chapter 133—A Missionary Field

Sanitarium, Cal., April 17, 1907.

Elder J. S. Washburn,

Dear Brother Washburn:

I have just received and read your letter, in which you tell me about your visits to the colleges in Nashville. I am so glad that you are beginning to understand why our work should be located in Nashville. A wide interest should be manifested for the colored people. We ought to have in Nashville a first-class sanitarium established for the colored people, that shall be conducted by physicians and workers who will do their work wisely. The colored people of the South are to become educated workers; through the reception of the gospel they are to become teachers of the gospel to their own people.

Brother Washburn, you and your colaborers should ever bear in mind that you are in a missionary field where a grand, all-round work is to be done for God. The heathen are right about you. Should you follow the course that has been pursued in the past toward the colored people, you would not fulfill your duty. The Lord calls for missionary work to be done. Those who make the South their field of labor are not to perpetuate the prejudice that has existed in the past against the colored people. The teachers of the truth are to labor for this neglected race, and by their efforts win the respect, not only of the colored people, but of the workers in other denominations. May the Lord bless you in this work, is my earnest prayer.

The words that Christ spoke to his disciples when he sent them forth the first time, will apply to the experiences of the worker today. "Behold," he said, "I send you forth as sheep in the midst of wolves." You will need to understand how to meet all classes. "Be ye therefore wise as serpents, and harmless as doves." "He that spared not his own Son, but delivered him up for us all (black as well as white), how shall he not," the apostle asks, "with him also freely give us all things?" Well might the apostle also ask, How shall we not all freely give him our most devoted service?

We need to study the life of him who, though he was rich, yet for our sakes become poor, that we through his poverty might be made rich. Then we shall not be unwilling to give kind, disinterested labor to those who need it.

Do not lose interest in the work for the colored people. Do not rest until sanitarium work is established for them, both at the Huntsville school and at Nashville. In the past much labor has been given to this people under the most trying circumstances; and you should not overlook what has been done by the hardest kind of labor. Do not ignore what has been done, but unite your sympathies with the sympathies and labors of those who have gone before you and prepared the way. God help you, and give you wisdom to know how to treat your fellow workers. Christian instrumentality is a wonderful thing. If its place in the divine economy is appreciated as it should be, the workers will appreciate more than they do what has been accomplished in the Southern field.

When I first visited the South, I learned many things regarding the work that has been done there, and when I can do so, I will have a history of that work published. Those who did not take part in it can not fully understand how much of self-denial and sacrifices is called for.

I hope you will follow up the work begun in Nashville, for there is much to be done for all classes in that city. Give special attention to the colleges established there. Much labor has been expended in educational lines of work by other denominations.

We must not treat the colored people as though God has not a message for them. Become acquainted with the teachers. Encourage them in their work, and take a part with them in their labors when this is possible. The gospel in its simplicity is to be presented to this people. If you will labor in the spirit of Christ, conversions to the truth will be the result of this work.

Ellen G. White.

Chapter 134—All Ye Are Brethren

Sanitarium, Cal., April 18, 1907.

Elder J. S. Washburn, Dear Brother:

I am sorry that you should make any excuse for withholding your sympathy from the workers in Madison. It is true that they have made some mistakes; but they have confessed their errors with brokenness of heart, and have done what they could to rectify their mistakes. After I had pointed out to them their wrong, and they had confessed it, we prayed together, and the Spirit of the Lord rested upon them. Then I could say to them, The Lord has pardoned your transgression.

My brother, you would have had evidence of this, if you had taken pains to see them often and bind up their sympathies with yours. It was your privilege, instead of judging them, to speak to them kindly; instead of treating them with suspicion, to give them your kindness and sympathy and love.

You have been represented to me as holding yourself aloof from these brethren. Had you gone to them in the spirit of Christ, and studied with them the needs of the field, you would have said, These brethren need some of the means we are handling. Had you inquired into their needs, and advocated the dividing with them of the means given for the work in that field, considering that "All ye are brethren," you would have done a work well pleasing to the Lord. Those who withdraw their sympathy and help from their fellow laborers, God will deal with in a way to show them his displeasure.

God does not require his servants all to work in precisely the same way. Each worker should thank God that he has a part in the Lord's vineyard, and each should believe that the Lord is leading his brother workers as verily as he believes that the Lord is leading him. The words of Christ, "All ye are brethren," should ever be kept in mind. The spirit that leads workers to measure themselves among themselves, and to estimate the value of the workers according to human judgment, is not the spirit of Christ.

Wherever you labor, come close to your brethren. Bear in mind that the Holy Spirit is the converter and sanctifier of the soul. The power of the Father, the Son, and the Holy Spirit is pledged to every believer, to preserve unity and love, and to sustain him in his labor for the recovery of lost souls. When we are with Christ, we will co-operate harmoniously for the salvation of souls. There is no miracle of mercy unperformed, no angel left undirected, that is necessary for the work of uniting God's people in the grand work of saving souls.

The Madison School needs our help just as truly as help was needed for the sanitarium. The brethren connected with that school have done excellent work. In their efforts to combine manual labor with other school work, all have gained a valuable experience. The Lord has not been pleased with your indifference toward the school.

The Madison School is in the very place to which we were directed by the Lord, in order that it might have an influence and make a right impression upon the people. The Lord has been dishonored by the indifferent treatment given to the workers in this school by their fellow workers. They need encouragement and good wholesome fellowship, and they are as verily deserving of it as are other workers in the Southern field.

Ellen G. White.

Chapter 135—The Work God Has Appointed

Loma Linda, Cal., May 14, 1907.

Prof. P. T. Magan,

Dear Brother Magan:

I bear positive testimony that you and your fellow workers in Madison are doing the work that God has appointed to you. There was at first in your mind a question regarding this, but as you have advanced, you have been able to see the way of the Lord more clearly.

The attitude of opposition or indifference on the part of some of your brethren has created conditions that have made your work more difficult than it should have been. You have not received from some many words of encouragement, but the Lord is pleased that you have not been easily discouraged.

Some have entertained the idea that because the school at Madison is not owned by a conference organization, those who are in charge of the school should not be permitted to call upon our people for the means that is greatly needed to carry on their work. This idea needs to be corrected. In the distribution of the money that comes into the Lord's treasury, you are entitled to a portion just as verily as are those connected with other needy enterprises that are carried forward in harmony with the Lord's instruction.

The Lord Jesus will one day call to account those who would so tie your hands that it is almost impossible for you to move in harmony with the Lord's biddings. "The silver and the gold is mine, saith the Lord, and the cattle upon a thousand hills."

You and your associates are not novices in educational work, and when you are in stress for means with which to advance the work, you are just as much entitled to ask for that which you need as are other men to present the necessities of the work in which they are engaged.

You have in the past done much to bring means into circulation in the work of God. And you need not now feel troubled about accepting gifts and free-will offerings; for you will need them in the work of preparing young men and women to labor in the Lord's vineyard. As you carry on this work in harmony with the Lord's will, you are not to be kept on a constant strain to know how to secure the means you need in order to go forward. The Lord forbids the setting up of walls and bands around workers of experience who are faithfully acting their God-appointed part.

Much precious time has been lost because man-made rules and restrictions have been sometimes placed above the plans and purposes of God. In the name of the Lord I appeal to our conference workers to strengthen and support and labor in harmony with our brethren at Madison, who are carrying forward a work that God has appointed them.

Ellen G. White.

Chapter 136—The Right of Way to the Footstool of Christ

Sanitarium, Cal., Aug. 29, 1907.

To Elder Geo. W. Reaser, and the Ministers in Southern Calif.

Dear Brother Reaser:

The Lord has revealed to me that in your work as president of the Southern California Conference, you are in danger of embracing too much responsibility. Some time ago the Lord showed me that if you were placed in office, you would attempt to rule in every branch of the work, but that this was not to be permitted, because you have not the judgment to deal with all lines of work, and because God has chosen especially qualified workers for certain lines of his work.

Because of a wrong comprehension of the duties of your office, the work in your field has become sadly confused in the past two years. You have accepted responsibilities that should not have been placed upon you. Because you were president of the conference, you considered yourself to be in a certain sense the manager of the work of the Loma Linda Sanitarium, and that it was your duty to see that matters there were conducted according to your ideas. I am bidden to say to you that you are not qualified to take the control of the sanitarium work.

Elder Burden has been given this work, and he has good helpers and advisers in the workers who are associated with him The Lord appointed Elder Burden to the position he occupies, and he is to bear his responsibilities in that position without interference. He is fully capable of doing the work that has been given him to do. The Lord has not told you to watch and criticize, and interfere with his work. He bids you, my brother, to stand out of the way. Elder Burden has proved in the past that he can do his work acceptably. He is to stand in his lot and place, exercising his God-given right to ask wisdom of Him who giveth to all men liberally and upbraideth not.

It is a mistake for a conference to select as president one who considers that his office places unlimited power in his hands. The Lord has instructed me to tell you that you do not know when to use authority, and when to refrain from using it unwisely. You have much to learn before you can do the work of a conference president intelligently. You are to bear in mind that in the cause of God there is a chief Director, whose power and wisdom is above that of human minds.

God will have nothing to do with the methods of working where finite men are allowed to bear rule over their fellowmen. He calls for a decided change to be made. The voice of command must no longer be heard. The Lord has among his workers men of humility and discretion; from these should be chosen men who will conduct the work in the fear of God.

It would be well if Elder Cottrell and at least one other worker of broad experience should be called upon the consult together and consider your plans that affect the medical work. God designs that his servants shall carry the responsibilities of the conference in a spirit of humility and dependance upon Him.

It is a dangerous work to invest men with authority to judge and rule their fellowmen. Not to you nor to any other man has been given power to control the actions of God's people, and the effort to do this must be no longer continued. God has been dishonored by the education that has been given to the churches in Southern California in looking to one man as conscience and judgment for them. God has never authorized any man to exercise a ruling power over his fellow workers; and those who have allowed a dictatorial spirit to come into their official work need to experience the converting power of God upon their hearts. They have placed man where God should be.

When men engage in labor for the souls of others, they are not to be made amenable to the will of their fellow laborers. God is well able to direct the course of action of those who work for Him. But when his laborers, instead of calling upon him, seek first, and regard as of first importance, the counsel and advice of human minds, he is dishonored. The method of sending one minister to another minister to learn his duty is a plan of working that should not be encouraged. Greater evils will result from such a course than finite and erring man can foresee.

My brother, God lives and reigns. Let your brethren have the right of way to the footstool of Christ. Encourage them to carry their burdens to the Lord, and not to any human being. Never take the responsibility of becoming conscience for another. As brethren, you can counsel together, and pray together, and seek instruction from the Source of all wisdom; but you are not to seek to direct another regarding his duty. Let all work of this character be done away. God forbids that this spirit shall again come into his work while time shall last.

Chapter 137—Go Not to Human Agencies

Sanitarium, Cal., Oct. 3, 1907.

Elder Reaser,

257 South Hill Street, Los Angeles, Cal.

My Brother:

I have read your letters, but can not possibly answer them fully now. You would misunderstand me if I should write. If I attend the Los Angeles meeting, I can then communicate to you and to others. I have much to say. Until then make no decided moves.

In the last few days I have written many letters to Australia, to Washington, and to other places. Not all that I have written has been sent. I am not able to sleep for the burdens I carry for the many places where souls are in peril. The cases of some have been especially urged upon me. Satan is playing the game of life for their souls. I can not let them make decisions that will place them in the power of Satanic agencies. By giving them a plain and decided message, God may use my words to save them.

For a long time I have seen the danger that was coming into our ranks in the tendency to look to human wisdom and to depend on human guidance. This will always prove a snare to souls, and I am bidden to lift the danger signal, warning my fellow workers against it, and pointing them to the Lord Jesus. The man or woman who leans upon the wisdom of the human mind, leans on a broken reed.

I am instructed to point those who are in need of wisdom to the Lamb of God which taketh away the sin of the world. "He was in the world, and the world was made by him; and the world knew him not. He came unto his own, and his own received him not. But as many as received him, to them gave he power to become the sons of God, even to them that believe on his name." "If any man lack wisdom, let him ask of God, that giveth to all men liberally and upbraideth not, and it shall be given him. But let him ask in faith, nothing wavering; for he that wavereth is like a wave of the sea, driven with the wind and tossed; for let not that man think that he shall receive anything of the Lord. A double-minded man is unstable in all his ways. Blessed is the man that endureth temptation; for when he is tried, he shall receive the crown of life, which the Lord hath promised to them that love him."

"Ask and it shall be given you," the Saviour declared; "Seek, and ye shall find; knock, and it shall be opened unto you; for everyone that asketh receiveth, and he that seeketh findeth, and to him that knocketh it shall be opened. Or what man is there, if his son ask bread, will he give him a stone: or if he ask a fish, will he give him a serpent? If ye then being evil know how to give good gifts unto your children, how much more shall your Father which is in heaven give good things to them that ask Him? Therefore whatsoever ye would that men should do to you, do ye even so then; for this is the law and the prophets.

"Enter ye in at the strait gate: for wide is the gate, and broad is the way, that leadeth to destruction, and many there be that go in thereat; because strait is the gate, and narrow is the way, which leadeth unto life, and few there be that find it."

Never should a worker encourage one who is in need of instruction and help to go first to human agencies for an understanding of his duty. It is our privilege as laborers to pray together and to counsel together; but we are individually to seek God to know what he would have us do. When the Lord impresses the mind of one of his servants that he is to go to a certain place to labor, that man is not under obligation to go to a human being to know if it is right for him to do this.

It is a wrong education to teach our people to lean on human aids, instead of going to the Lord in prayer. The enemy of souls has been the instigator of this, that minds might become obscured. The people are not to be instructed differently. God's people are to meet together in counsel, but no leader or worker is to take the position that God's children are to make no move until he is first consulted. Those who bear responsibilities in the work are to co-operate with heavenly angels in teaching men and women to look to God as the source of their strength.

"Wherefore (as the Holy Ghost saith, Today if ye will hear his voice harden not your hearts, as in the provocation, in the day of temptation in the wilderness, when your fathers tempted me, proved me, and saw my works forty years. Wherefore I was grieved with that generation, and said, They do always err in their heart; and they have not known my ways. So I sware in my wrath. They shall not enter into my rest) take heed, brethren, lest there be in any of you an evil heart of unbelief, in departing from the living God. But exhort one another daily, while it is called today; lest any of you be hardened through the deceitfulness of sin. For we are made partakers of Christ, if we hold the beginning of our confidence steadfast unto the end; while it is said, Today, if ye will hear his voice, harden not your hearts, as in the provocation. For some, when they had heard, did provoke; how-be-it not all that came out of Egypt by Moses. But with whom was he grieved forty years? Was it not with them that had sinned, whose carcasses fell in the wilderness? And with whom sware he that they should not enter into his rest, but to them that believed not? So we see that they could not enter in because of unbelief.

"God who at sundry times and in diverse manners spake in times past unto the fathers by the prophets, hath in these last days spoken unto us by his Son, whom he hath appointed heir of all things; by whom also he made the worlds; who being the brightness of his glory, and the express image of his person, and upholding all things by the word of his power, when he had by himself purged our sins, sat down on the right hand of the majesty on high. Being made so much better than the angels, as He hath by inheritance obtained a more excellent name than they.... But to which of the angels said He at any time, Sit on my right hand, until I make thine enemies thy footstool? Are they not all ministering spirits, sent forth to minister unto them that shall be heirs of salvation?"

The ministration of Christ is ever to be kept before the minds of the people; His efficiency is that to which they should ever be directed. Ministers in word and doctrine are not to seek in human wisdom to supply the necessities of these souls; they are not to direct and guide. By doing this, they educate the flock of God to depend on human beings who are liable to err. "If any man lack wisdom, let him ask of God, that giveth to all men liberally, and upbraideth not; and it shall be given him. But let him ask in faith, nothing wavering." Here is marked out a straight path to the world's Redeemer, which every soul may take. Christ tasted death that every man might be partaker of the blessings of the gospel. Then let all, experienced and inexperienced, be directed to the source of all efficiency and power. Christ has promised to be our wisdom, our righteousness, our sanctification and redemption.

Elder Reaser, my message to you is, Consecrate yourself to the Lord Jesus Christ. Seek the One who understands your every weakness, and who never makes a mistake. He is able to impart to you his rich grace. Looking unto Jesus, studying his Word, learn to humble your soul before God and to wrestle in prayer with him.

It is not the position you may hold in the work that determines your efficiency. A high position will not change the character or increase the moral worth. It is written, "Thou madest him a little lower than the angels; thou crownedest him with glory and honor, and dist set him over the works of thine hands; thou hast put all things in subjection under his feet. For in that he put all things in subjection under him, he left nothing that is not put under him. But we see Jesus, who was made a little lower than the angels, crowned with glory and honor; that he by the grace of God should taste death for every man. For it became him, for whom are all things, and by whom are all things, in bringing many sons to glory, to make the captain of their salvation perfect through sufferings. For both he that sanctifieth and they that are sanctified, are all of one; for which cause he is not ashamed to call them brethren, saying, I will declare thy name unto my brethren; in the midst of the church will I sing praise unto thee."

The all-sufficiency of the Saviour is brought to view in this Scripture. He experienced in his human nature all that we can possibly experience. Taking our nature, and in the strength that his humanity received from God, he coped successfully with the powers of Satan and fallen angels. He bids his servants learn of him. "Come unto me, all ye that labor and are heavy laden," He invites, "and I will give you rest. Take my yoke upon you and learn of me; for I am meek and lowly in heart, and ye shall find rest unto your souls. For my yoke is easy, and my burden is light." Learn of Christ. As you study his personal life, and practice his works you will find rest to your soul.

I am bidden to say to every professing child of God, Go not to human agencies to learn your duty. Take your case to the One who has tasted death for every man. "In all things it behooved Him to be made like unto his brethren, that he might be a faithful and merciful high priest in things pertaining to God, to make reconciliation for the sins of the people. For in that he himself hath suffered, being tempted, he is able to succor them that are tempted."

The worker who considers himself in a position of such high responsibility that he allows the members of the churches to look up to him to voice their decisions and control their actions, if educating men and women to wear a human yoke. They are not learning of the divine teacher. To the one who is being led to have such an experience, I would say, Go to Christ: ask Him to give you an experience; learn to emulate his faultless character, and do not look for experiences of guidance to any human being, who is as liable to err as yourself.

There are reasons why we should not put our trust in men who are placed in positions of large responsibility. It is often difficult for them to maintain a humble and teachable spirit. They suppose that their position gives them the power to control their fellows, and they flatter themselves, as did Peter, that they will not fall under temptation. When in the hour of his trial Christ declared to his disciples that they would all forsake him, Peter answered, "Lord, why can not I follow thee now? I will lay down my life for thy sake. Jesus answered him, Wilt thou lay down they life for my sake? Verily, verily I say unto thee, the cock shall not crow till thou hast denied me thrice." Throughout his trial Christ preserved his humility. Peter's self-confident assertion was tested, and he failed to endure the test. He denied his Lord in the hour of temptation.

I am instructed to present these words before the workers in Los Angeles and at Paradise Valley. Man is not to be depended on as a model in speech or in plans. If it is possible, there should be chosen to fill the responsible positions in a conference, men who will not lead others to depend upon them, but will lead all to make the life of Christ their study, and their pattern. Christ ever manifested a heavenly courtesy in dealing with human souls. His life was a life of constant self-denial and self-sacrifice. Those who are numbered with the overcomers will be those who have practiced the virtues of Christ. My heart has been made sick and sore when I have seen the example set by those who have loved to dictate and control; and I have said, If this wrong continues in spite of the warnings that have been given, I shall have no courage regarding their meeting successfully the great conflict that is before us.

Chapter 138—Health Reform Essential for These Times

Loma Linda, Cal., November 1907.

Dear Brother and Sister Kress:

... I have written out some instruction to ministers and physicians in regard to the subject of health reform. I have been shown that the example of some of our leading workers is not a healthful or praiseworthy example. They are losing ground, backsliding from the principles of health reform, and this is having its effect upon the church members. These brethren are very conscientious is some matters, but on points where they should be very strict, they are very slack. The Lord has instructed me to tell them that their example in the home and in the church and with those whom they visit, is causing the people to lose confidence in the light that God has given on this subject.

The light that God has given on the subject of health reform is very essential for these times. There is no one thing that men and women in these days need to be more earnestly impressed with than that of the importance of guarding the appetite. One of the reasons why we have our sanitariums is that we may bring the blessing of health before the world. O that we might see every representative of present truth exerting a wholesome influence in every line upon which light has been given.

Individually we have a work to do in our own borders. If each member of the body of Christ would attend to his God-given work, a much sweeter atmosphere would pervade our churches. The Lord is not pleased with the backslidden state of his people in regard to health reform. If they do not arouse to the need of heeding the light on health reform, they will soon fail to see the importance of other phases of the message.

When in Australia, Brother Kress, you lay trembling between life and death.-- Was the message given me for you, Return to a diet of flesh meats? No, no. God gave you directions regarding a healthful diet, which if diligently followed, would, mingled with the exercise of faith and prayer, save your life. The Lord foresaw that as a physician in one of our sanitariums, you would be a teacher of the principles of health reform. You were working hard, Dr. Kress, and you did not give yourself proper rest and nourishment. The Lord permitted you to come to the very brink of collapse that you might be guided by his instruction. He has never bidden any minister or physician to break down the barrier of correct eating in order to save life.

I feel very grateful for the light God has given me on health reform. In several cases when the adoption of health reform has been carried to extremes, and life has been endangered because of the limited supply of nourishment taken, the Lord has shown to me the course to follow in order to save life. Through his instruction telling me what to do, several lives have been saved, when physicians and nurses were unable to bring relief. When they have come to me for counsel, light has been given in the visions of the night. The prescriptions given were carried out, and the persons were raised up and lived for many years. The lives of some of those who were thus saved have been of a character to bring honor to the name of the Lord.

God permitted the flesh of dead animals to be eaten by the ancients, although he knew by so doing the lives of men would be shortened. But when he brought his chosen people from the land of Egypt, he did not give them flesh to eat, but fed them with the bread of heaven. When they murmured against their heaven-appointed food and asked for flesh, God sent them quails; but the consequence of their rebellion were speedily felt. They ate to excess of the meat thus provided, and while the flesh was yet between their teeth many of them died. Our people would do well to study this experience of the children of Israel, and learn the lesson that it teaches

Light has been given me that some of our ministers and leading workers are working against the light of health reform. They are indulging in the use of flesh meats and other harmful things. Those who for years have had the Testimonies before them are without excuse. Many need to make decided reforms, for those who have left our ranks make this an occasion of charging our people with unbelief in the Testimonies. God calls for thorough work on the part of professed believers, that he may be able to impress minds and hearts.

Ellen G. White.

Chapter 139—To Those Bearing Responsibilities in Washington and Other Centers

Elmshaven, Sanitarium, Cal., Jan. 6, 1908.

God has given me a message for the men who are carrying large responsibilities in Washington and other centers of the work. This is a time when the work of God should be conducted with the greatest wisdom, unselfishness, and the strictest integrity by every conference; a time when there should be the closest observance of the law of God on the part of every worker; a walking and working under the guidance of the Holy Spirit.

God needs men and women who will work in the simplicity of Christ to bring the knowledge of truth before those who need its converting power. But when a precise line is laid down which the workers must follow in their efforts to proclaim the message, a limit is set to the usefulness of a great number of workers. I am charged to speak, saying, God seeth not as man seeth. Those who occupy responsible positions need to place a lower estimate upon the value of human wisdom and to esteem more highly the sanctification of the Spirit revealed in the lowliness and gentleness of Christ. They need to have the Holy Spirit come into their hearts and minds, to control their wills and to sanctify their tongues. When soul and mind and body are converted to God, our physical strength and our desires will become working agencies for God. When the converting power of God transforms the life, we shall be educated by God himself to speak his words and work his works.

When soul and mind and body are converted to God, our physical strength and our desires will become working agencies for God. When the converting power of God transforms the life, we shall be educated by God himself to speak his words and work his works.

The law of God is to be magnified. Its claims must be presented by our workers, in our books and papers, and through the spoken word. The knowledge of its holy character is to become widespread. The message of Christ's righteousness must be proclaimed from one end of the earth to the other. Our people are to be aroused to prepare the way of the Lord. The third angel's message--the last message of mercy to a perishing world--is so sacred, so glorious. Let the light go forth as a lamp that burneth. Mysteries into which angels have desired to look, which prophets and kings and righteous men desired to know, the church of God is now to unfold.

An Illustration

Ezekiel writes: (Here is quoted Ezekiel 47:1-1.)

This presentation is an illustration of the way in which the truth for this time is to go. A large work is to be done by many who have commenced in a small way. Many souls will be reached, not through display, not through any devising on the part of man, but because of the working of the Holy Spirit on the hearts of the human agencies. The Saviour worked in this way. When His methods become the methods of his followers, his blessing will attend their labors. Let us always remember that our schools are not to be conducted after the worldly plan.

The Work of the Madison School

In the work being done at the training school for home and foreign missionary teachers in Madison, Tennessee, and in the small schools established by the teachers who have gone forth from Madison, we have an illustration of a way in which the message should be carried. I would say to the workers there, Continue to learn of Christ. Do not be daunted. Be free in the Lord; be free. Much acceptable work has been done in Madison. The Lord says to you, Go forward. Your school is to be an example of how Bible study, general education, physical education, and sanitarium work may be combined in many smaller schools that shall be established in simplicity in many places in the Southern states.

My brethren in responsible places, mourn not over the work that is being done at Madison to train workers to go forth into the highways and the hedges. It is the will of God that this work should be done. Let us cease to criticize the servants of God, and humble our own hearts before the Lord. Let us strengthen this company to continue the good work in which they are engaged, and labor to encourage others to do a similar work. Then the light of truth will be carried in a simple and effective way, and a great work will be accomplished for the Master in a short time.

When the Lord favors any of his servants with worldly advantages, it is that they may use those advantages for the benefit of the work. As laborers together with God, men are to keep constantly in mind the need of giving the message of Christ's soon coming to the people who have not been warned. In this we are not left to human intelligence alone, for angels of God are waiting to encourage us in a life of patience and self-denial. We are to learn to be content with simple food and clothing, that we may save much to be invested in the work of the gospel.

The gospel of Christ calls for entire consecration. The Christian sower is to go forth to sow. But many by their fretting and contentions are disqualifying themselves for labor. Their sluggish senses do not discern how feeble are their efforts, and how strong is their unbelief. Let our church members now arise to their responsibilities and privileges. Let them spend less on self-indulgence and needless adorning. The money thus expended is the Lord's, and is needed to do a sacred work in his cause. Educate the children to do missionary work, and to bring their offerings to God. Let us awake to our need of denying self. Let us awake to a sense of the spiritual character of the work in which we profess to be engaged.

I have said only a little in comparison with what might be said on this subject. But I call on our ministers, our teachers, and our physicians to awake out of sleep, and see the opportunities for work that are within their reach, but which for years have been allowed to pass unimproved.

Our lack of self-denial, our refusal to see the necessities of the cause at this time, and to respond to them, call for repentance and humiliation of heart before God. It is a sin for one who knows the truth of God to fold his hands and transfer his duty to another.

It is a sin for any to criticize and find fault with those who in their manner of working do not exactly meet their mind. Let none blame or censure the men who have labored at Madison. In the place of complaining at your brother's work, take up your own neglected work. Instead of picking flaws in your brother's character, search your own heart, confess your sins, and act honestly with God. Let there be condemnation of self for the work that lies undone all about you. Instead of placing impediments in the way of those who are trying to accomplish something in the South, let our eyes be opened to see that time is passing, and that there is much for you to do.

The Lord works through various agencies. If there are those who desire to step into new fields and take up new lines of labor, encourage them to do so. Seventh-day Adventists are doing a great and good work; let no man's hand be raised to hinder his brother. Those who have had experience in the work of God should be encouraged to follow the guidance and counsel of the Lord.

Do not worry lest some means shall go direct to those who are trying to do missionary work in a quiet and effective way. All the means is not to be handled by one agency or organization. There is much business to be done conscientiously for the cause of God. Help is to be sought from every possible source. There are men who can do the work of securing means for the cause, and when these are acting conscientiously and in harmony with the counsels of their fellow-laborers in the field which they represent, the hand of restraint is not to be laid upon them. They are surely laborers together with Him who gave his life for the salvation of souls.

Brethren Sutherland and Magan should be encouraged to solicit means for the support of their work. It is the privilege of these brethren to receive gifts from any of our people whom the Lord impresses to help. They should have means--God's means--with which to work. The Madison enterprise has been crippled in the past, but now it must go forward. If this work had been regarded in the right light, and had been given the help it needed, we should long ere this have had a prosperous work at Madison. Our people are to be encouraged to give of their means to this work which is preparing students in a sensible and creditable way to go forth into neglected fields to proclaim the soon coming of Christ.

The Lord directed Brethren Sutherland and Magan, as men of sound principles, to establish a work in the South. They have devised and planned and sacrificed in order to carry forward the work on right lines, but the work has been greatly delayed. The Lord guided his servants in the selection of the farm at Madison, and he desires that it be managed on right lines, that others, learning from the workers there, might take up a similar work and conduct it in a like manner. Brethren Sutherland and Magan are chosen of God and faithful, and the Lord of heaven says of them, I have a special work for these men to do at Madison, a work of educating and training young men and women for mission fields. The Spirit of the Lord will be with his workers if they will walk humbly before him. He had not bound about and restricted the labors of these self-denying, self-sacrificing men.

To those in our conferences who have felt that they had authority to forbid the gathering of means in certain territory I now say: This matter has been presented to me again and again. I now bear my testimony in the name of the Lord to those whom it concerns. Wherever you are, withhold your forbiddings. The work of God is not to be thus trammeled. God is being faithfully served by these men whom you have been watching and criticizing. They fear and honor the Lord; they are laborers together with Him. God forbids you to put any yokes on the necks of his servants. It is the privilege of these workers to accept gifts or loans that they may invest them to help in doing an important work that greatly needs to be done. This wonderful burden of responsibility which some suppose God has placed upon them with their official position, has never been laid upon them. If men were standing free on the high platform of truth, they would never accept the responsibility to frame rules and regulations that hinder and cramp God's chosen laborers in their work for the training of missionaries. When they learn the lesson that "All ye are brethren", and realize that their fellow-workers may know just as well as they how to use in the wisest way the talents and capabilities entrusted to them, they will remove the yokes that are now binding their brethren, and will give them credit for having love for souls and a desire to labor unselfishly to promote the interests of the cause.

The Character of the Work

The school at Madison not only educates in a knowledge of the Scriptures, but it gives a practical training that fits the student to go forth as a self-supporting missionary to the field to which he is called. In his student days he is taught how to build simply and substantially, how to cultivate the land, and care for the stock. To this is added the knowledge of being able to treat the sick and care for the injured. This training for medical missionary work is one of the grandest objects for which any school can be established. There are many suffering from diseases and injury, who, when relieved of pain, will be prepared to listen to the truth. Our Saviour was a mighty Healer. In his name there may be many miracles wrought in the South and other fields through the instrumentality of the trained medical missionary. Therefore it is essential that there shall be a sanitarium connected with the Madison school. The educational work at the school, and at the Sanitarium, can go forward hand in hand. The instruction given at the school will benefit the patients, and the instruction given to the sanitarium patients will be a blessing to the school.

The class of education given at the Madison School is such as will be accounted a treasure of great value by those who take up missionary work in foreign fields. My brethren, let no hindrance be placed in the way of men and women who are seeking to gain such an education as those at the Madison School are receiving. If many more in other schools were receiving a similar training, we as a people would become a spectacle to the world, to angels, and to men. The message would quickly be carried to every country, and souls now in darkness would be brought to the light

It would have been pleasing to God if, while the Madison School has been doing its work, other such schools had been established in different parts of the Southern field. No soul should be left in darkness if by any possible means he can be enlightened. There is plenty of land lying waste in the South that might have been improved as the land about the Madison School has been improved. The time is soon coming when God's people, because of persecution, will be scattered in many countries. Those who have received an all-round education will have the advantage wherever they are. The Lord reveals divine wisdom in thus leading his people to the training of all their faculties and capabilities for the work of disseminating truth.

Every possible means should be devised to establish schools on the Madison order in various parts of the South; and those who lend their means and their influence to help this work are aiding the cause of God. I am instructed to say to those who have means to spare; Help the work at Madison. You have no time to lose. Satan will soon rise up to create hindrances; let the work go forward while it may. This is no time for weakness to be woven into our experience. Do not spend your money for unnecessary things, do not waste it on story magazines and cheap literature, but take your surplus means and say, I will use this in employing men and women to give the last message of warning to the world.

When the Holy Spirit is allowed to mold our hearts and lives, there will be much more confidence expressed in the workers who are struggling with difficulties in hard places. Let everyone take his own individual case before the Lord, and study his own faults instead of the fancied shortcomings of his brother. We each need to realize our own weakness and be constantly on guard. Satan is watching to take us unawares, and many are ignorant of their own defects of character.

We need to read and understand the message of Ezekiel 2:-- (Here is quoted Ezekiel 2:1-8; and Ezekiel 3:17-21)

The Lord is calling for men and women to guard their own houses and families, and instead of watching their fellow-workers, regarding with jealousy their outgoing and incoming, to turn their attention to self. The Lord has a report to make of every soul who would restrict the liberty of another. There is a Watcher who is taking the measure of character, and who will judge accordingly. The jealousy revealed by some who claim to be in the truth, plainly reveals that unless their hearts are changed they will never be overcomers. Unless they respond to the subduing, sanctifying influences of the grace of God, they will never wear the crown of life.

Those who desire to wear Christ's yoke will heed the invitation "Come unto me, all ye that labor and are heavy laden, and I will give you rest. Take my yoke upon you, and learn of me; for I am meek and lowly in heart, and ye shall find rest unto your souls." To all who would mark out a certain course for their brother to pursue, the Lord says, Stand out of the way. Satan and his emissaries are doing enough of this kind of work. We are altogether too near the close of earth's history to seek to block the wheels of the chariot of truth. God's workers are to come into line, to pray together, to counsel together. And whenever it is impossible for them to gather for counsel, God will instruct through His Spirit those who sincerely desire to serve him.

Ellen G. White.

Chapter 140—An Appeal For the Madison School

March 25, 1908.

I am acquainted with the necessities of the work being done by Brethren Magan and Sutherland at Madison, Tennessee; for the Lord has presented this matter clearly before me.

In their efforts to build up the school at Berrien Springs, these brethren nearly sacrificed their lives. Those who took up the work of Emmanuel Missionary College after them had the benefit of their pioneer labors, and brethren Sutherland and Magan began work in a new and more difficult field.

Light had been given that a great work was to be done in and about Nashville. A printing plant was established there. This city was to hear the final gospel message to be given to the world.

When Brethren Sutherland and Magan were looking for a place where a school might be established, they found the place where the school is now located. The price was moderate, and the advantages were many. I was shown that we should secure the property for the school, and I advised them to look no farther.

In their work at Madison Brethren Sutherland and Magan and their associates have borne trial nobly. They have taught the students to raise their own crops, to build their own houses, and to care wisely for cattle and poultry. The students have been learning to become self-supporting, and a more important training than that they could not receive. Thus they have obtained a valuable education for useful labor in missionary fields.

There have been plenty of discouraging words spoken regarding the work at Madison, and compared with the importance of the work, very little help has been given. When I have heard words calculated to discourage the workers at Madison, I have felt it my duty to say to the workers there, Have courage in the Lord, and do your best. And in the results that have attended their efforts, the Lord has given evidence that his blessing has rested upon their labors. It has been demonstrated that at the Madison School an all-round education can be given that will fit the students for efficient work in other fields.

Now a modest sanitarium is being built, and a more commodious school building. These are necessary to carry on aright the work of education. In the past Brethren

Sutherland and Magan have used their tact and ability in raising means for the work in other places. They have worked and planned for the good of the cause as a whole. And the time has now come when these faithful workers should receive from their brethren, the Lord's stewards, the means that they need to carry on successfully the work of the Madison School and the little Madison Sanitarium.

I appeal to our brethren to whom the Lord has entrusted the talent of means. Will you now help the workers at Madison, who have been instrumental in raising means for many enterprises? As the Lord's messenger, I ask you to help the Madison School now. This is its time of need. The money which you possess is the Lord's entrusted capital. It should be held in readiness to answer the call in places where the Lord has need of it.

The necessities of the Madison School call for immediate help. Brethren, work while the day lasts; for the night cometh, when no man can work. We hope that no means will be drawn from you to help those who have gone out from us because they are not of us. There are many needy missionary fields that call for our help. The message of present truth must be carried to those who have never heard it. We pray that the Lord will give you wisdom to place your means where it will build up the cause of God in the earth.

There is another matter I desire to write about. I desire to secure means that I can use for the publication of my books. I have much matter written which should come before the Church and the world; but I have not the means with which to publish these writings.

I have been instructed to publish the early experiences of the cause of present truth, showing why we stand, as we do, a people separate and distinct from the world. Few of the men who led out in the proclamation of the message are now living; but I have kept in my diaries an account of many precious experiences. These are now being prepared for the press. Will someone loan me, at a low rate of interest, the means to help in doing this work that needs to be done in bringing these things before the people? While Satan is stirring up many to depart from the faith, I am bidden to republish the experiences of the past, and give the message of warning God sends, showing the dangers of the present time, and what will be in the future.

Ellen G. White.

Chapter 141—Backsliding in Health Reform

Sanitarium, Cal., March 29, 1908.

Elder A. G. Daniells,

Takoma Park Station, Washington, D. C.

Dear Brother:

I received your letter from Chicago, stating the need of a meeting-house in Takoma Park. It seems strange that the believers in Takoma Park have no suitable house of worship. I agree with you that provision should have been made for a good meeting-house in view of the large number of our people who are living there.

There is a decided work to be done in Washington. But some of the brethren there, who should be far advanced in the understanding of spiritual things, are not working out the plan of God, but are following their own inventions. The converting power of God needs to take hold of the workers in the school, in the publishing house, and in the churches. The leaders in the work need to understand the deep, earnest work that must be done before heavenly agencies can make the impressions upon the minds of the youth that will lead them to come to the Lord with their human wills broken, and seek him in true repentance.

The responsible workers in our schools in Washington and other places need to bear in mind that there are thousands upon thousands in the cities who need help in many ways. Let the workers bring to mind the words of Christ, "Ye are the light of the world; a city that is set on a hill can not be hid." "Ye are the salt of the earth; but if the salt have lost his savor, wherewith shall it be salted?" The Lord Jesus is a miracle-working God; we must let him be our dependence.

After Christ was received up into heaven and set at the right hand of his Father, his disciples went forth and preached the Word, and the record states that the Lord worked with them, confirming the word with signs following. Today the Lord is qualifying his servants to take up medical missionary work. He calls for men and women who are peaceable in spirit, who learn of Jesus, and are willing to follow his instruction, who day by day wait upon the Lord to know his will, prepared to go where he bids them go, and to take up the work which he requires.

I am instructed to bear a message to all our people on the subject of health reform, for many have backslidden from their former loyalty to health reform principles. The light God has given is being disregarded.

A true reformation needs to take place among the believers in Washington in the matter of healthful living. If the believers there will give themselves unreservedly to God, he will accept them. If they will adopt in the matter of eating and drinking the principles of temperance that the light of health reform has brought to us, they will be richly blessed. Those who have received instruction regarding the evils of the use of flesh meats, tea and coffee, and rich and unhealthful food preparations, and who are determined to make a covenant with God by sacrifice, will not continue to indulge their appetites for foods which they know to be unhealthful. God demands that the appetites be cleansed, and self-denial be practiced in regard to those things which are not good. This is a work that will have to be done before his people can stand before him a perfected people.

The Lord has given clear light regarding the nature of the food that is to compose our diet; he has instructed us concerning the effect of unhealthful food upon the disposition and character. Shall we respond to the counsels and cautions given? Who among our brethren will sign a pledge to dispense with flesh meats, tea, and coffee, and all injurious foods, and become health reformers in the fullest sense of the term?

If we could be benefitted by indulging the desire for flesh meats, I would not make this appeal to you; but I know we can not. They are injurious to the physical well-being, and we should learn to do without them.

In this experience of backsliding from the principles of health reform, our people have been repeating the history of the Children of Israel in the wilderness during their forty years of travel. Those who continue to follow their own course in this respect, eating and drinking as they please, will gradually grow careless of the instructions of the Lord regarding other phases of the present truth; they will surely reap as they have sown.

I have been instructed that the students in our schools are not to be served with flesh foods or with food preparations that will cause disturbance of the stomach. Nothing that will serve to encourage a desire for stimulants should be placed on the table.

I appeal to young and old and to middle-aged. Deny your appetite of those things that are doing you injury. Serve the Lord by sacrifice. Let the good work begin at Washington, and go forth from there to other places. I know whereof I am writing. If a temperance pledge providing for the abstinence from flesh foods, tea, and coffee, and some other foods that are known to be injurious, were circulated through our ranks, a great and good work would be accomplished. I ask you at this time, will you not circulate such a pledge? The means saved by such a sacrifice, if used for the furtherance of the cause of God, would be blessed to the salvation of many souls.

Let the children have a part in this work. We are all members of the Lord's family; and the Lord would have his children, young and old, pledge themselves to deny appetite and save the means for the building of meetinghouses and the support of missionaries.

I am instructed to say to parents, Place yourselves soul and spirit, on the Lord's side of this question. We need ever to bear in mind that in these days of probation we are on trial before the Lord of the universe. Will you not give up indulgences that are doing you an injury? Words of profession are cheap; let your acts of self-denial testify that you will be obedient to the demands God makes of his peculiar people. Then put into the treasury a portion of the means you save by your acts of self-denial, and there will be that with which to carry on the work of God.

There are many who feel that they can not get along without flesh meats; but if these would place themselves on the Lord's side, resolved to obey his requirements in this matter, they would receive strength and wisdom as did Daniel and his fellows. They would find that the Lord would give them sound judgment, and they would be surprised to see how much could be saved for the cause of God by acts of self-denial. And the small sums gained by deed of sacrifice will do more for the upbuilding of the cause than larger gifts will accomplish that have not called for denial of self.

I am sure if you will begin in Washington to do this work of reform--in the school, in the printing office, and among all our working forces,-- the Lord will help you to present a pledge that will help our people to return from their backsliding on the question of health reform. And as you seek to carry out the will of the Lord in this particular, he will give you clearer understanding of what health reform will do for you.

I have heard from several as I travel that Sister White has changed her view in regard to the reform diet. I would have all understand that Sister White has the same testimony to bear on this subject that she has ever borne.

There are those among us who occupy important positions of trust, and who should have stood on a high platform in the matter of health reform, who have refused to follow the light, and their course has been displeasing to God. Let these now turn to the Lord, that their example may no longer be a temptation to others.

Because of the example set by influential men in the indulgence of appetite, the truth has not made the impression on hearts that it might have done. I appeal to you now to set an example of self-denial. Cut off every needless indulgence, that God may bless you with his approval and acceptance.

"If any man will come after me," said Jesus, "Let him deny himself, and take up his cross daily, and follow me." Let us follow the Saviour in his simplicity and self-denial. Let us lift up the man of Calvary by word and by holy living. The Saviour comes very near to those who consecrate themselves to God. If ever there was a time when we needed the working of the Spirit of God upon our hearts and lives, it is now. Christ is speaking to us individually, saying, "I am he that holdeth thy right hand. I am he that liveth, and was dead; and, behold, I am alive forever more."

There is a decided message to be borne to our people upon the question of health reform. Let us come into line that our prayers be not hindered. God can not be glorified in the lives of ministers who give up these principles of reform; but he will reveal himself to every soul who will be clothed with the righteousness of Christ. We need now to arouse, and in all our schools follow closely the light that God has given on this question. Let the teachers in our schools return from their backsliding and educate themselves in a knowledge of the principles of healthful living. Let the students be taught to live these principles.

Cooking schools are to be established at many of our gatherings. Meetings are to be held where the children can be taught principles of temperance and the value of self-denial. In the year 1908 we are to do all in our power to advance the work of God in every line.

Ellen G. White.

Chapter 142—Home Schools

May 17, 1908.

(Partly included in "Counsels to Teachers." pp. 158 ff.)

As church schools shall be established in the future, there is a class of work to be done in connection with them that has not been done in the past. All who can should have the privileges of a home church school. It would be well if several families in a neighborhood would unite to employ a humble, God-fearing teacher to give to the parents the help that is needed in educating their children. This will be a great advantage, and a plan more pleasing to the Lord than that which has largely been followed of removing the youth from their homes to attend one of our larger schools. The church members, uniting, could erect an inexpensive building, and secure a wise teacher to take charge of the school.

Our small churches are needed. And the children are needed in their homes, where they may be a help to their parents when the hours of study are ended. The Christian home is the best place for young children; for here they can have parental discipline that is after the Lord's order. God would have us consider these things in all their sacred importance. It is the precious privilege of teachers and parents to co-operate in teaching the children how to drink in the gladness of Christ's life by learning to follow his example. The Saviour's early years were useful years. He was his mother's helper in the home; and he was just as verily fulfilling his commission when performing the duties of the home and working at the carpenter's bench, as when he engaged in his public work of ministry.

It is not required that all the youth rush off from home responsibilities to seminaries or higher schools in order to reach the highest round of the ladder. It should be remembered that right in the home there are generally young children to be instructed. The elder should ever seek to help the younger. Let the elder members of the family consider that this part of the Lord's vineyard needs to be cultivated, and resolve that they will put forth their best capabilities to make home attractive and to deal patiently with younger minds.

There are young persons in our homes whom the Lord has qualified to give the knowledge they have to others. Let these strive to keep spiritual lessons fresh in the mind, that they may impart the knowledge they have gained. If these older members of the family would become learners with the children, new ideas would be suggested and the hours of study would be a time of decided pleasure as well as of profit.

The tender years of childhood are years of sacred responsibility to fathers and mothers. Parents have a sacred duty to perform in teaching their children to help bear the burdens of the home, to be content with plain and simple, good and neat, and inexpensive dress. The requirements of the parent should always be reasonable; kindness should be expressed, not by foolish indulgence, but by wise direction. Parents are to teach their children pleasantly, without scolding or faultfinding, seeking to bind the hearts of the little ones to them by the silken cords of love. Let all, fathers, and mothers, teachers, older brothers and sisters, become an educating force to keep up every spiritual interest, and create a wholesome atmosphere in the home and school life that will train the younger children in the nurture and admonition of the Lord.

Our children are the Lord's property; they have been bought with a price. This thought should be the mainspring of our labors for them. The most successful methods of assuring their salvation, and keeping them out of the way of temptation, is to instruct them constantly in the Word of God. And as parents become learners with their children, they will find their own growth in a knowledge of the truth more rapid. Unbelief will disappear; faith and activity will increase; assurance and confidence will deepen as they thus follow on to know the Lord. Their prayers will undergo a transformation, become more earnest and sincere. Christ is the Head of his church, the dependence of His people; he will give the needed grace to those who seek him for wisdom and instruction.

I speak to fathers and mothers: You can be educators in your home churches; you can be spiritual missionary agencies. Let fathers and mothers feel the need of being home missionaries, the need of keeping the home atmosphere free from the influence of unkind and hasty speech, and the home schools a place where angels of God can come in and bless and give success to the efforts put forth.

Let parents unite in providing a place for the daily instruction of their children, choosing as teacher one who is apt to teach, and who as a consecrated servant of Christ will increase in knowledge while imparting instruction. The teacher who has consecrated self to the service of God will be able to do a definite work in missionary service, and will instruct the children in the same lines. Let fathers and mothers co-operate with the teacher, laboring earnestly for the salvation of their children. If parents will realize the importance of these small educating centers, co-operating to do the work that the Lord desires to be done at this time, the plans of the enemy for our children will be frustrated.

Ellen G. White.

Chapter 143—The Aim of Our School Work

May 15, 1908.

To the Teachers in Council:

We are rapidly nearing the final crisis in this world's history, and it is important that we understand that the educational advantages offered by our schools are not to be such as are offered by the schools of the world. Neither are we to follow the routine of worldly schools. The instruction given the Seventh-day Adventist schools is to be such as to lead to the practice of true humility. In speech, in dressing, in diet, and in the influence exerted, is to be seen the simplicity of true godliness.

Our teachers need to understand the work that is to be done in these last days. The education given, in our schools, in our churches, in our sanitariums, should present clearly the great work to be accomplished. The need of weeding from the life every worldly practice that is opposed to the teachings of the word of God, and of supplying their place with deeds that bear the mark of the divine nature, should be made clear to the students of all grades. Our work of education is ever to bear the impress of the heavenly, and thus reveal the excellency of divine instruction above that of the learning of the world. To some this work of entire transformation may seem impossible. But if this were so, why go the expense of attempting to carry on a work of Christian education at all? Our knowledge of what true education means is to lead us ever to seek for strict purity of character. In all our association together we are to bear in mind that we are fitting for transfer to another world; the principles of heaven are to be learned, the superiority of the future life to this impressed upon the mind of every learner. Teachers who fail to bring this into their work of education fail of having a part in the great work of developing character that can meet the approval of God.

The last earthly work of the prophet Elijah was to visit all the schools of the prophets of Israel, and to give the students divine instruction. This he did, and then ascended to the heavenly courts in a chariot of fire. As the world in this age comes more and more under the influence of Satan, the true children of God will desire more and more to be taught of him. Teachers should be employed who will give a heavenly mold to the characters of the youth. Under the influence of such teachers, foolish and unessential practices will be exchanged for habits and practices befitting the sons and daughters of God.

As wickedness in the world becomes more pronounced, and the teachings of evil are more fully developed and widely accepted, the teachings of Christ are to stand forth exemplified in the lives of converted men and women. Angels are waiting to co-operate in every department of the work. This has been presented to me again and again. At this time the people of God, the truly converted men and women, under the training of faithful teachers, are to be learning the lessons that the God of heaven values. The most important work for our educational institutions to do at this time is to set before the world an example that will honor God. Holy angels through human agencies are to supervise the work, and every department is to bear the mark of divine excellence. Let the word of God be made the chief book of study, that the students may learn to live by every word that Christ has given.

All our health institutions, all our publishing houses, and all our institutions of learning, are to be conducted more and more like the divine model that has been given. When Christ is recognized as the head of all our working forces, more and more thoroughly will our institutions be cleansed from every common, worldly practice. The show and the pretense, and many of the exhibitions that in the past have had a place in our schools, will find no place there when teachers and students seek to carry out God's will on earth as it is done in heaven. Christ, as the chief working agency, will mold and fashion characters after the divine order; and students and teachers, realizing that they are preparing for the higher school in the courts of God, will put away many things that are now thought to be necessary, and will magnify and follow the methods of Christ.

Into all to which the Christian sets his hand should be woven the thought of the life eternal. If the work performed is agricultural or mechanical in its nature, it may still be after the pattern of the heavenly. It is the privilege of the preceptors and teachers of our schools to reveal in all their works the leading of the Spirit of God. Through the grace of Christ every provision has been made for the perfecting of Christlike characters, and God is honored when his people in all their social and business dealings reveal the principles of heaven. The Lord gave an important lesson to his people in all ages when to Moses on the Mount he gave instruction regarding the building of the tabernacle. In that work he required perfection in every detail. Moses was proficient in all the learning of the Egyptians; he had a knowledge of God, and God's purposes had been revealed to him in visions; but he did not know how to engrave and embroider.

Israel had been held all their days in the bondage of Egypt, and although there were ingenious men among them, they had not been instructed in the curious arts which were called for in the building of the tabernacle. They knew how to make bricks, but they did not understand how to work in gold and silver. How was the work to be done? Who was sufficient for these things? These were questions that troubled the mind of Moses. Then God himself explained how the work was to be accomplished. He signified by name the persons he desired to do a certain work. Bezaleel was to be the architect. This man belonged to the tribe of Judah,--a tribe that God delighted to honor.

"And the Lord spake unto Moses, saying, See, I have called by name Bezaleel, the son of Uri, the son of Hur, of the tribe of Judah: and I have filled him with the spirit of God, in wisdom and in understanding, and in knowledge, and in all manner of workmanship, to devise cunning works, to work in gold, and in silver, and in brass, and in cutting of stones, to set them, and in carving of timber, to work in all manner of workmanship.

"And I, beheld, I have given with him Aholiab, the son of Ahisamach, of the tribe of Dan; and in the hearts of all that are wise-hearted I have put wisdom, that they may make all that I have commanded thee. The tabernacle of the congregation, and the ark of the Testimony, and the mercy-seat that is there upon, and all the furniture of the tabernacle, and the table and his furniture, and the altar of incense, and the altar of burnt offering, with all his furniture, and the pure candlestick with all his furniture, and the laver and his foot. And the cloths of service, and garments of Aaron the priest, and the garments of his sons to minister in the priest's office, and the anointing oil, and sweet incense for the holy place; according to all that I have commanded thee shall they do."

The Lord demands uprightness in the smallest as well as the largest matters. Those who are accepted at last as members of the heavenly court, will be men and women who here on earth have sought to carry out the Lord's will in every particular, who had sought to put the impress of heaven upon their earthly labors. In order that the earthly tabernacle might represent the heavenly, it must be perfect in all its parts, and it must be in the smallest detail like the pattern in the heavens. So it is with the characters of those who are finally accepted in the sight of heaven.

The Son of God came down to earth that in him men and women might have a representation of the perfect characters which alone God could accept. Through the grace of Christ every provision has been made for the salvation of the human family. It is possible for every transaction entered into by those who claim to be Christians to be as pure as were the deeds of Christ. And the soul who accepts the virtues of Christ's character and appropriates the merits of his life, is as precious in the sight of God as was his own beloved Son. Sincere and uncorrupted faith are to him as gold and frankincense and myrrh, the gifts of the wise men to the Child of Bethlehem, and the evidence of their faith in Him as the promised Messiah.

Ellen G. White.

Chapter 144—Is Man to be a Dictator

Sanitarium, Cal., May 26, 1908.

To the Officers of the General Conference, Washington, D. C.

Dear Brethren:

I have read a very encouraging letter from Prof. P. T. Magan to Prof. E. A. Sutherland regarding the recent council held in Washington. I am very thankful for the good report it brings regarding the council.

I was very thankful to hear of the efforts that are to be made in behalf of the Huntsville and Madison schools. They have long waited for the help they need, and an earnest effort should be made to redeem the time.

When I read the resolutions published in the Review, placing so many restrictions upon those who may be sent out to gather funds for the building up of institutions in needy and destitute fields, I was sorry for the many restrictions. I can but feel sad, for unless the converting grace of God comes into the conferences, a course will be taken that will bring the displeasure of God upon them. We have had, enough of the spirit of forbidding.

This morning I could not sleep after midnight. I awoke bearing this message to our leading men, Break every yoke that would hinder or limit the power of the Third Angel's message. The calls that have been made for large liberality, which have been responded to so nobly by our people, should lead to feelings of confidence and gratitude, rather than to the placing of yokes upon the necks of God's servants. Let your requirements ever be dictated by the Holy Spirit of God. When the officers of the General Conference allow such restrictions to be made, they give evidence that they need clearer spiritual eyesight, that the heavenly anointing is not upon them.

Representations have been made to me of a work that does not bear the divine credentials. The prohibitions that have been bound about the labors of those who would go forth to warn the people in the cities of the soon coming judgments, should every one be removed. None are to be hindered from bearing the message of present truth to the world. Let the workers receive their directions from God. When the Holy Spirit impresses a believer to do a certain work for God, leave the matter to him and the Lord. I am instructed to say to you, Break every yoke that would prevent the message from going forth with power to the cities. This work of proclaiming the truth in the cities will take means, but it will also bring in means. A much greater work would have been done if men had not been so zealous to watch and hinder some who were seeking to obtain means from the people to carry forward the work of the Lord.

The Lord's mercy and love are misrepresented by a policy that would hinder the message of his grace from going to any part of the world. Is man to be a dictator to his fellow man? Is he to take the responsibility of saying, You shall not go to such a place? Let us rather say to those who desire to labor, It is your privilege to work for souls on every occasion, and to make earnest request of God in their behalf. "And whatsoever ye do in word or deed, do all in the name of the Lord Jesus, giving thanks to God and the Father by Him." Put on charity which is the bond of perfectness. And let the peace of God rule in your hearts, to the which ye are also called in one body; and be ye thankful. Let the word of God dwell in you richly in all wisdom; teaching and admonishing one another in psalms and hymns and the spiritual songs, singing with grace in your hearts to the Lord." The Holy Spirit is working upon human minds. Those upon who the spirit lays the burden of labor, and who are of good report in the church, encourage them to enter new fields. Let the work of the Lord go forward with power. Let the people be encouraged to prepare the way of the Lord and to make straight in the desert a highway for our God.

The enemies of truth are working with all their unconsecrated powers to hinder the advance of the message. The churches of the world are being drugged with the opiates of error. The great deceiver is making determined efforts to becloud the understanding of the people. Let not those be discouraged who would go forth to warn a perishing world. The cause of God needs the labors of men who have faith, men who can pray, and who can open the Scriptures in simplicity to the people. It is the simplicity of true godliness that will speak of the love of God for souls ready to perish.

God requires much more of the men at the head of the work than they give him. Some give him long sermons, but this he does not require. Workers are needed just now who will explain the word of God in its simplicity. There is a fearful deception upon human minds. Even those who hold positions of trust are not all faithful. But do not allow yourselves to sleep. The light of truth must go forth as a lamp that burneth.

If our leaders realized the time of night, they could not leave our cities unwarned and be willing to do so little to change the present condition of things in the world. God requires that every soul who believes in Christ shall go forth and bear much fruit. He requires that they be in earnest in doing missionary work, faithful in their home life, in their student life, true to their church duties. Those who have pledged themselves by baptism to follow Christ, who have professed to put on the robe of Christ's righteousness, are to consider the words of the apostle Paul, "If ye then be risen with Christ, seek those things which are above, where Christ sitteth on the right hand of God."

Let there be less sermonizing and more humbling of the soul in prayer for the divine presence among us. Our meetings should be seasons of humble seeking after God. O, that we might sense our need of Christ and by living faith claim the promise of his presence!

There are some of our ministers who are true burden bearers, whose hearts go out in prayer to God, and who weep between the porch and the altar, crying, "Spare thy people, O Lord, and give not thine heritage to reproach." There are a few who are in earnest. But there are many who have but little sense of their great need of the divine blessing.

In visions of the night I was in a company where our ministers were assembled. A few were humbling themselves before God and confessing their sins. They were weeping, and pleading with God to spare his people and to give not his heritage to reproach. But with many there was no special burden to get near to the Lord. I looked for the burden bearers; but there were few who carried any genuine burden for souls. The very ones who needed to seek the Lord most earnestly were not coming to him with broken hearts and contrite spirits. While some of the ministers were brokenly calling upon the Lord, and were weighted down as a cart beneath sheaves, the hearts of many were untouched. What kind of account will those have to give who stand in holy places of trust, and yet have little or no burden for the souls of the perishing!

There is need of a great reformation in our ranks. The ministers who are drawing pay from the conference need to ask themselves the question, Am I a faithful worker? Am I a spiritual help to the church? There are those who demand high wages for their labors, but who bring few souls into the truth to stand steadfast and true to its principles. It is time for our ministers to humble their hearts before the Lord, and bear a straight, convincing testimony to the people. It is time for them to labor earnestly to increase the membership of the churches, leading all to a thorough understanding of the truth, for this time. The Lord wants living members in his church, men and women who will encourage one another in faithful service.

Ellen G. White.

Chapter 144.1—On Degrees

Oct, 29 1908 – W. C. White

Text unavailable.

Chapter 145—Work For Every Member of the Family

(Extract from the Northern Union Reaper, Dec. 29, 1908.)

We need to branch out more in our methods of labor; not a hand should be bound; not a soul discouraged; not a voice should be hushed; let every individual labor privately or publicly to help forward the work. Place the burden upon men and women of the church that they may grow by reason of exercise, and thus become efficient agencies in the hand of the Lord for the enlightenment of those who sit in darkness.

There has been so much preaching to our churches that they have almost ceased to appreciate the gospel ministry. The time has come when this order of things should be changed. Let the minister call out the individual church members to help him by house-to-house work, to carry the truth into regions beyond.

Mrs. E. G. White.

Chapter 146—Call Your Forces Into Action

Sanitarium, Cal., Oct. 26, 1908.

Elder R. A. Underwood, 2718 3rd Avenue, So., Minneapolis, Minn.

Dear Brother Underwood:

I am instructed to say to our people that when special advantages are offered for doing quickly and at a small expense a work that it is time for us to do, such as were recently offered in the school buildings near Chamberlain, S.D., that those who meet in Council and stand in positions of responsibility should be ready to accept them; for these are the Lord's openings for the rapid advancement of his work. Here was an opportunity for quick work that was neglected because of lack of faith and largeness of heart. I am more sorry for this than I can express. Such opportunities are given us that we may be enabled to carry out the commission Christ gave to his first disciples, "Go ye into the highways and hedges and compel them to come in, that my house may be filled." This message, which means so much to all people, is to reach out to highways and hedges. I fear that a door has been closed, an opportunity neglected, that will result in the loss of souls.

The work at our campmeetings should be conducted not according to man's devising, but after the manner of Christ's working. The church members should be drawn out to labor. The light is to be taken from under the bushel, that it may reach to the many that need it. I am instructed to say that the angels of God will direct in the opening of fields nigh as well as afar off, that the work of warning the world may be accomplished. God calls upon believers to obtain an experience in missionary work by branching out into new territory, and working intelligently for the people in the byways. To those who will do this, openings, for labor will come. The light of truth will shine forth to the (world through the) efforts of missionary workers.

I have a message for the leaders in Minnesota and Iowa. They need to call their forces into exercise by engaging actively in missionary work. Our brethren need to go forth as the first disciples did, to the byways and the highways, teaching the message of truth. They need to become laborers in the Lord's vineyard. God's servants must not be idlers, but must work diligently to win souls. One soul saved is of more consequence than all the riches of the world. Let our church members ask themselves the question, Do I improve my opportunities? What fruit am I bearing to the glory of God?

God forbid that there should be a large outlay of means in a few places without considering the needs of the many fields that have scarcely any help. Self-denial exercised by the brethren in favored localities in order that adequate help may be given to needy fields, will aid in accomplishing a work that will bring glory to God. None can afford to build a high tower of influence in one locality while they leave other places unworked. The Lord grant that our senses may be sanctified and that we may learn to measure our ideas by the work and the teachings of Christ.

To every church the instruction is given to gather in the ignorant and those who need help. The candlestick is to be brought from under the bushel and light given to all that are in the house. The Lord has men of opportunity in the world, and these will embrace the truth if proper labor is bestowed in their behalf. The Lord says, "I will open ways in the highway and in the desert." Let not large means be consumed in a few places while we begrudge the needed means to other localities. When opportunities arrive such as has recently come to us, it is for us to see and understand that the Lord is opening the way, that souls may be converted and become sowers of the truth of the gospel. I present this instruction to you as a servant of the Lord, and repeat, Take advantage of the providence of God. Then give the churches a chance to economize on their tables, in their homes, in their church expenditures, and to follow Christ's example of faithful, untiring labor. Again I say, Secure the Chamberlain place if you can. The Lord grant that you may not be too late.

Ellen G. White.

Chapter 147—A Division of Large Companies

Sanitarium, Cal., Sept. 10, 1908.

Elder R. A. Underwood:

Dear Brother Underwood:

There is a great work to be done at this stage of our history. I have been shown that there are places, away from our cities, where are buildings that it would be wise for us to secure for our schools. There are places that should be purchased, and every talent possible should be used to carry on the work that the Lord has given us to do.

We see determined efforts being made to establish the first day of the week as the Sabbath for all the world, in place of the Sabbath of the Lord. And while this is being done, a work is going forward in the councils of heaven to bring advantages to the people who believe and obey the word of the Lord.

The Lord is certainly opening the way for us as a people to divide and subdivide the companies that have been growing too large to work together to the greatest advantage. And this dividing should be done, not only that the students may have greater advantages, but that the teachers may be benefitted, and life and health spared. To establish another school will be better than further enlargement of the school at Lincoln. Let another locality have the advantage of one of our educational institutions. Secure for it the best talent, and guard against the dangers of an overcrowded school.

All parts of our country are to be warned of the time in which we live. As schools are established in new localities, many will become acquainted with the reasons of our faith. In planning our school work, we are to work to benefit both believers and unbelievers, that the truth may come to the homes of many who are now in ignorance of it.

Let the work of dividing be carefully and prayerfully considered. Properties will be offered for sale in the rural districts at a price below the real cost, because the owners desire city advantages, and it is these rural locations that we desire to obtain for our schools, that the students may be away from the temptations of city life. If in these places there is land to be worked and buildings to be erected, this work will be of great benefit to the students. When driven from the cities, or when sent to other countries, the trades learned in our school may be made an influence in favor of the truth.

As we divide our schools, we should seek to make them more and more like the schools of the prophets. More and more we are to make the Bible the great lesson book. Wherever our schools are established now, the students are to become most thorough students of the Bible. If they will become doers of the Word, if they will dig deep, laying their foundations sure to obedience to all the requirements of God, they will be preparing to graduate to the higher school.

Ellen G. White.

Chapter 148—The True Higher Education

Washington, D. C., May 7, 1909.

(Part of this are contained in "Counsels to Teachers," pp. 11 ff.)

To the Teachers in Union College,

Dear Fellow Laborers:

Here are the words I spoke to you Monday morning, April 19, with a few paragraphs from a letter written upon the subject a few days before our visit to College View:

"When then, as workers together with Him, beseech you also, that ye receive not the grace of God in vain. (For He saith, I have heard thee in a time accepted, and in the day of salvation have I succored thee: behold, now is the accepted time; behold, now is the day of salvation.) Giving no offense in anything, that the ministry be not blamed; but in all things approving ourselves as the ministers of God, in much patience, in afflictions, in necessities, in distresses, in stripes, in imprisonments, in tumults, in labors, in watchings, in fastings; by pureness, by knowledge, by longsuffering, by kindness, by the Holy Ghost, by love unfeigned, by the word of truth, by the power of God, by the armor of righteousness on the right hand and on the left, by honor and dishonor, by evil report and good report; as deceivers, and yet true; as unknown, and yet well known; as dying, and behold, we live; as chastened, and not killed; as sorrowful, yet always rejoicing; as poor, yet making many rich; as having nothing, and yet possessing all things.

"Be not unequally yoked together with unbelievers; for what fellowship hath righteousness with unrighteousness? and what communion hath light with darkness? and what concord hath Christ with Belial? or what part hath he that believeth with an infidel? And what agreement hath the temple of God with idols? for ye are the temple of the living God; as God hath said, I will dwell in them, and walk in them, and I will be their God, and they shall be my people. Wherefore come out from among them, and be ye separate, saith the Lord, and touch not the unclean thing; and I will receive you, and will be a father unto you, and ye shall be my sons and daughters, saith the Lord almighty."

There is constant danger among our people that those who engage in labor in our schools and sanitariums will entertain the idea that they must get in line with the world, study the things that the world studies, and become familiar with the things that the world becomes familiar with. This is one of the greatest mistakes that could be made.

We shall make grave mistakes unless we give special attention to the searching of the Word.

The question is asked, "What is the higher education? There is no education higher than that contained in the principles laid down in the words that I have read to you from the sixth chapter of Second Corinthians. Let our students study diligently to comprehend this. Through his own chosen messengers God has given us light and instruction as to what constitutes the higher education. There is no higher education to be gained then that which was given to the early disciples, and which is given to us through the Word. May the Holy Spirit of God impress your minds with the truth that there is nothing in all the world in the line of education that is so exalted as the instruction contained in the chapters to which I have referred. Let us advance just as far as the word will take us. Let our righteousness be the sign of our understanding of the will of God committed to us through his messengers.

It is the privilege of every believer to take the life of Christ and the teachings of Christ as his daily study. Christian education means the acceptance, in sentiment and principle, of the teachings of the Saviour. It includes a daily conscientious walking in the footsteps of Christ, who consented to lay off his royal robe and crown and to come to our world in the form of humanity, that he might give to the human race a power that they could gain by no other means. What was that power? It was the power resulting from the human nature uniting with the divine, the power to take the teachings of Christ and follow them to the letter. In his resistance of evil and his labor for others Christ was giving to men an example of the highest education that it is possible for anyone to reach.

The Son of God was rejected by those whom he came to bless. He was taken by wicked hands and crucified. But after he had risen from the dead, he was with his disciples forty days, and in this time he gave them much precious instruction. He laid down to his followers the principles underlying the higher education. And when he was about to leave them and go to his Father, his last words to them were, "I am with you always, even unto the end of the world." Christ will not forsake us.

Strong temptations will come to many who place their children in our schools, because they desire the youth to secure what the world regards as the most essential education. Who knows what the most essential education is, unless it is the education to be obtained from the Book which is the foundation of all true knowledge. Those who regard as essential the knowledge to be gained along the line of worldly education are making a great mistake,-- one which will cause them to be swayed by individual opinions that are human and erring. To those who feel that their children must have what the world calls the essential education, I would say, Bring your children to the simplicity of the Word of God, and they will be safe. We are going to be greatly scattered before long, and what we do must be done quickly.

The light has been given me that tremendous pressure will be brought upon every Seventh-day Adventist with whom the world can get into close connection. We need to understand these things. Those who seek the education that the world esteems so highly, are gradually led farther and farther from the principles of truth il they become educated worldlings. At what a price have they gained their education! They have parted with the Holy Spirit of God. They have chosen to accept what the world calls knowledge in the place of the truths which God has committed to men through his ministers and prophets and apostles. And there are some who, having secured this worldly education, think that they can introduce it into our schools. But let me tell you that you must not take what the world calls the higher education and bring it into our schools and sanitariums and churches. I speak to you definitely; this must not be done.

Upon the mind of every student should be impressed the thought that education is a failure unless the understanding has learned to grasp the truths of divine revelation, and unless the heart accepts the teachings of the gospel of Christ. The student who, in the place of the broad principles of the Word of God, will accept common ideas, and will allow the time and attention to be absorbed in commonplace and trivial matters, will find his mind becoming dwarfed and enfeebled. He will lose the power of growth. The mind must be trained to comprehend the important truths that concern eternal life.

I am instructed that we are to carry the minds of our students higher than it is now thought by man to be possible. Heart and mind are to be trained to preserve their purity by receiving daily supplies from the fountain of eternal truth. The divine Mind and Hand have preserved through the ages the record of creation in its purity. It is the Word of God alone that gives to us an authentic account of the creation of our world. This Word is to be the chief study in our schools. Here we may hold converse with the patriarchs and prophets; here we may learn what our redemption has cost One who was equal with the Father from the beginning, and who sacrificed his life that a people might stand before him redeemed from every common, earthly thing, and renewed in the image of God.

If we are to learn of Christ, we must pray as the apostles prayed when the Holy Spirit was poured upon them. We need a baptism of the Spirit of God. We are not safe for one hour while we are failing to render obedience to the Word of God.

I do not say that there should be no study of the languages. The languages should be studied. Before long there will be a positive necessity for many to leave their homes and work among those of other languages; and those who have some knowledge of foreign languages will thereby be able to communicate with those who know not the truth. Some of our people will learn the languages in the countries to which they are sent. This is the better way. And there is One who will stand right by the side of the faithful worker to open the understanding and to give wisdom. If you did not know a word of the foreign languages, the Lord could make your work fruitful. As you go among these people, and present to them the publications, the Lord will work upon their minds, giving them an understanding of the truth. Some who take up the work in foreign fields can teach the Word through an interpreter. As the result of faithful effort there will be a rich harvest gathered that you do not understand.

There is another line of work to be carried forward, the work in the large cities. There should be companies of earnest laborers working in the cities. Men should study what needs to be done in the places that have been neglected. The Lord has been calling our attention to the neglected multitudes in the large cities, yet little regard has been given to the matter.

We are not willing enough to trouble the Lord, and to ask Him for the gifts of the Holy Spirit. And the Lord wants us to trouble him in this matter. He wants us to press our petitions to the throne. The converting power of God needs to be felt in our ranks. The most valuable education that can be obtained will be found in going out with the message of truth to the places that are in darkness, just as the first disciples went out in obedience to the commission of Christ. The Saviour gave the disciples their directions in a few words. He told them what they might expect. "I send you forth," He said, "as sheep in the midst of wolves. Be ye therefore wise as serpents, and harmless as doves." These workers were to go forth as the representatives of Him who gave his life for the life of the world.

The Lord wants us to come into harmony with his spirit. If we will do this, his spirit can rule our minds. If we have a true understanding of what constitutes the essential education, and endeavor to teach its principles, Christ will stand by us to help us. He promised to his followers that when they should stand before councils and judges, they were to take no thought what they should speak. I will instruct you, He said, I will guide you. Knowing what it is to be taught of God, when words of heavenly wisdom are brought to our mind, we will distinguish them from our own thoughts. We will understand them as the words of God, and we will see in them life and power for us.

"I will give you tongue and utterance." Of all the precious assurances God has given me regarding my work, none has been more precious to me than this, that He would give me tongue and utterance wherever I should go. In places where there was the greatest opposition, every tongue was silenced. I have spoken the plain message to our own people and to the multitude, and my words have been accepted as coming from the Lord.

If we look to him, the Lord will help us to understand what constitutes true higher education. It is not to be gained by putting yourself through a long course of continuous study. In such a course you will get some things that are valuable, and many things that are not. The Lord would have us become laborers together with him. He is our helper. He would have us come close to him and learn of him with all humility of mind.

We are to educate the youth to exercise equally the mental and the physical powers. The healthful exercise of the whole being will give an education that is broad and comprehensive. We had stern work to do in Australia in educating parents and youth along these lines; but we persevered in our efforts until the lesson was learned that in order to have an education that was complete, the time of study must be divided between the gaining of book knowledge and the securing of a knowledge of practical work. Part of each day was spent in useful work, the students learning how to clear the land, how to cultivate the soil, and to build houses, in time that would otherwise have been spent in playing games and seeking amusement. And the Lord blessed the students who thus devoted their time to learning lessons of usefulness.

Do not regard as most essential the theoretical part of your education. Medical students will have to follow the prescribed studies. They will listen to many theories that are contrary to truth. The Lord would have our medical students connect closely with those who believe and teach the truth. And as helpers with them, they can learn how to treat the sick, and how to become faithful ministers to the sick. There are many ways by which the Lord would have us connect with those who honor and teach his Word, and he will give us through this connection a most valuable education.

You may say, The world will not acknowledge us. What if the world will not acknowledge you? It is the power of God that makes the impression upon human mind. Let it be more and more deeply impressed upon every student that everyone of us should have an intelligent understanding of how to treat the physical system. And there are many who would have greater intelligence in these matters if they would not confine themselves to years of study without a practical experience under the instruction of learned physicians and surgeons. The more fully you put yourself under the direction of God, the greater knowledge you will receive from God. As you keep yourself in connection with the Source of all power, and as you minister to the sick, suggestions will come to your mind how you can apply to the case in hand the principles learned in your student days. "Ye are laborers together with God." He is to be your Chief Instructor.

Ellen G. White.

Chapter 149—The Hillcrest School

Takoma Park Station, Washington, D. C., May 17, 1909.

During our visit to Nashville, I visited the Hillcrest School Farm, where Brethren Staines and Bralliar are laboring to establish a training-school for colored workers. This farm of ninety-three acres is about six miles from Nashville. The location is excellent. Here the students can be trained to erect buildings and to cultivate the land as a part of their education. At the same time they can be given instruction in Bible knowledge, and be fitted by general study of wisely selected books to know how to do the work to which they are called.

As I saw the different parts of the farm, my heart was glad. The hill land is suitable for the buildings, for the orchard, and for pasture, and the level land will be highly appreciated when faithfully worked. A beginning has been made in the erection of cottages for students. They are plain and inexpensive, but comfortable and convenient. More of these cottages are needed. One cottage that I visited had just been built with money given by Sister Marian Stowell Crawford. Those who are bearing the burden of this work should be encouraged, and not hindered by words that would dishearten them or dampen the faith of those who have been helping them.

My heart was filled with thanksgiving to God that a place has been provided here near Nashville where intelligent youth seeking to obtain an education that will fit them to help others, can have the advantages offered by the Hillcrest School. The Lord is indeed moving the hearts of his people, and leading them to aid in the establishment of training centers for the education of colored youth to labor among their own race. Hillcrest is a beautiful property, and gives opportunity to provide for many to receive a training for service. Let us thank God for this, and take courage.

Brother Staines and his associates are engaged in a good work. I believe that the Lord has led them, and will bless them in doing conscientiously that which they have undertaken. It is my prayer that the Lord will move upon the minds of his people to take hold of this work and help it forward. We must not let the criticism and unwise movements of some of the brethren dishearten the workers, and hinder the work. As the Lord has led Brother Staines to take up this work, so others will be led in various places to help. Men in different parts of the field, as laborers together with God, will search out promising colored youth, and encourage them to attend this school. And they will help in the providing of a suitable building with classrooms.

When we were ready to return to Nashville, the teachers and students all gathered in the classrooms, and I said to them:

"I am thankful that I have had the privilege of visiting this school. You all should appreciate it. Here you have high and low ground. You are to prepare the ground for the sowing of the seed; and in your efforts the blessing of the Lord will certainly be with you if you will walk humbly with God. Trust in him who understands the situation. Then he can work with you in all your efforts, and you will see the salvation of God.

"You will have our prayers and our help as far as we can give it. Our interests will go with you. And the Lord will help you in making this effort, not merely because of the good that may be accomplished in this school, but because of the many others who need the experience you are having. The work you do here may result in the salvation of hundreds of souls.

"If you will follow on to know the Lord, you may know his goings forth are prepared as the morning; and the blessing of the Lord will rest on parents and children. There is one point that we must be careful to remember. It is this, that the students in this school will carry away with them what they see and hear here. They will follow the example you give them.

"I am deeply interested in the work that is being done here, because special light has been given me regarding the neglect there has been to take up the work you are doing. I have specified in my writings what this work is. I have tried again and again to impress its importance on the minds of the people. I shall still talk of it wherever I go.

"You are not working alone. When you are tempted to become discouraged remember this. Angels of God are right around you. They will minister to the very earth, causing it to give forth its treasures.

"This is the instruction I am trying to give to our people. I want them to understand what could be accomplished if we would work according to the will of the Lord. It is the Lord who has given the instruction. Let us follow his direction."

After speaking these words of encouragement we bowed in prayer, and the blessing of the Lord rested upon me, giving assurance and hope regarding this work so humbly begun. I there decided to give one hundred dollars to help in equipping the school. And I now present to our people an invitation to join me in giving the means necessary to its work.

Let the teachers consider this message: "Fear thou not; for I am with thee: be not dismayed; for I am thy God: I will strengthen thee; yea, I will help thee; yea, I will uphold thee with the right hand of my righteousness."

Ellen G. White.

Chapter 150—To Our People in the Southern States

Washington, D. C., June 8, 1909.

Brethren Sutherland and Magan:

I am instructed to say to you, Be careful as to what moves you now make. You have had many hindrances to your work, and at times you have been greatly bound about by difficulties, so that at times it seemed almost impossible to advance in the work that the Lord desired you to do. You have had many discouragements, but the Lord's directing care has been over you. You need now to be careful that you do not take one step in a path where he is not going before you and guiding you. You should not leave your present field of labor unless you have clear evidence that it is the Lord's will for you to do so.

Brother Magan, your family is precious in the sight of God. Your wife and children should have your care. Your family can work harmoniously together.

I have words to speak to our people in the Southern field, Do not confine your work in any one place. The Lord will provide for the carrying forward of the work in many places, The work that Brethren Staines and Brailliar have begun is not to be in any way discouraged. The talents of many workers are to be used wisely and faithfully. "My reward is with me, to give every man according as his work shall be," the Saviour declares. Let the workers remember that their final reward will be in proportion to their development of Christian character. The Lord expects interest on the talents he has entrusted to his servants--interest in proportion to the gifts he has bestowed.

Christ's life of humiliation and death of shame has paid the price of the salvation of every soul. Eternal life in the kingdom of God is the highest inducement for consecrated service that he can hold out to men and women.

Capabilities have been entrusted to every soul. These are talents to be improved by faithful service, that Christ at his coming may receive his own with usury.

We hear much of the higher education as the world regards the subject. But those who are ignorant of the higher education as it was taught and exemplified in the life of Christ, are ignorant of what constitutes the higher education. Higher education means conformity to the terms of salvation. It embraces the experience of daily looking unto Jesus, and of working together with Christ for the saving of the perishing.

Idleness is sin; for there is a world to be labored for. Christ gave his life to the work of uplifting the fallen and the sinful. Though he was the prince of heaven, he lived and suffered and died under the abuse and scorn of fallen men; and this that he might prepare for the human family mansions in the heavenly courts. Christ imparted instruction of the highest order. Can we imagine a higher education than that to be gained in co-operation with him?

Now is our time to work. The end of all things is at hand; soon the night cometh in which no man can work. This night is much nearer than many suppose. Lift up the man of Calvary before those who are living in sin. By pen and voice labor to sweep back the false ideas that have taken possession of men's minds regarding the higher education. To every worker Christ gives the command, Go work today in my vineyard for the glory of my name. Represent before a world laden with corruption the blessedness of true higher education. Light is to shine forth from every believer. The weary, the heavy-laden, the broken-hearted and the perplexed, are to be pointed to Christ, the source of all spiritual life and strength.

The word is spoken to you and your students, Be faithful minutemen. Seek for the higher education, which is entire conformity to the will of God, and you will surely reap the reward that comes as the result of its reception. When you hourly place yourselves in that position where you can be the recipients of the blessing of God, the name of the Lord will be magnified through your lives.

Read carefully the fortieth chapter of Isaiah. Those who give their hearts to the Lord to learn his will and his ways are receiving the highest education that it is possible for mortals to receive. They are building their experience, not of the sophistries of the world, but on the pure and undefiled principles of the word of God. ...

Ellen G. White.

Chapter 151—W.C.W. The Work in the South

Elmshaven, Sanitarium, Cal., Sabbath afternoon, Aug. 15, 1914.

(Report of an interview held between Mrs. Ellen G. White and Elder W. C. White,

Finding Mother in the sitting-room about 2:30 P.M., I told her about the forenoon meeting at the Sanitarium chapel, and the home news.

After a few minutes' conversation, Mother asked me if there were any matters that I wished to present to her. I told her there was a testimony written in 1908, regarding the school work in the South, that I should like to have her consider. Then I brought forward the letter dated January 6, 1908, addressed, "To Those Bearing Responsibilities in Washington and Other Centers." (See pp. 419-425.) Slowly and distinctly I read this letter to her.

At the close of the reading, I referred to the fact that what she had written about the school work in the South and its need of help, had led several men representing small enterprises to feel that they were free to make a general canvass of our churches for donations, and that this was opposed by our brethren. I also stated that I had been thinking that we ought to have a board of seven or nine trustees appointed to receive gifts, and to dispense help where most needed.

Mother said: "That ought to be done. It has been presented to me several times that something like that should be done. If we would be sensible enough to counsel together kindly and courteously, the blessing of God would be seen in the work, and the grace of God in the action of the workers. Then God can make impressions on hearts.

"Unity of spirit and action, puts a trust-note in their hands regarding the receiving of means, and the whole line of work. An impression is made that can not be effaced from minds, that the work is to be perpetuated. It gives evidence that the work is based on truth and righteousness."

I said that a board of trustees could receive gifts, and appropriate a little here and a little there, where most needed.

Mother said: "It has been shown me several times that this ought to be done, and I have wondered that it has been so long before it was entered into.

"There ought to be a firm confidence established between brethren who are accepted to act a part in this work,--not a make-believe unity, but a solid, compact; that when questions arise, it can be shown that they were dealing not with supposition, but with truth."

I said that a board of trustees properly selected, would give confidence to our people, and that these trustees could give counsel to the workers.

Mother said: "That is the way it has been presented to me for a long time. Then if they see evils in the work, they can change matters. If handled at once, the changes can be made easily.

"We must show that we are walking on solid ground. If we are working in harmony with the principles of righteousness and truth, the angels of God will work with us. The people must see righteousness and consistency in the work. Righteousness and truth must work in perfect harmony. God will be with the workers, and prosperity will follow them, as they labor in simplicity and truth.

"It is our business to make sure that the work will go forward safely and as perfectly as possible. Men will see our determination to dig deep and lay a sure foundation, and the God of Israel will be our reward.

"One subject I must speak of:

"Those having families should not be called upon to bear undue hardships and privations. They should be allowed to deal with their families. We must not suffer the idea that those working hard to build up, shall be treated indifferently. The angels of God will be their dependence for surety and success.

"Let us draw in even cords,--not one pulling this way, and another that way. Then the angels of God will give success.

"These things will have to be repeated over and over again, in order that our brethren may draw in harmony and unity for uplifting,--not in themselves, but for uplifting in the presence of God. They are to labor in accordance with his word. Then the lessons given will be of a character that the students will understand them as "yea" and "amen" for the victory. It is because we do not walk steadily in sure tracks, that there are failures. But there is no need of failures, because God has spoken, and his will shall be fulfilled. Nothing will enable us to prevail like presenting to God the sure work of his promises. Then there is no failure.

"We do not talk faith one-half, no, not one-quarter as much as we should if we expect the victory. There is not one-quarter of the faith exercised that it is our privilege to exercise. We have honored the promises so little that we do not know where we are. We should prove the Lord, and see that he means just what he says. He is a God of mercy, knowledge, and power; and all these are for us, if we will take them.

"These words were spoken for me to speak to the people. If all will take hold by living faith, we shall see the salvation of God."

Here Mother rested for some time.

After this I spoke about our system of auditing all conference and institutional accounts, and stated that some of our brethren thought that the accounts of independent and self-supporting auxiliary enterprises which received gifts from our people, should also be audited. I also stated the objection to this.

Mother said: "I thought that was done. That ought to be done every time. The money they receive is God's money. According to the light given me, this should be done. If confidence in the brethren is shown, the people's gift will live and repeat themselves.

"God live and reigns. We must take God at his word. Then there will be wondrous works wrought. We are to magnify the Lord God of Israel in obeying his word; then glorify him because our expectations are fulfilled. We have a working God; therefore in full confidence we can open our lips and glorify him. And with our purses we can work for the saving of souls all around us."

Chapter 152—The Last Days of Mrs E. G. White

(On February 13, 1915, sister White met with an accident, the prelude to her death, which occurred friday afternoon, July 16, 1915. The following reports and articles contain her last instructions, given during this time.)

A Letter From Elder W. C. White

("Review and Herald", March 11.)

During the past few months Mother's general condition of health has been as favorable as could be expected of one of her age. She has stated that at no other period of her life has she been so free from physical pain. And while she has gradually become more feeble, yet she had not, prior to her recent accident, been obliged to spend a day in bed. She had been able to go up and down stairs without assistance, and in favorable weather, has taken pleasure in riding out once a day, and sometimes twice.

Her cheerfulness has never diminished. When referring to her age and physical condition, she has often expressed gratitude to God for his care. Her abiding trust in him has never wavered. Always thoughtful of others, she has manifested recently still greater solicitude regarding the welfare of her friends and associates. She has found great joy in reading the reports of progress in the review and in letters from her old friends. She has taken a deep interest in the work of preparing her manuscripts for publication.

Wednesday morning, January 27, I returned home after an absence of sixteen weeks in the east and south. I found mother cheerful and interested to hear about the work in the places that I had visited. She seemed to be about as well as when I left home early in October.

Friday afternoon, February 12, as I was leaving the office for A quick trip to st. Helena, mother came outdoors, and we spent ten minutes in walking about in the bright sunshine, and talking about the progress of the message in all the world.

Sabbath morning, mother appeared to be as well as usual. About noon as she was entering her study from the hallway, she tripped and fell. Her nurse, may walling, who was in the hall about twenty feet away, hastened to her assistance, and endeavored to help her onto her feet. When mother cried out with pain, may lifted her into a rocking chair, pulled the chair through the hall to Mother's bedroom, and got her to bed. Then may telephoned Dr. Klingerman at the sanitarium, and at once applied fomentations to the hip, where the pain seemed to be the greatest.

When the doctor came, he said that is was either a bad sprain or a fracture, and advised an X-ray examination at the sanitarium. This examination showed an "Intracapsular fracture of the left femur at the junction of the head and neck." Mother bore very patiently all the painful experiences of being carried from her room to the sanitarium and back again.

Sara mcenterfer, who was her traveling companion and secretary most of the time for thirty years, is with her; and so is may walling, who was brought up in her home, and who has been her faithful nurse for about two years. Mrs. Hungerford, a trained nurse from the sanitarium, is also with her.

Mother occupies her study, where for the last ten busy years she did most of her writing. Sometimes when half awake, she asks how long the journey will take, and when she will get home; and then, when fully awake, she says, "I am right here in my own room." In our seasons of prayer mother unites with her usual fervor and clearness of thought, expressing complete confidence and entire resignation.

Since her accident she has told me that she feels that her work is done, her battles ended, and that she is willing to lie down and sleep till the resurrection morning, unless there is yet some special work the Lord has for her to do.

This is not A new thought, but is in perfect harmony with Her frequent expressions during the past year. Regarding her constant faith and courage, brother C. C. Crisler wrote to me Dec. 23, 1914, as follows:—

"Even when exceedingly brain-weary, your mother seems to find great comfort in the promises of the word, and often catches up a quotation and completes it when we begin quoting some familiar scripture. At such times she seems to me to be even more spiritualminded than usual; that is, she dwells more at length on her personal experience and faith and hope, and recounts providences that cause her to renew her courage in God. At such times she also reaches out after spiritual comfort and help, and asks more frequently than at other times that we unite in prayer with her.

"I do not find her discouraged over her own case, nor do I find her discouraged over the general outlook throughout the harvest field where her brethren are laboring. She seems to have strong faith in God's power to overrule, and to bring to pass his eternal purpose through the efforts of those whom he has called to act a part in his great work. She rises above petty criticism, above even the failures of those who have been reproved, and expressed the conviction, born, apparently, of an innate faith in the Church of the living God, that her brethren will remain faithful to the cause they have espoused, and that the Lord will continue with them to the end, and grant them complete victory over every device of the enemy.

"Faith in God's power to sustain her through the many weaknesses attendant on old age; faith in the precious promises of God's word; faith in her brethren who bear the burden of the work; faith in the final triumph of the third Angel's message,—this is the full faith your mother seems to enjoy everyday and every hour. This is the faith that fills her heart with joy and peace, even when suffering great physical weakness, and unable to make progress in literary lines. A faith such as this would inspire anyone who could witness it."

W. C. White

Chapter 153—A Message For Our Young People

Wednesday morning, March 3, 1915.

(About ten o'clock this morning, mother began to talk with her nurse about selecting books for the young that would strengthen their minds. The nurse called me, and I wrote down, as fully as I could, what mother said to me. Here is that portion of what she said that is of general interest.—W. C. W. Published in review & herald of April 15, 1915.)

There are books that are of vital importance that are not looked at by our young people. They are neglected because they are not so interesting to them as some lighter reading.

We should advise the young to take hold of such reading matter as recommends itself for the upbuilding of Christian character.

The most essential points of our faith should be stamped upon the memory of the young. They have hade a glimpse of these truths, but not such an acquaintance as would lead them to look upon their study with favor. Our youth should read that which will have a healthful, sanctifying effect upon the mind. This they need in order to be able to discern what is true religion. There is much good reading that is not sanctifying.

Now is our time and opportunity to labor for the young people. Tell them that we are now in a perilous crises, and we want to know how to discern true godliness. Our young people need to be helped, uplifted, and encouraged, but in the right manner; not, perhaps, as they would desire it, but in a way that will help them to have sanctified minds. They need good, sanctifying religion more than anything else.

I do not expect to live long. My work is nearly done. Tell our young people that I want my words to encourage them in that manner of life that will be most attractive to the heavenly intelligences, and that their influence upon others may be most ennobling.

In the night season I was selecting and laying aside books that are of no advantage to the young. We should select for them books that will encourage them to sincerity of life, and lead them to the opening of the Word. This has been presented to me in the past, and I thought I would get it before you and make it secure. We can not afford to give to young people valueless reading. Books that are a blessing to mind and soul are needed.

These things are too lightly regarded; therefore our people should become acquainted with what I am saying.

I do not think I shall have more Testimonies for our people. Our men of solid minds know what is good for the uplifting and upbuilding of the work. But with the love of God in their hearts, they need to go deeper and deeper into the study of the things of God. I am very anxious that our young people shall have the proper class of reading; then the old people will get it also. We must keep our eyes on the religious attraction of the truth. We are to keep mind and brain open to the truths of God's Word. Satan comes when men are unaware. We are not to be satisfied because the message of warning has been once presented. We must present it again and again.

We could begin a course of reading so intensely interesting that it would attract and influence many minds. If I am spared for further labor, I should gladly help to prepare books for the young.

There is a work to be done for the young by which their minds will be impressed and molded by the sanctifying truth of God. It is my sincere wish for our young people that they find the true meaning of justification by faith, and the perfection of character that will prepare them for eternal life. I do not expect to live long, and I leave this message for the young, that the aim which they make shall not miscarry.

I exhort my brethren to encourage the young ever to keep the preciousness and grace of God highly exalted. Work and pray constantly for a sense of the preciousness of true religion. Bring in the blessedness and the attractiveness of holiness and the grace of God. I have felt a burden regarding this because I know it is neglected.

I have no assurance that my life will last long, but I feel that I am accepted of the Lord. He knows how much I have suffered as I have witnessed the low standards of living adopted by so-called Christians. I have felt that it was imperative that the truth should be seen in my life, and that my testimony should go to the people. I want that you should do all you can to have my writings placed in the hands of the people in foreign lands.

Tell the young that they have had many spiritual advantages. God wants them to make earnest efforts to get the truth before the people. I am impressed that it is my special duty to say these things.

Ellen G. White.

Chapter 154—"I Know My Work is Done"

Elmshaven, Sanitarium, Cal., March 7, 1915.

(A Circular Letter from W. C. White.)

Dear Friend:--

During the last week Mother has been sitting up three or four hours each day. The doctors say that she is holding up remarkably, considering her age.

Last Wednesday she said to Brother Crisler, "I need the prayers of all God's people." To her nurse she said, "Jesus is my blessed Redeemer, and I love him with my whole being."

Today in talking with Brother Crisler, she said, "My courage is grounded in my Saviour. I want that peace that abounds in Christ Jesus. My work is nearly ended. Looking over the past, I do not feel the least mite of despondency or discouragement. I feel so grateful that the Lord has withheld me from despair or discouragement, and that I can still hold the banner. I am very grateful that this is so. I know Him whom I love, and in whom my soul trusteth."

Speaking of death, she said, "I feel the sooner the better; all the time that is how I feel,--the sooner the better. I have not a discouraging thought, nor sadness. I have hoped that I should be able once more to speak to the people; but that is the Lord's business, not mine."

"I have light and faith and hope and courage and joy in the Lord, and that is enough. The Lord understands what I can endure, and he has given me grace to bear up under the discouragements that I have sometimes had to bear, and I feel thankful for this.

"I have nothing to complain of: I thank the Lord for all his goodness, all his mercy, all his love."

Pointing to and handling some of her books, she continued: "I appreciate these books as I never did before. I appreciate them. They are truth, and they are righteousness, and they are an everlasting testimony that God is true.

"I have nothing to complain of. Let the Lord take his way and do his work with me, so that I am refined and purified; and that is all I desire. I know my work is done; it is of no use to say anything else. I shall rejoice when my time comes, that I am permitted to lie down to rest in peace. I have no desire that my life shall be prolonged."

Following a prayer by Brother Crisler, she prayed: "Heavenly Father, I come to Thee, weak, like a broken reed, yet by the Holy Spirit's vindication of righteousness and truth that shall prevail. I thank Thee, Lord, I thank Thee, and I will not draw away from anything that shall prevail. Let thy light, let thy joy and peace, be upon me in my last hours, that I may glorify Thee, is my greatest desire; and this is all that I shall ask of Thee. Amen."

Following the prayer: "I did not know how it would be in the last, the very last, on account of the affliction. But I find that I can lean my whole weight on the promises of God; and I do not at all doubt or question his wisdom in any way. He has provided for me to be carried through; and I will rejoice just as long as I have tongue and voice."

Chapter 155—"I Go Only a Little Before the Others"

Review & Herald, June 17, 1915.

Under date of May 27. Elder W. C. White writes as follows:--

Tuesday morning, May 25, she was very weak, but her mind seemed clear; and when I asked if she was comfortable, she said:--

"I am very weak. I am sure that this is my last sickness. I am not worried at the thought of dying. I feel comforted all the time, the Lord is so near me. I am not anxious. The preciousness of the Saviour has been so plain to me. He has been a Friend. He has kept me in sickness and in health.

"I do not worry about the work I have done. I have done the best I could. I do not think I shall be lingering long. I do not expect much suffering. I am thankful that we have the comforts of life in time of sickness. Do not worry. I go only a little before the others."

Chapter 156—« Unto Him Be Glory »

Review & Herald, July 1, 1915.

At three o'clock Sabbath afternoon, May 29, 1915, Elder G. B. Starr visited Sister White. Elder Starr found her in her reclining chair, in the bay window of her room, looking out upon the trees and hills about her place. He remarked how glad he was to find her amid such pleasant surroundings, and stated that she looked much better than when he saw her the Tuesday before.

She replied that she was grateful for her pleasant surroundings, and that they had much improved in the years since she first came here.

Sister White then said: "I am pained at the lightness and frivolity that has come in. It seems to be everywhere. We must seek greater solemnity as a people, before we shall see the power of God manifested as it should be." This she repeated two or three times, almost word for word, and she seemed to be greatly pained over the matter.

She continued: "O, how much we need more of the Holy Spirit! There is a great work to be done, and how are we ever to accomplish it?"

To this Elder Starr said: "God is raising up hundreds of strong young men and women through our schools and sanitariums, and is putting his Holy Spirit upon them, and qualifying them to do a great and blessed work; and many of them are devoted, sober, earnest, and successful."

She replied: "I am so glad to hear that! You could not have told me anything more encouraging."

Continuing, she said:zxc "I wish that I might speak again to the people, and help carry the work; but they tell me I must not speak in public now."

She then inquired, "Where have you been keeping yourself so long?"

Elder Starr replied, "At Melrose, Mass., at the sanitarium where you said we ought to work."

"Oh yes," she answered, "I have always felt a great interest in the cause in the East, and have not lost it. The work there is not nearly finished; it is only just begun. There is a great work to be done. I wish that I might bear another testimony to our people, a strong testimony." Elder Starr said, "We are praying daily that God will raise you up and strengthen you to bear another testimony to his people, if that is his will."

"Keep on praying," she answered.

Elder Starr then asked if she should like to have him pray with her. She replied that she should be very glad to have him pray. He knelt close by her side, so that she could hear well, and after thanking God for his many blessings, in giving to us his truth, and the special part he had enabled Sister White to act in it, he repeated, word for word, very slowly, Paul's prayer recorded in Ephesians 3: 14-21, as follows: "For this cause I bow my knees unto the Father of our Lord Jesus Christ, of whom the whole family in heaven and earth is named, that he would grant you, according to the riches of his glory, to be strengthened with might by his Spirit in the inner man; that Christ may dwell in your hearts by faith; that ye, being rooted and grounded in love, may be able to comprehend with all saints what is the breadth, and length, and depth, and height; and to know the love of Christ, which passeth knowledge, that ye might be filled with all the fullness of God. Now unto him that is able to do exceeding abundantly above all that we ask or think, according to the power that worketh in us, unto him be glory in the church by Christ Jesus throughout all ages, world without end. Amen."

Sister White gave expression to several hearty amens during the quoting of this prayer; and when it was over, she expressed her gratitude for the call and the prayer, and requested Elder Starr to call again.

W. C. White.

Chapter 156.1—Longs For Rest

Review &. Herald, July 22, 1915.

A letter from Elder W. C. White, dated July 7, says: "Mother is slowly losing ground. She talks but little now and longs for rest. It is now 144 days since the accident. What a strange world this will be to me when mother is gone!"

Death of sister E. G. White

(Review & Herald, July 22, 1915)

We stop our Presses to announce the sad word of the death of Sister E. G. White, which occurred at her home, near St. Helena, Cal., Friday afternoon, July 16.

After a life of nearly eighty-eight years of faithful, untiring labor for God, and for her fellow men, a truly noble woman, a devoted servant of the Master, rests from her labors. The influence of her godly life will live on to gather with Christ till the final harvest.

Chapter 156.2—Extremes

The following, relating to extremists, was written by Elder James White to "A Brother at Monroe, Wisconsin," and printed as an editorial in the Review of March 17, 1868, Vol. 31, No. 14, p. 220.

Probably there has not been an important movement or reform for the benefit of fallen man, which would, if properly conducted, result in his own spiritual advancement, that has been free from extremes. There are always many who move too slowly, and that testimony necessary to urge them to duty, is always to be taken advantage of by some who have more zeal than caution. While Satan tempts the many to be too slow, he always tempts these to be too fast. Mrs. W's labors are made very hard, and, sometimes perplexing, by reason of the course of extremists, who think the only safe position is to take the extreme view of every expression she has written or spoken upon points where different views may be taken.

These persons will often hang upon their interpretation of an expression, and push matters at all hazards, and utterly disregard what she has said of the danger of extremes. We suggest that these loosen their hold of some of her strong expressions designed to move the tardy, and for a while suspend their whole weight upon some of the many cautions she has given for the benefit of extremists. In doing this, they will be more safe themselves, and will get out of her way, that she may speak freely to those who need urging to duty. Now they stand between her and the people, and paralyze her testimony, and are the cause of divisions.

Satan uses two classes to keep the body of the people behind their duty. First, those who are too fast, and second, the rebellious. The latter are usually either those who have been reproved for their haste, or those who have been turned aside by these hasty persons. Let these get out of the way, and let the body be moved forward unitedly by the testimony of the Lord. ...

Mrs. W. needs the help of all who can help in the cause of truth and reform. The people generally are slow to move, and hardly move at all. A few move cautiously and well, while others go too fast. The work of reform is not brought about in a single day. The people must be helped where they are. They can be helped better by one standing on the line of truth nearest them, than on the side the greatest distance from them. It is best for them to be taught on all points of truth and duty by persons of judgment and caution, and as fast as God in his providence unfolds them to his people. He who is but partly reformed himself, and teaches the people, will do some good. He who sees the duty of reform and is full strict enough in any case, and allows of no exceptions, and drives matters, is sure to drive the reform into the ground and hurt his own soul, and injure others. Such do not help Mrs. W., but greatly burden her in her arduous work. We invite, you, entreat, such to get out of the way and let Mrs. W. come to the people.

She works to this disadvantage, namely: she makes strong appeals to the people, which a few feel deeply, and take strong positions, and go to extremes. Then to save the cause from ruin in consequence of these extremes, she is obliged to come out with reproofs for extremists in a public manner. This is better than to have things go to pieces; but the influence of both the extremes and the reproofs are terrible on the cause, and bring upon Mrs. W. a three fold burden.

Here is the difficulty: What she may say to urge the tardy, is taken by the prompt to urge them over the mark. And what she may say to caution the prompt, zealous, incautious ones, is taken by the tardy as an excuse to remain too far behind.

We say to those who wish to help Mrs. W. in her work, you will not find her far ahead of the people, with a few extremists. No, she is back with the people, tugging away at the wheel of reform, and has to lift all the harder because of your extreme advance. Come back, good, whole-hearted souls, and stand by her side, and lift where she lifts. What can you do there at such a distance from the people?? Come back. You must meet the people where they are.--From Statements Concerning the Visions of Mrs. E. G. White. pp. 33 and 34

Chapter 157—We Are Laborers Together

Sanitarium, Cal., June 13, 1906.

Dr. C. E. Steward:

Dear Brother,--

I have received your letter, in which you inquire what is meant by the words "I", "We," and so on, in my testimonies. In my work, I am connected with my helpers, and I am also connected and in close touch with my Instructor and other heavenly intelligences. Those who are called of God should be in touch with him through the operation of his Holy Spirit, that they may be taught by him.

Of mine own self I can do nothing. I feel that all credit must be given to a higher Power whose will and word I am to carry out, in order that, united with heavenly intelligences, I may have a clear perception of spiritual and eternal things. Christ has said, "The Son can do nothing of himself, but what he seeth the Father do; for what things soever he doeth, these also doeth the Son likewise."

Again, God's way is to be practiced in every line of work, else the cause of truth, I am instructed, will bear the imperfections of the mold of men, and will be misrepresented. We are to become one with Christ, in harmony with his prayer: "Neither pray I for these alone, but for them also which shall believe on me through their word; that they all shall be one; as thou, Father, art in me, and I in thee, that they also may be one in us; that the world may believe that thou hast sent me. And the glory which thou gavest me I have given them; that they may be one, even as we are one: I in them, and thou in me, that they may be made perfect in one; and that the world may know that thou hast sent me, and hast loved them, as thou has loved me. . . . . O righteous Father, the world hath not known thee; but I have known thee, and these have known that thou hast sent me. And I have declared unto them thy name, and will declare it; that the love wherewith thou hast loved me may be in them and I in them."

I can not always say "I"! I am not accustomed to doing so. Without the special light and grace of Christ, I can do nothing. Furthermore, I am connected with my workers. During the night season I am often deeply impressed with representations passing before me, and usually, whatever the hour of the night may be, I arise at once, and write out the instruction that has been given me. This manuscript is placed in the hands of one of my copyists, who makes several copies on the typewriter. Then it is returned to me, and I carefully read it over to see if it is all correct. Matter written for publication is sometimes sent direct to one of our periodicals, and sometimes laid aside with other matter to be published later in book form or in some other way.

This is one reason why I often say "we". My helpers and I are co-workers in sending out the light given me to be a blessing to the world.

In the first chapter of the first epistle to the Corinthians we read: "Paul, called to be an apostle of Jesus Christ through the will of God, and Sosthenes our brother, unto the church of God which is at Corinth, to them that are sanctified in Christ Jesus, called to be saints, with all that in every place call upon the name of Jesus Christ our Lord, both theirs and ours: Grace by unto you, and peace, from God our Father, and from the Lord Jesus Christ.

"I thank my God always on your behalf, for the grace of God which is given you by Jesus Christ; that in every thing ye are enriched by him, in all utterance, and in all knowledge (this is a very broad statement); even as the testimony of Christ was confirmed in you: so that ye come behind in no gift, waiting for the coming of our Lord Jesus Christ; who shall also confirm you unto the end, that ye may be blameless in the day of our Lord Jesus Christ. God is faithful, by whom ye were called unto the fellowship of his Son Jesus Christ our Lord. Now I beseech you, brethren, by the name of our Lord Jesus Christ, that ye all speak the same thing, and that there be no divisions among you; but that ye be perfectly joined together in the same mind and in the same judgment."

"For the preaching of the cross is to them that perish foolishness; but unto us (notice the use of this word) which are saved it is the power of God. For it is written, I will destroy the wisdom of the wise, and I will bring to nothing the understanding of the prudent. Where is the wise? Where is the scribe? Where is the disputer of this world? Hath not God made foolish the wisdom of this world? For after that in the wisdom of God the world by wisdom knew not God, it pleased God by the foolishness of preaching to save them that believe.

"For the Jews require a sign, and the Greeks seek after wisdom; but we preach Christ crucified, unto the Jews a stumbling-block, and unto the Greeks foolishness; but unto them which are called, both Jews and Greeks, Christ the power of God, and the wisdom of God. Because the foolishness of God is wiser than men, and the weakness of God is stronger than men. For ye see your calling, brethren, how that not many wise men after the flesh, not many mighty, not many noble, are called; but God hath chosen the foolish things of the world to confound the things which are might; and base things of the world, and things which are despised, hath God chosen, yea, and things which are not, to bring to nought things that are; that no flesh should glory in his presence.

"But of him are ye in Christ Jesus, who of God is made unto us wisdom, and righteousness, and sanctification, and redemption; that, according as it is written, He that glorieth, let him glory in the Lord."

Read the second chapter of First Corinthians, and notice carefully how Paul uses the words, "I", "we", and "us".

In the third chapter we read: "Who then is Paul, and who is Apollos, but ministers by whom ye believed, even as the Lord gave to every man? I have planted, Apollos watered; but God gave the increase. So then neither is he that planteth any thing, neither he that watereth; but God that giveth the increase. Now he that planteth and he that watereth are one; and every man shall receive his own reward according to his own labor. For we are laborers together with God; ye are God's husbandry, ye are God's building."

Now if I say "we" and "us", you may understand what I mean; we are laborers together with God. The whole of the third chapter of First Corinthians needs to be carefully studied. Study every verse of this chapter; for it means to you and your associates, as well as to me.

"Know ye not that ye are the temple of God, and that the Spirit of God dwelleth in you?" Then why should not I say "we" in a peculiar and significant sense? I myself and you yourself must be united in mind, in heart, in soul, in strength, with heavenly agencies. This is our only hope of success. The less that is said of "I", the more correct will be our understanding of the great I Am.

"If any man defile the temple of God, him shall God destroy; for the temple of God is holy, which temple ye are. Let no man deceive himself. If any man among you seemeth to be wise in this world, let him become a fool, that he may be wise. For the wisdom of this world is foolishness with God. For it is written, He taketh the wise in their own craftiness."

I have been instructed that unless there is a decided changed in the religious experience of those who have refused to heed the warnings given them, but who, instead, remain willingly under the molding influence which now predominates at the Battle Creek Sanitarium, it will not be of the least use to explain everything that is presented as an objection to the visions. Some have been under his influence for years, and the many subterfuges and explanations that are resorted to there, will be taken up by those misled souls and used against the testimonies. So long as they refuse to heed the warnings given them, the spell that is upon them can not be broken. God has a work that must be carried forward purely and intelligently, in his own way, entirely separated from the influence of seducing spirits that some have communion with.

I am instructed to say to you, We are now living amid the perils of the last days. I am commissioned to bear my testimony, "Be ye also ready, for in such an hour as ye think not, the Son of man cometh."

Our God has given us, his people, a special work to do. The Son of God was manifest in human flesh, that man might receive knowledge intelligently from the divine-human Teacher. Christ came in the likeness of humanity, that he might draw all men unto himself. His followers must walk in the light of his glorious example.

At whatever sacrifice of ease of reputation, at whatever sacrifice of property of cost of labor, a Christian must maintain the reformative doctrine of the gospel. In short, if a man is risen with Christ by profession of faith in the Son of God as his Redeemer, he has made a most solemn pledge to maintain these reformative doctrines. As he advances in the Christian life, he will gladly accept the self-denial and self-sacrifice involved. "Ye are laborers together with God."

llen G. White.

Chapter 158—Who Has Told Sister White?

Sanitarium, Cal., Jan. 15, 1906.

Dear Brother Amadon:--

I have received your letter, I will send you copies of things taken from my diaries. These articles contain presentations and instructions given me, point by point. For instance, the evening after the Sabbath I retired, and rested well without ache or pain until half past ten. But I was unable to sleep. I had received instruction, and I seldom lie in bed after such instruction comes. There was a company assembled in Battle Creek, and instruction was given by One in our midst that I was to repeat and repeat with pen and voice. I left my bed, and wrote for five hours as fast as my pen could trace the lines. Then, I rested on the bed for an hour, and slept part of the time.

I placed the matter in the hands of my copyist, and on Monday morning it was waiting for me, placed inside my office door on Sunday evening. There were four articles ready for me to read over, and make any corrections needed. The matter is now prepared, and some of it will go in the mail today.

This is the line of work that I am carrying on. I do most of my writing while the other members of the family are asleep, I build my fire, and then write uninterruptedly, sometimes for hours. I write while others are asleep. Who, then, has told Sister White?--A messenger that is appointed.

If Elder Daniells is in Battle Creek, please place in his hands the manuscripts I send you. I have my work to do, to meet the misconceptions of those who suppose themselves able to say what is testimony from God and what is human productions.

If those who have done this work continue in this course, Satanic agencies will choose for them. At the Berrien Springs meeting, the richest blessing was proffered them. This blessing they could have had if they had let Christ help them, confessing their wicked obstinacy. But they refused to take the right course. The holy angels turned away, the evil angels have been holding sway over minds. Evil angels obtained the victory at that meeting. But there is no need for me to give the particulars of this.

If Brother Daniells is not in Battle Creek, please read to the church what I am sending you. I have many letters to write, and I can not add more to this now. There is just one thing the Lord calls for, and that is, for every man, minister, or physician, or lay member, to confess his own sins. Each one will have a hard battle to fight with his own perverse self. Those who have stood directly in the way of the people, having a clear realization of their perilous condition, will have an account to settle with God. Those who have helped souls to feel at liberty to specify what is of God in the Testimonies, and what are the uninspired words of Sister White, will find that they were helping the devil in his work of deception. Please read Testimony No. 33, single volume, page 211, "How to Receive Reproof". Or, Testimonies Vol. 5, p. 683.

Ellen G. White.

Chapter 158.1—The Integrity of the Testimonies to the Church

Remarks by W.C. White at College View, Neb., Sabbath morning, November 25, 1905.

For some time I have hoped for a favorable opportunity to state to our physicians and ministers facts regarding the Testimonies to the Church, which may answer questions that seem to be troubling many minds. Perhaps this morning is the opportunity.

Time is precious, and this subject is important; and I ask you to pray for me that I may speak to the point. My desire to speak about this matter is for the sake of the work.

As a body of Seventh-day Adventists, we believe that this church will stand until Christ comes. Those who have studied church history, know that each denomination which has come out from established bodies has proclaimed glorious truths. Men of God have started out with high motives and pure principles; and then, step by step, the enemy has undermined their integrity, until each church has fallen away from its first principles. The Seventh day Adventist church, we believe, will stand firm until the end, but it is by the power of God and obedience to his messages of warning that we hope to be kept from backsliding and the delusions that have crept into other churches.

The attack of the enemy upon this church has been along definite lines, the same lines as his attack upon our first parents, First of all, he got them separated, and then he deceived Eve with reference to obedience to God. So his strangest effort against this church has been the work of separation, a strange work against unity. Satan has sought to separate from the church the most precious part of its work. He has always opposed the united work of teaching the gospel and healing the sick. In many subtle ways has an effort been made to degrade the Sabbath, and to lead us to feel that humanitarian work was so valuable that in prosecuting it we could disregard the sacred claims of the Sabbath of Jehovah.

Most strenuous opposition has been brought against the means which God has selected for the strengthening and guidance of his church, an opposition manifest in efforts to unsettle confidence in the messages which God sends his people through ministers of the gospel, through teachers in our schools, and through the chosen agent whom he has appointed to give his special message of warning and counsel to the church. And finally the attack has been upon the Deity. An effort is being made to put man in the place of God; and if this be done, the work of apostasy is well nigh completed.

As you study the Testimonies of warning and counsel to this church, you will find the burden of these testimonies follows very closely the line of the enemy's attack. They have been full of warning against separation, against building up and elevating unduly one branch of the gospel work end binding everything possible to it. That ambitious work we may well be afraid of; it is not yet complete; it will continue in various forms; and in whatever form it is brought before us, we may be afraid of it.

The Scriptures say that a house divided against itself can not stand. But there has been a movement among this people for merry years for a divided house. And I am thankful to see in this assembly a body of people working together for a united house. Let us continue to work on these lines. But how shall complete union be accomplished? Several years ago Elder Irwin presented to Mother in Australia some of the perplexities we have had to meet, and I remember well her answer. "This controversy," she said, "will never be settled, until it is settled by our brethren and sisters working together in the field." And as time advances, I see more and more clearly that the field is the place of work for a settlement of the difficulties in the way of perfect union.

If those attending this convention go to their homes and unite every feature and branch of the work in our churches and conferences, light and power will come in. In working for humanity, the Saviour preached the gospel and healed the sick. If we would do more of this work, we would not need so much to be discussing plans in our committees and Councils.

Apparent Lack of Harmony

For years there has been perplexity in the minds of many of our people because of what seemed to be a contradiction in the teachings of the Testimonies. I might illustrate this by referring to what was written regarding the medical work before and after the General Conference in 1897. Before that conference, Mother read to me from time to time, many, many things that she was writing, which showed that the Lord had revealed to her as clear as day the movements that were going on at the center of the medical missionary work, in the criticism of the ministry and the church, and in exalting the medical work above all other branches. And it was outlined clearly what that would lead to.

After the Conference, it seemed that the time had come for these things to be printed, but, to my surprise, Mother would read these things and then lay them aside, and later she would send them privately to the leading physicians and their associates, warning them against their danger. She sent some privately to ministers. Then she wrote articles for the papers to be sent out broadcast to our people, reproving them for their backsliding and their failures to come up to a correct standard of health reform living.

She also reproved the ministers for not making the medical missionary work the work of the churches. Our people were sharply reproved for not standing by Dr. Kellogg and the Sanitarium.

Some of our people saw in this, what seemed to be a contradiction and some of them stumbled over it, and are stumbling today. Some said it must be a severe trial for Sister White to write testimonies of reproof to old personal friends. "It must be that when she comes to write out these things that the Lord has revealed to her regarding the medical work, that her years of friendship, her sympathy and her love for Doctor Kellogg are so strong that she has not the courage to put them out, and instead of that she puts out these appeals for the people to stand by him." I knew this was not the reason, but I could not discern at that time the real reason for the course that was followed,

This was indeed a sever perplexity to me at the time, as it was to others, but that very experience, as I look at it today, is one of the strongest evidences of the wisdom and power of God in directing and guiding his servant in the way that the testimonies are put forth. Some of the testimonies of warning, counsel, and entreaty, were sent out privately, and were given time to do their work. Others were put on file, and they show that the perils attending the medical work were often revealed by God to his messenger, long before the message was to be delivered.

Let us ask, What would have been the result if the warnings and reproof regarding errors in the medical work had been made public when first given? Many of our people were then so halfhearted in this work of health reform, that they would have dropped it, and turned their backs on the physicians and nurses, and many would have gong back with joy to their flesh pots, as some are doing today. There would naturally have followed a great denominational backsliding, on health reform.

The people were not ready for the things that were being sent to the leaders, therefore the messages needed by the leaders were sent to the leaders, and the people were sent those things which they needed. What has been the result? Through the mercy of God, a great victory has been gained, and our people have been led to take a decided stand as health reformers; hundreds have given themselves to the Christian help work, and plans have been devised by which many in the church are striving to do the untied work of healing and teaching. I thank God for his way of leading us, which to some has seemed mysterious.

There are many things in connection with the Testimonies, and the opposition to them, that have been sore trials to me, and in times of great perplexity I have thrown myself on my face before God in agony of soul and said, "0 God, why didst thou choose nay mother to be the instrument for this work? Why didst thou let so much perplexity come to us, so much distress?" It was at a time like this that I read the manuscript of those chapters in "Desire of Ages", in which is related the experiences of the disciples when they were distressed and perplexed, because their Master's teaching and manner of life seemed to leave the way open for misunderstanding and criticism. (Chapters 40-44) I said then, "Father, if it by thy will that thy people in all ages shall be perplexed and distressed, help me to enter into the experience meekly and intelligently.

Many tines I have come to things in the Testimonies, as also in the Bible, that I did not understand, that I could not explain and harmonize. These I have carried to the Lord and said, "Here, Lord, are some things that I can not understand. I leave them with Thee. Help me to go straight forward and do the work that has been given me to do; and when thy time comes, let me see clearly that thou shouldst have me to understand. Lord, take me by the hand and lead me in the strait and narrow way."

Many of the Testimonies I do not understand. In many cases, if I were commissioned to use any discretion in the matter, I would not send them out. But that is not my business. Many a thing passes through my hand and goes out to the people with a prayer that God may help those to understand it to whom it is sent, but I do not understand it. And is it not a fact that the message should mean more to the person to whom it is addressed, than to those who copy it, and more also then to the one who writes it?

Let me illustrate this point. At the General Conference when we reorganized the General Conference Association, and we were in great perplexity over the best method of work, Mother called together, in the committee room at the Tabernacle, conference presidents and managers of institutions, and read a testimony which was based upon Isaiah 8:12-14, which was a decided reproof to us regarding confederacy.

There were at that time, two plans for confederacy before us. One was our union with outsiders in the religious liberty work, and the other, the question of the scope of the work of the General Conference Association. Some applied the testimony altogether to the former. Some of us felt in our hearts that it should be applied to our plans for the General Conference association also. But instead of getting together and studying and praying over the matter until we comprehended what it meant to us, we called another meeting and asked Sister White to come in and explain the matter that perplexed us. We questioned her as to whether the message applied to what we were planning for in the reorganization of the General Conference Association. She said she could not answer that question. Then we said, "Of course it does not apply to that."

We did not study and pray about it till we received light, but carried out our own plans. About six or eight years afterwards it was opened up to Mother plain and clear that the testimony was given to us at that time to save us from going into those plans which resulted in binding together many lines of work in an unsatisfactory and unprofitable connection.

Often times when we go to Mother and ask her to explain the things that she has said or written, she will say, "I can not explain it; you should understand it better than I. If you do not understand it, pray to the Lord, and he will help you." Is not that the right way to get a correct understanding of the Testimonies?

Personal Influence

The question of personal influence is a matter that has perplexed many. The question is, Can persons go to Sister White and present their needs and their views, and, by presenting matters as they look at them, influence the character of the Testimonies and secure the bringing out of something in harmony with their minds?--No, indeed. If any believes this, let them be assured it is not so.

You know that in the '90's there was a work going on to build up the work at Battle Creek disproportionately. This was let by strong financiers, men who had a large influence with the president of the General Conference. In the face of the counsels given immediately after the Minneapolis Conference, and during the years that followed, there had been too much centralization of responsibility at Battle Creek; and in the face of the effort to distribute responsibility by dividing the field, and appointing district superintendents, there were men who labored untiringly to continue the work of centralization.

The work was one of binding things together, bringing the management of everything possible under the control of a few men at Battle Creek, and unduly enlarging the institutions in that place. Mother's testimonies were strongly against this. She sent many reproofs and carried a heavy burden on her heart regarding the wrong character being given to the work. I could not understand why Mother should continue to carry this burden after having written to the responsible men many times, and I pleaded with her to give her time and energies to the writing of her books.

For years I have felt that it was my privilege to do all I could to draw Mother's attention to the most cheerful features of our work, to the many hopeful experiences in our institutions and conferences. I reasoned that as the Lord has chosen Mother to be his messenger for the correcting of wrongs in the church, opening up to her the dangers, the mistakes, the errors, and the weaknesses and the wickedness of men, and as these revelations burden her heart almost to death, therefore it can not be wrong for me to gather up all the words of cheer, and all the good news that will comfort her heart, and every incident that will show the power of Christ working in the church, and that will make manifest the best side of the workings of men who are bearing heavy burdens in the work of the Lord; therefore I will endeavor to bring to her attention the bright side of things. When a brother speaks well of what another brother is doing, I will try to bring it to her attention. The criticisms and the accusations that are made by brother against brother, I must try to keep to myself. I know that this is very different from the representations that have often been made to some of you regarding the character and aim of my work, but I assure you that this is what I have endeavored to do.

Well, one day while we were living at Cooranbong, New South Wales, we received letters from the president of the General Conference, filled with cheering reports, telling us about the good campmeetings, and how that some of these business men who had been reproved by the Testimonies were going out to various states and speaking in the campmeetings, and that they were getting a new spiritual experience, and were a real help in the meetings.

We were made very happy by the reading of these letters. We were fairly overjoyed about it, and we united in praising the Lord for the good report. Imagine our surprise when in the afternoon of the next day Mother told me that she had been writing to these men of whom we had received the good report, and she then read to me the most far-reaching criticism, the most searching reproof for our bringing in wrong plans and principles in their work, that were ever written to that group of men. This was a great lesson to me in the matter of personal influence.

In recent years I have seen such experiences often repeated. Many persons have visited Mother at her home with the belief that personal representation of their work and plans would influence Mother to command them. They have been welcome in our home; we enjoyed their society, and were glad of their friendship; but when Mother came to write, it was what the Lord had taught her. Sometimes it was very encouraging, and sometimes it was like hot iron piercing the heart, because the spirit of wisdom discerned that there were results to follow the plans proposed, that would be detrimental to the cause of God, and the messenger was obliged to speak that which God had given her to speak.

How is it, then, that there are some who have had opportunity to present to Sister White their plans, who feel that she is influenced, and that sometimes she favors one side and sometimes another side? Brethren, the field of the controversy between right and wrong principles is broad, and extends far beyond our ordinary conception. There is weakness on all sides, and often when matters are opened to Mother's mind, it is presented to her that if a certain course is taken, that certain results will follow, and if such and such things shall be done, that other results will surely follow. With such a presentation of the field, the time and manner of sending out messages to the church depends largely upon the actual progress of the work.

When good strong men like the leading teachers in our schools are perplexed on some point, and they come and present to Mother their views regarding the dangers and duties of the hour, and ask her counsel, what does she do? Does she begin at the first of her interview to point out where they are wrong? No, indeed, she knows that these men are burdened with a great work that is not generally appreciated, and she knows that if she would help them most successfully she must show that she understands their motives and the weight of their burdens. Naturally the first thing is to express every word of confidence that she can sincerely express in the work they are doing; and to acknowledge the evils and dangers in the church which they see, showing to what extent these evils and dangers have been revealed to her. Then she often points out the weak points in their work and the dangers that attend their paths, and cautions them about matters that they may have overlooked.

A man representing another side of the work may talk with her of the same experience. She also expresses confidence in his efforts. She acknowledges the dangers that attend the work, and then she points out the weaknesses of his work, and the dangers that attend it.

Now, if these men go forth and remember clearly that which was said that is in harmony with their views, and forget that which was said to correct their faulty plans and work, their views and reports of Sister White's counsels will often differ.

In reference to my relation to Mother's work, a great many say W. C. White keeps close to his mother, and he makes suggestions and calls her out upon this and that, and thus largely influences her work. What are the facts? Often for weeks before a general meeting, and sometimes for months before a General Conference, the burden is laid upon Mother as to the character of the work she must do in the coming meeting. And as I meet her day by day, she speaks to me of what has been presented to her during the night, regarding the work before her in the coming meeting.

Before the Oakland Conference, she presented to me morning by morning, sometimes three or four mornings in succession, what she was writing; and then she would lay aside her writings and tell me the character of the issues and conflicts of that meeting. She would say, At that meeting there are going to be such and such movements, and if I attend, I shall have to bear strong testimony of reproof. She presented the dangers that might arise from the wrong views of the medical men, and the dangers to arise from the wrong views of General Conference men. And she would outline the positions she would be obliged to take at the meeting.

Often I was impatient to get away to the office and resume my regular work, but I felt that it was for a purpose that she related these matters to me, end so I offered the silent prayer, "Lord, help me to remember these things, so if at any time I ought to know them, they will come clearly to mind," As a result I had before the meeting a clear outline of the course she intended to follow at the General Conference.

When the General Conference was called, Mother often said that the burden would be so great that she dared not go, and sometimes we thought she did not have the strength to go. But the Lord gave her strength and courage, and she attended the meetings. Elders Danielle and Prescott, came, at her request, to talk with her about the progress of the meeting, and they presented their views, plans, and perplexities, and asked for counsel. Then Brethren Paulson and Sadler came, at her request, and presented their view of things. You will remember that Brother Sadler had been working with us in California. As Mother gave counsel and encouragement, I wondered if it were possible that the course of her talks to the Conference was going to be changed in any way from what she had planned, by the facts brought out by these interviews with the brethren.

When the time came for Mother to bear her testimony before the Conference, I yaw that every utterance was in perfect harmony with the outline that she had given me day by day, during the months before. I shall remember, as long as I live, that I could not discern that she varied a hair's breadth from the line laid down before the meeting. This is the result of my observation in the matter of personal influence.

The Integrity of Sister White's Writings

With reference to the integrity of the writings sent out from Mother's office, I can assure you that Mother is responsible, intelligently responsible, for the letters, manuscripts, and other documents that go out from her office over her signature.

The Lord has blessed Mother with good, conscientious helpers, tender-hearted people, God-fearing people, who would not for their lives venture in any way to temper with her Testimonies.

Mother writes very rapidly. She does much of her writing early in the morning. She often writes upon many subjects in one letter of manuscript, just as subject after subject is flashed upon her mind. These manuscripts she passes to one who is expert in reading her writing, to copy off on the typewriter, and then it is given back to Mother, and she examines it, making such corrections, changes, and additions as she sees fit. Then it is copied again, and sent out according to Mother's direction. Sometimes a long and personal letter will contain matter which she wishes to use in a more general letter to be sent to a group of workers. Sometimes it contains material for an article for one of our periodicals, or a chapter in a book.

Some of the most precious chapters of "Desire of Ages" are made up of matter first written in letters to mien laboring under trying circumstances, for the purpose of cheering and instructing them regarding their work. Some of these beautiful lessons about Christian experience illustrated in the life of our Saviour, were first written in letters to my Brother Edson, when he was struggling with many difficulties in his work in Mississippi. Some were written first to Elder Corliss, when he was holding a discussion with a wily Campbellite in Sydney.

Letter Received

Mother receives many letters. Some of these are reports or progress; some tell the story of the Lord's merciful dealings with His -people. Some letters cheer her heart and do her lots of good. Others are sad and discouraging. Some are from strangers, asking many questions that she can not answer, because the subjects upon which the Lord gives her light are seldom the subjects of her own choosing.

There are letters which come from men bearing heavy burdens, asking counsel regarding perplexing matters. Some have adopted the practice of sending their perplexing letter to me, asking that if it is reasonable and right, that I bring the matter to Mother's attention, but if she is feeble, or pressed with other burdens, to let the letter wait. Often these communications come to me when her mind is absorbed with some difficult subject, and I put them into a pigeon hole, to await a favorable time. It often happens that in the course of a week or two, I find her mind traveling over the subjects presented in some of these letters. She says, What is going on with reference to this matter? Then I tell her that I have several letters in the office on that subject, and, at her request, I bring them to her. At such times these letters do not burden her mind. When the Lord has directed her mind to any subject, it is not a burden for her to study into it deeply.

Information from Men

There is a part that men have to act, in bringing facts regarding the progress of events, by writing and by word of mouth, to the Lord's messengers. This is seen in the experience of Paul as recorded in First (Corinthians 1:11).

While we were in Australia, the plans on which our school work ought to be developed were clearly outlined to Mother, and she presented these thoughts to those connected with the school. We were surrounded with difficulties, and the work laid out before us seemed to be impossible. Some wanted to push forward the work very rapidly; others were cautions, and wanted to wait for assurances that we could complete what we began. We had our struggles.

At one important meeting I determined not to tell Mother of the perplexes connected with our work, but that I would tell the Lord all about them, and ask him to send us instruction according to our necessities. When I cam home from Board meetings, late at right, I laid the matter before the Lord, and asked him to help us, and send us messages as he would. Each morning I would go to Mother and say, Have you anything new for us this morning? Sometimes she would say, I do not know that I have; but I was in Council last night, and we were talking over such and such a matter. Sometimes what she told me did not seem to have any bearing upon the subject that was on my mind, and sometimes it would answer the very questions that I had laid before the Lord the night before. Many times what she said gave light that was direct answer to my prayer.

One morning after I had asked Mother if she had anything new for us, she said, "What are you doing in your Board meeting? What kind of a time are you having?" I answered, "I do not need to tell you; the Lord can tell you what you need to know, better than I can, and I might not tell it impartially." She said, "Willie White, you tell me what you are doing." I asked why. Then she said, "It is presented to me that you are having a hard time, and when you reach a certain point, I am to have something to say.' I want to know if you have reached that point." "Mother," I said, "we are having a hard time, but for several reasons I did not want to tell you about it." Then she insisted, and I told her the best I could from my standpoint about the status of our work. When I had finished she said, "That is all right. I do not believe I will go today, but I think you are getting pretty near the point when I must come over and bear my testimony."

In a day or two she came over and told us what had been presented to her.

Some have wondered why it is that sometimes when Sister White is speaking, toward the close of her remarks she will turn to me and say, "Have I covered the points, Willie?" And from this they have drawn the conclusion that I have been prompting Mother regarding what she shall say in meeting.

It often happens that Mother tells us a few days, or a few hours, before the meeting, the line of thought which she wishes to present, and she sometimes asks me to remind her if any essential point is left out. Then in closing her remarks she feels anxious to know if any essential features of what she intended to present have been overlooked.

A Misunderstanding

Some have wondered if W. C. White did not sometimes prompt his mother as to what she ought to say to ministers or business men regarding their duty and connection with the general work. I will relate an instance showing what I sometimes do, and how one good woman thought she had the clearest evidence that I had undertaken to tell Mother what she ought to say to a minister who was under deep trial, and who felt that he needed counsel and advice.

At the close of the General Conference held in Battle Creek in 1901, the brethren urged that Mother should go to Indianapolis and attend the general meeting appointed there, to consider the fanatical work carried on by a group of laborers who had been teaching the doctrine of the "holy flesh".

Mother was weary, and felt that she had not strength for this additional burden. She repeatedly told me and other members of the family that she did not feel able to attend that meting. She did not feel that she had strength to bear the testimony which she must bear if she attended the meeting. Then she told us many things which she would have to say to- the brethren who had been teaching the strange doctrines in Indiana. She repeated this several times, so that I remembered very distinctly what it was she said she must testify if she went to Indiana. Finally she decided to go. The Lord strengthened her for the journey, and she bore her testimony to a large congregation of our people in a clear, decisive way. After this she was requested to speak to a large public audience Sunday afternoon. This was a heavy draft on her strength, and at the close she was very weary.

Sunday afternoon I had a long talk with one of the ministers holding the strange doctrine against which Mother had borne her testimony, and he asked for an interview with Mother. I told him that Mother was weary. But when I saw that he would feel grieved and injured if the interview was denied, I told him I would to all I could to arrange for an interview early Monday morning.

I expected to see Mother Sunday evening and tell her of this brother's desire to see her in the morning, but committee work prevented me seeing her that evening.

Monday morning early I went to her room and found her very busy writing. Then she told me that an important subject had been opened up to her mind in the night and she greatly desired to write it out before anything came in to divert her mind from the subject. I told her then that I had promised one of the ministers that I would do my best to arrange for an interview with her early Monday morning. Mother said, "But my mind is now on this other subject. I have borne my testimony to our people, and my discourse to the large audience exhausted my strength, and now I have this new subject to write out. Why must I have a private interview with this brother?" Again I told her of his desire to have an interview with her, and she said, "But what can I say to Him?" Then I saw that the Sunday afternoon discourse and the new subject opened to her mind had taken her thoughts completely away from the matter of the holy flesh fanaticism, and so I repeated to her some of the things which she told us in Battle Creek that she would have to say to these brethren if she came to Indiana. After calling her attention to a few of the things that she had repeatedly told us she must say to these brethren if she came to Indiana, her mind took up that line of thought, and than I went to look for the brother.

During this conversation, a good sister in the next room had heard some of our words. I had spoken quite lowly to Mother, end the sister had heard my words without hearing, perhaps, what Mother said, and she was greatly surprised and shocked to hear W. C. White telling his mother what she should say to a brother in perplexity. Of course the matter was told to others, and the report was circulated far and wide for many months before it came to my attention. When Elder Harkins wrote to me about it, I explained to him the facts in the case, and I have heard nothing from it since; but this is an illustration of how what is fair and right may be misunderstood and regarded as serious error by those who but partially understood the facts in the case.

It has often happened that because of the instruction I have received from Mather, I have in committee meetings taken a position disagreeing with some of my brethren, and afterward, when Mother had occasion to write upon the subject, our brethren were shocked and surprised to find that she was upholding these things which I had stood for, and they drew the conclusion that I had been influencing Mother; whereas, I had been trying to represent in the committee that which she had been teaching and advocating. Her testimony agreed with those plans and policies which I had been taught by her.

W. C. White.

Chapter 158.2—A Sure Basis of Beliefs

Written in 1907.

"Jesus walked in the temple in Solomon's porch. Then came the Jews round about him, and said unto him, How long dost thou make us doubt? If thou be the Christ, tell us plainly. Jesus answered them, I told you, and ye believed not; the works that I do in my Father's name, they bear witness of me.' (John. 10:23-25)

Our attitude toward the serious charges that some are preferring against the writings of Mrs. E. G. White, must first be, of necessity a personal one. When we meet with things hard to be understood in connection with the Spirit of Prophecy, we are compelled to cast about for some sure foundation on which to anchor our faith and future believe in the divine source of these writings.

When in perplexity, we may attempt to relieve our minds by entering into a critical investigation of every seeming difficulty. Our opportunities for doing a thorough work may be all that could be desired. However, the result of such investigation may fail to afford relief. Sometimes, by no amount of reasoning and conjecture as to the probably explanation of the things we do not understand, can we remove every apparent difficulty.

In every instance we can come into the light regarding these matters, but often not until we begin to study from a point of view altogether different from that of a critical investigator. It is when we apply to the acceptance and understanding of the Testimonies the same principles that we apply to the acceptance and understanding of the Bible, that faith and confidence take the place of quibbling and questioning.

To illustrate: The surest and most satisfactory test by which one may establish his faith in the Word of rod, as revealed in the Bible, is the effect that this Word has upon life and character,--the transforming power of the Word seen in the lives of multitudes of men and women. It is difficult to define one's inmost faith. But God in his infinite mercy implants in the heart faith in him as the Creator, the Supreme Ruler, and faith in his Word. The operations of the Holy Spirit upon the human heart can not be explained; but a man may know that the Holy Spirit has worked on his heart, and that with the passing of time his faith in God and in the Bible is strengthening.

This fundamental faith comes not by any process of reasoning. Spiritual things are spiritually discerned. Faith in the Word comes through the Word itself; the Bible says so, and human experience proves it to be so. This fact admits of no explanation; it is, nevertheless, a fact. One's faith in the Bible, it is true, is strengthened by many external evidences as well.

The testimony of scientists who by their investigations are led to declare their belief in an unseen Intelligence directing the affairs of the universe; the mute testimony of ancient inscriptions giving historical records in accord with the Biblical record; the anticipation in the Bible of many of the greatest discoveries of scientists; the exact correspondence of history with prophecy,-these external evidences, and many moo ,tend to strengthen the faith of those who have been able to discern the divine origin of the Scriptures primarily on the basis of their internal beauty and of their spiritual, transferring power on the human heart.

When the faith of a believer in God's Word has been established by the influence it has had on his own mind and heart, as well as by many incontrovertible external evidences of genuineness, he is not troubled over the fact that certain portions of the Word are beyond his human understanding. Infidels may scoff at many statements and apparent contradictions found on the pages of Holy Writ; higher critics with their subtle insinuations and their erroneous conclusions may seek to undermine his confidence in the inspiration of certain portions of the Bible; but these things have no influence over him. His faith has been established on a sure foundation. He is firmly anchored, and is therefore unmoved by the tempest off criticism prevailing on every side. He is sustained throughout every trail of faith by his personal acquaintance with Holy Writ , by the transforming influence it is having on his life, and by the many external evidence of its genuineness that can not be gainsaid.

This is a sure basis on which to establish faith in the Testimonies of God's Spirit. There are many who for years have been powerfully influenced by the teachings of these writing.

Over the lives of thousands the Testimonies have been exercising a transforming power that the writings of no human being could ever have exercised. Aside from the Bible, nothing in literature can in any wise be compared with the Testimonies, with respect to the spirit and power accompanying them, as well as with respect to their scope--the depth and the breadth of thought found in them. Nowhere else can there be found anything that is similar to the closing chapters of "Great Controversy", or the opening chapter of "Desire of Aces", or the chapter in "Patriarchs" on "The Origin of Evil". Anyone who in conversant with the masterpieces of the world's literature, would be slow to concede that a human being, unaided by divine inspiration, could produce writings of such wonderful scope and depth of thought, and, withal, of such spiritual beauty and power.

Again: When we compare the Testimonies that were written sixty years ago, with those that were written under innumerable conditions and ever varying circumstances fifty years ago, forty years ago, thirty years ago, twenty years ago, and during the past decade; when we remember that the writer of these words has continually been burdened with perplexity and care, and that usually, when writing, she does not have access to many of the things she has written in former years; when , in the face of these circumstances, a critical comparison of all her writings on a certain subject reveals a marvelous harmony throughout, we are deeply impressed with the conviction that these writings have a higher source than that of a human mind. New conditions are continually developing; policies are changing; new men and mew measures are introduced during successive administrations; crises in distant lands are met without any opportunity for forethought and study; and yet the writings, during this long period of years, constantly set forth principles in which there can be found a beautiful harmony.

Throughout the writings of Sister White, there is a delicate adjustment of every varying condition and statement and admonition to the bread principles underlying the plan of redemption, the controversy of the ages, God's great plan for his people, the final consummation of this plan amid the scenes of the closing conflict, and the restoration of all things in the earth made new. These principles can not be lost sight of; they are constantly presented; in way innumerable, so naturally and easily that apparently no effort has been made to make possible this most wonderful adjustment of everything to the one great purpose God has in view for mankind. The more these writings are studied, the clearer becomes the view of broad vistas leading direct to the city of our God, the new Jerusalem.

As is often said of the Bible, so it may be said of the Testimonies: Lines of thought, like golden threads, run throughout the whole, and are inseparable interwoven with the instruction that has been given during a long period of time.

Still more wonderful is the fact that all the principles developed in these lines of thought are in perfect accord with the principles set forth in the Bible. Nothing in Sister White's writings is contradictory to Bible truth. The more the Bible is studied, the clearer the light in the Testimonies shines and the more it is appreciated; the more the Testimonies are studied, the clearer the light in the Bible shines and the more it is appreciated. This in itself is one of the strongest evidences of the divine source of these writings.

To the student of denominational history, another most interesting phase of this question is opened to view. The gift of the Spirit of Prophecy was restored to the Christian church shortly after the 1844 movement, about the time God's people saw clearly the Sabbath truth, the connection between the three angel's messages of Revelation 14, and the meaning of the disappointment in 1844. At once the humble instrument through which this gift was exercised began having visions of the scenes through to the close of time and the second coming of Christ. A clear line of truth was presented, and the entire history of the remnant church, from its beginning to its final triumph, was gradually unfolded, at a time when the commandment-keepers were a small, despised people. Throughout the years that have followed, these predictions of the trials and the victories that would await God's people, recorded in the volume known as "Early Writings", have been fulfilling. All that has been revealed to Sister White since these earlier revelations, has been simply a development of the principles outlined in the beginning.

The student of denominational history find unmistakable evidence of the validity of the Testimonies in many, many experiences through which God's people have passed.

The establishment of a firm platform, based on fundamental pillars of faith, during the earlier years of our message; the establishment and growth of our publishing work; the introduction of a divine system of organization a few years later; the development of the tithing system; the reaching out into the regions beyond, begun early in the seventies; and rapidly gathering strength with the passing of the years; the development of our institutional work as the direct outgrowth of instruction received through the Spirit of prophecy; the crisis at Minneapolis and the subsequent broadened policy in the conduct of mission work at home and abroad; the outlining of principles that finally culminated in the strengthening of the general cause at the time of the 1897 General Conference; the peculiar experiences of the 1901 General Conference with subsequent revelations of the infinite love and compassion and long-sufferance of God toward the erring;--all these experiences, and many, many more, are evidences that can not be gainsaid--evidences everyone of which strengthens faith in the divine source of the Testimonies.

In the light of personal knowledge regarding the transforming influence of the Testimonies on the individual heart and life; in the light of the transformations seen in the lives of others; in the light of the wonderful consistency existing throughout the tens of thousands of pages of writings covering a period of upwards of sixty years; in the light of denominational experiences that we as a people have passed through safely,--in the light of such knowledge, everyone who desires to believe can find abundant opportunity to establish his faith firmly on a sure foundation, as regards the heavenly origin and the absolute reliability of the Testimonies of the Spirit of Prophecy.

Having once found a firm basis on which to establish faith, we shall not be affected by any so-called evidences of the seeming unreliability of certain portions of the Testimonies. This position is not one that "higher critics" would regard as tenable. But it is as tenable as the position we hold with respect to the plenary inspiration of the Bible itself. Our faith in the Testimonies must rest on the same basic principles that underlie our faith in God's Word; and with a spirit of submission to God's inscrutable plan we should submit to his method of presenting truth in the Bible and in the Testimonies. God's messengers are human; these messages are affected by their individuality and their environment; nevertheless their messages to the church of God are inspired. The individuality of the writers of tie gospels is reflected in their writings; John's record of the life of the Saviour was influenced by his natural temperament and his view of spiritual things; likewise with Matthew and Mark and Luke. Granting all this, their messages bear the seal of God's approval, and are written for our admonition and spiritual uplift.

Clarence C. Crisler.

Chapter 159—A Messenger

Sanitarium, Cal., May 26, 1906.

Last night, in vision, I was standing before an assembly of our people, bearing a decided testimony regarding present truth and present duty. After the discourse, many gathered about me, asking questions. They desired so many explanations about this point and that point and another point, that I said, "One at a time, if you please, lest you confuse me."

And then I appealed to them saying: "For years you have had many evidences that the Lord has given me a work to do. These evidences could scarcely have been greater than they are. Will you brush away all these evidences as a cobweb, at the suggestion of a man's unbelief? That which makes my heart ache is the fact that many who are now perplexed and tempted are those who had abundance of evidence, and opportunity to consider and pray and understand; and yet they do not discern the nature of the sophistries that are presented to influence them to reject the warnings God has given to save them from the delusions of these last days."

Some have stumbled over the fact that I said I did not claim to be a prophet; and they have asked, "Why is this?"

I have had no claims to make, only that I am instructed that I am the Lord's messenger; that he called me in my youth to be his messenger, to receive his word, and to give a clear and decided message in the name of the Lord Jesus.

Early in my youth I was asked several times, Are you a prophet? I have ever responded, I am the Lord's messenger. I know that many have called me a prophet, but I have made no claim to this title. My Saviour declared me to be his messenger. "Your work," he instructed me, "is to bear my word. Strange things will arise, and in your youth I set you apart to bear the message to the erring ones, to carry the word before unbelievers, and with pen and voice to reprove from the Word actions that are not right. Exhort from the Word. I will make my Word open to you. It shall not be as a strange language. In the true eloquence of simplicity, with voice and pen, the messages that I give shall be heard from one who has never learned in the schools. My Spirit and my power shall be with you.

"Be not afraid of man, for my shield shall protect you. It is not you that speaketh; it is the Lord that giveth the messages of warning and reproof. Never deviate from the truth under any circumstances. Give the light I shall give you. The messages for these last days shall be written in books, and shall stand immortalized, to testify against those who have once rejoiced in the light, but who have been led to give it up because of the seductive influences of evil."

Why have I not claimed to be a prophet?--Because in these days many who boldly claim that they are prophets, are a reproach to the cause of Christ; and because my work includes much more than the word "prophet" signifies.

When this work was first given me, I begged the Lord to lay the burden on some one else. The work was so large and broad and deep that I feared I could not do it. But by his Holy Spirit the Lord has enabled me to perform the work which he gave me to do.

God has made plain to me the various ways in which he would use me to carry forward a special work. Visions have been given me, with the promise, "If you deliver the messages faithfully and endure to the end, you shall eat of the fruit of the tree of life, and drink of the water of the river of life."

The Lord gave me great light on health reform. In connection with my husband, I was to be a medical missionary worker. I was to act an example to the church by taking the sick to my home and caring for them. This I have done, giving the women and children vigorous treatment. I was also to speak on the subject of Christian temperance, as the Lord's appointed messenger. I engaged heartily in this work, and spoke to large assemblies on temperance in its broadest and truest sense.

I was instructed that I must ever urge upon those who profess to believe the truth, the necessity of practising the truth. This means sanctification, and sanctification means the culture and training of every capability for the Lord's service.

I was charged not to neglect or pass by those who were being wronged. I was especially charged to protect against any arbitrary or overbearing action toward the ministers of the gospel by those having official authority. Disagreeable though the duty may be, I am to reprove the oppressor, and plead for justice. I am to present the necessity of maintaining justice and equity in all our institutions.

If I see those in positions of trust neglecting aged ministers, I am to present the matter to those whose duty it is to care for them. Ministers who have faithfully done their work are not to be forgotten or neglected when they have become feeble in health. Our conferences are not to disregard the needs of those who have borne the burdens of the work. It was after John had grown old in the service of the Lord that he was exiled to Patmos. And on that lonely isle he received more communications from heaven than he had received during the rest of his lifetime.

After my marriage I was instructed that I must show a special interest in motherless and fatherless children, taking some under my own charge for a time, and then finding homes for them. Thus I would be giving others an example of what they could do.

Although called to travel often, and having much writing to do, I have taken children of three and five years of age, and have cared for them, educated them, and trained them for responsible positions. I have taken into my home from time to time boys from ten to sixteen years of age, giving them motherly care and a training for service. I have felt it my duty to bring before our people that work for which those in every church should feel a responsibility.

While in Australia I carried on this same line of work, taking into my home orphan children, who were in danger of being exposed to temptations that might cause the loss of their souls.

In Australia we also worked as Christian medical missionaries. At times I made my home in Cooranbong an asylum for the sick and afflicted. My secretary, who had received a training in the Battle Creek Sanitarium, stood by my side, and did the work of a missionary nurse. No charge was made for her services, and we won the confidence of the people by the interest that we manifested in the sick and suffering. After a time the Health Retreat at Cooranbong was built, and then we were relieved of this burden.

To claim to be a prophetess is something that I have never done. If others call me by that name, I have no controversy with them. But my work has covered so many lines that I can not call myself other than a messenger, sent to bear a message from the Lord to his people, and to take up work in any line that he points out.

When I was last in Battle Creek, I said before a large congregation that I did not claim to be a prophetess. Twice I referred to this matter, intending each time to make the statement, "I do not claim to be a prophetess." If I spoke otherwise then this, let all now understand that what I had in mind to say was that I do not claim the title of prophet or prophetess.

I understand that some were anxious to know if Mrs. White still held the same views as she did years ago when they had heard her speak in the Sanitarium grove, in the Tabernacle, and at the campmeetings held in the suburbs of Battle Creek. I assured them that the message she bears today is the same that she has borne during the sixty years of her public ministry. She has the same service to do for the Master that was laid upon her in her girlhood. She receives lessons from the same Instructor. The directions given her are, "Make known to others what I have revealed to you. Write out the messages that I give you, that the people may have them." This is what she has endeavored to do.

I have written many books, and they have been given a wide circulation. Of myself I could not have brought out the truth in these books, but the Lord has given me the help of his Holy Spirit. These books, giving the instruction that the Lord has given me during the past sixty years, contain light from heaven, and will bear the test of investigation.

At the age of seventy-eight I am still toiling. We are all in the hands of the Lord. I trust in him; for I know that he will never leave nor forsake those who put their trust in him. I have committed myself to his keeping.

"And I thank Christ Jesus our Lord, who hath enabled me, for that he counted me faithful, putting me into the ministry."

Ellen G. White

Chapter 159.1—The Discerning of Spiritual Things

(Six months ago I received an inquiry from an old friend in regard to the Testimonies, to which I made a somewhat extended reply. Recently I have become impressed that the Lord would be pleased to have me publish the essential portions of this letter. I do this with an earnest prayer that God may use it to his glory and the establishment of his truth.-David Paulson.)

Dear Brother:-

I have recently reread the stirring article you wrote nearly twenty years ago entitled, "Believe His Prophets, So Shall Ye Prosper." God at that time evidently gave you a new glimpse off this whole question of the spirit of prophecy.

If the principles you stated in that article were sound then, (and I find no flow in them), they are just as true today, even though you may shrink now from accepting them. If you are questioning the spirtuality and inspiration of the Testimonies, under which of these classes of doubters do you belong that you pointed out in that article?

Nearly twelve years ago, after years of most blessed experiences in studying the Testimonies in connection with the Bible, and teaching them to hundreds of our workers, and seeing definite results in their lives, I myself, from something I found in the Testimonies, began to get into a fog over this human side of Sister White's work.

Up till that time the prophets has "hewed me."--Hosea 6:5. After that I began to hew the prophets. Up till that time the Testimonies had judged me; then I began to judge the Testimonies. Mind you, I never for a moment doubted that Sister White was a genuine prophet. No doubt the devil would ultimately have brought me to that if it had not been for God's grace; but I simply began to do what you pointed out in your article,-- discard what I needed the most. It may be a surprise to you to learn what means God used to get me back on the right track. Ten years ago this fall I was in Washington attending the first council after the headquarters were moved from Battle Creek.

The first testimony regarding the "Living Temple" was received and read while we were there in session. In spite of the "new light" that I had received regarding the Testimonies, I had enough spiritual sense to appreciate that there was something in it that would have to be reckoned with either in time or eternity. A day or two later one of my intimate friends and myself spent a good share of one night earnestly seeking God for wisdom and for light, and it was during this experience that he was led to say in substance, "Doctor, this talk of the 'human side' of the Testimonies has been a snare to us. No doubt there is a human side to the Testimonies, but with all that there is so much more divinity in them there is in us that God will never permit us feeble mortals to show up or point out this human side. A weaker thing can never destroy a stronger thing. We must treat whatever comes from that source with the highest respect, and seek God for wisdom how to apply it to our lives and our course.

I saw in an instant that he had enunciated sound principles as to how to relate ourselves to the Testimonies, and I told him gratefully, "You have given me light, light that I needed." I went back to Chicago, where I was then at work, took up my Bible and my Testimonies, and on my bended knees began again to study them as before. I am free to say that it took me several years before I had entirely lost the blighting influence of the previous year of two of experience. I presume the Lord permitted that so that I might have much sympathy and forbearance with others who have yet that experience to go through before any latter rain can descend upon their parched souls.

You bring out a truthful observation in this article. "I have observed that whoever partially rejects the Testimonies discards what he needs most, and that every person who wholly rejects them eventually doubts the Scriptures also, and loses his spiritual life and his hold on God, though he may still hold on to the church." A friend of mine who has wholly rejected the Testimonies told me only recently he did not take any stock in some of the Bible stories. It is more important to love the Testimonies then it is merely to believe them. A man who only believes his wife, but does not love, will soon cease to believe in her.

As far as I know, everyone off the workers in the Hinsdale Sanitarium loves the Testimonies and is studying them in connection with the Bible. I have promulgated no theory about the Testimonies to those workers, simply because I know that truth carries its own credentials and convictions to the genuine truth-loving heart. I have tried with the help of God, in season and out of season, to have these workers yield their hearts to the demands of spiritual truths, and any men who will receive into his own heart God's spirit will have no difficulty in detecting that same spirit in the Testimonies. He who can not smell the spirit of God in them is a total stranger to its blessed influence in his own life. I have recently been reading the old "Spiritual Gifts" printed in '55, I have read again the early struggles of Brother and Sister White, the trials and sacrifices and privations, the fierce buffeting of Satan which they had to meet to establish this message. To a less degree Sister White has faced that sort of thing down to this day. The "visions" were opposed by self-seeking, professed Christians who had an abundance of foliage and little or no fruit in those days, just as Sister White's writings and experiences are opposed by the same classes today.

When I was in perplexity over this question, I wrote Sister White frankly and honestly regarding this human side question. Among other things, she referred me back to Testimonies, Vol. 5, page 67, the very chapter that you quoted from in your article years ago, where she says, "when I went to Colorado, I was so burdened for you that, in my weakness, I. wrote many pages to be read at your camp meeting. Weak and trembling, I arose at three o'clock in the morning to write to you. God was speaking through clay. You might say that this communication was only a letter, Yes, it was a letter, but prompted by the Spirit of God, to bring before your minds things that had been shown me. In these letters which I write, in the Testimonies I hear, I am presenting to you that which the Lord has presented to me. I do not write one article in the paper expressing merely my own ideas, They are what. God has opened before me in vision, the precious rays of light shining from the throne."

Dear brother, you can not build even a successful worldly career on a lie. The things that come from Sister White's pen, even down to Volume 9, her latest book stir my soul, bring me to my knees a humble wretch before God; they illuminate the Bible to me afresh just as much as what I read from her pen written years before I was born. And yet sensible, sane people who know that the business faker and crook can not last only a few short years, even in worldly business, will try to convince me that Sister White has been able to live a successful pretense and still continue for more than sixty years to have a spiritual message that cuts one to the very bone.

The real difficulty with the Testimonies is the same difficulty that the whole Christian world around us are having with the Bible. Spiritual things are spiritually discerned. Practically every up-to-date preacher in the outside churches believe the higher criticism of the Bible. With us the higher critic begins with the Testimonies, and one is just as sincere in his belief as the other, for we are living in a time when the professing people of God are to "believe a lie." 2 Thess. till. The same devil that is destroying faith in the Bible in the outside churches is as busily engaged in destroying faith in the Testimonies among us.

You have filled an important place among us, but don't forget a similar experience did not save David from a terrible backsliding in his later years. But when he heeded God's prophet in those days, God forgave his sin, while his son, who later on ignored prophets, plunged the nation into deepest darkness. The hour has struck for you to return to your first love, and then it will not be long before you will be found doing your "first works." The trouble with so many people today is that they are trying to do their works without having first love, and that is why they are making such a wretched failure out of it.

Chapter 159.2—The Use and Abuse of the Testimonies

From "The General Conference Bulletin," 2nd Quarter, 1899.

"As the end draws near, and the work of giving the last warning to the world extends, it becomes more important for those who accept present truth to have a clear understanding of the nature and influence of the Testimonies, which God in his providence has linked with the work of the third angel's message from its very rise." -- Testimonies for the Church, Vol. 5, p. 654 . Mark that this quotation does not raise the question of the importance of believing the Testimonies, but of understanding their nature and influence. Those who have made a deep and prayerful study of the Testimonies, have certainly realized in a most practical manner the words of the psalmist, "I have more understanding than all my teachers; for thy testimonies are my meditation." Psalm 119:99.

Hundreds of young men and women among us might have their former teachers for their present pupils, had they appreciated the living rays of light which have, through this channel, permeated into the darkest recesses of almost every branch of human knowledge. It has always been God's purpose that his people should especially be made to "lie down in green pastures." This is just as true in scientific knowledge and in methods of presenting and making a practical application of the same, as in the purely spiritual truths. The Bible is the fountain head of all truth, and any tree of knowledge whose root does not strike into the principles, will vanish away; for "every plant that my heavenly Father hath not planted shall be rooted up."

It is the work of the Testimonies not to enunciate new principles of truth, but to point out and bring to the surface God's eternal truth. Right here is where so much misunderstanding has arisen in reference to the Testimonies, as to whether they were to be placed on an equality with the Bible, in place of the Bible, or as an addition to the Bible. As a matter of fact the scope of the Testimonies fills none of these. The Lord has pointed out the exact position that they occupy, and no one need to stumble over it.

"The written Testimonies are not to give new light, but to impress vividly upon the heart the truths of inspiration already revealed." -Idem, Vol. 2, p. 605, In short, the Testimonies are to take the truths of God's Word and hold them up before the mind in such a manner that as lasting impression shall be made as was left upon our minds when perhaps our home burned down, or when we were an eye-witness of some frightful accident; or, in the words, of the quotation, to "impress vividly."

"Additional truth is not brought out; but God has through the Testimonies simplified the great truths already given."-Idem. Vol. 2, p. 605. In such a principle of truth as is stated in the words, "Glorify God in your body, and in your spirit," the casual reader perceives little; but when God shifts his great telescope, the Testimonies, to this verse, and adjusts the focus, we see how this test applies to habits of daily life, even to such simple things as clothing, diet, and exercise. In a drop of water that may hang on the point of a cambric needle, the ordinary eye discovers nothing, yet let the scientist put it under his microscope, and if it has been properly inoculated, it will reveal myriads of animal forms that are perfectly developed. Some would say, "Oh, the microscope added all that," and would perhaps argue for hours to prove that what they now see could not possibly have been in the water before; and apparently they may have the best of the argument.

In like manner I have frequently heard of many of our brethren spending a great deal of time arguing that certain things they see in the Testimonies could not possibly be in the Bible, for identically the same reason that others could not, with their naked eye, see the animal forms in the drop of water. Again, "The Testimonies are not to belittle the word of God, but to exalt it, and attract minds to it, that the beautiful simplicity of truth may impress all." Idem, Vol. 2, p. 606.

Then if the Testimonies are read in the proper spirit, the Bible will seem more exalted, the mind attracted to it as though it were a magnet; and where the truths expressed in the Bible seem hazy, the Testimonies bring them out in clear lines.

We often hear people say, "Don't do so and so, because it is condemned by the Testimonies. Bear in mind that this is not what makes it wrong; the particular thing is wrong in itself, and the Testimonies in love and tenderness only point out the fact. For instance, if I point out to a stranger who passes my door that the bridge over the creek below my house is unsafe for him to cross, my telling him that is not what makes the bridge unsafe; I am only pointing out that fact to him. Thousands of people have been driven away from the Testimonies, and the Bible too, for that matter, because those who used them did not recognize that the things which they condemned were destructive in their very nature.

There is no one who mingles much with our people but whose heart must be made to ache continually by the misquotations, to say nothing of misinterpretations, frequently made by well-meaning people who themselves try hard to believe the thought that their perverted quotation seems go convey, and insist that others must do the same, because "it is in the Testimonies."

Only recently a very prominent man who, with his wife, had just embraced the truth, came to me in great distress of mind, stating that his wife was completely discouraged and confused because during the day one of our sisters had visited her, and had told her of a most unreasonable thing that she said the Testimonies taught, and assured her she must believe it in order to be in harmony with this people, I was glad that I was able to deny that such an inconsistent thing could be found in any statement of God's revealed will. Only the day of God will fully show the harm that has come from garbling and misquoting the Testimonies. In order for anyone to absolutely avoid doing this, the proper plan to adopt is to have a book in which may be written the substance of what is likely to be used again, with the accompanying reference, classified under separate heads. Anyone who perseveringly follows this plan will find in a few years that he has accumulated, and has ready access to, the very choicest gems in the Testimonies.

To illustrate what I mean, I will turn at random to several pages of a book (Index Rerun) in which I thus began eight years ago to classify statements from the Spirit of Prophecy. Under subject of "Testimonies," I have written, as suggestive of the full quotations, "Should not be criticized or flippantly spoken of," Vol. 4, p. 443. Under subject of "Feeling and Emotions", "Satan can give feelings and impressions, therefore not safe guide." Signs of the Times, No. 19, 1884. Under subject of "Christ to us," "Takes our ungrammatical prayers, presents them graceful and perfect to the rather." Review and Herald No. 9, 1893, Under the subject of "Surrendering and Trusting," "If we could see the end from the beginning, would of ourselves choose to be led through the experience we pass through now." Desire of Ages, p. 225. Under subject of "Promises," "Not to be rashly claimed by those who violate laws of nature and disregard prudence; this is presumption," Vol. 4, p. 45.

Under each of these heads, and hundreds of others similar, there naturally accumulates, in the course of a few years, scores of grand and beautiful thoughts; and while perhaps the idea of the entire paragraph is condensed into the brief space of a line on a book, yet the accompanying reference enables one instantly to turn to the original source and refresh his mind with the full thought as well as the context. "Testimonies for the Church," Vol. 4, pg. 440, points out the case of one of whom it was said that he possessed so little spirituality he could not understand the value of the Testimonies nor their real object. May heaven save us as workers from falling into such a condition. The men and women in our ranks today who are keeping step with the message, and giving the trumpet a certain sound, are those whose volumes of the Testimonies are well worn, and the margins of whose Bible are liberally sprinkled with references to the Testimonies where they have shed glorious light on the opposite text. The worker who, as soon as the wrapper is taken from the Review, earnestly and prayerfully reads the first-page article, is the one who, upon the Sabbath day in the church, in the evening effort in the tent, or to a congregation of drunkards and harlots in the mission, is preaching a living gospel from the Bible.

David Paulson

www.ingramcontent.com/pod-product-compliance
Lightning Source LLC
Chambersburg PA
CBHW080857010526
44118CB00015B/2181